PRENTICE-HALL SERIES
IN INDUSTRIAL RELATIONS AND PERSONNEL

Dale Yoder, Editor

Compensation Administration

David W. Belcher
Thomas J. Atchison
San Diego State University

PRENTICE-HALL, INC., Englewood Cliffs, N.J. 07632

Library of Congress Cataloging-in-Publication Data

BELCHER, DAVID W.
    Compensation administration.

    (Prentice-Hall series in industrial relations and personnel)
    Includes index.
    1. Compensation management. 2. Wages.
I. Atchison, Thomas J. II. Title. III. Series.
HF5549.5.C67B45 1987   658.3′2   86–25494
ISBN 0-13-154790-9

Editorial/production supervision: Bernie Scheier and Mary Miller
Cover design: Photo Plus Art
Manufacturing buyer: Ed O'Dougherty

Previously published under the title of *Wage and Salary Administration*.

Printed in the United States of America

10 9 8 7 6 5 4 3 2 1

ISBN 0-13-154790-9   01

Prentice-Hall International (UK) Limited, *London*
Prentice-Hall of Australia Pty. Limited, *Sydney*
Prentice-Hall Canada, Inc., *Toronto*
Prentice-Hall Hispanoamericana, S.A., *Mexico*
Prentice-Hall of India Private Limited, *New Delhi*
Prentice-Hall of Japan, Inc., *Tokyo*
Prentice-Hall of Southeast Asia Pte. Ltd., *Singapore*
Editora Prentice-Hall do Brasil, Ltda., *Rio de Janeiro*

To
Betty A.
and
the Memory of
Betty B.

Contents

Preface

Compensation administration is an organizational process that determines the total remuneration of all the organization's employees due them for their services. The aggregation of these individual amounts creates the organization's total labor costs. Since labor costs represent 40 to 90 percent of the total costs of most organizations, the judicious determination and allocation of these costs can mean the difference between success and failure for any organization. The nature and practice of compensation administration is ever-changing. Each year new techniques are being developed, new technology is being applied (computers, for instance), the behavioral sciences are contributing new knowledge, and the government and society are placing new demands on how compensation is administered. Any book hoping to cover this topic must continually change to reflect these changes. Even so, by the time this book is in print there will be changes that will affect how compensation is practiced in organizations.

It is not the sole purpose of this book to reflect and codify the practice of compensation. More than just trying to tell the student and practitioner *what things are like*, we see our purpose in this book to show *what things can be like*. This is an expressly prescriptive role. We believe that the field of compensation administration must continuously change and improve or it will become obsolete. We hope to send out students who can see a better way to do things in the organizations that hire them. Likewise, we hope to inspire current practitioners to change and upgrade their practices.

We also attempt to integrate behavioral theory wherever we can in the discussion of compensation decisions. This is not only because we ourselves are academics but because, through the examination of theory, the effects of practice on the individual, group, and society are much more predictable. Behavioral theory has progressed greatly, and there is a body of concepts and experiments that have focused directly on compensation. We have tried to incorporate this research in this edition.

Compensation is a complex subject, partly because organizations wish it to do so many things. On the one hand, organizations and their employees want a process that creates rewards that are seen as fair and equitable. They also want a process that is competitive, so that employees are content to stay with the organization. In addition, a newer focus is on making employees more productive as well as being sure that all this is done legally. As in most circumstances where there are many goals, the actions that take place may be congruent with some goals and in conflict with others. In practice, compensation administration is at best a compromise of the various goals it seeks to serve.

Which goals are pursued actively are partly a function of organizational values. But they are also a function of the focus that society has currently placed on these goals. John Gardner in his book *Excellence: Can We Be Equal and Excellent Too?* points out the tension in our society between equality and competitive performance.[1] In a way, compensation administration is caught on the horns of this dilemma, and the approach and focus of the various editions of this book reflect something of the shift back and forth that Gardner claims is inevitable and healthy in our society. The last edition of this text was published in 1974. Through the 1960s and into the 1970s there was a deep concern with equality in our nation. Legislation such as the Equal Pay Act and the Civil Rights Act that directly affect compensation administration is a legacy of this era. The last edition of this book reflected that concern, with an outline that focused on equity.

At the end of the 1970s organizations became very concerned with keeping up with the market as inflation rates went into double digits for one of the few times in our history. Today, while preserving most of the progress made toward equality, organizations are much more concerned with productivity. This is a reaction to increased competition from foreign countries that makes us much more conscious of the high wage rates paid to American workers and the need to obtain the most from employees to counterbalance this foreign advantage. One of the areas being focused on to increase our productivity is the way employees are compensated.

Thus, this edition of *Compensation Administration* differs greatly from the previous edition. The book is organized in terms of the major decision areas that must be dealt with in compensating employees. These decisions center in the major systems developed to administer the ongoing compensation process. These systems and the decisions that activate them move from the broad system of establishing the organizational pay level, through developing the pay struc-

[1] J. W. Gardner, *Excellence: Can We Be Equal and Excellent Too?* (New York: Harper & Row, Pub., 1961).

ture, to the more specific decisions of the pay system designed to determine the pay rate for the individual employee. In addition, the book explores the supporting decisions of the form that pay takes (direct or benefits), pay treatment of specific employee groups, and the planning and control of compensation. In addition, there is more of a focus on performance-motivation models, although the equity model is still appropriate. The extent of these changes made it most convenient to start almost from scratch and rewrite large portions of the book.

Part I of the book adds a chapter on the environment of compensation. It is clear that what is happening outside the organization has a dramatic effect on how compensation is administered within. The chapters on wage structure (part III) have increased the discussion of establishing a wage structure and shortened the discussion of job evaluation. The discussion of pay systems (part IV) now includes a chapter on pay for performance, and the chapter on incentive plans includes a great deal more on gain sharing. Finally, the last chapter is on discrimination in pay, which has become a major issue and one that will not go away until there are some substantive changes in compensation administration practices and, more importantly, results.

This book has gone through revisions for 32 years now (it was first entitled *Wage and Salary Administration*). To acknowledge all the people who have suggested approaches and emphasis would be impossible. We hope that the scholars and practitioners with whom we have had contact both in person and through their writings will recognize that we are trying to use their best ideas. We only hope that we have given them credit where it was due. If we did not get it right, we take full responsibility.

A great deal of this book is the result of a friendship between the authors that has extended over 20 years and countless luncheons at which the book and more broadly the topic of compensation has been discussed in depth. Betty Ann Belcher was of great help in typing, editing, and transforming Dave's scribbling on yellow pads into finished manuscript for as long as she was able. Betty Atchison was critic, goad, and supporter when needed. But her major contribution was to obtain an IBM personal computer for Tom for Christmas some years ago. That gift has changed Tom's world.

The previous editions of this book were well received and used in a variety of courses in different college departments.

Professors who are examining this book for adoption in their course may note that this book does not contain many of the pedagogical features of numerous textbooks. This has been purposeful, since this book is used considerably as a reference by professionals. However, an instructor's manual is available, and it contains discussion and examination questions (essay and multiple choice) as well as exercises, cases, and term projects. It was also in evidence in the offices of many compensation practitioners throughout the country. We sincerely hope that this edition is as useful as past editions appear to have been.

David W. Belcher
Thomas J. Atchison

PART
I

THE THEORY
AND ENVIRONMENT
OF COMPENSATION
ADMINISTRATION

"What do we need to think about if we are going to set up a new pay plan for this division?"

"Does the low unemployment rate mean that we should raise wages to keep our employees from changing companies?"

"I don't see why we have to offer so much to these new college graduates; they ought to be thankful to have a job!"

"I think it's unfair that Jim makes more money than I do!"

"How do we get more production out of our employees?"

"You can't pay women less than men for the same job!"

These questions and comments reflect the types of decisions organizations have to make each day regarding how people are paid. In particular, they reflect the environment in which these decisions are made and the theory underlying them. These topics are the subject of part I (chapters 1–4) of this book. These first four chapters set a framework for the discussion in later parts of the way in which organizations make the wide variety of decisions concerning what would seem to be a rather simple thing—paying employees.

Chapter 1 develops a model of compensation administration that illustrates how these various decisions relate to each other. Chapter 2 describes the environments that compensation decision makers must consider, as opportunities or constraints. Chapters 3 and 4 deal with the applicable theories, economic and behavioral, of why compensation decisions can be expected to produce certain results.

1

A Model
of Compensation
Administration

Almost every worker receives a paycheck at some regular interval. The amounts of these paychecks vary enormously, from the minimum wage to the salary of the chief executive of a major corporation. Why the particular amount of each paycheck? If we asked the recipients, we might get answers like these:

> "I worked all week."
> "My job is very important."
> "I did a good job on that project."
> "I'm paid what I'm worth!"
> "This is the market rate for my job."
> "This job is boring and the work conditions are terrible!"

These answers are almost as diverse as the amount on the paycheck. People are paid for the work they do. They are also paid for their performance, their skills, their seniority, and a host of other factors. Their pay is influenced by the market value of labor, by unions, by social attitudes, and by other factors. The way the organization they work for sets pay rates also influences the size of the paycheck.

In other words, compensating people is a complex task requiring many decisions. This book is about this daily multitude of decisions and the influences on them both inside and outside the organization.

PAY AND WORK

In short, this book is about pay—how it is determined and managed. But pay, like a coin, has two sides: it represents income to employees, cost to the employer. What the employer provides the employee is called a *wage* or a *salary*. Often, the term *compensation* is used to indicate the various forms of pay—money, benefits, nonfinancial rewards.

What the employee provides the employer is labor service, usually called *work*. This labor service consists of many different kinds of employee behavior, for example: showing up regularly and on time, carrying out tasks dependably, cooperating with others, making useful suggestions.

So pay or compensation represents an exchange between employee and organization. Each gives something in return for something else.

Significance of Compensation

To an employee, pay is a primary reason for working. For some people, it may be the only reason. For most of us, it is the means by which we provide for our own and our family's needs. Few people refuse to accept pay for their work. Perhaps fewer would continue to work if they were told they would not be paid. Pay can represent status or recognition for accomplishment to an employee.

Compensation is also important to organizations. It represents a large proportion of expenditures. In manufacturing firms it is seldom as low as 20 percent; in service enterprises it is often as high as 80 percent. Even more important, organizations try to accomplish many goals with compensation—attracting and retaining people and motivating them to perform more effectively, for example.

Compensation is also significant in the operation of the economy. Salaries and wages account for about 60 percent of the gross national product. Compensation is the largest type of income.

COMPENSATION DOMAINS

So far we have established that compensation (1) represents an employment contract, and (2) is important to employees, organizations, and the economy. But what class of variable does it represent? In what scholarly discipline does it belong? What kind of theory is applicable to it?

An Economic Concept

Compensation is a price for a factor of production. As such it serves to allocate scarce human resources to productive uses. To the employer, compensation is the price paid for labor services. As an economic concept, compensation is governed by the same logic as any other purchase by a firm—to get the greatest quantity and the highest quality for the money. By the same logic, the worker is selling labor services to obtain income and holds out for the highest price obtainable. The actions of these buyers and sellers are supposed to set the price and to allocate labor (employee services) to its most productive use.

But the market for labor services differs in many ways from the market for commodities. Labor service is perishable. If today's labor is not purchased today it has no value tomorrow. Also, labor service may vary from hour to hour and day to day because it varies with the ability of a person to work. Furthermore, the labor supplier cannot be separated from the labor services supplied: he or she can change the quality and quantity of those services.

This variability of supply has advantages and disadvantages to the employer. Through various personnel policies and practices, the quality and quantity of labor services may be enhanced. Also, the labor supplier can quickly fill the needs of the organization as they change. This flexibility of labor supply permits the employer to vary his or her demands.

Because the employer's demand for labor services is derived from the demand for the goods and services the organization supplies, any change in demand may change the labor services needed. These changes and the variety of labor supplies needed at any one time are evidence of how organizations depend on the variability of labor supplies.

But this variability is also a disadvantage. The variability of both demands and supplies makes it difficult for the purchaser to quote a price. The real cost of labor services to the purchaser is the cost per unit of output. But the seller requires that a price be quoted in advance. Hence, the purchaser must offer a price before the bargain is made. This price must come from estimates of the value of average quality and quantity of labor services in this exchange. This value is in turn derived from cost per unit of product or service.

The supplier of labor service likewise experiences difficulty in deciding what price to accept. The labor supplier can, at best, know only the range of "going rates" for particular jobs. Other aspects of the employment exchange—design of the job, working conditions, supervision, work associates, personnel policies and practices—are typically unknown before the person is hired. Translating these elements into money terms is not easy.

The *labor market* is assigned the task of making sense out of these forces. It brings together purchasers and sellers of labor services, sets prices, and seeks to allocate labor to its most productive uses. Many labor markets exist, corresponding to the many types of labor service and the many types of employees of labor services. Neither a balance between demands and supplies nor a single price is likely to emerge for a single type of labor service. A single price, when it does appear, is usually caused by restrictions on the market mechanism—a strong union.

If compensation for labor services were influenced only by economic forces, pay for similar work would be equal. Differences in pay between occupations would reflect only scarcities that the market had not had time to adjust or actual differences in ability.

This brief description of compensation as an economic variable shows that economic analysis is essential in any study of compensation. But the differences between labor markets and other markets suggest that economic analysis alone is not sufficient.

A Psychological Concept

Compensation (pay) represents the psychological contract between the individual and the organization. An organization's reward practices have consequences only through this contract. Thus pay as a psychological concept is pay viewed from the standpoint of the individual.

The situation and the needs, perceptions, and attitudes of the individual determine behavior. But the situation and the individual are not independent, because the situation is that perceived by the individual. Needs are felt states both influencing and influenced by perceptions. Means for satisfying needs are those perceived by individuals and interpreted as such through attitudes (categories of past experiences). One need may be satisfied by a number of means, and one means may satisfy a number of needs.

The psychological contract between the individual and the organization attains reality through perceptions. Rewards offered by the organization enter the contract only if the individual perceives them. In fact, both organizations and employees often speak and act as if they believe that employees work only for money. But even carefully controlled laboratory experiments of simple employment contracts show that many other rewards are operating. Pay is perceived by most people as a means of satisfying many kinds of needs. But many other factors (interesting work, congenial associates, competent supervision, and security, for example) may also be perceived as rewards.

Rewards are offered by organizations to motivate many types of behavior. Which rewards motivate what kinds of behavior, and how rewards operate are functions of perceptions and attitudes. Motivation is a complex phenomenon only partially understood. All rewards appear to follow the law of diminishing returns. It is therefore necessary to determine whether a particular reward motivates, and if so, within what range.

Thus pay is a psychological concept much involved with motivating the behavior of individuals in organizations. As such it complements the economic perspective by emphasizing the perceptions of individuals.

A Sociological Concept

Pay is a status symbol within organizations and society. In less complex societies, the status of individuals is a product of many standards of judgment—their families, friends, occupations, educations, and religious and political affiliations, for example. In large, mobile societies, many of these standards are harder to measure and become less significant. Income as a symbol of status does not present this problem.

Organizations create status structures of jobs. Status differences are measured by both organizations and individuals in terms of pay differences. In fact, employees learn to place associates in the status structure of the organization according to how much they are paid.

Because pay is such a universal measure of status in organizations, it is easy to understand why even small differences in pay assume great significance. Also explained is the symbolic significance of methods of payment and frequency of payment. *Salary* may imply a status different from that of *wage*, and a yearly salary a higher status than a monthly or weekly salary. This symbolic significance adds another dimension to the importance of compensation to individuals. As pay acquires more meanings, its importance increases.

Compensation viewed as a status measure helps to explain the force of custom and tradition in pay determination. The protection of present status and the desire to improve it appear to be universal human values. Protection of present status gives force to custom defined as "what is right." Custom and tradition require that change be justified. The force of custom is conservative. When changes are made they call forth numerous other changes based on traditional relationships.

These values operate within an organization as well as in society in general. In designing the status structure of jobs and pay, an organization is influenced by what pay the job commanded in the past and what other organizations are paying at present. The force of outside influences varies with the kind of people hired, their attachment to the organization, and the similarity of the organization's jobs to those found elsewhere. If the organization can create unique jobs, hire only for beginning jobs, and do its own training for higher-level jobs, outside influence is minimized. But customary relationships that are just as conservative soon arise inside the organization. Groups within the organization struggling for status and pay bring forces at least as powerful as traditional forces from outside the organization.

Unions are as subject to these forces as employing organizations. In fact, unions tend to serve as channels through which customary relationships are made or restored. Both unions and employing organizations are subject to group pressures. Both hesitate to violate customary relationships.

Viewing compensation as a sociological concept focuses neither on the organization nor on individuals but on the relationship between them. This mutual influence of individuals and organizations and of groups within and without constitutes another dimension of compensation.

A Political Concept

Compensation as a political concept involves the use of power and influence. Organizations, unions, groups, and individual employees all use their power to influence pay. Unions exert influence at the time the contract is bargained and during the life of the contract through the grievance procedure. Similarly, compensation in unionized organizations influences that in nonunion organizations.

Organizations exert power in the same situations. In addition, some choose to be *pay leaders* and thus become major forces in labor markets. Within organizations, groups try to use their power to enhance their influence and pay. As organizations acquire more differentiated but interdependent units, more and more individuals achieve power to influence compensation. Highly skilled individuals in demand by other employers also have the power to influence their pay.

Compensation as a political concept involves no notion that the parties have equal power. Nor does all the power reside on the side of the organization. The political perspective stresses accommodating the influence of all the parties.

An Equity Concept

Few discussions of compensation are conducted without repeated appeals to fairness. Phrases such as "a fair day's pay" or "the just wage" are common. In both cases, the equity sought is distributive justice—the idea that returns should be proportionate to contributions.

But problems occur in the definition of contributions. Not everyone agrees on what contributions are being sought or obtained. As a consequence, there are no universal standards of equity.

Because people have different ideas of what to measure and how to measure, opinions differ widely on what justice, fairness, and equity mean in pay. Everybody agrees that justice in distribution should be based on merit of some sort. But people do not understand the same thing by merit.[1]

This probably means that equity is best viewed from the eyes of the beholder. This in turn may mean that although equity in compensation can exist for both the organization and the individual, this situation is unlikely unless it results from bargaining and a relatively complete specification of the terms.

Viewing compensation as an equity concept means analyzing pay from the separate viewpoints of the parties. Ideally, compensation will be adjudged fair by all of them.

A Multidiscipline Concept

Compensation has thus been studied selectively by those in separate disciplines. Economists have focused on the price (wage) of a factor of production and abstracted employee behavior into labor units employed (typically in terms of working hours). Psychologists have focused on the needs of individuals and the means by which they may be met by organizations, emphasizing less the needs of the organization. Sociologists, political scientists, and philosophers have not often studied compensation per se, but concepts they have developed for other purposes may be usefully applied to the study of pay.

THE PARTIES

Our attempt in the previous pages to pin down the appropriate domain for the study of compensation assumes the existence of certain organizations, groups, and individuals involved in compensation decisions. It will be useful now to enumerate these parties. The employing organization may be a private profit-seeking organization, a nonprofit entity, or a government agency. Through pay policies and practices, all of these organizations seek to obtain the participation of the types, number, and quality of employees needed. They may also use pay policies and practices to elicit certain types of employee behavior. Profit-seeking private organizations range from marginal operations very sensitive to changes in labor markets to large, closed bureaucracies relatively isolated from labor-market influences. Nonprofit entities and government agencies can vary in exactly the same way.

---

[1]See the excerpt from bk. V of Aristole's *N Ethics* in *Man and Man: The Social Philosophers*, ed. S. Commins and R. N. Linscott (New York: Random House, 1947), pp. 87–92.

Employees of organizations fall into several categories: (1) production employees (those who work on the products or provide the services of the organization), (2) clerical employees, (3) sales employees, (4) technical employees, (5) professional employees, (6) supervisors, and (7) managers. Although the pay of these employee groups is determined on similar grounds and administered in similar ways, these determinants are not identical. Pay determinants may be weighted differently for different employee groups. One reason for this is that the numbers and types of employees change with changes in technology.

Unions, as representatives of employees, are parties to both pay determination and pay administration. One or several unions may represent production employees. Where clerical employees are organized, they are often represented by the same union as production employees. Some technical and professional employees are organized, usually in a separate union. It is conceivable that changing production technology could foster unionization of employee groups now primarily not organized.

The public is a party to compensation determination. But public participation seldom occurs except through the pressure of public opinion and through government policy. Consumers are very much concerned with pay questions, but no mechanism exists for their voice to be heard. Individuals on fixed incomes (pensions, for example) are much concerned with possible inflationary effects of pay increases.

Federal, state, and municipal governments are also parties to compensation determination. Public policy directly influences pay decisions, as does the less direct policy influencing collective bargaining.

Other parties, of course, may be involved in pay determination. For example, suppliers and industrial customers of large corporations may indirectly influence or be influenced by a pay dispute.

Under our system, all of these parties either have a voice in or are influenced by compensation decisions. Making pay decisions serve this variety of interests is not easy.

A MODEL OF COMPENSATION DECISIONS

We have said that compensating employees necessitates a series of decisions. The product of these decisions is a pay rate for each employee in the organization. The decisions to be made consist of three core decisions—those involving *pay level, pay structure,* and *pay system.* Supporting these are three other decisions, concerning *pay form, pay treatment* for special groups, and *pay administration.* All these decisions are influenced by a number of environmental and organizational variables, such as the *economic, social/cultural,* and *legal environments* and the *organization's structure* and *work force.* All these variables are represented in figure 1–1 and described in the pages that follow.

The broadest of the core decisions is the *pay level* decision. This decision determines how much the organization will pay for labor services, or what its average pay will be. *Pay level* refers to the average pay for jobs, for departments, or for the entire enterprise. An average pay must be set that will secure and keep a productive work force. Major considerations in the pay level deci-

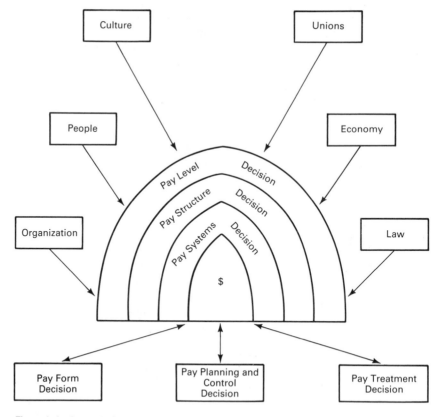

Figure 1–1 A model of compensation decisions and determinants

sion are (1) public policy, (2) pay for comparable work in the community or industry (usually called the "going rate"), and (3) company response to economic, political, and social issues. These considerations may be weighed unilaterally or together with the union(s) representing employees.

The second core decision is the *pay structure* decision, which focuses on the relationships between jobs within the organization and thus pay. Pay structure decisions usually involve arraying jobs in a hierarchy and setting pay for these jobs relative to their status within the hierarchy.

Together the pay level and pay structure decisions determine the *pay for jobs*. In addition, they involve external and internal standards. Presumably, pay level decisions ensure that the organization is in line with the requirements of the external environment, and pay structure decisions ensure that the pay for jobs is internally consistent.

Although pay level and pay structure decisions have been cited as providing external and internal equity,[2] it might be more accurate to relate pay

[2]G. T. Milkovich and J. M. Newman, *Compensation* (Plano, Tex.: Business Publications, 1984).

level to external competitiveness and pay structure to internal equity (fairness). If equity is synonymous with fairness, it seems meaningless in economic decisions.

The third core decision involves determining the pay of individual employees on the same job. Of course, it is possible for all employees on the same job to get the same pay, in which case no decision is needed. But once a decision is made to differentiate the pay of employees on the same job, two further decisions are required: (1) how to differentiate among employees, and (2) whether to pay for time or for output. We can label the first of these decisions as *individual pay determination* and the second as the *pay method* decision. Adopting the designation of *pay system* for both decisions makes sense.[3]

The first supporting decision is *pay form*, the composition of the pay the individual receives. The major part is money, or take-home pay. But a large proportion is in benefits of several kinds.

The second supporting decision involves the *pay treatment* of some special employee groups. Although the organization wants similar behavior from all employee groups, compensation policies and practices may differ somewhat for salespeople, professionals, and managers.

The final supporting decision involves ensuring that pay achieves organization and individual objectives and meets public policy goals. Those responsible for *compensation planning and control* seek answers to questions of efficiency, effectiveness, and legality (discrimination in pay is a particularly important issue today).

Compensation administration as defined by this book is the organizational process of arriving at the decisions just described. Actually, the separation of pay determination and management into these six decisions is an analytical convenience to aid understanding. It is quite possible though, for an organization to use one set of procedures in two or more decisions. Also, each of these decisions affect the other decisions. Perhaps a bit more detail on each decision would be useful.

Pay Levels

The level of pay of an organization is a response to the changing pressures of the labor market. If it is too low, the organization may have difficulty attracting and holding qualified people. There may also be legal penalties from those charged with administering minimum-wage and public-contract laws. Unions within or seeking entry into the organization may exert pressure. If the pay level is too high, on the other hand, the competitive position of the firm in the product market may suffer. In times of wage controls, too high a level may bring government sanctions.

An organization's pay level is decided after consideration of many factors, among them are (1) public policy on pay, (2) going wages for comparable work in the community and/or industry, (3) union wage policy and collective bargaining, and (4) management's philosophy on proper pay levels as reflected in its reaction to the economic, social, and legal environment.

[3]H. G. Heneman and D. P. Schwab, *Perspectives on Personnel/Human Resource Management*, 3rd ed. (Homewood, Ill.: Richard D. Irwin, 1986), p. 234.

Pay Structure

Relationships between the pay of different jobs within the organization may be more important to employees than pay level. Although the pay level may attract qualified employees, inequitable pay relationships may do the opposite. If, for example, Herb is earning less money than Jim, on a job he believes is worth more than Jim's, he is likely to consider the situation unfair and will likely do something about it.

Preventing such inequities and correcting them if they do occur are two of the objectives of pay structure decisions. Pay structures may be set up by management judgment or constructed through collective bargaining. The technique most often used, however, is formal or informal *job evaluation.*

Although there are several methods of job evaluation, they all involve the following steps. First, jobs are analyzed and job descriptions written. Then the factors on which pay will be based are identified; such factors as skill, effort, and responsibility are typical. Next, jobs are evaluated on the basis of these factors. The result is a logical *job structure.* The final step is assigning pay rates that relate to the job structure. These rates constitute a *wage structure.*

At this final step, pay level and pay structure decisions come together. Often, a *wage survey* is used as an aid in both decisions. Ideally, the pay rates not only meet the test of internal consistency but are in tune with the external environment. But as we will see, some of the most difficult pay decisions involve correlating these two separate standards. Figure 1–2 offers a useful way of distinguishing pay levels and pay structures. Pay level is the height of the line above the x-axis. Pay structure is the slope of the line. (Line b represents a higher pay level than line a, but its structure is the same.)

Pay System

Pay level and pay structure provide a decision on the pay for jobs. It is individuals who are paid, however, and a decision is now required as to whether all individuals on the same job shall receive the same pay. Most organizations decide that employees on the same job will get different pay. Some or-

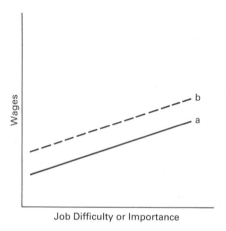

Figure 1–2 Pay level and pay structure comparison

ganizations pay high-seniority employees more than low-seniority employees, presumably because they are concerned with keeping senior employees. Most organizations state that higher performers are paid more than lower performers. These pay systems are called *merit systems*. Often pay differences among people on the same job are based on a combination of performance and seniority, on the assumption that the organization wants to reward both membership and effectiveness.

Actually, a decision by the organization to pay for performance of employees can be actuated not only by a merit system but by an *incentive system*. The difference is that although merit systems attempt to *relate* pay to performance, incentive systems *tie* pay to performance. Under an incentive system, the usual practice is to set a base rate for the job and to vary individual pay with some measure of output. Logically, the applicability of an incentive system depends on technology. Practically, however, it depends more on tradition and custom. Incentive systems involve substantial administrative costs but often are associated with raising productivity above costs. Incentive plans can be based on group or plantwide output as well as individual output.

Pay Form

Pay form refers to the makeup of the pay an individual receives. As noted, most of an employee's pay is cash in the form of take-home pay. But a growing portion is indirect, in the form of benefits. At least one third of an average employee's pay consists of benefits. Some are required by legislation; others are voluntarily provided by the employer or are required by union agreement. The growth of benefits, employee differences in benefit needs, and greater individualization of organization benefit programs are important issues in pay form decisions.

Another way of viewing pay form is to recognize that in most organizations employees receive three forms of pay: membership pay, job pay, and performance pay. *Membership pay* is given employees as a consequence of their joining and remaining in the organization. *Job pay* is based upon accepting a particular job and performing at a satisfactory level. *Performance pay* is contingent upon differential employee behavior. In this sense, all forms of pay are contingent on some form of employee work behavior.

Pay Treatment

Although the objectives of an organization's pay are likely to be quite similar for all employee groups, pay programs and practices may differ for some of them. Ideally, where pay decisions and programs are differentiated they are based on differences in employee behavior requirements and pay systems designed to meet them. Salespeople, professionals, and managers are examples of groups deserving separate pay analysis.

Pay Administration

The final pay decision is whether the previous ones are achieving the goals of the organization and of employees. The primary question is economic: is the firm really getting the employee contributions that it is paying for? In most organizations, pay is expected to obtain many different kinds of employee behavior. Is the organization getting the value it is paying for? Are employees getting the rewards they want for their contributions?

Other questions are legal: are the pay programs meeting legal requirements? Do regular audits show that pay programs do not discriminate against members of protected groups?

Determinants of Compensation Decisions

Compensation decisions are not made in a vacuum: they must consider a number of environmental and organizational variables. As indicated earlier in this chapter, compensation is at least partly an *economic* concept: economic conditions are a major influence upon what an employee is paid. Tied to this economic environment is the impact of *unions* on the wages, both industry wide and in each organization.

Likewise, the *social* environment has an impact on compensation decisions. Members of a society have ideas about the "worth" of different jobs, and these ideas need to be taken into account. The social environment has been changing dramatically along with the changing views of women in the work force. These views have spurred probably the strongest recent impact on compensation decisions, changes in *law*.

Compensation decisions are also affected by the dynamics of the particular organization. Employee pay must be consistent within the *organization's structure*. The *organization's culture* helps determine the priority to be placed upon various compensation goals. The organization's *work-force characteristics* influence the success of different compensation programs.

THE PLAN OF THIS BOOK

In this book, compensation administration is viewed as a set of organizational decisions subject to a set of environmental and organization influences. The remainder of part I examines these influences. Chapter 2 deals with the environments of compensation decisions in the 1980s. Chapters 3 and 4 explore the economic and behavioral theories concerning these environmental influences. Part II covers the pay level decision. Part III analyzes the pay structure decision. Part IV covers the last core decision, concerning the pay system. Part V focuses on the pay form decision, specifically benefits. Part VI describes special pay programs for sales, professional, managerial, and international employees. Part VII consists of a chapter on the planning and control of compensation programs and a chapter on the primary issue in compensation today, discrimination in pay.

2

The Environments of Compensation Administration

The decisions outlined in chapter 1 are reached within economic, social, legal, union, and organizational environments. Let us consider each in turn.

THE ECONOMIC ENVIRONMENT

Compensation decisions are made by a multitude of employers and apply to millions of employees. Employing organizations may be classified in varying ways. One classification consists of private profit-seeking enterprises, not-for-profit organizations, and government entities—a classification that seems to result in smaller differences in employment practices over time. Another classification is by size, measured in several ways, all of which result in significant wage differences. Another is by industry, which results in wage and occupational differences at least as large as differences by size. Still another is by industrial sector—manufacturing or service, with the latter representing over 60 percent of employment but different (often lower) wage levels. There are also differences in the location of employing organizations—section of the country and size of the community, all of which affect wage decisions and levels. For our purposes, the thread that runs through all of these classifications is the presence of employers with employees who demand pay if they are to continue to work. Even volunteer organizations must provide some rewards to their members.

Employees differ—by occupation, skill level, age, sex, and minority or majority status—in the compensation they are willing to accept. These differences affect their reward preferences, and their views about what they contribute to the organization.

Employers use compensation as the primary magnet for attracting employees, and the amount offered is a strong consideration for employees in choosing jobs. These employment exchanges are made in a multitude of labor markets that vary greatly and are not very efficient.

The approaches to solving compensation issues come from labor markets and are supplemented by rules imposed by employers, unions, and governments. Market forces and the imposed rules may or may not conflict.

Labor markets do some things well and others poorly. They are reasonably effective in determining relative wage rates for different jobs and in raising wages and living standards with increases in productivity and national output. Labor markets also do reasonably well in determining relative wage levels for different occupations, establishments, industries, and regions. Labor markets sort millions of workers with varying skills and interests into thousands of different jobs and employers—a task that perhaps couldn't be done administratively without a great loss in personal freedom.

But labor markets do a poor job of regulating working conditions and personnel policies. They still set limits, because workers can quit if conditions become too unsatisfactory. But the limits are quite wide, because it is difficult for the worker to determine these conditions before employment. Perhaps the major reason labor markets do poorly in regulating working conditions and personnel policies is that most workers regard changing employers as a last resort rather than an opportunity and typically try to stay with their present employer and to change that employer's behavior through a union. Also, labor markets almost always contain more people seeking jobs than jobs seeking workers: they do not *clear* (balance supply and demand). These shortcomings of labor markets are major reasons for the employer, union, and government rules that supplement the operation of market forces.

In the following sections we attempt to broadly describe the "real world" economic environment of compensation determination and management. Markets consist of supplies and demands. This holds for labor markets, although they differ from other markets because of the relatively long duration of employment relationships.

Labor Supply

The quantity of the labor supply is termed the *labor force*. A person is included in the labor force if he or she is 16 years of age or older, is able to work, and is either working or looking for work.

The size of the labor force is determined by the population and the number in the labor force (termed the *labor-force participation rate*). Population growth increases the potential labor force. The "baby boom" (roughly 1946–1956) greatly increased today's labor force. The labor-force participation rate has been changed by the greatly increased participation of adult women and the lower rates of participation by people under 20 and over 65. Some of the changes predictable into the 1990s are fewer young entrants, a bulge in the 25-to-44 age bracket, more women, more older workers, more part-time employment, and more moonlighting.[1]

Unemployment influences labor-force participation in two opposite ways: additional family members look for work when the major breadwinner is unemployed, and discouraged workers leave the labor force believing no jobs for them exist. The latter force is greater.

The quantity of the labor supply is also determined by the number of hours labor-force members want to work. Desired hours per week or per year are affected by the hourly wage rate and other income received by the family. Working hours have been declining over time, especially per year. Much variation exists among the hours people want to work.

Labor-force quality is determined by the formal education, on-the-job training, and experience of the labor force. This quality (termed *human capital*) has been increasing relative to physical capital in the United States.

Labor Demand

Our labor force is employed in many thousands of specific jobs, in specific locations, with specific employee requirements. The pattern of employment is constantly changing. The labor force is constantly being reshaped to fit changes in the demand for labor. This constant change is due to changes in product demand, work methods, and the location of organizations. It is also a response to cyclical fluctuations in demand, the birth and death of organizations, the entrance and exit of labor-force members, and the search for better jobs.

Foreign competition and changes in consumer tastes have resulted in shifts in the relative importance of industries. One notable change has been the rise in the service sector which now employs over 60 percent of the labor force with the proportion still rising. These shifts have changed the occupational distribution. The demand for professional and technical skills has increased greatly, for example. The demand for clerical workers has also increased. Each of the occupational categories (unskilled, semiskilled, skilled, clerical, technical, professional, managerial) imply different levels or skills, each containing a wide range of jobs in terms of the skill and training required. Further, these differences in skill requirements within and between categories are increasing. There is a current trend toward demand for both employees with high skills and low skills, with the traditional blue-collar skilled worker in lower demand.

Labor demand also varies by area. Job demand may be increasing in some areas (such as the Sunbelt) while declining in others (such as the Snowbelt). This rising demand in growing regions is met largely by migration from declining areas.

When labor demand shifts, people learn the jobs in demand and move to where these jobs are. The more the demand shifts, the more workers will have to change jobs. Workers regard enforced job changes as disasters rather

[1]C. Kerr and J. Rosow, eds., *Work in America: The Decade Ahead* (New York: Van Nostrand Reinhold, 1979).

than opportunities. Much movement raises unemployment. Also, displaced workers may not have the qualifications to fill vacancies among the jobs in demand.

Labor Markets

The demand for and supply of specific skills meet in labor markets. This meeting determines wage rates for particular jobs and brings together employers who need workers and workers who need jobs.

The term *market* usually means an area within which buyers and sellers are in sufficiently close communcation that price tends to be the same throughout the area. The size of the area may vary from the neighborhood to the whole world. Labor market size varies with skill, both type and level. Managers and professionals, for example, have a national or international market. For most manual, clerical, and technical jobs, labor markets are local, often defined by commuting distance. A locality contains many specialized markets for various occupations and skills; these markets are linked by the possibility of transfer between occupations.

In fact, each organization can be considered a separate labor market for two reasons. First, the organizations usually promote from within rather than filling positions from the outside labor market. Second, they create jobs that are organizationally specific—ones where the organization trains the person so that the skills obtained have little transferability to the outside labor market. These actions by the organization create what is called the *internal labor market.*

Neither workers nor employers have sufficient information about labor markets and must seek it in order to make decisions about wages and employment. Both unemployment and job vacancies exist at the same time, usually more of the former. Moreover, workers are reluctant to quit their jobs and employers are aware of their investment in present employees.

Labor markets may be viewed as a flow of people from unemployment to job vacancies where both are being constantly renewed. But the two "pools" are related in that a change in one creates forces that change the other. The flow during the year is much larger than the net change over a year.

Employers can cut their costs of seeking labor market information (recruitment) by paying above-average wages, hoping to attract a pool of applicants. They can also attempt to keep present employees and to recruit friends of present employees. But the favored method is to use internal labor markets as a source of employees so that only a few jobs are filled from external labor markets.

A consequence of the use of internal labor markets is that an employee who has moved up the job hierarchy is more reluctant than usual to quit. Moving to another employer means starting at the bottom.

Because employers have hiring standards that they attempt to meet through employee selection, the labor supply of the enterprise includes only those people the employer is willing to consider. Since employers tend to raise and lower hiring standards with general unemployment rates, they are in effect changing the labor supply.

Workers also seek labor market information. Employees may look for a better job, either within the organization or outside. Managers and professionals usually have another job before leaving and thus suffer less unemployment. Workers at lower levels, because they have less free time to search and because employers discourage job switching, may quit to look full-time for a better job if unemployment is low and if they have transferable skills.

Job seekers include those who have quit, those who have been laid off or discharged, and those who are entering or reentering the labor force. A job search involves costs of lost income and benefits of information on better job openings. Information on which organization is offering what wage rate and which organizations are hiring may result from the hunt, but the worker typically has only one offer at a time and must decide quickly. The decision usually involves a comparison of the costs of continued unemployment and the possible gain from continuing to search. As time goes on, expectation of gains falls and the cost of unemployment rises. Eventually, a job is found that meets the worker's minimum standards. The state of the labor market greatly influences the time involved in this search.

This employment-seeking process is one reason for different wage rates for the same skill in the same labor market. These differences would be eliminated only if workers continued to search as long as wage differences remained.[2]

In summary, the economic environment in which compensation takes place is unique. Employment exchanges are made in hundreds of thousands of labor markets. Labor markets almost never set one price, do not clear (balance supplies and demands), and are constantly in flux. Both organizations and workers must search to find an acceptable employment exchange.

The economic environment of compensation administration, it is generally agreed, has the strongest impact on the outcome—the pay of individual workers. But other environments also influence compensation determination and management.

THE SOCIAL ENVIRONMENT

The social environment in which compensation administration is practiced may be discussed in terms of work and workers. This section examines the major forces that shape work in our society and the people who do the work. Much current discussion focuses on how both work and workers have changed, issues that must be faced by our society.

Work

Defining work is not as easy as it appears. Work is what most of us do to earn a livelihood, but it is also done by members of volunteer organizations. To many of us, work consists of activities performed for others, but this would exclude the self-employed. Perhaps work is best described as sustained activity whose purpose is the accomplishment of goals. If we add "for rewards" (usually pay), this definition is sufficient for our purposes.

Most of us work both because we have to and because we want to. Our collective survival is no longer dependent on whether we choose to work. Al-

---

[2]G. J. Stigler, "Information in the Labor Market," *Journal of Political Economy,* supplement, October 1962, pp. 94–105.

though many projections have appeared about the future of work, few have projected a workless society. The future of work is determined by numerous forces: the goods and services we demand (want and can afford), the number and qualifications of workers, and the technologies available, for example. Rising expectations of workers make relative incomes a driving force. Rising levels of education lead us to expect greater challenges and skill requirements in our jobs. Technologies however, may constrain the realization of our expectations.

Although rising per capita income might suggest that fewer workers and less work time are available, this has not been the case. The length of the workweek has remained stable for almost 50 years. The proportion of the population in the labor force has increased, largely because of the increased participation of women. However, we are working shorter work years, because of longer vacations, more holidays, and more part-time employment.

Changes in Work

Today's jobs differ from yesterday's jobs. The most visible change is the shift toward white-collar and service employment. The proportion of unskilled jobs has declined steadily, and the most boring and punishing tasks have disappeared or are done by machines. True, there haven't been uniform gains in skill requirements, and threats of displacement of low-skilled workers through automation persist.

The growth of the service sector has been the most pervasive change in work. Agriculture, manufacturing, and mining no longer represent the typical workplace in the United States or any other industrial country. The shift toward service employment is in many ways a result of rising incomes and technological advance. The surge of women in the labor force has strengthened the demand for personal services. The growth of the service sector has destroyed traditional links between work and physical effort. Increasingly we work with symbols instead of tools and produce reports instead of goods.

Paralleling the growth of the service sector is the change from blue-collar to white-collar employment. By 1981 slightly more than half of the work force held white-collar jobs. Managers and professionals today outnumber unskilled laborers five to one. Artisans and semiskilled workers constitute nearly 90 percent of the blue-collar work force. This growth in professional and managerial jobs reflects in part the size and complexity of organizations. It also reflects the growing importance of research and managerial functions in the use of advanced tehcnologies. Reduction of middle-management positions in many organizations in the early 1980s may lead us to question whether all jobs are essential.

It seems important to recognize that white-collar and blue-collar designations are not necessarily made on the basis of job skills. A wide range of skill levels, work environments, and job attributes occur in both groups. Many blue-collar jobs actually require more skill and provide more challenge than white-collar jobs. Although clerical workers may enjoy a more pleasant environment, the tasks of a skilled factory worker may demand more talent. Many service workers enjoy less status and lower pay than workers on assembly lines.

But structural changes in jobs point in many directions. Professionals and managers historically have required high skills and were awarded high status. The jobs of clerical workers and many service workers have required less skill and hold ambiguous status. The evidence of occupational shifts or fluctuations in skill levels fails to prove that there have been either uniform improvements or deterioration in the quality of work. Some jobs are now cleaner, safer, or more interesting, but others offer less freedom and demand fewer skills. Although many more professional and technical jobs exist, so do stifling and menial work.

A driving force behind occupational change is the continuing process of technological innovation. Its impact on work quality fosters continual debate. Many present-day workplaces are safer and more comfortable. Many automated technologies have reduced requirements for physical labor. But skill requirements have not uniformly improved, and automation may even decrease variety and the opportunity for creativity.

Whether microprocessors and robots will significantly change the nature of most jobs is not known at this time. Although it has been estimated that the current generation of robots could perform about one third of existing factory jobs, the pace of innovation will depend on the relative costs of labor and robots, as well as the supply of and demand for goods and services.[3] Projections of the impact of microprocessors on office employment are even more problematic. It is generally recognized that office technologies will be changing, but there is little agreement on the effects on employment or design of jobs.

Predictions of immediate and massive job losses from microprocessor applications tend to ignore the market and other forces that slow the pace of technological change. The size of the required investment, capacity utilization, and customer and worker attitudes raise barriers to rapid change. If past experience is any guide, work is here to stay.

It is doubtful that automation will have a uniform impact on the quality of work. The worst jobs may disappear as robots march into factories and assume the most dangerous and unpleasant tasks. Computerized technology can offer significant job upgrading—more freedom, more job challenge—but it can also easily do the opposite. Button pushing and machine watching are not very challenging. Computerized technologies also give managers greater ability to monitor worker performance, thus increasing job pressures. Automation can create new health hazards (eyestrain from computer terminals) as well as insecurities aroused by change.

The most serious threat, however, is the possible disparity between skills needed by jobs and worker skills. It seems unlikely that the skills of workers in declining industries will fit the skill requirements in new growth areas. It is equally unlikely that unskilled workers will find jobs in an automated society if preferential treatment is given displaced workers.

The service sector presents a different picture. Here there is an increasing demand for relatively unskilled jobs that provide little discretion. This increasing demand for low-level service skills on one hand and an increasing skill demand in professional areas on the other leads to different predictions about future labor force requirements.

These adjustment problems represent only a part of the occupational shifts and technological changes faced by our labor force due to the growing

[3]*Business Week,* August 3, 1981, p. 62.

size and interdependence of today's markets. The movement toward a world economy will continue to reshape domestic industries and the occupations within them. As in the past, our work force must adjust to changes in requirements.

As we will see in the following discussion of workers and worker values, demographic and value changes have given our labor force more choices. Also, to a considerable extent, the economic system provides a basis for determining if a job is worth doing: employers decide what they are willing to pay, and workers what they are willing to accept. Increasing choice among our labor force means that the work society chooses to accomplish will be determined increasingly by what workers want to do, as well as by what tasks society wants done.

Workers

In recent years, projected changes in our labor force have received even more attention than forthcoming changes in work. Much of this attention has focused on demographic changes and their impact. But a spirited debate about whether worker values have changed—whether we have a "new breed" of workers—appears to be continuing.

QUANTITATIVE CHANGES.   Both greater numbers and larger proportions of the population have entered the labor force in recent years. The ratio of workers to the working-age population has been growing, driven by rising expectations and an interest in relative income gains. Much more important, however, have been demographic forces.

The Baby Boom.   The so-called baby boom (1946–1956) greatly changed the age structure of the labor force. In the mid 1960s, the number of younger workers began increasing rapidly, almost doubling the normal yearly growth in the labor force. Much of the growth in the labor force of younger workers occurred among the college trained until the 1970s, when the supply of college graduates outstripped demand. The ensuing drop in college enrollments undoubtedly increased the labor-force participation rates of young people.

Women.   An even more important demographic change in the labor force was the extraordinary increase in female participation. More than three fifths of the growth in the total work force from 1947 to 1976 was the result of increased female participation. Much of this growth was accounted for by married women. In more than 60 percent of all marriages today, the husband is not the sole breadwinner. In 1981, slightly more than 50 percent of all wives held paying jobs outside the home.

The explanation for the tremendous increase in the labor force participation of women is not as simple as the explanation for the increase in younger workers. Part of the explanation may be technological: housekeeping consumes less time today. Also, the number of children in the home has declined. Economic need is another partial explanation. Women provide substantial proportions of family income and are the sole wage earners in a rising percentage of families. Thus, many families could not maintain their economic status without the woman's income.

But economics is only a partial explanation of the increased participation rate of women. It does not explain, for instance, why the participation rate increases with overall family income. Perhaps the strongest explanation of the increased labor force participation of women is sociological. Proper roles for women have been redefined, and women work for the same reasons that men do—a sense of identity and self-esteem.

Of course, women would not have been able to increase their numbers in the work force without favorable labor market conditions. The expanding labor requirements in the growing service sector made women's increased participation possible. Now our economy is dependent on female labor to meet our needs for a labor force. A large return of women to the home would bring our economy to its knees.

Older Men.   Another change in our labor force has been the reduced participation of older men. In the past 30 years, the labor force participation of men has dropped about ten percentage points due to earlier retirement. Much of the explanation is economic—improvements in Social Security benefits. Interestingly, older women's participation has increased rather than decreased.

Part of the explanation is attitudinal. Retirement has acquired a more positive social image along with improved public and private pensions.

The permanence of this reduced labor force participation of older men is in question. Inflation, the extension of protected labor market status to age 70 by the 1977 amendments to the Age Discrimination in Employment Act, and the ongoing debate on Social Security and recent changes in that system, may have begun to reverse the trend to early retirement.

Black Men.   The other segment of society that has been reducing its labor force participation is black men. In the past 30 years, the participation of black men of all ages has dropped almost 15 percent. Unfortunately, this decrease appears best explained by discouragement of black men with their labor market prospects. Poor job opportunities and higher unemployment rates have reduced the attractiveness of participation; transfer payments and the underground economy may be as remunerative as work.

Poverty and Unemployment.   Almost half of all people with incomes below the poverty level continue to work. The unemployed must maintain their labor force attachment to be counted as unemployed. Both of these facts seem to testify to the attractiveness of labor force participation in our society. Even with increasing national unemployment rates over the past two decades, labor-force participation rates grow each year.

Tomorrow's Workers.   Although these quantitative changes in the American work force apparently have more than one explanation, it is possible to make some predictions about our future labor force.[4] Obviously, those based on demographic factors are the most solid.

---

[4]These predictions are made by R. R. Freeman, *Labor Economics*, 2nd ed. (Englewood Cliffs, N.J.: Prentice-Hall, 1979).

Youth Shortage.   Because of the low birth rates of the 1960s, the absolute numbers of young workers must fall sharply in the 1980s. Between 1975 and 1990, the people aged 16 through 24 in the labor force will decline by over one million. One consequence of this should be improved relative earnings for this shortage group. Another should be reduced youth unemployment, which has been especially severe for blacks. The employment prospects for the less qualified young people will improve greatly. The only force that can soften this shortage of youth will be a large inflow of immigrants.

Surplus of Prime-Age Workers.   Also predictable on demographic grounds is a surplus of workers in the 25-to-44 age group. From 1975 to 1990 this "baby boom" group will increase by over 20 million persons, or 55 percent. The consequences of this bunching imply a more rapid rate of economic growth but a fierce competition for promotions. Members of this group will suffer career disappointment and low relative income for their entire working lives. The potential personnel and labor-relations problems resulting from this surplus of prime-age workers present unpleasant prospects in this decade and the next.

A More Educated Labor Force.   Today's workers bring more schooling to the workplace than their predecessors. Tomorrow's young people are more likely to go on to college to improve their career opportunities. Because these workers will be in short supply, their potential return from more education will increase. But because of the increased education of older workers, the rate of increase in average years of schooling in the labor force will decline. Educated workers in the surplus 25-to-44 age group are likely to have problems in getting jobs that require their educational attainment.

As Americans in all occupations enter the labor market with more education, these educational gains may outpace skill requirements. Most of the increase in educational levels has occurred independently of the technical requirements of the labor market. There are rational explanations for the continuing rise in educational attainment, though. For the individual worker, education continues to pay off. Although the income advantage of a college degree is not as great as it used to be, it still broadens employment options and enhances individual earning potential. Because employers rely on formal education as a screening device, the growing number of college graduates forces others to seek higher education in order to compete.

Increased Female Participation.   Female labor force participation is expected to increase by all forecasts. The sectors of the economy that tend to hire relatively many women are likely to grow. If the movement of women into previously male occupations continues, there may be an increased diffusion of women across occupations and industries. In fact, any weakness in demand in traditionally female occupations will create additional pressures for movement into traditionally male jobs. It seems safe to predict that self-employment and management responsibilities for women will continue to grow. Women may even become a majority of those gainfully employed.[5]

[5]L. Harris, "Our Changing Structure of Values," in *Working in the Twenty-First Century,* ed. C. Sheppard and D. C. Carroll (New York: John Wiley, 1980), pp. 123–36.

WORKER VALUES. Much recent discussion of workers has been concerned with their attitudes and values. It has been suggested, for example, that
today's workers are less work-committed, that the usual work incentives have
lost their effectiveness, that a "new breed" of worker has emerged who rejects
traditional values. It is useful to identify three kinds of attitudes, which are not
completely separable: (1) the importance of work to people (job involvement),
(2) what a person wants, needs, or expects from a job (work values), and (3)
how much a person likes or dislikes a job (job satisfaction).

Job Involvement. This attitude, which is often called *work commitment,* is
particularly hard to isolate. That more and more people want jobs is obvious,
but only 13 percent of all working Americans find their work more important
to them than their leisure pursuits.[6] Wanting a job and being willing to work
hard are clearly separable and undoubtedly differ more for some segments of
our work force than others.

Work Values. Work values have been found to vary by occupation, education, sex, and age. Blue-collar workers fit the stereotype of the economic
man. White-collar workers emphasize such intrinsic factors as interesting work
and opportunities to develop abilities somewhat ahead of economic factors.
However, the differences between occupational groups are not very great and
are associated largely with education level. Sex has been found to be associated
with work values: women have generally ascribed greater importance to social
and emotional considerations than men. There is evidence that young workers
place more importance than older people on intrinsic factors such as degree of
challenge, diversity, and freedom.

Yankelovitch insists that a "new breed" of American worker exists
whose work values are different from the traditional definition of a good job—
steady work, good pay, comfortable and safe working conditions, and possibly
an opportunity to get ahead.[7] This new breed takes these things for granted
and demands, in addition, freedom, interesting and challenging work, and a
voice in what goes on. These people believe they are entitled to a good job. But
millions of them who have jobs find the incentive systems so unappealing that
they are not motivated to work hard.

According to Yankelovitch, in the 1970s self-fulfillment was severed
from success for a majority of Americans—the younger, better-educated and
most affluent.[8] A small minority reject success and opt out of the system. Most
value success but find it wanting. They assume that self-fulfillment is to be
found *within* the self. Thus they demand the freedom to express impulses, to
enjoy life now, to call desires entitlements. Leisure has become more important
than family or work. For new-breed women a paid job has become a symbol of
membership in the larger society and a badge of self-worth. In the new value

[6]D. Yankelovich, "Work Values and the New Breed," in *Work in America,* ed. Kerr and
Rosow, p. 3–26.
[7]D. Yankelovich, "Yankelovich on Today's Workers," *Industry Week,* August 6, 1979,
pp. 60–68; and D. Yankelovich, "The New Psychological Contracts at Work," *Psychology
Today,* May 1978, pp. 46–50.
[8]See D. Yankelovich, *New Rules* (New York: Random House, 1981).

system, the individual is more than the role. Being recognized as an individual is more important than having interesting work.

Some consequences of these new values need emphasis. First, there is a strong consensus that a job paid at a fair rate should be guaranteed to everyone who wants to work. Given the demographics of the labor force discussed previously, the competition for jobs, at least in the 1980s, will be fierce. Second, work incentives must be revised to meet the new work values. Employers must recognize that the motivation to take a job and the motivation to work hard are independent and require different approaches. The new values of individualism will require different incentives for different employee groups and perhaps for different individuals. Nonfinancial rewards have become more important to employees and can be used as work incentives.

The proponents of the new-breed hypothesis and the traditional view of American workers are probably both partly right and partly wrong, depending on which worker they are talking about.

Job Satisfaction.   How well a person likes his or her job depends on the discrepancy between an individual's work values and what the job provides. Some of the conclusions from numerous studies of job satisfaction are these: about 80 percent of workers describe themselves as quite satisfied with their jobs. Job satisfaction can be broken down into satisfactions with job features (typically pay, promotional opportunities, supervision, co-workers, and the work itself). Average job satisfaction is lower for disadvantaged minorities. Men and women have about equal job satisfaction. Younger people have lower job satisfaction. Job satisfaction tends to be higher among the more highly educated if their education is used. The connection between job satisfaction and job performance is low.[9]

Information on trends in job satisfaction is less complete and somewhat controversial. A review by the United States Department of Labor in 1974 found 15 national surveys on this topic conducted between 1958 and 1973. In these surveys the percentage of satisfied respondents ranged from 81 to 92. The authors of the review concluded that job satisfaction levels have not changed.[10]

Others disagree. Gallup, Jr., finds lower job satisfaction among youths. Opinion Research Corporation surveys indicate a growing gap between managerial and nonmanagerial employees. The Survey Research Center found lower satisfaction among older workers in 1977 than in 1973 and a greater decline among blue-collar than among white-collar employees.[11]

On balance it may be said that levels of job satisfaction remain high, and that impressions of decline may be exaggerated. But job satisfaction may be declining in certain segments of the labor force, and satisfaction with certain aspects of work may be rising while satisfaction with other aspects may be falling. Because our labor force brings a wide variety of needs and expectations to

[9]R. A. Katzell, "Changing Attitudes toward Work," in *Work in America,* ed. Kerr and Rosow, pp. 35–57.

[10]R. P. Quinn, G. L. Staines, and M. R. McCullough, "Job Satisfaction: Is There a Trend?" *Manpower Research* Monograph #30, U.S. Dept. of Labor, Washington D.C., U.S. Government Printing Office, 1974.

[11] Ibid.

the workplace, their satisfaction is a composite of many reactions to many job attributes.

Nor is it wise to generalize about what factor does or does not increase job satisfaction. A 1977 opinion survey showed that more than three quarters of responding workers would prefer a 10 percent raise to more interesting work. Sociological studies of the most trying work settings have shown that people can find pleasure at work even when they fail to derive satisfaction from the content of their jobs.[12]

THE LEGAL ENVIRONMENT

The legal environment in which compensation administration is practiced consists of federal and state legislation and the regulations imposed by executive branches of these governments. In the case of some developing legal concepts, case law (court decisions) represents the public position. In these three forms, governments are stating public intentions or guides to decision makers. Although private organizations tend to characterize these laws, regulations, and court decisions as constraints, they may also represent opportunities. It is difficult to portray this environment briefly, but in essence the "rules" state that compensation must not be too low or (at times) too high, but that within these limits compensation decisions should be left to the parties at interest. Also, in the interests of fairness, certain groups have been protected and all must be paid when due.

Unfortunately, governments have not labeled the laws, regulations, and cases according to categories of compensation. Nor indeed have they limited them to compensation matters. Because our concern is with compensation, we will focus on the guides of concern to compensation decision makers.

The Wage Legislation

THE FAIR LABOR STANDARDS ACT. The Fair Labor Standards Act (FLSA), often called *the wage and hour law,* has four provisions that affect compensation programs. They concern minimum wages, overtime pay, record-keeping requirements, and equal pay.

Minimum Wages. Minimum-wage provisions set a floor on the amount of pay an employee must receive. The minimum wage per hour starting January 1, 1981, was $3.35. In general, Congress has raised the minimum wage by amending the FLSA whenever the floor falls below about 50 percent of average hourly earnings.

Coverage of the act has also been extended. Today almost all employers are covered by the minimum-wage provisions. Formally, covered employers are those with at least two employees engaged in interstate commerce, producing goods for interstate commerce, or having employees who handle, sell, or otherwise work on goods or materials produced for or moved in interstate

---

[12]S. A. Levitan, and C. M. Johnson, *Second Thoughts on Work* (Kalamazoo, Mich.: W. E. Upjohn Institute for Employment Research, 1982), p. 85.

commerce. Not surprisingly, this has been interpreted to cover almost all employers. Retail or service establishments with annual gross sales of $362,000 (as of January 1, 1982) are covered as well as employers of domestic workers who are paid at least $100 per year. Construction companies, laundries, dry cleaners, and private hospitals and schools are covered regardless of volume of business. Practically speaking just about every business is covered unless it qualifies for one of the special exemptions (very small retailers, fishing and fish processing, seasonal amusement and recreational establishments).

Not all employees are covered, however, and many employers distinguish between exempt and nonexempt employees in their personnel programs. Exempt employees are not covered; nonexempt employees are. The major group of exempt employees are executives, administrative and professional employees, and outside sales personnel whose jobs match the definitions provided by the Wage and Hour Division of the Department of Labor. Placing people on salary does not make them exempt, but where the match between an organization's job and the WH definitions leaves some room for question, amount of weekly pay decides. (See the Wage and Hour Division definitions in table 2–1.) Employers may seek permission to pay less than the minimum to apprentices, handicapped workers, or full-time students.

Table 2–1   Definition of Executive, Administrative, Professional Employees and Outside Salesman

---

541.1 EXECUTIVE

The term "employee employed in a bona fide executive . . . capacity" in section 13(a) (1) of the act shall mean any employee:

(a) Whose primary duty consists of the management of the enterprise in which he is employed or of a customarily recognized department of subdivision thereof; and

(b) Who customarily and regularly directs the work of two or more other employees therein; and

(c) Who has the authority to hire or fire other employees or whose suggestions and recommendations as to the hiring or firing and as to the advancement and promotion or any other change of status of other employees will be given particular weight; and

(d) Who customarily and regularly exercises discretionary powers; and

(e) Who does not devote more than 20 percent, or, in the case of an employee of a retail or service establishment who does not devote as much as 40 percent, of his hours of work in the workweek to activities which are not directly and closely related to the performance of the work described in paragraphs (a) through (d) of this section: *Provided,* That this paragraph shall not apply in the case of an employee who is in sole charge of an independent establishment or a physically separated branch establishment, or who owns at least a 20 percent interest in the enterprise in which he is employed; and

(f) Who is compensated for his services on a salary basis at a rate of not less than $225 per week beginning February 13, 1981 and $250 per week beginning February 13, 1983 (or $180 per week beginning February 13, 1981 and $200 per week beginning February 13, 1983, if employed by other than the Federal Government in Puerto Rico, the Virgin Islands, or American Samoa), exclusive of board, lodging, or other facilities: *Provided,* That an employee who is compensated on a salary basis at a rate of not less than $320 per week beginning February 13, 1981 and $345 per week beginning February 13, 1983 (or $260 per week beginning February 13, 1981 and $285 per week beginning February 13, 1983, if employed by other than the Federal Government in Puerto Rico, the Virgin Islands or American Samoa), exclusive of board, lodging, or other facilities, and whose primary duty consists of the management of the enterprise in which the employee is employed or of a customarily recognized department or subdivision thereof, and includes the customary and regular direction of the work of two or more other employees therein, shall be deemed to meet all the requirements of this section.

Table 2–1 (continued)

541.2 ADMINISTRATIVE

The term "employee employed in a bona fide . . . administrative . . . capacity" in section 13(a)(1) of the act shall mean any employee:

(a) Whose primary duty consists of either:

(1) The performance of office or nonmanual work directly related to management policies or general business operations of his employer or his employer's customers, or

(2) The performance of functions in the administration of a school system, or educational establishment or institution, or of a department or subdivision thereof, in work directly related to the academic instruction or training carried on therein; and

(b) Who customarily and regularly exercises discretion and independent judgment; and

(c) (1) Who regularly and directly assists a proprietor, or an employee employed in a bona fide executive or administrative capacity (as such terms are defined in the regulations of this subpart), or

(2) Who performs under only general supervision work along specialized or technical lines requiring special training, experience, or knowledge, or

(3) Who executes under only general supervision special assignments and tasks; and

(d) Who does not devote more than 20 percent, or, in the case of an employee of a retail or service establishment who does not devote as much as 40 percent, of his hours worked in the workweek to activities which are not directly and closely related to the performance of the work described in paragraphs (a) through (c) of this section; and

(e) (1) Who is compensated for his services on a salary or fee basis at a rate of not less than $225 per week beginning February 13, 1981 and $250 per week beginning February 13, 1983 ($180 per week beginning February 13, 1981 and $200 per week beginning February 13, 1983, if employed by other than the Federal Government in Puerto Rico, the Virgin Islands, or American Samoa), exclusive of board, lodging, or other facilities, or

(2) Who, in the case of academic administrative personnel, is compensated for services as required by paragraph (e)(1) of this section, or on a salary basis which is at least equal to the entrance salary for teachers in the school system, educational establishment, or institution by which employed: *Provided,* That an employee who is compensated on a salary or fee basis at a rate of not less than $320 per week beginning February 13, 1981 and $345 per week beginning February 13, 1983 ($260 per week beginning February 13, 1981 and $285 per week beginning February 13, 1983, if employed by other than the Federal Government in Puerto Rico, the Virgin Islands, or American Samoa), exclusive of board, lodging, or other facilities, and whose primary duty consists of the performance of work described in paragraph (a) of this section, which includes work requiring the exercise of discretion and independent judgment, shall be deemed to meet all the requirements of this section.

541.3 PROFESSIONAL

The term "employee employed in a bona fide . . . professional capacity" in section 13(a) (1) of the act shall mean any employee:

(a) Whose primary duty consists of the performance of:

(1) Work requiring knowledge of an advanced type in a field of science or learning customarily acquired by a prolonged course of specialized intellectual instruction and study, as distinguished from a general academic education and from an apprenticeship, and from training in the performance of routine mental, manual, or physical processes, or

(2) Work that is original and creative in character in a recognized field of artistic endeavor (as opposed to work which can be produced by a person endowed with general manual or intellectual ability and training), and the result of which depends primarily on the invention, imagination, or talent of the employee, or

(3) Teaching, tutoring, instructing, or lecturing in the activity of imparting knowledge and who is employed and engaged in this activity as a teacher in the school system or educational establishment or institution by which he is employed; and

Table 2–1   (continued)

541.3 PROFESSIONAL

(b) Whose work requires the consistent exercise of discretion and judgment in its performance; and

(c) Whose work is predominantly intellectual and varied in character (as opposed to routine mental, manual, mechanical, or physical work) and is of such character that the output produced or the result accomplished cannot be standardized in relation to a given period of time; and

(d) Who does not devote more than 20 percent of his hours worked in the workweek to activities which are not an essential part of and necessarily incident to the work described in paragraphs (a) through (c) of this section; and

(e) Who is compensated for services on a salary or fee basis at a rate of not less than $250 per week beginning February 13, 1981 and $280 per week beginning February 13, 1983 ($225 per week beginning February 13, 1981 and $250 per week beginning February 13, 1983 if employed by other than the Federal Government in Puerto Rico, the Virgin Islands, or American Samoa), exclusive of board, lodging, or other facilities: *Provided,* That this paragraph shall not apply in the case of an employee who is the holder of a valid license or certificate permitting the practice of law or medicine or any of their branches and who is actually engaged in the practice thereof, nor in the case of an employee who is the holder of the requisite academic degree for the general practice of medicine and is engaged in an internship or resident program pursuant to the practice of medicine or any of its branches, nor in the case of an employee employed and engaged as a teacher as provided in paragraph (a)(3) of this section: *Provided further,* That an employee who is compensated on a salary or fee basis at a rate of not less than $320 per week beginning February 13, 1981 and $345 per week beginning February 13, 1983 (or $260 per week beginning February 13, 1981 and $285 per week beginning February 13, 1983 if employed by other than the Federal Government in Puerto Rico, the Virgin Islands, or American Samoa), exclusive of board, lodging, or other facilities, and whose primary duty consists of the performance either of work described in paragraph (a) (1) or (3) of this section, which includes work requiring the consistent exercise of discretion and judgment, or of work requiring invention, imagination, or talent in a recognized field fo artistic endeavor, shall be deemed to meet all of the requirements of this section.

541.5 OUTSIDE SALESMAN

The term "employee employed . . . in the capacity of outside salesman" in section 13(a) (1) of the act shall mean any employee:

(a) Who is employed for the purpose of and who is customarily and regularly engaged away from his employer's place or places of business in:

(1) Making sales within the meaning of section 3(k) of the act, or

(2) Obtaining orders or contracts for services or for the use of facilities for which a consideration will be paid by the client or customer; and

(b) Whose hours of work of a nature other than that described in paragraph (a) (1) or (2) of this section do not exceed 20 percent of the hours worked in the workweek by nonexempt employees of the employer: *Provided,* That work performed incidental to and in conjunction with the employee's own outside sales or solicitations, including incidental deliveries and collections, shall not be regarded as nonexempt work.

Source: WH Publication 1281, U.S. Department of Labor, Revised June 1983.

Overtime. The FLSA requires that nonexempt employees be paid 150 percent of regular pay for all hours in excess of 40 per week. The workweek is defined as a period of 168 hours during seven consecutive 24-hour periods. An employer may arbitrarily decide the day and the hour the workweek begins. Hours cannot be shifted from one week to another. An exception to this rule is that a hospital may use 14-day work periods and an 80-hour breakpoint. Another exception is that some employers are permitted week-to-week balancing under a collectively bargained guaranteed-wage plan.

Calculating overtime pay is straightforward for employees paid by the hour. For employees on a wage incentive plan, the base rate is average hourly earnings. Salaried employees' base rate is determined by (1) converting monthly to weekly salary (divide by $4\frac{1}{3}$) and (2) computing the hourly rate (divide by 40).

As implied in our dicussion of minimum wages, employees who are exempt from minimum-wage provisions are exempt from overtime provisions. Employers may, of course, pay overtime to these exempt employees but are not required to do so. Additional exemptions from overtime provisions of the FLSA are agricultural employees, truck drivers, railroad and air-carrier employees, seamen, some local delivery people, and taxi drivers.

Record Keeping.   Under the FLSA, employers must collect and keep certain wage and hour information on nonexempt employees. In general, the purpose of these record-keeping requirements is to permit the Wage and Hour Division to enforce the minimum-wage and overtime provisions of the FLSA. Such information as the following is required: employee's name, address, occupation, sex; definition of workweek; total hours worked each workday and workweek; basic pay; regular hourly rate; overtime pay; deductions and additions to pay; total wages for period; pay date and period; and special information—estimated tips, payments in kind.

Equal Pay.   The Equal Pay Act of 1963 was passed as an amendment to the FLSA. It prohibits wage differentials between men and women employed by the same establishment in jobs that require equal skill, effort, and responsibility, and that are performed under similar working conditions. The act requires that all three factors (skill, effort, and responsibility) must be substantially equal for the jobs to be adjudged equal. Likewise, working conditions must differ significantly if pay differentials are to be justified. Actually, case law has accepted "substantial equality" between jobs as sufficient for equal pay.

The equal-pay provisions do specifically approve some conditions as justifying lower pay for women than for men. Wage differentials resulting from legitimate seniority systems, merit systems, or any system that ties earnings to quantity or quality of production are permissible. Wage differentials also may be based on factors other than sex (education required by the job, profitability to the employer). Part-time workers need not be paid the same as full-time workers. Differentials paid to family heads are permitted if both male and female heads of families are paid the differential.

Employers may not lower pay to correct violations of equal-pay provisions. Instead, the pay of the affected group must be raised to that of the favored group. There are no exempt employees under the equal-pay provisions of the FLSA. Nearly all employers are covered by the act, as are unions that negotiate for covered employees. Most states have had equal-pay laws predating the federal statute, but they vary greatly in provisions and method of enforcement.

STATE MINIMUM-WAGE LAWS.   Most states have minimum-wage laws and laws concerning overtime. Some of these laws apply to all workers, others only to workers not covered by federal law. The state laws include exemptions that usually parallel those under the federal law. Quite a number of states empower state labor agencies to set minimum wages.

PREVAILING-WAGE LAWS.   Both federal and state governments have laws requiring contractors supplying goods or services to the government to pay "prevailing" rates. The Davis-Bacon Act of 1931 requires the secretary of labor to determine prevailing rates applicable to government construction contracts in excess of $2000. The law is controversial primarily because the secretary has used union rates in the geographical area as the prevailing rate. Employers argue that the law does not require the secretary to use union rates and that doing so raises wages and government expenditures. Labor leaders argue that changes in administration of the law would weaken unions and union contractors.

The Walsh-Healy Public Contracts Act of 1936 applies to employers that are a party to federal contracts for materials, supplies, and equipment in excess of $10,000. It requires these employers to pay prevailing wages in the industry as determined by the secretary of labor. Walsh-Healy also requires covered employers to pay overtime at one and a half times the base rate for all hours in excess of 8 in a day or 40 in one workweek, whichever is greater.

The McNamara-O'Hara Service Contract Act of 1965 extends Davis-Bacon concepts to government contracts for services. Contractors holding service contracts of $2500 or less must not pay service employees less than the minimum wage. Contractors holding service contracts in excess of $2500 must pay employees no less than the wage rates and benefits found by the Department of Labor to be prevailing in the area, or no less than the compensation (pay and benefits) found in the previous contractor's collective-bargaining agreement.

EFFECTS OF WAGE FLOORS.   The effects of wage floors (both minimum-wage laws and prevailing-wage laws) have long been a matter of controversy. Economic theory shows that wage floors may reduce employment by in effect prohibiting the employment of individuals not worth the floor. Economic theory also suggests that such floors may contribute to inflation by providing targets against which noncovered employers may be compared and by restoring customary relationships when they are raised.

A contrary view is that wage floors reduce poverty by keeping wages above subsistence levels. It is also argued that wage floors prevent exploitation of employees and may in fact improve employer utilization of labor training programs to make employees worth what they must be paid.[13]

WAGE CONTROLS.   Although wage floors have existed as part of our legal environment for over 40 years, wage ceilings have usually been avoided. During times of strong inflationary pressures, however, attempts have been

---

[13]S. A. Levitan, and Richard S. Belous, "The Minimum Wage Today: How Well Does It Work?" *Monthly Labor Review*, June 1979, pp. 17–21.

made to slow wage and price advances. During World War II, a War Labor Board was charged with devising and administering controls over wage changes. During the Korean War, a Wage Stabilization Board was created to control wage and price advances. Although evaluations of their effectiveness are mixed, wartime wage controls were generally adjudged to be necessary and somewhat effective, especially during World War II.

Peacetime controls have been more controversial and less effective. The effectiveness of the wage-price guidelines of the 1960s in the Kennedy and Johnson administrations remains debatable. The more stringent controls in the Nixon administration were adjudged no more effective. The weaker controls under the Carter administration were probably even less effective.

The wage-control techniques tried in the United States have been: (1) a wage-price freeze for a limited period, (2) guidelines and "jawboning" by the administration, and (3) a wage-price review board. Another strategy, suggested but untried, is to tax organizations that exceed guidelines. Objections to controls that they are either ineffective or harmful to the economy depends on the technique used. But the more effective the controls, the more harmful to the economy.

Problems with wage and price controls have appeared throughout the industrial world. These controls, called *income policies,* are designed to improve the trade-off between wage and price stability and unemployment (the Philips curve) by political means. Although these policies have not been notably effective economically, they can achieve political effectiveness for short periods. Obtaining and keeping a consensus among various segments of society that their interests are being served is an unsolved problem.

ASSURANCE OF PAYMENT. A final type of wage legislation is the requirement that workers be paid the wages due them. State legislation typically specifies that wages be paid at regular intervals (one week or two) and that they be paid in cash or its equivalent. Payment in scrip (private currency) is usually prohibited, as is paying employees in barrooms. These laws also specify immediate payment if an employee is discharged.

There are also laws that limit the ability of creditors to attach the wages of employees, called garnishments, and to assign wages. These laws regulate the collection of debts from employees by restricting the amount of wages that may be deducted for such debts and by prohibiting employee discharge for a single garnishment. The Consumer Credit Protection Act of 1968, for example, restricts garnishments on worker earnings to the lesser of either (1) 25 percent of the debtor's disposable earnings for the workweek or (2) the amount by which the debtor's disposable earnings for the work exceed 30 times the minimum hourly wage ($3.35). Disposable earnings are defined as compensation less legally required withholding (for Social Security and income taxes).

Under this law, garnishment restrictions do not apply to federal and state tax debts, alimony and child support, or orders under bankruptcy proceedings. Federal law preempts state law on garnishment amounts unless state law requires smaller garnishments. The 1968 federal law also forbids firing debtors for a single garnishment but not for subsequent ones.

The federal antikickback statute—the Copeland Act of 1934—makes it illegal to require that the employees return a part of their earnings to employers or others for the privilege of working. The act applies to all federal projects and contracts. Several states have such laws to ensure that employees receive the agreed-on rates.

Social Legislation

Just as minimum- and prevailing-wage laws place a floor under wage rates, so Social Security, unemployment insurance, and worker's compensation can be interpreted as placing a floor under benefits. Likewise, the Employee Retirement Income Security Act of 1974 and the 1980 amendments of it applying to multiemployer pensions can be considered assurance-of-benefit-payment laws.

OASDHI.   The Old Age, Survivors, Disability and Health Insurance Program (OASDHI) is at least as significant to employee benefits as the FLSA is to wages. More than nine out of ten workers are covered by its provisions, which form the base of most benefit programs. The only workers not covered are federal civilian employees in the federal retirement system (as of now), state and local government employees who have chosen not to participate, some agricultural and domestic workers, and employees of some nonprofit organizations who have not arranged coverage. The programs under this label provide retirement, survivors, and disability insurance; hospital and medical insurance for the aged and disabled; black-lung benefits for coal miners; supplementary security income; unemployment insurance; and public assistance and welfare services.

SOCIAL SECURITY.   Retirement, survivors, and disability insurance and hospital and medical insurance for the aged and disabled are paid for by a tax on employers and employees. These taxes, authorized by the Federal Insurance Contributions Act of 1936, constitute the FICA deductions noted on paychecks. Employer and employee taxes and the earnings subject to tax have been rising along with benefits. As of 1982, they were 13.4 percent of the first $32,400 of each employee's earnings. Social Security also imposes some recordkeeping and reporting requirements on employers: amounts and dates of wage payments; amount of tips received; name, address, occupation, periods of employment; and Social Security number of each employee receiving wages. The W-2 form that each employer must provide each employee by January 31 for the previous calendar year is a requirement of Social Security.

UNEMPLOYMENT INSURANCE.   This is a state-administered program operating under general requirements set out by OASDHI. Its function is to provide partial income replacement when a worker loses a job through no fault of his or her own. Unemployment insurance is funded by a tax levied by states on employers. In a few states, employees also contribute to unemployment insurance. The employer's tax depends on benefit levels in the state and the employer's record. The standard tax is 3.4 percent of the first $6000 earned by a worker in a calendar year. Most of this tax (2.7 percent) goes to the state benefit fund; 0.7 percent goes to the federal government for administration.

The employer's tax is adjusted up or down from the standard tax depending on the employer's record or *experience rating*. States vary somewhat in the way they compute the experience rating, but in all of them, the greater the number of successful UI filers, the higher the tax. Successful filers must register at a public employment office and file for UI. The worker's previous job must have been covered, and an earnings or employment test met. To draw UI, workers must be able to work, be available for work, actively seek work, and be willing to take a suitable job. Workers must have lost jobs through circumstances beyond their control: (they cannot quit without good cause, and cannot have been discharged for cause). In almost all states, workers may be unemployed because of a labor dispute in which they are participating. Both workers and employers have the right to appeal UI-eligibility decisions. Employers concerned with their experience ratings challenge claims they deem inappropriate and carefully document discharges.

WORKER'S COMPENSATION.   Worker's compensation varies from state to state depending upon state laws. Because worker coverage, benefits to workers, and costs to employers vary tremendously from state to state, several national commissions have suggested federal standards. The goal of worker-compensation laws is to provide medical care and income to workers who are injured on the job or who acquire an industrial illness, and to provide support to dependents if a worker is killed; it is essentially an insurance program covering work-related injuries and illnesses. States vary in whether employer self-insurance is permitted, and whether a state insurance fund must be used or whether private insurance carriers are acceptable. Benefits are usually based on a worker's wages at the time of injury and the number of his or her dependents. Maximum and minimum payments for specified injuries and total claims are typically specified by law, as are time limits for benefit payments. Costs to employers are influenced by the provisions of the state law as well as by the employer's accident record.

ERISA.   The Employee Retirement Income Security Act of 1974 was passed to ensure that pensions offered by employers met certain standards and were received by employees. ERISA does not require employers to offer pension programs but it does require that those who do follow certain rules if they want favorable tax treatment for both their contributions and for their employees' deferral of income.

ERISA applies to all employees 21 years or older who have completed one year or more of service. Workers under a collective-bargaining agreement where pension benefits are subject to negotiation may be excluded. But tax benefits apply only to ERISA-qualified pension plans. ERISA prohibits pension plans set up to benefit management only, stipulating that a qualified plan cover (1) 70 percent of all employees of the organization, or (2) 80 percent of eligible employees where at least 70 percent of all employees are eligible, or (3) some fair share of employees in a plan that does not favor officers, shareholders, or highly compensated employees.

Under ERISA, an employee gains ownership of accrued pension rights through a period of employment. These ownership rights obtain even if the employee leaves the organization before retirement. The process of acquiring ownership through employment time is called *vesting*. An organization can use any of three vesting methods under ERISA. In the simplest method, the employee is fully vested after ten years of service. In a second method, the employee is 25 percent vested after five years, gains 5 percent a year through 10 years, and gains 10 percent through 15 years of employment. The third method, *the rule of 45,* requires 50 percent vesting when the employee's age plus years of service (at least five) equal 45, then 10 percent vesting for each year of service. The rule of 45 further requires 50 percent vesting after 10 years' service and 100 percent after 15.

ERISA also has requirements for accrual of pension benefits. Under *the 3 percent rule,* the employee must accrue for each year of service at least 3 percent of the benefit payable under the plan if the employee began at the earliest age and retired at the normal retirement age. Under *the $133\frac{1}{3}$ rule,* the annual rate of accrual cannot exceed the accrual rate for a prior year by more than one third. Under *the fractional rule,* the benefits accrued for any one year of service should equal the employee's projected benefit at the normal retirement age prorated for years of service. Thus if the plan is based on 40 years of service and an employee has accumulated 20 years of service, he or she should have accrued 50 percent of expected benefits.

ERISA-qualified plans must provide an option for employees to receive a 50 percent joint and survival annuity to benefit employee dependents. Further, plans must be funded each year with a minimum contribution equal to a normal cost, i.e. that required to cover the year's liability, plus amortization over 30 years of unfunded accrued liabilities for all plan benefits.

To insure that vested benefits are paid to employees in spite of employer default, the Pension Benefit Guarantee Corporation (PBGC) was created. A covered employer pays $2.60 per plan participant per year into the PBGC as an insurance premium. Vested benefits of up to $750 per month are guaranteed to participants.

ERISA places a ceiling as well as a floor on pension benefits. Benefits may not exceed $15,000 per year or 100 percent of the employee's compensation for the highest three consecutive years, whichever is lower. This is another provision designed to discourage weighting the pension plan in favor of highly paid people.

In addition to these technical requirements under ERISA, there are several record-keeping and reporting requirements. The latter include reports to employees about pension plans. These reports represent an opportunity to the employer to inform employees about an important portion of their compensation.

In 1980 parts of ERISA dealing with employer obligations under multi-employer pension plans were amended by the Multiemployer Pension Plan Amendments Act. These amendments require that an employer, once in such a plan, must assume the liabilities for the fund, even upon withdrawal. Because multiemployer pension plans are typically the result of collective-bargaining agreements and because pensions are mandatory bargaining items, it is conceivable that employee benefits and employer liabilities could be completely unrelated.

Rules Concerning Equal Employment Opportunity and Affirmative Action

Equal employment opportunity (EEO) rules and affirmative action (AA) guidelines are to be found in several laws, a number of executive orders, and some case law. The principal federal laws are the Civil Rights Act of 1964. Section VII; the Equal Employment Opportunity Act of 1972; the Age Discrimination in Employment Act of 1967 and its 1978 amendments; the Vocational Rehabilitation Act of 1973; and the Vietnam Era Veterans Readjustment Assistance Act of 1974. The Equal Pay Act discussed previously may also be considered EEO legislation. State laws on civil rights matters have been in effect longer but have been superseded by federal laws. Executive orders 11246 of 1965 and 11375 of 1967 are the foundations of affirmative action programs. The most important legal cases will be cited shortly.

These rules and guides apply to two separate types of programs. EEO programs prohibit discrimination based on race, color, sex, religion, age, or national origin in any of the terms of employment stipulated by employers, employment agencies, or labor unions. The Equal Employment Opportunity Commission issues guides for employer actions, record keeping, and reports that represent compliance with EEO. AA programs call for positive steps to correct the results of past discrimination. Government contractors are the major group required to have AA programs, and the executive orders just mentioned spell out most of the requirements. AA programs also require employer activities, record keeping, and periodic reports. The handicapped and Vietnam veterans are covered by both EEO and AA requirements. Employer coverage varies somewhat under the different legislation and regulation.

One useful way to view EEO and AA rules in their entirety is to use the concept of protected groups. Since compensation decisions constitute important terms and conditions of employment, they are covered by law. If compensation differentials exist between the majority employees and members of protected groups, the employer must be prepared to justify them. All compensation policies, programs, and practices of an organization should be examined as steps intended to guarantee that no discrimination against protected groups has occurred or can occur.

Comparable Worth

Comparable worth is an undeveloped legal concept that has become an important issue. It flows from the observation that women are paid less than men. More specifically, advocates of comparable worth call for equal pay for jobs of equal value. Note that this is different than equal pay, under which the jobs must be substantially equal.

Three major court cases may serve to illustrate the issue. One involved nurses employed by the city of Denver.[14] The nurses charged that they were being discriminated against in pay because of their sex. They showed that they were paid a lower wage than parking-meter repairers, tree trimmers, and sign painters. They argued that these wage differentials did not reflect any differences in type or value of work but were due rather to society's tendency to pay women less for their work than men.

The nurses based their case on the Equal Pay Act and the Civil Rights Act. The former was inappropriate because the jobs compared were different. But the latter appeared to apply, because jobs dominated by women were paid less than jobs dominated by men even though the jobs were of equal or comparable worth.

[14]Lemons v. City and County of Denver, Colorado, 1978 620 F2d 225.

The federal district court agreed with the nurses that occupations dominated by women could have historically been paid less than occupations dominated by men. It also agreed that such discrimination could in fact lead to a violation of a comparable worth criterion of fairness. But the court found against the nurses by citing the market rather than comparable worth as the proper standard. In fact the court commented, "This is a case which is pregnant with the possibility of disrupting the entire economic system of the U.S. . . . ."

In the second case, a union charged that Westinghouse Corporation had historically established classes of jobs for wage-setting purposes that discriminated against women.[15] They demonstrated that Westinghouse had segregated "women's" jobs from "men's" jobs and set lower rates for the former. The federal district court decided that such a practice discriminated against women and ordered it stopped.

In the third case, jail matrons doing work similar to but not equal to that of prison guards charged that they were being discriminated against because the difference in pay between the two jobs was much greater than the difference between the jobs themselves.[16] In this case the Supreme Court ruled that women who file lawsuits charging sex discrimination in pay matters may have valid claims under civil rights law.

All three of these cases have questioned the adequacy of the market as a criterion of job worth. Proponents of comparable worth argue that because women have been "crowded" into certain occupations, the labor market discriminates against them.[17]

Job evaluation as a formal method of comparing jobs is logically a potential solution. To the extent, however, that different job-evaluation plans are used for men's and women's jobs, the crucial job comparisons are not made. Also, to the extent that job-evaluation plans are developed on the basis of market wage rates for key jobs, job evaluation and market rates are not separate criteria.[18]

The issue of comparable worth will arise at several points in this book. At present it seems best to label it an undeveloped legal concept that may be settled by further court cases or by legislation. As an issue for compensation administrators, it seems important to recognize that wage decisions under our system are made for decentralized units. Thus, the issue is whether jobs and/or people in the organization are being paid on a nondiscriminatory basis. The larger issue of differences between men's and women's pay is beyond the control of the organization's decision makers.

Laws Affecting Collective Bargaining

The legal environment of compensation administration would seem to include the rules of the game in collective bargaining. These rules specify col-

---

[15]I.U.E. v. Westinghouse Electric Corporation, New Jersey, 1979 620 F2d 228.

[16]Gunther v. County of Washington, 1981 U.S. Supreme Court 451 U.S. 161.

[17]See, for example, Helen Remick, "Strategies for Creating Sound, Bias-Free Job Evaluation Plans," in *Job Evaluation and EEO: The Emerging Issues* (New York: Industrial Relations Counselors, 1978).

[18]See E. R. Livernash, ed., *Comparable Worth* (Washington, D.C.: Equal Employment Advisory Council, 1980).

lective bargaining as the method of determining compensation (as well as other terms and conditions of employment) if employees prefer it. They also offer guidelines for collective bargaining when it is used. But with very minor exceptions (union security clauses and discrimination matters) they leave the decisions to the parties. If employers and employees prefer to strike individual bargains, the rules are those we have been discussing.

Tax Laws

Tax laws are an obvious part of the legal environment of compensation administration. Anyone who has ever received a paycheck is aware of income-tax withholding.

Less obvious, however, is the influence of tax laws on benefits and, especially, on executive compensation. Not all benefits are taxed; many are bargains in part because they aren't. Some benefits provide deferred income that is not taxed until the employee receives the benefit. These provisions constitute many of the real benefits of pensions, profit-sharing plans, and employee stock-ownership plans. Equally important is the influence of tax laws on employer benefit costs. These laws often encourage certain kinds of benefit programs and discourage others.

Under the present internal revenue code certain benefits are not taxed; health and life insurance are examples. Other services or perquisites may or may not be taxed. For example, services or perquisites provided only to executives are considered taxable. Under the last several federal tax laws, Congress has declared a moratorium on changes in the tax status of fringe benefits until a certain date. What this means about future taxation of benefits is difficult to forecast.

Many forms of executive compensation appear, expand, and even disappear in response to changes in tax laws. Stock options, for example, seem to expire or acquire new life in this way. Various forms of deferred income and restricted stock also seem to vary in this way.

For all of these reasons, tax laws are an important part of the legal environment of compensation administration. Understanding tax laws is a prerequisite to designing compensation programs. As this book goes to press, Congress has passed legislation to overhaul the tax system and instigate changes which will have a major impact on both take-home pay and benefits.

THE UNION ENVIRONMENT

Unions and collective bargaining represent an important part of the environment in which compensation administration is practiced. Compensation decisions by both union and nonunion organizations are affected by unions—the former directly and the latter through the "threat" effect.

Unions attempt to regulate every kind of managerial action that directly affects the welfare of their membership or their own strength and security. The substantive provisions of union contracts may be said to encompass three main groups: job tenure and job security; work schedules, work speed, and production methods; and amount and method of compensation. All three influence wage costs and decisions. Methods of hiring, promotion, and layoff influence labor costs indirectly. Work speeds and production methods strongly influence labor costs. The decisions on compensation—wages and benefits—bear directly on costs.

Unions try to influence employers' hiring, placement, and retention decisions in part to ensure jobs for their members and in part to influence the wages paid by reducing the labor supply. Their interest in union security, training programs, use of seniority in promotion and transfer, and discipline and discharge decisions is tied to getting and keeping jobs and employment opportunities for their members. Although unions have always showed concern with demand for labor, there is evidence that their concern for job security may be increasing. A not unusual quid pro quo for wage concessions in the recession of the early 1980s was an increase in job-security guarantees.

The unions' interest in work schedules, work speeds, and production methods represents their concern with the effort bargain. As pointed out in chapter 1, the cost to employers of employment is labor cost per unit of output. Thus employers want as much output as possible for their wage costs. The unions' concern with work speeds, timework versus incentive plans, production techniques, and work rules represents their desire to prevent exploitation of members, conserve employment opportunities, and make life on the job more pleasant for members.

Unions try to influence all of the compensation decisions affecting their members. For example, they try, often successfully, to reduce wage differences among unionized companies in the same industry. This principle of the "standard rate" for workers doing comparable work stems partly from considerations of equity and partly from political pressures within the union. But a better explanation is that a uniform wage level for companies operating in the same product market "takes wages out of competition."

Application of this principle varies with the geographic scope of the product market. In local-market industries there is a tendency toward wage equalization within the city but often much variation in wage levels between cities. In manufacturing industries where firms compete on a regional or national basis, there is a tendency toward uniformity in wage levels throughout the country.

Although attempted equalization of hourly rates is most common, equalization of other measures has been sought by various unions at various times. For example, equalization of the rate for common labor, all job rates in a plant, piece rates, or labor cost per unit may be attempted. Equalizing one of these measures, though, will not produce equality in the others. More important, these objectives have different consequences. Imposing uniform hourly rates may result in serious hardship to an inefficient plant or company, whereas uniform piece rates would not. Equalizing labor cost per unit of output would be most difficult.

The wage-paying ability of companies or plants may differ because of variations in technical efficiency, management ability, or geographic location. Unions attempt to determine if low-paying firms are paying as much as they are able to pay. Organizations may assert their inability to pay, and unions may require convincing evidence. One of the effects of concession bargaining in the early 1980s has been that firms now provide more information on their condition and prospects.

Union pressure frequently forces management to increase efficiency and thus the firm's ability to pay. Where this "shock effect" cannot occur because of unchangeable economic conditions or company conditions, some of the less efficient plants may be forced from the industry. If union members in a particular plant become convinced that forcing wage equalization will cost them their jobs, they will usually vote to accept a lower wage and keep the plant in operation. This is more likely to occur when the plant is geographically isolated and members would have to travel some distance to find new employment. In such cases even national union officers may be willing to accept some departure from wage equality. In general, however, unions emphasize the principle of the standard rate rather than the principle of ability to pay.

Whether the last statement is still true after the rash of concession bargaining in the recession of the early 1980s is a matter of debate. Some authors insist that pattern bargaining is dead, that the ability to pay of each employer will drive the bargaining.[19] Others believe that concessions and other unusual union behavior will disappear with improved economic conditions.[20] The latter may argue that whether a given organization followed the "pattern" has always depended on the economic survival of the firm.

Unions in different industries face different conditions that may enhance or reduce their influence. Such factors as skill mix of the labor force, geographic location, proportion of female or minority employees, percentage of the industry organized, profitability, rising product demand, productivity increases, industrial concentration, oligopolistic product market, and large size have been shown by research to influence the degree of success of union bargaining efforts.

Much of this research has been designed to determine whether unionism makes a difference in wages. In the process it has been necessary to try to measure and adjust for the factors just mentioned in order to isolate the independent effect of unionism. Most of these studies have found that unionism has a moderate effect—on the order of 15 percent. The effect is greater in times of recession and much less in periods of inflation. Apparently the serious recession of the early 1980s was no exception, and the union–nonunion differential has been growing in spite of the lower proportion of the work force represented by unions.

An interesting question left by such research is why, given the tremendous differences among industries in favorability of economic conditions for union gains, the union–nonunion differential has been so modest. One possible answer is the politics of unionism, which forces union leaders to keep up with wage changes but holds out little incentive for them to lead. Another is that equity and reasonable wage relationships act as conservative forces. Still another is that market forces limit the relative wage differences among industries, which would permit all of them to attract and keep a work force.

It is true that unions in some industries have raised relative wages of

[19]For example, A. Freedman and W. E. Fulmer, "Last Rites for Pattern Bargaining," *Harvard Business Review*, March-April 1982, pp. 30–48.

[20]For example, J. T. Dunlop "Remarks by Former Secretary of Labor Dunlop on 1982 Wage Developments before Conference of Business Economists," *Daily Labor Report*, February 23, 1982, pp. D1–D2; and D. J. B. Mitchell, "Is Union Wage Determination at a Turning Point?" in *Proceedings of the 35th Annual Meeting, IRRA*, (1983), pp. 35–61.

their members more than unions in other industries. This may be partially explained by favorable economic conditions, but not always. A better explanation may be that large-scale, highly concentrated industries are easier to organize and to win gains from, for several reasons. Large plants may mean less costly organizing. Workers in large organizations have lower job satisfaction and are more union-prone. Large organizations are visible to the public, and antiunion activities would be also. Large plants represent high fixed investments; their parent firms cannot run away. But this explanation is also incomplete. Some industries are made up of small firms whose business is such that they are confined to a location that the union controls when organization is complete.

Another possible explanation is the nature of the union and its leaders. The skill mix of an industry has an effect on whether craft or industrial unionism is the norm. But type of union has an independent effect. A strong case can be made that the industrial unions in autos and steel changed the wages and benefits of tens of millions of American workers through innovative bargaining. If, as seems likely, their influence has been eliminated by structural changes in the economy, and if no other union(s) assumes their former leadership role, the union environment of the United States will be greatly changed.[21]

Unions may change occupational differentials in the industries that they organize, and they may do so through their influence on how general increases are made in a company. By organizing blue-collar workers in certain industries they may have raised their wages relative to clerical, professional, and managerial workers. Also because the least-skilled and lowest-paid workers are nonunion and often in the service sector, the wages of these people may be relatively lower because of unionism. Within organizations, unions that obtain general wage increases have an effect on occupational differentials. But those that obtain flat cents-per-hour increases (primarily industrial unions, for political reasons) reduce occupational differentials.

Craft unions, however, are more likely to maintain customary differentials, and thus occupational differentials would not change. However, union policy may dictate raising the lower rates to protect the total structure. Even in industrial unions, customary differentials are usually protected by membership sentiment and threats by skilled people to form their own union.

On balance, a decline in the earnings of skilled and semiskilled relative to unskilled workers has been a general tendency in the United States. Unionism may have aided this tendency, but not very much. The decline in the occupational differential has varied by industry.

The principle of the "standard rate" suggests that unions attempt to eliminate the differential among regions and communities of varying size. But this depends on the market structure of the industry and the scope of bargaining. Where competition is limited to a locality and bargaining is conducted locally, there is no reason to expect wage equalization among localities. Thus, where unions have organized high-wage regions and communities, they may have widened geographic differentials in such industries.

In manufacturing industries selling in a national market, unionism may reduce or eliminate geographic differentials. Economic pressures work in this direction. So do political pressures from union members. Although employers

[21]E. M. Kassalow, "Concession Bargaining: Something Old, but Also Something Quite New," in *Proceedings of the 35th Annual Meeting, IRRA*, (1983), pp. 372–82.

tend to favor paying wages that are in line with the community level, national bargaining may be able to achieve equalization.

Geographic equalization is more likely in industries that are highly unionized and concentrated and in which plants in low-wage areas are subsidiaries of companies in high-wage areas. In some industries unions fail to reduce or eliminate geographic differentials because their strength varies from region to region. On the other hand, strong unions may achieve equalization among regions even where there is no reason for it in the product market.

Unions in most industries have had little effect on geographic differentials, because of either local markets or lack of strength. Where differentials have been reduced, industry location may be affected. Wage leveling reduces inducements to move on the grounds of labor costs, at least in small, labor-intensive industries.

Unions also influence the employment exchange by trying to influence legislation. Union support for minimum-wage laws is well known. Unions have also been in the forefront in reducing hours of work. Less evident is their interest in restricting immigration. All of these efforts have probably had the effect of reducing the labor supply and thereby increasing the general level of real wages.

Unions also attempt to influence the makeup of the reward package by pushing for benefits that improve the security of employees and the amenities at the workplace. The widespread existence of some benefits is probably due to union innnovation.

Unions also greatly influence personnel policy and practice in organizations. With the exception of selection and training of new employees, all personnel programs for unionized agreements are jointly determined. In fact, the erosion of the "employment at will" doctrine in the 1980s stems at least in part from the protection against arbitrary discharge that unionism provides.

There is evidence that concession bargaining in the early 1980s has resulted in a change in union concerns and bargaining tactics. One such effect has been a demand for gain sharing, including profit sharing. More significant, perhaps, is increased union concern with employment levels. Where in the past unions have usually bargained wages and left decisions on employment levels to the employer, now unions granting wage concessions often demand detailed information on company operations. Further instances of union concern with employment levels include wage concessions in return for employment guarantees, union involvement in management decisions, advance notice to unions before plant closures or work transfers, and strengthening of supplementary unemployment benefits, severance-pay provisions, and employee rights to transfer to still-open plants.[22]

These trade-offs appear to involve important management prerogatives. Probably the most important is the unions' insistence on their right to be informed of company decisions that affect the organization's prospects and thus its work force. Apparently pricing policy, cash-flow decisions, and new investment decisions have all been discussed in concession bargaining.

Whether these are permanent changes in collective bargaining and whether they will spread to industries in which they do not now appear cannot

[22]P. Cappelli, "Concession Bargaining and the National Economy," in *Proceedings of the 35th Annual Meeting, IRRA,* (1983), pp. 362–71. See also Kasslow, op cit.

be foreseen. They seem quite foreign to the ideology of American workers and to management tradition. But it is hard to believe these innovations will disappear without having some effects.

THE ORGANIZATIONAL ENVIRONMENT

Compensation administration is practiced within organizations. For this reason, it may be said that the organization's goals and its incumbents represent the most pertinent environment of compensation administration.

Organizations may be classified as private for-profit, not-for-profit, and government entities. Although there are differences among these types of organizations in cost consciousness and accounting practices, they are of degree and are becoming smaller.[23] As a result, these differences appear to be among the least important to compensation administration.

But the economic, social, and legal environments of the organization have substantial effects. So do the maturity, size, number of businesses engaged in, number of organization levels, centralization versus decentralization decisions, technology, information and control systems, and management style of organizations.[24]

Economic conditions place limits on organizations. These limits, however, vary among organizations and over time. An organization's wage levels have maximum and minimum limits, which are set by its position in the product and labor markets. The organization could not go below the minimum and hold enough employees to meet organization goals, and it cannot exceed the maximum for budgetary reasons. But these limits are not clearly defined unless the organization believes it is close to either limit and in danger of being pushed beyond it. Furthermore, these limits depend on the period under consideration. The organization can exceed either limit for short periods, but for longer periods the range between them is narrower.

The maximum and minimum are determined by different forces, and there is not necessarily a connection between them. The maximum is set by conditions in product markets and the organization's ability to operate within them in terms of costs and prices. The minimum is determined by conditions in labor markets, which result in part from supply and demand for labor, but at least as much from customary relationships, legal pressures, union pressures, and pressures from other organizations.

Other organizations affect employer wage decisions in two directions. Other organizations in the community exert downward pressure to keep the employer from "upsetting the market." Other organizations in the industry may exert upward pressure to forestall "unfair competition" in wages. Thus an organization in a high-wage industry in a low-wage community must somehow balance these opposing forces.

Social, legal, and union environments affect an organization through the kinds of employees it hires and retains. Forces bearing on these organizational members will be outlined later in this section.

[23]D. Q. Mills, *Labor-Management Relations* (New York: McGraw-Hill, 1978), p. 38.

[24]E. E. Lawler III, *Pay and Organizational Effectiveness: A Psychological View* (New York: McGraw-Hill, 1971).

Although some organizations are seriously restricted in at least some compensation decisions by the environments in which they operate, the typical organization has a good deal of leeway in compensation decisions. It can adjust its compensation administration system according to its structure and incumbents.

Size

An organization's size can serve to free or restrict its compensation decisions. Small size, if combined with limited economic resources, may restrict the range of compensation levels. But the flexibility permitted by small size may be an advantage in most other compensation decisions. Pay relationships may be less important because each member can arrange his or her contract with the owner. Unique pay arrangements with individuals may be worked out to attract needed individuals. Pay increases may be closely tied to performance visible to all members. Profit-sharing and gain-sharing plans may have performance-motivation effects in small organizations but not in large ones. Communication regarding pay may be more open.

Large organizations, on the other hand, may have more economic slack and thus be less restricted in determining wage levels. But in other compensation decisions they are typically more restricted. More attention must be paid to internal pay relationships. The possibility of conflict between internal equity and external competitiveness becomes more severe. More serious is the difficulty of relating pay and performance. Lower-level managers in large organizations have the information on performance, but permitting them to make pay decisions often promotes inconsistency. Also, the needed attention to pay relationships may serve to hide the pay-performance relationship. A common result appears to be that large organizations need to relate pay to performance more, but use this relationship less, than small organizations. Communication of the pay system is probably also vulnerable to differences in organization units. As is well known, large organizations have difficulty integrating the differentiated units that come with increased size. Thus, seeing that the pay system accords with other systems is a continuing problem.

Age

The age of an organization may be associated with its size, because almost all organizations attempt to grow. But age may also be considered an independent influence. New organizations and plants may be designed around a homogeneous work force and a particular management style and innovate in pay systems. With increasing age and diversity of the work force, new and different pay plans may be required. Just as product life cycles dictate different management approaches, organization life cycles seem to require different pay systems.

Multiple Businesses

Although, as mentioned, product markets drive the maximum wage levels, organizations engaging in several businesses often have only one compensation system. Perhaps the major reasons are their desires for a consistent approach and more ease in transferring employees. Whereas an organization in a single business can have a single pay system regardless of location, a multiple-business enterprise would be unwise to do so. The needs of each business should determine the pay system—pay levels, pay structure, pay-system plans, and pay forms.

This influence often becomes important when an organization diversifies into a new business. Attempting to use the previous pay system in the new business may cause serious equity and performance problems.

Perceived inequities can probably occur if more than one business is operated out of a single installation. Moving to separate locations seems a better solution than trying to operate with one pay plan.

Number of Management Levels

Just as large size (more jobs and more incumbents) requires different compensation systems, so do more management levels. More attention to job and pay relationships is usually called for in multiple-level organizations. At least in management jobs, reporting level has been found to explain almost 90 percent of the variance in pay.[25] Also, jobs at different management levels require that different variables be measured in performance-pay plans.

Centralization versus Decentralization

The degree of centralization should influence the pay system because it determines the level at which performance information is gathered, the point where important decisions are made, and the technical competence of decision makers. If only centralized measures are available, measuring plant or other unit performance may be impossible. If decisions are made at corporate levels, unit managers can not be rewarded for unit performance. If the competence to measure and reward performance does not exist at the local level, performance-based pay plans at that level won't work.

Technology

The technology of an organization has a strong influence on its pay system. Technologies differ in job design and the kind of job incumbents that predominate. Jobs in the different technologies differ in cost structures, measurability of performance, interdependence and thus need for cooperation, and number and level of skills needed.

Organizations engaged in process production (as opposed to mass production and unit production) usually have lower labor-cost ratios and thus more freedom in decisions on wage levels.[26] But in process technology (such as chemical plants), operations are much more interdependent and individual performance is much more difficult to measure. Thus, process industries, although in a position to pay well, are limited in designing pay to motivate performance at the level of the individual. Plans measuring performance at the level of the group, plant, or company may, however, make good sense. On the other hand, organizations in process industries, often have relatively few employees and thus enjoy the advantages of small size.

[25]K. Foster, "Job Evaluaton: It's Time to Face the Facts," *Working Papers.*

[26]J. Woodward, *Industrial Organization: Theory and Practice* (London: Oxford University Press, 1965).

Unit or mass production usually requires less interdependence and a more simple form of it. Thus, these two types of production often permit paying for individual performance. Appropriate pay-for-performance plans, however, usually differ between unit and mass production.

Service industries can usually be classified in the same way and would seem to be subject to the same variables. Many service organizations specify high interdependence among employees. But many do not. In some service industries, identifying performance may require more effort. But many service organizations are small and enjoy the advantages that this entails. Also, many have high proportions of highly skilled jobs.

Another useful way of classifying technologies for pay-system purposes emphaszies the different types of employees as typical rank-and-file members.[27] Obviously, organizations composed chiefly of semiskilled production workers, skilled workers, engineers and other professionals, or technically trained managers would call for quite different pay systems. For example, the first two would be expected to resist performance-pay plans and the latter two to demand them.

Information Systems

The information system of an organization often determines if a performance-pay plan is appropriate and, if so, the level at which it must operate. Performance-pay plans require a good performance-measurement system. Equally important, the organization level to which these measurements apply (individual, group, plant, or organization) determines the appropriate type of performance–pay plan.

Influence Systems

Whether an organization is basically authoritarian or is open to substantial influence by its members has a strong effect on its pay system. Because authoritarian organizations limit information to members and member trust is unlikely, severe limits are placed on the pay system. Pay information will be secret or limited. Employee input in pay decisions will be unlikely. As a consequence, pay decisions must be objectively based to achieve employee acceptance.

In contrast, organizations permitting more member influence on decisions are more likely to exhibit employee trust in management. In such organizations more pay information will be provided employees. Also, employee participation in committees making pay-related decisions is more likely. Because employee acceptance is the ultimate test of the equity of a compensation system, such organizations have more leeway in choosing a pay system that fits the organization.

Organization Members

Pay systems must fit the people who work in the organization. People differ in capabilities, needs, and values. As mentioned in our discussion of technology, they differ by occupation. They differ in age, sex, and family situation.

[27]C. Perrow, *Organizational Analysis: A Sociological View* (Belmont, Calif.: Wadsworth, 1970).

They also differ in reward preferences, attitudes toward work, and involvement in work groups.

These differences affect the appropriateness of a compensation system. Members of different occupational groups expect to be treated differently. Age, sex, and family differences often result in different reward preferences. Attitude and value differences may encourage or discourage a performance-pay plan or the form it takes.

Perhaps even more important to pay systems are forthcoming changes in work forces. As suggested in the section on the social environment, the work force is becoming more heterogeneous. Organizations can expect to employ more minorities, more women, and more older people. This means more differences in values, lifestyles, and family situations. In turn this means greater differences in preferences for and attitudes about compensation.

Another suggestion that flows from the rising expectations noted in the social-environment section is that people are placing more importance on pay. If this is true, pay-system design and operation become even more crucial.

Still another suggestion flows from what appears to be an increase in rights consciousness. It appears that workers are becoming increasingly conscious of their right to a fair process of pay, promotion, and dismissal decisions. This means additional attention to the equity of compensation systems.

Compensation Policy

Perhaps the most important aspects of the organizational environment are an organization's intentions and goals with respect to compensation. What the organization intends to do about rewards and what goals it seeks to accomplish with the pay system tell managers and employees what to expect. It should also provide stability, consistency, and the credibility the compensation system needs in order to work.

Organizations should probably determine and state their policies in the following areas: (1) purposes of the compensation system, (2) communication, (3) who will make what compensation decisions, (4) intended market position, (5) intended equalization or differentiation of organization units (together with the rationale), (6) intended mix of cash and benefits, and (7) the basis of individual pay decisions.

Because there is no objectively correct answer to pay issues, each organization must design its own compensation system to fit its situation. Carefully considering these strategic issues and taking and stating a position on them tells members what to expect and decision makers what to do.

SUMMARY

In most areas of management today there is a greater concern with the environment. Compensation is no exception. This chapter has examined the major aspects of the environment that affect the manner and outcome of compensation decisions, including the economic, social, legal, union, and internal organizational environment.

The economic environment has been affected recently by major changes both in the supply of and demand for labor. On the supply side, there has been an increasing participation rate, particularly on the part of women. Men, on the other hand, have shown some decline in participation, especially older men and minorities. These changes, coupled with changes in the attitudes of younger workers, has created a significant transformation in the nature of today's labor force. The demand for labor is likewise changing. The move to a service society makes many of the traditional middle-class skills obsolete. There is an increasing dichotomy in the demand for labor between the highly skilled and the low-skilled, such that movement from one to the other becomes more and more difficult. Matching these diverse trends is the job of the labor market. This market is clearly an imperfect one, both theoretically and practically.

The legal environment continues to become more structured and demanding for the organization. While the basic laws in compensation were a result of the depression years, the new legislation is a function of the demands for social justice of the past 20 years. The issue of *comparable worth* will probably be the major concern in compensation for the next decade. But this is just the latest manifestation of the overall trend to assure that *all* personnel decisions in organizations are considered *fair* to all employee groups. In the field of benefits, there is a continuing trend toward legislation to protect employees' investment in their benefits.

The balance of power between management and labor unions has changed dramatically in the past few years. Union power has been eroded by the poor economy, losses in union membership, changing composition of the work force, and changing attitude by management and the government. However, the impact of unions on compensation decisions, while lessened, has not disappeared. Some of the more dramatic changes in compensation, such as *two-tiered pay systems,* are a result of the changing balance of power in union-management negotiations. It would appear that, for a time anyway, unions are going to be more interested in security than in increasing wages greatly.

One of the least considered influences on compensation decisions is the organization itself. The size, age, type of business, management structure and philosophy, technology, and power structure all influence the compensation program that the organization requires. There needs to be a fit between the type of organization and the type of compensation program.

It can be seen from these environmental factors that the organization is limited in the type of compensation program that it develops. In contrast to that, different organizations, since they are in different environments, can be expected to have different compensation programs.

3

Economic Theories of Compensation

The multiple influences on compensation decisions discussed up to this point suggest that compensation theorists face a huge task. This task is to specify the factors that determine compensation, the manner in which they do so, and the relative and absolute importance of each. Although this goal has not been accomplished, some progress is being made. Economists continue their long-term interest in wage theory. Psychologists, through their study of motivation and other aspects of organizational behavior, are contributing to compensation theory. Sociologists, through their study of work and exchange relationships, have added to our understanding of compensation. Because these three disciplines have different focuses, there is no one interdisciplinary compensation theory. But all three agree that the proper focus of study is an exchange relationship between employers and employees—an employment exchange.[1]

Compensation policies and practices are based on theories of compensation determinants and relationships, whether those who make policy or design techniques are aware of it or not. Improved theories are shortcuts to improved understanding and practice. If we knew precisely what conditions or factors determine compensation, it would be far easier to agree on the means

[1]See D. W. Belcher and T. J. Atchison, "Compensation for Work," in *Handbook of Work, Organization, and Society*, ed. R. Dublin (Chicago: Rand McNally, 1976), pp. 567–611.

of solving compensation issues. Such an understanding would indicate the relative usefulness of various policies and practices and the relative advantages and disadvantages of each alternative.

Economists have long been concerned with compensation theory. They have viewed employment as an exchange of labor services for payment in money or in kind. They have distinguished labor markets from other markets. They have shown how labor markets determine wages. Wage theories designed to explain the determinants of wages and wage relationships have been developed by economists for over two centuries. Wage theory has changed with changes in the economy and with changes in pertinent wage issues. A major change in wage theory came from the understanding that different kinds of wage theory were required for different types and levels of wage problems. The general wage level of the economy, for example, may require an explanation different from those required by the average wage in an enterprise, wage rates for particular jobs, and wage structures or relationships.

In recent years, economists interested in labor markets and thus wages have largely separated themselves into two fields. Labor economics is a branch of economics concerned with theory and measurement. Industrial relations (sometimes called institutional economics) is an interdisciplinary field that draws on sociology, psychology, law, and personnel management as well as economics. Industrial relations is largely an applied field that deals with workers or their union in a particular organization.[2]

This chapter sets out theories from both camps. First, historical wage theories are selectively reviewed from the perspective of today's wage issues. Then, the most developed models of labor economists will be reviewed. Finally, some of the work of institutional economists will be covered.

Chapter 4 reviews the work of psychologists and sociologists that bears on compensation. The substantial research on the psychology of pay and on motivation and job satisfaction are interpreted as compensation theory. Also, some sociological contributions to compensation theory are covered.

HISTORICAL THEORIES

Although most historical theories of wages are economic, the oldest is essentially sociological. The *just-price theory*, followed in the Middle Ages, involved setting wages in accordance with the established status distribution. Wages were systematically regulated to keep each class in its customary, and hence "right," place in society. Higher-status persons got higher wages. This emphasis on equity, the tying of wages to status, and the preservation of customary relationships, although developed in preindustrial times, has a modern ring. *Coercive comparisons,* in which unions and employees insist on the correctness of comparisons designed to preserve customary relationships, seem to reflect this theory. So do today's organizations' pay policies, which call for supervisors to be paid more than subordinates. Equity theory, developed in the next chapter, also seems based in part on such thinking. As we will discover in our discussion of

---

[2]For more on these two fields of economics see A. Rees, *The Economics of Work and Pay,* 2nd ed. (New York: Harper & Row, Pub., 1979).

wage relationships (structures), customary relationships continue to exert a powerful force.

During the Industrial Revolution, market forces became dominant and laissez-faire principles were invoked to free market forces from custom and regulation. Adam Smith set the stage for what is now called *classical wage theory* by providing a plausible explanation of the relation between the price of goods and the amount of labor required to secure them. Although he did not develop a wage theory, he made a number of observations pertinent to wages. His labor theory of value, which concluded that the full value of any commodity is the amount of labor it will buy, may be considered a theory of labor demand. But his observations on wage differentials speak to today's wage issues. He suggested that people choose the employment that yields the greatest net advantage. Five characteristics, he proposed, are used to differentiate jobs and thus net advantage: (1) hardship, (2) difficulty of learning the job, (3) stability of employment, (4) responsibility of the job, and (5) chance for success or failure in the work. He also identified two quite different standards for comparing things of value: use value and market value. *Use value* refers to the value anticipated from use of the item. It varies among individuals and over time. *Market value* refers to the price something will bring. In a free market where demand and supply are equal, use value will equal market value. Because, as pointed out in the previous chapter, labor markets do not clear, use value and market value would be expected to differ.

It was Thomas R. Malthus's theory of population that provided the raw material for the first economic wage theory. Population, according to the theory, is limited by the means of subsistence: it increases geometrically whereas the means of subsistence increases arithmetically. David Ricardo translated Malthus's theory into the *subsistence theory* of wages. According to this theory, wages in the long run tend to equal the cost of reproducing labor—the subsistence of the laborer. This theory, often called *the iron law of wages,* indicated that little could be done to improve the lot of the wage earner because increasing wages leads only to increasing the number of workers beyond the means of subsistence.

The subsistence theory was an explanation of the general level of wages in terms of labor supply. Any increase in the wage rate above the subsistence level would induce an increase in the birth rate and therefore in the supply of labor. The expanded labor supply would force the wage rate back to the subsistence level. Any decrease in the wage rate below the subsistence level would result in starvation and a reduction in the labor supply. Although the market price of labor might temporarily climb above or fall below the natural price, the two would converge in the long run.

In the industrial world, the theory erred in two ways: (1) improvements in technology have greatly increased the means of subsistence, and (2) cultural forces have limited birth rates. Although Ricardo recognized the potential effects of the second factor, he believed that labor supply rather than labor demand would determine the general wage level in the long run.

Although the iron law of wages seems to have been repealed in the industrial world, it appears to be still in effect in many other parts of the world. Population growth holds back economic development in many developing countries. Famine is still part of the world scene. High unemployment in most of the industrial world and the previously mentioned effects of the "baby boom" on the American labor force suggest further that Ricardo had a point.

The short-term version of classical wage theory was the *wages-fund theory*. As described by John Stuart Mill this theory explained the short-term variations in the general wage level in terms of (1) the number of available workers and (2) the size of the wages fund. The wages fund was thought to come from resources accumulated by employers from previous years and allocated by them to buy labor currently. Employers were thought to have a fixed stock of "circulating capital" for the payment of wages. Dividing the labor force (assumed to be the population) into the wages fund determined the wage.

The theory erred in assuming that a fixed fund for the payment of wages exists and that it accounts for labor demand. Most workers are paid out of current production. Employers balance labor costs against other costs in determining labor demand. Both employers and workers, however, often talk as if such funds exist and as if they determine the amount of labor services needed. They may also accept the implication of the theory that any gain to one group is a loss to others.

Francis A. Walker's *residual claimant theory* may be thought of as an American version of the wages-fund theory. Here, the workers demand for wages represents the residual claimant on output after rent, interest, and profit have been independently determined and deducted. Assigning wages rather than profits as the residual seems curious, but it does suggest that distribution of income is a matter of decision. It also permitted Walker to suggest that if labor increased its productivity without the use of more capital or land, its residual would increase—the germ of a productivity theory.

The economic and social climate that produced classical wage theory perhaps inevitably produced *Marxian wage theory*. Marx accepted the subsistence and the wages-fund theories. He interpreted Smith's and Ricardo's labor theory of value as meaning that labor is the sole source of economic value. His explanation of the wage-setting process was that the entrepreneur collects the value created by labor but pays labor only the cost of subsistence. The difference is surplus value, roughly equivalent to profit. The existence of surplus value means exploitation of labor. Competition among capitalists, Marx argued, results in the accumulation of labor-saving capital ("jellied labor"). This substitution of capital for labor results in technological unemployment and a reserve army of unemployed. Because labor is the only source of value, substituting capital for labor results in a falling rate of profits. The only solution for capitalists is to spend relatively more on capital and relatively less on labor. In this way, surplus value can be maintained by further exploitation of labor. This exploitation of labor in turn results in a class conflict which would, according to Marx, result in the demise of capitalism.

Although Marx's assumptions and predictions were faulty, his arguments are still voiced in parts of the underdeveloped world and by radical economists in the United States. Capital produces value, but it can be defined as embodied labor. Land also produces value. In the industrial world, labor's absolute and relative share of the fruits of production has continually increased and real wages have risen. Although many of Marx's objectives have been realized without revolution, his argument that income distribution depends on social decisions as well as economic forces remains valid.

We have seen that historical theories of wages hold some implications for modern wage issues. But their emphasis on the general level of wages leaves many particular wage decisions without guidance. Further, it is instructive that neither the theories that emphasize labor supply nor those that emphasize labor demand were sufficient to provide a comprehensive model of the labor market. In fact, the theories emphasizing noneconomic variables seem to yield more complete answers. The just-price theory, with its sociological explanation of wages, and the Marxian implications of the influence of the social system on wages may have more to say to wage decision makers than classical economic theory.

But the values that flow from classical and Marxian wage theory continue to influence current thought. For example, the beliefs that attempts to improve the lot of the worker are self-defeating and that unions aid their members at the expense of nonunion members seem to be a legacy of classical wage theory. Also, the fear of "exploitation of labor" may be a bequest from Marx.

CONTEMPORARY LABOR ECONOMICS THEORIES

As mentioned, labor economists in recent years have developed some precise models of economic variables that bear on labor markets and have tested them empirically. The requirements of careful testing have meant that models of parts rather than of labor-market operation as a whole have been developed. Thus wage theory includes the quite well verified models of labor supply, labor demand, the search process, collective bargaining, wage structures of various kinds, benefits, and the general level of money wages.[3]

Some of these models have been elaborately developed and carefully tested over time. Others have been less well developed and subjected to fewer empirical tests. In either case, we shall attempt to discuss them in a nontechnical manner.

Labor Supply

Labor economists now define labor supply as the amount of work supplied by a given population. From this definition, four dimensions of labor supply are usually noted: (1) the labor force participation rate, (2) the number of hours people are willing to work, (3) the amount of effort workers exert at work, and (4) the level of training and skill of workers.

The concept of the labor force and labor force participation rates was discussed in chapter 2. Labor force participation rates depend on labor-supply decisions within the household that are made only partially on economic grounds. These rates vary by age, sex, race, and educational attainment as well as somewhat over time. The labor force participation rate has been shown to vary in the same direction as labor demand. This conclusion comes largely from studies of labor-force response to unemployment. The added worker response is less than the discouraged-worker effect.[4]

[3]See Rees, op. cit.

[4]W. G. Bowen and T. A. Finegan, *The Economics of Labor Force Participation* (Princeton, N.J.: Princeton University Press, 1968), p. 482.

Variation in hours of work offered by the labor force is explained by the theory of choice between work and leisure. This theory shows how a rational decision maker would respond to opportunities for work and leisure. Models may be constructed relating hours of work and household income under various assumptions. Such an analysis separates the *substitution effect* (an increase in the price of leisure which encourages longer hours) and the *income effect* (the ability to buy more of everything which encourages shorter hours). The sum of these two effects is the total effect of income changes on hours of work. This type of analysis may be applied to the effect of wage changes, the effect of income or payroll taxes, effects of competition in labor and product markets, personal preferences, productivity changes, nonwork income, and overtime and shift premiums. Empirical work based on these analyses shows that the income effect is greater than the substitution effect—that wage increases reduce preferred hours, but not as much as nonlabor income increases. Worker preferences are shown to have a powerful influence on working hours. Worker preferences are not uniform among individuals. Overtime premiums make most workers eager to work overtime. Shift premiums are usually too small to encourage work at unusual hours.

The theory of supply of effort is much less developed. The pace of work should be faster where hours are short. There should be an increase in the intensity of effort as real wages rise, because of a better diet and better medical care. In industrialized countries the primary effect of level of wages on effort operates through supervision and incentive-pay plans. But custom serves to set limits in work pace.

The quality of labor supplies is explained by *human capital theory*. Experience, schooling, and on-the-job training are forms of investment in human capital. So are expenditures designed to improve worker health and the costs of migration to labor markets offering better employment opportunities.

Human capital theory analyzes the effects of additional experience, education, and on-the-job training on the quality of the labor force. It also analyzes employee and employer decisions on investment in human capital.

Private investment in schooling is analyzed by comparing the age-earnings profiles of individuals having differing amounts of schooling. The costs of continued education to the individual include costs of foregone earnings (the larger) and direct costs. To be worthwhile, an investment in additional education must yield lifetime earnings in excess of these costs. The analysis usually includes discounting additional earnings at some rate of interest to yield the present value of that investment.

Such analyses show that continued-education returns are greater at completion points than in intermediate years. They also show, not surprisingly, that these investments made later in life yield a lower return. Furthermore, a high rate of return could attract many more college entrants and eventually eliminate the return. Such calculations should be made after taxes. Some of this effect of increased education was noted in chapter 2.

An additional potential individual return to additional education is preferred placement in the queue for scarce, highly paid jobs. To the extent that employers use education as a selector, private returns to education are increased.

Calculations of human capital from age-earnings profiles are complicated by the productivity effects of continued experience. Another difficulty is the correlation between amount of education and ability, although the effect of ability on rate of return has been found to be slight.[5]

Human capital analysis can also be applied to training in the multiple skills required in an occupation by employing age-earnings profiles of occupations. The same kind of analysis can be applied to formal apprenticeship.

Human capital theory may yield even more information on the qualitative dimension of labor supply when applied to on-the-job training. Training within organizations involves costs. To minimize those costs, organizations usually try to hire and keep experienced employees.

On-the-job training can be usefully divided into general and specific training.[6] General training provides skills useful to the organization providing it and to other organizations. Specific training provides skills useful to the former alone. Employers expect to and do pay for specific training by paying trainees more than they are worth during training. This cost can be recouped over the period of employment by paying the workers slightly less than they are worth after the training is completed. General training, however, must be paid for by the worker through lower wages during the training period.

Some conclusions about labor supply can now be stated. Decisions on labor-force participation, hours of work, and investment in human capital are interrelated. Individuals who expect to be in the labor force all of their lives have a stronger economic incentive to invest in education. People receiving on-the-job training may work longer hours. Workers with large investments in human capital are less likely to retire early. But all of these decisions are influenced by wages, costs of training, taxes, and other income.

Supply curves of employee hours can be drawn at the level of the occupation, the industry, the area, or the economy as a whole. The horizontal axis is employee hours at all levels; the vertical axis is relative wages, except at the economy level, where it is real hourly wages. The supply curve for any particular occupation, industry, or area must be forward-sloping when measured against the wages in this employment relative to wages elsewhere. The reason is that a higher relative wage attracts labor into the activity for which it is paid. For unskilled occupations, labor supply can be almost flat, even in the short run. For occupations requiring specialized skills demanding a long period of training, the short-run supply curve can be almost vertical. Over time, if changes in relative wages attracted more people to training, the slope would decrease unless training places were fixed or people left the employment as fast as new ones were added.

The supply of labor to an occupation will have an upward slope even in the very long run, for a number of reasons. Some occupations call upon innate talents. Others have nonpecuniary advantages and disadvantages that different people value differently. As an occupation expands, it must eventually recruit people who dislike it and demand higher earnings to enter it.

In general, both short-run and long-run supply curves for occupations requiring training slope upward to the right. Short-run supply curves are not perfectly vertical (inelastic). Long-run supply curves are not perfectly flat (elastic).

A labor-supply curve for the economy as a whole in developed countries may be downward-sloping (or *backward-bending*). This occurs because of

[5]G. S. Becker, *Human Capital* (New York: National Bureau of Economic Research, 1964).
[6]Ibid.

the tendency for hours per year to be reduced as real income rises with the labor force participation rate unchanged.

Labor Demand

The theory of labor demand explains how much labor employers want to employ at different wage rates. As such, it is a major component of wage theory in situations where market forces have influence.

The generally accepted theory of demand for labor is an application of the *marginal-productivity theory* of the demand for any factor of production where two or more factors cooperate. Because the demand for labor is derived from the demand for a product or service, it is almost always employed in combination with other productive factors. A demand schedule for labor is a functional relation between a price (wage) and the quantity of labor demanded. Demand alone does not determine the wage except where the supply schedule is perfectly vertical (inelastic)—a very unusual situation. Demand has no effect on the wage where the supply curve is perfectly flat (elastic), but it does determine employment. In all other cases, wages and employment are jointly determined by supply and demand.

Quantity of labor demand may be expressed in working hours if it is assumed that wages represent the total costs of employment and that labor productivity is independent of the length of the workweek. Demand for labor in competitive markets is derived from a production function representing for an unchanging technology all possible combinations of labor and capital inputs. Selecting a particular production function to produce maximum output at some fixed level of capital inputs produces the short-run marginal (additional)-product schedule of labor (see figure 3–1).

The downward-sloping portion of this curve shows how the marginal-productivity schedule determines the quantity of labor demand in the short run. This downward slope represents the law of diminishing returns. Assuming that all units of production are sold at the same price (which they are under competitive conditions), the marginal-productivity schedule times price is the short-run demand for labor.

Deriving the long-run demand for labor involves assuming that the nature of capital services can be varied. Since it is possible to substitute capital for

Figure 3–1   Short-run, marginal product schedule of labor

labor through changes in the amount and kind of capital equipment, the long-run demand curve for labor is flatter (more elastic). In the still longer run, technology can be influenced by relative factor prices, so that new technologies are devised that shift production functions, resulting in more output for given quantities of inputs.

Under competitive conditions, where product prices are assumed constant, an organization's demand for labor is the product of marginal physical product times price to get the value of marginal product (VMP). The demand curve for a labor market is the sum of the demand curves for the firms included in that market.

Since the demand for labor is derived from the demand for products or services, a shift in the demand for the products will produce a shift in the demand for labor in the same direction. Likewise, even under competitive conditions, an increase in costs in one industry may result in substitutions in production and, if price must be increased, substitution by consumers. Thus, the slope of the demand curve for product (elasticity) and ease of substitution by the producer affect the shape of the labor-demand curve. In fact, demand for labor will have more slope (more inelasticity), if it is harder for producers and consumers to substitute. Smaller ratios of labor cost to total cost (unless the producer can substitute more easily than the consumer) and more slope (more inelasticity) in the supply of other factors have the same effect.

A labor-demand curve for the entire economy can be constructed for competitive conditions by assuming that the aggregate demand for all the factors remains unchanged. This demand curve will still slope downward but will have less slope than curves at lower levels of aggregation.

The demand for labor in markets that are not perfectly competitive is derived by dropping the assumption that product or labor markets are competitive. Dropping the assumption that product markets are competitive results in a downward-sloping demand for product. In this case, the demand curve for labor is the marginal-revenue product (MRP is the marginal physical product times marginal revenue). Labor is demanded up to the point where the wage is equal to the marginal revenue product. Since in product markets that are not perfectly competitive marginal revenue is always less than price, MRP must always be less than VMP. Thus a profit-maximizing monopolist, confronted with a given wage, will employ labor up to the point where the cost of another hour of labor is equal to the marginal-revenue product (see figure 3–2).

Restoring the assumption of product-market competition but dropping the assumption of labor-market competition gives us a situation in which a *labor monopsonist* (single buyer) is confronted with an upward-sloping supply curve for labor. Because (1) the upward-sloping curve represents the supply of homogeneous labor, (2) the employer must pay higher wages to get more workers, and (3) all workers must get the same wage, the employer faces a steeper upward-sloping marginal-labor cost (MLC) curve (see figure 3–3). This means the monopsonist sets employment where MLC crosses VMP but pays the wage specified by S at that employment. Note that a minimum wage above W_o would increase employment.

A monopsonist hiring each worker at the worker's own supply price (a discriminating monopsonist) would pay unequal wages for equal work. A perfectly discriminating monopsonist would pay competitive wages and set em-

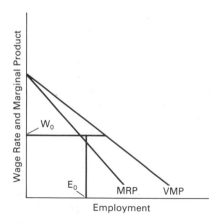

Figure 3–2 Demand for labor under imperfect competition

ployment at the competitive level, but would be earning profits on employees who are worth more than their supply price. Such a policy is more possible for professional and managerial employees under a policy of pay secrecy.

Another possibility is collusive monopsony, resulting from an agreement among employers not to raise wages or pirate each other's employees. Such a policy requires loose labor markets and the policing of pay policies other than those concerning pay levels.

Abandoning the assumption of homogeneous labor would permit an employer to hire the best workers first and then add the less able. This would result in a more steeply sloped MRP curve and reduced employment.

Marginal-productivity theory assumes that the demand schedule is independent of the wage rate. It is sometimes argued that this assumption is

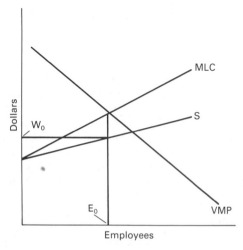

Figure 3–3 Wages and employment under monopsony

incorrect—that a wage increase can increase the efficiency of workers or of management. The assumption that the demand schedule is independent of the wage rate probably has little merit in developed countries. The opposing argument, called *shock theory*, assumes that all organizations have slack and that when threatened increase their efficiency. Thus a new, higher marginal-productivity curve is created. Shock theory is most plausible when applied to a newly unionized employer.

Up to this point it has been assumed that the cost of labor to the employer consists only of the hourly wage. Dropping this assumption permits recognition that there are fixed costs of employment that vary less than proportionately with the hours an employee works. There are turnover costs, for example, including recruitment, selection, and training costs as well as severance pay and increased unemployment-insurance costs. Other costs, such as some taxes on employment plus contributions to health and welfare plans, are unrelated to hours of work. Other benefits are not fixed costs unless they are based on hours worked.

Many turnover costs are related to employee skill level, and employers are more reluctant to lose skilled employees. Employer provision of greater stability of employment for skilled employees may be largely explained by these fixed costs. A similar distinction is often made between manual and white-collar employees.

If employers keep workers in site of a drop in demand because of their investment in them, the effect is to pay them above their current marginal product. This is done on the assumption that their marginal product will exceed their wage over a longer period of time.

The fixed costs of employment also motivate employers to try to cut voluntary turnover. Thus employers find it to their advantage to tie some benefits and layoffs to seniority and to consider seniority in promotions.

Organizations that make extensive use of internal labor markets and have few ports of entry, are especially likely to emphasize promotion from within to protect their investment in training. Markets for workers with specialized training cannot be highly competitive, and employers can be expected to try to cut turnover in order to spread the fixed costs of employment over a long tenure.

The fixed costs of employment also partially explain the growth of temporary-help agencies. The employer pays an hourly rate above the prevailing rate for permanent employees. The worker gets less to cover fixed costs and agency fees, but can work the hours he or she prefers.

An additional employer decision affected by the fixed costs of employment concerns demand for overtime hours. Overtime hours involve payment of a premium and often losses of efficiency. But adding workers instead of assigning present employees overtime increases the fixed costs of employment. Because, as discussed, fixed costs increase for skilled workers, the rising level of skill increases these costs and may encourage overtime.

Search in Labor Markets

Analysis of search in labor markets explains how workers and employers search for and find each other. Because labor markets differ from other markets, the way in which they operate must be considered. As mentioned in chapter 2, labor markets usually do not clear (demand doesn't equal supply), in part because wages do not respond fully to changes in the supply and demand factors. This is particularly true in surplus labor conditions, which lead to the comment that wages are "sticky on the downside." The quantity of labor supplied is composed of employment and unemployment. The quantity demanded consists of employment and job vacancies. It is useful to think of a labor market as a flow of people from unemployment to job vacancies where both pools are constantly being renewed. Although the pools are related, they are subject to different forces.

SEARCH BY INDIVIDUALS.   Because of differences among workers and jobs, even within an occupation, and because employment usually involves an important, long-term transaction, search is required by both parties. Furthermore, the search is required each time an employment exchange is made. Large differences in terms offered may occur, and substantial costs of search may be justified.

Even an experienced unemployed worker looking for a job in his or her usual occupation is unlikely to know which employers are hiring without searching. Employers will be offering different wages. Because accepting the first offer would be unlikely to produce the best bargain, the worker must search. Costs of search involve the worker's own time (the most important) and direct costs.

As more openings are found and investigated, the probability of getting a better offer decreases. Eventually, the worker decides that further search will cost more than it will gain and accepts the best offer still open. The possibility that the job has been filled or that the employer's time limit for acceptance or rejection has been exceeded increases search costs.

If unemployment is very high, a worker may accept the first job offered. The search may be long and costly before any offer is received. Frictional unemployment (that generated by the search process) is thus related to labor demand.

Job seekers include not only the unemployed but those who are dissatisfied with their job and are looking for a better one. High-level employees usually find another job before leaving their present one. In this case, the chief cost of search is the loss of leisure time.

Accepting or rejecting job offers does not turn exclusively on the wage offered. Job security, commuting costs, advancement opportunities, benefits, and other less tangible factors are considered. If, however, the wage rate is the only certain information, it may be decisive.

When job seekers enter the market with a minimum acceptable wage from the last job or information from others, the search may take longer. But this lower limit is revised by offers received until an acceptable one is found.

EMPLOYER SEARCH.   Employers with vacancies are also engaged in search. If they find their vacancies are hard to fill, they improve wage offers or lower their hiring standards. Employers can cut search (recruitment) costs by paying above-average wages, hoping to attract a pool of applicants. They can also attempt to keep present employees and to recruit friends of present employees. Most commonly, they use internal labor markets as a source of present employees, so that only a few jobs are filled from external labor markets.

Large employers hiring substantial numbers of people for jobs are less likely to change wage offers. They are most likely to widen their area of search, use more varied recruitment methods, or lower their hiring standards. Low-wage employers must search longer, spend more on recruitment, and perhaps lower hiring standards more often. High-wage employers can often choose from among a pool of applicants and spend less on recruiting. Employers who frequently use internal labor markets must look for promotion potential as well as present skills.

Employers also must decide how long to continue their search. If applicants do not meet the organization's hiring standards, the cost of lowering standards is compared with the costs of further recruiting and leaving vacancies unfilled. If the latter costs are too high, hiring standards are lowered and the best applicants are hired. When unemployment is low, search costs go up.

If the organization finds outside recruiting too costly and decides to fill the job from within, this can lead to numerous moves within the organization. Because only the remaining lower-level job is eventually filled from outside, external search costs will be lower, but the costs of the internal moves must be considered.

The search process varies by skill level in recruitment methods and in distance covered. Employers broaden their search for incumbents for higher-level jobs. Applicants for these jobs also employ a broader search. Higher-skilled job seekers, especially managers and professionals, are often willing to move to other areas for higher wages or better jobs. But this movement is not enough to equalize wages in different areas.

Unemployment affects the search process, as mentioned. But the type of unemployment is also important. Demand-deficiency unemployment, which results from sluggishness in the economy, has different effects than frictional, structural, and seasonal unemployment. *Frictional unemployment* occurs because it takes time for employers and workers to find each other, even though they occupy the same markets and the same places. *Structural unemployment* involves a mismatch between worker skills and job requirements, or the existence of workers and jobs in different places. *Seasonal unemployment* is exactly what the term implies. Unemployment may also be differentiated as voluntary and involuntary. Voluntary unemployment involves workers who have been offered a job they can fill but who continue to search for a better one. Involuntary unemployment means that willing, qualified workers can't find jobs. Voluntary unemployment is frictional; involuntary, demand-deficient.

The relationship between job vacancies and unemployment may be analyzed formally. For any given structure of the labor market the relationship is curvilinear and negative. Improving the functioning of the labor market by retraining workers or by relocating workers and jobs reduces both. But such analysis also shows that the balance between unemployment and job vacancies is different for each possible structure of the labor market. Also, such analysis shows that if it is assumed that wages are rigid downward and that wages will rise in any market having more vacancies then unemployed, the average level of wages will rise as long as there is excess demand in any labor market. Finally, such analysis shows the difficulty of separating the different types of unemployment. If, as we emphasized in chapter 2, there are thousands of labor markets, however, structural unemployment must be larger than frictional unemployment.

Structural unemployment varies by place, industry, occupation, and type of worker. Much of it is consistent with fixed costs of employment. Unemployment rates are higher for mature women as a result of their less continuous labor-force participation. They are lower in high-skill occupations. Teenage workers have higher unemployment rates. Some of minority unemployment reflects differences in educational attainment and occupations.

The seriousness of unemployment depends on its duration. Cyclical and structural unemployment are longer than frictional. Teenage workers have the most unemployment but also the shortest. Because one of the purposes of our unemployment compensation system is to make possible a longer search, improving benefits raises frictional unemployment.

Unions and Collective Bargaining

Economic analysis by labor economists attempts to determine how unions and collective bargaining affect labor-market variables—labor supplies, labor demand, wages, and employment. Because unions are both economic and political entities, formal models are of limited usefulness. The following discussion of the economic functions of unions excludes their social and political functions. The final section of this chapter, covering the contributions of institutional economists, takes up some of these.

Because leaders and members of unions share power and because any union gains go to members and not the union, it is impossible to model a union as a maximizer of anything. Thus, assuming a union to be a monopolistic seller of labor is meaningless, because unions have no profit to maximize. The assumption that unions attempt to maximize the wage bill is even worse, because it involves setting a wage below the supply price of labor. Assuming that unions try to increase membership and the wage level is more promising, but the weight attached to each of these goals varies from union to union. Assuming that wages and employment are union goals and imperfect substitutes for each other not only varies among unions but may pit the goal of union membership against either.[7]

Union wage policy is best explained by the critical role of the current money wage when compared with other goals, such as size of membership or amount of employment. Unions sometimes grant wage concessions to employers (especially when union-management relations are good and when such concessions are not visible to other employers). But wage concessions are always fought. Union demands are strongly influenced by comparisons with other groups of workers, but the comparisons emphasized are those that would justify a wage increase. A union definition of equity usually involves a comparison with a more highly paid group doing comparable work. In the long run the importance given to claims for relative wage increases is influenced by labor-market conditions.

It has been assumed that when unions emphasize wage demands they expect that employers will set employment on their labor-demand curve. Some unions, however, force employers to use more labor than they need at the union wage; this in turn forces them off the demand curve to the right. This

[7]A. M. Cartter, *The Theory of Wages and Employment* (Homewood, Ill.: Richard D. Irwin, 1959), ch. 2–4.

practice, called *featherbedding,* is more prevalent in craft than in industrial unions. Formal analysis of featherbedding rules shows that at some point in union demands no labor will be employed, that these rules do not increase total employment, and that they may force employers to change factor proportions.

Economic analysis of bargaining power shows that union power is based largely on the strike. Lesser sources are political action, boycotts, and control of the labor supply. Employer bargaining power involves the ability to replace strikers, the capacity to carry on production, and financial resources. The balance of power differs greatly among bargaining situations.

Developing formal models of the collective bargaining process has been difficult. In most situations the parties are forced to deal with each other on terms both parties accept, a power concept. Nor are the parties dealing with a set of fixed parameters: prices may be raised or employment may be cut, for example. In collective bargaining, there are always pressures from other sources, such as the public. Also, the bargaining involves many variables, only some of which may be quantified.

A formal bargaining theory applicable to wages has been developed. Its central proposition is that each party compares its probable gain from a strike with the expected costs. The present value of the expected gains over the contract period is compared with the expected costs. Unfortunately, the expected gains and costs cannot be known in advance. Also, a matter of principle or equity is sometimes involved. During a strike a combination of rising costs and improved information brings the parties closer together and eventually produces a settlement. The cost of a strike to a union is higher when business is bad; the cost to management is higher when business is good.

Labor economists have also measured the effects of unionism on relative earnings. This is a difficult task, because the comparison must be between union and nonunion workers who are as much alike as possible. These differentials may be biased, however, since nonunion employers often raise wages when unions win increases.

The direct effect of unions on nonunion wages is called the *threat effect.* Indirect effects occur in tight labor markets, when nonunion employers must increase wages to compete with union employers for employees.

Comparing wages in union and nonunion firms tends to understate union effects because of the threat effect. Comparing wages as a function of the percentage of workers covered by union contracts is more useful in comparing product markets. Such measurements show that the effect of the proportion of workers organized is nonlinear. When only a small percentage of the market is organized, the union has little effect. But the union effect approaches its maximum well before 100 percent organization, because of the threat effect. The union effect in all comparisons may be overstated if employers respond to higher union wages by hiring more qualified workers.

It is also possible to make wage comparisons over time between the unionized sector of the economy and other sectors (agriculture, domestics, small firms). These comparisons lower the union effect to the extent that union wages reduce employment in the union sector and thus increase labor supplies in nonunion sectors.

Collective bargaining raises wages. It also makes them more rigid, because labor contracts are for fixed periods. Thus the union effect is greater in depressions and quite small in periods of rapid inflation. But union effects vary by the type of union and the skill level of those organized as well as by differences in product markets. Unions of skilled workers facing an inelastic labor demand may win large wage increases with little reduction in employment. This is especially true when their wages represent a small part of total costs and where they bargain independently. However, these effects cannot occur if all crafts bargain together or follow a pattern that spreads to all crafts. In general, craft unions have not been as effective in raising wages as industrial unions, perhaps because union wage policy often calls for reducing wage differentials and political forces often result in the largest absolute increases for the least skilled.

The question of whether strong unions gain more in competitive or monopolistic product markets has not been answered. Although the answer depends on the elasticity of demand for a product, unions bargaining with monopolists may lose more employment with a given wage increase than when they bargain with a competitive firm. Also, monopolists or oligopolists that administer prices may raise prices by more than the increase in labor costs and blame the price increase on the union.[8]

Because unions change relative wages, they also affect the allocation of labor among sectors of the economy and may cause losses in total output from misallocation of labor. This effect results when workers move from the union sector to the nonunion sector because the union sector becomes more capital-intensive and the nonunion sector more labor-intensive. In this move, the productivity of labor goes down. This effect, although, has been found to be very small.

Although one of the goals of unions has been to increase labor's share of the national income, there is no evidence that they have done so. Although labor's share has risen over the years, this rise can probably be attributed to a decline in the relative price of capital goods and an increase in investment in training and education.

Wage Structure

Wage structure theory seeks to explain the many structures of wage differentials: occupational, industry, geographical, by race and sex, and within groups. Particular differentials seldom appear in pure form. Also, the economic significance of some wage structures is greater than that of others.

OCCUPATIONAL DIFFERENTIALS.   Occupational wage differentials reflect differences among workers in levels and kinds of skill and in conditions of work. In a perfectly competitive market almost no industry differentials except those that flow from different occupational mixes would be expected.

The forces that determine the wage level of an occupation change greatly with the period considered. In the very short run, the number of people qualified for all but the lowest-skill occupations is fixed, and if the demand for labor in an occupation rises, wages will rise. Thus the short-run supply is inelastic and demand determines the wage. If the time period is lengthened to

---

[8]A. Rees, "Wage–Price Relations in the Basic Steel Industry, 1945–48," *Industrial and Labor Relations Review,* January 1953, pp. 195–225.

include time for training people, the supply depends on tastes, training costs, and expected career earnings. Thus the long-run supply could be highly elastic, with the wage determined largely by the height of the supply curve and employment by demand.

The long-run wage structures of any two occupations may be differentiated by training requirements, worker tastes, nonpecuniary advantages, worker expectations about future earnings, and the rate used to discount future earnings. If there are no differences except in training requirements, the long-run supply curve of the higher-skill occupation will be perfectly elastic at a constant differential that when discounted just covers the cost of training. If nonpecuniary advantages are not equal and workers prefer the higher-skill occupation, the wage differential will not cover training costs. If workers prefer the lower-skill occupation, the differential will have to be more than enough to cover training costs.

Differences among workers in tastes and expectations would cause the long-run supply curve for the higher-skill occupation to slope upward (it would be more inelastic). For constant training costs, larger differentials would be needed to attract those whose tastes and expectations differed most from those who like the occupation the most.

The advantages of an occupation include the pay and other amenities that go with it plus its prestige and the satisfactions of working in it. But worker tastes differ. If workers are arrayed in order from those who like an occupation the most to those who like it the least, they will form an upward-sloping supply curve. When wages are measured relative to other occupations requiring the same amount of training, then if everyone dislikes an occupation there must be a positive wage differential, but the size of the differential will depend on demand.

This compensating differential, however, may not be required if there is substantial demand-deficiency unemployment or if there are many unemployed immigrants or minority workers. These latter groups may bid down the wage for disagreeable work that requires little skill until it is no more than the wage for agreeable work requiring no more skill.

Occupational wage differentials may also be rents for scarce natural talents. In the case of most athletes, actors, and artists, such rents account for the differentials in earnings between the most successful and the average. If average earnings in these fields are above those in others requiring as much training but less ability, the difference also represents costs. If, however, many people of modest talent enter the occupation and fail, the result can be low pay and frequent unemployment. Such entrants might even drive average wages below those of other skilled occupations in which ability is less important.

The most important component of occupational wage differentials is the return on investment in acquiring skills. To acquire new entrants a skilled occupation must return the private costs of training over the entrants' working life discounted at their rate of return.

The historical tendency for percentage occupational differentials to decline is best explained by lower private costs of training. Governments have reduced such costs through compulsory school attendance laws and free and subsidized public education. If all the costs of training needed to acquire skill were paid by the public, occupational differentials would be much smaller and would be based on compensation for the nonpecuniary disadvantages of occupations and on rents for scarce abilities. Restricted immigration earlier in this century has also been a force in narrowing occupational differentials.

In the short run, skill differentials narrow during labor shortages. This results from more individuals shifting to higher-skill and presumably more pleasant jobs and from the lowering of hiring standards for skilled jobs.

Changes in unionism have also affected skill differentials. When the labor movement was dominated by craft unions there were wider differentials between the skilled and unskilled. Industrial unionism, however, narrows skill differentials through across-the-board absolute increases.

The process of correcting unjustified occupational differentials works differently when they are too large than when they are too small. When the relative wage of an occupation is too high, it is almost never cut and for long periods more people train for the occupation than there are openings. When the relative wage for an occupation is too low, the most likely result is higher starting pay and faster promotions. Thus the adjustment process falls heavily on expanding occupations and the difference between the pay for new recruits and that for longer-service employees is compressed.

Occupational differentials, as mentioned, account for many industry differentials. They also account for many regional differentials. A major factor is the skill mix in the industry or region.

RACE AND SEX DIFFERENTIALS.   Economic analysis of wage differentials between men and women and among the races seeks to explain the forces that cause them. It is well known that such differentials exist. Men earn more than women. Minorities earn less than whites. These differentials arise in part from discrimination in labor markets and in part from productivity differences, some of which may be traced to past discrimination in the labor market and in education.

The most common forms of discrimination are refusing to hire women or minorities in jobs for which they are qualified, employing them at lower wages, or insisting on higher qualifications at the same wage. All of these practices by an employer are illegal under federal law. But demanding higher qualifications from women and minorities for doing the same work or excluding them from certain jobs still occurs. Also, because employers in the same market pay different wages for the same occupation, minorities and women are overrepresented among employees of low-paying employers. Occupational distributions suggest that discrimination is greater in higher-level occupations, but differences in educational attainment is a partial explanation. Women are overrepresented in white-collar (especially clerical work) and service occupations and underrepresented in blue-collar occupations, especially the crafts. Although women form a higher proportion of professional and technical occupations than men, the higher-paid professional occupations are heavily male.

Discrimination in labor markets may also be traced to prejudice by the employer to an employer's belief that his or her employees or customers are prejudiced. Discrimination in labor markets may arise from the belief that minorities are less productive than they in fact are. A theory of discrimination developed by Becker asserts that a discriminator behaves as though the wage required to hire a woman or a minority member includes a positive discrimination coefficient based on prejudices.[9] Such an employer is willing to sacrifice profits to indulge these beliefs. The wage differential between equally competent blacks and whites in a competitive labor market depends upon the distribution of employers by extent of discrimination and the size of the minority group. The more discrimination in a market and the larger the supply of minority workers, the lower the relative wage.

If employers believe that employees and customers are prejudiced, a different analysis is required. If most skilled workers are white and they prefer to work with white unskilled workers, the employer who hires blacks must pay his or her skilled workers a premium (assuming the wage of unskilled blacks is below that of unskilled whites).

The prejudice of whites against having a black supervisor or of men against a female supervisor may require an even larger premium. Assuming a correlation between education and supervisory potential, this force lowers the return on education for blacks and women.

Unions have affected the racial wage differential. Many craft unions used to exclude black members, thus shifting skilled minority workers into the nonunion sector and lowering wages. Industrial unions have not excluded black members, but some locals have, especially at higher occupational levels. The overall effect of unionism on black-white differentials is to reduce the differential; the effect is greater where the proportion of black union members is smaller. Because fewer women are union members unions have probably widened the male-female differential. As mentioned in chapter 2, unions and women are discovering each other, and the effect of this will be to reduce this differential.

Consumer prejudice can operate in occupations where workers have contact with customers. Although it operates in both directions, the net effect may be to lower the relative incomes of minorities and women. This result would be expected if white males determine policy and whites have higher purchasing power.

Sex and race wage differentials are also due to productivity differences. The clearest source of these is education, which may differ in both quality and quantity. Low educational attainment is an independent source of wage differentials. But until recently there was more discrimination against educated blacks, which lowered their return on their education and their investment in education.

Blacks also receive less on-the-job training than whites—a result of higher unemployment for blacks and less experience. Also, blacks have been underrepresented in occupations where experience has the greatest value.

Women's relative wages suffer from the same productivity forces and some additional ones. Although few jobs today require heavy physical work, the fact that women typically have less strength and the survival of laws that limit what they can lift keep women out of work they could do. Cultural expectations toward women affect their investment in education. When they have young children they may work part-time and be out of the labor force for a time. These forces lower women's return to education, labor-force experience, and on-the-job training. Productivity-related factors, however, do not explain

[9]J. Becker, *The Economics of Discrimination* (Chicago: University of Chicago Press, 1957).

all of the sex differential in wages. Moreover, reduction in discrimination by increasing women's incentives to invest in education and careers would reduce productivity differences.

Economic analysis of the effect of antidiscrimination laws differs somewhat by law and by employer familiarity and enforcement efforts. The effect of equal-pay laws is to reduce employment of women previously encouraged by pay differentials, assuming the barrier to employment is on the demand side. If equal-pay laws are better understood and enforced than equal-opportunity laws, the effect could be reduced employment of minorities and women. If the opposite is true, such employment could be increased. But such laws change attitudes. An early study of state fair-employment laws showed that both relative wages and employment increased after their enactment.[10]

WAGE DIFFERENTIALS WITHIN GROUPS. Economic analysis has also been applied to wage differences within groups. There is always substantial variation in earnings within each group. A careful early study attributed about 75 percent of the variance in male earnings in the United States to occupational difference and the rest to variations within occupations.[11]

Economic theories that attempt to explain within-group differences focus on the effect of training, the interaction of separate abilities, and the hierarchial structure of large organizations. Assuming that all people have the same ability and that there are no nonpecuniary advantages or disadvantages in any employment, without investment in human capital all workers would receive the same earnings. If we now assume that two forms of investment in human capital are possible—education beyond the minimum and general on-the-job training—paid for in part by private means, those with the easiest access to capital will invest the most. People getting on-the-job training will earn less than the untrained during training. Those completing training will be more productive than the untrained and receive sufficient additional income over their working life to recoup their investment plus interest.

The effect of on-the-job training interacts with the variation in earnings by age. Earnings typically rise with age, level off in middle age, and are lower for older workers. The peak comes earliest in the lowest-skill occupations. Some of the dispersion in earnings below the earnings peak is due to differing on-the-job training and some is due to changes in ability due to aging. But there can still be substantial dispersion in earnings of people with quite similar education.

Another model of intragroup wage differentials permits differences in ability. This will further increase the spread in earnings if ability is used in part to select for scarce training slots. Those with the greatest ability will tend to get more training and to have higher earnings after training. But it is difficult to decide how much ability affects earnings on its own and how much it does so through additional investment in human capital.

Models that consider ability directly recognize that several different kinds of abilities affect earnings. It has been shown that if each relevant ability

[10]W. M. Landes, "The Economics of Fair Employment Laws," *Journal of Political Economy,* 76 (July/August 1968), pp. 507–52.

[11]H. Lydall, *The Structure of Earnings* (Oxford: Clarendon, 1968).

is normally distributed but if earnings vary with the product of two or more uncorrelated abilities, then the logarithms of the earnings are normally distributed.[12] Although this distribution fits actual earnings quite well, it is inadequate in explaining very high earnings. Economic analysis of the process whereby ability is translated into earnings shows that the process of choosing careers to accommodate tastes and talents would tend to produce dispersion and skewness in earnings distributions even if all abilities were normally distributed. Very able people would receive high earnings, which are in part a rent for specialized ability and in part a return on specialized training.

Benefits

Economic analysis of employee benefits explains how this portion of compensation affects labor markets. Employee benefits are defined as any part of compensation not paid currently in money to individual employees, but paid by employers on behalf of employees. Some of these benefits are required by law. Others are provided unilaterally by employers or as a result of collective bargaining.

As usually provided, benefits determine part of the consumption pattern of employees. They may even be useless to some employees. This is in contrast with cash, which permits workers to spend their income as and when they wish.

Economies of scale in providing benefits may permit an employer to cater to the tastes of particular groups of employees in order to cut the costs of recruiting and keeping employees. If all employers provide the benefit, however, this result may not accrue.

Benefits sometimes represent employer attempts to influence the consumption patterns of employees. Subsidized cafeterias, for example, may be motivated in part by the assumption that employee productivity is enhanced by a good lunch.

Employers who give employees a choice in benefits (cafeteria plans) take the risk that employees will not provide for themselves. For this reason, governments mandate benefits and employers develop a core of benefits that cover all employees.

Many benefits either escape income taxation or are taxed on more favorable terms than cash wages. Tax considerations do much to explain the growth in benefits over time and their positive correlation with earnings levels. In fact, the growth of benefits is explained more by tax treatment than by all other causes combined.

As noted in our discussion of human capital theory, employers who give their employees specific on-the-job training want to keep their employees to recover their investment. One way of doing so is tying benefits to length of service. Because specific training probably correlates positively with wages, attempts to keep employees help to explain the positive correlation between benefits and wage levels.

Unions have contributed to the growth of employee benefits. Unions may be better judges of what employees want than employers. Also, union lead-

---

[12]A. D. Roy, "The Distribution of Earnings and of Individual Output," *Economic Journal*, 60 (1950) pp. 489–505.

ers may get more credit from members by bargaining for new benefits than by bargaining for the equivalent in cash.

Unfortunately, the most favorable benefits have gone to workers who already had the most. Employees of large, high-pay companies and members of the strongest unions get the most benefits. Employees of small employers usually have only government-mandated benefits, and some employees (of very small employers) get none at all.

The General Level of Money Wages

Economic analysis of the money-wage level of the economy rests heavily on what happens in labor markets. As such, the general wage level in a depression is treated separately from those in more prosperous periods.

In a depression, wage rigidity means that wages are not reduced. Keynes argued that a wage reduction in a depression is undesirable because it would force a reduction in worker consumption expenditures, which in turn would lead to a further reduction in aggregate demand.[13] Such cuts could also generate expectations of further reductions of wages and prices. Keynes saw the downward rigidity of money wages as an acceptable feature of industrial economies.

Given the downward rigidity in money wages, a decline in demand cannot lower all wages and prices proportionately. Therefore, it must lower real output and employment. If some product prices go down, a decrease in aggregate demand may even raise the real wages of those still employed.

The mechanism whereby the general level of money wages in a depression is determined assumes that the aggregate demand curve shifts to the left. If the supply curve does not change and the general wage level does not come down, employment is reduced by the amount of decreased demand. In this new position the wage is above the supply curve and calls attention to the involuntary demand-deficiency unemployment.

Money wages are rigid downward because union contracts fix wages for the contract period and because unions resist wage cuts. But downward wage rigidity has existed in the United States much longer than strong unionism. One reason for this is the reluctance of employers to lose employees who have been given specialized training. Another is that workers strongly resent a wage cut. Thus nonunion employers fear that a wage cut will result in lowered productivity or a union organization drive. Both reasons mean that during a depression the employed and the unemployed are noncompeting groups.

Cuts in real wages resulting from price rises are not resisted with the same force as cuts in money wages. They aren't personal and can't be blamed on the employer. Moreover, they don't involve changes in relative wages.

The general level of money wages rises every year in relation to economic activity. The rise responds to strong demand and other forces, including collective bargaining. The most common explanation of the increase in the level of money wages is the *Phillips curve*,[14] which relates the percentage change

[13]J. M. Keynes, *The General Theory of Employment, Interest, and Money* (New York: Harcourt, Brace, 1936).

[14]A. W. Phillips, "The Relation between Unemployment and the Rate of Change of Money Wage Rates in the United Kingdom 1861–1957," *Economica*, November 1959, pp. 283–99.

of money wages (the vertical axis in figure 3–4) to unemployment (the horizontal axis). The argument underlying this formulation is that excess demand will cause money wages to rise, and the greater the amount of excess demand, the faster the rise. Employers raise money wages when they are short of labor. Of course, the response of employers to an excess of job vacancies is somewhat sluggish.

The Phillips curve is convex as viewed from the origin. Frictional unemployment prevents it from ever reaching the vertical axis. Wages would be expected to rise very rapidly if demand were strong enough to push unemployment below normal frictional levels. At the left of the curve, duration of job search is falling faster than the quit rate is rising. At its far right the curve is flattened by the downward rigidity of money wages. This means that the average wage will rise as long as there is excess demand in any market. This can occur even when total unemployment is quite high.

When the curve is fitted to United States data it is found to be much less convex than the theoretical curve. However, such comparisons usually include the effects of a change in the unemployment rate and changes in retail prices, and both improve the fit with the theoretical curve. This suggests that the actual adjustment process involves more than just excess demand. Price changes change labor demand but may also affect wages directly. The effect of the unemployment change is for wages to rise faster when unemployment is falling.

The Phillips curve has strong implications for national economic policy on wages and prices. If productivity changes are assumed to be constant, any given wage change changes unit labor costs. If we further assume that prices are proportional to unit labor costs, then a given price change corresponds to each rate of change in wages. Thus the vertical axis in figure 3–4 can be changed to rate of price change.

In this form, the Phillips curve represents economic policy choices between rate of change in prices and unemployment. Choosing either high inflation or high unemployment is not attractive. Thus attempts are made to shift the curve to the left. One approach is to attempt to lower frictional and struc-

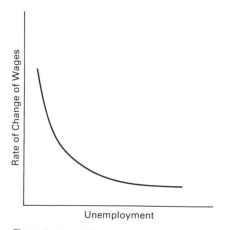

Figure 3–4 A Phillips curve

tural unemployment by improving the public employment service or by retraining or relocating the unemployed. Another is to attempt to lower the rate of wage and price increases.

The short-run impact of a given unemployment rate on the rate of wage increase will differ from the long-run effects. If workers expect a higher rate of inflation, they demand larger wage increases. The higher the wage increase corresponding to a given unemployment rate, the steeper the curve in the long run. The Phillips curve for the United States may have shifted to the right and become steeper in part because of the changed composition of the labor force.

CONTEMPORARY INDUSTRIAL RELATIONS THEORY

As mentioned early in this chapter, industrial relations scholars, or the institutional approach to wage theory and analysis, use a variety of disciplines. The distinction between labor economics and industrial relations is not a hard-and-fast one. But institutionalists, by and large, distrust static analysis and attempts to limit conclusions to a limited set of variables. For example they have long complained of the myopia of traditional economic theory when it is applied to labor markets. Their observations of wage determination in the real world, with numerous sizes and types of employing organizations and unions, have convinced them that wage theory was attempting to answer the wrong questions and was neglecting important variables. Thus, they stress the range of variables—political, psychological, social, and ethical, as well as economic—that impinge on wage determination. Also, they have been more interested in learning about the behavior of employers and workers and their unions than in developing and testing theories. The theories they have developed speak to wage decisions encountered by the parties rather than to abstractions and tendencies.

The institutional approach is heavily empirical. The details of wage experience, the variability of wage relationships, the latitude available to decision makers, the dimension added to wage determination by collective bargaining—all are regarded as important matters requiring explanation.[15] The wage rate is seen as inseparable from considerations such as timing, amount, and distribution of wages, union recognition, labor efficiency, other wage bargains, lower-wage competitors, recruitment problems, company reputation, strikes, control over discharge, and job prospects. Institutionalists' distrust of marginal-productivity analysis focuses on what they consider to be neglect of or abstraction from important variables. They approach wage decisions as involving a variety of choices that depend on weights assigned to varying and perhaps conflicting considerations. The alternatives available to the decision makers are considered as important to study as the determinants of wages and wage relationships. The effects of wage changes, in their view, must also be considered, because the parties can alter wages by administration.

The institutional approach questions the usefulness of static analysis, wherein changes are studied singly while other considerations are held con-

---

[15]G. W. Taylor and F. C. Pierson, eds., *New Concepts in Wage Determination* (New York: McGraw-Hill, 1957).

stant, on the grounds that the relationships among changes are the more important issues. The observation of wage-decision making suggests that (1) a variety of results are possible, (2) the system of relationships is itself changing, and (3) results may be cumulative rather than self-correcting. Moreover, analysis limited to one point in time may hide forces that change and interact with one another over time and the influence of past decisions and future expectations.

Even the definition of wages may be an issue. Conceptually, the wage agreement in collective bargaining may be defined as all of the clauses that hold cost implications. As such, it could include, besides the effect on labor costs, the present and ultimate costs of benefits, tactical considerations involving how and when wage increases are granted, continuing bargaining in the grievance procedure, and the way various agreement clauses are administered.

Also of importance in institutional analysis are the influences exerted by institutions and their leadership. Institutional forces are seen to modify, and at times possibly even to overshadow, economic forces. Unions, for example, are observed to have a wage philosophy with strong ethical overtones. They may stress certain standards of health, safety, and decency regardless of cost. Union leaders typically do not regard cost relationships as static and unchanging. They are skeptical about predicted economic effects of wage increases. Unions differ in philosophy and type of leadership. The impact of tradition on labor markets and the psychological makeup of union leaders may be as important as economic forces.

Employers are also observed to be influenced by forces other than economic ones. The large employer may be just as concerned with the status of the organization as a dependable supplier, a considerate employer, and a wage leader, as with economic necessity. Management may treat wages and prices as institutional decisions rather than as reactions to economic forces. Both may be based in part on company convenience. In large organizations, organizational slack may permit wage increases to be absorbed until prices or efficiency can be increased. Observation suggests that wage rates and benefits are paid because other organizations do so or because they are settled by collective bargaining rather than determined by cost considerations. Employers as well as unions differ in philosophy and type of leadership. Perhaps differences in size come closest to requiring an economic explanation.

Economic forces, institutional analysis tends to show, set rather broad limits on wages, leaving a range of discretion. But the amount of discretion varies with the type of wage rate or wage relationship under analysis. For example, the internal wage structure of a company is largely under the control of the decision makers, the external wage structure is only partially under their control, and the general wage level in the economy is beyond their control.[16] Wage uniformity, where it appears, usually results from conscious decisions rather than from market forces. One of the strongest forces is custom.

The observation that a wide latitude exists for wage decisions prompts study of the effects of wage changes based on the reasoning that anticipated and actual effects influence wage decisions. These effects depend on noneco-

[16]A. M. Ross, "The External Wage Structure," in *New Concepts in Wage Determination*, ed. Taylor and Pierson, pp. 173–205.

nomic considerations as well as economic ones. For example, organizational goals, union-management relations, employee attitudes, employee comparisons, communications of wage decisions, and seniority policies represent a short list of noneconomic considerations.

Institutional analysis has resulted in some theories that have attempted to explain the effects of some of the wide range of forces with which institutional analysis deals. Because such theories attempt to incorporate the conclusions of institutional analysis of labor markets and collective bargaining, they emphasize wage structures (relationships) within organizations.

A *range theory* of wage differentials developed by Lester employs what he calls anticompetitive, impeditive, and competitive variables.[17] The anticompetitive factors include institutional and ethical considerations used to restrict or prevent competition for jobs. The impeditive factors include historical, psychological, and institutional considerations that present obstacles to market adjustments by creating frictions and personal preferences of workers. The competitive forces are those that affect hiring and pay.

Taylor explained wage determination in all sizes and types of organizations in terms of *consequences of nonagreement*.[18] The upper and lower limits of the negotiating area are the points at which the employer and the employee or the employee's representative consider the cost of settlement prohibitive. Although these limits are set by economic forces, they are not precise. They are variously conceived at the start of negotiation, they change at critical points during negotiations, and they are influenced by the bargaining tactics and skills of the parties. Using only this one variable—consequences of nonagreement—Taylor explains wage determination in situations involving individual bargaining, management-administered wage determination, and wage determination under collective bargaining.

Taylor's formulation defines wages as all clauses in the contract affecting labor costs. It also recognizes that these clauses are affected by what goes on in preparation for negotiation, the bargaining, and the effectuation of the agreement.

Dunlop's theory of wage structure seems to provide some theoretical underpinnings for two common techniques of compensation administration—wage surveys and job evaluation.[19] In this formulation, the structure of wage rates within a company, within an industry, and among different industries and regions is assumed to be a system. There are two elements in the system—a job cluster and a wage contour. A *job cluster* is a stable group of jobs within an organization linked together by technology, administrative arrangements, and social custom. Wage rates of jobs in a cluster are related more closely to one another than to jobs elsewhere in the firm. The structure of wage rates within a cluster consists of one or more *key rates* and a group of associated rates. The wage structure of a firm (or establishment in a multi-plant firm) is made up of

[17]R. A. Lester, "A Range Theory of Wage Differentials," *Industrial and Labor Relations Review,* (July 1952), 483–500.

[18]G. W. Taylor, "Wage Determination Processes," in *New Concepts in Wage Determination,* ed. Taylor and Pierson, pp. 83–113.

[19]J. T. Dunlop, "The Task of Contemporary Wage Theory," in *New Concepts in Wage Determination,* ed. Taylor and Pierson, pp. 117–39.

a number of clusters. Rates of key jobs in each cluster are related to one another through technology, organization, and custom.

A *wage contour* is a stable group of companies linked together by a common product market, labor market, or custom so that they have common wage-making characteristics. The wage rates of particular occupations in a company are related more closely to the wage rates of some firms than to those of others. A contour for a particular group of occupations is defined in terms of both the product market and the labor market. A wage contour has three dimensions—occupational, industrial, and geographic. The organizations that form a contour belong to a particular product market and may either be located in one labor market or be broadly dispersed geographically. Wage contours do not have sharp boundaries. The product market of a company may place it in several wage contours. The contour is often composed of a wage leader and a group of associated firms, and operates through wage comparisons.

Wage-making forces operate on key rates in job clusters. These rates spread externally through the operations of wage contours and internally through the relation of key job rates to one another and to associated rates.

Salkever has offered a more varied list of wage structure determinants.[20] Social inertia resulting from employment consciousness rather than wage consciousness and resistance to change is one example. Employer judgments of the relative importance of tasks and the learning curve associated with these tasks constitute another. Once created, wage differentials persist because employees reinforce these judgments. A third determinant is the cost to workers of acquiring skills. A fourth is the immobility resulting from noncompeting groups and the labor reserves associated with these groups. Insulation from market pressures in different product markets may affect differentials. Worker willingness to undergo training and employer ability to take advantage of the learning curve affect differentials, as do differential unemployment rates of separate occupational groups.

Hildebrand explains the variation in forces operating in labor markets by characterizing them as (1) union-oriented, (2) market-oriented, (3) internally determined, and (4) union- and product-market-oriented.[21] Although he found nonmarket forces operating in labor markets, he concluded that the influence of the product market was not sufficiently emphasized.

SUMMARY

This chapter has reviewed the contribution of economists to wage theory. Economists have been studying wages longer than anybody else. Historical theories of wages were reviewed for their contributions to wage issues. Labor economists' application of the tools and concepts of economic analysis to labor markets was presented as contemporary wage theory. This model building and testing shows how economic variables determine the relative wage rates of par-

[20]L. R. Salkever, *Wage Structure Theory* (New York: Humanities Press, 1964).

[21]G. H. Hildebrand, "External Influence and the Determination of the Internal Wage Structure," in *Internal Wage Structure,* ed. J. L. Meij (Amsterdam: North-Holland Pub. Co., 1963), pp. 260–99.

ticular occupations, wage relationships, and the general level of money wages. Finally, the contributions of institutional analysis (industrial relations scholars) to wage theory were reviewed.

Although economists have contributed a great deal to our understanding of wages, it is apparent that noneconomic factors are also operating. As Barbara Wooten has concluded, "the contemporary wage and salary structure [is] the accumulated deposit laid down by a rich mixture of economic and social forces . . . . [These forces] act and react upon one another to produce a result which is quite inexplicable if either is left out of the reckoning."[22]

---

[22]B. Wooten, *The Social Foundations of Wage Policy* (London: Allen & Unwin, 1955), p. 252.

4

Behavioral Theories of Wages

No one questions the interest of economists in wages. After all, wages are a form of price. But why are psychologists and sociologists interested in pay? What concepts link the interests of these behavioral scientists to pay?

THE EMPLOYMENT EXCHANGE

The most obvious concept is the concept of exchange that economists, psychologists, and sociologists use to study behavior. It is useful to think of employment as involving an exchange of work for pay. Economists treat employment as an exchange of time, effort, and ability for payment in money or in kind. Psychologists view employment as an exchange of behavior and attitudes for money and other sources of satisfaction. Sociologists approach employment as a broad exchange of tangible and intangible inputs and outputs among people whose behavior influences one another and in turn influences and is influenced by other segments of society.

      The parties to the exchange most commonly are the individual and the organization. If a union is involved, the exchange is between the union and the organization. The parties do not have to have equal power, but they must be able to influence the other party for the exchange to take place.

Exchange is a double input-output system in that each party is contributing something to the exchange and in return is receiving something. The input of one party is the output of the other, and vice versa.

The exchange process works because it is perceptual: each party perceives the value of the rewards received as greater than the contributions made. There can be varying perceptions of the exchange by the two parties. However, the exchange still takes place, because the two parties place different values on what is being exchanged. Individuals enter the employment exchange because they perceive their rewards as greater in value than their contributions. Likewise, the organization enters the exchange because what the organization receives has more value to it than what it contributes.

Exchanges intended to be short-term tend to be carefully specified; continuing exchanges tend to be less well defined. Most employment exchanges are expected to be long-term. Although in some exchanges hours of work and sometimes production standards are specified on one side and pay rates and benefits on the other, in most the definition of work is left to job descriptions, supervision, and work rules and the definition of rewards to starting pay. In most exchanges there are long-term expectations by both parties that extra inputs will eventually result in extra rewards.

Often, what we have been calling the employment exchange is referred to as an *employment contract*. The contract is implicit except in the case of a labor agreement. But in all cases compensation in its various forms (cash, benefits, and nonfinancial rewards) is central to it. We assume that neither party enters into or continues in the employment exchange unless they perceive that the rewards are equal to or exceed the required contributions. Logically, the exchange includes contributions (anything provided that is recognized and considered relevant), rewards (anything received that is recognized and considered relevant), a comparison process (comparing rewards with contributions and with some standard), and results (attitudes and behavior). Although it is possible to study the employment exchange in terms of rewards, contributions, comparison standards, and results pertinent to both parties, our major focus is on the rewards to employees.

Required Employee Behaviors

Although the employment contract usually leaves the definition of work to job descriptions, supervision, and work rules, it is useful to specify the kinds of behavior the organization requires from employees. Organizations require that individuals (1) join and remain with the organization (membership), (2) carry out job assignments dependably, (3) achieve organization objectives beyond the job assignment through innovative and spontaneous behaviors, (4) cooperate with others, (5) protect the organization against disaster, (6) make creative suggestions, (7) carry out self-training, and (8) create a favorable climate.[1] Unfortunately, organizations appear to believe that they obtain all these behaviors merely by hiring the employee. Although compensation could be used to encourage all these behaviors, it typically concentrates on the first two. As we will see, organizations would be wise to focus separately in compensation

---

[1] D. Katz, "The Motivational Basis of Organizational Behavior," *Behavioral Science*, 9 (1964) 131–46.

administration on attraction, retention, and performance; it can obtain other specific behaviors through compensation policies and programs.

Perhaps the most explicit statement of the distinction between membership and performance behaviors required by organizations and the quite different sources of these behaviors was made by March and Simon.[2] They carefully distinguish the motivation to acquire and keep organizational membership (their term is *motivation to participate*) from productivity (the *motivation to perform*). Membership motivation results from a favorable inducements–contributions balance. That is, applicants must perceive that what they get from the organization at least balances what they must give to it. Employees must perceive a continuing favorable balance if they are to remain members. The motivation to perform represents a much more complex psychological contract between the individual and the organization involving perceived alternatives, perceived consequences of these alternatives, and individual goals.

Organizations have no choice but to provide membership motivation if they wish to remain organizations. But if providing motivation to perform is too costly or too much trouble, the organization may choose other routes to organizational goals, such as designing jobs so that prescribed job performance is sufficient.

MOTIVATION THEORY

The most visible contribution of behavioral scientists to compensation theory is motivation theory.[3] Motivation theory seeks to explain all kinds of motivated behavior in all kinds of situations, including behavior in organizations. In the following discussion of motivation theory, we will argue that some theories seem to fit better with organization-required behaviors of several types, but primarily membership and performance.

Compensation administration is an application of motivation theory. For this reason, motivation theory can be considered a form of compensation theory. Although motivation is complex and much remains to be learned about it, enough may be known to guide organizations in designing and managing compensation programs.

Most behavior is in some sense motivated. People are strongly influenced by their environment. This means that organizations can influence people's behavior by changing environments and rewards.

But motivation is not the sole determinant of behavior. Ability and knowledge of what one is supposed to do combine with motivation in determining behavior in organizations. Also, an organization's tasks vary in their composition of ability versus motivation. Thus motivation can make little or much difference in performance, depending on the task.

Psychologists studying motivation have focused on two psychological processes: arousal and choice. The first is concerned with why people do anything at all. The second involves the choices they make in what to do. A similar

[2]J. G. March and H. A. Simon, *Organizations* (New York: John Wiley, 1958).

[3]Much use is made in this section of T. R. Mitchell, "Motivational Strategies," in *Personnel Management*, ed. K. M. Rowland and G. R. Ferris (Boston: Allyn & Bacon, 1982), ch. 10.

way of classifying motivation theory is to distinguish content and process theories. Content theories focus on the factors that motivate behavior. Process theories explain how these factors operate.

Content Theories

Content or arousal theories center in needs or drives. Several physiological and social needs have been identified and studied. Need classifications have been offered.

A need for *competence* in mastering the environment is supposedly aroused when individuals are faced with new, challenging situations; it dissipates after mastery. Closely related are *curiosity* or *activity* needs: people need and enjoy a stimulating environment, but they differ on this need and become adapted to certain levels of stimulation.

The need for *achievement* and the work of McClelland on it are well known.[4] Individuals have been found to differ in their need for achievement. The need can be increased by training. People with a high need for achievement prefer moderate risks and immediate feedback and enjoy doing tasks for a sense of accomplishment. Productivity is posited to be related to this need.

A need for *affiliation* has been suggested but not carefully studied. There may be an innate need for contact and a tendency for people to congregate during a crisis. Separately identifying this need appears to be a problem.

A need for *power* has been suggested as a requirement for success in organizations. Effective managers may have a high need for power.[5]

One problem with predicting behavior from individual needs is that people seem to have differing degrees of them at different times of their lives. Classifications of needs can be considered a response to this finding.

Maslow's *hierarchy of needs* represents the first major attempt to classify needs that are relevant to organizational behavior.[6] His classification—physiological, safety, belonging, esteem, and self-actualization—is well known. Maslow argues that these needs constitute a hierarchy. Most normal people move upward in the hierarchy as lower level needs are satisfied. Thus, the greater the fulfillment of a particular need, the less it is a motivator. Because in American society the first two needs are presumably satisfied, higher-order needs should be better motivators. Empirical tests of the theory have not supported the categories, their order, or the suggestion that one need must be satisfied before the next one is activated. But the implications of the theory that there are higher-order as well as lower-level needs and that different people want different things were major contributions.

Alderfer's *ERG theory* postulates three categories of needs: existence, relatedness, and growth.[7] Although this classification also represents a hierarchy,

---

[4]D. C. McLelland, "Managing Motivation to Expand Human Freedom," *American Psychologist,* 33 (1978), 201–10; and D. C. McLelland, *The Achieving Society* (Princeton, N.J.: Van Nostrand, 1961).

[5]D. C. McLelland and D. H. Burnham, "Power is the Great Motivator," *Harvard Business Review,* 54 (1976), 100–110.

[6]A. H. Maslow, *Motivation and Personality* (New York: Harper, 1954).

[7]C. P. Alderfer, *Existence, Relatedness and Growth: Human Needs in Organizational Settings* (New York: Free Press, 1972).

the theory does not state that one need is more important than another or that only unsatisfied needs arouse behavior. All three motives may be working to some degree at one time, and the growth needs may grow with satisfaction. Although empirical data seem to fit this classification better than Maslow's, little research has been done to test the theory.

McGregor's *theory X–theory Y*[8] and Herzberg's *motivators and hygienes*[9] flow from Maslow's higher- and lower-order needs. The empirical evidence does not support Herzberg's conclusion that only the motivators provide job satisfaction and motivated employees. Hygienes and motivators don't operate in the same way for everyone. Moreover, his results are influenced by his method of data collection. But Herzberg's work contributed to an understanding of the conditions that lead to job satisfaction and the reasons that different people are motivated by different rewards.

An evaluation of the motivation theories based on needs would probably focus on their limitations. Empirical studies have provided only modest support for them, and the proportion of the variance in performance explained has been low.

Another content motivation theory is the *job characteristics model*.[10] In this model characteristics of the job (skill variety, task identity, task significance, autonomy, feedback) cause psychological states that in turn cause motivation and performance. The model suggests that enriched jobs motivate people with high growth needs. Empirical tests of the model suggest that job enrichment affects satisfaction more than performance and quality more than quantity. Also, growth needs affect satisfaction more than performance.

Consistency theory suggests that people choose jobs and behaviors based upon the consistency between their self-image and the demands of the job or the expectations of friends.[11] Arousal is caused by inconsistency.

A final content theory suggests that *social cues* stimulate behavior as a result of (1) the presence of others, (2) wishes to be evaluated favorably by others, and (3) desires to conform to the opinions of co-workers. Empirical work shows that social cues do affect performance.[12]

Process Theories

Process or choice theories explain the operation of motivation, or the factors that influence an individual to choose one action rather than another. Process theories can be subdivided into cognitive and noncognitive approaches. *Cognitive theories* see behavior as involving some mental process. *Noncognitive theories* see behavior as caused by environmental contingencies.

[8]D. McGregor, *The Human Side of Enterprise* (New York: McGraw-Hill, 1960).

[9]F. Herzberg, *Work and the Nature of Man* (Cleveland: World Publishing, 1966).

[10]J. R. Hackman and G. R. Oldham, "Motivation through the Design of Work: Test of a Theory," *Organizational Behavior and Human Performance*, 19 (1976), 250–79; and J. R. Hackman and G. R. Oldham, "The Job Diagnostic Survey: An Instrument for the Diagnosis of Jobs and the Evaluation of Job Redesign Projects," *Journal of Applied Psychology*, 60 (1975), 159–70.

[11]A. K. Korman, "Hypothesis of Work Behavior Revisited and an Extension," *Academy of Management Review*, 1 (1976), 50–63.

[12]S. E. White and T. R. Mitchell, "Job Enrichment versus Social Cues: A Comparison and Competitive Test," *Journal of Applied Psychology*, 64 (1979), 1–9.

COGNITIVE THEORIES.   The major cognitive theories are equity theory, goal-setting theory, and expectancy theory. All of them focus on perceptions of the outcomes that flow from behavior.

Equity Theory.   This theory suggests that motivated behavior is a form of exchange in which individuals employ an internal balance sheet in determining what to do. It predicts that people will choose the alternative they perceive as *fair.* The components of equity theory are inputs, outcomes, comparisons, and results. Inputs are the attributes the individual brings to the situation and the activities required (investments and costs). Outcomes are what the individual receives from the situation. The comparisons are between the ratio of outcomes to inputs and some standard. Results are the behaviors and attitudes that flow from the comparison.[13]

In Adams's application of the theory to organizations, the comparison is with co-workers. But other standards of comparison, including oneself in a previous situation, seem equally probable. The idea is that people look at their inputs and the payoff they receive and compare the latter with what they think their comparison standard is getting. If a state of equity exists—that is, if they perceive the situation as in balance (fair)—then they are comfortable with the situation and no change is predicted to occur.

When, however, inputs are seen as too great relative to outcomes, underreward inequity is experienced. To remove this inequity people can (1) reduce their inputs (actually or perceptually), (2) increase their outcomes (actually or perceptually), (3) change their comparison standard, or (4) leave the situation. If outcomes are too great compared with inputs, a state of overreward inequity exists. To correct this situation the individual may (1) increase inputs, (2) decrease outcomes, or follow step 3 or 4 above.

Empirical tests of equity theory have in general accorded with predictions regarding over- and underreward. In addition, perceptions of inequity have been shown to be related to absenteeism and turnover.[14] Reduced performance following feelings of inequity resulting from lower compensation for the same job has also been reported.[15]

But equity theory, at least as stated by Adams, contains several unsolved problems. Little is known, for example, about how people select a comparison standard. It is also difficult to define inputs and outcomes. How people combine inputs and outcomes and how these factors change over time are likewise unexplained.[16]

[13]J. S. Adams, "Inequity in Social Exchange," in *Advances in Experimental Social Psychology,* ed. I. Berkowitz (New York: Academic Press, 1965), pp. 267–299.

[14]J. E. Dittrich and M. R. Carrell, "Organizational Equity Perceptions, Employee Job Satisfaction and Departmental Absence and Turnover Rates," *Organizational Behavior and Human Performance,* 24 (1979), 29–40.

[15]M. R. Carrell, "A Longitudinal Field Assessment of Employee Perceptions of Equitable Treatment," *Organizational Behavior and Human Performance,* 21 (1978), 108–18; and R. G. Lord and J. A. Hohenfeld, "A Longitudinal Field Assessment of Equity Effects on the Performance of Major League Baseball Players," *Journal of Applied Psychology,* 64 (1979), 19–26.

[16]P. S. Goodman, "Social Comparison Processes in Organizations," in *New Directions in Organizational Behavior,* ed. B. M. Staw and G. R. Salancik (Chicago: St. Clair Press, 1977), pp. 97–132.

Also, the definition of equity employed by individuals has been challenged. Some people are apparently a little more comfortable with a slight advantage over their comparison other.[17] Salaried employees have been found to prefer equality rather than equity; hourly employees prefer equity.[18] In some cases, people follow a winner-take-all strategy. Finally, equity ratios and resolution strategies have been found to vary with culture, family orientation, and personal values.[19]

Another version of equity theory was developed by Elliot Jaques of Great Britain. Jaques' *theory of equitable payment* holds that individuals have an intuitive knowledge of their capacity, the level of their work, and the fairness of their pay. When their capacity is properly utilized in their work and when their pay matches their level of work, they achieve psychological equilibrium.[20] When, however, pay is less or more than that justified by the level of their work, individuals perceive inequity and react to it.

Jaques believes that level of work can be measured by determining an individual's *time span of discretion*—the maximum period of time the individual's work is permitted to go unreviewed. He reports measuring time span of discretion at all levels of work and measuring *felt fair pay*—the amount of pay the individual perceives as fair for his or her level of work. Operationalizing the theory requires measuring the individual's level of work and providing the proper pay for that level of work. Equity is achieved when felt fair pay equals actual pay or deviates from it by less than minus 10 percent or plus 20 percent.

Measuring time span of discretion is the major problem with the theory. Although Jaques reports no difficulty, he has offered several methods of doing this. His present method is apparently that developed by Atchison—asking supervisors the duration of the most extended task assigned to subordinates.[21] Atchison and Richardson were able to measure both time span of discretion and felt fair pay,[22] but others question the stability and measurability of both of these concepts.[23]

A number of studies of equity in operating organizations have been

[17]R. D. Middlemist and R. B. Peterson, "Test of Equity Theory by Controlling for Comparison Co-worker Efforts," *Organizational Behavior and Human Performance*, 15 (1976), 335–54.

[18]L. Larwood and J. Blackmore, "Fair Pay: Field Investigations of the Fair Economic Exchange," *Proceedings of the Academy of Management*, August 1977, pp. 162–64.

[19]K. E. Weick, M. C. Bougan, and G. Maruyama, "The Equity Context," *Organizational Behavior and Human Performance*, 15 (1976), 32–65.

[20]E. Jaques, *Equitable Payment* (New York: John Wiley, 1961); and E. Jaques, *Time Span Handbook* (London: Heinemann, 1964).

[21]T. J. Atchison and W. French, "Pay Systems for Scientists and Engineers," *Industrial Relations*, October 1967, pp. 44–56.

[22]R. Richardson, *Fair Pay and Work* (Carbondale and Edwardsville: Southern Illinois University Press, 1971).

[23]See, for example, G. T. Milkovich and K. Campbell, "A Study of Jaques' Norms of Equitable Payment," *Industrial Relations*, May 1969, pp. 269–79; and P. S. Goodman, "An Empirical Examination of Elliott Jaques' Concept of Time-Span," *Human Relations*, May 1967, pp. 155–70.

made by the authors.[24] These studies use concepts from both streams of equity theory. An instrument has been developed that reliably measures the perceived importance of a rather large number of potential rewards and contributions. It also measures perceived discrepancy between the existing rewards and contributions and respondent preferences as well as comparison standards and preferred response to perceived inequity.

The rationale of these studies has been to test the validity of equity theory as an aid in designing organization compensation programs. Although they are subject to the limitations of survey research, the results support equity theory and its components and yield suggestions for improving compensation programs. People can and do perceive a large number of inputs and outcomes as relevant. They can compare what exists and what they want. Both the rewards desired and contributions seem to be culturally based and to vary occupationally and demographically. From the studies it seems useful to classify outcomes as (1) extrinsic rewards, (2) intrinsic rewards, and (3) rewards provided by the organization that it is not aware of providing. Likewise, inputs can be usefully classified as (1) job-related contributions, (2) performance-related contributions, and (3) personal inputs—contributions that are not obviously required by the job but that individuals believe are relevant to the organization.

We lean heavily toward equity theory as a useful explanation of membership motivation. If individuals perceive the situation as equitable, they are likely to join the organization and continue their membership. An individual's decision that equity exists seems to represent the attitudinal counterpart of March and Simon's inducements–contributions balance.

Goal-setting Theory. This theory argues that employees set goals and that organizations can influence work behavior by influencing these goals.[25] The major concepts in the theory are intentions (targets), goals (performance standards), goal acceptance (the degree the goal becomes the conscious intention), and goal commitment (effort expended). These concepts are assumed to be the motivation. Hard goals, when accepted, are postulated to be better than easy ones. Participation in goal setting should increase commitment and acceptance. Individual goal setting should be more effective than group goals because it is the impact of goals on intentions that is important. The more specific the goal, the greater its impact.

In goal-setting theory the crucial factor is the goal. Although incentives or rewards may affect goal acceptance and commitment, they are not the critical element. They are important only as they affect the goals.

---

[24]T. J. Atchison and D. W. Belcher, "Equity, Rewards, and Compensation Administration," *Personnel Administration*, March-April 1971, pp. 32–36; D. W. Belcher and T. J. Atchison, "Equity Theory and Compensation Policy," *Personnel Administration*, July-August 1970, pp. 22–33; and D. W. Belcher and T. J. Atchison, "Compensation for Work," in *Handbook of Work, Organization, and Society*, ed. R. Dubin (Chicago: Rand McNally, 1976), pp. 567–611.

[25]E. Locke, "Toward a Theory of Task Motivation and Incentives," *Organizational Behavior and Human Performance*, 3 (1968), 157–89.

Tests of the theory show that goals lead to higher performance than situations without goals and that difficult goals lead to better performance than easy ones.[26] But participation in goal setting, though it may increase satisfaction, does not always lead to higher performance. Assigned goals may work as well as participation in goal setting. Rewards and social pressure have been found to affect performance independent of goals. Difficult, accepted, specific goals combined with feedback and rewards for goal attainment should result in highly motivated employees.

Expectancy Theory.   This theory argues that people choose the behavior they believe will maximize their payoff. It states that people look at various actions and choose the one they believe is most likely to lead to the rewards they want the most.

The elements in the theory are expectancies that certain outcomes will occur and the valence (anticipated satisfaction) of those outcomes. Although the formal elements are expectancies and valences, in most formulations expectations are divided into two types: *expectancy* (the expectation that effort will lead to performance) and *instrumentality* (the expectation that performance will lead to reward).

The earliest statement of expectancy theory was made by Vroom, who developed a model both to predict choice of occupation and how much effort will be expended on the job.[27] In this model each expectancy is multiplied by its valence and the products are summed. The theory predicts that the individual will choose the alternative with the highest expected return.

Later formulations, by Lawler, summed the product of expectancy (E→P) and the sum of the products of each instrumentality (P→O) and its valence (V). Therefore, a person will behave in whatever way results in the highest score in this equation: $(\Sigma[(E{\rightarrow}P) \times \Sigma[(P{\rightarrow}O)(V)]])$.[28] This means that there is only one probability of effort leading to performance but several possible outcomes from performance, each with a separate valence.

Expectancy theory has been tested extensively.[29] The usual approach is to obtain expectancies, instrumentalities, and valences by questionnaire or interview and to relate these responses to self-reported or measured choices, such as occupational choice, job satisfaction, effort, or performance. It has been found that expectancy theory can do an excellent job of predicting occupational choice and job satisfaction and a moderately good job of predicting effort on the job.

Expectancy theory implies that the anticipation of rewards is important as well as the perceived contingency between the behaviors desired by the organization and the desired rewards. The theory also implies that since different people desire different rewards, organizations should try to match rewards with what employees want.

[26]See, for example, T. R. Mitchell, "Organizational Behavior," *Annual Review of Psychology*, 30 (1979), 243–81.

[27]V. H. Vroom, *Work and Motivation* (New York: John Wiley, 1964).

[28]E. E. Lawler III, *Pay and Organizational Effectiveness* (New York: McGraw-Hill, 1971).

[29]See, for example, T. R. Mitchell, "Expectancy-Value Models in Organizational Psychology," in *Expectations and Actions: Expectancy-Value Models in Psychology*, ed. N. Feather (Hillsdale, N.J.: Lawrence Erlbaum Associates, 1980), pp. 293–312.

Although these implications suggest that following the requirements of expectancy theory will lead to performance motivation in organizations, organizations should be aware of possible difficulties. For example, employees may not want more of the rewards offered by organizations. Or they may believe that in order to get more of one reward (pay) they must give up another reward (security or pleasant social relationships). Again, employees may not believe that good performance does in fact lead to more desired rewards, and convincing them may require more changes than the organization is prepared to make. Or employees may not believe that performance always reflects their efforts. Many factors that are beyond employee control may affect performance. Poor selection and training of employees, for example, even with maximum effort, results in poor performance.

It should be apparent that the possibility of securing performance motivation through the application of expectancy theory varies by employee group and the technology of the organization. Although for most people money is one thing of which more is better, there may be some who don't value it highly. Some employees may want other rewards the organization doesn't want to provide (autonomy for a file clerk, for example). In some jobs, the relationship between effort and performance is beyond the control of employees. For many types of employees (and in many organizations) the relationship between performance and rewards is in fact very low and it is impossible to convince employees that high performance leads to high rewards.

Finally, it should be noted that the components of expectancy theory are beliefs that require a good deal of information and a rather complex cognitive process in determining action. Some employee groups do want the rewards the organization has to offer, do want to believe that greater effort results in improved performance, and do want to believe that better performance leads to greater rewards. For such groups expectancy theory seems the preferred route to performance motivation. But for groups who lack these beliefs because of lack of information or whose behavior is guided by habitual actions or by what they see others do, a noncognitive approach would seem superior.

NON-COGNITIVE THEORIES.   Non-cognitive theories do not dwell on what goes on in the person's head. Instead, they claim that it is the environment that determines the behavior of the person. Therefore, to control behavior, one must control the person's environment.

Behavior Modification.   This theory of operant conditioning is such an approach. The components of the theory, which is based on the work of Skinner, are the ideas of reinforcement and environmental determinism.[30] Human beings are assumed to emit two types of behavior: respondent and operant. *Respondent behaviors* are controlled by instincts and direct stimulation; sneezes are an example. *Operant behaviors* are emitted in the absence of any apparent external stimulation. But whenever an operant behavior is followed by a consequence that changes the likelihood that the behavior will recur, the event or consequence is called a *reinforcer*. Consequences that increase the frequency of behavior are called *positive reinforcers*. Ones that decrease the frequency are *negative reinforcers*. When it is discovered that a consequence serves as a positive or

[30]B. F. Skinner, *Beyond Freedom and Dignity* (New York: Knopf, 1971).

negative reinforcer for a particular behavior, the frequency of the behavior can be manipulated by using the reinforcer.

Skinner argues that no cognitive processes are involved. The behaviorist believes that operant behavior is caused by environmental events. Current behavior is caused by the history of their reinforcement.

One of the issues in the use of operant conditioning is the optimal schedule of reinforcement. Skinner suggests that continuous reinforcement produces more immediate change but that variable reinforcement produces changes that are more lasting. A study by Latham showed a 33 percent increase for a continuous schedule and none for the control group.[31] Studies using variable schedules have conflicting results. Tests of the theory show that there is little difference in performance between the types of schedules but a big difference between reinforcing and not reinforcing.

Implementing a behavior modification program involves a number of steps.[32] The first one is specifying the behavior to be changed. Next, its present frequency (the *base rate*) must be measured. Then various outcomes contingent on the desired behavior are administered and changes in frequency observed. Most programs include frequent reports and feedback. The result is a determination of the rewards that work best and the best reinforcement schedule.

Operant conditioning and approaches based on expectancy theory are similar. Both argue that the contingency between the behavior and the reward is crucial. The major difference is the presence or absence of mental processes—cognition.

One criticism of the operant approach is that the results found are due not to reinforcement but to the feedback used, to the goals, or to some other confounding variable.[33] A practitioner and a former student of the authors applied behavior modification over five years and found that feedback can produce a performance improvement of up to 18 percent but that reinforcement results are much greater.[34]

Recently the issue of whether behavior modification is entirely noncognitive has arisen. It has been suggested that behavior can be (1) traced to beliefs or perceptions (expectancy theory), (2) traced to reinforcement (operant conditioning), or (3) learned from the experiences of others.[35] Called *social learning theory,* this proposal seems to bridge cognitive and noncognitive motivation theory.

In summary, motivation theory contains directives for compensation policies and programs. Although, for reasons given, we prefer equity theory as an explanation of membership motivation and operant conditioning and ex-

---

[31]G. P. Latham, "The Effect of Various Schedules of Reinforcement on the Productivity of Tree Planters" (paper presented at the annual meeting of the American Psychological Association, New Orleans, 1974).

[32]F. Luthans, "An Organizational Modification (O. B. MOD) Approach to O. D." (paper presented at the annual meeting of the Academy of Management, Seattle, 1974).

[33]E. A. Locke, "The Myths of Behavior Modification in Organizations," *Academy of Management Review,* 2 (1977), 543–53.

[34]C. H. Henry, Personal communications.

[35]A. Bandura, *Principles of Behavior Modification* (New York: Holt, Rinehart & Winston, 1969).

pectancy theory as explanations of performance motivations, all of the theories carry useful precepts. The need theories, for example, show that different people want diffrent things from the employment exchange. Clear, specific, agreed-upon goals are important motivators. Equity theory shows that pay and pay programs must be perceived to be fair if they are to work as intended. Operant conditioning and expectancy theory show the importance of the contingency between performance and reward. Note that all the approaches require that management know what performance the organization needs and wants.

That there is some validity in each of the approaches suggests that combining them should increase performance. Equally important, organizations are seen to have choices among approaches that fit their employee groups and their situation.

SOCIOLOGICAL CONTRIBUTIONS

Sociologists study the relationships between individuals and how these relationships channel behavior. Much of the work of sociologists has implications for compensation programs. For example, sociologists have studied the process by which people learn the rewards to expect from work and the expected behavior at work. They learn the former as a result of the socialization process that occurs in the family and in school. As a consequence, when individuals enter employing organizations they have a reasonably good idea of what rewards to expect. When they join a particular organization, they learn the rewards offered by that organization.[36] Pay is only one of a long list of rewards available in organizations.

Motivation

To sociologists, motivation is built into the social system. We learn that it is highly appropriate to earn a living, "get ahead," and provide financial and other security for one's family. By the time people go to work, they carry these fundamental motivations appropriate to being an employee. When they join an organization they have already learned the appropriate channels in which their behavior can be directed. These motivations are given specific form in the organization. Labor unions operate within the motivational system of society. They are concerned not with changing this system but with influencing management decisions within it.[37]

Forces outside the organization shape work conduct and the pattern of social relationships inside the organization. For example, the meanings assigned to work are influenced by group identifications. Different groups have different cultural values about the significance of work.

Self Theory

This theory helps explain group differences. It suggests that people learn the meanings of events and objects along with language. These meanings

---

[36]R. Dubin, *The World of Work* (Englewood Cliffs, N.J.: Prentice-Hall, 1958).

[37]R. Dubin, *Working Union–Management Relations* (Englewood Cliffs, N.J.: Prentice-Hall, 1958), p. 16.

are solidified through associations in groups important to the individual. Motivation is imbedded in the attitudes, values, and roles of individuals in various groups.[38]

Labor Markets

Sociologists study labor markets and occupations in order to show the different expectations of different occupational groups and the social forces making for these diverse expectations.[39] That a typical organization is drawing members from several different sociological labor markets helps to explain some of the problems faced by organizations in maintaining consistent internal pay relationships.

BUREAUCRATIC LABOR MARKET. The bureaucratic labor market is a useful benchmark in comparing sociological labor markets because bureaucracies are assumed to fill all jobs but the entry one from within the organization. A bureaucracy is a rationally organized hierarchy of positions designed without reference to the individuals who occupy the positions. It is insulated from external labor markets because its labor supply is recruited at the bottom of the hierarchy and promoted from within through training and experience. The labor-supply problems in bureaucracies involve primarily the individuals it cannot train itself—professionals, for example. Labor demand is also controlled by the bureaucracy, except for entry positions.

In theory, wage determination in a bureaucracy is an administrative decision based on the principle that the rank order of wages follows the rank order of training and experience required by positions. Both qualifications and pay for positions with similar work and responsibility must be equal. Nonfinancial rewards, such as tenure, are further rewards for membership.

In practice, few bureaucracies are sufficiently closed to fit the theory. Some occupational groups cannot be trained by the bureaucracy and must be brought in from outside. In these cases, economic forces, historical accidents, and political pressures operating in external labor markets may force the bureaucracy to pay the new entrant at a rate that varies from the rational calculation of the worth of his or her qualifications. Even the requirements that differences in qualifications be reflected in differences in pay may be difficult to follow in large organizations with many occupations.

PROFESSIONAL LABOR MARKET. Once it becomes apparent that few organizations can operate as closed bureaucracies, the characteristics of sociological labor markets from which the organization must recruit members become important. Perhaps the market that differs the most from the bureaucratic labor market is the market for professional services. In theory, each professional is unique and the value of his or her service is unmeasurable. Supply is fixed in the short run and may decrease with increased demand if professional societies increase admission standards. Demand is highly variable. This fixed supply and varying demand permit professionals to fix their price and determine its bases.

---

[38]C. A. Hickman and M. H. Kuhn, *Individuals, Groups, and Economic Behavior* (New York: Dryden Press, 1956).

[39]See, for example, T. Caplow, *The Sociology of Work* (Minneapolis: University of Minnesota Press), 1954.

Historically, the basis has been the client's ability to pay. More recently, some professional associations have adopted a policy of standard minimum prices and restricted price competition. Professional work is defined by professional training and professional norms. Because some professionals are independent practitioners and some are employees of varying sizes and types of organizations, the fit of the model varies. But all professionals seem usefully defined as those with theoretical, research-based training usually strongly controlled by the profession itself.

CRAFT LABOR MARKET. Next to the professional market, the labor market least within the control of the organization is the craft labor market. In theory, the labor supply of a craft is fixed and the demand is variable. Identification is with the craft rather than the employer. Because fluctuating labor demand and a fixed labor supply could mean fluctuating wages and cutthroat competition, craft unions emerge to distribute work, control labor supply, and bargain the price.

Craft control of the conditions of sale of craft labor serves to preserve the system of selling labor in standardized units and to prevent the employer from modifying either the system or the attractiveness of work. The crafts determine the contents of craftwork, decide who is qualified to do it, and try to collect a standard rate for all levels of it.

Craft markets are essentially local, and craft controls operate locally. This feature of the craft labor market is the most useful distinction between it and professional labor markets.

The building trades, with their tradition of apprenticeship and often a highly homogeneous membership in terms of ethnic, racial, and religious backgrounds, represent the best fit with the craft model. The new crafts, such as automobile, computer, and television repairers, may or may not turn out to fit the model.

SEMISKILLED LABOR MARKET. The market for semiskilled labor, in theory, is a close fit with the bureaucratic model. Labor supply depends on the local labor force. Demand and competition for workers are determined by employers, who design the jobs, provide training, and promote from within. In practice, however, many semiskilled workers are represented by unions, and thus labor supply and wages are determined by collective bargaining.

As in bureaucracies, jobs are designed by the organization and employees are affiliated with the organization. But wages are not determined solely by employee qualifications, even in the absence of a union. Custom strongly affects wages for the semiskilled in that wage changes are usually determined with reference to wages previously paid and to wages paid by other employers in the industry or area. Wage differentials among jobs in an organization are also influenced by custom. These differentials, although assumed to be related to the skill required, are at least as likely to be correlated with skill once required by the job, group power, and seniority of the job incumbent. Transfers and often promotions are based on seniority.

Perhaps the most important characteristic of semiskilled work is that the job is designed by the employer. This often means that the worker is not hired for the job but is assumed to be trainable for the jobs that exist in the organization. But even if semiskilled workers are not represented by unions, the impersonal conditions of bureaucracy seldom prevail. Work groups always arise and influence organization decisions. In very small organizations, semiskilled workers are often key employees.

UNSKILLED LABOR MARKET. The market for unskilled labor, if such labor is defined as requiring no skill or training, has almost disappeared. But casual labor is still employed. The supply of unskilled labor is highly variable. Demand is fairly constant in the long run but highly variable in the short run. Minimum wage laws and public opinion prohibit the wide range of wages that could be possible in this labor market. The secondary labor market, as described in chapter 3, is analogous to the unskilled labor market.

WHITE-COLLAR LABOR MARKET. The market for white-collar workers has some similarities to the bureaucratic model. The organization designs the job, often hires at the bottom, and promotes from within. Workers are typically affiliated with the employer.

But the requirement for impersonal and organizationally rational decisions is no more likely here than it is with semiskilled workers. In fact, many clerical workers today have jobs hardly distinguishable from semiskilled factory jobs. They run machines to produce a product, and their contacts are limited to other employees and supervisors. One possible difference for these workers is that a good portion of their basic skills are acquired in school.

A second type of white-collar worker—receptionists and salespeople— have contacts with customers and clients. This seems to be the type that is expanding. Because social interaction is a large part of these jobs and success or failure depends on the way the interaction is handled, such jobs are difficult to standardize.

MANAGERIAL LABOR MARKET. The market for managers is the most diverse of the sociological labor markets. In some ways, it is a close fit with the bureaucratic model. Affiliation is with the organization and success is defined by the organization. There is a strong tendency to hire at the bottom and promote from within. Pay is geared to status in the organization. But the rational-impersonal dimension of the bureaucratic model is not met, especially at higher levels of the organization. Although the organization designs low-level managerial jobs, above this level the manager is expected to have a voice. Like the second type of white-collar worker, managers must interact with various publics. Interactions with superiors, peers, and subordinates also influence the definition of managerial work.

UNIQUE SERVICES LABOR MARKET. Although there is a strong tendency to fill managerial positions by hiring at the bottom and promoting from within, higher levels of management may be treated as a market for unique services. In such markets the supply is one individual and the value of the service is difficult to measure. This market is only partially like the market for free professionals, in that the price is set by individual bargaining.

Sociological analysis of various labor markets emphasizes the different forces operating in each. The typical large employer deals with all these markets and must reconcile their various forces in designing compensation policies and programs.

Social Stratification

Processes of social stratification locate an individual within the social system and thus should influence the determination of who gets what rewards. Status differences have been found to rest primarily on occupations.[40] Occupation is not only the most meaningful indicator of status but is indicative of and closely related to other measures of status, such as education and income.

A number of characteristics of occupations have been found to contribute to their position in status rankings. One is based on the nature of the work performed—whether it involves manipulating physical objects, symbols, or other people. In general, manipulation of physical objects provides the least status and manipulating symbols the most. But occupations involving social manipulation (such as managers) also carry high status. Occupations involving solely symbol manipulation (artists, writers, scientists) generally have lower status than occupations involving both symbols and people. The present edition of the *Dictionary of Occupational Titles* bases occupational level on measures of manipulation of data, people, and things.[41]

Another indicator of occupational status is prerequisites for entry—amount of education and experience. Another is whether the tasks are performed by an individual or a group, with the former carrying higher status. Occupations involving supervision have higher status than those whose occupants are supervised. Occupations of higher responsibility have higher status, and responsibility for social and symbolic activities yields higher status than responsibility for physical objects. Work situations are also status indicators, with factories carrying lower status than an office or research laboratory. Within a community, business organizations in different industries carry different statuses, as do other organizations. Even public employment, private employment, and self-employment are status indicators, with self-employment the highest, private employment next, and public employment the lowest.

Because the status of an occupation is related to the rewards of incumbents of that occupation, social stratification theory would seem to be useful in designing pay structures within organizations. Unfortunately, although a number of determinants of occupational status have been proposed, a coherent theory has not been agreed upon. The functional theory of stratification proposes as variables the differential importance of positions in society, variations in the requirements of positions, and differences in the kinds of abilities needed in these positions, but does not suggest measurements or weights.

Work Groups

Work groups form as a result of the organization of work, develop attitudes and norms, and influence the behavior of group members and the re-

---

[40]R. H. Hall, *Occupations and the Social Structure* (Englewood Cliffs, N.J.: Prentice-Hall, 1969).

[41]U.S. Employment Service, *Dictionary of Occupational Titles* (Washington, D.C.: U.S. Government Printing Office, 1966).

ward structure of organizations.[42] Semiskilled jobs are the most susceptible to group actions. Uncertainty about the value of the job because these jobs are not well defined in external labor markets and ambiguity of status and skill requirements make for successful pressures to follow group norms.

These group pressures are an important influence on the rewards and status of jobs. The semiskilled worker adopts an occupational orientation in spite of the ambiguity of semiskilled work and behaves as if he or she belonged to a highly specific occupational group. Work groups rank certain jobs as more important or desirable and expect these jobs to carry higher pay. Over time group pressures force a correlation between job rank and pay. The union as well as management responds to these pressures.

Reference Groups

Reference group theory argues that individuals take the values and standards of other individuals and groups as a frame of reference in evaluating themselves and their situations. The choice of reference groups is influenced by rationality and tradition. Comparisons take on a moral tone, yielding "what is right."

Reference group theory argues that individuals and groups that are subordinate to the same authority use one another as reference groups. But workers in large-membership groups such as a union are likely to use abstract groups such as skilled workers. In an open society, the choice of reference groups is broader than in a more rigid society, where intragroup comparisons are more likely. Unions and probably employers can modify the choice of reference groups, but only in the direction perceived to be legitimate. But consequences of efforts to change reference-group comparisons may not coincide with intentions.

Social Norms

Workers apparently have feelings about which factors employing organizations should pay for; these feelings are a function of group norms. An early study presented respondents with an organization chart representing direct and indirect supervision, provided a salary in one of the boxes, and asked respondents to supply the others.[43] The results showed that the respondents (students) employed indirect over direct supervision and number of subordinates as compensable factors. An unpublished study done by a graduate student at San Diego State University used the same approach to determine whether education, job title, performance ratings, experience, and demographic factors were used by students and managers in determining salary. The two groups were consistent in their use of these factors except for a reversal of education and job title.[44] Mahoney subsequently employed this technique to determine cultural perceptions of the necessary relation between manage-

---

[42]L. R. Sayles, *Behavior of Industrial Work Groups* (New York: John Wiley, 1958).

[43]J. L. Kuethe and B. Levinson, "Conceptions of Organizational Worth," *American Journal of Sociology,* November 1964, pp. 342–48.

[44]C. H. Henry, "Weighting of Input Factors for Equity in Pay" (Master's Thesis, San Diego State University, 1972).

ment levels and found approximately 33 percent to be the norm.[45] A more recent study involving one of the authors found a somewhat lower distance between management levels (20 percent) and revealed that the input factors related to jobs and training were higher for the upper organizational level. The subordinates, of course, saw the performance factors as higher for the subordinate level.[46] All these findings suggest that there are cultural values concerning the employee contributions that organizations should pay for.

A summary of sociological contributions to compensation theory would show that sociologists have not offered a wage theory. But sociological concepts of motivation, labor markets, social stratification, work groups, reference groups, and social norms seem useful in understanding compensation issues. In addition, sociologists have carefully developed the concept of behavior as an exchange.[47]

SUMMARY

Chapter 4 has continued the presentation, begun in chapter 3, of concepts and theories that seem pertinent to compensation issues and decisions. The fact that economic theory was presented in chapter 3 and behavioral science theory in chapter 4 suggests that they are unrelated. Such an impression, if received, is untrue. The employment exchange model that begins this chapter shows that both chapters are attempting to explain the same phenomena. Also, the classification of psychological motivation theory into theories of arousal and choice could have been used with economic models as well. But perhaps as useful as either arousal or choice theories is search theory, discussed in chapter 3. Chapter 3, in a broad sense, can be thought of as explaining organizations' search for the information and choices they need to make compensation decisions. Likewise, chapter 4 can be thought of as explaining the search process of individuals in the case of psychology and of groups and society in the case of sociology.

[45]T. A. Mahoney, "Organizational Hierarchy and Position Worth," *Academy of Management Journal,* 22 (1979), 726–37.

[46]P. Wright and T. J. Atchison, "Salary Differentials as a Function of Hierarchical Rank: A View from the Bottom Up" (paper presented to the Academy of Management, Reno, 1986).

[47]See, for example, P. M. Blau, *Exchange and Power in Social Life* (New York: John Wiley, 1967).

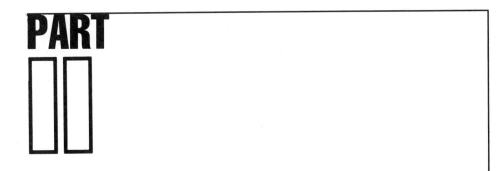

PART
II

THE WAGE LEVEL
DECISION

> "How much do we have to pay in order to attract more machinists for the new project?"
>
> "The policy of this company is to be 10 percent above the market. You make sure that we are!"
>
> "But this survey in our professional journal indicates that we are 15 percent behind the market. How can you say we are paying market rates?"
>
> "Boy, this pay raise isn't even up to the cost of living!"
>
> "Who should we compete with for workers?"
>
> "Do we need the best workers, or can we get along with average ones?"

All these questions and comments have to do with the wage level of the organization and how it is arrived at. The wage level is the average wage paid to employees. This has two implications. The first is external: how does the organization compare with other organizations? This question is a strategic one of how the organization wishes to position itself in the marketplace. The second implication is internal. The average wage is a reflection of the total wage bill of the organization. Labor is one of the claimants on organizational resources. The size of the wage bill is a reflection of *who gets what* within the organization.

This section of the book contains three chapters. The first, chapter 5, defines wage level and deals with the strategic question of the organization's pay policy compared with that of other organizations. Chapter 6 covers wage surveys, the method used to determine the market rate. Chapter 7 deals with other considerations and determinants of the organization's decision regarding pay level.

5

Wage Level Strategies

We are now ready to discuss wage decisions in organizations. The decision on wage level(s)—how much will the organization pay?—may be the most important pay decision the organization makes. As mentioned in chapter 1, the potential employee's acceptance usually turns on this decision and a large segment of the employer's costs are determined by it.

ORGANIZATION WAGE DECISIONS

Chapter 1 briefly outlined the decisions organizations must make in determining and managing compensation. Analysis of these decisions requires separate treatment. Although organizations are under no constraint to separate these decisions, a book is. In practice, most organizations make the decision on wage level (how much to pay) and wage structure (wage relationships) at the same time. Thus one approach would be to follow the chronological steps used by organizations in making wage decisions.

Because, however, the wage level decision may be considered the most important one for organizations, in terms of both employee attraction and cost considerations, it is considered first. Also, it seems essential to recognize that wage level decisions can never be completely separate from job-mix and hiring-standard decisions, and internal labor markets are powerful determinants. For these reasons, wage level decisions are emphasized in chapters 5–7. We hope that separate analysis of wage level and wage structure decisions will not result in unnecessary repetition.

The term *wage level* simply means the average wage paid to workers at some level of analysis—the job, the department, the employing organization, an industry, or the economy. Our discussion of economic theory emphasized the wage level of the job. Our discussion of the various environments in which compensation administration is practiced usually concerned the wage level of the organization.

The importance of the wage level decision to organizations rests on its influence in getting and perhaps keeping the desired quantity and quality of employees. If the wage level is too low, the applicant pool may dry up and recruitment efforts may meet with little success. Equally serious, some employees (often the wrong ones) may leave. At the extreme, the organization may experience difficulties with state and federal regulatory bodies administering minimum wage laws and prevailing wage laws. Also, the organization may be confronted with concerted organizing drives if no union is present, or pressing wage demands from existing unions. It is less apparent, but equally real, that a low wage level may attract only less efficient workers, with the result that labor costs per unit of output rise.

If, on the other hand, the wage level is too high, equally undesirable results are likely. The competitive position of the firm may suffer. Turnover rates may drop below some desirable minimum so that the organization tends toward inflexibility or stagnation. Also, if during periods of wage controls by federal authorities wage and salary levels are too high, trouble may be forthcoming from these officials.

Changes in wage level have the most drastic effects on total payroll. Of course, other wage decisions have payroll effects, but usually not nearly as great. Substantial sums of money can be involved, and for this reason alone an organization must pay close attention to wage levels.

Nor are employees and their representatives any less concerned with wage level decisions. It is here that the absolute amount of the wage or salary rate is determined. Also, it is here that unions exert their major effect, and here that member loyalty is built or lost.

Finally, consumers and the general public have major interests in wage level decisions—the consumer because wages are a major element in prices, and the general public because wages and salaries represent the major portion of national income. Also, too frequent or too drastic changes in wage levels affect the health of our economy.

The environment chapter (2) and the theory chapters (3 and 4) pointed out the considerations organizations use in making wage level decisions and some suggestions about how they do so. This chapter begins the discussion of how organizations go about making wage level decisions.

STRATEGIC WAGE LEVEL DECISIONS

Most of us are aware that some employers pay more than others for the same type of skill in the same market.[1] The actual cost to employers of employee ser-

---

[1]This section relies heavily on L. G. Reynolds, *Labor Economics and Labor Relations,* 7th ed. (Englewood Cliffs, N.J.: Prentice-Hall, 1978).

vice is total hourly compensation—average hourly earnings plus benefits. But, as mentioned in chapter 1, the employer is interested primarily in labor cost per unit of output—total hourly compensation divided by output per employee hour.

Unfortunately, labor cost per unit is not information that is easily obtained by employers. It must be estimated from in-house information on the average productivity of employee groups and organization units and the average pay of these groups.

The information available on what other employers pay comes only as a result of search. This search takes the form of wage surveys conducted or purchased by the organization. These surveys invariably show a range of wages paid for the same job by different employers. This range tends to be narrower for the skilled occupations and wider for the semiskilled. One reason for this is the difficulty of job comparisons. Another is differences in employee quality. But these differences are never as wide as wage differences. A major reason for finding out what others are paying for jobs is to decide how to position your organization in relation to others and the labor market.

High-Wage Employers

High-wage organizations tend to share a number of characteristics: larger size, higher profits, a lower ratio of labor costs to total cost, few industry competitors, and unionization. Larger organizations tend to pay higher wages and benefits for a number of reasons.[2] One is that they usually are able to. Large organizations tend to have some organization slack, which they can use in various ways. Another reason is that they may be willing to pay more to make it possible to expand employment without increasing pay rates, and to attract a pool of competent applicants. Still another may be a perceived obligation to counter lower job satisfaction. Finally, those large organizations that are not unionized are continuing targets of union organizers.

Higher-profit organizations are better able and perhaps more willing to pay. They may be willing to pay more for the reasons just cited for larger organizations.

A lower ratio of labor costs to other costs may mean that high wages are a less significant cost item. As a consequence, organizations with such a ratio can pay high wages in the hopes of forestalling labor problems and devote their attention to high-cost items.

Few industry competitors may mean that the organization faces an inelastic demand for its product or service, so that it can pass on cost pressures as price increases without reducing sales. Also, especially under union conditions, the few competitors may tend to pay equal wage rates to "take labor out of competition."

Because of their policy of the "standard rate," unions try to equalize wages in the same product market. As described in chapters 2 and 3, this policy is based upon equity considerations as well as practical ones.

Note that all of these reasons, except for size, suggest that high-wage employers tend to group by industry (product market). Thus there is a wage

---

[2]R. Lester, "Pay Differentials by Size of Establishment," *Industrial Relations*, October 1967, pp. 57–67.

hierarchy among companies that is related at least partially to the industry to which the companies belong.

The high-wage employer may be part of a national organization whose major wage decisions are made at the corporate level. Also, unionized employers may have a uniform wage scale, dictated by the labor agreement, in all company establishments.

Quite naturally, high-wage employers hope to gain several advantages from their high-wage position: higher worker quality as a result of higher hiring standards, ability to insist on higher performance standards, lower quit rates, time savings for management because wage changes do not have to be considered as frequently, insurance against unionization, fewer labor disputes in unionized companies, and company prestige. It is conceivable that the last of these (which appears to be noneconomic) may bear more weight than economic advantages.

Low-Wage Employers

Low-wage employers tend to be relatively small, to occupy competitive product markets, and to have low profit margins, and they are typically nonunion. They have low wage-paying ability because of the constraints of their product market. Most of their wage decisions may be explained by this low ability to pay.

Low-wage employers may gauge their position by comparing themselves with the largest and most visible employers. Using wage surveys, they usually pay attention to rates for specific jobs for which there is an active outside market. The starting rate for new production workers may be particularly significant. The jobs on which attention is focused obviously varies by industry.

The minimum feasible wage is one that will obtain just enough employees to maintain desired employee levels for some period—typically six months. But often organizations pay above this minimum, hoping to obtain employees of higher quality, lower their quit rates, and lower their recruitment, hiring, and training costs.

Market Rate Employers

Probably the most common wage level strategy followed by organizations is to "pay the market." These organizations wish to treat their employees fairly and yet not to raise their costs significantly more than their competitors. In short, these organizations are trying to average out the advantages and disadvantages of the high- and low-paying strategies by staying in between. This strategy should enable the organization to recruit and retain an adequate but not outstanding work force. In a tight labor market they are likely to be affected more like the low-paying organization and need to engage in concerted recruitment activities to obtain new employees. At the same time, internal adjustments must be made to retain current employees. Often this adjustment is made after some of the best employees have already left.

The types of organizations that choose to pay the market rate are harder to identify than high- and low-paying organizations. Many organizations with the characteristics identified with high-paying organizations will choose to pay the market instead since this strategy will still supply them with an adequate work force. High-paying organizations are more likely to be those in which it is clear to management that human effort can make a difference in organizational success. Low-paying organizations may wish to pay market rates but often are unable to do so.

To pay the market rate an organization must engage in collecting wage data and determining from that data exactly what the market rate is. As we shall discuss in succeeding chapters, this determination is at best a judgment. This strategy can be characterized as being reactive to the market, so the organization needs to keep constantly in touch with other organizations to find out what changes are occurring in what groups of employees are paid. This strategy also requires that the organization carefully identify where to obtain wage information, that is, the organization must identify what the market is.

Because employing organizations differ in employment-expansion plans, nonwage characteristics of jobs, quit rates, and recruitment and training efforts, wage levels differ from company to company. As will be detailed in chapter 6, they differ tremendously in their use of wage-survey information.

Labor Markets and Wage Level Strategies

Labor markets fluctuate in terms of the number of employees and employee hours needed. These swings in labor demand affect employer wage decisions and wage differentials among companies. High-wage employers are less affected by these swings because their wages are high enough above the area level so that they are little affected by short-run changes. They try to limit wage level changes to once a year and tend to set prices by a percentage markup over average unit costs of production.

Low-wage organizations adjust to changes in labor demand by deciding how far they can lag behind high-paying organizations. During an economic upswing, high-wage employers will be increasing wages and employment. Low-wage employers, to hold down turnover and to increase employment, will have to raise wages more than high-paying firms. The wage gap between high-paying and low-paying firms thereby narrows during an upswing.

During a downswing, high-wage firms stop hiring and may lay off employees. Low-wage firms find that they have more and better applicants and few quits. This means they can lag further behind the wage leaders and that the intercompany differential widens.

But although these swings in labor demand compress and expand the differential, it never disappears. The reason is that although some labor markets are tight in upswings, most are quite loose (they have more unemployment than job vacancies) most of the time.

Fluctuations in demand also change hiring standards. When an employer's pool of applicants begins to dry up, the employer may raise wages or lower hiring standards. Pressure to lower hiring standards is felt first by low-wage firms. During a downswing, hiring standards are raised. It is usually easier and quicker and perhaps less costly to change hiring standards than to change wages. As a result employers may prefer changing hiring standards in the short run to changing wages.

Obviously, swings in labor demand have their greatest effects on the less-preferred members of the labor force. Tight labor markets increase the hiring of these groups. Loose labor markets discourage it. Organizations paying market rates can expect to have to react to most of these changes like the low-paying organizations but not to the same degree.

An employer's wage level is typically, in the final analysis, a matter of policy. Organizations take positions in labor markets and try to maintain them—at the market or so much above or below it. Most companies most of the time pay more than they would need to in order to meet their employment objectives, but they ration jobs through hiring standards. Preferred groups are hired first, less-preferred groups next. Many firms can quickly expand employment at present wage levels by merely announcing openings. In this way, employees can flow from lower-wage to higher-wage employers and sectors with no change in differentials.

During an upswing, low-wage employers will try to expand employment just as high-wage employers do. People are attracted from low-paying to high-paying firms. At some point, the low-wage employer must raise wages and probably also lower hiring standards. Eventually all employers must do the same. The reverse process occurs in a downswing.

INTERNAL LABOR MARKETS

So far we have been describing the process of determining or adjusting the (average) wage level of an organization. But most companies have many different jobs, each with its own wage rate. Some kinds of employees are hired from an outside market—typically for jobs at the bottom and top of the skill ladder and for standard clerical jobs. But most employers have only a limited number of entry points. Most jobs are specific to the industry or company and are filled from within. These jobs have no outside market, and their wage rates are determined by administrative decision or collective bargaining.

It is useful to describe employers as having either open or closed internal labor markets. Employers with open markets (construction companies, for example) fill most jobs from the outside. Employers with closed markets fill most jobs from within. Open markets are strongly influenced by all the forces in the environment that bear on the organization. Closed markets, in the final analysis, like closed bureaucracies, can determine wages administratively by manipulating both demand and supply. Obviously, open and closed internal labor markets constitute not a dichotomy but a continuum. But most organizations tend toward closed internal labor markets, because they are advantageous to both employers and employees.

A closed internal labor market does not mean that the organization does not have to have a wage level policy. Entry-level jobs are exceedingly important to this type of organization and they must be competitive in the labor markets from which they recruit their organizational entrants. Failure to be competitive at this point will lead to sub-standard hires, and this deficiency will stay with the organization for many years as these employees move within the organization. Closed internal market organizations pay close attention to wage survey trends both to recruit through their entry points and to retain current employees who are moving upward in the organizational hierarchy.

Early paragraphs in this chapter pointed out that wage levels can be too low and they can be too high. The floor is determined by what labor-market competitors are paying to attract people to their jobs. Thus employers with relatively open internal labor markets need to attend to the hiring rates of relevant labor-market competitors for almost all jobs. Employers with relatively closed internal labor markets, however, need be concerned only with the hiring rates of jobs they fill from the outside.

Ceilings on wage levels are another matter. Employers in the same product market (industry) must not exceed the labor cost per unit (wage costs divided by productivity) of competitors if they wish to remain competitive. But such information is not available. Average wage rates for jobs and organizations are, but not productivity. One suggestion is to use the average wage of product-market competitors using similar technology.[3] Employers with relatively open internal labor markets could use this figure as a ceiling and adjust, if necessary, by changing their job mix (substituting lower-paid jobs for higher-paid jobs) or recruiting in lower-wage markets. Employers using global surveys (exchanging payroll data with frequency distributions of jobs) may be using the job-mix approach. Employers with relatively closed internal labor markets could meet the average wage of product-market competitors by setting rates for entry jobs at the external-market level and controlling the rates of internally filled jobs to compensate.

Of course, the importance of the product market as a ceiling depends on competition in the product market. In highly competitive industries, organizations follow the practice of low-wage employers discussed earlier. In less competitive industries, the high-wage employer serves as a useful reference point.

Product-market competitors could also seek competitive advantage through increased productivity of employees. Although wage levels alone are not expected to achieve increased productivity, they may attract better candidates and encourage them to stay.

WAGE LEVEL STRATEGIES
FOR EMPLOYEE GROUPS

As indicated, a wage level strategy may be for an organization or for any subpart thereof, such as groups of employees. The discussion in this chapter has focused on the overall organizational wage level strategy but an organization may have a number of wage level strategies for different organizational units, locations, or employee groups. The importance of the organizational unit or group of employees may call for a wage level strategy higher than that of other parts of the organization. The characteristics of particular labor markets or competitors may call for a selective wage level strategy in parts of the organization. Loose labor markets, where there is a constant supply of adequate employees, encourages a low-paying strategy for those employee groups. All these conditions can apply in a single organization, making it useful to have a number of policies rather than a single one. A major concern in employing different wage level strategies within an organization is to ensure that the differences do not create discrimination in wage rates within the organization. Establishing

[3]T. A. Mahoney, "Compensating for Work," in *Personnel Management,* ed. K. M. Rowland and G. R. Ferris (Boston: Allyn & Bacon, 1982), pp. 227–61.

low-paying strategies only for employee groups that are predominantly minority or female can lead to charges of discrimination.

SUMMARY

First, organizations must decide how important human resources are to the accomplishment of organizational goals. This decision is reflected in the wage level strategy that the organization employs. As seen in this chapter, organizations may choose to pay the market, or above or below the market. This decision is a function of a number of factors including the job mix of the organization, hiring standards, product markets, competition in the labor market, the use of the internal labor market, and the requirements for employee productivity.

Employers set overall wage rates by reference to the market and thus must have considerable information as to what the market is paying. This data collection is done through the technique of wage surveys, the topic of the next chapter. Since market conditions are one of a number of influences on the pay level decision, chapter 7 concludes this section by discussing a number of the other considerations in wage level decisions.

6

Compensation Surveys

By all odds the most common practice in compensation administration is the collection, analysis, and use of information on compensation paid by other employing organizations. This chapter examines this practice. Although we intend to focus here on wage level decisions, it will be seen that compensation surveys are a multipurpose tool used in all aspects of compensation determination and management.

This emphasis on compensation surveys should surprise no one. Analysis at both theoretical and practical levels would suggest it. Wages are prices of labor services. Because labor markets are different from other markets, both employing organizations and workers must search for information and choices. An important target of employer search is "going wages"—what other organizations are paying for similar labor. The information sought is also of great interest to employees and potential employees. Most people are likely to accept the paying of market wages as "fair."

For most organizations, the way to start determining a workable wage or salary level or diagnosing other existing or potential wage problems is to discover "going wages" in the area or the industry or both. The particular "going wage" used may apply to all organizations in the area, all organizations in the same industry in the area, all organizations in the same industry without regard to area, or some combination. The information is usually obtained from some form of wage survey.

There is no way of estimating the number of wage surveys made each year. They undoubtedly run into the thousands. They are made by governments, trade and professional associations, consultants, voluntary associations of employers, and individual employers.

Such voluminous data collection suggests that an enormous need exists. Why are wage surveys necessary? Part of the answer has already been given: it seems fair to both employers and employees to have wages related in some fashion to wage rates for comparable work in the area or in the industry. Equally important, the information needed is not available in other ways. True, the Bureau of Labor Statistics publishes occupational-wage data in three separate programs—industry wage surveys, area wage surveys, and the national survey of professional, administrative, technical, and clerical pay. Government efforts have contributed greatly to wage-survey techniques. But most employers, even while using government occupational-wage statistics, do not find them sufficiently timely and specific to fill their needs.

What the employer wishes to know are specific wages for specific occupations in specific markets as defined by the organization. This information must be complete, up-to-date, and comparable in terms of organizations and jobs included.

The lack of occupational-wage information appears at first glance to be a major omission in wage statistics. But the needs for wage information by employing organizations are so specific, varied, and continuous as to preclude their satisfaction solely through government programs.

Organizations requiring wage-survey data have several choices: (1) a government wage survey may be used if one is available that appears applicable; (2) union wage-rate data may be available; (3) surveys made by a trade association to which the employer belongs may be available; (4) surveys made by professional associations or consultants may be purchased; (5) an informal group of employers may make surveys; (6) an organization can make its own survey. Providing the needed information is obtained and careful methods followed, the choice may be made on the basis of cost (the preceding possibilities are listed in probable order of increasing cost). But because questionable information may be useless, useful data and exacting procedures are more important than costs.

SURVEYS CONDUCTED BY THE ORGANIZATION

Examining how an organization designs and conducts its own survey provides information useful in appraising surveys made by others. The steps involved may be outlined as follows:

    A. Planning the survey
        1. Determining the purpose of the survey
        2. Determining the jobs to be included
        3. Determining the markets to be surveyed
        4. Determining the firms to be surveyed
        5. Determining the information to be obtained

  6. Making the schedules
  7. Determining the survey method
 B. Conducting the survey
  1. Insuring job comparability
  2. Collecting information
 C. Tabulating, analyzing, and presenting results

Planning the Survey

Even when a firm decides to conduct its own survey there is much to be said for attempting to interest other organizations in co-sponsoring the effort. If this is possible, the costs may be shared. The joint effort may also result in an informal group of firms that will see the advantage of periodic surveys.

Whether or not other organizations accept co-sponsorship, a steering committee of some of the firms certain to be included is a good idea. These committee members will be helpful in planning the survey and in securing cooperation.

DETERMINING THE PURPOSE OF THE SURVEY. This will be useful in determining the jobs, markets, and firms to be included and the information to be obtained. It also determines the accuracy needed and the time limits of the survey. Obviously, if information is needed on only one or two jobs or an overtime policy, a much less elaborate survey is called for than if a picture of an area or industry market is to be sought.

DETERMINING THE JOBS TO BE INCLUDED. The jobs on which pay data are sought must be selected. For a number of reasons wage surveys do not attempt to obtain information on all of an organization's jobs. First, some jobs are unique to the organization and unlikely to be found elsewhere. Second, many jobs are always filled from the internal labor market and market data may not be needed. Third, compensation policy and practice in most organizations are based on a limited number of key jobs.

Key jobs are reference points in the job structure. In most wage and salary surveys a limited number of them (25 to 30) are chosen to represent the entire range of jobs. It should be noted, however, that organizations placing more emphasis on external competitiveness tend to survey a larger number of jobs—sometimes as many as 80, if possible.

Key jobs are selected on a number of criteria. They should represent the entire range of jobs in the organization or as determined in the purpose of the survey. They should be numerically important in terms of surveyed firms having them and in terms of organizational positions. They should be readily definable. They should be relatively stable in content. They should represent good reference points in the job structure in terms of difficulty and responsibility. They should be well known to managers and labor leaders. They should be jobs that at least some organizations fill from external sources.

Using these criteria, the organization or the steering committee will choose the jobs to be surveyed. Obviously, jobs involving recruitment or turnover problems will become key jobs in the survey.

DETERMINING THE MARKETS TO BE SURVEYED. The next step is determining the relevant labor markets for these jobs. Both the normal recruiting area for the jobs concerned and the area within which employees have been lost to competitors are apropos. The relevant labor-market area is the area where the labor supply for the jobs is most likely to be found.

As mentioned in chapter 2, the labor supply for some jobs is local, for others regional, and for still others national or international. Most companies confine their wage and salary surveys to local or regional markets. Surveys containing regional, national, or international data are usually secured from trade or professional organizations or from consultants.

Most white-collar and blue-collar employees are hired locally, and the labor-market area is defined as normal commuting distance. For these employees normal commuting distance, if in question, can usually be determined from the addresses of employees presently filling these jobs.

Technical, administrative, and professional employees may be attached to the local area. But often they come from and go to other areas of the state or even adjacent states. Some managers and professionals operate in national or even international markets. Obviously, local surveys are of limited usefulness for these jobs.

DETERMINING THE FIRMS TO BE SURVEYED. Given the geographic area of the survey, the next step is to choose the organizations to be surveyed. An attempt is first made to obtain firms in the same industry. Such organizations are more likely to have all of the jobs of the surveying organization and usually have similar wages.

Organizations hiring similar skills is another criterion. An attempt is made to include firms hiring substantial numbers of employees for jobs being surveyed.

A third consideration is organization size. Compensation varies by company size. Ideally, the survey will include a balance of organizations of varying size. But very small firms may represent noncomparable labor markets.

If possible, organizations selected should have formal compensation systems administered by a compensation professional. A plus would be organizations using pay systems similar to that of the surveying organization.

The number of organizations included in the survey is very much a function of the purpose of the survey. If only a limited number of firms are adjudged to represent an organization's labor-market competition, including only these firms makes sense. If, however, the objective is to achieve a realistic picture of the labor market in the area (or industry), a representative and balanced sample is called for. The latter approach would call for a census of establishments in the universe to be sampled and a sample drawn for representativeness and reliability. The Bureau of Labor Statistics follows this approach.

In most surveys made by companies or groups of companies, the participants are usually chosen on the criteria of (1) industry, (2) comparable work, (3) competition for workers, and (4) size. In most private-company surveys, the number of cooperating establishments is limited to a small number on the assumption that these organizations represent the pertinent labor-market competitors.

DETERMINING THE INFORMATION TO BE OBTAINED. This determination is driven by the purpose of the survey. Although it is possible to obtain information on pay and benefits as well as pay policies in one survey, the need for cooperation from other organizations argues against such an approach. A better practice is to make separate surveys of wages and benefits and perhaps of average wage changes.

But wage surveys require some information on pay policies and practices to permit interpretation of wage data, and sufficient organization-identification data to permit decisions on organization comparability. The latter information consists of location, industry, size (usually number of employees), and union or nonunion status. Information sought on wage and salary policy and procedures may be limited to general increases, wage structure adjustment, and individual pay change. Alternatively, information on job-evaluation plans, number of wage structures, incentive-plan usage, hours and work schedules, and general benefit policy may be sought.

The major information contained in wage surveys is pay information on specific jobs. Here, the major requirement besides job descriptions or job briefs is for careful definitions of the data sought. For example, base rates for regularly employed day workers are defined as *not* including overtime, shift differentials, or nonproduction bonuses, but including cost-of-living increases. These rates should be reported prior to deductions for Social Security, other taxes, and any employee contributions to benefits.

Directions for calculating base rates for employees on incentive or salary should be specified. Incentive base rates are obtained by dividing earnings by hours worked, increasing the hours to remove overtime premiums. Monthly or weekly salary is reduced to a common period.

Hiring rates should reflect the starting wage rates for particular jobs and classes of employees. Minimum, standard, and maximum rates are usually sought. Actual wage rates may be sought, together with the number of incumbents at each. The actual minimum and maximum paid for the job are usually obtained.

Benefit surveys are usually conducted separately. The information sought is quite detailed but usually applies to all employees or broad employee groups. The purpose is usually to determine the prevalence of benefits and benefit practices rather than costs, but some benefit surveys attempt to obtain the latter as well.

Some surveys are concerned only with wage changes since the last survey. Thus they carefully specify the method of calculating the information sought.

MAKING THE SCHEDULES. After it has been decided what information to seek, the next step is making the schedules to be used in collecting the data. The schedules are designed to permit recording the data as conveniently as possible and to permit rapid tabulation and analysis.

Normally two schedules are prepared, one for information about the organization and wage policy and procedures and another for wage data. Only one of the former is required per organization. But one wage-data schedule is required for each job included in the survey. A common practice is to present the job description or job brief in the schedule prior to specifying the wage information sought. Exhibits 6–1 and 6–2 are examples of such schedules. Obviously, both schedules could be shortened or lengthened depending upon the information called for.

Exhibit 6–1   General Information: Policies and Practices Affecting Compensation

Name of organization participating in the survey: _____

Address: _____   Industry: _____

Code No.: _____   Date this form was completed: _____

Data furnished by: Name _____   Title _____

1. Briefly describe major products (or services) of your reporting unit: _____
   _____
   _____
   _____
   _____

2. Employment:
   Total number of employees in company, division, or plant for which survey data is reported:
   Hourly   _____
   Nonexempt salaried   _____
   Exempt salaried   _____
   Total   _____

3. General increase and structure adjustments:
   a. During the past twelve months, has your firm granted a general increase to employees in the following classifications?
      Hourly   _____ No _____ Yes Amount or %_____ Date _____
      Nonexempt salaried _____ No _____ Yes Amount or %_____ Date _____
      Exempt salaried   _____ No _____ Yes Amount or %_____ Date _____
   b. During the same period, did you have a structure adjustment?
      Hourly   _____ No _____ Yes Amount or %_____ Date _____
      Nonexempt salaried _____ No _____ Yes Amount or %_____ Date _____
      Exempt salaried   _____ No _____ Yes Amount or %_____ Date _____

4. Merit increases:
   a. Does your firm maintain a merit increase budget for granting pay increases during a time period?
      Hourly   _____ No _____ Yes
      Nonexempt salaried _____ No _____ Yes
      Exempt salaried   _____ No _____ Yes
   b. If no, what was the approximate salary increase for the last period?
      Hourly $_____
      Nonexempt salaried $_____
      Exempt salaried $_____
   c. If yes (if you have a merit increase budget), it is:

	Merit	Promotion	Total
Hourly	_____·__%	_____·__%	_____·__%
Nonexempt salaried	_____·__%	_____·__%	_____·__%
Exempt salaried	_____·__%	_____·__%	_____·__%

   d. What are the dates of your current budget year?
      From _____ to _____, inclusive.

Exhibit 6–1 (continued)

5. Union? _____ Yes _____ No
   If yes, list by name: _____
   _____
   _____
   _____

6. Cost of Living:
   Do you grant a cost-of-living allowance? _____ No _____ Yes
   If yes, what is the current amount and group involved? _____
   _____

7. Are any employee groups on automatic progression? _____ No _____ Yes
   If yes, groups, frequency, and amount: _____
   _____

8. Does your firm grant pay increases on an anniversary date or fixed calendar date(s)?

	Anniversary Date	Fixed Calendar	Date(s)
Hourly	_____	_____	_____
Nonexempt	_____	_____	_____
Exempt	_____	_____	_____

9. What is the frequency of your salary increases?

Times per Year

	1	2	3	Other
Hourly	___	___	___	_____
Nonexempt	___	___	___	_____
Exempt	___	___	___	_____

10. Any additional information that might help us interpret your pay data: _____
   _____
   _____
   _____
   _____

Exhibit 6–2 Wage and Salary Information

Company name: _____
Job title: _____   Date: _____
Job description or brief:

Modifier:
_____ W (survey job brief is perceptibly *weaker* than your job)
_____ M (survey job brief *matches* your job very well)
_____ S (survey job brief is noticeably *stronger* than your job)
Number of employees: _____
Rate range: Minimum _____ Mid _____ Max _____
Actual rates paid: Low _____ High _____
Weighted average: _____
Cost-of-living: $_____ per hour
Level (within a job family): _____ of _____
FLSA:
   Hourly   _____
   Nonexempt _____
   Exempt   _____

DETERMINING THE SURVEY METHOD.   Wage and salary surveys may be made by telephone, by mail, by visit, and by group meeting. Telephone surveys may be used to acquire some wage policy and practice data and wage information on a very few jobs when both the caller and the respondent are well-acquainted compensation professionals. Such surveys may be common practice in well-defined industry groups where job comparability has been recently established or can be easily accomplished. But outside such informal networks such surveys can be unproductive or dangerous.

Mailed surveys may be safely used for securing wage policy and practice data. But although this is the most common survey method, assuring job comparability and thus useful wage data is a continuing problem. Careful construction of schedules and precise definitions help. But the quality of the data always depends on the qualifications of the respondent and the general press of business. As in the case of telephone surveys among professionals in the same industry, reliable data may be secured. In fact, organizations surveying a widely dispersed industry may have no other choice. But local surveys, unless job comparability by some other method has recently been assured, should probably not be done by mail.

It is usually agreed that the most productive method of gathering accurate wage data is a visit by qualified personnel. Because determining job comparability is the key to obtaining useful occupational-wage data, the visit is probably best conducted by trained personnel using a standardized data-collection method on site, at least in the original survey. These people can compare the survey job descriptions with company job descriptions. They can question compensation professionals. They may talk to job incumbents. They may apply a standard job-evaluation scale. They collect wage data only after personally verifying job comparability. They interview the proper person to obtain information on wage policies and procedures.

Some wage surveys, usually local ones, are made in group meetings. The job descriptions or job briefs of survey jobs are distributed in advance. At the meeting compensation professionals thrash out problems of job comparability and provide the surveying organization with wage data. Although this method seems superior to mailed surveys and is much less costly than visit surveys, some questions about it can be raised. For example, in large organizations with hundreds of jobs can even the most competent professional answer questions of comparability with survey jobs in the meeting? Does high turnover among compensation professionals have any effect on the reliability of the data?

From this discussion of survey methods it should be obvious that determining *job comparability* is the Achilles' heel of wage surveys. Job comparability can be improved by personal visits, group meetings, use of common job-evaluation plans, and use of job-scope data. But cost and coverage requirements probably ensure that many surveys will continue to be made by mail. Does this mean that survey reliability and validity depend on the conscientiousness and time pressures of respondents? Foster argues that developing Z-scores from the range midpoints of benchmark jobs and the mean and standard deviation of the company's overall range-midpoint distribution provides a useful measure of job comparability among reporting organizations.[1] These job-value indexes (JVI) can be supplemented by policy-capturing statistical techniques (such as multiple-regression analysis) and then used to explain how and why different firms value key jobs differently. Measures such as a JVI would permit much quicker and easier determination of job comparability than would use of a common job-evaluation plan.

Conducting the Survey

The survey method in large part determines the steps in conducting the survey. Regardless of the method, however, it is useful to separate the initial contact from the collection of the data. The initial contact is made to ensure the participation of the firms selected for the survey. It usually involves providing information on (1) the purpose of the survey, (2) the jobs covered, (3) the information sought, (4) the survey method, and (5) the report of the results. Participation is invited. Confidentiality of the data is assured. A copy of the report is offered. The latter is usually enough to secure cooperation if the potential participant has a use for the information. Participating in a survey is much less costly than conducting your own.

In mailed surveys obtaining wage policy and practice information, determining job comparability, and obtaining wage data depend largely on the schedules developed. Constructing the schedules with ease of completion in mind pays off in rate of return and ease of tabulating results.

In other survey methods the wage policy and practice schedule can be mailed back to the surveying organization without loss of accuracy. In visit surveys, they are usually completed before the visit is made.

In both the group meeting and the visit survey job comparability is determined by discussion between the representative of the surveying organization and a company compensation professional. In the latter method wage data may be secured from the payroll department by the surveying company's representative.

Tabulating, Analyzing, and Presenting Results

When the data from all cooperating organizations are in, they are tabulated, summarized, and presented in the form of results. All information is edited for comparable terminology and units before tabulation. Consolidating the data involves separate tabulations for wage data and wage policy and practice data.

WAGE DATA.   There are several ways to tabulate and present wage data, depending on the purpose of the survey. Data summaries in surveys focusing on separate jobs, as is usually the case, differ from summaries in surveys focusing on the job structure.

In most surveys data are presented separately for each job. Table 6–1 illustrates this approach. One of the advantages of this method is that it permits

---

[1]K. E. Foster, "Measuring Overlooked Factors in Relative Job Worth and Pay," *Compensation Review,* first quarter 1983, pp. 44–55.

Table 6–1 Wage and Salary Data by Job Title

COMPANY NO.	JOB-MATCH MODIFIER	No. OF EMPLOYEES	RANGE			% SPREAD	CURRENT RATES PAID			% COL	LEVEL	CLASS
			Min	Med	Max	Min–Max	Low	High	Wt Avg			

Weighted averages:
Simple averages:

comparisons with other companies individually or collectively. Organizations may, if they wish, exchange code numbers and custom-build their comparisons. The method also has the advantage of presenting several measures of actual rates and ranges in one tabulation.

Somewhat less common is a frequency distribution presenting the total number of incumbents at each wage rate or class for each job. This is the method used by the Bureau of Labor Statistics in its area surveys. See table 6–2. This method has the advantage of presenting sufficient detail to permit the user to calculate several summary measures. But it has the disadvantage of lacking means of identifying specific company data. Other information, such as hiring rates or ranges, can be tabulated in the same way.

If the major purpose of the survey is to compare job structures rather than individual jobs, graphs may be used. See figure 6–1. In this approach, a graph depicts a summary wage line, made up consolidating all the information in the survey, and a company wage line. The chief advantage of this method is the possibility of each organization's comparing its wage level and structure with the summary wage line and the wage line of each participant. A disadvantage is the averaging necessary to develop the graph.

Constructing such graphs is facilitated when the participating organizations are using the same job-evaluation plan. But the method does not depend upon this. Any consistent method of plotting the jobs on the horizontal axis will do.

WAGE POLICY AND PRACTICE DATA. Many variations are also possible in the tabulation of wage policy and practice data. They may be presented in narrative form. They may be tabulated question by question following the schedule used. For maximum usefulness of wage-survey data it is advantageous

Table 6–2 Wage-Rate Frequency Distribution

Job: Electronics assembler—repetitive

DOLLARS PER HOUR	NUMBER OF EMPLOYEES
3.50 and under 3.70	33
3.70 and under 3.90	66
3.90 and under 4.10	72
4.10 and under 4.30	94
4.30 and under 4.50	198
4.50 and under 4.70	201
4.70 and under 4.90	450
4.90 and under 5.10	268
5.10 and under 5.30	118
5.30 and under 5.50	79
5.50 and under 5.70	39
	1618

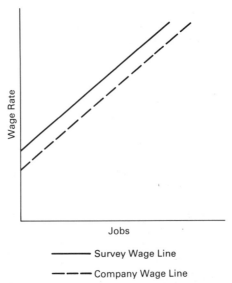

Figure 6–1   Comparison of wage survey data and company wage structure

to use company codes for wage policy and practice data. In this way unusual wage positions may be interpreted by reference to wage policy and practice information.

SURVEYS CONDUCTED BY OTHERS

As mentioned, making its own survey is usually the most costly choice for an organization. Thus many organizations must rely on wage and salary surveys conducted by others. In some cases, the reports they receive as participants in surveys conducted by other organizations provide sufficient information. They may obtain surveys conducted by the U.S. Bureau of Labor Statistics. They may purchase wage surveys made by industry groups, professional societies, or private organizations. They may join an informal group whose purpose is to conduct surveys.

BLS Surveys

The Bureau of Labor Statistics (BLS) publishes three surveys of occupational-wage data: area-wage surveys, industry-wage surveys, and the national survey of professional, administrative, technical, and clerical pay.

Each year the BLS makes a large number of area surveys of Standard Metropolitan Statistical Areas (SMSAs) and other areas—74 geographic areas in all—for the Department of Labor and other government agencies. These surveys collect data on a limited number of jobs in a wide variety of manufacturing and nonmanufacturing industries. Some of the surveys permit administering the Service Contract Act of 1965 and limit the number of jobs. Those made for SMSAs survey a larger number of jobs: office, professional, and technical; material-movement and custodial; and maintenance, toolroom, and power-plant jobs. For some areas, earnings and some benefit data are available for banks and savings and loan associations, and union wage rates for the building trades, printing trades, local transit operations, local truck drivers and helpers, and grocery store employees. In addition to earnings data, these surveys provide information on weekly work schedules; paid holidays and vacations; and health, insurance, and pension benefits. Shift-operation data and shift differentials are provided for plant workers. Minimum entrance rates for inexperienced office workers are furnished. Data are classified by industry as well as by occupation and are presented in frequency distributions showing the number of people in each wage-rate class.

The occupations covered in area surveys are limited to those that are common to a variety of industries. They do not include processing jobs that are specific to particular industries.

Industry-wage surveys provide data for selected occupations in 50 manufacturing and 20 nonmanufacturing industries nationally and are performed on a three- and five-year cycle, depending on the industry. These surveys provide data on straight-time first-shift rates for workers in selected occupations; weekly work schedules; shift operations and differentials; paid holidays and vacations; and health, insurance, and pension benefits. Although industry surveys provide data that could be highly useful to employing organizations, their long-term time cycle attenuates their usefulness.

The national survey of professional, administrative, technical, and clerical pay (the PATC survey) provides salary distributions and measures for occupations that fit into these categories. Definitions for the occupations covered provide for classification of employees by work levels. This survey was designed to aid in pricing specific pay grades of federal civil service employees. In addition to salary data, weekly hours are presented as well as industry salary differences. The PATC survey appears to be widely used by employing organizations, both public and private.

Although probably few organizations are able to rely solely on BLS surveys for occupational wage data, the BLS survey methodology is designed to yield highly reliable information. Definitions of data collected are specific. The job descriptions, though short, seem sufficient to identify the skill, difficulty, and responsibility requirements. Job comparability is established by trained people. Sampling principles are followed in selecting organizations to be included.

Industry, Professional, and Private Surveys

A large number of trade associations, industry groups, professional societies, and consulting organizations conduct wage and salary surveys. These surveys are often specialized in terms of occupation, industry, or locality. Some are free to members of associations. Others cost as much as several hundred dollars. There is no comprehensive listing of all these surveys, but the Prentice-Hall Compensation Service, the Bureau of National Affairs, and the Commerce Clearing House present numerous sources.

The Merchants and Manufacturer's Association of Los Angeles, for example, conducts regular surveys. One well-known industry survey is that of the American Electronics Association. The Wyatt's Executive Compensation Service is also well known. Surveys of computer personnel by A. S. Hansen, Inc., are examples of surveys of professional employees. Most professional societies conduct pay surveys. The Hay group; Towers, Perrin, Forster and Crosby; and Hewitt Associates are examples of consulting firms that conduct surveys for clients. See appendix 1 at the end of the book for a more extensive list of government agencies, industry groups, and consultants who conduct wage surveys.

Informal Group Surveys

What may be a growing practice in some areas is the formation of informal groups to conduct pay surveys of members. Such surveys have the advantages of obtaining the information the members need when they need it, at quite reasonable cost. An example is the Compensation Practices Association of San Diego County. Membership consists of manufacturing organizations with at least 200 employees, including a compensation professional. Three surveys per year are conducted—an occupational survey of over 100 jobs, an average-pay survey, and a comprehensive benefits survey. Job comparability is established in group meetings of compensation professionals. Perhaps the greatest advantage to members is the rapidity with which the data are disseminated: the report is in members' hands within two weeks after the information is collected. An example of such a report appears in table 6–3.

Non-Occupational Surveys

The difficulty of determining job comparability in wage and salary surveys has prompted the development of survey methods not dependent on this process.

THE GLOBAL APPROACH. One of the best known of these is the global approach, which asks for pay data and number of employees by function. Respondents are asked either to provide data on all job levels in the function or to provide a frequency distribution of number of individuals in each of a number of salary classes.[2]

Such surveys are most valuable when conducted within an industry where the occupations are known to be similar but where organizations may differ in occupational distributions. Some compensation professionals conduct their own global surveys to judge the representativeness of data from occupational surveys.

MATURITY CURVES. An even better known nonoccupational approach, the maturity curve is typically used in salary surveys of professional employees. Many professional societies collect and publish salary data by scholarly discipline, degree level, supervisory status, and years since degree. Such

---

[2]See K. E. Foster, G. F. Wajda, and T. R. Lawson, "Global Plan for Salary Administration," *Harvard Business Review*, September-October 1961, pp. 62–66.

Table 6-3 A Wage-Survey Report by an Informal Group:
Aggregate Data on Compensation Practices of San Diego County—August 1985

POSITION	NUMBER OF FIRMS	NUMBER OF EMPLOYEES	RANGE ($)			CURRENT RATES PAID ($)		
			Min	Mid	Max	Low	High	Wt. Avg.
2320 Buyer, junior (highest level nonexempt)	28	33	1409	1778	2148	1473	1521	1531
2330 Buyer	42	153	1675	2156	2637	1770	2333	2018
2340 Senior buyer	38	94	2013	2597	3181	2351	2781	2528
2342 Purchasing supervisor	27	33	2399	3044	3689	2875	3115	3005
2350 Production control planner (highest level)	33	98	1765	2289	2812	1945	2445	2192
2352 Production control supervisor	29	47	2082	2666	3250	2530	2797	2639
2360 Master scheduler (highest level)	8	9	1722	2211	2700	2096	2327	2211
2370 Manufacturing methods planner (highest level)	11	25	1543	1989	2435	1813	2038	1932
2372 Maintenance supervisor	25	58	2040	2638	3236	2502	2882	2659
2378 Manufacturing engineer (entry level)	27	78	1985	2532	3080	2246	2859	2534
2380 Manufacturing engineer (highest level)	29	81	2387	3006	3626	2878	3281	3084
2390 Industrial engineer (entry level)	22	17	1931	2496	3061	2446	2651	2517
2400 Industrial engineer (highest level)	24	27	2398	3016	3634	2937	3065	3000
2410 Quality control supervisor	31	67	1881	2413	2944	2241	2546	2388
2418 Quality assurance engineer	30	74	1955	2517	3078	2218	2590	2412
2420 Senior quality assurance engineer	31	85	2387	3017	3648	2809	3193	3012

Source: Compensation Practices Association of San Diego County.

data are presented as frequency distributions of number of individuals at each salary level for each year since obtaining the degree. Separate distributions are provided for the different degree levels and for supervisors and nonsupervisors. Some graphs of these data designate years since the degree as the horizontal axis and monthly salary as the vertical axis and plot several computed measures (medians, quartiles, trends)—hence the term *maturity curve*.

Maturity curves represent substitutes for pay information about specific jobs. Actually what they represent is a picture of progress in the profession of professionals classified in various ways.

COMPUTER DATA BANKS. An interesting development in salary surveys is the data bank that organizations may query by computer. An example that has been around for some years is the Salary Information and Retrieval System developed by the System Development Corporation and now operated by Industrial Relations Counselors. The data bank consists of both occupational-salary data and maturity-curve data that subscribers may tap to make their own survey. The Hay group has recently developed a data-base system for its clients. As the use of computers of all kinds expands and costs come down, such custom surveys may at some point become the least costly approach.

USE OF SURVEY DATA

The effort and money expended by organizations on obtaining wage data suggest a great need. Moreover, informal discussion with compensation administrators suggests that the information is heavily used. But knowledge about how information is and should be used is meager.

An early study found that employers attach different meanings to "keeping up" with their area or industry.[3] Another study found that organizations use industry and area surveys differently, placing greater emphasis on the former and using the latter to determine trends.[4] Logic suggests that the analysis and use of survey data depend heavily on the problem(s) that called for making or purchasing the survey.

A study performed by one of the authors attempted to obtain more information on how organizations analyze and use wage-survey data.[5] Compensation professionals in 34 organizations were interviewed at length (almost all over an hour) about what they did with wage-survey information. Thirty-one of the firms were in manufacturing, with two thirds of them in high technology (mostly electronics). They ranged in size from under 350 employees to over 1000, with 16 of them in the latter category. About one third of the firms were unionized. The interviews were taped and later transcribed.

The strongest conclusion was the dependence of these compensation professionals on wage and salary surveys. Most of them reported that surveys carried over 50 percent of the weight in most compensation decisions, and a

---

[3]L. G. Reynolds, *The Structure of Labor Markets* (New York: Harper & Brothers, 1951).

[4]W. A. Groenkamp, "How Reliable Are Wage Surveys?" *Personnel*, January-February 1967, pp. 32–37.

[5]D. W. Belcher, M. B. Ferris, and J. O'Neill, "How Wage Surveys are Being Used," *Compensation and Benefits Review*, (1985), 34–51.

few asserted that compensation administration would be impossible without surveys.

But by all odds the most surprising finding of the study was the time, energy, and imagination that was expended in analyzing survey data. Apparently, search theory as outlined in chapter 3 applies equally forcibly to labor-market information. The variety of methods of analysis applied to the same survey and the variations in analyzing different surveys were amazing (97 separable approaches in the 34 firms).

Some of the methods of analysis, such as adjusting the data for time lag (over 90 percent did this) are quite understandable, but the variety of methods used seems less so. Perhaps less justified, given the variety of survey methods, is the practice of combining surveys, which was reported by one third of the firms. But most of the analyses involved eliminating some firms, selecting others for comparison, recalculating measures, arbitrarily weighting some of the data, or custom-building a minisurvey from the data. Various forms of statistical analysis were employed, including graphic analysis, calculation of trends, and even some regression analysis. The picture that emerged was multiple attempts to get the data to answer the questions posed by the analyst. Equally surprising, each organization seemed to employ its own analysis. No significant differences in analytical aproach by size, industry, or unionization appeared.

Perhaps the major lesson from this variety is that compensation professionals prefer wage data presented by job and responding organization so that they can design their own comparisons. Many organizations, for example, make separate analyses of industry and area competitors. Only a third of the organizations included maturity-curve data in their analysis. But some of them had methods of forcing a comparison of job and maturity data.

Except for maturity-curve data, there was no evidence in this study that organizations were obtaining more wage-survey data than they use. Most of the organizations made some use of all of the information in their survey.

This chapter began by assuming that the major use of wage surveys is to determine wage levels. But among the 48 separate reported uses of wage-survey data found by the study, only 17 could be classified as involving pay levels. Eleven of the uses involved building or adjusting wage structures. Although wage level and wage structures are related, as we have seen, the wage-structure uses found by the study involved changing pay relationships on the basis of external data.

Seven of the uses involved individual wage determination. Nineteen organizations, for example, use surveys to determine the merit budget. Four use them as a signal to speed up or slow down individual increases. Six use surveys to drive special pay adjustments to individuals. One uses surveys to move discretionary money among groups.

Perhaps the most interesting aspect of the survey uses found was that some uses are not easily classified into level, structure, and individual pay decisions. Six firms, for example, reported using surveys to guide their entire compensation program. An equal number reported that they use them to control turnover. Two use surveys to point out potential recruiting problems. One firm uses surveys to determine the training budget. One uses them as a ritual (presumably to tell employees the organization is keeping up with the market). One organization uses surveys as a criterion of turnover levels. One firm uses surveys as an indicator of changing labor demands. One uses surveys made by others as an aid in designing its own survey.

Because this study was confined to surveys of occupational-wage data, no information was received on analyses and uses of wage policy and practice or benefit data. Presumably, in both of the latter cases a major use is to determine whether certain benefits or practices are prevalent.

ANTITRUST AND COMPENSATION SURVEYS

During the early 1980s some litigation suggested that compensation surveys held antitrust (price-fixing) implications. The issue apparently arose in connection with industry-specific surveys. Many organizations were advised by their attorneys to (1) exchange only historical (not prospective) data; (2) not meet to jointly discuss survey information; and (3) not identify companies with the data supplied. Another suggestion was that participation be limited to surveys made by third parties.

Our discussion of the use of wage-survey data would seem to show that any antitrust implications of compensation surveys are unfounded. Given the variety of labor markets faced by organizations, the various methods employed to analyze survey information, and the many uses to which the data are put, suggestions of collusion seem ludicrous.

SUMMARY

Developing, analyzing, and using wage surveys is probably the most common practice in compensation administration. Organizations use wage surveys as the measurement of the labor market. Given the importance and common use of wage surveys, planning their design and use is of utmost importance. Developing a wage survey consists of making a series of decisions starting with the purpose of the survey, what jobs to include, what markets and organizations to obtain information from, what information to seek, and how to obtain the information.

The major issue in wage surveys is the comparability of the organization's jobs to those being surveyed. It is difficult to ensure this comparability in any way other than analyzing the jobs in both organizations. While the process of collecting data through wage surveys is well defined, the analysis of those data is done in a myriad of ways. This lack of commonality in data analysis makes the statement that wage surveys measure the labor market questionable.

Organizations may choose to use wage surveys developed by others or to participate in groups that develop wage information. These methods cut down on the time expended and may provide the organization with a broader range of information. However, the question of comparability becomes greater with surveys developed by others; in some cases, large organizations may have to consider antitrust implications of joining in groups that collect wage data.

7

Other Determinants of Wage Level

Both the theory chapters (3 and 4) and the wage-survey chapter (6) point up the wide range of discretion that organizations have in setting wage levels. Although organizations seek and use information on what other employers pay, this information is only one of the determinants of wage levels. This chapter attempts to set out some of these other wage determinants and the manner in which they may be used. Although no claim is made that all wage-level determinants have been identified, it is hoped that enough have been discovered to illustrate the process used and the factors considered when an organization decides how much to pay.

THE VARIETY OF WAGE DETERMINANTS

Chapter 5 and the study of company analyses of wage-survey data discussed at some length in chapter 6 suggest that numerous forces operate as wage determinants. These might be roughly classified as economic, institutional, behavioral, and equity considerations. Because wage decisions appear to be made by comparison to labor markets, many of the determinants appear to be economic. But because the meaning and force of economic variables are interpreted by organization decision makers, these determinants are tempered by institutional, behavioral, and ethical variables.

There is no doubt that wage determinants operate through labor markets and that they include economic forces.[1] More profitable organizations tend to pay higher wages for the same occupations than less profitable organizations. Capital-intensive organizations tend to be more profitable usually because additional capital increases productivity. Small organizations tend to pay lower wages often because those wages are all they can afford. Service industries that tend to be labor-intensive, low-profit, and low-wage are often composed of small organizations.

Local labor markets vary in wage levels, depending on industrial composition. Communities in which a large proportion of organizations are in high-profit industries tend to be high-wage communities. Communities with a high proportion of organizations in low-profit industries tend to be low-wage. Sometimes communities experience short-run increases in wage levels because labor demands increase relative to labor supply or decrease because of an increase in labor supply without a proportional increase in demand.

Differentials among local labor markets are limited by a tendency for workers to leave low-wage communities and for organizations to locate new plants in low-wage areas. Unions sometimes attempt to eliminate these differentials by making a concession in work rules affecting productivity. The cost of living tends to be higher in high-wage areas.

Wage levels tend to increase faster in good times both because profits increase and because workers tend to become more demanding and more mobile. Unions reinforce this tendency by insisting on using gains made elsewhere to make their comparisons. But even in good times less efficient organizations get by, by paying less and lowering standards of employability.

But even though good times, high profits, and increasing productivity tend to increase an organization's wage-paying ability, organizations may or may not be willing to pay higher wages. Some of them do so to simplify recruiting problems and to forestall turnover. Others do so because above-average profits whet the appetites of workers and their unions. Most organizations tend to adopt a position in the wage structure of the community and attempt to maintain that position.

Thus economic forces operate on wage decisions through the actions of decision makers. If decision makers believe that adjustments in wages are necessary or desirable on economic or other grounds, they make them. If they believe that the organization's present wage-paying position is prudent and acceptable, they do not.

In the remainder of the chapter we classify wage level determinants on the basis of (1) employer ability to pay, (2) employer willingness to pay, and (3) employee (or potential employee) acceptance. Although some of these considerations have been used by arbitrators and wage boards, little is known about how they are used by wage-paying organizations or unions. We therefore emphasize how and when these determinants could be used by organizations.

EMPLOYER ABILITY TO PAY

Ability to pay influences the wage levels of organizations. In fact, a Prentice-Hall survey conducted for the American Compensation Association (ACA)

[1]H. M. Douty, *The Wage Bargain and the Labor Market* (Baltimore: John Hopkins, 1980).

found that ability to pay is the most significant factor in changing pay rates: six out of ten respondents ranked it first or second in their list of pay determinants.[2]

As reported, more profitable firms tend to pay higher wages, whether their profitability is based on the product market, technical efficiency, management ability, size, or some other factor. Likewise, in the early 1980s concession bargaining in which unions often accepted pay cuts showed the significance of inability to pay.

In a very real sense wage determination by the organization is an assessment of its ability to pay. The weight attached to other wage determinants may be determined by this estimate. Wages are labor costs to employers, and these costs are high or low depending on what the employer gets for the wage—the results of effort. What the employer actually pays is labor cost per unit of output—wage costs divided by these results (termed *productivity*). A prospective wage increase may or may not increase labor cost per unit, depending on anticipated changes in productivity. A wage increase that would be offset by increases in productivity does not increase labor costs and meets the requirement of ability to pay. A wage increase that increases labor costs, however, requires determining whether the increase can be passed on to customers or offset by a reduction in other costs. Success in either effort again meets the requirements of ability to pay.

Similarly, a union presumably attempts to estimate an organization's ability to pay before making its demands. High current profits or favorable future prospects signal ability to pay and strengthen the union's bargaining power.

Some early union contracts tied wages to ability to pay. For example, a 1919 printing agreement tied wages to economic conditions in the industry. Contracts covering motion picture operators have based wages on the seating capacity of theaters. Coal industry agreements have tied wages to the productivity of coal fields. *Sliding-scale agreements* have geared wages to selling prices.[3] Both the United Steelworkers and the United Auto Workers attempted (unsuccessfully) to secure agreements tying prospective wage increases in their industries to company profits.[4]

Although employers profess to use ability to pay (or inability to pay) as a wage determinant, little is known about how they measure it. An early study found a number of organizations that estimated ability to pay by inserting a projected wage increase into the latest income statement.[5] This definition accords closely with the definition contained in a glossary of compensation terms

---

[2]ACA/P-H Survey, *Compensation Practices,* American Compensation Association (Englewood Cliffs, N.J.: Prentice-Hall, 1982).

[3]Z. Dickinson, *Collective Wage Determination* (New York: Ronald Press, 1941), pp. 189–210.

[4]R. R. Nathan, O. Gross, and G. G. Johnson, *Economic Factors Relating to Wage Negotiations in the Steel Industry for 1947* (Pittsburgh: United Steelworkers of America, 1947); and W. P. Reuther, *Purchasing Power for Prosperity: The Case of the General Motors Workers for Maintaining Take-Home Pay* (Detroit: UAW–CIO, General Motors Department, 1945), pp. 55–76.

[5]L. G. Reynolds, *The Structure of Labor Markets* (New York: Harper & Brothers, 1951), ch. 6.

published by the American Compensation Association: the ability of a firm to meet a union wage demand while remaining profitable.[6]

Although no other published studies of how organizations measure their ability to pay have been found, the study of uses of wage surveys reported in chapter 6 suggests that they do so in a variety of ways. Over a quarter of the firms participating in that study reported that they used wage surveys to evaluate their ability to pay. If by *evaluate* they meant *determine,* this would be somewhat surprising, because surveys would logically determine willingness to pay.

A recent attempt to determine how organizations measure ability to pay by surveying a local compensation-practices group suggests much less use of ability to pay than the ACA/P-H survey cited previously.[7] Less than one third of the questionnaires were returned, and none of the respondents offered a measurement method. One compensation professional insisted that ability to pay is irrelevant—that organizations must pay what the market requires. Almost half of the responses mentioned profit targets and one mentioned ability to compete in the product market. Over half referred to labor markets and union rates, suggesting that willingness to pay is a more important determinant for these organizations.

Actually ability to pay is a composite of the economic forces facing a firm. As such it involves decisions on how profits should be measured, against what standard (net worth or sales), and over what period. It also involves determining an appropriate rate of return and resolving the issues, such as product development, product mix, and pricing policy, that most affect profits.

These considerations illustrate that although employing organizations and unions may cite ability to pay or inability to pay as a primary reason for wage decisions, no one suggests that it be used as the sole determinant. Such a strict application of ability to pay could lead to very undesirable results.

It would, for example, completely disorganize wage relationships. Wage levels would bear no relationship to the going rate in the labor market. Organizations in the same industry could have vastly different wage levels. Wages would fluctuate widely along with profits. Any semblance of industry wage uniformity (usually strongly desired by unions) would disappear. Low-profit firms employing a high proportion of highly skilled people could have lower wage levels than high-profit firms employing only unskilled labor. In this way unskilled labor could receive higher wages than highly skilled labor.

Strong limits, moreover, would be placed on economic efficiency. Under a system wherein increases in profits are absorbed by wages, an efficient management would have nothing to gain from increased effort and inefficient management would be subsidized by low wages. Nor could employees leave inefficient organizations for more efficient ones, because expansion of output and employment in efficient firms would be forestalled by the paying out of increased profits in wages to present employees. Incentives for management to improve efficiency would be seriously impaired. Possibilities of expansion would be limited.

[6]M. J. Wallace, *Glossary of Compensation Terms* (Scottsdale, Ariz.: American Compensation Association, 1984).

[7]B. Ferris, "Informal Survey of San Diego County Compensation Practices Group" unpublished paper, 1985.

For these reasons strict application of ability to pay is likely to hold little attraction for the parties. On the other hand, the general economic environment of the economy, the industry, and the firm is important in wage determination. When the demand for the product or service of an organization is strong, when potential employees are relatively scarce, and when prices can be increased without reduction in sales, unions are likely to point to ability to pay and management is unlikely to plead inability to pay. When economic conditions facing the economy, the industry, or especially the organization are unfavorable, management estimates of inability to pay may set a low limit to wage increases.

Union reactions to situations in which a company faces financial hardship are pragmatic: although they are strongly opposed to subsidizing inefficient organizations, the many cases of concession bargaining in the 1981–1982 recession show the strong influence of evidence of company inability to pay.

Although, as mentioned, organizations report using ability to pay as a wage determinant in collective bargaining, such use is subject to strongly held opinions. Most union leaders consider ability to pay irrelevant unless high profits are apparent. Most employers consider it no business of the union.

The force of ability to pay is probably best seen at the extremes—in judging whether a wage adjustment apparently justifiable on other grounds can or cannot be met. Strong evidence of favorable prospects causes employers to resist less strongly a prospective increase in wage levels. Similarly, strong evidence of unfavorable prospects reduces pressure for a wage increase, especially if it is feared that such a wage adjustment might cause loss of jobs, and greatly increases employer resistance.

Ability to pay is an expression of the economic forces that bear on wage determination. Although it is a determinant beset by measurement and forecasting problems, search theory suggests that organizations are able to estimate it when a decision calls for it.

Productivity

Productivity was used earlier in this section as a shorthand term for what the employer gets in return for the wage. Thus wage level determination is often referred to as *the effort bargain.*

Actually, as will be seen, productivity is a result of the application of human and other resources. As such it is a prime determinant of ability to pay. If production increases in the same proportion as wage costs, labor cost per unit remains unchanged. If, however, an increase in the wage level is not matched with a proportional increase in productivity, labor costs per unit rise. At some point this mismatch runs the risk of exceeding the employer's ability to pay.

Although productivity is not widely used as an explicit wage level determinant, it is always present in the form of the effort bargain. If the employer gets more output for each unit of input, the organization's ability to pay is increased. For this reason, productivity deserves some discussion as part of the concept of ability to pay.

What is productivity? How is it measured? Productivity refers to a comparison between the quantity of goods or services produced and the quantity of resources employed in turning out these goods or services. It is the ratio of output to input. But output can be compared with various kinds of inputs—hours worked, the total of labor and capital inputs, or something in between. The results of these different comparisons are different, as are their meaning, and different comparisons are appropriate to different questions.

Two main concepts and measurements of productivity are used, but for different purposes. The first, output per hours worked or labor productivity, answers questions concerning the effectiveness of human labor under the varying circumstances of labor quality, amount of equipment, sale of output, methods of production, and so on. The second, output per unit of capital and labor, or total factor productivity, measures the efficiency of labor and capital combined. This second measure gauges whether efficiency in the conversion of labor and capital into output is rising or falling as a result of changes in technology, size, and character of economic organization, in management skills, and in many other determinants. It is more complex and more limited in use.

The first measure—output per hours worked—is the appropriate measure to employ in wage questions. It reflects the combined effect of changes (1) in the efficiency with which labor and capital are used, (2) in the amount of tangible capital employed with each hour of labor, and (3) the average quality of labor. It is these three factors that have been found to best explain the long-term trend in the general level of real wages.

It should be emphasized that labor productivity measures the contributions not just of labor alone but of all the input factors. In fact, the potential for estimating the contribution of various factors makes measures of labor productivity at various levels appropriate or inappropriate for use as wage standards.

Output per hours worked can be measured at the job, plant, industry, or economy level. At the job level it is possible to measure worker application and effort separately from other inputs as the basis for incentive plans. At the plant level estimates of the source of productivity increases can be made the basis of gainsharing plans. But at the industry level productivity improvements cannot be traced separately to the behavior of workers, managers, and investors in the industry. Nor can the contributions of one industry to another industry's productivity be separated. Finally the use of industry productivity as a wage determinant would have adverse economic consequences. For these reasons plus predictable adverse economic consequences, industry productivity is seldom suggested as a wage determinant. At the level of the economy changes in labor productivity have been suggested as appropriate for wage determination. In fact, the improvement factor in labor contracts employed in the automobile industry from 1948 until the early 1980s is an example of such a use.

The wage–price guideposts of the 1960s were based on the argument that wage increases in organizations should be determined by economywide advances in productivity. This formula use of productivity for wage determination has advocates and opponents. Advocates point out that increasing wage levels in specific organizations in accordance with annual increases in productivity in the economy insures that productivity gains get distributed. They also argue that distributing these gains through price reductions may contribute to economic instability.

Opponents point out that although there is a long-term relationship between productivity and wages, the short-term relationship is highly variable, which suggests that other wage-determining forces are more pertinent. They also argue that tying wages to productivity yields stable prices only when productivity increases are accepted as a limit to wage increases. Obviously, when the cost of living is increasing, limiting wage increases to productivity increases would be unpalatable to employees. Even more unacceptable would be wage cuts when economywide productivity declines, as has sometimes occurred.

In auto contracts the improvement factor was accompanied by a cost-of-living escalator clause and other wage increases. The guideposts broke down when price increases made the limiting of wage increases to economywide productivity increases impractical. The effect, of course, is to build higher prices into the cost structure.

The inflationary potential of productivity formulas that are not accepted as limits is enhanced by a tendency to seek a productivity measure that makes larger wage increases feasible. Increases in industry productivity, for example, may be higher, but industry indexes are less reliable and more variable. Such indexes may also conceal the contribution of one industry to another's productivity. Even indexes of national productivity may overstate noninflationary wage-increase possibilities by failing to measure the effects of transfers of workers from lower- to higher-productivity industries and other sources of increase in labor quality.

Perhaps enough problems have been cited to argue against raising wages in strict accordance with productivity increases. The difficulty of securing acceptance of wage increases based on national productivity as a limit argues against the use of such a formula. Different industries and organizations have such varying rates of change in productivity as to throw wages based solely on productivity completely out of line with other wage considerations. Higher-productivity industries would be penalized for their higher productivity, and this would harm the economy.

If, however, productivity is interpreted to mean that increases in labor productivity at constant wages lower labor cost per unit, it operates through ability to pay. If employed in the narrower sense that a productivity increase attributed to increased performance by employees calls for an equivalent increase in pay (as with merit increases and incentive plans), it is also applicable. Although productivity increases are often mentioned in wage level determination, especially in labor negotiations, their effect as a separate consideration is probably minimal.

Whether the slowdown in economywide productivity since 1973 and the actual declines in the early 1980s will change the emphasis on productivity as a wage determinant is controversial. Lewin argues that concession bargaining in the public sector is evidence that more emphasis is being given to productivity.[8] A special report on productivity at the workplace offers a catalog of programs designed to increase productivity.[9] At least two publications purport to show organizations how to measure company productivity.[10]

---

[8]D. Lewin, "Public Sector Concession Bargaining: Lessons for the Private Sector," *IRRA: Proceedings of the 35th Annual Meeting* (1983) pp. 383–93.

[9]"Productivity at the Work Place," *ILR Report,* 21, no. 1 (Fall 1983), pp. 6–27.

[10]I. H. Siegel, *Company Productivity: Measurement for Improvement* (Kalamazoo, Mich.: W. E. Upjohn Institute, 1980); and Leon Greenberg, *A Practical Guide to Productivity Measurement* (Washington, D.C.: Bureau of National Affairs, 1973).

EMPLOYER WILLINGNESS TO PAY

Employer willingness to pay may be a more powerful wage determinant than employer ability to pay. Chapter 6 explained how organizations obtain and use information on what other employers pay. Such information is undoubtedly the most-used wage level consideration. Sometimes considered as well is the cost of living. Another determinant of employer willingness to pay consists of the state of supply of particular skills and the presence of tight or loose labor markets. This section devotes some attention to each of these wage determinants.

Comparable Wages

Comparable wages constitute, without doubt, the most widely used wage determinant. Not only are the wages and salaries of federal employees keyed directly to comparable wages in labor markets, so are those of most public employees in other jurisdictions. Also, unions emphasize "coercive comparisons" and private organizations consciously try to keep up with changes in going wages. Perhaps the major reason for this widespread use of the concept of comparable wages is its apparent fairness. To most people, an acceptable definition of a fair wage is the wages paid by other employers for the same type of work. Employers find this definition reasonable because it implies that their competitors are paying the same wages. In essence then, labor costs become even across the industry. Another reason for the popularity of the concept is its apparent simplicity. At first glance, it appears quite simple to "pay the market."

As we saw in chapter 6, however, this illusion of simplicity vanishes once we try to "determine the market rate." Precise techniques, carefully employed, are required to find comparable jobs and comparable wage or salary rates. Numerous decisions must be made on which organizations and which jobs shall be compared and how. Equally important are decisions concerning how to analyze the data and use them. Wage comparisons may involve other organizations in the area or in the industry, wherever located. An important question is when differences in competitive conditions in the product market are so significant as to warrant a different wage level regardless of labor-market influences.

The going wage is an abstraction—the result of numerous decisions on what jobs and organizations to include, what wage information is appropriate, and what statistical methods to employ. Some employers decide to pay on the high side of the market, others on the low side. The result is a range of rates, to which various statistical measures may be applied. Various interpretations of the going rate may be made and justified.

To rely on comparable wages as a wage determinant is to rely on wages as income rather than as costs. Comparable wage rates may represent entirely different levels of labor costs in two different organizations. Setting wage levels strictly on the basis of going wages could impose severe hardships on one organization but a much lower labor cost on another.

Chapter 6, however, showed that these difficulties are not insurmountable: many employers lean heavily on wage and salary surveys. Also, as that chapter's section on analysis and uses of surveys shows, employer choices on what surveys to acquire and use, what benchmark jobs to attend to, and how to analyze, interpret, and use the data suggest that reasonable accommodation to "the market" is usually possible.

In addition to offering a certain measurability, following comparable wages contains a good deal of economic wisdom. Wages are prices. One function of prices in a competitive economy is the allocation of resources. Use of comparable-wage data operates roughly to allocate human resources among employments.

Furthermore, comparisons simplify the task of decision makers and negotiators. Once appropriate comparisons are decided upon, difficulties are minimized. A wage level can be set where the wage becomes satisfactory as income and operates reasonably well in its allocation function. Wages as costs are also satisfied because unit labor costs can differ widely between two organizations having identical wage rates and can be identical in two organizations having widely different wage rates. That unit labor costs fluctuate more than wage rates and are capable of variation through employer action permits satisfactory adjustment to some level within the range of going rates.

Comparable wages also operate as a force for generalizing changes in wage levels, regardless of the source of change. Unfortunately, however, although changes in going wages tell what occurred, they don't tell why it occurred. The changes may represent institutional, behavioral, or ethical considerations more than economic ones.

On balance, however, comparable wages probably operate as a conservative force. Because wage decisions involve future costs, employers are understandably unwilling to outdistance competitors. In a tight labor market, changes in going wages may compel an organization to get and keep a labor force, especially of critical skills. But in more normal periods, where unemployment exceeds job vacancies, employers will more likely focus on equalizing their labor costs with those of product-market competitors. In other words, comparable wages are followed as long as other considerations are not more compelling.

Cost of Living

Cost of living is emphasized by workers and their unions as a wage level consideration when it is rising rapidly. In such times they pressure employers to adjust wages to offset the rise. In part these demands represent a plea for increases to offset reductions in real wages (wages divided by the cost of living). In part they represent the recognition that when the cost of living is rising rapidly the economic position of most employers is changing in the same direction. Although wage pressures resulting from changes in the cost of living fluctuate with the rapidity with which living costs rise, price rises in most years since 1940 have produced employee expectations of at least annual pay increases. To employees a satisfactory pay plan must reflect the effect of inflation on financial needs.[11]

Employers understandably resist increasing pay levels on the basis of increases in the cost of living unless changes in going wages fully reflect these changes—which they seldom do. Although increases in the cost of living are

---

[11]L. Dyer, D. P. Schwab, and J. A. Fossum, "Impacts of Pay on Employee Behaviors and Attitudes," *Personnel Administrator,* January 1978, pp. 51–58.

partially translated into wage increases by most employers through payment of comparable wages, long-term contracts with unions have fostered other methods of incorporating cost-of-living changes. One such method is the re-opening clause, which permits wages to be renegotiated during a long-term contract. Another is the deferred wage increase, an attempt to anticipate economic changes at the time the contract is signed. A third is the escalator clause by which wages are adjusted during the contract period in accordance with changes in the cost of living. In this third method, living-cost changes are measured by changes in the Consumer Price Index.

Escalator clauses vary in popularity from year to year in accordance with the rapidity of cost-of-living changes during the period immediately preceding the signing of the contract and with anticipation of subsequent rises. In some recent years as many as 60 percent of workers under large union contracts were covered by escalator clauses. Reduced inflation, however, tends to reduce their popularity.

Nonunion employers are much less likely to adjust wage levels in accord with changes in the cost of living. But some do by granting general increases based at least in part on these changes. For example, in the late 1970s double-digit inflation prompted many nonunion employers to make cost-of-living adjustments. Most employers, however, while painfully aware of the effects of inflation on the real income of employees, based wage level changes on changes in going wages.

Employing the cost of living as a wage level determinant is somewhat controversial. Wage rates do tend to follow changes in the cost of living in the short run. Tying wages to changes in the cost of living provides a measure of fairness to employees by assuring them that their real wages are not devalued.

But using the cost of living as a determinant also implies a constant standard of living—a treadmill. Historically, unions have opposed the principle for this reason. Methods that provide the same absolute cost-of-living adjustment for all employees may actually impair fairness to employees. Such flat adjustments imply that everyone's cost of living is the same and has changed by the same amount. Unfortunately, technical problems in measuring changes in the cost of living may make such effects inequitable.

A cost-of-living index measures changes over time in the prices of a constant bundle of goods and services. The bundle of goods and services (called a *market basket*) is obtained by asking a group whose cost of living is to be measured to keep a record of their purchases and then sample from it.

The Bureau of Labor Statistics (BLS) has been publishing such an index since 1921—the Consumer Price Index. The CPI was developed to measure the cost of living for families of urban wage earners. As such it became the basis of escalator clauses in union contracts.

Like any general index the CPI is an abstraction that rarely corresponds with the actual living-cost changes for any given family. Differences in consumption patterns among family units due to differences in family composition, age, income, tastes, and other characteristics mean that the CPI varies greatly in its ability to measure cost-of-living changes for various groups. Moreover, consumption patterns change over time, as does the quality of products.

The BLS has made changes to improve the index over time and to meet specific problems. At present two indexes are published—the CPI-U, which measures the cost of living for all urban consumers, and the CPI–W, the traditional index. The latest change involved substituting a rent equivalent for home ownership because high interest rates had skewed upward the cost of home ownership.

Obviously, such technical problems mean that tying wage levels to the CPI varies in fairness to different groups. Moreover, at least in unions and perhaps in most organizations, fairness seems to suggest the same cost-of-living adjustment for everyone. A compressed wage structure resulting from flat cost-of-living increases may produce difficulties in recruiting and keeping higher-level employees. It seems that changes in the cost of living do not closely parallel changes in the supply–demand situation of any specific employee group. Also, particular organizations and industries may face competitive situations in product markets that run counter to changes in living costs.

It also seems that wage increases that fully reflect living-cost increases build inflation into the economy. Fortunately, although escalator clauses do narrow the time gap between price and wage changes in an inflationary period, they have been found to yield only about 57 percent of a year's inflation, and they apply to only about ten percent of nonagricultural civilian employment.[12] Although labor contracts containing wage reopeners, deferred increases, or escalators are prevalent in the United States, the fact that most wage level decisions are widely decentralized and give heavy weight to comparable wages may provide enough lag between price and wage changes to prevent more inflationary effects.

In summary, the cost of living as a wage level determinant usually operates indirectly. Although attractive to employees, unions, and some employing organizations in periods of rapidly rising prices, it should never be used as the sole standard of wage adjustment. When influences in the labor market are stronger than those in the product market, cost-of-living considerations may increase an employer's willingness to pay. But when an employer is faced with strong competition in the product market, employees may have to choose between maintaining their real wages and maintaining their jobs. In inflationary periods, the cost of living reinforces going wages through employer willingness to pay.

Labor Supplies

One consideration always present in wage level determination is the ability of the organization to obtain and hold an adequate work force. The wage level must be sufficient to perform this function or the organization cannot operate. Effectiveness of recruitment efforts, refusal of offer rates, and labor turnover levels may be considered in wage level decisions. Wage level is only one determinant of recruitment effectiveness and labor turnover. But it is an important one in that it is usually agreed to be the major element in job choice.

Some organizations experience serious shortages of certain skills. Labor-force demographics predicting a shortage of young labor-force entrants in the 1990s may bring this experience to many organizations. In the face of

[12]V. J. Scheifer, "Cost of Living Adjustment: Keeping up with Inflation?" *Monthly Labor Review*, 102, no. 6 (June 1979) pp. 14–17.

such shortages organizations may feel that they have no choice but to raise wages to attract the needed skills.

If, however, the organization experiences no recruitment or turnover problems, it may presume that the present wage level is adequate to permit securing and holding a labor force. But quality issues require answers. Is the quality of the labor force being maintained, or have employees of lower efficiency been the only ones available at the present wages? Is the quality of the present labor force adequate? Is it more than adequate? Is a change in standards of employability a good idea? Can such a change be accomplished at present pay levels?

Such questions emphasize the point that it may be more important to maintain the quality of a labor force than the quantity. A labor force of low quality at a given wage level may be more costly to the organization than a labor force of higher quality obtained at a higher wage level but resulting in lower unit labor costs. If an employer can lower unit labor costs by raising the wage level and standards of employability, such a course may deserve careful consideration.

This approach partially explains the existence of wage leaders. Organizations that pay "on the high side" may do so in the hope of attracting a higher-quality labor force. Wage leadership may not only permit "skimming the cream" off the present labor force, it may ensure a continuing supply of high-quality personnel from new entrants. Some companies always have a waiting list of applicants, whereas others must continually use an aggressive recruitment program. Labor-market studies have consistently shown that most employees find jobs by applying at the gate and by obtaining information from friends and relatives. Such practices work to the advantage of those firms known as high-paying organizations.

Wage level decisions based on labor-supply considerations must be made in light of the prospects of the organization and the industry. Firms in declining industries may be forced to allow wage levels to drop with reduced productivity and to plan on less efficient and lower-paid work forces. An expanding organization, on the other hand, may want to upgrade the quality of its work force by paying above the market and raising standards of employability.

The extent to which labor-supply considerations affect wage levels apparently varies greatly among organizations. Organizations in high-wage industries in low-wage areas experience few labor-supply problems. But those in low-wage industries may face serious labor-supply problems. Although most organizations fill most of their jobs from within, it is doubtful that any organization lacks labor-supply problems for at least some skills.

As emphasized in chapter 2, most organizations operate in numerous labor markets. Not only does the extent of the market (local, regional, national, or international) vary for different skills, the use of internal labor markets varies among organizations. Those with relatively open internal labor markets fill most jobs from outside. Those with relatively closed internal labor markets fill almost all jobs from within.

Obviously, labor-supply considerations affecting wage levels vary with labor markets. Jobs filled externally must meet or exceed the going rate. Jobs filled internally are constrained only by organization decisions. In both situations the organization is able to vary its pay levels and hiring standards on the basis of its willingness to pay.

EMPLOYEE ACCEPTANCE

The considerations employers use in determining wage levels obviously meet their test in employee or potential-employee acceptance. If employees are unwilling to accept the wages offered, the employment contract and the effort bargain are not completed. This statement suggests that all of the factors discussed in the environmental chapter (2) are potential wage level determinants. For example, employee expectations, employee definitions of equity, and employee satisfaction or dissatisfaction with pay become pertinent considerations. So do the demands of unions and society (through laws and regulations). Ideally, these considerations find their way into employers' decisions regarding their ability and willingness to pay.

SUMMARY

Organizations must be both able and willing to pay wages at particular levels. The labor market tells the organization what others are doing but the determination of what the organization will do is based on these factors of ability and willingness. The ability to pay is a major influence on the wage level decision and one that has come to have increasing importance in the past few years with changes in economic fortunes of organizations and the increasing competition from foreign firms. Since the early 1980s organizations have focused on relating the organization's wage level to worker productivity.

Since most organizations are not operating so close to the wire that the ability to pay is the only consideration in establishing the organization's wage level, the willingess to pay is also a factor in establishing the wage level. Willingness is more a matter of equity and competition in the marketplace. Organizations wish to pay wage rates that are considered *fair*. Thus they pay particular attention to wage surveys in terms of identifying comparable wage rates for their jobs. A broader measure of fairness used in the late 1970s was the cost of living. This measure, while fraught with problems, is one which employees see and can make comparisons with readily. From an organizational standpoint the willingness to pay certain wage rates is most likely a calculation that these wage rates are required to attract and retain the desired quality of employees.

THE WAGE STRUCTURE DECISION

"How many different jobs do we have?"

"How can they decide to pay that job over there more than our job?"

"What criteria should we use to decide what different jobs are worth to us?"

"How do we decide what to pay this job when there is no market rate?"

"How many and what kinds of pay grades should we have, considering the kind of organization this is?"

"I have a lot more responsibility than she does. Why aren't I making as much as she is?"

The wage structure decision has to do with determining the *wage rates for jobs*. It combines the external marketplace considered in the pay level decision with the relative value that different jobs have to the organization. The organizational value of a job is determined through job evaluation, which in turn needs job analysis to produce the information required for the evaluation. The organizational and market values of jobs are integrated through the development of a wage structure, which defines job levels or grades, and assigns wage rates to those grades by reference to market rates.

The concepts of the wage structure decision are covered in chapter 8. Job analysis is the starting place in developing a wage structure, and chapter 9 covers this topic. Chapter 10 discusses the methods of job evaluation, and chapter 11 describes how all the information and decisions collected thus far are combined into a wage structure that sets the wage rate or range for each organizational job.

8

Wage Structure Concepts

In most organizations wage and salary rates are assigned to jobs. The relationships among the pay for jobs involve pay structure decisions. In chapter 1 and the introduction to chapter 5, we observed that although organizations often make pay level decisions (how much to pay) and pay structure decisions (pay relationship) at the same time, these decisions and the process by which they are reached require separate treatment.

Actually, wage structures represent wage relationships of all kinds. Analysis of wage differentials of any kind—geographic, industry, community, or occupation—deals with wage structure issues.

But because our primary focus is on pay decisions in organizations, our concern is with pay differences between jobs. In fact, determining the pay structure of an organization may be usefully described as putting dollar signs on jobs. Decisions on wage relationships among jobs within an organization are largely within the control of its decision makers. Wage level decisions are usually influenced more by forces external to the organization than are wage structure decisions.

Some organizations pay for skills possessed by employees rather than for the jobs employees hold. The rationale is usually serious and continual skill shortages experienced by the organization. But most organizations measure employee contributions first in terms of the jobs employees hold.

One interesting analysis of organizational compensation decisions is that pay structure decisions are intended to achieve retention of employees through prevention of dissatisfaction and encouragement of employee cooperation.[1] Pay level decisions, in this analysis, are intended to attract employees. To this analysis could be added the statement that wage structure decisions are intended to encourage employees to make a career with the organization and to accept training in preparation for higher-level jobs.

DETERMINANTS OF THE WAGE STRUCTURE

Chapter 3 (economic theories of wages) contained a number of explanations of occupational differentials. Chapter 4 (behavioral theories of compensation) used a number of suggestions from psychologists and sociologists to explain occupational pay differences. This section of the chapter focuses on these factors in wage structure decisions.

Economic Determinants

Adam Smith's explanation of occupational wage differentials in terms of (1) hardship, (2) difficulty of learning the job, (3) stability of employment, (4) responsibility of the job, and (5) chance for success or failure in the work is a theory of wage structure.[2] But his standards of worth are equally useful in explaining the complexity of wage structure decisions. The *market value* of an item is the price it brings in a market where demand and supply are equal. *Use value* is the value an individual buyer or seller anticipates through use of the item. Use value obviously varies among individuals and over time.

These two concepts of worth and the concept of internal labor markets combine to explain important differences among employers in wage structure decisions. Organizations with relatively open internal labor markets (organizations in which most jobs are filled from outside) make much use of market value. They also make much use of wage and salary surveys in wage structure decisions.

Conversely, organizations with relatively closed internal labor markets (most jobs are filled from inside) emphasize use value. Their analysis of job worth relies more heavily on perceptions of organization members of the relative value of jobs.

Some other wage structure determinants derived from economic analysis may be noted. Training requirements of jobs in terms of length, difficulty, and whether the training is provided by society, employers, or individuals constitute a primary factor in human-capital analysis and thus job worth. The interaction of ability requirements with training requirements can yield different job values depending on the scarcity of the ability required and the number of people who try to make it in the occupation and fail.

Employee tastes and preferences are another economic factor. People differ in the occupations they like and dislike. In like manner, occupations have nonmonetary advantages and disadvantages of many kinds.

[1]T. A. Mahoney, "Compensating for Work," in *Personnel Management,* ed. K. M. Rowland and G. R. Ferris (Boston: Allyn & Bacon, 1982), p. 227–61.

[2]See the discussion of Adam Smith in chapter 3.

Worker expectations of future earnings strongly influence occupational choice and thus labor supplies. Unfortunately, labor-market information is far from perfect, and responses to labor-market shortages are likely to be more prompt than responses to oversupplies.

Industrial as opposed to craft unionism has also been shown by economic analysis to affect wage structures. Industrial unions, with their heavy proportions of semiskilled members, are more likely to favor absolute increases. Although large organizations where employees are represented by industrial unions may have a highly differentiated wage structure, they pay less attention to percentage differentials than they would in the presence of craft unions.

Another economic determinant is discrimination. Although wage differentials based on sex or race are unlawful, they still exist. The extent to which such differences are based on productivity differences or represent discrimination is very much a wage structure issue.

Industrial Relations Explanations

Industrial relations scholars' explanations of wage structures tend to be different from those of labor economists. For instance, an employer concerned with the status of his or her organization as a dependable supplier, a considerate employer, or a wage leader is more likely to base wage structure decisions on organization criteria than on economic forces. A short list of noneconomic considerations on wage structures emphasized by industrial relations scholars would include organization goals, the health of union–management relations, employee attitudes, employee comparisons, communication of pay decisions, and seniority policy. Also emphasized by these analysts is the force of custom.

One powerful analysis of considerations in wage structure decisions argues that wage structures keyed solely to the labor market are likely to be few, to result from very tight labor markets, and to be characteristic of organizations well insulated from product-market competition, unions, and technological change. One author classified organizations as having wage structures that are primarily oriented toward unions, markets, internally, or union-and-product. Union-oriented organizations basically have craft unions, and union-and-product oriented organizations basically have industrial unions. This classification suggests that in only one of the four, market-oriented organizations, does the labor market drive the wage structure.[3]

Social Determinants

In chapter 3, we saw that the *just-price theory* advocated setting wages in accordance with the preestablished status distribution: wages were to be systematically regulated to keep each class in its customary place in society. The theory emphasized equity, the tying of wages to status, and the preservation of customary relationships.

Although we have described the just-price theory as historical, an eminent contemporary labor economist, E. H. Phelps-Brown, has made a similar

---

[3]G. H. Hildebrand, "External Influence and the Determination of the Internal Wage Structure," in *Internal Wage Structure,* ed. J. L. Meij (Amsterdam: North-Holland Publishing Company, 1963), pp. 260–99.

argument.[4] Brown argues further that one determinant of the fair rate is the requirements of the work. He interprets job evaluation as a pains-taking application of the way in which people continually think and argue about relative pay.

Another sociological view of wage structure is that different jobs have different statuses to which the structure of pay should conform. Generally a group is ranked according to the difficulty of attaining proficiency in the job. By this reasoning the criterion of a fair wage is that it shall enable the recipient to keep up a position in the class to which the job assigns him or her.

Since both the assessments of the requirements of a job and the esteem due incumbents can only be subjective, in practice they lean much on custom. When rates of pay remain unchanged for a century and differentials between two jobs remain proportionately constant over even longer periods, the force of custom rather than supply and demand seems a better explanation.

In fact, to those involved in pay decisions social forces may be more apparent than economic ones. The arguments used are mainly ethical. A wage is claimed because it is fair and just. A differential is justified because it is right and proper.

But whereas social forces generally operate to maintain what is customary and accepted, market forces have been operating to narrow differentials. Market forces usually operate through the shifting of labor supplies. One reason that social forces seem to predominate is the slow reaction of supply to price. Supply shortages are more effective in raising pay than supply surpluses are in lowering it.

Organizational Determinants

Organizations develop jobs to get their work done. Labor services acquire specific economic meaning only in relation to the particular jobs in which they are performed. In our economic system, the organization typically designs jobs and selects employees to fill them. The jobs the organization designs are the source of the contributions provided by employees and a primary determinant of their rewards. Through these jobs and pay decisions about them, the organization is structuring the market for labor services.[5]

Other organizations differing in technology, management competence, competitive economics, and collective bargaining are also designing jobs. As a consequence, it is quite unlikely that the jobs designed by one organization will be identical to those of other organizations. Furthermore, the decisions that go into job design are not made once and for all but are subject to revision as market conditions, technology, and institutional influences change.

One of the strongest influences on job design is technology. But technology seldom provides rigid job boundaries. Although it may be useful to assume that organizations in the same industry have designed jobs and job structures similarly, they have not necessarily done so. On the other hand, if two quite similar jobs are found in different industries, it would be safe to assume that they hold different significance or value to their respective organizations.

[4]E. H. Phelps-Brown, *The Economics of Labor* (New Haven: Yale University Press, 1962), ch. 5.

[5]See Hildebrand, "External Influences." op. cit.

In one industry it may represent an organization's most essential task. In another the job may be peripheral.

A recent study queried compensation practitioners in 37 organizations on what information they used to design or adjust wage structures in their organization.[6] Thirty-one kinds of information were reported, some by all 37 firms, some by only 1. Although the most-used information involved wage surveys and job evaluation data, the balance was almost too varied to classify.

Employee Acceptance

The discussion in chapter 4 of the employment exchange and of equity theory suggests that a primary criterion of organization wage structures is employee acceptance. Both the employment exchange and equity theory strongly suggest that employees' decisions to acquire and retain organization membership are based on their perception of a favorable ratio of rewards to contributions. The most visible employee contribution is the job to which he or she is assigned.

Most organizations base wage structures primarily on the work content of jobs and the value of that work to the organization. Work content is determined by job analysis. Relative value of work is determined by job evaluation. Equity theory postulates that both processes must be accepted as fair by employees if they are to achieve their purposes.

There is some tendency to equate pay fairness or equity with pay satisfaction. This is unfortunate because, although related, they are quite different concepts. It has been shown that people can believe that their pay is fair but not be satisfied with it. Also, people can be satisfied with their pay but believe it to be unfair.[7] Pay satisfaction has been shown to be a multidimensional concept in which satisfaction with pay level is independent of satisfaction with benefits. Satisfaction with pay structure, although apparently another dimension, is not independent of administration of compensation.[8]

INFLUENCES ON THE WAGE STRUCTURE

From the last section it is clear that organizations determine the pay for jobs by taking a number of considerations into account. Furthermore, they have considerable choice as to how much emphasis to place on various determinants. These choices lead in turn to variations in the wage structures that organizations create. But organizations do not have total freedom in the design of wage structures. Besides the determinants so far considered there are a number of other influences on the design of wage structures that will be considered in this section. These influences are often indirect in that they influence the design of

[6]D. W. Belcher, N. B. Ferris, and B. Dalton, "Building or Adjusting a Pay Structure" (working paper, San Diego State University, 1984).

[7]D. W. Belcher, "Pay Equity or Pay Fairness?" *Compensation Review*, second quarter 1979, pp. 31–37.

[8]H. G. Heneman III and D. P. Schwab, "Pay Satisfaction: Its Multidimensional Nature and Measurement," (working papers, University of Wisconsin, 1983).

jobs and therefore the way the organization is likely to evaluate it in relation to other organization jobs. These influences are society, the labor market, unions, and the organization structure.

Society

People and institutions both have a hand in structuring jobs and wage structures. Craft unions, for example, determine the kinds of work their members do and expect employing organizations to adjust to this decision. Jobs for clerical workers are structured by the institutions that train them, with the result that clerical jobs are often quite similar in different organizations. Professional employees and managers insist on having a say in the design of their jobs, and the result is influenced in part by the institutions that train them. At the other extreme are semiskilled factory employees. Organizations employing these workers are subject to little influence on job design by either employees or unions, except in job-redesign decisions. Unions of semiskilled factory workers typically insist, however, on participating in the latter decisions. This participation is guided by customary relationships among and within employee groups. Custom also operates in nonunion situations to resist change in job design.

A further societal influence on jobs and wage structures is the technology used by the organization and changes in that technology. But as we have noted, technology seldom provides rigid boundaries. It typically provides choices within which management, unions, and competitive pressures can operate in designing jobs and job relationships.

The Labor Market

The labor market influences the wage and salary structure basically through the supply of labor. But often only a few of an organization's jobs are highly market-oriented, since the labor supply for most jobs is provided from within the organization. As discussed in chapter 5, most organizations replace the external labor market with an internal labor market that makes decisions by administrative means rather than according to supply and demand. These organizations have restricted ports of entry, which are highly sensitive to the labor market but rely on the organization's internal labor supply to fill most job openings.[9] The exception occurs when there is an internal and external shortage of people to fill vacancies for specific skills. In fact, any job for which qualified people are in short supply becomes a market-sensitive job. But given relatively adequate labor supplies, only those groups wherein the labor market is structured by unions, is otherwise well organized, or is designed to be filled from the outside by the organization are oriented to the labor market.

Shortages in the labor market provide those who are qualified to fill the jobs an opportunity to negotiate better terms of employment. A part of this negotiation is for a relative increase in pay greater than other groups are obtaining. This, of course, runs into the problem of customary relationships already discussed. But another part of the negotiations is for a "better job."

[9]O. E. Williamson, M. L. Wachter, and J. E. Harris, "Understanding the Employment Relation: The Analysis of Idiosyncratic Exchange," *Bell Journal of Economics*, Spring 1975, pp. 250–78.

Workers in jobs where there is a shortage of qualified workers will demand changes in job content that will increase the job's value to the organization and in the eyes of other workers. Computer programmers are an example of a group of workers with a skill in short supply in a new and expanding industry. The independence of action and discretion allowed this group of employees is based, at least partially, on the continuing shortage of this skill.

The product market also affects wage structures through cost-oriented jobs. Such jobs exist where profit margins are sensitive to changes in unit labor cost. If the ratio of unit labor cost to price is critical, the jobs involved become cost-oriented jobs and organizations will strongly resist changes in their wage rates, especially changes not made by other organizations. Organizations that compete in the same product market, those whose prices are interrelated, or those experiencing or anticipating increased competition or decreased demand may regard any increase in unit labor costs as a threat, especially when labor cost is a significant proportion of total costs. On the other hand, employees in these areas often recognize the advantageous position they are in and seek maximum advantage.

Unions

Unions affect wage structure, but the differential effects of craft and industrial unionism and the type of bargaining relationship are considerable. Craft unions tend to determine craft rates for all organizations employing members of the craft, as well as the design of craft jobs. The limit of craft rates is the cost–price resistance of employers. Industrial unions, on the other hand, are more concerned than craft unions with employing organizations, but less concerned with product markets because they often bargain with organizations in many product markets. Thus, industrial unions may attempt to impose a common wage structure on organizations with which they deal that clashes with product-market realities.

Within organizations, industrial unions are concerned with equalities and differentials among particular groups of jobs. They often serve to reinforce custom and tradition in jobs and wage structures and to resist changes that might decrease employee security. If the industrial union deals with organizations in a common product market, it may attempt to impose a common job design and wage structure by comparing rates of a number of reasonably comparable jobs. But even in such cases, the influence of industrial unions on wage structure is light compared with that of craft unions.

Unions also affect wage structures by resisting lower wage rates for jobs downgraded by technological change and by demanding that increased productivity arising from any source results in wage increases. Typically this means that wages of changed jobs are not cut but often increased when the changes result in increased productivity. Such job rates distort rational job and wage structures, and a series of them can so impair an organization's cost–profit position that management is forced to fight for a revised, rational wage structure.[10]

Union strategy with respect to general increases can also affect wage

[10]A. Thomson, "The Structure of Collective Bargaining in Britain," in *Handbook of Salary and Wage Systems,* 2nd ed., ed. A. M. Bowey (Aldershot, England: Gower Pub. Co. 1982), pp. 37–54.

structures. As mentioned in chapter 7, flat cents-per-hour or dollars-per-month increases maintain absolute differentials but compress the structure in relative terms, whereas flat percentage increases maintain relative differentials and increase absolute differentials. Industrial unions especially may follow a policy of cents-per-hour increases because most of their members are in lower-paid groups. But unions cannot maintain this strategy in the face of opposition from higher-paid groups. In fact, worker preferences and resulting labor-supply shortages force restoration of relative differentials in both union and nonunion situations.

But probably the strongest influence of unions on wage structures is the quality of the union–management relationship. As mentioned, some unions take an active part in job evaluation, and their interest in a rational wage structure results in reduced grievances over wage inequities. Other unions, most of them craft unions, seek to preserve customary relationships and job security, resist changes in job content and structure, and are uninterested in the employer's problems of maintaining economic efficiency. Still other unions seem totally uninterested in job designs and wage structure of the organization and (1) insist on no wage cuts when job content changes, (2) demand wage increases for all increases in job productivity, (3) strongly resist job-content and other changes calculated to increase productivity, and (4) encourage wage-inequity grievances. In such cases job and wage structures become chaotic and correcting the irrationalities may require long and bitter strikes, which are often prolonged by political struggles within the union resulting from the wage inequities.[11]

The Organization

Organization decisions on job and wage structures represent a balancing of the aforementioned forces. But the strength of these forces varies by organization type and within organizations by job clusters. Organizations made up largely of members of craft unions have wage structures almost completely determined by the union. Organizations in construction, printing and publishing, the railroads, longshoring and maritime work, and entertainment offer examples of union-oriented wage structures.

Organizations whose members come largely from a well-organized and competitive labor market but are not unionized have what might be called market-oriented wage structures. Organizations of this type have only limited choices because jobs are easily identified and are quite uniform throughout the market. Banks, insurance companies, department stores, and restaurants are organizations with primarily market-oriented wage structures. Professionals are groups of employees whose jobs have been designed largely by the educational process they have been through. This makes for a commonality between organizations in the design of professional jobs.

Organizations having many specialized jobs, dealing in labor markets too disorganized to provide adequate grading and pricing, and lacking unionization have primarily internally determined wage structures. Such wage structures may be influenced by product markets, but only if labor cost is high relative to total cost. Internally determined wage structures result from management decisions and may range from highly rational structures flowing from

[11]See Thomson, op. cit.

job evaluation to a system of personal rates. Organizations in small towns, isolated locations, or nonunion communities provide examples, as do unique organizations in larger communities, and government employment.

Most large, unionized organizations have what might be called union-and-product-oriented wage structures. In these organizations wage structures represent management decisions shaped and restrained by technology, unions, and cost–price relationships and the product market. Technology provides some uniformity in job structures in organizations engaged in common lines of production. Unions, through their insistence on traditional relationships, establish some key jobs and job clusters and provide an upward thrust to the entire structure. Cost–price relationships and the product market compel the organization to resist this upward push and to make changes in jobs and job relationships in line with such resistance. Low ratios of labor cost to total cost and inelastic product demand, however, reduce competitive pressures on organizations. Organizations in many branches of manufacturing, in mining, and in some service industries are examples of organizations with union-and-product-oriented wage structures. Recent events have shown that organizations with this kind of wage structure can eventually get into a competitive bind.[12]

Organizations with internally determined or union-and-product-market-determined wage structures leave large portions of wage structure decisions to management. Wage structure determination in these organizations follows closely Dunlop's theory of key jobs, job clusters, and wage contours (see chapter 3). Key jobs acquire their status from labor markets, product markets, and comparisons with other organizations, often fostered by unions. Job clusters come from technologies and employee skill groupings. Wage contours originate in customary comparisons with other organizations, again often fostered by unions. Custom strongly influences all three.[13]

But although organizations can be classified as having wage structures that are oriented primarily in one of the four ways just outlined, organizations of any considerable size have job clusters that fall more comfortably into one or more of the other categories. Organizations employing artisans, unless they are members of an industrial union, are usually forced to develop a union-oriented wage structure for this job cluster. All organizations employ clerical workers, and the wage structure of the clerical job cluster is largely market-oriented. Professional employees (such as engineers and scientists) have salary structures that combine market orientation and internal determination, regardless of the major activity of the organization. Managerial salary structures are primarily internally determined except in very tight labor markets, without regard to organization type.

Thus the typical organization develops and administers at least four or five of the following separate wage structures: shop, clerical, craftsmen and technicians, administrators, engineers and scientists, sales, supervision, and executives. Although, obviously, there will be relationships among these separate wage structures, the strength of these relationships varies by organization and over time.

---

[12]L. Iacocca, *Iacocca* (New York: Bantam, 1984).

[13]J. T. Dunlop, "The Task of Contemporary Wage Theory," in *New Concepts in Wage Determination*, ed. G. W. Taylor and F. C. Pierson (New York: McGraw-Hill, 1957), pp. 117–39.

JOB EVALUATION

Organizations usually begin the process of designing a wage structure by determining their *job structure*. Two often-cited principles of compensation are (1) equal pay for equal work, and (2) more pay for more important work. Both imply that organizations pay employees for contributions required by jobs.

Most organizations utilize job assignment as a major determinant of employee contributions. A formal wage structure, defined as a rate or range of rates established for job classifications, seems to be standard organization practice, except in very small organizations. Formal job evaluation or informal comparison of job content is the almost universal base of pay rates.

Job evaluation is the process of methodically establishing a structure of jobs within an organization based on a systematic consideration of job content and requirements. The purpose of the job structure or hierarchy is to provide a basis for the pay structure. The job structure, as seen in previous sections of this chapter, is only one of the determinants of the wage structure. But it is an important one, often used.

Job evaluation is concerned with *jobs*, not *people*. A job is a grouping of work tasks. It is an arbitrary concept requiring careful definition in the organization. Job evaluation determines the relative position of the job in the organization hierarchy. It is assumed that as long as job content remains unchanged, it may be performed by individuals of varying ability and proficiency.

The Job Evaluation Process

Although the next two chapters spell out the process and procedures involved in job evaluation, it is useful at this point to understand the steps in the process. The first step is a study of the jobs in the organization. Through *job analysis*, information on job content is obtained together with an appreciation of worker requirements for successful performance of the job. This information is recorded in the precise, consistent language of a *job description*.

The next step is deciding what the organization "is paying for"—that is, what factor or factors place one job at a higher level in the job hierarchy than another. These *compensable factors* are the yardsticks used to determine the relative position of jobs. In a sense, choosing compensable factors is the heart of job evaluation. Not only do these factors place jobs in the organization's job hierarchy, they serve to inform job incumbents which contributions are rewarded.

The third step in job evaluation is to select a method of appraising the organization's jobs according to the factor(s) chosen. The method should permit consistent placement of jobs containing more of the factors higher in the job hierarchy than jobs involving lesser amounts.

The fourth step is comparing jobs to develop a job structure. This involves choosing and assigning decision makers, reaching and recording decisions, and setting up the job hierarchy.

The final step is pricing the job structure to arrive at a wage structure. Strictly speaking, this step is not part of job evaluation. As seen earlier in this chapter, many wage structure determinants are used by organizations. The job structure is only one of these.

This view of job evaluation implies that its major purpose is to classify jobs and establish a job hierarchy based on job content. Other perspectives are that job evaluation (1) links external and internal markets, and (2) is a process used to gain consensus and acceptance of a pay structure.[14] Perhaps these views could all be accommodated by the recognition that job structures and wage structures are separate concepts and that the relationship between them is a decision that varies among organizations.

Objectives of Job Evaluation

The general purpose of job evaluation may include a number of more specific goals:

1. to provide a basis for a simpler, more rational wage structure;
2. to provide an agreed-upon means of classifying new or changed jobs;
3. to provide a means of comparing jobs and pay rates with those of other organizations;
4. to provide a base for individual performance measurements;
5. to reduce pay grievances by reducing their scope and providing an agreed-upon means of resolving disputes;
6. to provide incentives for employees to strive for higher-level jobs;
7. to provide information for wage negotiations;
8. to provide data on job relationships for use in internal and external selection, personnel planning, career management, and other personnel functions.

Background of Job Evaluation

Job evaluation developed out of civil service classification practices, job analysis applied to time study and selection, and some early employer job and pay classification systems. Whether formal job evaluation began with the United States Civil Service Commission in 1871[15] or with Frederick W. Taylor in 1881,[16] it is about 100 years old. The first point system was developed in the 1920s. Employer associations have contributed greatly to the adoption of certain plans. The spread of unionism has influenced the installation of job evaluation in that employers gave more attention to rationalized wage structures as unionism advanced. The War Labor Board during World War II encouraged the expansion of job evaluation as a method of reducing wage inequities.

Job evaluation has received a good deal of attention in recent years as a result of social concern regarding discrimination. A study of job evaluation as a potential source of and/or a potential solution to sex discrimination in pay was made by the National Research Council under a contract from the Equal Employment Opportunity Commission.[17] The study suggested that jobs held

[14]G. T. Milkovich and J. M. Newman, *Compensation* (Plano, Tex.: Business Publications, 1984), pp. 92–95.

[15]J. A. Patton, C. L. Littlefield, and S. A. Self, *Job Evaluation: Text and Cases*, 3rd ed. (Homewood, Ill.: Richard D. Irwin, 1964).

[16]A. M. Pasquale, *A New Dimension to Job Evaluation* (New York: American Management Association, 1969).

[17]D. J. Treiman, *Job Evaluation: An Analytical Review* (Washington, D.C.: National Academy of Sciences, 1979, (mimeographed).

predominantly by women and minorities may be undervalued. Such discrimination may result from the use of different plans for different employee groups, from the compensable factors employed, from the weights assigned to factors, and from the stereotypes associated with jobs. Although the preliminary report failed to take a position on job evaluation, the final report concluded that job evaluation holds some potential for solving problems of discrimination.[18]

Prevalence of Job Evaluation

Job evaluation is used throughout the world. Although recent evidence is not available, it appears that job evaluation is more prevalent in the United States than elsewhere. However, a 1982 International Labor Office publication states that in centrally controlled economies or in economies where wage or income controls exist, job evaluation is frequently used.[19]

Holland has had a national job evaluation plan since 1948 as a basis for its national wages and incomes policy. Sweden and West Germany have a number of industrywide plans. Great Britain, like the United States, usually employs job evaluation at the plant or company level. Australia and some Asian countries have installed some forms of job evaluation. The USSR and East Germany make wide use of job classification.

The evidence on use of job evaluation in the United States consists of surveys made at different times and locations. A 1976 survey found that three quarters of the responding companies (117) had one or more formal job evaluation plans.[20] Thirty-eight percent of the companies used more than one plan. A 1979 survey found that 80 percent of the 325 companies responding had formal job evaluation plans, over one third had two, and 42 percent had three or more. This survey found smaller companies somewhat less likely to use job evaluation.[21] Almost all government jurisdictions employ some form of job evaluation.

Responsibility for Job Evaluation

The installation and operation of job evaluation involves certain responsibilities. Several possibilities for implementing the process are apparent. One or more committees may be selected, a department may be set up or an existing one assigned, or a consulting organization may be brought in. These possibilities are not mutually exclusive.

Committees have the potential of gaining acceptance and understanding of job evaluation. Support for the program is essential because installation of it involves commitments of time, effort, and money. Such support is usually obtained by securing top management approval and the collaboration of other

[18]D. J. Treiman and H. I. Hartman, eds., *Women, Work, and Wages: Equal Pay for Equal Jobs of Equal Value* (Washington, D.C.: National Academy Press, 1981).

[19]H. Pornschlegel, *Job Evaluation and the Role of Trade Unions* (Geneva: International Labour Office, 1982).

[20]M. G. Miner, *Job Evaluation Policies and Procedures*, Survey No. 113 (Washington, D.C.: Bureau of National Affairs, 1976).

[21]*Personnel Management-Compensation*, pp. 152, January 10, 1979 (Englewood Cliffs, N.J.: Prentice-Hall), p. 317.

managers and organization members. Often this approval is obtained through a committee set up for this purpose. Or such a committee may already exist. This committee is given an explanation of job evaluation, the purposes it is expected to accomplish, a rough time schedule, and perhaps an estimate of the cost of the program. The committee makes the decision to install job evaluation, decides on the scope of the project, and assigns responsibility for the work.

The actual work of job evaluation is usually done in committee in both large and small organizations, whether the task is accomplished by organization members alone or with the help of a consultant. Committees have the advantage of being able to pool the judgment of several individuals. They serve the even more important function of communication. The committee usually selects the compensable factors, determines weighting, chooses the method of comparing jobs, and evaluates jobs.

The chair of the committee is usually a compensation professional, although a consultant, if employed, may assume the chair for part of the work. Other members are typically other managers selected for their analytical ability, fairness, and commitment to the project. Representation of broad areas of the organization aids in communication and in gaining acceptance. But job evaluation committees should be kept small to facilitate decision making. Five members may be optimum, ten a maximum. A common procedure is to invite supervisors to committee meetings when jobs in their department are under study.

In union-management installations union members are regular members of the committee. Where the union is not involved employee representation is often rotated. Employee representation in committees seems to aid in securing acceptance and in communication.

Committee job ratings are a result of pooled judgments. This usually means either that ratings made individually are averaged or a consensus is reached as a result of discussion.

Committee members must be trained. Much of this training involves following the steps in the process. But training on how to guard against personal bias and the common rating errors is advisable.

Consultants are sometimes employed to install job evaluation plans. Successful consultants are careful to ensure that organization members are deeply involved in installing the plan and are able to operate the plan on their own.

Consultants are most likely to be employed in small organizations where no member has the necessary expertise. They are also more likely to be employed when a complex rather than a simple plan is to be installed. Consultants often have their own ready-made plans. Sometimes consultants are brought in to insure objectivity in union-management installations. It is also common to hire consultants to evaluate management jobs, because the objectivity of committee members rating jobs at levels higher than their own may be questioned.

It is quite possible for the organization to assign installation and operation of a job evaluation plan to the compensation department. Sometimes the compensation professional heading the unit and a number of job analysts carry out the task.

Those who favor this last approach emphasize the technical nature of the task. They may also be reacting to the difficulty of getting operating managers to devote the time that the program requires. While they may recognize the education and communication advantages of committees, they believe these advantages can be provided in other ways. It is doubtful that this position can be justified, though. Input by operating managers and perhaps employees during job evaluation installation is probably essential to acceptance of the results. Once the program is installed, however, there seems to be no reason why a department cannot operate it with proper provision for settling grievances.

Union Involvement in Job Evaluation

Union involvement has the same rationale as that offered in our discussion of job evaluation committees. Acceptance and understanding are the expected results of involvement.

In practice, union participation in job evaluation has varied greatly. Some unions profess to formally evaluate an organization's jobs independently and then use the information as an aid in collective bargaining. Some job evaluation plans have been installed and maintained as a joint venture. A well-known union-management job evaluation plan exists in the basic steel industry. Less well known is the joint plan in the West Coast paper industry. At AT&T, union-management task forces are reported to be working on a new job evaluation system. There is evidence that joint plans are more successful than unilateral plans. But this is not always the case.

Perhaps most unions in organizations with job evaluation plans review the findings after installation by management and either present grievances on individual jobs or insist on bargaining the wage structure. In the latter case, the bargained wage structure may follow the job structure resulting from job evaluation or represent a compromise.

Some unions have ignored job evaluation plans installed unilaterally by management. Some employers prefer this arrangement, insisting that job design and evaluation are management prerogatives. Other employers invite union participation in the hopes of obtaining understanding and acceptance of the plan.

If a union rejects an invitation to participate in job evaluation and ignores the plan, the employer installs the plan unilaterally, recognizing the need for a logical hierarchy of jobs. The findings are used in negotiating the wage structure.

There is probably no way of knowing which form of union involvement in job evaluation is typical. But a 1978 study by Janes of union views of job evaluation found that job evaluation plans were included in 64 percent of labor agreements.[22] This study compared a 1971 and a 1978 survey of union opinions of job evaluation. One of the findings was a modest increase in the acceptance of jointly designed job evaluation plans. While the proportion of unions reporting satisfaction with their organization's job evaluation plan decreased from 1971 to 1978, the proportion dissatisfied also decreased. Those neutral increased 24 percent.

[22]H. D. Janes, "Union Views on Job Evaluation: 1971 vs. 1978," *Personnel Journal*, February 1979, pp. 80–85.

Unions have criticized job evaluation on several grounds: (1) that it restricts collective bargaining on wages, (2) that wages shouldn't be based solely on job content, (3) that supervisors do not or cannot explain the plan to employees, (4) that management doesn't administer the plan the way it explained it, and (5) that it is subjective.

Janes found a substantial decrease in resistance by unions to job evaluation over the period 1971–1978 and an increase in the use of the grievance-arbitration procedure to challenge the system. However, less than 5 percent of the grievances concerned job evaluation. Slightly over 50 percent of union comments regarding job evaluation voiced approval while expressing the right to criticize. Janes states that unions have very seldom really opposed job evaluation, provided it is not used as the sole criterion for establishing wages or as a substitute for collective bargaining. In fact, several unions report that job evaluation, especially of factory jobs, has helped both management and unions.

Employee Acceptance

Job evaluation is usually adjudged successful when employees, unions, and organizations report satisfaction with it. Most surveys report organization satisfaction levels at 90 percent or better. The union opinions just reported were moderately favorable.

Employee acceptance is the primary criterion organizations use in determining the success of a job evaluation plan. This is reflected in the increasing use of employees on job evaluation committees and in the communication steps accompanying job evaluation installations.

SUMMARY

The discussion in this chapter showed that the development of a wage structure is the result of a number of influences. These factors vary from ones over which management has a great deal of control to ones in which management must simply be responsive. Given the variety of influences it is also not likely that organizations will always be able to develop optimum structures and that current structures will need adapting in the future.

While the economics of the labor market is a major consideration it is not the only determinant to influence the design of wage structures. Most organizations must consider labor-cost ratios, product market competition, and union demands as well in determining their wage structure. Furthermore, many labor markets are abstractions that do not provide a close fit for any organization's jobs or wage-paying ability because dissimilar organizations design these structures and, within limits, control them and decide the place of jobs within their own structures.[23]

Wage structures have to do with the internal alignment of jobs in a wage hierarchy. To do this there must be a hierarchy or structure of jobs within the organization. Determining the internal job structure is the task of job evaluation. This process compares jobs, not people, in terms of a set of criteria, called compensable factors, to establish the job hierarchy. Job evaluation is a

[23]C. T. Stewart, Jr., "Wage Structures in an Expanding Labor Market: The Electronics Industry in San Jose," *Industrial and Labor Relations Review,* October 1967, pp. 73–91.

major tool that organizations use to make job comparisons when determining the relative equity of jobs within the organization. In job evaluation there is an interesting conflict. On one hand, like wage surveys, this process requires technical expertise of a compensation professional. On the other hand, acceptability of job evaluation results relies on the perceptions of management and workers so that their participation would seem to be a necessity in job evaluation.

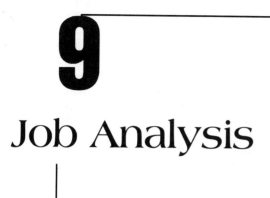

9

Job Analysis

The job evaluation process begins with securing information about jobs. Failure to secure complete job facts has been cited as a primary reason for job evaluation failure.[1] Later steps in job evaluation become virtually impossible without adequate job information.

Information about jobs is obtained through a process called job analysis. The goal of this process is to secure whatever job data are needed.

Job analysis is a tool of many uses, of which job evaluation is only one. For example, organizations use information obtained by job analysis for such personnel programs as recruitment, selection, and placement; organization planning and job design; training; grievance settlement; and job evaluation and other compensation programs.

Job evaluation represents the major use of job analysis. It is also our focus in this chapter. Because the job information needed for various uses may differ, some organizations make a specialized study for each specific use. Another approach is to obtain all the needed job information at once. In fact, a 1983 review of job analysis defines it as a procedure for gathering, documenting, and analyzing information about three basic aspects of a job: content,

[1]J. L. Otis and R. H. Leukert, *Job Evaluation*, 2nd ed. (Englewood Cliffs, N.J.: Prentice-Hall, 1954).

requirements, and context.[2] The authors of this review strongly imply that such a job analysis would be sufficient for all purposes.

But the different uses of job information may require specialized job descriptions. Job evaluation requires information that permits distinguishing jobs from one another, usually on the basis of work activities and/or job-required worker characteristics. Recruitment and selection require information on the human attributes a successful jobholder must bring to the job. Training requires information on the knowledge and skills that the successful jobholder must evidence. Job design may require identifying employee perceptions of intrinsic and extrinsic rewards. Although there is overlap among these different requirements, arguments for separate job analysis for separate purposes are understandable.

BACKGROUND

Job analysis as a management technique was developed around 1900.[3] It became one of the tools with which managers understood and directed organizations. Frederick W. Taylor, through his interest in improving the efficiency of work, made studying the job one of his principles of scientific management.[4] Early organization theorists were interested in how jobs fit into organizations: they focused on the purpose of the job.[5] But this early interest in job analysis disappeared as the human relations movement focused on other issues and it was not until the 1960s that psychologists and other behavioral scientists rediscovered jobs as a focus of study in organizations.

But the organization with the greatest long-term interest in job analysis has been the United States Department of Labor (USDL). The United States Employment Service (USES) of the USDL's Training and Employment Administration has developed job analysis procedures and instruments over many years. These procedures probably represent the strongest single influence on job analysis practice in the United States. The USDL's *Guide for Analyzing Jobs* and *Handbook for Analyzing Jobs* show the development of job analysis procedures over almost 50 years.[6] In part through their responsibility for publishing *The Dictionary of Occupational Titles (DOT)*[7] and in part through their policy of helping private employers install job analysis programs, the USDL has led in the development of what is often called the conventional approach to job analysis.

[2]S. E. Bemis, A. H. Belensky, and D. A. Soder, *Job Analysis* (Washington, D.C.: Bureau of National Affairs, 1983).

[3]J. E. Zerga, "Job Analysis: A Resume and Bibliography," *Journal of Applied Psychology*, (1943), 249–67.

[4]F. W. Taylor, *The Principles of Scientific Management* (New York: Harper & Brothers, 1911).

[5]L. H. Gulick and L. Urwick, eds., *Papers on the Science of Administration* (New York: Institute of Public Administration, 1937).

[6]U.S. Department of Labor, *Guide for Analyzing Jobs* (Washington, D.C.: U.S. Government Printing Office, 1946); and U.S. Department of Labor, *Handbook for Analyzing Jobs* (Washington D.C.: U.S. Government Printing Office, 1972).

[7]U.S. Employment Service, *Dictionary of Occupational Titles* (Washington D.C.: U.S. Government Printing Office, 1965).

The last ten years has seen a resurgence of interest in job analysis. The basis of this resurgence lies in the passage of civil rights legislation. Job analysis is required in the field of staffing since any predictor used to select a person must be job-relevant. Determining job relevance requires having a knowledge of what is happening in the job, usually through job analysis. Likewise, in compensation the requirements of the Equal Pay Act requires that jobs that are substantially similar be paid the same. The determination that two jobs are substantially similar is done through job analysis.

JOB ANALYSIS IN THE 1980s

The 1980s appear to be a period of ferment in the field of job analysis. As indicated, it is as if the concept has been rediscovered after lying fallow for many years. Actually, what has become apparent is that jobs are more complex than had been realized. There has been no agreement, though, on what information to collect or on how to collect it.

A Deficient Theoretical Base

A good part of the difficulty is due to an almost complete lack of theoretical bases on what information about jobs is needed, useful, and worthy of study. Some models of the kinds of information needed for various purposes and the methods likely to yield such information are called for.

Several models of job analysis now exist, but as we will see shortly, each leaves something to be desired. The job analysis formula outlined by the USDL in 1946 is a simplified but complete model of obtaining information on work activities. The formula consists of (1) what the worker does, (2) how he or she does it, (3) why he or she does it, and (4) the skill involved in doing it. In fact, providing the what, how, and why of each task and the total job should constitute a functional description of work activities for compensation purposes.

By 1972, however, this formula had been expanded by the USDL to encompass five models as described in exhibit 9–1. Note that work activities in the 1946 formula become worker behaviors identified through the use of functional job analysis.[8] Models 2 and 3 are elaborations of the how question in the

---

Exhibit 9–1   Five Types of Job Descriptors

---

1. *Worker Functions.* The relationship of the worker to data, people, and things.

2. *Work Fields.* The techniques used to complete the tasks of the job. Over 100 such fields have been identified. This descriptor also includes the machines, tools, equipment, and work aids that are used in the job.

3. *Materials, Products, Subject Matter, and/or Services.* The outcomes of the job or the purpose of performing the job.

4. *Worker Traits.* The aptitudes, educational and vocational training, and personal traits required of the worker.

5. *Physical Demands.* Job requirements such as strength, observation, and talking. This descriptor also includes the physical environment of the work.

Source: U.S. Department of Labor, *Handbook for Analyzing Jobs* (Washington, D.C.: U.S. Government Printing Office, 1972).

[8]S. A. Fine and W. W. Wiley, *An Introduction to Functional Job Analysis* (Kalamazoo, Mich.: W. E. Upjohn Institute of Employment Research, 1971).

original format. The fourth model is an elaboration of the why (purpose) question in the original formula. Finally, worker traits or characteristics represents an additional type of job information.

Thus the 1972 approach implies that the job information needed has changed from work activities (tasks) to worker behaviors. It also suggests that the how and why of work activities (but not the work activities themselves) are more important. Finally, worker characterisitcs are added to the job information required. No explanation is provided for the change in needed information. In fact, it is assumed that worker behaviors (functions), work fields, tools, and products and services represent work performed. The 1972 approach seems to represent neither a consistent model of job information needed nor a method of obtaining such information.

McCormick classifies job descriptors as follows:

1. work activities
   a. job-oriented activities
   b. worker-oriented activities
2. machines, tools, equipment
3. work performed
4. job context
5. personnel requirements[9]

This classification suggests that job analysis can yield six kinds of useful job information. These descriptors presumably flow from McCormick's model of the operational functions basic to all jobs—sensing (information receiving), information storage, information processing, and decision and action (physical control or communication). These functions vary in emphasis from job to job. It is not clear how the five descriptors flow from this model, however.

Risher suggests that the following job information is needed by organizations: (1) job content factors; (2) job context factors; (3) worker characteristics; (4) work characteristics; and (5) interpersonal relations (internal and external).[10] Although this is an interesting approach, the rationale for obtaining these types of information is not clear.

None of these models has provided a rationale for all the descriptors they mention. In fact, the grounds for collecting some of the types of information do not appear to be clear. For example, are worker behaviors synonymous with work activities? It seems that managers are more likely to use the term *work activities* and organizational psychologists the term *worker behaviors*. We believe they are separate concepts. The former refers to formal work-devoted acts; the latter would include informal activities not all of which are pertinent to work goals.

Since the job is the connection between the organization and the employee, it may be useful to develop a model based upon this common connection. We can say that both the organization and the employee contribute to the job and expect to receive something from it. In order for these results to come

---

[9]E. J. McCormick, *Job Analysis* (New York: American Management Association, 1979).

[10]H. Risher, "Job Analysis: A Management Perspective," *Employee Relations Law Journal*, Spring 1979, pp. 535–51.

about something has to happen inside the job. This dual systems-exchange model is illustrated in figure 9–1.

The vertical dimension of the model is the person–job relationship. The person brings his or her abilities and effort to the job (cell 1). These are used in activities, which are divided into physical, mental, and interactional types (cell 3). The results, for the person, are the rewards and satisfaction received from working on the job (cell 5). These rewards can be both intrinsic and extrinsic. The latter are the basic subject of this book.

The horizontal dimension of the model is the organization–job relationship. The organization brings to the job resources needed to perform the job and ways to do the job that coordinate with organizational needs; the latter are perceived as constraints (cell 2). These resources and constraints determine the way the job activities (cell 3) are carried out. The organizational results are some product created or service performed by the employee; these outcomes are in the form of a change in data, people, and/or objects (cell 4). These results can be defined in terms of quantity, quality, and time. This model suggests that information, descriptors of jobs, can be collected on the purpose of the job (cell 4), the activities of the job (cell 3), the worker requirements of the job (cell 1), the organizational context of the job (cell 2), and the rewards of the job to the worker (cell 5).

Levels of Analysis

By titling the concept we are discussing *job analysis* we imply that the unit of analysis is the job. Actually, the level or unit of analysis represents a decision that is worthy of discussion.

The lowest level is *employee attributes*—the knowledge, skills, and abilities required by the job.[11] Some of the models discussed in the previous section suggested this level of descriptor.

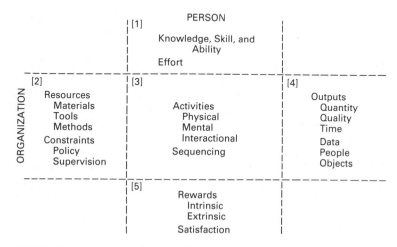

Figure 9–1   Systems exchange model of job analysis

[11]K. Perlman, "Job Families: A Review and Discussion of Their Implications for Personnel Selection," *Psychological Bulletin* (1980), 1–28.

One level up is the *element*. An element is often considered the smallest division of work activity apart from separate motions, although it may be used to describe singular motions. As such, it is used primarily by industrial engineers.

The next level is the *task*—a discrete unit of work performed by an individual. A task is a more independent unit of analysis. It consists of a sequence of activities that completes a work assignment. As such it has all the aspects of the model in figure 9–1.

When sufficient tasks accumulate to justify the employment of a worker, a *position* exists. There are as many positions as employees in an organization.

A *job* is a group of positions that are identical in their major or significant tasks—that are sufficiently alike, in other words, to justify being covered by a single analysis and description. One or many persons may be employed on the same job.

Jobs found in more than one organization may be termed *occupations*. Finally, occupations grouped by function are usually referred to as *job families*.

Obviously, the level or unit of analysis chosen may influence the decision of whether the work is similar or dissimilar. By law (the Equal Pay Act of 1963) if jobs are similar, both sexes must be paid equally; if jobs are different, pay differences may exist.

As suggested in the previous section, the unit of analysis used in practice differs among organizations. Although the procedure is called job analysis, organizations using it may collect data at several levels of analysis. The more detailed the analysis, the more likely that differences will be found. Research has shown that jobs can be similar or dissimilar at different levels of analysis.[12]

METHODS OF OBTAINING JOB INFORMATION

After deciding on descriptors and the level of analysis, the organization must determine which method is to be used to collect job information. Although there are a number of methods of obtaining job information (observation, interviews with job incumbents or experienced personnel and supervisors, structured and nonstructured questionnaires, diaries kept by workers, data on critical incidents, and work sampling), they are perhaps best understood if we classify them as (1) conventional procedures, (2) standardized instruments, (3) task inventories, and (4) structured methods.

This classification is only marginally satisfactory. It will be seen that these job analysis methods differ in descriptors, levels of analysis, and methods of collecting, analyzing, and presenting data. We will evaluate these approaches in terms of purpose, descriptor applicability, cost, reliability, and validity.

Conventional Procedures

Conventional job analysis programs typically involve collecting job information by observing and/or interviewing job incumbents and preparing job

---

[12]E. J. Cornelius III, T. J. Carron, and M. N. Collins, "Job Analysis Models and Job Classification," *Personnel Psychology* (1979), 693–708.

descriptions in essay form. Much of the conventional approach comes from the long experience of the United States Employment Service in analyzing jobs. As mentioned in our discussion of models, the original job analysis formula of the USDL provided for obtaining work activities. The USDL's 1972 revision of this schedule requires the job title, job summary, and description of tasks (these were referred to as work performed in the 1946 formula) as well as other data.

Conventional job analysis treats work activities as the primary job descriptor. As a consequence, the use of the conventional approach by private organizations focuses largely on work activities rather than on the five types of descriptors used in the USDL job analysis schedule (exhibit 9–1).

Because job evaluation purports to distinguish jobs on the importance of work activities to the employing organization, this descriptor seems primary. As we noted, in fact, using the USDL's original job analysis formula (what the worker does, how the worker does it, why the worker does it) as the model for the job summary and each task may provide reasonable assurance that all the work activities are covered. One of the functions of this model is to require the analyst to seek out the purpose of the work.

In some private use of the conventional approach, worker attributes required by the job are also sought. Ratings of education, training, and experience required may be obtained as well as information on contacts required, report writing, decisions, and supervision. In part these categories represent worker attributes, and in part they represent a search for specific work activities.

Some conventional job analysis programs ask job incumbents to complete a preliminary questionnaire describing their jobs. The purpose is to provide the analyst with a first draft of the job information needed. It is also meant to be a first step in obtaining incumbent and supervisor approval of the final job description. Of course, not all employees enjoy filling out questionnaires. Also, employees vary in verbal skills and may overstate or understate their work activities. Usually, the job analyst follows up the questionnaire by interviewing the employee and observing his or her job. Exhibit 9–2 (p. 164) is an example of a job analysis schedule to use as a guide to the job analysis interview.

RESPONSIBILITIES AND DUTIES.   We should not leave this section on conventional job analysis techniques without a word about two commonly used terms—responsibilities and duties. The omission has not been accidental. While job descriptions are often organized around these concepts, we feel that they are not useful terms in identifying job content. Both terms move the analyst away from thinking about what is done and how. When done well, descriptions of duties and responsibilities describe why work is done adequately. But few of these descriptions do even this well. This leaves the job incumbent with some vague statement about why he or she is doing something but little knowledge of what it is or how to do it. The supervisor has a statement that provides little comparison with the activities of the job so that determining performance levels is difficult. And the job evaluator has a collection of words that provide little help in determining the relative worth of jobs in the organization. Adjectives become the main determinant of job level. It is this kind of job description that has lead many personnel directors to decry the futility of job analysis and job descriptions.

Exhibit 9–2   Job Analysis Schedule

1. Establ. JOB TITLE ___INFORMATION DESK CLERK, receptionist-clerk___

2. Ind. Assign. ___ret. tr.___

3. SIC CODE(s) AND TITLE(s) ___5311 Department Stores___

4. JOB SUMMARY:

Answers inquiries and gives directions to customers, authorizes cashing of customers' checks, records and returns lost charge cards, sorts and reviews new credit applications, and requisitions supplies, working at Information Desk in department store Credit Office.

5. WORK PERFORMED RATINGS:

                (D)   (P)   T

Worker Functions	Data	People	Things
	5	6	7

Work Field ___282—Information Giving,   231 Recording___

M.P.S.M.S. ___890—Business Service___

6. WORKER TRAITS RATINGS:
   GED   1 2 (3) 4 5 6
   SVP   1 2 (3) 4 5 6 7 8 9

   Aptitudes G3 V3 N3 S4 P4 Q3 K4 F3 M4 E5 C5

   Temperaments D F I J (M) (P) R S T (V)

   Interests   1a (1b) (2a) 2b 3a 4a 4b 5a 5b

   Phys. Demands (S) L M H V 2 3 (4) (5) 6

   Environ. Cond. (I) O B 2 3 4 5 6 7

7. General Education

   a. Elementary __6__ High School __none__ Courses _____

8. Vocational Preparation

   a. College __none__ Courses _____

Exhibit 9–2 Job Analysis Schedule (continued)

b. Vocational Education __none__ Courses _____

_____

c. Apprenticeship __none_____

_____

d. Inplant Training __none_____

e. On-the-Job Training __3 to 5 weeks by Credit Interviewer_____

f. Performance on Other Jobs __none_____

9. Experience __none_____

10. Orientation __1 week_____

11. Licenses, etc. __none_____

12. Relation to Other Jobs and Workers

Promotion: From__this is an entry job__ To__CREDIT INTERVIEWER_____

Transfers: From __none_____ To __none_____

Supervision Received__CREDIT MANAGER_____

Supervision Given__none_____

13. Machines, Tools, Equipment, and Work Aids
Impressing Device—Small hand-operated device, of similar construction to stapler, with a nonmoving base and a moveable upper arm containing inked rollers which are moved by a lever in the upper arm. Charge card is placed in a groove in the base, stand-up print facing up, and paper or bill positioned over card; then the upper arm is brought down and lever depressed to bring inked rollers over paper to make impress of card's print.

14. Materials and Products
none

15. Description of Tasks:

a. Answers inquiries and gives direction to customers: Greets customers at Information Desk and ascertains reason for visit to Credit Office. Sends customer to Credit Interviewer to open credit account, to Cashier to pay bills, to Adjustment Department to obtain correction of error in billing. Directs customer to other store departments on request, referring to store directory. (50%)

b. Authorizes cashing of checks: Authorizes cashing of personal or payroll checks (up to a specified amount) by customers desiring to make payment on credit account. Requests identification, such as driver's license or charge card, from customers, and examines check to verify date, amount, signature, and endorsement. Initials check, and sends customer to Cashier. Refers customer presenting Stale Date Check to bank. (5%)

Exhibit 9–2 Job Analysis Schedule (continued)

c. Performs routine clerical tasks in the processing of mailed change-of-address requests: Fills out Change-of-Address form, based on customer's letter, and submits to Head Authorizer for processing. Files customer's letter. Contacts customer to obtain delivery address if omitted from letter. (10%)

d. Answers telephone calls from customers reporting lost or stolen charge cards and arranges details of cancellation of former card and replacement: Obtains all possible details from customer regarding lost or stolen card, and requests letter of confirmation. Notifies Authorizer immediately to prevent fraudulent use of missing card. Orders replacement card for customer when confirming letter is received. (10%)

e. Records charge cards which have inadvertently been left in sales departments and returns them to customer: Stamps imprint of card on sheet of paper, using Imprinting Device. Dates sheet and retains own records. Fills out form, posting data such as customer's name and address and date card was returned, and submits to Authorizer. Makes impression of card on face of envelope, inserts card in envelope, and mails to customer. (5%)

f. Sorts and records new credit applications daily: Separates regular Charge Account applications from Budget Accounts. Breaks down Charge Account applications into local and out-of-town applications and arranges applications alphabetically within groups. Counts number of applications in each group and records in Daily Record Book. Binds each group of applications with rubber band, and transmits to Tabulating Room. (10%)

g. Prepares requisitions and stores supplies: Copies amounts of supplies requested by Credit Department personnel onto requisition forms. Submits forms to Purchasing Officer or Supply Room. Receives supplies and places them on shelves in department store storeroom. (10%)

16. Definition of Terms
    Stale Date Checks — More than 30 days old

17. General Comments
    none

18. Analyst ___A. Yessarian_____ Date___7/25/70___ Editor___M. Major___ Date ___7/26/70_____

Reviewed By _____John Milton_____ Title, Org. _____Credit Manager_____

National Office Reviewer _____W. Irving_____

Source: U.S. Department of Labor, *Handbook of Analyzing Jobs* (Washington, D.C.: U.S. Government Printing Office, 1972), pp. 37–41.

RELIABILITY AND VALIDITY. Conventional job analysis is subjective. It depends upon the objectivity and analytical ability of the analyst as well as the information provided by job incumbents and other informants. Measuring reliability (consistency) and validity is difficult because the data are nonquantitative. Having two or more individuals analyze the job independently would provide some measure of reliability but would also add to the cost. Perhaps the strongest contributor to both reliability and validity is the common practice of securing acceptance from both job incumbents and supervisors before job descriptions are considered final. Cost is also an issue here.

COSTS.   Conventional job analysis takes the time of the analyst, job incumbents, and whoever is assigned to ensure consistent analysis and form. In the authors' experience people with moderate analytical skills can be taught to analyze jobs on the basis of the job analysis formula (what, how, why) in a few hours.

An early survey found some dissatisfaction with conventional job analysis, especially with its costs and with the difficulty of keeping the information current.[13] McCormick's review of job analysis, while concluding that the continued use of conventional methods testifies that they serve some purposes well, suggests more attention to a comprehensive model and more quantification.[14]

As suggested earlier in the chapter, a good deal of research is presently being devoted to job analysis. The work to date suggests to us that work activities represent the primary descriptor in job analysis for job evaluation purposes. However, these data take considerable effort to obtain and are of questionable reliability. It would be desirable to develop a standardized quantitative approach that retains the advantages of conventional job analysis, while permitting a less costly and time-consuming approach.

Standardized Instruments

Quantitative job analysis instruments do exist. The best known is the Position Analysis Questionnaire developed by McCormick and associates at Purdue University. Some others much less well known are the Occupational Analysis Inventory developed by Cunningham and associates at North Carolina State University and the Management Position Description Questionnaire.

THE POSITION ANALYSIS QUESTIONNAIRE (PAQ).   The PAQ is a structured job analysis questionnaire containing 194 items called job elements.[15] These elements are worker-oriented; using the terminology of the USDL's 1972 job analysis formula, we would call them worker behaviors. The items are organized into six divisions: (1) information input, (2) mental processes, (3) work output (physical activities and tools), (4) relationships with others, (5) job context (the physical and social environment), and (6) other job characteristics (such as pace and structure). Each job element is rated on six scales: extent of use, importance, time, possibility of occurrence, applicability, and a special code for certain jobs.

The PAQ is usually completed by job analysts or supervisors. In some instances managerial, professional, or other white-collar job incumbents fill out the instrument. The reason for such limitations is that the reading requirements of the method are at least at the college-graduate level.

Data from the PAQ can be analyzed in several ways. For a specific job, individual ratings can be averaged to yield the relative importance of and

[13]J. J. Jones, Jr., and T. A. DeCottis, "Job Analysis: National Survey Findings," *Personnel Journal* (1969), 805–9.

[14]E. J. McCormick, *Job Analysis*, (New York: American Management Association, 1979).

[15]See P. R. Jeanneret and E. J. McCormick, *The Job Dimensions of "Worker Oriented" Job Variables and of their Attribute Profiles as Based on Data from the Position Analysis Questionnaire*, Report no. 2, Occupational Research Center, Department of Psychological Sciences, Purdue University (West Lafayette, Ind., 1969).

emphasis on various job elements, and the results can be summarized as a job description. The elements can also be clustered into a profile rating on a large number of job dimensions to permit comparison of this job with others. Estimates of employee aptitude requirements can be made. Job evaluation points can be estimated from the items related to pay. Finally, an occupational prestige score can be computed. Analysts can have PAQ data computer-analyzed by sending the completed questionnaire to PAQ Services.

The PAQ has been used for job evaluation, selection, performance appraisal, assessment-center development, determination of job similarity, development of job families, vocational counseling, determination of training needs, and job design.

The PAQ has been shown to have a respectable level of reliability. An analysis of 92 jobs by two independent groups yielded a reliability coefficient of .79.[16]

If our earlier analysis of job descriptors is correct, then in spite of the successful use of the PAQ for job evaluation purposes its use of worker behaviors instead of work activities as descriptors may serve to limit its acceptability to employees. So might its lack of employee involvement, as well as its use of only 9 of the 194 job elements when used in job evaluation.

THE OCCUPATIONAL ANALYSIS INVENTORY (OAI). The Occupational Analysis Inventory, although similar to the PAQ, was developed as a way of describing and classifying occupations for educational purposes. It consists of 602 elements grouped into the following categories: information received, mental activities, work behavior, work goals, and work context. Although most items are worker-oriented, as in the PAQ, a large number of job-oriented items associated with particular activities are also included. The items in the inventory are rated on significance to the job, extent of occurrence, and applicability.[17]

The OAI has been used to estimate human-ability requirements of jobs. There appears to be no reason the inventory cannot be used for other purposes. Like the PAQ, the OAI has been subjected to systematic analysis.

The OAI would seem to have largely the same advantages and disadvantages that the PAQ has. No information is readily available on costs, but this can presumably be obtained from Dr. William J. Cunningham at North Carolina State University.

THE MANAGEMENT POSITION DESCRIPTION QUESTIONNAIRE (MPDQ). The MPDQ is a structured questionnaire for describing, classifying, and evaluating managerial positions. It was developed from a predecessor, the Executive Position Description Questionnaire. The latter instrument was found to be too lengthy and complex, and it lacked credence with managers. The MPDQ contains fewer items, and managers were included in its development. The items are categorized as follows: (1) general information, (2) financial and human re-

[16]See Jeanneret and McCormick, op. cit.

[17]J. W. Cunningham, T. C. Tuttle, J. R. Floyd, and J. A. Bates, *The Development of the Occupational Analysis Inventory: An "Ergonomic" Approach to an Educational Problem*, Research Monograph no. 6, Center for Occupational Education, North Carolina State University (Raleigh, N.C., 1971).

source responsibilities, (3) decision making, (4) planning and organizing, (5) supervising and controlling, (6) consulting and innovating, (7) coordination, (8) monitoring business indicators, (9) know-how, (10) overall rating, and (11) reporting relationships. Respondents are asked to indicate the significance of items, in terms of both importance and frequency, on a five-point Likert scale.[18]

Task Inventories

The task inventory emphasizes work activities. In this approach a list of tasks pertinent to a group of jobs is developed. Then the tasks involved in the job under study are rated on a number of scales by incumbents or supervisors. Finally the ratings are manipulated statistically, usually by computer, and a quantitative job analysis is developed. Actually any method of job analysis, even narrative job descriptions, could be termed a task inventory if an analysis of the data can provide quantitative information from appropriate scales.

THE COMPREHENSIVE OCCUPATIONAL DATA ANALYSIS PROGRAM (CODAP). Undoubtedly the best-known task inventory is the one that has been developed over many years by Raymond E. Christal and his associates for the United States Air Force.[19] The heart of the program is a list of tasks involved in a particular job. After the task list has been prepared by incumbents, supervisors, or experts, incumbents are asked to indicate whether they perform each of the tasks. They are then asked to indicate on a scale the relative amount of time spent in performing each particular task. Other ratings are also obtained, such as training time required and criticality of performance.

The ratings are then summed across all tasks and an estimated percentage of time on each task derived. The total percentages account for the total job. The relative times are then used to develop a group job description.

Computer programs are used to analyze, organize, and report on data from the task inventory. The programs are designed to provide information for a variety of applications. For example, the CODAP can describe the types of jobs in an occupational area, describe the types of jobs performed by a specified group of workers, compare the work performed at various locations or the work performed by various levels of personnel, and produce job descriptions. The program can process data on 1700 tasks for each of 20,000 workers.

Obviously the CODAP is most useful for large organizations and is relatively costly. The descriptor employed is work activities, and the output of the analysis is the work performed. Worker requirements must be inferred, as in conventional job analysis. Data developed by this method have been used in selection to identify training needs and design training programs, to validate training completion as a training criterion, to restructure jobs, and to classify jobs. The CODAP is used in all branches of the military and by the federal and some local governments.

[18]L. R. Gomez-Mejia, R. C. Page, and W. W. Tornow, "A Comparison of the Practical Utility of Traditional, Statistical, and Hybrid Job Evaluation Approaches," *Academy of Management Journal*, December 1982, pp. 709–809.

[19]R. E. Christal and J. J. Weissmuller, *New Comprehensive Occupational Data Analysis Programs (CODAP) for Analyzing Task Factor Information*, Interim Professional Paper no. TR-76-3, Air Force Human Resources Laboratory (Lackland Air Force Base, Lackland, Texas, 1976).

Like most computer-driven systems, the technique is as good as the input. Computer analysis cannot correct for inaccurate or incomplete information. Using trained personnel to develop inventories of specific tasks is therefore a requirement of the method. Given a complete and accurate task inventory, statistical analysis of the distribution of the ratings provides some indications of reliability and validity.

THE WORK PERFORMANCE SURVEY SYSTEM. Task inventories are also being used in private organizations. Drawing on his experience with the CODAP program and his development of a task inventory for AT&T, Sidney Gael has recently published a step-by-step guidebook for developing and using task inventories for job analysis.[20] The book includes rules for developing task statements and inventories, methods of developing and distributing questionnaires, computer programs for analyzing the questionnaires, and methods of interpreting and using results. Gael calls his approach the Work Performance Survey System.

Gael's guidebook also offers a shortcut procedure for small organizations. This procedure, though, seems to require at least a medium-sized organization. Task lists are still required, although preliminary versions may be developed by job analysts. Group meetings for further developing task lists and the questionnaire are still required, although shortened. Rating scales are simplified, as are methods of analysis. Computer analysis is not called for. On balance, however, the shortcut version, while also furnishing work activities as the raw material for job descriptions, may still be too costly for small organizations.

THE JOB INFORMATION MATRIX SYSTEM (JIMS). Although the JIMS could be classifed as a standardized basis for gathering and recording job information, the heart of the procedure consists of task inventories.[21] The procedure is designed for specific occupational groups. It provides information on (1) what the worker does on the job, (2) what the worker *uses*, (3) what *knowledge* he or she must have, (4) his or her *responsibilities*, and (5) the *working conditions* of the job.

The information on what the worker does on the job is obtained through a standardized task inventory for a specific occupational area. Provision is made for describing the major (most time-consuming) tasks.

In addition, the JIMS provides a list of active verbs that permit elaboration of the *data* and *people* hierarchies of functional job analysis. Each of these verbs is defined so as to permit standardization.

A list of machines, tools, equipment, and other work aids is furnished to standardize the information on what the worker uses and what he or she must know. Lists of types of responsibilities are also provided. The procedures for obtaining information on working conditions parallel the procedures used in the 1972 USDL job analysis schedule.

As mentioned, the JIMS approach must be developed for each occupational group. As of now it is incomplete; developing it for a broad range of uses would be a large project.

[20]S. Gael, *Job Analysis* (San Francisco: Jossey-Bass, 1983).

[21]C. H. Stone and D. Yoder, *Job Analysis, 1970* (Long Beach: California State University, 1970, Mimeographed).

However, the idea of using a standardized task list is intriguing: such a list would permit expeditious job analysis and processing and storage of job information. The descriptor emphasized, as in the 1946 USDL approach, is work activity. In fact, the JIMS seems to be an elaboration of the USDL approach.

OTHER STATISTICAL APPROACHES.   Any job information in numerical form may be analyzed statistically for similarities and differences among jobs. Cluster analysis, analysis of variance, and factor analysis have been applied to job data.

For example, an approach employing cluster analysis was developed by Carr.[22] Called the Systematic Approach to Multidimensional Occupational Analysis (SAMOA), it groups jobs on technical, organizational, and communicational dimensions. The technical dimension rates jobs on work activities. The organizational dimension rates jobs on work context. The communicational dimension seems to be another rating of work activity. The approach was developed from data obtained from Navy enlisted personnel. Its use would seem to be primarily the development of job families.

Structured Methods

Quite a number of job analysis methods have been developed in recent years that represent either different concepts of what to look for in jobs or complete systems purporting to better accomplish given purposes. For these reasons they are classified as structured job analysis methods. This section briefly describes and attempts to evaluate a number of these approaches. Because of the renewed interest in job analysis, new methods are appearing all the time and will most likely have appeared by the time this book is published.

FUNCTIONAL JOB ANALYSIS (FJA).   Functional Job Analysis is usually thought of in terms of the familiar "data, people, things" hierarchies used in the *Dictionary of Ocupational Titles.* Developed by Sidney A. Fine and associates, this comprehensive approach has five components: (1) identification of purposes, goals, and objectives, (2) identification and description of tasks, (3) analysis of tasks on seven scales, including three worker-function scales (one each for data, people, and things), (4) development of performance standards, and (5) development of training content.[23]

FJA data are developed by trained job analysts from background materials, interviews with workers and supervisors, and observation. The method provides data for job design, selection, training, and evaluation and could be used at least partially for most other personnel applications. It has been applied to jobs at every level.

The major descriptor in FJA is work activity. A number of task banks have been developed by Fine and his colleagues as a means of standardizing

[22]M. J. Carr, *The SAMOA Method of Determining Technical, Organizational, and Communicational Dimensions of Task Clusters,* Technical Bulletin STB-68-5, U.S. Naval Personnel and Training Research Laboratory, San Diego (1967).

[23]S. A. Fine, A. M. Holt, and M. F. Hutchinson, *Functional Job Analysis: How to Standardize Task Statements* (Kalamazoo, Mich.: W. E. Upjohn Institute for Employment Research, 1974).

information on this descriptor. FJA is rigorous, but it does require a heavy investment of time and effort.

THE CRITICAL INCIDENT TECHNIQUE (CIT). The Critical Incident Technique is a method of determining the specific work behavior necessary for successful performance on a job. Developed by John C. Flanagan, the method involves securing instances of effective and ineffective behaviors on a job from supervisors, incumbents, and others in a position to observe worker behavior.[24] The incidents may be collected through individual or group interviews, observation, or questionnaires. They must be specific and concrete and represent successful or unsuccessful behavior.

Applications have included job design, selection, training, and especially performance evaluation. The CIT does not provide a complete description of the job but only those worker behaviors that distinguish successful from unsuccessful performance.

THE JOB ELEMENT METHOD (JEM). The Job Element Method, developed by Ernest Primoff, focuses on collecting from workers and supervisors the knowledge, skills, abilities, and other worker characteristics required by a job.[25] The respondents also rate these characteristics for their importance in successful performance of the job. The JEM was developed as an aid in selecting employees for the federal government.

Because the JEM originally did not provide for identifying job content or linking worker requirements to content data, Primoff has supplemented it with FJA and the CIT.[26] This change enabled the JEM to meet the requirements of the Uniform Guidelines for Employee Selection Procedures for content validity and will probably make the method useful for other personnel applications.

THE HEALTH SERVICES MOBILITY STUDY (HSMS). The Health Services Mobility Study was developed in response to personnel shortages in the health-care field. Its underlying premise is that worker skills can be developed to alleviate these shortages.

The HSMS involves collecting and analyzing information about tasks and about skill and knowledge requirements through interviews and observation by individuals trained in the method.[27] It includes a set of skill scales and a knowledge scale. It also uses a number of computer programs to develop job structures and job ladders. Its major application is the use of these job ladders for personnel planning, training, and performance evaluation.

[24]J. C. Flanagan, "The Critical Incident Technique," *Psychological Bulletin* (1954), 327–58.

[25]E. S. Primoff, *How to Prepare and Conduct Job-Element Examinations,* Technical Study 75-1, U.S. Civil Service Commission (Washington D.C.: U.S. Government Printing Office, 1975).

[26]E. S. Primoff, "The Use of Self-Assessments in Examining," *Personnel Psychology* (1980), 283–90.

[27]E. Gilpatrick, *The Health Services Mobility Study Method of Task Analysis and Curriculum Design—Writing Task Descriptions and Scaling Tasks for Skills and Knowledge: A Manual,* Research Report no. 11, vol. 2 (Springfield, Va.: National Technical Information Service, 1977).

Because of the method's complexity, its major area of applicability would seem to be a group of organizations for which it could establish training goals and curricula. It could also be used by a single organization, but this would be costly and time-consuming.

GUIDELINES ORIENTED JOB ANALYSIS (GOJA). This method was developed specifically to meet fair employment practice rules.[28] There are three versions of the approach—full, brief, and simplified.

The full version obtains task descriptions rated for importance and criticality; knowledge skills, and other worker characteristics; and the physical characteristics of the work. Information is obtained from a group of job incumbents and supervisors. The result is a fully documented job description. Full GOJA takes about 20 hours per job.

Brief GOJA includes an instruction booklet and work sheets on which incumbents write their own job descriptions. Analysts review the data for inconsistencies and insure that job differences are real. The brief approach takes four to six hours per job.

Simplified GOJA employs a semistructured form completed by the incumbent but reviewed and perhaps modified by supervisors and analysts. The form calls for information on (1) machines, tools, and equipment, listed and rated for frequency of use; (2) kinds of people supervised and supervisory tasks, listed for checking; (3) types and frequency of contacts; (4) work activities and results; (5) knowledge, skills, and abilities; (6) physical and other requirements; and (7) characteristics that differentiate levels of performance. The simplified version takes two to four hours per job.

GOJA employs work activities, worker requirements, and work context as descriptors. It seems applicable to all personnel uses. The brief and simplified versions require college-level reading ability and probably some training in the method.

THE BEHAVIOR CONSISTENCY METHOD (BCM). The Behavior Consistency Method was designed to help analysts identify worker competencies that could be used in the selection of experienced professional and managerial applicants for mid-level government jobs.[29] It is essentially an elaboration of the Critical Incident Method. Trained personnel specialists describe the work activities. Supervisors in structured group meetings identify the critical knowledge, abilities, skills, and other characteristics (KASOS), then rate them on six scales. Average ratings are computed for the KASOS.

Although it emphasizes critical worker requirements the BCM appears to yield higher reliabilities and validities than other methods of determining worker requirements. But it is time-consuming and therefore costly.

THE WORK ELEMENTS INVENTORY (WEI). This inventory, developed at the University of Chicago by Melany E. Baehr and associates, purports to measure the basic dimensions of jobs in terms of underlying worker behaviors

[28] R. E. Biddle, *GOJA Manual,* 3rd ed. (Sacramento: Biddle & Assn., 1976).

[29] F. I. Schmidt, J. R. Caplan, S. E. Bemus, R. Decuir, L. Dunn, and L. Antone, *The Behavioral Consistency Method of Unassembled Examining* (Washington, D.C.: U.S. Office of Personnel Management, 1979).

and the relative importance of these dimensions.[30] The dimensions are organization, leadership, personnel, and community. Developed from factor analysis, these dimensions are the basis of a job description instrument that when scored yields a profile of the job in which the importance of each dimension is recorded. In terms of our discussion of job descriptors earlier in this chapter, the WEI records worker behaviors.

✝ **THE VERSATILE JOB ANALYSIS SYSTEM (VERJAS).** This system was developed with the idea of obtaining all the job information needed for all personnel purposes with one method and at one time.[31] Information is collected on work activities, worker requirements, and job context (these are defined as typical job evaluation factors).

In this approach managers analyze the jobs of subordinates, although job analysts may do so through observation and interviews. The steps involved in the VERJAS are: (1) writing an overview of the job, describing its purpose and primary duties; (2) describing the action, purpose, and result of each task, rating its importance, and identifying training requirements; (3) describing the context of the job—its scope, effect, and environment; (4) identifying basic worker competencies needed for minimal acceptable performance of the job's tasks; and (5) identifying the special worker competencies that make for successful job performance.

The VERJAS uses the USDL concepts, including FJA. Its job context factors are taken from the Factor Evaluation System, the job evaluation system used by the federal government.

If an organization decides to obtain job information for all personnel uses at one time and if managers really know the jobs under them, this method may produce highly reliable and valid data at nominal cost. Whether the job context is appropriately defined by the method, however, seems to be a decision the organization must make.

Two Other Methods

Two more methods may serve to round out the various approaches to job analysis. Physical Abilities Analysis, developed by Edwin A. Fleishman and associates, examines jobs in terms of nine physical abilities, using a seven-point scale for each.[32] The second method, not detailed here because it is the subject of the next chapter, is job evaluation. Most versions of job evaluation analyze jobs in terms of specific factors and scales for each factor.

JOB ANALYSTS

Employees, supervisors, and job analysts perform the tasks of collecting and analyzing job information. Job incumbents have the most complete and accurate information, but getting this information and making the results consistent re-

[30]M. E. Baehr, *Skills and Attributes Inventory* (Chicago: University of Chicago Industrial Relations Center, 1971).

[31]Bemis, Belensky, and Soder, *Job Analysis*.

[32]E. A. Fleishman, "Evaluating Physical Abilities Required by Jobs," *Personnel Administrator* (1979), 82–92.

quires attention to data-collection methods. Also, employee acceptance of the results is a priority, and employee involvement in data collection and analysis tends to promote this.

Supervisors may or may not know the jobs of their subordinates well enough to be useful sources of job information. If they do know the jobs well enough, a great deal of time and money can be saved.

Job analysts have been trained to collect job information. They know what to look for and what questions to ask. They also know how to standardize the information and the language employed. People with various educational backgrounds have been trained as job analysts. Most organizations train their own job analysts by having them work with experienced analysts. Experience suggests that limited training suffices to provide these skills.

Some organizations place new personnel staff as job analysts as an early assignment. This approach permits new incumbents to learn something about the organization's work and provides a pool of trained analysts.

When supervisors and job incumbents are used in job analysis, some training is required. As repeatedly emphasized, involvement by employees and supervisors increases the usefulness and acceptance of the data and personnel process which use these data.

Ideally, the increased interest in job analysis mentioned previously will result in methods that will make job analysis easier for all involved. In the meantime, the more people who can analyze jobs consistently and accurately, the better the personnel decisions based on the information thus obtained.

JOB DESCRIPTIONS

Regardless of who collects job information and how they do it, the end-product of job analysis is a standardized job description. A job description describes the job as it is being performed. In a sense, a job description is a snapshot of the job as of the time it was analyzed. Ideally they are written so that any reader, whether familiar or not with the job, can "see" what the worker does, how, and why. *What* the worker does describes the physical, mental, and interactional activities of the job. *How* deals with the methods, procedures, tools, and information sources used to carry out the tasks. *Why* refers to the objective of the work activities; this should be included in the job summary and in each task description.

An excellent set of prescriptions of writing style for job descriptions is offered by the *Handbook for Analyzing Jobs*.[33] These include a terse, direct style; present tense; an active verb beginning each task description and the summary statement; an objective for each task and no unnecessary or fuzzy words. The handbook also suggests how the basic task statement should be structured: (1) present-tense active verb, (2) immediate object of the verb, (3) infinitive phrase showing the objective. An example would be: (1) collects, (2) credit information, (3) to determine credit rating.

Unfortunately, many words have more than one meaning. Perhaps the easiest way to promote accurate job description writing is to select only active verbs that permit the reader to see someone actually doing something.

[33]U.S. Department of Labor, *Handbook for Analyzing Jobs* (Washington, D.C.: U.S. Government Printing Office, 1972).

Conventional job descriptions typically include three broad categories of information: (1) identification, (2) work performed, and (3) performance requirements. The identification section distinguishes the job under study from other jobs. Obviously industry and company size are needed to describe the organization, and a job title is actually used to identify the job. The number of incumbents is useful as well as a job number if such a system is used.

The work-performed section usually beings with a job summary that describes the purpose and content of the job. The summary is followed by an orderly series of paragraphs that describe each of the tasks. Job analysts tend to write the summary statement after completing the work-performed section. They find that the flag statements for the various tasks provide much of the material for the summary statement.

The balance of the work-performed section presents from three to eight tasks in chronological order or in order of the time taken by the task. Each task is introduced by a *flag statement* that shows generally what is being done followed by a detailed account of what, how, and why it is done. Each task is followed by the percentage of total job time it requires.

The performance-requirements section sets out the worker attributes required by the job. This section is called the *job specification*. Job descriptions used for job evaluation may or may not include this section. An argument can be made that worker attributes must be inferred from work activities. This would require the job analyst not only to collect and analyze job information but to make judgments about job difficulty.

Managerial job descriptions differ from nonmanagerial job descriptions in what are called *scope data*. For example, financial and organizational data are used to locate managerial jobs in the hierarchy. The identification section of managerial job descriptions is usually more elaborate and may include the reporting level and the functions of jobs supervised directly and indirectly. The number of people directly and indirectly supervised may be included, as well as department budgets and payrolls. The work-performed section of managerial job descriptions, like that of nonmanagerial job descriptions, includes the major tasks but gives special attention to organization objectives. Writers of managerial job descriptions need to remember that "is responsible for . . ." does not tell the reader what the manager does.

Careful writing is a requirement of good job descriptions. The words used should have only one possible connotation and must accurately describe what is being done. Terms should not only be specific but should also employ language that is as simple as possible.

Obviously, when job descriptions are written by different analysts coordination and consistency are essential. These are usually provided by having some central agency edit the job descriptions.

For two examples of job evaluation–job description, see exhibits 9–3 and 9–4.

SUMMARY

Wage structures deal with the relationship between jobs within the organization. In developing a wage structure the developer must have information about the jobs of the organization. This is the task of job analysis—the collec-

Exhibit 9–3   Nonmanagerial Job Description

JOB TITLE: Sales Clerk

JOB SUMMARY: Serves customers, receives and straightens stock, and inspects dressing rooms.

TASKS

   1. *Serves customers to make sales and to provide advice:* Observes customers entering store, approaches them and asks to help, locates desired articles of clothing, and guides customers to dressing rooms. Decides when to approach customers and which articles of clothing to suggest. Sometimes gets suggestions from other sales clerks or supervisor. Rings up purchases on cash register and takes cash or check or processes credit card. Decides whether check or credit-card acceptance is within store policy. (80%)

   2. *Receives and arranges stock to attractively exhibit merchandise:* Unpacks boxes, counts items, and compares with purchase orders. Reports discrepancies to supervisor. Arranges and inspects new and old merchandise on racks and counters. Removes damaged goods and changes inventory figures. Decides where to place items in the store, within guidelines of supervisor. Twice a year helps with taking inventory by counting and recording merchandise. (15%)

   3. *Inspects dressing rooms to keep them neat and discourage shoplifting:* Walks through dressing area periodically, collecting clothing left or not desired. Remains alert to attempts to shoplift clothing from dressing area. Decides when security needs to be called in. Rehangs merchandise on sales floor. (5%)

Exhibit 9–4   Managerial Job Description

JOB TITLE: Branch Bank Manager

JOB SUMMARY: Promotes bank in community and supervises branch operations and lending activities.

TASKS

   1. *Promotes bank services in the community to increase total assets of the bank:* Engages in and keeps track of community activities, both commercial and social. Identifies potential customers in community. Analyzes potential customer needs and prospects, plans sales presentation, and meets with potential customers to persuade them to use bank services. (40%)

   2. *Supervises branch operation to minimize cost of operation while providing maximum service:* Plans work activity of the branch. Communicates instructions to subordinate supervisors. Observes branch activity. Discusses problems with employees and decides or helps employees decide course of action. Coordinates branch activities with main office. Performs personnel activities of hiring, evaluating, rewarding, training, and disciplining employees and financial activities of budgeting and reviewing financial reports. (35%)

   3. *Evaluates and processes loan requests to increase revenues of the bank:* Reviews and analyzes loan requests for risk. Seeks further information as appropriate. Approves (or denies) requests that fall within branch lending limits. Prepares reports to accompany other loan requests to bank loan committee. Keeps up with changes in bank lending policy, financial conditions, and community needs. (25%)

---

tion and organization of information about jobs. The end product of job analysis is a job description, an instrument that is used by most aspects of personnel administration. Carefully done job analysis is becoming more important in personnel administration with the requirements of civil rights laws.

   There is little commonality as to what information to record in job analysis or how to collect the information. We have suggested in this chapter that the information collected needs to focus on what the job is, how it is done, and why it is done. For these purposes, understanding the activities the worker engages in on the job is very important. Worker traits, on the other hand, are a derivative of understanding the job and not the job itself.

The methods for collecting data about jobs are numerous and range from very informal to highly structured questionnaires. Despite this variety, the use of a job analysis interview is still the major method of obtaining job information. The flexibility provided outweighs the advantages of consistency and analytical power of the more structured techniques. The future may provide useful tools for more carefully collecting information that provides the worker, supervisor, and the compensation specialist with adequate information for their diverse purposes.

10

Job Evaluation

We began our discussion of job evaluation in chapter 8. The process was briefly described, as were its objectives. We looked at the background and prevalence of job evaluation. The assignment of responsibility for the process and the question of union involvement were also discussed. Finally, employee acceptance of the results was reiterated as the major criterion of job evaluation success.

Chapter 9 dealt with the first step in the job evaluation process—what information to collect and available methods of doing so. We are now ready to look more closely at the remainder of the process.

DETERMINANTS OF JOB STATUS

The next step in job evaluation is to determine what the organization is "paying for"—what aspects of jobs place one job higher in the job hierarchy than another job. These yardsticks are called *compensable factors*.

In the previous chapter we suggested that the job information needed for job evaluation consists of work activities and worker requirements. But what aspect or aspects of work activities and/or which worker requirements are to be used? Logically the choice of yardstick will strongly influence where a job is placed in the hierarchy.

179

We also noted in the last chapter that some methods of job analysis require analysts to describe jobs in terms of preselected factors. This practice seems to assign to job analysts not only the analysis but the evaluation of jobs. A legitimate question is whether this combination of information gathering and evaluation may introduce bias to job evaluation.

Some job evaluation methods (to be described later) are classified as whole-job methods, implying that compensable factors are not used because "whole jobs" are being compared. If this means that one broad-based factor rather than several narrower factors is employed, no problem occurs. But if *whole job* means that jobs can be compared without specifying the basis of comparison, the result may be a different basis of comparison for each evaluator. If this reasoning is correct, then useful job evaluation must always utilize one or more compensable factors.

To be useful in comparing jobs, compensable factors should possess certain characteristics. First, they must be present in all jobs. Second, the factor must vary in degree. A factor found in equal amounts in all jobs would be worthless as a basis of comparison. Third, if two or more factors are chosen, they should not overlap in meaning. If they do overlap, double weight may be given to one factor. Fourth, employer, employee, and union viewpoints should be reflected in the factors chosen; consideration of all viewpoints is critical for acceptance. Fifth, compensable factors must be demonstrably derived from the work performed.

The factors must be observable in the jobs. For this reason responsibility is a hard factor to use. Compensable factors can be thought of as the job-related contributions of employees. Documentation of the work-relatedness of factors comes from job descriptions. Such documentation provides evidence against allegations of illegal pay discrimination. It also provides answers to employees, managers, and union leaders who raise questions about differences among jobs.

Finally compensable factors need to fit the organization. Under our system organizations design jobs to meet their goals and to fit their technology and their culture and values. Organizations may also choose what they pay for in jobs.

METHODS OF DETERMINING COMPENSABLE FACTORS

Many organizations adopt standard job evaluation plans and thus the factors on which they are based are predetermined. Perhaps more organizations adjust existing plans to their own requirements. The factors in most existing plans tend to fall into four broad categories: skills required, required effort, responsibilities, and working conditions. These factors are used in numerous job evaluation plans. They are also the factors written into the Equal Pay Act of 1963 and used to define equal work.

Definitions and divisions of these factors vary greatly. Years of education required by the job is a common definition of skill, as is experience required. Skill is likewise often divided into mental and manual skills. In this way, a job evaluation plan may be tailored to the needs of the organization.

In most job evaluation plans the factors are chosen by a committee, as described in chapter 8. Broad representation on the committee helps to insure acceptance of the factors chosen.

One of the best-known job evaluation plans, the National Electrical Manufacturers (NEMA) plan, was designed by a group of 25 experienced people who knew much about the jobs to be evaluated. These people were asked to review the job descriptions of 50 key jobs and to list all the job characteristics, requirements, and conditions that in their opinion should be considered in evaluating the jobs. The group came up with 90 job attributes, which were finally reduced to 11 within the four broad categories just mentioned.

Perhaps the best-known union-management job evaluation plan (the steel plan) was developed by a committee of union and management representatives. Such joint determination of compensable factors is presently being used in the communication and utilities industries. Employees' acceptance of factors tends to be enhanced by their involvement in determining them.

Another possible method of determining compensable factors is to ask employees what factors they deem important. A questionnaire developed and tested by the authors has proved capable of determining what contributions employees believe they should be rewarded for.

Some job evaluation plans determine compensable factors statistically from quantitative job analysis. For example, the factors in the Position Analysis Questionnaire (PAQ) used for job evaluation were obtained by finding those elements most closely related to pay.[1] Statistical techniques may help ensure that the factors chosen are related to the work and are legally defensible. But factors derived statistically are not always accepted by employees as applicable to their jobs.

Use of the Managerial Position Description Questionnaire at Control Data Corporation resulted in eight factors derived by statistical analysis. The managers, however, did not believe that the factors reflected their jobs. Only after those factors were merged with factors developed by committee judgment were they accepted, even though both sets resulted in the same job structure.[2]

The major advantage of the statistical aproach is that it can determine how reliably the factors measure the jobs. The funds and the expertise needed to conduct statistical analysis are not always available, though. The committee or the questionnaire approach may yield equally useful compensable factors if based on adequate job descriptions.

NUMBER OF PLANS

Whether to employ a single plan to evaluate all the organization's jobs or a separate plan for each of several job families must also be decided. There is a strong tendency for organizations, especially large ones, to use multiple plans. Using different compensable factors for different job families may be justified in several ways. The organization may be paying for different things in differ-

[1]P. R. Jeannert, "Equitable Job Evaluation and Classification with the PAQ," *Compensation Review*, first quarter 1982, pp. 32–42.

[2]L. R. Gomez-Mejia, R. C. Page, and W. W. Tornow, "Development and Implementation of a Computerized Job Evaluation System," *Personnel Administrator*, February 1979, pp. 46–52.

ent job groups and different wage level policies followed. The wages of different job families do not always move together and in equal amounts.

Equally important, Livernash has shown that job-content comparisons are strongest within narrow job clusters and weakest among broad job clusters.[3] Employees in the same job family are likely to make job comparisons. Job relationships are likely to be influenced by custom and tradition as well as by promotion and transfer sequences.

For all these reasons, organizations commonly have separate job evaluation plans for different functional groups—production jobs, clerical jobs, professional and technical jobs, and management jobs, for example.

There is evidence that equal employment opportunity rules are causing organizations to reexamine their choice of single or multiple plans. Obviously, comparing all jobs within an organization for evidence of discrimination based on sex or race suggests employing a single plan. The National Academy of Sciences study for the Equal Employment Opportunity Commission argued strongly in its interim report (but not the final report) for a single plan for the organization.[4]

Although a number of organizations are opting for a single plan, defining compensable factors that are applicable to all jobs and acceptable to employees is difficult. As a consequence, there may be a growing tendency for organizations to use fewer plans keyed to job groups whose incumbents are balanced by gender and race. One alternative would be (1) a plan for service or production and maintenance jobs paid primarily for physical skills, (2) a plan for office and technical jobs paid primarily for mental skills, and (3) a plan for exempt jobs (managerial and professional) paid primarily for discretionary skills.

Another possible approach is a common set of compensable factors along with a set of factors unique to particular functional areas. The latter tend to make the plan more acceptable to employees and managers. Where more than one job evaluation plan is used, it is common when questions of bias are raised to evaluate the job in question with the other plans and compare results. Organizations that employ more than one job evaluation plan should identify a series of jobs that can be evaluated on two plans to ensure consistency of results across plans.

METHODS

The next step in the job evaluation process is to select or design a method of evaluating jobs. Four basic methods have traditionally been said to describe most of the numerous job evaluation systems: ranking, classification, factor comparison, and the point plan. The dimensions that distinguish these methods are (1) qualitative versus quantitative, (2) job-to-job versus job-to-standard-comparison, and (3) consideration of total job versus separate factors that when summed make up the job. These four methods as listed here, may be thought

[3]E. R. Livernash, "The Internal Wage Structure," in *New Concepts in Wage Determination*, ed. G. W. Taylor and F. C. Pierson (New York: McGraw-Hill, 1957), pp. 140–172.

[4]D. J. Treiman and H. I. Hartmann, eds., *Women, Work, and Wages* (Washington, D.C.: National Academy Press, 1981).

of as increasing in specificity of comparison. Ranking involves creating a hierarchy of jobs by comparing jobs on a global factor that presumably combines all parts of the job. The classification method defines categories of jobs and slots jobs into these classes. Factor comparison involves job-to-job comparisons on several specific factors. The point method compares jobs on rating scales of specific factors.

These four basic methods are pure types. In practice there are numerous combinations. Also, there are (as mentioned) many ready-made plans as well as numerous adaptations of these plans to organization needs. The following sections describe these basic plans and provide some examples.

Job Ranking

As its name implies, this method ranks the jobs in an organization from highest to lowest. It is the simplest of the job evaluation methods and the easiest to explain. Another advantage is that it usually takes less time and thus is less expensive.

Its primary disadvantage is that its use of adjacent ranks suggests that there are equal differences between jobs, which is very unlikely. Other disadvantages flow from the way the method is often used. For example, ranking has been done without first securing good job descriptions. This approach can succeed only if evaluators know all the jobs—virtually impossible in an organization with many jobs or with frequently changing jobs.

Another disadvantage is that rankers are asked to keep the "whole job" in mind and often merely to rank the jobs. This undoubtedly results in different bases of comparison among raters and permits raters, whether they realize it or not, to be influenced by such factors as present pay rates, competence of job incumbents, and prestige of the job. This difficulty can be overcome by selecting and defining one or more compensable factors and asking raters to use them as bases of job comparison. Even then, unfortunately, factor definitions are often so general that rankings are highly subjective.

If the ranking method is used in accordance with the process described in the next section it may yield the advantages cited and minimize the disadvantages.

Developing a job ranking consists of the following steps:

1. Obtain Job Information.   As we have noted, the first step in job evaluation is job analysis. Job descriptions are prepared, or secured if already available.

2. Select Raters and Jobs to Be Rated.   Raters who will attempt to make unbiased judgments are selected and trained in the rating procedure. Less training is required for ranking than for other methods of job evaluation. If job descriptions are available, it is unnecessary to select as raters only those people who know all the jobs well; this is probably impossible anyway except in very small organizations.

If all the jobs in the organization are to be ranked, it may be wise to start with key jobs. Another approach is to rank jobs by department and later dovetail the rankings.

3. Select Compensable Factor(s). Although ranking is referred to as a "whole-job" approach, different raters may use different attributes to rank jobs. If judgments are to be comparable, compensable factors must be selected and defined. Even as broad a factor as job difficulty or importance is sufficient, if carefully defined in operational terms. Seeing that raters understand the factors on which jobs are to be compared will help ensure that rankings are made on that factor.

4. Rank Jobs. Although straight ranking is feasible for a limited number of jobs (20 or less), alternation ranking or paired comparison tends to produce more consistent results. *Straight ranking* involves ordering cards (one for each job) on which job titles or short job briefs have been written. In case more information is needed by raters it is useful to have the actual job description at hand. *Alternation ranking* provides raters with a form on which a list of job titles to be ranked are recorded at the left and an equal number of blanks appear at the right. The raters are asked to record at the top of the right-hand column the job title they adjudge the highest, and cross out that title in the list to the left. Then they record the lowest job in the bottom blank and the remaining jobs in between, crossing out the job titles from the left-hand list along the way. In *paired comparison,* raters compare all possible pairs of jobs. One way to do this is with a pack of cards on which job titles have been recorded, as in straight ranking. Raters compare each pair of jobs at least once. The card of the job adjudged higher is checked after each comparison. After all comparisons have been made the raters list the jobs, starting with the job with the most check marks and ending with the job with the least. A similar approach is to use a matrix like the one in figure 10–1. For each cell in the matrix, the raters provide a check if the job listed on the left is higher than its counterpart on the top. The number of times a job is checked (tabulated in the "Total" column on the right) indicates its rank. Although this method of comparing pairs of jobs is less cumbersome, the number of comparisons increases rapidly with the number of jobs. The number of comparisons may be computed as $(n)(n-1) \div 2$.

5. Combine Ratings. It is advisable to have several raters rank the jobs independently. Their rankings are then averaged, yielding a composite ranking that is sufficiently accurate.

Although job ranking is usually assumed to be applicable primarily to small organizations, it has been used in large firms as well. Computers make it possible to use paired comparison for any number of raters, jobs, and even factors. But the other disadvantages remain. Unless job ranking is based on good job descriptions and at least one carefully defined factor, it is difficult to explain and justify in work-related terms. Although the job hierarchy developed by ranking may be better than paying no attention at all to job relationships, the method's simplicity and low cost may produce results of less than the needed quality.

Job Classification

The classification method involves defining a number of classes or grades of jobs and fitting jobs into them. It would be like sorting books among a series of carefully labeled shelves in a bookcase. The primary task is to de-

	Cost Clerk	File Clerk	Addresso- graph Opr.	Ledger Clerk	Junior Typist	Order Clerk	Mes- senger	Total
Cost Clerk								
File Clerk								
Addresso- graph Opr.								
Ledger Clerk								
Junior Typist								
Order Clerk								
Messenger								

Figure 10–1   A job comparison matrix

scribe each of the classes so that no difficulty is experienced in fitting each job into its proper niche. Jobs are then classified by comparing each job with the class description provided.

This method of comparing jobs has the major advantage that most organizations, and employees as well, tend to classify jobs. It may therefore be relatively easy to secure agreement about the classification of most jobs. The classification method also promotes thinking about job classes among both managers and employees. If jobs are thought of as belonging in a certain grade, many problems of compensation administration become easier to solve. In fact most organizations classify jobs into grades to ease the task of building and operating pay structures. When jobs are placed into grades or classes subsequent to job evaluation by any method, or even by informal decision or agreement, those grades often become the major focus of compensation administration. When jobs change or new jobs emerge, they may be placed in the job structure by decision or negotiation. It may be necessary to use formal job evaluation only infrequently, if agreement cannot be reached without it.

Perhaps the greatest advantage of the method is its flexibility. Although classification is usually said to be most useful for organizations with relatively few jobs, it has long been used successfully by the largest organization in the world—the United States government. In fact, it is the primary job evaluation method of most levels of government in the United States as well as of many large private organizations. In these applications millions of kinds and levels of jobs have been classified successfully.

Advocates of classification hold that job evaluation by any method involves much judgment. They also believe that classification can be applied flexibly to all kinds and levels of jobs but is sufficiently precise to achieve management and employee acceptance and organization purposes. Although the federal government adopted the Factor Evaluation System (a point-factor method, discussed later) in 1975 as an easier way of assigning jobs to GS grades 1–15, many local governments continue to use the classification method.

Disadvantages of classification include (1) the difficulty of writing grade level descriptions and (2) the judgment required in applying them. Because the classification method considers the job as a whole, compensable factors, although used in class descriptions, are unweighted and unscored. This means that the factors have equal weight, and a little of one may be balanced by much of another. Terms that express the degree of compensable factors in jobs are depended on to distinguish one grade from another. It is quite possible that a given grade could include some jobs requiring high skill and other jobs requiring little skill but carrying heavy responsibility.

It is even possible under the federal classification system for a job to fit into one grade on one factor but a different grade on another. In fact, the system employs both the use of higher levels of a factor and additional factors in descriptions of higher grades. These features cause little trouble because of the federal career system. But private organizations would probably have trouble justifying and gaining acceptance of such results.

Classification methods customarily employ a number of compensable factors. These typically emphasize the difficulty of the work but also include performance requirements. The terms used in grade descriptions to distinguish differing amounts of compensable factors necessarily require judgment. For example, distinguishing among simple, routine, varied, and complex work and among limited, shared, and independent judgment is not automatic. While the judgment involved in such distinctions may produce the flexibility just cited as an advantage, it may also encourage managers to use inflated language in job descriptions and job titles to manipulate the classification of jobs.

Developing a job classification system requires these steps:

1. Obtain Job Information.   If it is to function properly, classification, like all other job evaluation methods, must start with job analysis. A description is developed for each job. Sometimes key jobs are analyzed first and their descriptions used in developing grade descriptions; then the other jobs are analyzed and graded.

2. Select Compensable Factors.   Job descriptions are reviewed to distill factors that distinguish jobs at different levels. This is often done by selecting key jobs at various levels of the organization, ranking them, and seeking the factors that distinguish them. Obviously, the factors must be acceptable to management and employees.

3. Determine the Number of Classes.   The number of classes selected depends upon tradition, job diversity, and the promotion policies of the organization. Organizations tend to follow similar organizations in this decision. Those favoring more classes argue that more grades mean more promotions and employees approve of this. Those favoring fewer classes argue that fewer grades permit more management flexibility and a simpler pay structure. Obviously, diversity in the work and organization size increases the need for more classes.

4. Develop Class Descriptions.   This is a matter of defining classes in sufficient detail to permit raters to readily slot jobs. Usually this is done by describing levels of compensable factors that apply to the jobs in a class. Often, titles of benchmark jobs are used as examples of jobs that fall into a grade.

Writing grade descriptions is more difficult if one set of classes is developed for the entire organization than if separate class hierarchies are developed for different occupational groups. More specific class description eases the task of slotting jobs but also limits the number of jobs that fit into a class. A committee is usually assigned the writing of class descriptions. It is often useful to write the descriptions of the two extreme grades first, then those of the others.

5. Classify Jobs. The committee charged with writing grade descriptions is often also assigned the task of classifying jobs. This involves comparing job descriptions with class descriptions. The result is a series of classes each containing a number of jobs that are similar to one another. The jobs in each class are considered to be sufficiently similar to have the same pay. Jobs in other classes are considered dissimilar enough to have different pay.

Classification systems have been used more in government organizations than in private ones. Most are designed to cover a wide range of jobs and are based on the assumption that jobs will be relatively stable in content. Although classification tends to produce more defensible and acceptable job structures than ranking, it may substitute flexibility for precision. It is easy to understand and communicate, but its results are nonquantitative.

Factor Comparison

This method, as the name implies, compares jobs on several factors and obtains a numerical value for each job as well as a job structure. Thus it may be classified as a quantitative method.

Factor comparison itself is not widely used: it probably represents less than 10 percent of the installations of job evaluation plans. But the concepts on which it is based are incorporated in numerous job evaluation plans, including the one that is probably used the most—the Hay plan.

Factor comparison involves judging which jobs contain more of certain compensable factors. Jobs are compared with each other (as in the ranking method), but on one factor at a time. The judgments permit construction of a job comparison scale of key jobs, with which other jobs may be compared. The compensable factors used are usually (1) mental requirements, (2) physical requirements, (3) skill requirements, (4) responsibility, and (5) working conditions. These are considered to be universal factors found in all jobs. This means that one job-comparison scale for all jobs in the organization may be constructed, and this practice is often followed upon installation of factor comparison. However, separate job-comparison scales can be developed for different functional groups, and other factors can be employed.

Factor-comparison concepts employed in other job evaluation plans should be noted. Job-ranking plans using two or more compensable factors and weighting them differently are essentially factor-comparison plans. The practice of assigning factor weights statistically on the basis of market rates and the ranking of jobs on the factors employs a factor-comparison concept. The use of universal factors in the Hay plan and a step called *profiling* (to be discussed later) are factor-comparison ideas. Finally, the use of job titles as examples of factor levels in other job evaluation plans is a factor-comparison concept.

ADVANTAGES.   A major advantage of factor comparison is that it requires a custom-built installation in each organization. Such a plan may result in a better fit with the organization. Another advantage, according to its developers, is that comparable results accrue whether the plan is installed by management, employee representatives, or a consultant.[5]

The type of job comparisons utilized by the method is another advantage. Since relative job values are the results sought, comparing jobs with other jobs seems logical. Limiting the number of factors may be another advantage in that this tends to reduce the possibility of overlapping and the consequent overweighting of factors.

Still another advantage would seem to be the job-comparison scale. Once employees, union representatives, and managers have been trained in the use of the scale, visual as well as numerical job comparisons are easily made. The use of a monetary unit in the basic method has the advantage of resulting in a wage structure as well as a job structure, thus eliminating the pricing step required in other plans. It is questionable, however, whether this advantage offsets the disadvantage of possible bias introduced by monetary units.

DISADVANTAGES.   One disadvantage of the method is its use of "universal" factors. Although, as mentioned, it is quite possible for an organization to develop its own compensable factors, factor comparison uses factors with common definitions for all jobs. For those who question the use of the same factors for all job families, another disadvantage is apparent.

The definition of key jobs may be another disadvantage. A major criterion of a key job in factor comparison is the essential correctness of its pay rate. Since key jobs form the basis of the job-comparison scale, the usefulness of the scale depends on the anchor points represented by these jobs. But jobs change, sometimes imperceptibly. When jobs change and when wage rates change over time, the scale must be rebuilt accordingly. Otherwise users are basing their decisions on what might be described as a warped ruler.

The use of monetary units may represent a disadvantage if, as is likely, raters are influenced by whether a job is high-paid or low-paid. An unnecessary possibility of bias would seem to be present when raters use the absolute value of jobs to determine their relative position in the hierarchy.

The complexity of factor comparison may be a serious disadvantage. Its many complicated steps make it difficult to explain and thus affect its acceptance.

THE BASIC METHOD.   Several variations in the basic method of factor comparison have appeared in response to one or more of these disadvantages. Understanding these modifications requires an understanding of the basic method. For that reason, it is discussed first.

1. Analyze Jobs.   As in other job evaluation methods, the first step is to secure job information. Sometimes only key jobs are analyzed prior to construction of the job-comparison scale. But all jobs to be evaluated are eventually subjected to job analysis.

[5]E. J. Benge, S. L. H. Burk, and E. N. Hay, *Manual of Job Evaluation* (New York: Harper & Brothers, 1941).

Job descriptions are written in terms of the five universal factors. Factor definitions such as those in exhibit 10–1 (p. 190) are used, and job descriptions are written on a form similar to table 10–1 (p. 191). Note that the factors and their definitions govern the job description. For this reason, the organization will want to determine if its jobs can be described in these terms. It will do this by analyzing some key jobs and deriving compensable factors.

2. Select Key Jobs. With job information at hand, the job evaluation committee selects 15 to 25 key jobs. This step is critical because the entire method is based upon these jobs. The major criterion for selection, as we have noted, is the essential correctness of the wage rate. However, the jobs should represent the entire range of jobs to be evaluated and be stable in content.

3. Rank Key Jobs. Next, key jobs are ranked on each of the five factors. Committee members individually rank the jobs, then meet as a committee to determine composite ranks. Table 10–2 (p. 192) illustrates the results of such rankings. Note that the jobs are called *tentative* key jobs. They remain tentative until they are eliminated in later steps or become "true" key jobs.

4. Distribute Wage Rates Across Factors. The next step is to decide for each key job how much of its wage rate should be allocated to each factor. This should be done individually and the results merged into one committee allocation (table 10–3, p. 192).

5. Compare Vertical and Horizontal Judgments. This involves cross-checking the judgments in steps 3 and 4. If a key job is assigned the same position in both comparisons, the judgments reinforce each other. If they do not, that job is not a true key job. Making this comparison may involve ranking the money distribution as well and then comparing the two ranks (table 10–4, p. 193). This table identifies jobs that are not true key jobs and that will therefore be eliminated from the scale, and indicates adjustments in the money distribution that would permit sufficient similarity in rankings to retain a job as a benchmark.

6. Construct the Job-Comparison Scale. The job comparison scale incorporates the corrected money distribution allocations to the key jobs (table 10–5, p. 194).

7. Use the Job-Comparison Scale to Evaluate the Remainder of the Jobs. This is done by comparing the job descriptions of nonkey jobs, one factor at a time, with jobs on the scale to determine the relative position. The evaluated wage for each nonkey job is the sum of the allocations to the five factors. Once evaluated, a nonkey job becomes another benchmark to use in evaluating the balance of the jobs.

VARIATIONS OF THE BASIC METHOD. We have seen that factor-comparison concepts are used in other job evaluation plans. The potential bias from the use of dollar-and-cent units, for example, has been met by multiplying monetary values by some constant, resulting in points.

Exhibit 10–1 Factor Definitions Used in Factor Comparison

MENTAL REQUIREMENTS

When we speak of mental requirements, we have in mind those activities of a job which call upon the use of the intellect; also those personal traits required by the job such as judgment, patience, ability to work with others, etc. The individual that has these job requirements brings them to the job and does not have to acquire them later.

In addition, most jobs call for a certain amount of education. A job may call for the ability to read and write and do simple addition. On a job specification, this is indicated by a certain number of years of education. It does not mean that the individual must have attended school for that length of time, as he may have taught himself without the actual formal education.

Another sub-division of the mental requirement is work knowledge. If you were to hire a person to do messenger work throughout the city, you would want someone who knew the streets and how to go between specific points. This is an example of what we mean by work knowledge. It is basic information that a person must have relative to job requirements before he would be considered for the job.

SKILL REQUIREMENTS

Skill is the experience factor and is developed by actually doing the job. A person might learn what all the duties of a job are, but merely knowing the duties does not mean that he can do them speedily and accurately until he has had the necessary experience.

One type of skill is manual skill. This is the ability to develop muscular coordination by repetitive use of the hands, feet, arms, etc., as required on a job. A person must develop skill in such simple things as lifting, shoveling; as well as in more complex operations such as using a typewriter. They all take practice to do them properly, and practice simply means that muscles are trained to do that type of work.

Generally manual skills are learned fairly rapidly—some take a few hours and others a few weeks to gain the necessary speed and accuracy to do the work properly.

Another type of skill is what is termed sensory. Certain jobs require that certain senses such as sight, hearing, taste, touch, and smell be developed above the average to do the job properly. As an example, an auto mechanic learns to diagnose motor trouble by the sound of the running motor. A crane operator, through training his sense of sight, knows how to swing out the boom to proper position in order to place or pick up material without any lost time. This type of skill is generally more difficult to learn than a manual skill.

The third type of skill may be called mental skill. It is the type of skill which is used in making decisions based on past experience. It differs from mental requirements, which as pointed out, are those mental abilities which a person brings to the job with him.

Mental skill can be seen in the decisions a supervisor makes in a given situation in order to get a certain piece of work out on time. From experience he knows how long it will normally take to do a job, given a certain number of workers, and he assigns them with this in mind. He has learned how to do these things by experience on the job; hence we term his ability "mental skill." It is very complex and is a higher type of skill than the other two.

Sub-divisions of the skill factor include necessary prior experience and time to learn and to become proficient.

PHYSICAL FACTORS

This factor refers to the demands of a job upon the human body. We will try to determine the exertion of bodily power, either in single actions or in a continued series of activities directed toward doing the job. We will consider whether the job demands standing, walking, sitting, lifting, bending, carrying, etc., and endeavor to break down total work time into the percentage spent on each type of physical effort.

The matter of comparing physical effort exerted on different jobs should not offer any great difficulty, and we will leave to committee discussions any clarifications of this factor. We might point out here that we are not trying to measure physical effort scientifically, but are endeavoring to arrange jobs in their relative positions with regard to this factor.

Exhibit 10–1 Factor Definitions Used in Factor Comparison (continued)

RESPONSIBILITIES

There are certain responsibilities in every job for which the worker is accountable and must answer for nonperformance or wrong performance of his duties. Responsibility is evaluated in terms of the cost of failure to perform the duties properly, assuming the man is properly trained. Obviously, it is also assumed that he is not crazy or angry, or a saboteur who would willfully destroy.

Job specifications will endeavor to set out responsibilities in each job. We will specify whether the job calls for responsibility for equipment and whether it is for maintenance, operation of such equipment, or other factors relative to these. Also, we will consider responsibilities for tools and materials—for purchases, sales, sorting, storing, etc. Another division of responsibility is record-keeping, and others are supervision of men, directing and instructing others, money, methods, and public contact.

WORKING CONDITIONS

Under this factor, consideration is given to those influences which tend to make the job pleasant or disagreeable. It includes such terms as place of work, whether it is indoors or outdoors, whether the job conditions are dirty, crowded, damp, hot, cold, or otherwise unpleasant.

Under working conditions also are considered the hazards of a job, and type of accidents that may be inherent in the job.

Source: Benge Associates, Management Engineers. Used by permission.

Table 10–1 Factor Comparison Job Description

Job Title:		Department:		Date:
		Requirements		
MENTAL	SKILL	PHYSICAL	RESPONSIBILITY	WORKING CONDITIONS
Years general education:	Kind:	Kind of physical effort	Equipment:	Workplace:
Special education:			Materials:	Type of work:
Work knowledge:	Desirable prior experience:	% Standing: % Walking: % Sitting:	Methods:	Surroundings:
Math used:	Time and proficiency:	Strength: Fatigue:	Records:	Conditions:
Records prepared:	Jobs which train for this:	Sex:		
Personal traits required:	This job leads to:	Eyesight requirements:	Supervisory:	Hazards:
	Other skill factors:	Other physical factors:	Other:	

Table 10–2 Average Ranks of 16 Tentative Key Jobs as Assigned by Committee

JOB	AVERAGE RANK				
	MENTAL REQUIRE- MENTS	PHYSICAL REQUIRE- MENTS	SKILL REQUIRE- MENTS	RESPONSI- BILITY	WORKING CONDITIONS
Gauger*	2	13	2	3	15
Pattern Maker†	1	12	1	1	16
Common Laborer†	16	1	16	16	1
Power Shear Opr.†	11	11	9	5	4
Plater†	10	6	6	12	9
Riveter†	12	3	12	14	8
Blacksmith*	13	2	8	13	7
Punch Press Opr.†	14	4	13	15	5
Automatic Screw Machine Opr.†	4	8	3	2	13
Casting Inspector*	3	7	4	4	10
Millwright‡	9	10	5	6	11
Tool Crib Attendant†	7	16	14	10	14
Arc Welder*	8	9	7	9	3
Electric Truck Operator†	6	15	11	8	12
Crane Operator†	5	14	10	7	6
Watchman†	15	5	15	11	2

Table 10–3 Average Distribution of Present Wages

JOB	AVERAGE CENTS PER HOUR ASSIGNED					
	MENTAL REQUIRE- MENTS	PHYSICAL REQUIRE- MENTS	SKILL REQUIRE- MENTS	RESPONSI- BILITY	WORKING CONDITIONS	PRESENT RATE
Gauger*	3.60	1.90	5.10	2.55	2.25	15.40
Pattern Maker†	4.50	1.95	5.65	3.00	1.15	16.25
Common Laborer†	0.90	3.00	1.05	0.70	2.50	8.15
Power Shear Opr.†	2.05	2.10	2.55	2.40	2.10	11.20
Plater†	2.20	2.55	2.95	1.50	1.65	10.85
Riveter†	1.95	2.80	2.05	0.52	1.65	8.97
Blacksmith*	1.65	2.95	3.40	1.35	2.40	11.75
Punch Press Opr.†	1.50	2.70	1.50	1.15	1.90	8.75
Aut. Screw Mach. Opr.†	3.10	2.40	4.90	2.85	1.20	14.45
Casting Inspector*	3.15	2.50	3.10	2.50	1.45	12.70
Millwright‡	2.40	2.25	4.50	2.35	1.35	12.85

Table 10–3 Average Distribution of Present Wages (continued)

JOB	AVERAGE CENTS PER HOUR ASSIGNED					
	MENTAL REQUIRE-MENTS	PHYSICAL REQUIRE-MENTS	SKILL REQUIRE-MENTS	RESPONSI-BILITY	WORKING CONDITIONS	PRESENT RATE
Tool Crib Attend.[†]	2.65	1.30	1.45	1.75	1.20	8.35
Arc Welder[*]	2.50	2.35	2.65	1.80	2.20	11.50
Elec. Truck Opr.[†]	2.85	1.60	2.20	1.90	1.30	9.85
Crane Operator[†]	3.00	1.80	2.50	2.25	1.80	11.35
Watchman[†]	1.00	2.65	1.15	1.60	2.25	8.65

Table 10–4 Difficulty Rank (D) versus Money Rank (M)

JOB	FACTORS									
	MENTAL REQUIREMENTS		PHYSICAL REQUIREMENTS		SKILL REQUIREMENTS		RESPONSIBILITY		WORKING CONDITIONS	
	D	M	D	M	D	M	D	M	D	M
Gauger[*]	2	2	13	13	2	2	3	3	15	4
Pattern Maker[†]	1	1	12	12	1	1	1	1	16	16
Common Laborer[†]	16	16	1	1	16	16	16	16	1	1
Power Shear Opr.[†]	11	11	11	11	9	9	5	5	4	6
Plater[†]	10	10	6	6	6	7	12	12	9	10
Riveter[†]	12	12	3	3	12	12	14	14	8	9
Blacksmith[*]	13	13	2	2	8	5	13	13	7	2
Punch Press Opr.[†]	14	14	4	4	13	13	15	15	5	7
Automatic Screw Machine Opr.[†]	4	4	8	8	3	3	2	2	13	14
Casting Inspector[*]	3	3	7	7	4	6	4	4	10	11
Millwright[‡]	9	9	10	10	5	4	6	6	11	12
Tool Crib Attendant[†]	7	7	16	16	14	14	10	10	14	15
Arc Welder[*]	8	8	9	9	7	8	9	9	3	5
Electrical Truck Operator[†]	6	6	15	15	11	11	8	8	12	13
Crane Operator[†]	5	5	14	14	10	10	7	7	6	8
Watchman[†]	15	15	5	5	15	15	11	11	2	3[§]

[*]These are *not* true key jobs.

[†]These may be accepted as key jobs.

[‡]This job has a higher rank in money on the skill factor and a lower rank in money on the working-conditions factor. This means that the job has been given too much for skill and too little for working conditions. In this case the committee may want to make an adjustment.

[§]When a tie in money rank occurs, the difficulty ranking decides which ranks first.

Table 10–5 Job-Comparison Scale

WAGE ALLOCATION, CENTS	MENTAL REQUIREMENTS	PHYSICAL REQUIREMENTS	SKILL REQUIREMENTS	RESPONSIBILITY	WORKING CONDITIONS
5.65			Pat. Mkr.		
4.90			ASM Opr.		
4.50	Pat. Mkr.		Millwright		
3.10	ASM Opr.				
3.00	Crane Opr.	Com. Labor.		Pat. Mkr.	
2.95			Plater		
2.85	El. Tr. Opr.			ASM Opr.	
2.80		Riveter			
2.70		P. Pr. Opr.			
2.65	To. Cr. Att.	Watchman			
2.55		Plater	Po. Sh. Opr.		
2.50			Crane Opr.		Com. Labor.
2.40	Millwright	ASM Opr.		Po. Sh. Opr.	
2.35				Millwright	
2.25		Millwright		Crane Op.	Watchman
2.20	Plater		El. Tr. Opr.		
2.10		Po. Sh. Opr.			Po. Sh. Opr.
2.05	Pow. Sh. Opr.		Riveter		
1.95	Riveter	Pat. Mkr.			P. Pr. Opr.
1.90				El. Tr. Opr.	Crane Opr.
1.80		Crane Opr.		To. Cr. Att.	
1.75					Riveter
1.65					Plater
1.60		El. Tr. Opr.		Watchman	
1.50	P. Pr. Opr.		P. Pr. Opr.	Plater	
1.45			To. Cr. Att.		Millwright
1.35					El. Tr. Opr.
1.30		To. Cr. Att.		Riveter	To. Cr. Att.
1.20					ASM Opr.
1.15			Watchman	P. Pr. Opr.	Pat. Mkr.
1.05			Com. Labor.		
1.00	Watchman				
.90	Com. Labor.				
.70				Com. Labor.	

The Percentage Method. This is a more fundamental modification of basic factor comparison. It meets the disadvantage of monetary units and may be used in case of doubt about the corrections of wage rates for key jobs. The percentage method employs vertical and horizontal comparisons of key jobs on factors, as does the basic method. In fact, the two methods are identical in their first three steps. At this point percentages are assigned to the vertical rankings by dividing 100 points on each factor among the key jobs in accordance with their ranks. The money distribution in the basic method becomes a horizontal ranking of the importance of factors in each job. This ranking is also translated into percentages by dividing 100 points among the factors in accordance with their ranks. Comparison of vertical and horizontal percentages involves expressing each percentage as a proportion of a common base. Then either the horizontal or the vertical percentage for each factor in each job, or an average of the two, forms the basis of the job-comparison scale. In practice, the percentages recorded in the scale are usually adjusted from a table of *equal-appearing intervals* of 15 percent. Hay, who developed the percentage method, argued that 15 percent differences are the minimum observable in job evaluation.[6] The job-comparison scale in the percentage method is a ratio scale (equal distances represent equal percentages) but is used in the same way as that in the basic method.

Profiling.   A profile is a distribution in percentage terms of the importance of factors in a job by distributing 100 percentage points in accordance with their horizontal rankings. This distribution is used like the percentage method already described.

The Use of Existing Wage Rates to Weight Factors.   This can now be considered a concept derived from basic factor comparison. The well-known Steel plan, for example, was developed by deriving factor (and degree) weights statistically by correlating job rankings by factors with existing wage rates of key jobs.[7]

The Hay Guide Chart—Profile Method.   Undoubtedly the best-known variation of the factor comparison, this plan is reportedly used by more than 4000 profit and nonprofit organizations in some 30 countries.[8] It is described by the Hay Group (a team of management consultants) as a form of factor comparison for the following reasons: it uses universal factors, bases job values on 15 percent intervals, and makes job-to-job comparisons. The plan is tailored to the organization. Profiling is used to adjust the guide charts and to check on the evaluation of jobs. The plan may be used for all types of jobs and is increasingly used for all jobs in an organization.

The universal factors in the Hay plan are know-how, problem solving, and accountability. These three factors are broken down into eight dimensions. Know-how (skill) involves (1) procedures and techniques, (2) breadth of management skills, and (3) person-to-person skills. The two dimensions of problem solving are (1) thinking environment and (2) thinking challenge. Accountability has three dimensions: (1) freedom to act, (2) impact on results, and (3) magnitude. A fourth factor, working conditions, is sometimes used for jobs whose hazards, environment, or physical demands are deemed important.

[6]E. N. Hay, "Four Methods of Establishing Factor Scales in Factor Comparison Job Evaluation," in *The AMA Handbook of Wage and Salary Administration* (New York: American Management Association, 1950), pp. 56–65.

[7]P. M. Edwards, "Statistical Methods in Job Evaluation," *Advanced Management,* December 1948, pp. 158–63.

[8]A. D. Bellak, "The Hay Guide Chart—Profile Method of Job Evaluation," in *Handbook of Wage and Salary Administration,* 2nd ed., ed. M. Rock (New York, McGraw-Hill, 1983), pp. 384–412.

The heart of the Hay plan is its guide charts (appendix 2, p. 444) use of 15 percent intervals. Although these charts appear to be two-dimension point scales, the Hay Group insists that except for the problem-solving scale they may be expanded to reflect the size and complexity of the organization. It also states that the definitions of the factors are modified as appropriate to meet the needs of the organization.

Profiling is used to develop the relationship among the three scales and to provide an additional comparison with the points assigned from the guide charts. Jobs are assumed to have characteristic shapes or profiles in terms of problem-solving and accountability requirements. Sales and production jobs, for example, emphasize accountability over problem solving. Research jobs emphasize problem solving more than accountability. Typically, staff jobs tend to equate the two.

Installation consists of (1) studying the organization and selecting and adjusting guide charts, (2) selecting a sample of benchmark jobs covering all levels and functions, (3) analyzing jobs and writing job descriptions in terms of the three universal factors, (4) selecting a job evaluation committee consisting of line and staff managers, a personnel department representative, often employees, and a Hay consultant, and (5) evaluating benchmark jobs and then all other jobs.

Point values from the three guide charts are added, yielding a single point value for each job. Profiles are then constructed and compared on problem solving and accountability as an additional evaluation.

Note that the Hay plan is independent of the market. Also an organization using the plan must rely heavily on an outside consultant for both installation and maintenance.

Point-Factor Method

The point-factor method, or point plan, involves rating each job on several compensable factors and summing the scores on each factor to obtain a point total for a job. A carefully worded rating scale is constructed for each compensable factor. This rating scale includes a definition of the factor, several divisions called *degrees* (also carefully defined), and a point score for each degree. The rating scales may be thought of as a set of rulers used to measure jobs.

Designing a point plan is complex, but once designed the plan is relatively simple to understand and use. Numerous ready-made plans developed by consultants and associations exist. Existing plans are often modified to fit the organization.

ADVANTAGES. Probably the major advantage of the point method is the stability of the rating scales. Once the scales are developed, they may be used for a considerable period. Only major changes in the organization demand a change in scales. Job changes do not require changing scales. Also, point plans increase in accuracy and consistency with use.

Because point plans are based on compensable factors adjudged to apply to the organization, acceptance of the results is likely. Factors chosen can be those that the parties deem important.

Point plans facilitate the development of job classes or grades. They also facilitate job pricing and the development of pay structures.

Carefully developed point plans facilitate job rating. Factor and degree definitions can greatly simplify the task of raters.

DISADVANTAGES.   As mentioned, developing a point plan is complex. There are no universal factors so these must be developed. Then degree statements must be devised for each of the factors chosen. All this takes time and money. Further, point plans take time to install. Each job must be rated on the scale for each factor, usually by several raters, and the results must be summarized and agreed to. Considerable clerical work is involved in recording and collating all these ratings. Much of this time and cost, however, can be reduced by using a ready-made plan.

The steps in building a point-factor plan are as follows:

1. Analyze Jobs.   As in all other job evaluation methods, this step comes first. All jobs may be analyzed at this point, or merely a sample of benchmark jobs to be used to design the plan. A job description is written for each job analyzed.

2. Select Compensable Factors.   When job information is available, compensable factors are selected. Although the yardsticks on which jobs are to be compared are important in all job evaluation methods, they are especially important in the point method. Because a number of factors are used, they must be the ones the organization is paying for on these jobs.

3. Define Compensable Factors.   Factors must be defined in sufficient detail to permit raters to use them as yardsticks to evaluate jobs. Such definitions are extremely important because the raters will be referring to them often during their evaluations.

When the factors chosen are specific to the organization, the task of defining them is less difficult. Also, it is often argued that definitions may be more precise when the plan is developed for one job family or function. There seems to be a growing tendency to define factors in more detail. See exhibit 10–2 (p. 198) for such an example.

4. Determine and Define Factor Degrees.   As we have noted, the rating scale for each factor consists of divisions called degrees. Determining these degrees would be like determining the inch marks on a ruler. It is necessary first to decide the number of divisions, then to ensure that they are equally spaced or represent known distances, and finally to see that they are carefully defined. The number of degrees depends on the actual range of the factors in the jobs. If, for example, working conditions are seen to be identical for most jobs, and if jobs that differ from the norm have very similar working conditions, then no degrees of the factors are sufficient. If, on the other hand, seven or even more degrees are discernible, that number of degrees is specified.

A major problem in determining degrees is to make each degree equidistant from the two adjacent degrees. This problem is solved in part by select-

Exhibit 10–2   A Compensable-Factor Definition

FACTOR: KNOWLEDGE

A. Formal Education: Considers the extent or degree to which specialized, technical or general education, as distinguished from working experience, is normally required as a minimum to proficiently perform the duties of the job. Credit for general education or technical and specialized training beyond high school must be carefully substantiated—that it is required and not merely preferred, and that it can be shown to be job related (what the education equips the job holder to do, not what the specific degree or course is).

B. Work Experience: Consider the minimum amount of experience normally required on the job and in related or lower jobs for an average qualified applicant to become proficient.

Statements of experience requirements for jobs involving promotions or transfers from other jobs *in the Company* should be made in terms indicating the average, typical, or ordinary periods of time *actually required* in the lower job to qualify for entrance to the job being analyzed (*not* the average length of time before promotional opportunities occur in the job being analyzed and not the time it took the present incumbent to reach the job).

Similarly, in jobs requiring experience in the same or related jobs gained *outside the Company,* both the kind and length of such previous experience should be specified.

In determining experience for a particular job, consider only the nature and extent of experience actually required for the proper understanding and performance of all elements of the job. For example, the average employee acquires a general knowledge of many procedures which are not necessary for the particular job. Care must be taken to include under experience required only the type and amount of experience *actually required* to become proficient on the job.

NOTE: When Education and Experience can be substituted one for the other, total combined years should be distributed for rating purposes on the basis of the division of the time which can be best justified (which represents the most probable "mix").

CAUTION: Although the Knowledge factor closely resembles standards used by companies in setting employment or hiring standards, it should be noted that the evaluation process is a process of comparing relative knowledge requirements between jobs and is not refined to an adequate degree to set hiring standards. In addition, hiring standards are frequently related to equal employment policies and the availability of personnel in the labor market which are not considered directly by the evaluation plan. The plan is concerned only with job values and not the placement of individuals into specific jobs.

Source: Hansen's Job Evaluation Plan for Clerical, Technical, and Production Jobs.

ing the number of degrees actually found to exist and in part by careful definition of degrees. Decision rules such as the following are useful:

1. Limit degrees to the number necessary to distinguish among the jobs.
2. Use terminology that is easy to understand.
3. Use standard job titles as part of degree definitions.
4. Make sure that the applicability of the degree to the job is apparent.

Table 10–6 is an example of degree definitions.

5. Determine Points for Factors and Degrees.   Only rarely are compensable factors assigned equal weight. It is usually determined that some factors are more important than others and should bear more weight.

Table 10–6 A Job Evaluation Degree Statement

FACTOR: KNOWLEDGE

A. Formal Education

Evaluate the requirements for formal education or its equivalent to perform the duties of the job. Training obtained on company time at company expense should be included as experience rather than formal education.

B. Work Experience

Evaluate the amount of work experience normally needed, as a minimum, for an average qualified applicant to become proficient. Note: Only *minimum* requirements for adequate or average performance are credited. When education and experience can be substituted one for the other, total combined years should be distributed between the two dimensions based on the combination best suited to the job requirements.

Degree	A	B	C	D	E	F	G	H	I	J
	0	1/4	1/2	1	2	3	4–5	6–7	8–10	10
1	0	3	6	10	15	20	25	31	40	50
2	4	7	10	14	19	24	29	35	44	54

(Experience, years)

- Degree 1: Elementary reading, writing, and arithmetic skills; knowledge equivalent to completing a general high school curriculum or a substantial portion thereof.
- Degree 2: Basic reading, writing, and arithmetic skills, supplemented by a basic knowledge of specific techniques; knowledge equivalent to completing a high school curriculum including courses in specific subject areas such as bookkeeping, equipment operation, basic vocational skills.

Table 10-6 A Job Evaluation Degree Statement (continued)

FACTOR: KNOWLEDGE

A. Formal Education

B. Work Experience

Degree		A	B	C	D	Experience, years E	F	G	H	I	J
		0	¼	½	1	2	3	4–5	6–7	8–10	10
• Basic reading, writing, and arithmetic skills, supplemented by a command of specific techniques or subject areas; knowledge equivalent to completing high school post-graduate or vocational school program typically lasting 3 months to 6 months.	3	12	15	18	22	27	32	37	43	52	62
• Basic reading, writing, and arithmetic skills, supplemented by a command of specific techniques or subject areas; knowledge equivalent to completing high school post-graduate or vocational school program typically lasting 6 months to 1 year.	4	20	23	26	30	35	40	45	51	60	70
• Broad educational background including well-developed verbal, written, and mathematical skills, equivalent to a 2 year Associate's degree or formal high school post-graduate curriculum requiring 2 to 3 years.	5	28	31	34	38	43	48	53	59	68	78
• Broad educational background including advanced verbal, written, and mathematical skills, equivalent to a Bachelor of Arts degree in a non-technical field.	6	40	43	46	50	55	60	65	71	80	90
• Extensive knowledge in a highly technical field, equivalent to a Bachelor of Science degree in Science or Engineering discipline or an M.A. in a non-technical field.	7	52	55	58	62	67	72	77	83	92	102
• Advanced knowledge in a technical field equivalent to a Master of Science degree, Law degree or MBA.	8	68	71	74	78	83	88	93	99	109	120

Source: Hansen's Job Evaluation Plan for Clerical, Technical, and Production Jobs.

Factor weights may be assigned by committee judgment or statistically. In the *committee approach,* the procedure is to have committee members (1) carefully study factor and degree definitions, (2) individually rank the factors in order of importance, (3) agree on a ranking, (4) individually distribute 100 percent among the factors, and (5) once more reach agreement. The result is a set of factor weights representing committee judgment. The weights thereby reflect the judgments of organization members and may contribute to acceptance of the plan.

The committee may then complete the scale by assigning points to factors and degrees. Next a decision is usually made on the total points possible in the plan—say 1000. Applying the weights just assigned to this total yields the maximum value for each factor. For example, a factor carrying 30 percent of the weight has a maximum value of 300 points. Thus the highest degree of this factor carries 300 points. Assigning points to the other degrees may be done by either arithmetic or geometric progression. In the former, increases are in equal numbers of points from the lowest to the highest degree. In the latter, increases are in equal percentage of points. Arithmetic progression is found in most point plans, especially those designed for one job family rather than the entire organization. But just as different factors usually have different numbers of degrees, some factors may employ geometric progression.

Because it is usually assumed that all jobs include some of a factor, the lowest degree is usually assigned some points. A simple way of assigning points to degrees is as follows:

1. Set the highest degree of a factor by multiplying the weight of the factor by the total possible points.
2. Set the minimum degree of the factor using the arithmetic or percentage increase figure.
3. Subtract these two figures.
4. Divide the result by the number of steps (numbers of degrees minus one).
5. Add this figure successively to the lowest degree.

The result of this procedure is an arithmetic progression. Using logarithms and following the same calculations produces a geometric progression.

In the *statistical approach* to weighting factors, benchmark jobs are evaluated and the points assigned are correlated with an agreed-upon set of wage rates. Regressing this structure of pay rates on the factor degrees assigned each job yields weights that will produce scores closely matching the agreed-upon wage rates. Factor weights were developed statistically in the Steel plan, which we mentioned in our discussion of factor comparison. The same approach is used to develop weights for factors derived from quantitative job analysis. The statistical approach is often called the *policy-capturing approach.*

Whether developed by committee decision or by the statistical method, the rating scales are often tested by evaluating a group of benchmark jobs. If the results are not satisfactory, several adjustments are possible. Benchmark jobs may be added or deleted. Degrees assigned to jobs may be adjusted. The criterion—the pay structure—may be changed. Or the weights assigned to factors may be changed. In any of these ways, the job evaluation plan is customized to the jobs and the organization.

6. Write a Job Evaluation Manual. A job evaluation manual conveniently consolidates the factor and degree definitions and the point values—the yardsticks to be used by raters in evaluating jobs. It should also include a review procedure for cases where employees or managers question evaluations of certain jobs. Usually the compensation specialist conducts such reevaluations, but sometimes the assistance of the compensation committee is called for.

7. Rate the Jobs. When the manual is complete, job rating can begin. Raters use the scales to evaluate jobs. Key jobs have usually been rated previously in the development of the plan. The others are rated at this point.

In smaller organizations, job rating may be done by a compensation specialist. In larger firms committee ratings developed from independent ratings of individual members are usual. As jobs are rated, the rating on each factor is recorded on a substantiating data sheet (see exhibit 10–3). This becomes a permanent record of the points assigned to each factor and the reasons for assigning a particular degree of the factor to the job. Substantiating data come from the job description.

Offshoots and Other Plans

The four basic methods of job evaluation have evolved into almost innumerable job evaluation plans. The similarity among these numerous plans has been noted. But even though plans may have similar factors, the factor weights may differ (see tables 10–7 and 10–8). The National Electrical Manufacturers Association (NEMA) plan has been widely adopted with varying degrees of modification. The National Position Evaluation Plan, which evolved from the original NEMA plan, is another commonly used plan. It was developed by NMTA Associates, a group of 11 consulting associations. The plan uses common factors but four separate manuals, which can be used to evaluate all the jobs in an organization. The manual for Unit I is used to evaluate manufacturing, warehousing, service, distribution, and maintenance jobs. Unit II was designed for nonexempt, clerical, technical, and administrative jobs. Unit III is used to evaluate exempt professional, technical, administrative, sales, and supervisory jobs. Unit IV is designed for executive jobs.

In addition, many consultants have modfied the original NEMA plans for plant and office jobs. The popularity of the point method is probably due in large part to the availability of such ready-made plans.

As mentioned in the section on determining compensable factors, job evaluation plans vary in the number of factors they employ. Nine to 11 factors are not unusual, but single-factor plans also exist. Jaques' Time Span of Discretion (the time before submarginal performance becomes evident) may be considered a single-factor plan, although Jaques insists that it represents measurement.[9] Charles's single-factor plan is based on problem solving.[10] Patterson's decision-band method is another single-factor plan.[11]

[9]E. Jaques, *Equitable Payment* (New York: John Wiley, 1961).
[10]A. W. Charles, "Installing Single-Factor Job Evaluation," *Compensation Review*, first quarter 1971, pp. 9–21.
[11]T. T. Patterson, *Job Evaluation: A New Method* (London: Camelot Press, 1972).

Exhibit 10–3 Substantiating Data Sheet

OFFICE JOBS
_____

Job Title: Code No. _____
Education   Degree   Points

_____

Job Knowledge
_____

Supervision Exercised
_____

Trust Imposed
_____

Errors
_____

Nature of Work
_____

Contacts with Others
_____

Physical-Mental Strain
_____

Date Rated _____ Date Re-rated _____ Total Points _____
_____

Table 10–7 Factors and Weights for Hourly Point Plans

FACTORS	NEMA–NMTA	APPLIANCE MFGR.	STEEL PLAN	AIRCRAFT MFGR.	ELECTRIC UTILITY
Skill					
Education	14		2.4		8
Experience	22			23.8	
Initiative	14				
Training			9.3	23.8	21
Knowledge		32			
Manual Dexterity			4.7		10
Judgment		10			
Mental Skill			8.1		
Mentality				12.0	13
Total	50	42	24.5	59.6	52

Table 10–7 Factors and Weights for Hourly Point Plans (continued)

FACTORS	NEMA–NMTA	APPLIANCE MFGR.	STEEL PLAN	AIRCRAFT MFGR.	ELECTRIC UTILITY
Effort					
Physical	10	15	5.8	7.0	10
Mental and/or Visual	5	5	5.8	6.0	5
Total	15	20	11.6	13.0	15
Responsibility					
General			15.1		
Equipment or Processes	5	5	9.3	12.0	5
Material or Product	5	5	23.3		5
Safety of Others	5	5	4.7		5
Work of Others	5	5			3
Total	20	20	52.4	12.0	18
Job Conditions					
Working Conditions	10	6.8	7.7	10	
Unavoidable Hazards	5	8	4.7	7.7	5
Total	15	18	11.5	15.4	15
Grand Total	**100**	**100**	**100.0**	**100.0**	**100**

Table 10–8 Factors and Weights for Salaried Point Plans

FACTORS	NEMA	EMPLOYER'S ASSN.	CONSULTANT	TRADE ASSN.	APPLIANCE MFGR.
Education	17.5	10.6	15.0	12.3	
Experience	29.0	16.0	9.0	19.0	10.1
Training			9.0		10.1
Complexity	14.5	10.6		12.3	
Mental Skill			27.0	3.3	48.2
Responsibility for:					
Function		10.6	22.0		
Procedures		6.3			
Confidential Data		4.2		3.3	
Assets		8.0			
Errors				11.0	11.6
Monetary Responsibility	8.8				
Contacts	8.8	8.0	7.0	11.0	10.8
Working Conditions	3.8	3.7	5.0	3.3	9.2
Hazards		7.0			
Types of Supervision	8.8	7.5	3.0	11.0	
Extent of Supervision	8.8	7.5	3.0	13.5	
Total	**100.0**	**100.0**	**100.0**	**100.0**	**100.0**

It is still usual for organizations to have more than one job evaluation plan. The plan may have quite different factors or merely different definitions for the same factors. In the former case, factors such as responsibility and decision making are used for executive jobs, physical demands and skills for manual jobs, and accuracy and amount of supervision for clerical and technical jobs. The rationale for different plans for different job families is that the organizations pay for different things in different job families.

A number of plans are designed to evaluate all the jobs in an organization. Elizur's Scaling Method of Job Evaluation is one such method.[12] It reportedly has the additional advantage of meeting the requirements of a Guttman scale. The Factor Evaluation System (FES) developed for federal pay grades 1–15 can also be considered a total organizational plan.[13] Such plans can be expected to become increasingly popular, in view of the conclusion of a National Science Foundation study that they permit the job comparisons needed to eliminate pay discrimination.[14]

An apparently increasingly popular job evaluation technique is to use a standardized job analysis questionnaire. For example, the Position Analysis Questionnaire (PAQ)[15] discussed in the previous chapter, has been used in numerous organizations by policy capturing the job dimensions by regressing them against wage rates for jobs. Although only nine of the PAQ elements are typically used for job evaluation, they are very similar to those found in traditional plans. Nationwide Insurance developed a job-content questionnaire and used it in this way.[16] Pact, Inc., of Glendale, California, has developed a comprehensive questionnaire called EvaluRate. The Management Position Description Questionnaire (MPDQ) has been used as a job evaluation plan in a number of organizations. Interestingly, however, Gomez-Mejia, Page, and Tornow found with 657 positions that traditional job evaluation systems were at least as valid and more accepted by supervisors and job incumbents.[17]

The expanding use of computers has undoubtedly encouraged such plans. One consultant (Newpher and Company of Oakbrook, Illinois) offers a standardized job analysis questionnaire with 100 variables and a choice of four job evaluation plans derived from the data base provided.

Some job evaluation plans actually rely almost entirely on labor-market information. The guideline method of job evaluation, for example, collects market-pay information on a large proportion of the organization's jobs and compares the "market rate" with a schedule of pay grades constructed on 5 percent intervals. The schedules include midpoints and ranges of 30 to 60

[12]D. Elizur, "The Scaling Method of Job Evaluation," *Compensation Review*, third quarter 1978, pp. 34–41.

[13]———, *Instructions for The Factor Evaluation System* (Washington, DC: United States Civil Service Commission, 1977).

[14]Cited in Treiman and Hartmann, eds., *Women, Work, and Wages*.

[15]E. J. McCormick, *Job Analysis* (New York: AMACOM, 1979).

[16]D. M. Van DeVoort, J. J. McHenry, and N. Elisabeth Fried, "A Policy-Capturing Approach to the Valuing of Managerial Jobs" (paper presented at the Academy of Management National Meeting, Dallas, 1983).

[17]L. R. Gomez-Mejia, R. C. Page, and W. Tornow, "A Comparison of the Practical Utility of Traditional, Statistical, and Hybrid Job Evaluation Approaches," *Academy of Management Journal*, December 1982, pp. 790–809.

percent. Job evaluation consists of matching market rates to the closest mid-point. Adjustments of one or two grades may be made to accommodate internal relationships. Key jobs are placed into grades and the remaining jobs positioned by comparison with them.[18] Evalucomp, used by the Executive Compensation Service, is similar.[19] So is Project 777.[20]

Kenneth Foster of Towers, Perrin, Forster, and Crosby has developed a job evaluation plan for executive positions based on factors that can be measured in organizations rather than subjectively evaluated. For example, his accountability, decision-impact, and job-complexity factors are based on factual evidence validated by regression analysis. Foster reports that his plan explains almost all of the variance in executive pay.[21]

ACCEPTANCE, RELIABILITY, AND VALIDITY OF RESULTS

In this chapter we have frequently mentioned the importance of acceptance of job evaluation results by employees and managers. One way of testing acceptance is a formal appeals process whereby anyone questioning the evaluation of his or her job may request a reanalysis and reevaluation. Organizations would be wise to include such a process in their job evaluation system. A second method would be to include questions about job evaluation in employee-attitude surveys.

Although evaluating jobs involves a good deal of judgment, few organizations have determined whether different evaluators produce similar results. Not much research has been conducted on the reliability of job evaluation. Early research found that job rating could be improved by a reduction in overlap among factors, good job descriptions, and rater training. Higher reliabilities result when scale levels, including the use of benchmark jobs, are carefully defined. Familiarity with the jobs also seems to increase reliability.[22] A recent study using a common point system confirmed the importance of training raters but found that consensus rating by groups produced reliabilities as high as those of independent ratings in other studies. This study also found that noninteracting groups produced very similar ratings and that access to information besides job descriptions improved the consistency of the ratings.[23] These findings suggest that consistent ratings of jobs are much less susceptible to administrative conditions than was previously thought.

---

[18]A. M. Pasquale, *A New Dimension to Job Evaluation*, AMA Management Bulletin 128 (New York: American Management Association, 1969).

[19]See Appendix 1 for the address of the AMA's Executive Compensation Service.

[20]Project 777 is performed by Management Compensation Services, Inc., Scottsdale, Arizona. (See Appendix 1, p. 443).

[21]K. E. Foster, "Measuring Overlooked Factors in Relative Job Worth and Pay," *Compensation Review*, first quarter 1983, pp. 44–55.

[22]R. C. Smyth, "Job Evaluation Failures" (address to the National Meeting of American Compensation Association, Scottsdale, Az. 1965).

[23]D. P. Schwab and H. G. Heneman, III, "Assessment of a Consensus Based Multiple Information Source Job Evaluation System" (working paper, University of Wisconsin, 1984).

The question of which method is the most valid (yields the best results) depends on the circumstances. Ranking methods yield results in less time and at less cost, but work-relatedness may be difficult to defend and inconsistencies among organizational units are quite possible. Factor comparison involves high cost, complexity, and explanation difficulties. The point and classification methods seem more acceptable to managers and employers.

The question of whether the different methods yield similar results has not been finally answered. Studies suggest that different methods yield similar job hierarchies,[24] but a review by Schwab found substantial differences.[25]

COSTS

Job evaluation involves costs of design and administration and the increased labor costs of installation. Labor-cost effects vary for each installation. Design and administrative costs also vary with the type of plan, the time spent by organization members, and with consulting fees (if any). Setting up a program has been estimated at 0.5 percent of payroll, and administering it, 0.1 percent per year.

DISCRIMINATION ISSUES

Although jobs and logically job evaluations are both color-blind and sexless, job evaluation has been cited as both a potential source of and a solution to discrimination against women and minorities. Discrimination may result from multiple job evaluation plans in the organization, from the choice or weighting of factors, and from stereotypes attached to jobs.

While more research is needed, the evidence so far does not establish the existence of discrimination in job analysis and job evaluation. A 1977 study found no evidence of sex discrimination in the use of the PAQ.[26] A study at San Diego State University replicating the 1977 study but using other methods of job analysis found no sex bias either.[27] Other studies, however, have found influence from sex stereotyping and sex composition of jobs.[28]

[24]R. Richardson, *Fair Pay and Work* (Carbondale and Edwardsville: Southern Illinois University Press, 1971); and L. R. Gomez-Mejia, R. C. Page, and W. W. Tornow, "Development and Implementation of a Computerized Job Evaluation System," *Personnel Administrator,* February 1979, pp. 46–52.

[25]D. P. Schwab, "Job Evaluation and Pay Setting: Concepts and Practices," in *Comparable Worth,* ed. E. R. Livernash (Washington, D.C.: Equal Employment Advisory Council, 1980), p. 49–78.

[26]R. D. Arvey, E. M. Passino, and J. W. Lounsbury, "Job Analysis Results as Influenced by Sex of Incumbent and Sex of Analyst," *Journal of Applied Psychology,* 62, no. 4, (1977), 411–16.

[27]M. E. Marcus, "Discrimination by Sex in Job Analysis and Job Description" (Master's Thesis, San Diego State University, 1981).

[28]T. A. Mahoney and R. H. Blake, "Occupational Pay as a Function of Sex Stereotypes and Job Content" (paper presented at the annual meeting of the National Academy of Management, Atlanta, 1979); and R. Grams and D. P. Schwab, "A Female Experimental Investigation of Evaluation Biases that May Influence Job Salaries" (working paper, University of Minnesota, 1982).
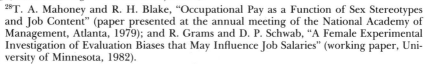

The National Science Foundation study cited previously maintains that job evaluation may be a solution to problems of pay discrimination.[29] But it suggests that single rather than multiple plans would help and that factors should represent all jobs and be defined without bias. It also suggests some ways of weighting factors to remove potential sex bias. These views will be discussed in more detail in chapter 20.

SUMMARY

Job evaluation is the process by which the organization develops a job structure, the first step in arriving at a wage structure. The job structure is the hierarchy of jobs within the organization ordered according to their value and importance to the organization. Job evaluation involves comparing jobs to each other, or to a standard and ranking, or by rating them by this standard of organizational importance.

The first decision to be made in developing a job evaluation plan is to decide on the factors which account for the importance of jobs to the organization, called compensable factors. Second, a decision must be made as to what jobs will be placed into the job evaluation plan—all jobs in the organization or some sub-set of jobs. Third, a decision needs to be made as to the type of job evaluation plan that will provide the organization with the best results. Here the organization has a number of choices which have been reviewed in this chapter.

Job evaluation plans are categorized as being either non-quantitative or quantitative. Non-quantitative plans, ranking or classification, rate the job as a whole, clearly rely on the judgments of the evaluator and are generally simpler and more flexible. These non-quantitative plans are used mainly in small organizations and governmental units. Quantitative plans, factor comparison and point factor, evaluate the job by the use of factors. These are more difficult to set up, provide a basis for determining their accuracy, and are more popular in industry.

Job evaluation has a basic dilemma. On one hand, it is a technical function which requires training and expertise to perform. On the other hand, the usefulness of job evaluation depends on the acceptance by management and employees of the job structure that results from the process. The best way to obtain acceptance is to allow managers and employees a role in the decision-making that creates the job structure. Too often, job evaluation is seen by managers and employees as some mysterious, incomprehensible process which has a considerable impact on their wages.

[29]Treiman and Hartmann, eds., *Women, Work, and Wages.*

11

Designing Wage Structures

Wage level decisions (chapter 5) are concerned with the labor costs of all jobs in the organization or all jobs in a cluster or family. In the last chapter we explained how job structures are developed through the use of job evaluation. Wage and salary structures are concerned with the rates for specific jobs and the relationships among these rates, and they represent a combination of the wage level and job structure decisions. Obviously wage levels, job structures, and wage structures are related, but because wage structure decisions involve determining pay rates for specific jobs, they involve considerations beyond those of wage level and job structure decisions. In this chapter we discuss the development and administration of wage structures.

DEVELOPING A WAGE STRUCTURE

Wage structures result from pricing job structures. Job structures, in turn, result from the application of formal or informal job evaluation to an organization's jobs (see chapter 10). In order to price a job structure it is necessary to use dollar amounts from either current pay rates or the market data collected from wage surveys (see chapter 6). A wage structure, then, is a combination of the job structure, the labor market, and the organization's decisions regarding the wage level.

The pricing of job structures is subject to the influences discussed in chapter 8 plus some technical ones. For example, the manner in which job relationships were determined may influence job pricing. If a formal job evaluation plan was employed, the type of plan has an effect. The extent of union involvement in a formal job evaluation program may also influence job pricing. If informal job evaluation was used to determine the job structure, the pricing process may be influenced by whether the informally derived job structure makes use of pay grades or separate jobs. Both unions and management tend to favor simplification of pay structures, however, and this agreement reduces the variation in pricing procedures.

The present wage and salary rates in an organization will clearly influence any changes made in its current wage structure. The current rates represent a series of decisions about all aspects of the program, including past market rates, organizational differentials, and customary differences that have survived.

Most often, however, the job structure is priced out through the use of market rates. This means the employment of wage surveys (chapter 6). Wage survey results are often employed as an important, but not the only, consideration in pricing job structures. One reason for this is that surveys usually secure data on a limited number of key jobs that vary in importance and cost significance from one organization to another. A second reason is that evaluated rates may easily be above market rates for certain jobs. Hence, market rates are only one consideration in job pricing. As will be seen, however, if market rates are higher than evaluated rates, market rates are often followed.

The cost consequences of jobs often influence job pricing just as much as market rates do. In most organizations there is a fairly well defined group of jobs that represents an important segment of the total labor costs of the company.[1] It is important to note that although some organizations are more restricted by labor cost considerations than others, prices assigned this group of jobs may greatly affect an organization's competitive position. Rates assigned these jobs during job-structure pricing largely determine the wage level of the firm, and wage structure relationships are built around this cost center.

Pricing a Job Structure

The job structure presents the compensation decision maker with a hierarchy of the jobs in the organization. Ordinarily, this hierarchy has been developed by the use of job evaluation and represents the organization's relative rating of its jobs. A dollar value now needs to be placed on this hierarchy. This dollar value is available in the current wage rates paid for the jobs and in the wage survey data representing the labor market. These two sets of data are combined into a matrix that is used to create a scatter diagram (see figure 11–1). The dollar values occupy the vertical axis and the organizational rankings the horizontal axis. Thus, pricing a job structure involves a series of techniques and decisions regarding the vertical, horizontal, and regression-line dimensions of the scatter diagram.

---

[1]E. R. Livernash, "The Internal Wage Structure," in *New Concepts in Wage Determination*, ed. G. W. Taylor and F. C. Pierson (New York: McGraw-Hill, 1957), pp. 140–72.

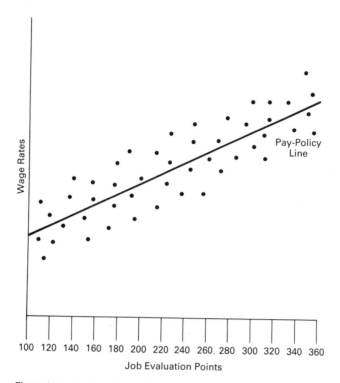

Figure 11–1   Scatter diagram for a wage structure

THE VERTICAL DIMENSION.   The vertical axis of the scatter diagram is simply a set of dollar figures from low to high. It is not the dollar figures themselves that are important but the dollar amount attached to the job so that a point in the scatter diagram can be recorded. This amount may come from either (1) the current pay rate or range for the job within the organization or (2) the value placed upon the job in the market survey.

When current pay rates are used, an initial concern is the exact pay rate to assign to each job. If there is a single job incumbent and/or a single pay rate for the job, then the particular dollar amount paid the job incumbent could be used, although this person could be paid high in the pay range. But if there is a pay range and a number of incumbents, then the exact figure to use must be determined. If the average pay of the incumbents is used, the pay for the job may be overstated or understated depending on how long the incumbents have been on the job or what their performance has been. The alternative is to use the midpoint of the pay range. This gives a good indication of the relative value of the job and not the incumbents.

Another concern is whether to use the current pay or to adjust current pay to changes that have occurred since that rate was established. All pay rates can be adjusted by multiplying them by a constant percentage reflecting changes in the labor market, cost of living, productivity, or whatever other standard the organization decides to adopt.

When wage survey data are used, the figures need to be adjusted in a number of ways. First, the wage data do not provide a single rate but a range of figures. Therefore the best single figure to use, such as the mean or median, needs to be determined. This set of decisions was dealt with in chapter 6.

Second, any data collected in the wage survey predate the effective date of the wage structure presently being built. Thus, the data need to be updated to the effective date of the new wage structure. This is usually done by multiplying the figures from the wage survey by some constant percentage based upon estimated changes in wage data during the interim or upon changes in a figure such as the cost of living.

Third, the organization's strategy toward the labor market requires a wage level decision, since the new wage structure is going to be in operation over time. This decision involves determining how competitive the organization wishes to be while the wage structure remains in effect. There are three basic strategies: lag the market, lead-lag, and lead the market.

Lag the Market. In this strategy the organization updates the wage survey data to the current date and then installs the new wage structure. If a change in the labor market of 10 percent is assumed for the next year, then the only time the organization will be competitive with the market is at the beginning of the year. By the end of the year any decisions based upon the wage structure will be 10 percent behind the market.

Lead-lag. Here the organization takes account of the 10 percent estimated change in the market but wishes to be on average with the market. It does this by starting the year at 5 percent above the market rate. Provided the increase is steady over the year, this strategy will place the organization ahead of the market the first half of the year and behind it the second half.

Lead the Market. In this strategy the organization wishes to pay above the market rate and does so by starting the year at 10 percent above the wage survey data. By the end of the year the organization will be paying the market rate.

These three strategies are illustrated in figure 11–2.

THE HORIZONTAL DIMENSION. The horizontal axis is the hierarchical ranking of all the organization's jobs. The pricing process may work with either individual jobs or pay grades. In fact, if the organization is to employ rate ranges with differential pay rates for individuals on the same job, it may save time by making decisions on the pay-policy line, pay grades, and rate ranges at the same time. (Discussion of pay grades and rate ranges will start later in this chapter and continue in chapter 12.) This is especially true if pricing makes use of both present rates and wage survey results, because the latter always represent a sizable range.

The major question involving the horizontal dimension is how the hierarchy of jobs was arrived at. There are three possibilities: market rates, job evaluation rates, and negotiated rates.

Market Rates. The organization may assume that it wishes to pay strictly market rates for its jobs and may therefore place dollar values on both

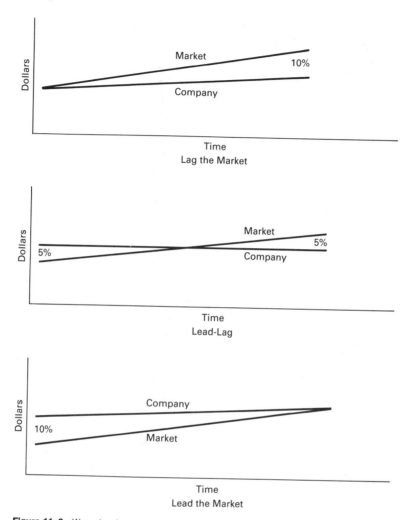

Figure 11–2   Wage level strategies for adjusting wage structures

axes, making a totally consistent structure. Clearly this alternative assumes that there is a market rate for all of the organization's jobs and that this rate is satisfactory, given all the other factors discussed so far in this chapter.

Job Evaluation Rates.   The most common alternative for the horizontal axis is the set of ratings developed through job evaluation. Depending upon the method of job evaluation used, these ratings may consist of a ranking of jobs from low to high, a series of classification levels, or a range of points.

Negotiated Rates.   Where there is a union, the hierarchy of jobs may be a negotiated ranking based upon custom or the relative power of a group of unions.

DEVELOPING THE PAY-POLICY LINE. Once the horizontal and vertical dimensions of the scatter diagram have been settled upon, all the jobs or the key jobs can be plotted by their value on both axes. Figure 11–1 uses the current wage rates of jobs and the average of each pay grade as the plotting points. To create a smooth progression between pay grades, a *pay-policy line* is fitted to the plotted points. The line may be straight or curved and may be fitted by a number of different methods. When plotting job structures of single job clusters, a straight line is usually employed. The most frequently used types of lines are the low–high line, the freehand line, and the least-squares line.

Low–High Line. This is a straight line connecting the highest and the lowest of the plotted points (these are often called *anchor points*). The rates of all intervening jobs are made to fall on the line. The low–high line appears especially useful in union bargaining of the wage structure because of its flexibility. When a final bargain is reached, it may be implemented by raising either end or both ends in such a way as to reflect the contract. Figure 11–3 is an example of a low–high line.

Freehand Line. After the points have been plotted the trend of the data can often be easily visualized. In this case it is possible to draw a freehand line that best describes the plotted points. In drawing such a line, it is useful to follow the principle that vertical deviations from the line are minimized if the line follows the obvious slope of the data. Although the line may be straight or curved, its advantages are greatest when it is straight. The obvious advantages of using a freehand line are that it is easy to plot and simple to explain. Figure 11–4 is an example of a freehand line.

Least-squares Line. The least-squares line follows the principles specified for the freehand line but is determined mathematically. It may be fitted by calculating the equation for the line and plotting the line obtained from the

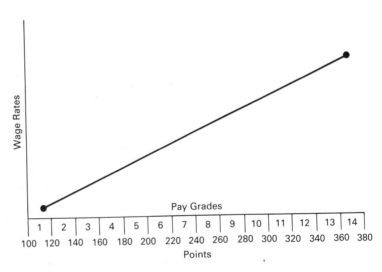

Figure 11–3 High-low pay policy line

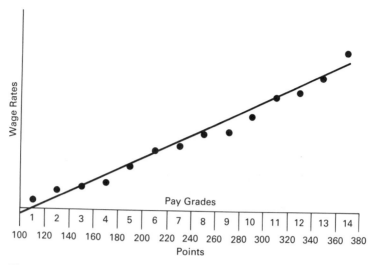

Figure 11–4 Freehand pay policy line

solution. Any standard statistics textbook provides instructions for computing a least-squares line.[2]

Experience suggests that the additional accuracy of the least-squares line, compared with that of a freehand line, is seldom sufficient to offset the added difficulty of explaining the method involved to the statistically unsophisticated. It may be useful to test wage lines developed by simpler methods against a least-squares line. Professionals or other statistically sophisticated groups, however, may prefer a wage line calculated by least squares.

In most cases, a low–high (anchor-point) line or a freehand line achieves all the accuracy inherent in job evaluation results. Furthermore, both permit adjustment to achieve agreement of committee members or union and management on wage determinations.

In using wage survey results instead of present rates in determining the wage line it is useful to employ a chart such the one in figure 11–5 (p. 216), in which survey results have been presented as quartiles representing the pay grades of the organization. When compared with present rates, such data enable the parties involved to make decisions on the wage structure. The medians (midpoints) or averages of survey results may, of course, be used in place of present wage rates in determining the wage line. But the inevitability of a range of rates (a minimum of 50 percent) raises questions about the usefulness of any single figure. Recognition of this may account for the practice of establishing rate ranges at the same time as standard rates for pay grades when wage survey results are used to price job structures. The starting rate of a pay grade must be sufficient to attract employees to those jobs, and wage survey results provide evidence of what that rate must be.

If the organization already has a series of pay grades in place, jobs may be slotted into the appropriate pay grade on the basis of the market rates that

[2]The equation for a straight line is $Y = a + bx$, where a is a point where the line crosses the Y axis and b is the slope of the line.

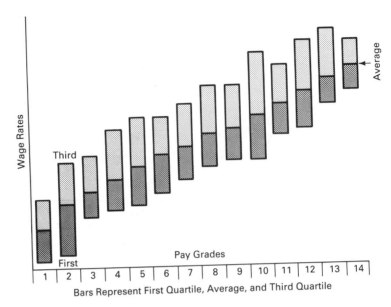

Figure 11–5 Graph of wage survey results

have been determined in the wage survey. This system can be called a *rank-to-market* job evaluation.[3] It is similar to the classification method of job evaluation but does not incorporate the rules or grade-level descriptions of the latter.

Wage Structure or Structures?

So far in this section we have spoken only of a single wage structure. Actually, of course, an organization may have several wage structures—one for each broad job cluster, for instance. The choice may depend on whether job evaluation is formal or informal and, if the former, on which type of method is used. We saw in chapter 10 that the ranking, classification, and factor-comparison methods can, if desired, derive one job structure for the organization. Even these plans, however, are often applied to distinct job clusters. The point method is more likely than any of the other three to be designed for a single job cluster.

Organizations having more than one wage structure most commonly have separate structures for exempt and nonexempt groups of jobs. Exempts are often divided into professional and managerial groups, and nonexempts into production workers and office staff. There seem to be two reasons for these breakdowns. One, it may be difficult to compare these different types of jobs, in which case the horizontal axis of the scatter diagram is not useful. Second, and more important, the slope of the pay-policy line for these groups may be very different. At opposite extremes would be the blue-collar workers, with a very flat slope, and the managerial group, with a very steep slope. Further, the pay-policy lines will start and stop at different places, so that there will be little overlap between them.

[3]J. Schuster, *Management Compensation in High Technology Companies* (Lexington, Mass.: Heath, Lexington Books, 1984).

One problem can occur in constructing these separate structures—discrimination. If one or two of the groups contain all or many of the female- or minority-dominated jobs, then the division may appear discriminatory. All job clusters that constitute a wage structure need to be examined for their sex and minority composition. If minorities and women are segregated, then the composition of jobs in all groups will have to be balanced by race and sex.

Completing the Wage Structure

Theoretically, at this point the wage structure consists of a horizontal dimension and a vertical dimension with a pay-policy line derived from the plotting of jobs on them. Every job in the organization could be plotted on the pay-policy line to determine its pay rate. For the sake of convenience and practicality most wage structures group data on both the horizontal and vertical dimensions. On the horizontal dimension, jobs are grouped into pay grades; on the vertical dimension, money is grouped into rate ranges.

PAY GRADES. If job structures of individual jobs are developed, as is done through job evaluation, it is possible to assign a dollar value to each job. As pointed out, however, simplified wage and salary structures are being encouraged by both management and unions. One of the results of this trend is a tendency to group jobs that are close together in the hierarchy into *grades* for pay purposes. This way, in large organizations at least, much time and effort are saved. Dealing with ten pay grades rather than hundreds of job rates, for example, is convenient for both unions and management. Where job rates are used, even small changes in duties may require changes in pay rates.

A pay grade is defined as a group of jobs that have been determined by job evaluation to be approximately equal in difficulty or importance. If a point plan is employed in job evaluation, a pay grade consists of jobs falling within a range of points; if factor comparison is used, a range of evaluated rates; if ranking is used, a number of ranks. In the classification method of job evaluation, a pay grade consists of all jobs that are comparable to the level description.

There appears to be no optimum number of pay grades for a particular wage structure. In practice, pay grades vary from as few as 4 to as many as 60. If there are few grades, the number of jobs in each will be relatively large, as will the increments from one grade to another. If, on the other hand, there are many pay grades, the number of jobs in each grade and the increments between grades will be relatively small.

Although organization practice varies greatly, there has been a tendency to reduce the number of pay grades. Ten to 16 grades for a given job structure appears to be common. Ten grades for nonsupervisory factory jobs is typical, as is 13 for clerical job structures.[4] Broader wage structures, of course, contain more grades. For example, salary plans that encompass clerical, professional, and administrative employees average 16 grades. Pay distance between grades is commonly 5 to 7 percent for hourly and clerical jobs and 8 to 10 percent for professional and administrative jobs.

[4]R. M. Story, "Trends in Wage Administration," *Business Studies* (Denton, Tex.: North Texas State University), Fall 1967, p. 114.

The actual establishment of pay grades is a decision-making process designed to (1) place jobs of the same general value in the same pay grade, (2) ensure that jobs of significantly different value are in different pay grades, (3) provide a smooth progression, and (4) ensure that the grades fit the organization and the labor market. Examination of job evaluation results may yield natural cutoff points.

Before determination of pay grades, it may be wise to determine both how many jobs and how many employees are affected by the number of grades and the division chosen. This can be done by plotting each employee on the wage structure matrix and noting whether there is a spread of employees over the matrix. Since large numbers of employees may be affected by small changes in pay grades, great care and fairness must be used in determining pay grades. Grievances can be avoided by seeing that pay grades with large numbers of employees are not placed in a grade that greatly changes their pay rate.

Because jobs in a pay grade are treated as identical for pay purposes, it is extremely important that grade boundaries be accepted. For this reason, it is often useful to move jobs that are very close to the maximum cutoff point into the next higher grade. There are a number of ways of grouping jobs into a limited number of grades. Let's examine four of them.

Cluster Approach. The simplest approach is to make a scatter diagram of the organization's jobs, as is done in establishing the pay-policy line. When this is done it can often be observed that the jobs tend to cluster rather than scattering evenly. This effect can be taken advantage of by encasing the clusters horizontally and vertically, as illustrated in figure 11–6. This provides all three dimensions, but none of them is arrived at consistently, nor are they likely to be symmetrical. This may have a negative impact on salary and career progression in the organization.

Clustering has the advantages of simplicity and flexibility: it can be changed each time the wage structure is adjusted. It tends to be used with ranking or slotting methods of job evaluation, so small organizations are most likely to use this approach.

Division Approach. Another relatively simple approach is to use the horizontal dimension of the wage structure—the job evaluation points—to determine the number of pay grades. This is done most easily by determining a set number of points for each pay grade and, starting with the least number of points, marking off the lines between adjacent grades. In figure 11–7, each pay grade is 40 points "wide." An alternative to using a set number of points for each grade is to use increasing numbers of points as we move up the scale. This would reflect the difficulty experienced in job evaluation of determining exact differentials between jobs higher in the hierarchy. In the division approach the job rate for each grade should be set by placing the range midpoint at the point where a vertical line from the point value in the middle of the grade, say 200 points for level 3 in figure 11–7 (p. 220), meets the pay-policy line. This method can be used sucessfully with a point system of job evaluation and can also be adapted to other systems, such as classification.

Midpoint-Progression Approach. This method is a little more sophisticated and allows for broader definition at higher grades. It focuses on the pay-policy line and the vertical axis of the wage structure. This time the number of pay grades is obtained by determining a standard distance between the midpoints of adjoining grades. In figure 11–8 (p. 221), 10 percent is the distance decided upon between grades. Starting at the midpoint of the lowest grade, we place the midpoint for each succeeding grade 10 percent higher than the lower one. The dividing line between grades is halfway between the two midpoints. As can be seen, the horizontal dimension—job evaluation points—widens with each higher grade.

This approach is often combined with increasingly broad rate ranges to make the wage structure balloon out at the higher levels. The rationale is that at higher levels, positions are harder to define and evaluate accurately and greater variation in performance is possible.

Continuum Approach. Here, in essence, each job evaluation point on the horizontal axis has its own rate range; there is no grouping of jobs. The pay-policy line constitutes the midpoints. A standard maximum and minimum

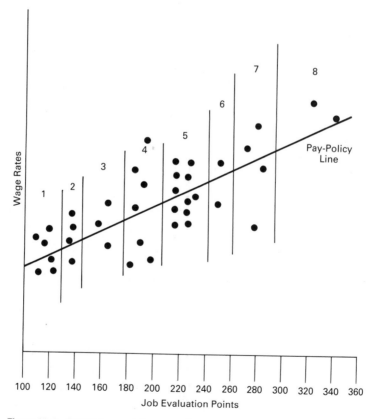

Figure 11–6   Cluster approach to pay grades

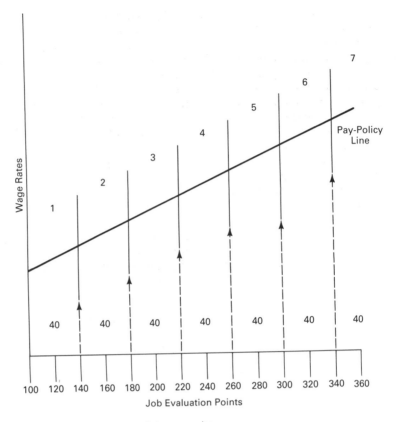

Figure 11–7   Division approach to pay grades

which are a set percentage above and below the midpoint are defined. As can be seen in figure 11–9 (p. 222), these lines widen as the wage level rises, making the range broader at the top than at the bottom.

The continuum approach has gained popularity with the Hay system (see chapter 10), which uses it. As noted, a system such as this requires a lot of confidence in the job evaluation system. It is likely to engender considerable argument over small differences in the number of points assigned to jobs. Small, technically oriented organizations are most likely to use this method.

RATE RANGES.   Just as it is useful to group jobs on the horizontal axis, it is useful to use a range of pay for each pay grade created. A range of pay allows an organization to move beyond pay for the job to pay for the person. Since this is the topic of the next part of this book (see chapters 13 and 14) it will not be covered in depth here. Factors important in rewarding people for other than the job, such as performance, can be accommodated by a rate range. Since the data from which a job rate is taken comprises not a point but a range, using a single job rate may create an aura of accuracy that is unwarranted. Also, since a pay grade incorporates a range of job evaluation points, it is useful to have some range of pay for the grade.

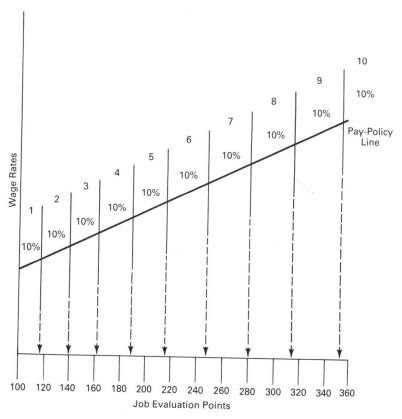

Figure 11–8 Midpoint progression approach to pay grades

Ordinarily the midpoint of the range will be the *job rate,* the mean or median of the wage survey data. The other points to define are the minimum and maximum of the range. The *range spread*—the distance from minimum to maximum—varies greatly but is usually within a 25 to 60 percent range. Many large wage structures with a variety of jobs are narrow at the bottom and spread out at the higher levels.

Once pay grades and rate ranges are designed, the wage structure is complete (see figure 11–10, p. 223).

The process described here is not the only way a wage structure can be established. In a study in which one of the authors participated, compensation specialists at 37 organizations were queried about how they went about establishing their wage structures. The findings showed that there were 19 separable approaches, and that only 2 were performed in as many as 5 organizations. These two were a comparison of market benchmarks with an internal ranking of benchmarks and a comparison of job evaluation with market benchmarks.[5]

[5]D. W. Belcher, N. B. Ferris, and B. R. Dalton, "Building a Pay Structure", (paper presented at the Western Region Conference of the American Compensation Association, San Diego, 1984).

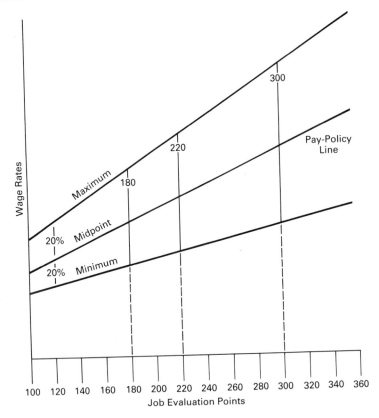

Figure 11–9   Continuum approach to pay grades

ADMINISTERING THE WAGE STRUCTURE

The wage structure developed in the first half of this chapter is designed to take the organization one step closer to the goal of figuring out what to pay the individual employee by defining a pay rate or range to be paid the job. The implementation of the structure involves a number of issues and problems, which we will deal with in the remainder of the chapter.

Issues in Administration

Decisions about the design of the wage structure affect the paycheck of all employees. From the standpoint of equity within the organization it is important that the way in which these decisions were arrived at is clearly understood and accepted by all parties. From an external perspective the organization must deal with the question of its competitiveness in the labor market compared with its values and customs. The issues to be dealt with in this section focus on these two aspects of equity.

RESPONSIBILITY FOR WAGE STRUCTURE PRICING.   If the job structure is determined through formal job evaluation, pricing responsibility depends heavily on whether the organization has a union and on how extensively the

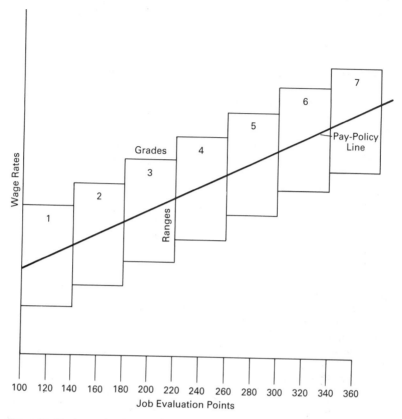

Figure 11–10   A completed wage structure

union participates in the job evaluation program. If job evaluation is a union-management venture, the union is obviously represented on the committee that prices the job structure. If job evaluation is conducted by the employer alone, the union in collective bargaining may accept the job structure developed, accept it in part, or ignore it. In each of these cases the pricing process is the result of collective bargaining, at least on key jobs and possibly on all jobs.

To some organizations the process of pricing a job-evaluated job structure by collective bargaining is disturbing, because the resulting wage structure may perpetuate or produce inequities that the job evaluation plan was designed to eliminate. To others collective bargaining is seen as introducing needed flexibility into the system. Some organizations insist that they need a logically developed job structure to prepare for bargaining. In nonunion organizations pricing the job structure derived from formal job evaluation is the responsibility of the committee or individuals charged with the program.

Informal job evaluation is priced through collective bargaining in unionized organizations and by management in nonunion organizations. In fact, pay-grade pricing is usual in both formal and informal arrangements.

PRICING JOBS.   When pay grades are used, the rate for a job is that attached to the pay grade in which the job is located. A system of code numbers identifying the jobs and their proper pay grade facilitates control and record keeping.

Some organizations prefer to work with a job structure composed of individual jobs rather than pay grades. Such organizations may have difficulty convincing managers that cutoff points are necessary and that efforts to move borderline jobs into higher pay grades destroy the usefulness of the system. And for small organizations in particular, pay grades may result in little savings. In still other cases, the union or unions involved may prefer job-rate structures.

If a job structure of individual jobs is to be priced, the procedures are largely the same as those we have covered. The essential difference is that adjustments are made to accommodate the different job evaluation plans. If a point plan is used, points and rates for separate jobs may be plotted on scatter diagrams. With factor comparison, evaluated rates instead of points are plotted and a choice may be made between plotting only key jobs in the pricing process or plotting all jobs. In a ranking plan, jobs are recorded by rank and job-rate adjustments are made to correspond with the ranking.

MARKET RATES VERSUS EVALUATED RATES.   In chapter 8 a number of wage structure considerations were discussed. One of these considerations was the labor market, or, more correctly, the numerous labor markets in which the typical organization deals. Because of the possibilities of conflict between market rates and rates that accord with job evaluation, it may be useful to highlight them here.

Job evaluation is an attempt to substitute rationality for a variety of nonrational influences on wages and salaries by appraising jobs in terms of their contribution to the organization. The process presumably produces a hierarchy of jobs that accords with both organizational requirements and employee values, including customary relationships. This internally developed job structure is logically, at least, somewhat different from that of any other organization.

Market rates, on the other hand, represent an agglomeration of prices paid by organizations of every size and type. Some jobs are never filled from the labor market but rather are occupied by employees trained by the organization. Some organizations are almost completely insulated from most labor markets, except in the case of jobs for which they cannot provide training. Even if jobs in different organizations are identical, the chance of their occupying the same position in the job hierarchy is small. Even highly skilled jobs may vary in importance to the various employing organizations.

Thus no job-evaluated wage structure is immune to conflict with market rates. The only way an organization could avoid such conflict would be to pay at or above the market on every job. But the severity of the conflict varies considerably from one organization to another. Low-wage organizations may experience conflict on many jobs. Organizations employing largely semiskilled workers and promoting from within have less conflict than organizations employing many highly skilled workers who must be hired from the outside for these jobs. If there is unemployment in the local labor market, less conflict between market rates and evaluated rates occurs, even in low-wage organizations.

Geographically isolated organizations or those with large numbers of unique jobs experience less conflict.

That the position and meaning of the same job rate vary from organization to organization makes it easier to solve the conflict. If the job is a hiring-in job, the organization may have no choice but to pay the market rate. If not, the importance of the conflict depends on the position of the job within a job cluster. If the job is related more strongly to associated jobs than to the market, the market rate is much less important. If jobs that are keyed to the market are at or above market rates, internal relationships are likely to prevail.

Some job clusters are market-oriented, usually because the organization cannot provide the training needed or because the union discourages intra-organization comparisons. Other job clusters are essentially insulated from the market, except for hiring-in jobs. But tight labor markets tend to market-orient any job cluster in which the organization does not provide its own labor supply by promotion or transfer from within. Although changes in market rates vary in amount and even direction for separate job clusters, in periods of generally tight labor markets there is some similarity among these movements.

The basic solution to conflict between market rates and evaluated rates is to develop a number of wage structures. In this way, a job cluster that must be tied closely to the labor market will not seriously disturb other wage and salary structures. A less preferable solution is to exempt certain jobs or job clusters from job evaluation. This approach is difficult to defend and endangers internal relationships. A third solution is the guideline method of job evaluation, which in effect determines internal relationships by market relationships.

Wage structure decisions as outlined in this chapter attempt to balance internal considerations and external considerations (market rates). Most organizations achieve this by developing a number of separate wage structures and by emphasizing flexibility in pricing job structures. Low-wage employers in competitive industries, especially those operating in tight labor markets, may have to abandon their interest in internal relationships and concentrate on keeping jobs filled by paying market rates. In fact, they may have to lower their hiring standards as well.

Solution to conflicts between market rates and evaluated rates may be made easier or more difficult by unionism. If the job evaluation plan is a joint one or if the union is interested in consistent internal relationships, solution is facilitated. Craft unionism, rival unionism, and lack of interest in internal relationships make solution more difficult.

Problems in Administration

Decisions concerning internal wage structures must contend not only with the numerous considerations discussed in this chapter but also with continuous change in employees, jobs, and organizations. Jobs change by the addition or subtraction of tasks according to the needs of the organization. Jobs also change as a result of changes in technology, with consequent changes in method and equipment. New jobs are added and old ones disappear. Employees also change, by leaving the organization and being replaced by others, and through transfer and promotion to different jobs. Organizations also change in response to these internal changes and to changes in the external environment—product markets, labor markets, legal changes, and the union or unions representing employees.

Responding to these changes involves wage structure maintenance. This section examines a number of problems related to administering a wage structure.

OCCUPATIONAL DIFFERENTIALS.   Job evaluation is ostensibly a device for maintaining occupational differentials. Whether this result has been achieved is not known. One study found that job evaluation plans often provide for an increase in skill differentials and suggests that there has been less occupational narrowing where the proportion of skilled workers is high.[6] The job evaluation plan in the basic steel industry has maintained occupational differentials. One of the announced purposes of the Dutch national job evaluation plan was to preserve occupational differentials.[7]

Most economists contend that there has been a long-term tendency for occupational differentials to decline, although it has been pointed out that the facts on this issue are ambiguous. It is generally agreed that in the short run, occupational differentials change little during normal periods but contract sharply during periods of very high employment.[8]

To the extent that job evaluation serves to maintain relative occupational differentials, it gives employees an incentive for accepting or undergoing training to enhance their skills and in the long run contributes to the supply of skilled people. Although wage differentials are certainly not the sole motive for acquiring additional skills, a latent function of job evaluation may be to preserve occupational differentials, especially during periods when employees, unions, and organizations have little reason for maintaining them.

JOB CHANGES AND JOB DESCRIPTIONS.   Job changes call for changes in job descriptions and job evaluations to ensure that the changed jobs carry the appropriate pay rate. New jobs call for job analysis and job evaluation to determine the appropriate rate. Both cases represent additional effort for busy supervisors and managers, even if the analysis and evaluation are done by others. As such, there may be a tendency for managers to neglect these chores.

However, consistent wage structures require that these changes be made and made promptly. In addition, under union conditions failure to make such changes can foreclose the organization's right to make job changes. In a number of cases, management has lost a considerable portion of its right to make job changes by failing to make prompt changes in job descriptions. By custom and practice, employees may acquire the right to do certain work and to refuse to do work not called for in job descriptions. Major union-

[6]S. H. Slicter, J. H. Healy, and E. R. Livernash, *The Impact of Collective Bargaining on Management* (Washington D.C.: Brookings Institute, 1960), p. 582.

[7]H. M. Douty, "The Impact of Trade Unionism on Internal Wage Structures," in *Internal Wage Structures,* ed. J. L. Meeij (Amsterdam: North-Holland Publishing Co., 1963), p. 238.

[8]M. Reder, "Wage Differentials: Theory and Measurement," in *Aspects of Labor Economics,* (Princeton, N.J.: Universities-National Bureau Committee for Economic Research, 1962) pp. 257–318.

management problems have been caused by laxity in wage administration, such that custom has come to limit management's rights to make changes.

Much of the problem can be attributed to failure to educate managers on pay administration. Unless managers realize the importance of keeping pay structure changes in tune with job changes, any program of pay structure maintenance is likely to degenerate into detective work.

EMPLOYEE CHANGES RESULTING IN RECLASSIFICATION.

When employees change jobs and when new employees are assigned to jobs, employee classification determines the job description that applies to the work the employee is doing and the appropriate pay rate. A pay rate cannot be assigned an employee until he or she has been classified as performing a certain job.

Classifying new employees properly and changing classifications when employees change jobs are essential to maintaining consistent pay structures. But, like job changes, they represent additional work for busy managers. Again, unless managers understand that employee misclassification destroys pay relationships and creates vested interests that are difficult to change, they are likely to neglect reporting employee changes and to inappropriately classify employees. The extent of the problem is illustrated by the case of an organization that conducted an employee audit bimonthly and still found mistakes in 2 to 4 percent of the classifications.

TECHNOLOGICAL CHANGE.

Technological change affects wage structures by making changes in jobs. As mentioned, when jobs change their place in the job structure may change.

The issue of whether automation brings an upgrading or downgrading of jobs has become a lively controversy in the literature. Although most observers have predicted that automation will bring a general upgrading, the evidence from actual cases has been mixed. Evidence of upgrading and downgrading has been reported, as well as increased tension and better working conditions. Skills, at least sometimes, are of a different kind rather than more or less.[9]

Experience shows that adjustments in job and wage structures resulting from automation have been less troublesome than expected. Skill levels in affected jobs have not been significantly raised or lowered. The Steel plan, with its 50 percent weight on responsibility, has accommodated automated jobs without apparent difficulty. Others report that present job evaluation plans can allow adjustment to the changes.

It appears to have been established, however, that automation reduces the number of separate job classifications. Broader job classifications take account of the interdependence of automated jobs and the tendency to move people from job to job.[10]

[9]L. E. Davis and J. C. Taylor, "Technology, Organization, and Job Structure," in *Handbook of Work, Organization, and Society,* ed. R. Dubin (Chicago: Rand McNally, 1976), pp. 379–420.

[10]J. Bezler, "Effects of Automation on Some Areas of Compensation," *Personnel Journal,* April 1969, pp. 282–85.

Broader job classifications mean broader job descriptions and less frequent changes in employee classification. Thus if the broad job descriptions represent reality, problems of maintaining wage structures may be reduced.

In practice, few jobs are actually downgraded as a result of automation. This may mean that job changes resulting from technological change do not reduce job-related contributions. It may also mean that automation creates new rather than changed jobs. A third possibility is that some jobs do require fewer contributions but organizations do not choose to evaluate them downward. There is no evidence that downgrading is more frequent in nonunion than in unionized organizations.

Technological and other changes over time may require basic revision of the job evaluation plan—in factors, weights, or both. If the model of the employment exchange used in this book is correct in implying that many employees want to make more contributions than organizations have chosen to recognize, these desires plus technological change may require such revision. A careful audit of job evaluation plans and pay structures at least every three years would be a good way to carry this out.

ENVIRONMENTAL CHANGES. Product markets, labor markets, legal requirements and union–management relationships also change and require adjustment of job and pay structures. Product-market changes may change the labor cost associated with jobs and force organizations to husband their economic resources. Labor-market changes may produce shortages of certain employee groups and compress pay structures. Changes in unions, in the internal politics of unions, in collective-bargaining agreements, and in union–management relationships may foster or inhibit union interest in internal wage structures and may make wage structure administration easy or difficult. Unions can aid or hinder organizations in making the adjustment in wage structures that environmental changes require.

In the United States in recent years, union contracts and the practice of nonunion organizations with regard to white-collar employees have resulted in yearly changes in the pay rates of jobs in response to environmental changes. Union contracts often call for deferred increases on a yearly schedule. Organization practice with respect to clerical, administrative, and professional employees is to make yearly adjustments.

The most pressing and dynamic recent change has been in the legal requirements placed upon the organization to not discriminate against women, racial groups, and, in certain circumstances, age, religious, and handicapped groups. The current pressure today is that of *comparable worth,* which will be discussed in chapter 20. As indicated, an organization should be careful that any wage structure it establishes has a balance of sex and racial groups and is not isolating these groups into a wage structure that treats them differently.

Maintenance Procedures

Problems of wage structure administration emphasize the importance of job evaluation maintenance. Maintenance, at a minimum, consists of (1) keeping job descriptions and job ratings up to date, and (2) seeing that employees are actually performing the jobs outlined in the job descriptions. The Compensation Department may be assigned to (1) analyze new or changed jobs, (2) see that job changes are reported, (3) see that old descriptions and evaluations are still adequate, (4) see that identical jobs have identical job titles, and (5) receive and process appeals and grievances with respect to job ratings.

Supervisors are normally responsible for advising the Compensation Department of any changes in job content that they are planning to make or have made. They are likewise responsible for seeing that employees are assigned to tasks and duties included in their job descriptions. To facilitate carrying out these responsibilities, supervisors may be required to review regularly with each employee the description of his or her job and, if the job description is not adequate, to request a new analysis and evaluation.

Some organizations require that approval for job changes be obtained before such changes can be made. It is doubtful that this practice can be justified in a dynamic organization. If job changes are reported and consequent reevaluations are made promptly, such rigidity would not seem to be called for. If, however, supervisors are guilty of shifting duties in order to manipulate pay rates, some method must be found to discourage the practice.

In addition to supervisory requests for job restudy, other methods may be used to maintain the job evaluation system. The Compensation Department may be set up to audit jobs in all departments on a continuing basis. Thus, each department's jobs would be subject to regular audit. Interim checks might be made, however, by regularly checking departmental job lists against a list of standard job titles.

Another device is to limit the life of job descriptions. Thus a job description would be valid only for a certain period, after which the job would have to be restudied.

A further check on the adequacy of job information and the correctness of job values is the grievance or appeal procedure. Employees should be encouraged to appeal whenever they believe their job description or job rating is incorrect. If the organization is unionized, the regular grievance procedure may be used. If the organization is nonunion, an appeal procedure may be devised. In either case, a request for restudy of the job is made early in the procedure. If the matter is still not settled after the wage department reevaluates the job, it is sent up the line until agreement is reached.

Standard job titles are an essential part of job evaluation maintenance. Such standard titles should apply to all jobs that entail identical duties and responsibilities, wherever they are found in the organization. The compensation group polices the use of these job titles to see that they are used only where they apply.

SUMMARY

The wage structure is a combination of the job structure of the organization and the market rates for those same jobs. A graph representing the wage structure usually starts with the job structure on the horizontal axis, represented by the job evaluation values given to the jobs. The vertical axis represents the market rates expressed in monetary terms. Each job, or those jobs for which there is a market comparison, can be represented by a point on the graph. A line of *best fit* can then be drawn that creates the *pay-policy line* for the organization.

The pay-policy line is the starting point for creating the wage structure. The values of both dimensions need to be grouped in order to make compensation administration more manageable. The horizontal axis, the job structure, is grouped into *pay grades*. This grouping may be done in a number of ways as discussed in this chapter. The vertical axis is grouped for each pay grade into a *rate range*. The methods for doing this will be discussed further in the next chapter, as this provides the opportunity for the organization to pay differential amounts to people on the same job or on jobs in the same pay grade.

The wage structure is the place in compensation administration where the labor market meets the internal values of the organization. This juncture is not always congruent. Organizations have a structure of jobs that depends not only on market value but on a range of organizational, psychological, and sociological factors. Often these factors are represented in a collective bargaining situation. The requirement of organizations to respond to the labor market differs considerably, so settling any conflict between organizational and market values is a matter of judgment in the organization. Any wage structure is only useful for a limited period of time. Changes in both the labor market and the organization make redoing the process over time a necessity.

PART IV

THE WAGE SYSTEM DECISION

> "I don't understand why she got a 10 percent raise and I only got a 5 percent raise!"
>
> "Where in the range will we have to start these new employees to keep them and not have the old employees mad at us?"
>
> "I've been at the top of the range for three years without a pay raise. Don't they care about keeping people around here?"
>
> "How can we get people to focus on getting their work done on time?"
>
> "We need a plan that makes the employees aware of the fact that this company must make a profit to survive!"

The wage system decision moves the focus of compensation from payment for the *job* to payment for the *person*. This part of the book examines this topic from two perspectives. The first is pay for the person within the context of the wage structure discussed in Part III. This is covered in chapters 12 and 13. These chapters progress from describing the mechanisms within the wage structure that allow for variable payment to individuals to showing how to pay for performance within this framework. Our second perspective on pay for the person concentrates on incentive plans, the topic of chapter 14. Incentive plans constitute a method of payment outside the confines of a formal wage structure.

12

Individual Wage Determination

From the viewpoint of the employee, the end product of any compensation program is a paycheck. The decisions discussed in this book thus far cannot, by themselves, deliver a paycheck to the employee. The structure must be personalized by making a further set of decisions—the subject of this part of the book. The first major compensation decision, the wage level, is an external organizational decision that determines the organization's competitive posture toward its human resources. The second major compensation decision is an internal organizational decision involving the structuring of the jobs within the organization. Putting these two decisions together in a wage structure provides the wage or range of wages that the organization perceives as equitable for each of its jobs.

Although pay rates are determined for jobs, it is people who receive paychecks. So the next decision to be made is whether all people on a particular job are to receive the same pay or different pay; and if different, on what basis and how? These are not trivial questions. The great majority of workers are paid through systems that provide for variable payment for the jobs. Such systems reflect the realization by management and employees that it is important to reward more than just minimal performance on the job. Thus management seeks to reward performance through merit-based systems and incentive plans and employees and their unions seek to have learning, proficiency, and seniority rewarded. In this chapter—the beginning of our examination of pay systems that accomplish these variable goals—we look closely at pay (rate) ranges.

233

BACKGROUND

In chapter 4 we described the two basic decisions that people make in their relationship with organizations. The first, according to March and Simon,[1] is the participation decision, more commonly called the *membership decision* today. The second decision is that of being productive—the *performance decision*. These two decisions provide a useful format for discussing why organizations need to move beyond establishing pay rates just for the job.

The Decision to Participate

The decision to participate assumes maintenance of an equilibrium between the inducements the organization offers and the contributions the person is asked to make. The organization must maintain, as a minimum, a balance of these two in the mind of the person, and, more realistically, a balance in the person's favor.

These ideas of March and Simon have been translated into equity theory, described in chapter 4. Pay system decisions can be regarded as focusing on individual equity. Equity theory states that a person compares his or her inputs or contributions with the outcomes from participation (I/O ratio). When this is hard to do directly, the person compares his or her I/O ratio with some "other" I/O ratio. Anything the person perceives as relevant goes into these input and output considerations.

INPUTS AND OUTPUTS. The compensation decisions discussed thus far have focused upon the value of the job, both in the marketplace and within the organization. Although these are critical input factors, neither organizations nor individuals would be satisfied by making the employment exchange solely on this basis. We suggest that inputs can be classified into three general areas—job, performance, and personal.[2] Pay system decisions must now incorporate the performance and personal factors into compensation in order to provide a regular paycheck perceived as equitable to the employee.

EQUITY AS A COGNITIVE PROCESS. The feeling of equity is a *cognitive* process. People's perceptions determine whether their pay situation is equitable. Not all individuals within an organization are likely to perceive their pay situation the same, nor is the organization, through its management, likely to see the situation the same as the employees. This makes the creation of equity in the organization a difficult and recurring problem, not one that is determined once and for all.

INFLUENCE. Organizations are not powerless in this cognitive process. They can influence the perceptions of the person in a number of ways. First, they can define clearly the inputs required of the person. This allows the person to accept or decline the exchange in the way that a student stays or leaves a course after the professor hands out a syllabus. Second, organizations can af-

[1] J. G. March and H. A. Simon, *Organizations* (New York: John Wiley, 1963).
[2] D. W. Belcher and T. J. Atchison, "Compensation for Work," in *Handbook of Work, Organization, and Society,* ed. R. Dubin (Chicago: Rand McNally, 1976).

fect through communication and influence the inputs and outcomes the person focuses on. Third, they can make certain responses to inequity more likely to occur than others. If an organization wishes to retain people, it may make quitting an unattractive way to solve feelings of inequity.

The Decision to Produce

Katz claims that organizations seek three things from employees: (1) membership, (2) role behavior, and (3) innovative and spontaneous behavior.[3] Membership includes remaining with the organization and being present for work regularly. It provides consistency to the organization's labor force and reduces staffing and training costs. The theoretical basis of membership was treated in our discussion of equity theory.

Role behavior consists of doing the job as it is described and/or assigned. This is also needed for consistency and coordination of activities within the organization. To the extent that role behavior is explicitly spelled out and is seen as the basis for the person's input to the organization, this requirement is also covered under the decision to participate. However, not all required role behavior is easily spelled out in jobs, and all jobs have areas of discretion that allow the person freedom in accomplishing tasks.[4]

Innovative and spontaneous behavior addresses the organization's need for the person to adapt what he or she is doing, and how it is being done, to the constantly changing circumstances within the organization. Clearly this requirement is not covered in the decision to participate.

The decision to produce, then, moves the person beyond the minimum required just to maintain membership. It is what most managers call *motivating their employees*. A useful framework for this decision is provided by expectancy theory (see chapter 4).[5] This theory has three basic parts: (1) valence, (2) the performance–reward connection, and (3) the performance–effort connection.

VALENCE. In expectancy theory *valence* means the strength of a reward. Does the person want the reward the organization is offering? Since this book deals with pay, we can be confident that the answer is yes—but not the same size yes for all people. People differ in how valuable money is to them compared with other things on and off the job (see the discussion of Adam Smith in chapter 3). The content theories described in chapter 4 help us understand how different people's need for money may be very different. The advantage of pay as reward, though, is that it is seen as a path to many different types of need satisfaction.

How much increase or difference in pay does it take to make the person respond? This is the difficult question of the proper *size of a meaningful pay increase* (SMPI).[6] The organization must worry not only about whether pay is a motivator but also about whether it is offering enough to make it worthwhile

[3]D. Katz, "The Motivational Basis of Organizational Behavior," *Behavioral Science*, April 1964, pp. 131–33.

[4]E. Jaques, *Equitable Payment* (New York: John Wiley, 1961).

[5]See also V. Vroom, *Work and Motivation* (New York: John Wiley, 1964).

[6]L. A. Krefting and T. A. Mahoney, "Determining the Size of a Meaningful Pay Increase," *Industrial Relations*, 1977, pp. 83–93.

for the person to produce beyond the minimum. As with the value of pay, the appropriate SMPI differs with a number of characteristics of the person, including current pay, age, experience, and type of job.[7]

THE PERFORMANCE–REWARD CONNECTION.   This may be the most important part of the decision to produce, since if the individual does not see the rewards he or she wants as being contingent on the behaviors or outcomes the organization wants, then the organization is not likely to obtain those outcomes. This connection would seem to be obvious, but in fact it is not. Managers find it difficult to always define the results and behaviors they desire. Also, it is difficult to measure and/or appraise whether these outcomes have occurred. In short, the definition of performance is difficult in and of itself.

The individual must understand what is requested and see its connection with the reward. This, like all understanding based on communication, is hard to realize perfectly. Most organizations claim they have a merit system of pay, but in most of them the employees do not perceive that merit is the primary basis on which pay adjustments are made. In some cases this perception is valid in that the organization says it uses merit but does not; in other cases the organization is rewarding merit but is not accurately communicating this fact to the employees.

THE PERFORMANCE–EFFORT CONNECTION.   People must feel that their efforts will affect their performance. This connection may seem a truism but it is not. There are many jobs in which variations in performance are impossible or inconsequential. To try to connect performance to reward in such jobs frustrates the incumbent. Also, individual effort is not a useful gauge in the many jobs whose tasks take two or more people to accomplish. Finally, the effort-performance connection highlights the fact that the person must perceive that he or she can adequately perform the task. All of these caveats must be taken into account in designing a pay system.

RATE RANGES

The major way in which organizations allow for factors other than the job to enter into the determination of an individual's pay is to develop a range of pay for each job or grade of jobs. A rate range is a range of pay determined by the organization to be appropriate for anyone who occupies a particular job. A rate range consists of a minimum pay rate (the beginning hire rate), a midpoint (the market or job rate), and a maximum (the highest rate the organization is willing to pay for the job). This section will cover single-rate wage systems, the rationals for rate ranges, two types of rate ranges and the manner in which a pay rate is set for individuals within a range, and the dimensions of range rates.

Single-Rate Wage Systems

Before discussing various aspects of rate ranges we should first consider the situation in which there is no range. There a single rate is paid for

---

[7]F. Krzystofiak, F. Newman, and L. Krefting, "Pay Meaning, Satisfaction, and Size of a Meaningful Pay Increase," *Psychological Reports*, 1982b, pp. 660–62.

the job and the individual receives just that rate. This pay rate is the market rate and may be paid to either a job or a pay grade. This is illustrated in figure 12–1, option *a*. If a job rate is used, the wage line provides the job rate. The individual is paid in accordance with the number of points assigned the job by the job evaluation system. Where the grade rate prevails, the individual is paid in accordance with the grade level assigned to the job.

This type of system is useful where performance variation and/or other personal characteristics are nonexistent or unimportant. Not all jobs allow for a significant difference in performance. Some assembly-line positions and lower-level service positions have very little discretion, so concern with differences in output or behavior are minimal. Other circumstances that lead to use of single-rate systems are (1) a strict technology that controls the output and (2) jobs for which the training time is short—a couple of hours or so—thereby making a learning curve inoperative. The individual in this type of system is paid for his or her time on the job and for completion of the job as directed.

Single-rate systems are simple to administer: once the pay rate of a person's job is identified, no further decisions need be made as to how much he or she is to be paid. The system can operate successfully if (1) there is little variation in output and (2) it is acceptable to the parties involved. Unions often like single rates because they eliminate judgment-based differences in pay.

Rationales for Rate Ranges

Any time individuals on the same job differ significantly in performance or personal characteristics that are perceived as relevant to either the organization or the person, differentiation by means of rate ranges may be in order. One study reported that the rationale for rate ranges in most large organizations was the need for performance differences, but in some cases industry practice was a major reason.[8] Thus labor-market demands may also be a significant factor.

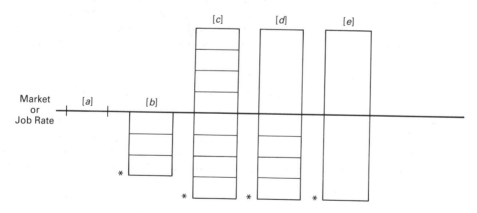

*Starting Rate

Figure 12–1 Alternative types of rate ranges

[8]U.S. Department of Labor, *Salary Structure Characteristics in Large Firms*, Bulletin no. 1417 (1963).

Rate ranges can serve other purposes for organizations. Retention is one of the most important of these. Experienced personnel can be made difficult to hire away by paying them above the market rate for the job. This is seen by the person as a significant reward for membership. Where there is a significant quality variation among people on the job, a rate range may represent an attempt by the organization to retain the best employees by paying them on the basis of quality.

Although performance is the reason most often given for rate ranges, this rationale should be scrutinized. Is movement in the range in fact related to performance? One major study challenged this assumption and found that performance was a very poor predictor of pay rate.[9] There must be more than just an actual connection between pay rate and performance: there must also be a perception by the individual that this connection exists. The need for this perception makes communication very important in pay systems.

A further rationale for rate ranges is employee expectations. Few people are content to keep making the same wage and being dependent for changes only on the changes in the total wage structure. In particular, they may see that length of time on the job is an important input and expect a reward for it. But they may also see a number of factors other than performance as relevant to movement within the range. Personal factors having to do with the job are a good example. For instance, many employees who are going to school part-time perceive that they should receive something for this. Employees may also perceive that they should receive more pay for a variety of non-work-related factors. Some of these factors, such as the birth of a new baby may be very important to the person but seen as irrelevant by the organization. Others, such as the person's sex, may be illegal to use as a differentiator of pay. It should also be noted that although some employees perceive the need for a rate range, they do not feel that performance should be the basis for this range.[10]

A final rationale for rate ranges may be collective bargaining. In contract negotiation the organization may agree to rate ranges or to an expansion of rate ranges as an alternative to a general increase. The union is likely to bargain for ranges in terms of movement within the range by seniority. The connection of performance and reward is not well served in this case.

Types of Ranges

Having made the argument that rate ranges are useful and expected, we turn to how to develop rate ranges.

STEP RANGES. A common form of pay range consists of a series of steps, usually a specified distance apart, either in percentages or flat amounts.[11] Step ranges may vary considerably in number of steps and the total range the

[9]M. Haire, E. E. Ghiselli, and M. E. Gordon, *A Psychological Study of Pay,* Journal of Applied Psychology Monograph no. 636 (1967).

[10]L. D. Dyer, D. P. Schwab, and J. A. Fossum, "Impacts of Pay on Employee Behaviors and Attitudes: An Update," *Personnel Administrator,* January 1978.

[11]Much of this discussion of types of rate ranges uses information from R. J. Greene, "Which Pay Delivery System is Best for Your Organization?" *Personnel,* May-June 1981, pp. 51–57.

steps cover. Clearly these two in combination will determine the size of each step. The point is that there are three variables present, and the determination of any two will decide the third.

Two basic types of step ranges are common. The first consists of a job rate (assumed to be the market rate), as in the single-rate system, and a starting rate. New employees are brought in at the starting rate and then moved up to the job rate in a series of steps. If done properly, this movement corresponds with the learning curve of the job. The market rate is the maximum since it is assumed that once the person has learned the job, performance differentials are minimal. This kind of system is illustrated in figure 12–1, option *b*. In this situation there would be a number of steps, most commonly three, between the starting rate and the job rate. This type of step system is most common in semi-skilled blue-collar jobs.

The second type of step system places the market rate not at the top of the range but in the center of it. Other places, such as the one-third point or the two-thirds point, are also possible, but the middle is the most common. Employees are hired at the starting rate, as in the other step system, and progress to the midpoint over time is on the basis of learning job proficiency. Thus, a person at the midpoint of the range is assumed to be a satisfactory performer. Movement above the midpoint is assumed to be for performance, or other characteristics beyond the normal or average. This type of system is illustrated in figure 12–1, option *c*. It is used in a wide variety of office nonexempt jobs and lower-level exempt jobs where performance is important but not critical.

These two types of rate ranges are not mutually exclusive in an organization. Lower-level pay grades may have the type of range that ends at the midpoint while higher grades have ranges extending beyond. The rationale for such a system is that the discretion in higher-level jobs in the organization allows for performance differences not permitted in lower-level jobs.

Movement within grades will be discussed later in the chapter, but one point should be made here. A person who is moved from one step to the next usually retains the new step even when the overall wage structure is changed. In this way, adjusting the wage structure to meet labor-market changes automatically becomes a general increase for employees in a step system.

There is a further consequence of this type of system: all people tend to move to the top of the grade over time. Even if movement is by performance, a person can eventually reach the top and stay there regardless of future performance. This phenomenon in turn has a dramatic effect on the total wage bill. In a period of normal growth and turnover the average wage for the job classification will probably match the market rate as people start to climb the ladder while others leave. But in a low-turnover, no-growth situation the organization may soon be paying above market rate even if it sets the midpoint of the range at the market, because all the employees in the job are in the top steps.

OPEN RANGES. In order to focus more clearly on performance and to avoid the problems of step ranges, more and more organizations are using an open pay range. In this system the organization defines the midpoint, the maximum, and the minimum of the range. Any one employee may be paid anywhere within this defined range. The function of the midpoint, as in the second type of step system, is that the average performer would be paid at this rate. Also as in the second step system, new employees would start at the bottom and move to the midpoint as they learned the job and became average performers. Payment above the midpoint can be reserved for above-average performance.

Unlike the second step system, the person's wage is not automatically adjusted when the wage structure is adjusted. At this point the person's performance is reviewed and adjustment is made in relation to that performance. The exact system for this is covered in chapter 13. Figure 12–1, options *d* and *e*, illustrate two types of open pay ranges. Option *d* has a series of steps up to the midpoint and an open range above the midpoint; option *e* has an open range from minimum to maximum.

With the increased emphasis on performance in organizations, open-range systems are becoming more popular. They provide more flexibility than a step system in granting pay increases and are more resistant to automatic increases. Finally, open ranges not only may make it easier to reward performance but are also useful when criteria other than performance are to be used.

Dimensions of Ranges

Any wage structure has a number of rate ranges and pay grades. This number can be a matter of the policy of the organization. Small organizations tend to have a small number of pay grades accompanied by wide pay ranges, broad definition of job titles, a great deal of movement within pay grades, little overlap between grades, and limited promotion to higher grades. Some organizations have many grades, which tends to create an opposite set of characteristics. When examining pay ranges we can determine the total wage structure with the help of three characteristics: the breadth of the rate range, the number of pay grades, and the overlap (see figure 12–2). If one knows the bottom and top of the wage structure, the slope of the pay line, and any two of the three characteristics just cited, the third will be determined.

Range Breadth

The breadth of the rate range is the distance from the top to the bottom of the range—*a* to *b* in figure 12–2. It is the vertical dimension of the range. The breadth may be stated in dollar amounts or in percentages. The latter is more common and will be used here.

The breadth of the range should vary with the criteria for movement within the range. Assuming that performance is the criterion, the breadth would represent the opportunity for performance differences in the job. Where ranges are narrow the assumption is that performance differences are narrow, and vice versa. In practice, hourly jobs have ranges of 10 to 20 percent, office jobs 15 to 35 percent, and managerial jobs 25 to 100 percent.

Factors other than potential performance differences may also affect range breadth. Organizations that promote intentionally fast encourage narrow ranges, since people do not stay within one grade very long. A wide range is encouraged if adjustments need to be large to be noticed by employees. Higher grade levels tend to have broader ranges for this reason. Broad ranges can

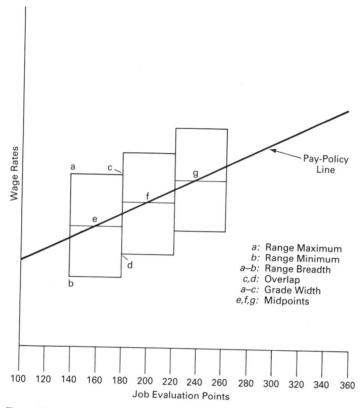

a: Range Maximum
b: Range Minimum
a–b: Range Breadth
c,d: Overlap
a–c: Grade Width
e,f,g: Midpoints

Figure 12–2   Parts of a wage structure

accommodate a wide variety of jobs and variable starting rates among jobs, and they indicate that the process of determining the market rate is not a precise one.

Establishing range maximums is particularly difficult. There is some logical maximum value for any job, regardless of how well it is performed. Ideally when this point is reached the person is promoted, either to a new job or by upgrading the tasks of the present job. Unfortunately, this may not be possible at the appropriate time. Realistically the person should be told that this is as high as he or she can go in the rate range and that any further salary adjustments will come from general increases.

Some organizations provide steps beyond the maximum of the range. There are usually two rationales for this—seniority and recruiting. Long-term employees who will never be promoted and whose performance remains good are sometimes granted longevity increases beyond the maximum of the range. These usually take place after five or ten years at the top of the grade. Trouble in recruiting and retaining professional and managerial employees can be ameliorated by starting these people quite a ways up in the rate range; in order to retain them the organization must go beyond the maximum to provide any significant movement in grade.

NUMBER OF PAY GRADES. The total number of pay grades in the wage structure can be either a result of other calculations—mainly range breadth and overlap—or a conscious decision that forces the other two variables to adapt. The number of pay grades is reflected in the horizontal dimension of figure 12–2 (*a* to *c*). At one extreme, a structure with a single pay grade would have a minimum and maximum embracing the total wage structure and would include all jobs. At the other extreme, each job evaluation point on the horizontal axis would constitute a separate pay grade. In the latter circumstance two jobs would occupy the same pay grade only if they had identical job evaluation points—a situation that would assume a very accurate job evaluation plan. (See chapter 11 for the design of pay grades.)

A large number of pay grades often coincides with a narrow range, permitting a large number of promotions and multiple classifications in job families in the organization. A small number of pay grades allows for flexibility in that it assigns people to a wide range of jobs without changing their pay grade. Not surprisingly, number of pay grades is associated with size and number of levels in the organization. It also seems reasonable that organizations with a fluid, organic structure would have a minimum of pay grades whereas more structured and bureaucratic ones would have more.

Clearly there is no optimum number of pay grades for a particular job structure. In practice, the number of pay grades varies from as few as 4 to as many as 60. But 10 to 16 seems to be most common. With few grades there are many jobs in each grade and the increments from one grade to another are quite large. The presence of many grades has the opposite characteristics.

A number of considerations help to determine the appropriate number of grades. One is organization size: the larger the organization, the more pay grades. A second is the comprehensiveness of the job structure. A structure that covers the whole organization will tend to have more pay grades than one that deals only with one job cluster. Third, the type of jobs in the structure make a difference. Production jobs whose pay policy line is relatively flat will tend to have fewer pay grades than a managerial structure that has a steep slope. The last determinant is the pay-increase and promotion policy of the organization. A large number of pay grades allows for many promotions but entails narrow ranges and a narrow classification of jobs. A small number of pay grades is accompanied by wide ranges, making in-grade adjustments common and broad job classifications and promotion opportunities rare.

OVERLAP. The final pay range determinant is the degree of overlap between any one pay grade and the adjacent grade (*c* to *d* in figure 12–2). Overlap allows people in a lower pay grade to be paid the same as or more than those at a higher grade. The rationale for such a phenomenon is that a person at a lower pay grade whose performance is very good is worth more to the organization than a new person at the higher pay grade who is not yet performing effectively. This reasoning seems to work: seldom are there complaints about overlap.[12]

As with the number of grades, overlap can be either a determining variable or the determined variable. Overlap will work well where there are

---

[12]For a discussion of the proper overlap see B. R. Ellig, "Pay Inequities: How Many Exist in Your Organization," *Compensation Review*, third quarter 1980.

many wide pay grades. A conscious decision to keep overlap to some maximum (such as 50 percent) will reduce one of the other two variables. Some overlap is desirable, but there are problems. The main one comes about in promotions. A person high up in a rate range who is promoted may start in the new rate range higher than the job rate of the new grade. But not to give the promoted person a pay raise is hardly to have promoted him or her. Organizations generally set some policy that any promotion be accompanied by some specified minimum increase, such as one step in the new rate range or a specified percentage. The designers of career paths in some organizations reduce this problem by placing the next job in the sequence more than one pay grade above the present one.

MOVING EMPLOYEES THROUGH RATE RANGES

Rate ranges make possible different pay rates for individuals in the same job and/or grade level. Operating such ranges calls for some method that differentiates between employees. Such a method must provide a decision framework for positioning each person within the range.

Open rate ranges facilitate a *pay-for-performance* approach to individual pay determination. Since this topic will be discussed in detail in the next chapter, the present section will focus on movement within grades in a step system. It should be noted, though, that an open range system can also accommodate the methods of progression discussed in this section.

Step Rates

Most government and some private organizations divide their entire rate range into a number of steps. This number is a function of the breadth of the rate range, the time required to achieve proficiency in the job, whether there are to be steps beyond the market rate, and a determination of the size of a meaningful pay increase. At least three steps are almost always used. A general step system is illustrated in figure 12–1, option *c*.

Step rates facilitate the granting of pay increases by determining the amount that any increase will take. Of course, it may be possible to move a person two steps, but this is always done in predetermined amounts. Such increases can be considered a disadvantage as well as an advantage. Many organizations prefer to be able to grant a wide variety of increases to better relate pay to their pay-increase policy.

Methods of Progression

All methods of progression specify how a person moves from the bottom of the range to the top of the range. The major difference among them is the criteria for movement. The major methods are automatic progression, a combination of merit and automatic progression, and merit progression. An organization does not have to restrict itself to only one method; it may use different methods for different jobs or even different methods for a single job at different parts of the rate range.

AUTOMATIC PROGRESSION. This type of progression (sometimes referred to as *scheduled increases*) consists of wage increases based automatically on length of service. In some situations, such as basic industries, there are a small number of increases often in rapid succession (every three months) to the maximum rate for the job. These are jobs in which proficiency can be gained in a short time. On the other hand, some governmental organizations may have many steps (five or more) and grant increases once a year. In these situations longevity on the job leads to higher proficiency and the organization wishes to reward continuity of employment.

A major source of variation in automatic plans is the nature of the maximum rate—whether it is the market rate or an above-market rate. Organizations that move only to the market rate tend to have rate ranges with a small number of steps and a short time frame for progression. They are interested not so much in rewarding longevity as in encouraging learning the job. Organizations that move beyond the market rate are specifically rewarding longevity on the job; they tend to spread out the progression to the top of the grade over a long period.

Automatic progression does not have to be totally automatic. A fully automatic progression plan is actually a variation of the single-rate or flat-rate system. If all employees can expect to reach the maximum of the rate range after a given period on the job, the assumption is that the maximum is the real rate for the job. Variation can be introduced in two ways. First the time period may vary from step to step. For instance, some systems move people rapidly to the midpoint and then much more slowly; the extended steps beyond the midpoint are clearly tied to longevity. The second variation introduces a little merit into the system by either denying movement to the next step for poor performance or giving good performers a double-step jump or shortening the time period between step increases.

Merit considerations in automatic plans should not be overemphasized. The system is designed to be automatic, and variations are seen as exceptions and not the rule. In most systems that allow either movement ahead or denial of increases, these alternatives are rarely used: the problems they pose for administration of the workplace are not perceived by supervisors to be worth the advantages they offer. Unions commonly accept rate ranges but insist on automatic progression and encourage maximum rates that are above the market rate.[13]

Organizations make much more use of automatic progression than might be assumed. Studies indicate that in most areas of the country and in most industries automatic progression is the norm and not the exception.[14] But this may be changing. The emphasis on productivity in the United States is translating itself into a search for ways to make employees more productive. Focusing on performance instead of longevity is part of this trend.[15]

[13]S. H. Slichter, J. J. Healy, and E. R. Livernash, *The Impact of Collective Bargaining on Management* (Washington, D.C.: Brookings Institution, 1960).

[14]U.S. Department of Labor, Bulletin no. 1625-90.

[15]E. E. Lawler, *Pay and Organizational Development* (Reading, Mass.: Addison-Wesley, 1981).

COMBINATIONS OF AUTOMATIC AND MERIT PROGRESSION. We have just seen that some introduction of merit is possible even in automatic progressions that focus on longevity. It is possible also to design progressions that try to balance merit and longevity. These usually provide for focusing on different criteria at different places in the pay range.

Probably the usual combination is automatic progression to the midpoint—the market rate—and progression beyond the midpoint on the basis of merit. The rationale for this method of progression is that all employees can be expected to reach average proficiency within a certain time on the job; this period matches the automatic movement to the midpoint. However, not all employees exceed average performance on the job, and movement from the midpoint on should be based on performance that is above average. If the organization does a good job of matching time taken to reach the midpoint with time taken to reach proficiency in the job, then labor costs are equalized; if these are out of balance, then labor costs are higher or lower than is optimum.

The rate range can take one of two forms in this case. The first looks like option *c* in figure 12–1, with a series of steps from bottom to top and the market rate as the middle step. The distinguishing feature of this form is how movement is determined after the midpoint has been reached. In the second form there is a series of steps up to the midpoint but an open range from that point on with movement of any degree possible and decided by merit. This form is illustrated in figure 12–1, option *d*.

Another method is to combine longevity and merit at all points in the range. Under this arrangement all employees receive an automatic adjustment but those with above-average performance receive more, such as a two-step jump. It is also possible to *hold back* those who are not performing well. The latter action is rare but can be effective in probationary situations.

The areas of prevalence of these different methods are hard to determine. It appears that automatic methods are most typical of factory jobs and combination methods most typical in office situations.[16]

Automatic-progression methods are simple to administer since they are purely mechanical adjustments made by time in grade. Introducing merit complicates the pay decision by adding a judgment about how well the person is doing the job and developing a way to incorporate this judgment into a wage increase. This makes administration more complex and, if the judgments are perceived as arbitrary, raises concerns about the equity of the system. The advantage is that a connection is made between performance and reward, and this may be worth the trouble.

MERIT PROGRESSION. A pure merit progression employs an open rate range with only the minimum, maximum, and midpoint defined, as in option *e* in figure 12–1. Movement within the range is based strictly on performance and there are no adjustments for general increases. This pay-for-performance system requires an integration of performance appraisal with pay determination, a process to be described in the next chapter. What we cover here is movement between steps of a pay grade, as in figure 12–1, option *c*, on the basis of

[16]U.S. Department of Labor, Bulletin no. 1417.

merit. The rationale for merit progressions is that the movement to proficiency is actually an improvement in performance and should be treated as such; people differ in their rate of improvement to proficiency, and this should be taken into account; and it is performance that the organization wants and should pay for.

In practice, a merit progression is usually a combination of merit and longevity. The initial decision to move a person from say, step 3 to step 4 is based on performance, but from that time on the person retains step 4 when adjustments to the wage structure are made, thereby remaining at the same relative position in the range. If step 4 is one step above the midpoint, the assumption is that this person is always above average in performance, but actually the person needs only to maintain a level of performance that will not result in termination. Further, unless the performance-appraisal system is tied consistently to the merit pay adjustments, either the system tends to be seen as arbitrary or supervisors tend to grant the same increase to all employees and thus destroy the performance–reward connection.

In all step systems most employees eventually get to the top of the pay range. In a merit progression method the good performer should get there faster than the average or poor performer. This phenomenon of getting to the top of the range tends to be hidden when the organization is growing and times are good. But when growth stops, then promotions slow up, employees stay on their current job, movement to the top of the range is accelerated, and the organization finds that all employees are at the top of the range. Labor costs thus become very high at exactly the time the organization can least afford them. From the employee's perspective, the only pay increases received are those that occur through wage structure adjustments, and these are likely to decrease in these circumstances. This lack of wage increases makes the potential for feelings of inequity increase considerably.

Most organizations and their management claim that they use a merit progression system. But studies show that up to 80 percent of employees are at the top of their rate range.[17] The problem is compounded when management mixes up general pay increases with merit pay. Granting all employees the same pay increase and announcing it as a merit increase destroys the concept of merit. Lower-level supervisors, in particular, find it uncomfortable to deal with merit pay, which requires him or her to make competitive distinctions between employees. For these supervisors it is often cooperation and not competition that is important. Because of the inflation of the late 1970s, annual pay increases are almost institutionalized in organizations today. This makes merit progression something of a misnomer, especially where organizations simply call all pay adjustments merit increases.

Unions generally do not support merit-progression systems. They question the objectivity of performance criteria and see the supervisor rewarding things other than getting the job done. Further, they are interested in getting their members to the top of the rate range as fast as possible. Unions can complicate the merit system through grievances. Some unions will automatically file a grievance if all members do not receive an adjustment or if they do not re-

---

[17]B. K. Scanlon, "Is Money Still the Motivator?" *Personnel Administrator*, July-August 1970, pp. 8–12.

ceive the maximum adjustment. This not only increases administrative costs but considerably burdens the performance-appraisal system.[18]

Unions also have an indirect effect on pay increases. Nonunionized people in the organization look at what happens to union members, and management knows this. Therfore, management tends to give those not in the union what union members received and maybe a little more. Organizations do try to deal with their nonunion sectors more on a merit basis than on a longevity basis, and to the degree that above-average employees receive more, the merit principle does work.[19]

Rate Ranges and Recruitment

To this point we have assumed that the organization has been hiring people who are just qualified and moving them up in the range as they learn the job. But what if it hires a person who can do the job from the beginning? Clearly this person should be hired at the market rate (the midpoint). In actuality, then, people are likely to be brought into the organization anywhere up to the midpoint of the range, based upon their qualifications. Thus a system that ends at the market rate becomes a flat rate for hiring fully qualified employees.

The labor market may complicate the rate range when there is a shortage of applicants. When it is hard to recruit, one way organizations adjust is to raise the starting pay to wherever in the range it must go in order to obtain people. This may result in hiring rates at the top of the rate range or above. This extreme situation makes any upward movement within the grade difficult or impossible for the person. A person who is then expected to stay in the grade for three or more years before promotion has nothing but general increases to which to look forward.

Correcting Out-of-Line Rates

The rate range defines the minimum and maximum that a person may be paid for a given job. For a number of reasons an individual's pay may be more or less than the prescribed range. The organization needs policies for dealing with these out-of-line rates.[20]

UNDERPAID EMPLOYEES.   A person paid below the minimum of the rate range for his or her job is said to carry a *green-circle rate*. This situation usually occurs when the wage structure is changed upward and the individual was at the bottom of the rate range. Little question exists regarding the appropriate response: the underpaid employee should have his or her pay raised to the minimum of the range, immediately if possible or in a couple of steps. If the person is performing adequately, the difference between his or her rate and the minimum of the range is an account payable of the employer.

Of course it is possible, for a number of reasons, that the employee is not worth the minimum of the range. Even so, there are usually adjustments that can be made. For instance, if the labor market is very tight and marginal

[18]Slichter, Healy, and Livernash, *Impact,* p. 604.
[19]Ibid.
[20]See Ellig, "'Pay Inequities."

workers must be hired and retained, a lower classification involving job redesign to accommodate the person's skills would be in order. This same reasoning could apply to older and handicapped employees who cannot fully carry out their jobs. On the other hand, redesign may be unnecessary where there is already a lower-level job to which the person can be assigned. Or if the situation is a learning one, a trainee rate may be appropriate.

Usually there will be a few underpaid employees, and a policy of bringing into line immediately the rates of those who are underpaid protects the integrity of the pay system. But if many employees are underpaid, a careful review is required: not only may the costs of adjustments be high but also equity between the newly raised employees and other employees on the job may require a phasing in of increases. Also, all underpay situations should be examined for racial or sexual discrimination.

OVERPAID EMPLOYEES. A person paid above the maximum of the range for his or her job is said to receive a *red-circle rate*. Other names for this situation are *ringed*, *flagged*, or *personal rates*, *red allowances*, *overrates*, and *personal out-of-line differentials*. The variety of terminology suggests that this is a common problem in organizations, that it stems from a number of sources, and that it is more difficult to deal with than the problem of underpaid employees.

Solutions to overpay vary from doing nothing to reducing the pay to the top of the range. Both approaches can cause equity problems, both in others and in the person affected.[21] The most common solutions are the following:

1. Freeze the pay until general increases catch up with the current pay.
2. Transfer or promote the person to a job in an appropriate pay grade.
3. Freeze the pay for a limited period, such as six months. Then attempt either of the previous strategies. If this is unsuccessful, reduce the pay at the end of the period.
4. Red-circle the job and not the person.
5. Eliminate the differential after a period such as a year or gradually over time.

A number of less common arrangements also exist. One, the adder, is a payment to the employee in quarterly installments of the difference between his or her rate and the maximum of the range. The employee is given 100 percent of the differential the first year, 75 percent the next year, and so on until there is no differential. The advantage of the adder is that the top rate for the job is made clear and both the person and the organization are aware of the exceptional and temporary character of the differential.

Another possible solution is a lump sum payment. For example, the employee may be paid the difference times 2080 hours and have his or her pay rate brought immediately into line.

[21]G. W. Torrence, "Correcting Out-of-Line Rates of Pay," *Management Record*, September 1960, pp. 10–13.

Any solution to overpay involves questions of equity. Overpayment is usually not the fault of employees, and any reduction in pay will be seen as unfair by them. On the other hand, there is also the perception of equity by other employees, so some action is always called for. All the actions just described try to balance these two perceptions in arriving at an equitable solution. Failure to correct red-circle rates means that range maximums are meaningless; people may be paid more than their job and performance are worth to the organization; and organizational resources are being diverted into paying these rates rather than rewarding others' good performance.

ADMINISTRATION OF INDIVIDUAL PAY DETERMINATION

The pay rate of an individual reflects a number of considerations, of which performance is only one. Other variables found to influence pay are the person's performance appraisal, pay history, present position in the range, and experience; the time since the last pay increase; the amount of that increase; pay relationship within the work area and other parts of the organization; labor-market conditions; the financial condition of the company; and of course the previous decisions regarding wage level and structure. The interaction of these forces determines whether a person receives an increase, and if so the amount of that increase.

Linking Pay to Performance

Judging from this list of variables, it is clear that an organization claiming use of a merit system is likely to be exaggerating somewhat. Although almost all companies would claim that performance is the primary variable in their determination of individual pay, not many have a system that directly links pay to performance. One study of a large organization showed that "the careers that people make for themselves in large-scale organizations attenuate the role of pure performance in pay."[22] However, it is becoming increasingly important that organizations do connect performance with pay. In the next chapter we will focus on programs that aim toward this goal.

Linking pay and performance is difficult at certain times. During the late 1970s, when inflation was running rampant, an organization had to offer very large increases to be seen as rewarding merit and not just keeping its employees up with inflation. Even if an organization is committed to pay for performance, its employees are the ones who have to perceive the relationship.

COMPRESSION. One particularly sticky problem is that of wage compression. This occurs when new people are brought into a pay grade at the same, a higher, or even a somewhat lower rate than people currently in it. This is most obvious in the case of new hires who are brought in at pay rates almost the same as those of employees who have been there a year. Rates for new hires

[22]T. H. Patten, "Merit Increases and the Facts of Organizational Life," *Management of Personnel Quarterly,* Summer 1968, pp. 33–38.

are determined by the external labor market, but current employees have their wages set by the internal labor market, which is an administrative decision. As we have noted, the particular pay rate for an individual is a complex of a number of factors, of which the market is just one. The result is that new hires make *too much* in relation to those already working.

Compression is also likely to occur with first-line supervisors of non-exempt employees who are paid overtime; in sales managers' jobs, whose sales staff can make more selling than the manager; and in middle management, who are squeezed between top management and the increases given to lower-level employees. The last is very evident in government jurisdictions. All three examples differ somewhat from the case of new hires in that they involve a hierarchy and the perception of unfairness is related to an inadequate distance between organizational levels.

Solutions to compression depend upon what type it is and how serious it appears to management. One obvious solution is to ignore it. This is possible if people are moving rapidly and the problem is mostly one of timing. The person feeling the inequity can be told that it will disappear shortly. A second possible solution is to adjust the internal structure more completely to the external realities. This may be an expensive alternative but may be necessary if the organization is experiencing turnover and employee discontent. In the set of three examples just cited the most likely solution would be a policy statement that a particular distance—say 15 percent—be maintained between levels. Rather than change the rate range for the supervisory jobs, however, organizations often pay this differential as a bonus based upon the wages of the subordinates.[23]

Integration of The Wage Structure and Individual Pay Determination

Changing the wage structure results in more money being spent on wages by the organization. This usually translates into pay adjustments for employees. But there needs to be some way for these two disparate events to come together. The vehicle for this is the budgeting process. On the wage structure side what is required is an indication of how much of a change is to be made in the structure and what money that will take. That money in turn becomes the organizational input data for individual pay determination. The question now is how to allocate the money provided by the wage structure adjustment.

BUDGET ALLOCATION.   The design decisions discussed in this chapter provide a framework for deciding how the budgeted money is to be spent. Where a single-rate system is used, the pay adjustment is a general increase. The basic question then becomes one of timing. When should the general increase be granted? If at the first of the budget period, then the percentage of the wage structure movement is the same as the general increase. But if the general increase is held off, the percentage can be larger and still fall within the budget. Remember, however, that this larger percentage is built into the next year's budget.

[23]For some problem statements and solutions see R. Kemp, "Salary Compression Workshop," in *Regional Conference Proceedings, 1978* (Scottsdale, Ariz.: American Compensation Association, 1978).

In organizations using an automatic-increase system the change in the wage structure changes all steps in all grades. But there is an additional cost—the movement of people from one grade to the next. So the total increase in the wage bill will be more than the increase in the wage structure. The exact difference depends on the timing of the step increases and on estimates of turnover. If all step increases are granted at one time then the impact is even, but if they are staggered by some criterion such as anniversary date then the organization needs to prorate the increases depending on when in the year they are granted. For instance, a 5 percent step increase given a person on July 1 is a 2.5 percent change for the year. But again, these adjustments increase the total wage bill beyond the cost of the wage structure adjustment. On the other hand, turnover tends to reduce the total wage bill since replacements are ordinarily hired at steps lower than those occupied by the people who left.

Merit-progression systems add another layer of complexity to the problem. In automatic systems the increases can be planned because the variables are known. Performance—the merit system variable—is less predictable. Organizations deal with this by developing a budget for a sector that shows how much it can spend to increase the wage bill in that sector. The same kind of considerations now go into the planning of each of the other sectors. The major complication is that the increase amounts will vary considerably among people. Last, a decision needs to be made as to whether all increase funds will be allocated on the basis of merit or whether there will be a general increase and a merit pool. This budgeting process is considered in more detail in chapter 19.

DECISION MAKERS. In a merit-progression program the supervisor becomes a key person in the pay decision, for it is he or she who decides upon the performance of the individual. Thus the pool of money available for wage adjustments is ordinarily controlled by the supervisor, to be dispensed within the guidelines provided by the compensation specialist. This supervisor must really believe in the value of a merit program for it to work. There are considerable pressures upon him or her not to allocate this money on the basis of merit. In brief, validating this decision in the minds of employees is difficult and may lead to feelings of inequity. In addition, supervisors are often much more concerned with cooperation than they are with outstanding performance.

An advantage of simpler individual pay determination is that the decision making can be more centralized and does not involve as much judgment. In this way consistency of treatment is maintained, which leads to feelings of equity. In an automatic-progression system the compensation specialist can make all the appropriate decisions and implement the program without having to coordinate their efforts with line management at all. This is convenient, but the program then becomes that of the compensation department and line management feels divorced from the compensation program, perceiving that they have little ability to motivate their employees.

Even if line management has a say in this determination of the exact amount people are to be paid, there is a series of other decisions framing this decision and limiting its impact. These decisions start with the wage-level determination, the form and shape of the wage structure, and the design of individual pay determination.

PAY-FOR-KNOWLEDGE PLANS

A nontraditional method of compensation that is gaining popularity is that of paying for the job knowledge of the employee rather than the job.[24] The focus of these plans is not the specific job the person is currently performing but the range of jobs the person can perform. This form of compensation has been made popular by some of the experiments in quality of work life, such as that undertaken by the Gaines pet food plant in Topeka, Kansas.[25] In this type of system employees are hired at a base rate that is determined by the labor market. Movement in pay then occurs as the employee learns new tasks used in creating the product. The top rate is for those employees who can do all the jobs in the work unit.

There are essentially two types of knowledge-pay systems. The first is a multi-skill plan. Here pay is linked to the number of different skills the employee learns and can perform. The second is an increased-knowledge plan, wherein the employee's pay is related to the increased knowledge required by a particular job category. The latter is a more appropriate plan where the jobs have a progression of difficulty and the employee can learn them over time. Top rates in this type of plan are for those employees who can act as trouble-shooters and trainers of others. The increased-knowledge program is similar to the type of compensation system developed for professionals (see chapter 17).

Administrative Issues

A number of issues are important in establishing a pay-for-knowledge compensation plan. Let's briefly consider some of them.

PROGRESSION OR PROMOTION.   When a person learns a new or improved skill, is this to result in a promotion or an in-grade increase? If the latter, then there would have to be very few grade levels and very wide rate ranges to accommodate the number of skills to be learned. If the former, then there would have to be a large number of grade levels since the person would move up a grade with each new skill. Each grade level could be a single rate.

PERFORMANCE.   In a pay-for-knowledge system performance can be considered the same as learning. But what about those who learn better than others? If the progression is by grade and not by promotion, then a range can be included in each grade that can be used for variation in performance, which is defined as doing the task better. Furthermore, a person's skills may deteriorate over time if he or she does not use them. Some organizations provide for retesting or refresher sessions to keep skill levels up.

WHOM AND WHAT.   Which employees and jobs to include in the system is always a problem in pay-for-knowledge systems. The ideal situation for

---

[24]G.D. Jenkins and N. Gupta, "The Payoffs of Paying for Knowledge," in *Labor–Management Cooperation Brief*, U.S. Department of Labor, Bureau of Labor–Management Relations and Cooperative Programs, 1985.

[25]R. E. Walton, "How to Counter Alienation in the Plant," *Harvard Business Review*, November-December 1972, pp. 70–81.

such a plan is a clearly defined production unit that produces a discrete product through tasks that all employees can learn. But even here there are positions around the edge, including that of the supervisor, on which inclusion decisions need to be made.[26] Even if the whole production unit is included, there may be some tasks that all employees are not able to learn. The tasks that constitute a pay increase must also be delineated.

MAINTAINING STABILITY. Pay-for-knowledge plans require job rotation. This can unsettle the production process if there are more employees learning new roles than employees well trained in their roles. Also, bottlenecks in rotation can prevent employees from moving up when they desire. In these situations special rates that hold the person until an opening occurs can be used.

MAXING OUT. As in all pay systems, there is the problem of the person who reaches the top of the range, or in this case who has learned all the jobs. The only increases available to this person are those granted across the board. There is no real answer to this problem except for those employees who move up from their current roles.

Advantages and Disadvantages

Pay-for-knowledge plans can have significant benefits, but they are not suited for all situations. Here are some of the advantages and disadvantages.

FLEXIBILITY. It is clear that organizations can obtain increased employee flexibility from this type of plan. The employee looks forward to learning and changing. Changes in demand can be adapted to more readily since employees can be moved to whatever task needs to be done at the moment. Staffing can be leaner since employees can fill in for one another, and not as much slack is required. It is further argued that this flexibility leads to a higher quality of output since the employees know all of the tasks and can therefore focus on the overall product rather than on the specialized task.

EMPLOYEE SATISFACTION AND COMMITMENT. Lawler's studies seem to indicate that employees in a pay-for-knowledge setting have higher levels of job satisfaction, particularly satisfaction with their pay.[27] This would seem to match our comment about the employment exchange that employees emphasize their personal contributions more than the organization does. This higher satisfaction is claimed to lead to lower absenteeism and turnover.

COSTS. The disadvantages are basically that the system is more expensive to operate. First, hourly labor costs are higher since the person is being paid for skills not currently being employed. Second, there are training costs, both in the design of the training and in the fact that trainees are performing the tasks. Finally, there are the administrative costs of keeping track of where

[26]E. E. Lawler and G. E. Ledford, *Skill Based Pay*, Working Paper no. 84–18, Center for Effective Organizations, University of Southern California (Los Angeles, 1984).
[27]Lawler, *Pay and Organizational Development*.

these employees are and what pay rate they should have, given the training they have received.

ORGANIZATIONAL INTEGRATION. Pay for knowledge has often been associated with a broader program of quality of work life in the organization. These programs are usually considered experiments and as such are separated from the rest of the organization. The success of this type of plan, as with all new ideas, depends in large part on how top management views it. If it is supported, the probabilities of success are increased. But these types of plans are often perceived as threatening by top-level staff, and this can lead to the demise of the program. A major consideration is the equity question with other employee groups, the supervisors, and the labor market. Higher wages of pay-for-knowledge employees may not accord with the equal pay for equal work doctrine, create compression with supervision, and pay above-market rates for labor.

SUMMARY

Organizations wish to pay for more than just the job that the employee does. Employees contribute both in terms of membership (staying on the job) and being productive while on the job. Both of these sets of contributions need to be rewarded by the organization. Wage structures deal with rewarding these sets of contributions by establishing *rate ranges* for jobs. This allows for variable pay rates for employees on the same job and/or in the same pay grade.

The breadth of the rate range (distance from top to bottom) is a matter of judgment for the designer of the wage structure. Further, the decision is interrelated with other factors in the wage structure, namely the distance from top to bottom of the entire wage structure, the number of pay grades, and the amount of overlap between grades.

The design of rate ranges may vary from a structured set of steps a given percentage apart to an open range in which only the minimum, maximum, and midpoint are defined. Picking the type of range depends largely on the factors that the organization wishes to reward. Step systems do a good job of rewarding membership and seniority. Open ranges allow the organization to more clearly recognize variable performance. There is an aspect of rewarding both in either case so the choice is one of emphasis and not of kind.

Administering the movement of employees within rate ranges faces a number of problems. Recruitment in the labor market may require the organization to hire new employees at advanced position on the range. This in turn can lead to compression as current employees are paid less than new employees. Keeping employees within the rate range is a constant problem. One of the most pervasive problems is keeping the focus of increases within the grade on performance; supervisors and employees alike are more comfortable with seniority increases. Last, while other aspects of compensation administration are often centralized in the hands of compensation staffs, the determination of pay increases within grade must involve all supervisors in the organization.

This chapter also examines a radically different type of pay system, that of *pay-for-knowledge*. In this system employees are paid for the range of skills that they bring to the job that are useful in performing the job. As employees learn more skills they are paid more. These types of plans can provide the organization with a well-trained work force flexible as to work assignments and interested in the work. It can also be more costly, have too many people in training, and be difficult to integrate with the more traditional wage structure of the organization.

13

Pay for Performance

A major goal of any compensation program should be to motivate employees to perform their best. This goal has gained importance in the past few years as American industry has begun to realize that it is in danger of losing its markets to foreign industry both here and abroad. Many programs have been launched to elicit employee cooperation and increased effort on the job in order to make American products better and more competitive. This chapter discusses the resurgence of merit pay, a technique that is not new but that fits industry's current need to focus on employee performance. The new terminology for merit pay is *pay for performance,* which specifies the intended focus of a merit program. As practiced, this type of program falls within the boundaries of the wage structure and rate range programs discussed in previous chapters. So the term *pay for performance* is intended to imply not that performance is the only criterion for pay determination but that at least one component of movement within the pay range is relative performance.

DESIRABILITY

The idea of relating pay directly to performance is highly attractive to most managers—so much so that almost all organizations claim that they have pay for performance in the form of a merit pay system. But there is a great deal of evidence that pay for performance is not easy to implement, not always desirable, and not as prevalent as the surveys would indicate.

Both management and employees agree that tying pay to performance is desirable. Studies such as that by Dyer, Schwab, and Theriault show that managerial employees feel that their level of performance should be the most important variable in establishing the amount of a pay increase.[1] Not all groups of employees rank performance that highly, but people consider it a significant indicator of how much pay they should receive.

Organizations clearly perceive that pay for performance is important. Most organizations surveyed claim that they do connect pay with performance in setting pay rates for employees.[2] Furthermore, the practice is spreading to more employee groups. Whereas managers have always worked under merit pay systems, the emphasis for other employee groups has usually been equity. But more and more emphasis on performance is extending to such nontraditional groups as teachers.[3]

Despite its obvious appeal, not all aspects of pay for performance are desirable. First of all, a focus on performance often conflicts with the compensation goal of equity: in a pay-for-performance system employees in the same work group doing the same work may be earning different pay rates. Feelings of inequity can always arise in this situation, especially if the program is not well designed and communicated or where people do not perceive performance as a proper variable on which to set pay.

A second reason that pay for performance may not be desirable stems from the first one. The program implicitly or explicitly puts people in competition with each other. Yet what is needed for the work of the organizational unit to be accomplished is cooperation. Where everyone has to work together differential pay can have a divisive effect that may produce lower and not higher performance for the group as a whole. This may explain why first-line supervisors are often not as enthusiastic about pay for performance as higher-level managers.

A third reason that pay for performance may not be desirable is administrative.[4] As will be seen in this chapter, pay for performance takes managerial time and effort and must be designed and administered carefully. Failure to put forth the managerial and staff effort required will lead to a program that does not in fact tie pay to performance and will make employees distrust management.

This leads to the fourth and last reason that pay for performance may not be desirable—lack of trust. Pay for performance most often relies on the judgments of managers about the level of performance of employees. Unless

[1]L. Dyer, D. P. Schwab, and R. D. Theriault, "Managerial Perceptions Regarding Salary Increase Criteria," *Personnel Psychology*, 29:1976, pp. 233–42.

[2]W. A. Evans, "Pay for Performance: Fact or Fable," *Personnel Journal*, September 1970, pp. 726–29.

[3]D. S. White, "Can Merit Pay Work in Education?" *American Educator*, Winter 1983, pp. 8–11.

[4]C. W. Hamner, "How to Ruin Motivation with Pay," *Compensation Review*, third quarter 1975, pp. 88–98; and H. H. Meyer, "Pay for Performance Dilemma," *Organizational Dynamics*, Winter 1975, pp. 71–78.

employees trust the judgment of the manager and perceive that it is in fact their performance that is being rewarded, there is a good possibility that they will see the program as manipulation of employees by management. The problem is that trust cannot be entirely created by the compensation program. Although a good program can enhance the feeling of trust, it must be present throughout the management process.

PREREQUISITES

A pay-for-performance program requires a compatible organizational situation if it is to succeed. To examine the feasibility of having pay for performance, it is useful to review the three components of expectancy theory specified in chapter 4.

Valence

The first part of expectancy theory says that people must feel that the reward being offered—in this case money—is important in satisfying their needs. Although an argument can be made that money is the most universal instrument for need satisfaction, it is clear that its value to different people is different. A pay-for-performance program is going to work best where pay is highly valent to the people covered by it.[5] This valence cannot be assumed but must be determined by research.

As an example, a researcher was called in to a company where a group of women seemed unable to meet production standards despite the attractiveness of the incentives provided. He discovered that this was a group of traditional women who believed they should not make more money than their husbands and felt guilty about not being at home when their children got out of school. The researcher suggested to management that the women be allowed to go home as soon as they had met their standard for the day. The suggestion was accepted and the productivity of the group improved immediately[6]. These workers were not completely motivated by money. Lawler suggests that programs such as pay for performance be installed only in units where the employees clearly have a high need for money.[7] In circumstances where management wants the motivational force of pay for performance then it is useful to select people who clearly have a need for money.

The Performance–Reward Connection

It should be obvious that for pay-for-performance to work there must be a connection between pay and performance. This is easy to say but very difficult to achieve. Organizations are complex social systems whose members are subject to many influences on their performance at any one time. To isolate a

[5]E. E. Lawler and L. Porter, "Perceptions Regarding Managerial Compensation," *Industrial Relations*, 3:1969, pp. 41–49; and A. Maslow, *Motivation and Personality* (New York: Harper, 1954).

[6]D. C. Feldman and H. J. Arnold, *Managing Individual and Group Behavior in Organizations* (New York, McGraw-Hill, 1983, pp. 296-301.

[7]E. E. Lawler, *Pay and Organizational Effectiveness* (New York: McGraw-Hill, 1971).

simple pay–performance connection is not possible. A number of problems increase the complexity of the connection.

First of all, as we saw in our discussion of the goals of compensation in chapter 1, any compensation program tries to achieve a number of things at the same time, but these goals are not always consistent. Second, even if the program does make the connection, the employees must perceive the connection. Hamner states that secrecy in pay leads employees to guess at this connection, usually inaccurately.[8] The connection is not always a comfortable one to employees, who may therefore try to assume it does not exist. Third, pay-for-performance is only as good as performance appraisal—the system that defines "good" performance. A perception that the performance-appraisal system is biased or does not appraise actual performance destroys the connection for the employee. Performance appraisal will be discussed in the last section of this chapter.

A serious complication is that management and employees may not agree on the performance level of the latter. Meyer studied a number of occupational groups and found that people tend to rate their performance higher than management is likely to.[9] Specifically, he found that over 95 percent of his respondents rated their performance above average; 68 percent thought they were in the top 25 percent in performance. If we compare such findings with the assumption of pay-for-performance that performance is a normal distribution, then we can see that a great many employees are not going to perceive that their pay is related to their performance.

The Performance–Effort Connection

Employees must perceive that their effort leads to performance. A pay-for-performance program assumes that performance varies among employees and that this difference is observable. But in many jobs variation is impossible or is so little that it is unrealistic to try to measure it for pay purposes. Even if there *are* differences, measuring them or attributing them to the effort of the employee may be difficult. For instance, the efforts of an individual in a group project may not be able to be divorced from the efforts of the other members of the group. The employee may not feel he or she controls the important measures of performance. Teachers, for example, realize that for them the important measure is student learning, but they feel only minimal control over that variable.

The main point of this section is that pay for performance is not a solution for all motivation and performance problems in organizations. It can be very effective where the requirements of expectancy theory can be met. But in many circumstances its application is likely to lead to frustration and other problems within the organization.

PROGRAM DEVELOPMENT

A pay-for-performance program is a particular method for determining the movement of employees within a pay range. The goal of the program is to

[8]Hamner, "How to Ruin Motivation with Pay."
[9]Meyer, "Pay for Performance Dilemma."

match employee performance level with position in the pay range over time. This idea is illustrated in figure 13–1. Movement upward in the rate range occurs only if the employee's wage rate is lower in the rate range than his or her performance is on the performance scale. Employees whose wage rate exceeds their performance standing receive no increase. Pay-for-performance allows the organization to move high performers upward in the rate range very fast by giving large increases to these employees. It also allows movement downward in the rate range if the employee's performance level goes down by freezing the wage rate at the current level. A pay-for-performance program requires the use of an open rate range, a good performance appraisal system, and a guide chart for pay increases.

Open Rate Range

A pay-for-performance program relies on an open rate range. As we saw in chapter 12, such a rate range defines only the minimum, the maximum, and the midpoint. This rate range needs to be broad enough so that it is possible to give large pay increases to good performers. Movement within the pay grade is determined strictly by the performance of the employee, and the position of the employee within the range is maintained only by good performance over time. Having reached a particular point in the range, the employee may slip back the next time the pay structure is adjusted if his or her performance is not as good as in the present period.

The starting point for determining a pay increase is the position of each employee in the rate range after a pay structure adjustment has been made. This is illustrated in figure 13–2. In this illustration there are three employees—A, B, and C. Before the structure adjustment A was between the first

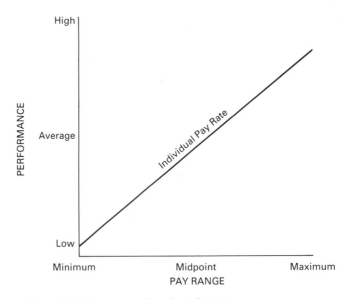

Figure 13–1   The concept of pay for performance

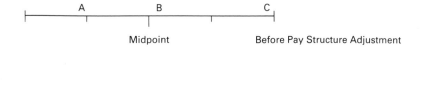

Figure 13–2 Pay structural adjustment in a pay-for-performance system

and second quartiles, B was just above the midpoint, and C was at the top of the pay grade. After the adjustment A is at the bottom of the pay grade, B is in the second quartile, and C is between the third and fourth quartiles. It is the latter positions that are the starting points for determining the pay increases for the next period.

Performance-Appraisal Rank

It must be possible to place each employee upon a distribution of performance. This distribution is assumed to be divisible into segments such as quartiles, and each individual can be identified as being within a particular segment. This system does not allow for everyone being rated high or low; it assumes that there is an even spread of performance—a normal distribution. If this distribution does not appear in the ratings, it must be developed by spreading out the ratings along a continuum.

Guide Chart

Rate range and performance rank are combined in a guide chart as illustrated in table 13–1. The horizontal dimension of this chart is the present position of an employee in the rate range. The vertical dimension is the performance ranking of the employee. Each employee can be placed in a box on the guide chart if these two dimensions are known about him or her.

The boxes in a guide chart indicate the appropriate percentage of increase that should be given to any employee in the current period. The amounts are determined by the budgetary process and the amount of adjustment that has been made in the wage structure. As an example, suppose that the wage structure adjustment illustrated in figure 13–2 was 6 percent. If employee C's performance during the period just ended was outstanding, then we would want to move her wage rate again to the top of the rate range, a 6 percent increase. If B's performance was below average no increase would be called for. Finally, if A's performance was outstanding then a maximum increase should be granted: 12 percent according to table 13–1. Note that even this increase would probably not fully equate A's salary with his current performance. A continued high level of performance would lead to more large in-

Table 13–1 Example of a Pay-for-Performance Chart

PERFORMANCE RATING	FIRST QUARTILE	SECOND QUARTILE	THIRD QUARTILE	FOURTH QUARTILE
Outstanding (1)	12%	10%	8%	6%
Exceeds Position Requirements (2)	10%	8%	6%	No Increase
Meets Position Requirements (3)	8%	6%	No Increase	No Increase
Meets Minimum Requirements (2)	Special Consideration	No Increase	No Increase	No Increase
Does Not Meet Requirements (1)	No Increase	No Increase	No Increase	No Increase

creases and a matching of performance rating and position in the rate range. In general, then, employees whose combination of wage rate and performance places them on the left upper portion of table 13–1 will receive above-average increases while those in the lower right areas will receive small increases or no increase.

The example in table 13–1 is a simple one: it varies only the amount of the pay increase with performance and place in the rate range. Rather than having a set percentage increase, as illustrated here, each of the boxes could have a range, say 11 to 14 percent, so that finer adjustments could be made for those close to the boundaries of the boxes. Even more movement for good performers and less for poor performers can be allowed by altering the time period between adjustments such as giving increases to good performers every six months while granting lower performers increases every eighteen months. Such alterations allow the top percentages to not appear so large when in fact they may be even larger and the percentages at the bottom to appear larger than they are in reality.

Operational Considerations

The ability of a pay-for-performance program to connect performance and reward is a function of the design and administration of the performance appraisal system of the organization. The rest of this chapter discusses the design of performance appraisal systems, but there are a couple of other points that need to be made about the operation of performance appraisal in conjunction with pay increases. A pay-for-performance program puts a lot of pressure on the supervisors doing the appraisals. At best, performance appraisal is an uncomfortable thing for supervisors. They often feel like they are "playing god".[10] In addition, the employees know that pay is a direct outcome of this evaluation and will put as much pressure as possible on supervisors to receive a positive rating. In other words, performance appraisal puts the supervisor's employees in a competitive position while the supervisor is trying to obtain co-operation and coordination. This leads supervisors to attempt to ameliorate the harshest effects of the system.

One other difficulty was illustrated to the authors by a personnel director recently. The flow is supposed to be from performance appraisal to pay adjustment, not the opposite. This personnel director noted that the first time the program operated there was a large discrepancy between performance and place in the rate range. The second time around, the discrepancy had almost disappeared—a much greater change than the initial adjustments would have accounted for. Research showed that the second time around, the supervisors made out their performance appraisals with an eye on where the person was presently in the rate range. This situation was particularly bad since many of the top performers the first time around were women whose pay was toward the bottom of the rate range.

PERFORMANCE EVALUATION METHODS

Evaluating performance is a necessary organizational process that takes place naturally in the act of managing. For certain purposes this process must be systematized. That is, the way in which it is to be done should be specified and the results of the process recorded in such a way that employees can be compared with one another.[11] Performance evaluation is a part of most personnel activities in an organization. As such it has a number of functions. These functions are not necessarily congruent with one another, so there is a great deal of trouble in developing performance evaluation systems that are equally useful for all purposes to which organizations wish to put them. In particular, there is a constant tension between the feedback and behavior-change goals on one hand and the personnel systems goals, such as merit-pay increases, on the other hand. This section will examine performance evaluation methods from the standpoint of their value to a pay-for-performance program.

Differential Performance

Differential performance is assumed to occur in organizations. It is usually desired but is also restricted by the way jobs are designed. Assembly-line jobs are often designed so that variation in performance is impossible or irrelevant to the desired outcomes. Variation in performance where tight coordination of activities is necessary creates trouble and not increased productivity. On the other hand, jobs such as sales, engineering, and managerial jobs have a great deal of latitude in their effects on outcomes.

There is also an intermediate position between these two extremes that may be very common in organizations. Most raters can identify those few

[10]D. McGregor, "An Uneasy Look at Performance Appraisal," *Harvard Business Review,* May-June 1957, pp. 89–94.

[11]W. F. French, *The Personnel Management Process,* 5th ed. (Boston: Houghton Mifflin, 1982).

employees who are doing an outstanding job. Likewise, they can identify those few who are doing very poorly. But most performance-appraisal systems ask that performance distinctions be made among all employees. It is very likely not only that making distinctions in the middle of the performance scale is difficult but that the differences are so small as to not warrant differentiation.

Differential performance is not just an ideal; it is a fact. Some people are capable of producing two or three times what others are, and the best as much as five or six times the worst.[12] One careful investigation found a variation of over 100 percent in routine work and concluded that a larger range of variation could be expected in less routine work.[13] These findings indicate that the reward system of organizations could create much higher levels of performance and therefore productivity in employees if it were clear to the employees that they would be rewarded for the increased productivity. But it should be kept in mind that not all jobs permit differences in performance and not all organizations require or desire them.

The preceding comments assume that *good performance* means higher output. This is certainly an important definition of good performance, but it is not the only one. How the job is done may also be very important. The organization may wish to reward a series of behaviors as well as the productivity of the employee. A focus strictly on the outcomes of work, such as sales volume, allows the organization to pay directly for those outcomes. This type of payment system—an incentive system—is the topic of the next chapter. If the organization wishes to focus on more than just outcomes or finds it difficult to measure the outcomes, then performance appraisal comes into play and the pay-for-performance programs discussed in this chapter are appropriate. The distinction between these two systems can also be seen as that between measurement and appraisal.

Measurement of Performance

Incentive plans pay employees for actual results as compared with expected results. Hence, they require determination of expected results (called *production standards*) and methods of measuring actual results. Development of production standards is normally the task of industrial engineers using work-study techniques. A work study is a detailed examination of the procedures, operations, and behaviors required to accomplish a task. It can take a number of forms, but all require an extensive measurement of the work activity itself to determine a production standard.[14]

The requirements for measurement as opposed to appraisal are strict. Essentially performance measurement requires a ratio scale, the most demanding type. A ratio scale requires a zero point. Without this we would not be able to conclude, for example, that one person had produced twice what another

[12]M. W. Richardson, "Forced-Choice Performance Records," *Personnel*, November 1949, p. 207.

[13]H. M. Douty, "Some Aspects of Wage Statistics and Wage Theory," *Industrial Relations Research Association: Proceedings of the Eleventh Meeting*, 1958, p. 201.

[14]S. J. Carroll and C. E. Schneier, *Performance Appraisal and Review Systems* (Glenview, Ill.: Scott, Foresman, 1982).

person had.[15] We would be able to say only that one had produced so much more than the other.

In work measurement the activities, often down to simple movements required to perform a task, are recorded as well as the time required to complete each motion. Outside influences, such as down time, delays, and fatigue, are built into the calculations and a standard time developed for completing the task cycle. This technique moves beyond being descriptive when it rearranges the order of activities to attain a more efficient sequence of work (that is, a sequence that takes less time). This is often called a *time-and-motion study*—a very descriptive phrase but one that has many negative connotations based upon restricting the employee's method of doing the work and applying tight standards.

Activity-ratio studies consist of recording a series of observations of activities. These observations are made on a sampling basis, and ratios between the different types of activities involved in the work cycle are calculated. Using this procedure, one can determine within some specified limits of accuracy the distribution of activities over a day or week.

Production standards consist of standard times obtained by these methods, plus allowances. Quality levels must also be built into the determination of outcomes so that the standard comprises both quantity and quality of production. Measuring performance then becomes comparing actual times against standard times. Units of production may also be the way in which the actual and the standard are developed. Payment is ordinarily based upon some base rate for meeting the standard and a bonus for exceeding it.

This brief explanation of the process of measuring performance under an incentive plan serves to point out (1) the specific and limited definition of performance under these plans, (2) the complexity of the process, (3) the subjectivity remaining despite the attempts to make the process objective, and (4) the importance of production standards in the process. Although this discussion has emphasized production jobs, performance measurement can be applied to a wide variety of other jobs in organizations.

Appraisal of Performance

For most jobs and in most organizations employee performance is appraised rather than measured. Performance appraisal is a formal method of evaluating employees. It assumes that employee performance can be observed and assessed even when it cannot be objectively measured. The performance that is evaluated may take the form either of outcomes of the work or the activity and behavior involved in it.[16]

Most organizations have some form of performance appraisal. But some employee groups are more likely than others to be covered. Most white-collar jobs, such as clerical, managerial, and professional, use performance appraisal. Recent studies of the use of performance appraisal indicate that from 75 to 90 percent of all companies surveyed have some form of formal

---

[15]F. G. Brown, *Principles of Educational and Psychological Testing,* 2nd ed. (New York: Holt, Rinehart & Winston, 1976).

[16]Carroll and Schneier, *Performance Appraisal.*

performance appraisal.[17] Performance appraisal is used less among blue-collarworkers than among white-collar workers. This lesser use may reflect the use of job-rate pay plans, rate ranges where movement is based upon seniority, and incentive plans. Union pressures may also be an influence, since unions typically do not like the use of performance appraisal.

Performance appraisal works by comparing an employee's contribution with some standard. The standard may be a set of criteria or some other person. The methods of comparison vary considerably and will be discussed at length shortly. Whereas performance measurement demands the ratio scale, with its precise requirements, performance-appraisal scales may be nominal, ordinal, or interval.

Performance Standards

Both measurement and appraisal require a comparison with a performance standard. It is the performance standard that defines what the organization considers to be performance. As pointed out, this is rather restricted in the case of measurement but may consist of a wide variety of outcomes or behaviors in appraisal.

The job description is the place to find the important performance standards for the job. The description should state the tasks required by the job and the purpose of those tasks. The next step is to define how well the task must be performed to represent acceptable performance. Depending upon the type of appraisal or measurement system used, this may be done through employee–supervisor conferences, analysis of records, committee work, or work measurement. The more objective the standard, the easier the rating task.

Appraisal systems are often weak in specifying performance standards. However, there is sufficient experience with developing standards to show that they can be established for almost any job. Some statement about expected quantity, quality, and time can usually be made. The statement is preferably quantitative but may be qualitative, and it should be verifiable by records. There has recently been a trend, however, to include performance standards in performance appraisal systems. The popularity of management by objectives (MBO) has encouraged organizations to add goals to their standard performance appraisal instruments.

Methods of Appraisal

Although there seems to be a large number of performance-appraisal methods, there are only two basic types, comparison with a standard and comparison with another person. The first approach requires a well-developed standard and allows direct comparisons on it throughout the organization. The second does not require a strong performance standard and under certain conditions can provide more reliable results.

COMPARISON WITH A STANDARD. This approach has a number of variations.

[17]Bureau of National Affairs, *Performance Appraisal Programs,* Personnel Policies Forum Survey No. 135 (Washington D.C., 1983).

Rating Scales.   The most common form of rating against a standard is the rating scale. Estimates indicate that about half of all large organizations use a rating scale in performance appraisal.[18] Very often, however, rating scales are used in conjunction with some other method, usually management by objectives. A rating scale defines a number of factors or criteria; the rater is asked to appraise the *degree* for each of these factors that best describes the employee's performance. Ordinarily the factors and degrees are defined so as to permit point values to be assigned to each degree statement and thus a total score calculated for the employee.

Rating scales may be described as rulers against which employees are compared. A ruler is developed for each factor to be rated. Then each ruler is divided into "inch marks" or degrees. But the analogy should not be carried too far. A ruler is a ratio scale, since it contains a zero point. A performance-appraisal scale, if well designed, is an interval scale—one whose units (inches, in our example) are equivalent.[19]

Rating scales typically provide a line for each factor, along which the degrees are arrayed in either increasing or decreasing order. Exhibit 13–1 is an example of a scaled factor. The rater may mark anywhere on a scale that is assumed to be a continuum. On other scales, however, the rater must pick the box that best represents the employee's performance. In these scales the line represents a set of steps instead of a continuum of performance.

The most common performance rating scale is the *graphic rating scale.* This scale follows the format just described. The factors or criteria are usually those that are organizationally important in determining performance. The reason that the consideration is organizational and not job-related is that a single graphic rating scale is typically used for a variety of jobs within the organization. At best the factors are outcomes (such as quantity of work) or behaviors (adaptation to change, for instance). At worst they are personal characteristics (such as a good personality). The degree statements can also range from

Exhibit 13–1   A Factor in a Graphic Rating Scale

QUALITY OF WORK—ACCURACY

How would you rate this individual with respect to the quality of the work he turns out, the neatness and accuracy evident in the job he does?

☐ Careless worker. Tends to repeat some types of errors.	☐ Work is sometimes unsatisfactory because of errors or untidiness.	☐ Usually turns out acceptable work. Not many errors.	☐ Checks and observes his work. Quality can be relied upon.	☐ Work is of highest quality. Errors extremely rare, if any. Little wasted effort.

COMMENTS _____

---

[18]C. W. Downs and P. Moscinski, "A Survey of Appraisal Processes and Training in Large Corporations," Proceedings of the National Academy of Management, Atlanta, 1979).

[19]Brown, *Principles.*

descriptions such as those in exhibit 13–1 to simply a scale from "Most" to "Least" with no explanation of what these terms mean.[20]

A newer rating scale that has attempted to eliminate the worst features of graphic rating scales is the *behaviorally anchored rating scale* (BARS). This type of scale is job-specific, or at least occupationally specific. The factors and the degree statements are arrived at through a complex system in which a group of experts who know the content of the job sort out behavior statements.[21] The format itself is little different from that of a graphic rating scale, except that the BARS dimensions and steps have been carefully arrived at. Exhibit 13–2 is an example of a BARS. It was expected that BARS, with its procedure and job-specific nature, would allow raters to make better judgments. However, the re-

Exhibit 13–2 A Behaviorally Anchored Rating Scale

POSITION: Chemical Equipment Operator
JOB DIMENSION: Verbal Communication

7 ☐ This operator could be expected to:
check verbal instructions against written procedures, always check to make sure he heard others correctly, brief his replacement quickly and accurately, giving only relevant information.

6 ☐ This operator could be expected to:
inform superiors immediately if problems arise, listen to others carefully and ask questions if he does not understand, give information, instructions, etc., in calm, clear voice.

5 ☐ This operator could be expected to:
always inform others of his location in the plant, avoid discussing non-work-related subjects when relating plant status to others, inform others of all delays that took place on the shift.

4 ☐ This operator could be expected to:
give others detailed account of what needs to be done, but not to establish priorities, mumble when speaking to others, not face the person communicating with him and act disinterested.

3 ☐ This operator could be expected to:
fail to relate all necessary details to those relieving him at break or shift change, not seek information and only offer it when asked, guess at status of pots when relaying information, not check to be sure he has heard others correctly but rely on what he thought he heard, leave out information about his own errors when talking to others.

2 ☐ This operator could be expected to:
never ask for help if unsure of something or if errors are made, refuse to listen to others, continually yell at others and use abusive language.

1 ☐ This operator could be expected to:
not answer when he is called, refuse to brief his replacements, give person relieving him inaccurate information deliberately.

Source: Beatty and Schneier, *Personnel Administration,* © 1981; Addison Wesley Publishing Co. Inc., Reading, MA; p. 129, Form 8. Reprinted with permission.

[20]W. F. Cascio, *Applied Psychology in Personnel Management,* 2nd ed., (Reston, Va.: Reston Publishing Co., 1982).
[21]Carroll and Schneier, *Performance Appraisal.*

sults have not been very encouraging: the use of BARS does not seem to significantly reduce the rating errors found in graphic rating scales.[22]

The research into BARS has led in turn to at least two other types of rating scales, the *behavioral observational scale* (BOS) and the *behavioral discrimination scale* (BDS). These scales are developed like the BARS but are themselves different. A BOS states a behavior and asks the rater to indicate where on a scale the employee's performance falls, as illustrated in exhibit 13–3. The BDS is more complex: for each of the behaviors—generic ones in this case—the rater is asked to judge three areas: (1) opportunity to exhibit the behavior, (2) satisfactoriness of exhibiting the behavior, and (3) level of performance of the behavior.[23]

Since rating scales are the most common performance appraisal method they have the advantage of familiarity. The graphic rating scale also has the advantage of being applicable to a large part of the employees of an organization. When well designed, it provides a clear definition of the criteria the organization considers to constitute "good" performance. This definition enables managers to discuss the relative performance of an employee against a known standard.

The preceding statement assumes that there is agreement about the meaning of factors and their degrees among managers and between managers and employees. If there is no such agreement, the "standard" is an illusory one and becomes a disadvantage. The advantage of commonality can also be seen as a disadvantage if in fact there is a great deal of difference among the performance factors required in different jobs. Different jobs may really require that different factors be used. This is a basic argument for the use of BARS. A third disadvantage centers in developing a total score for employees. The summation of a number of factors always assumes that a deficiency in one can be made up for by strength in others. Where this is not true the summated scores are not useful.

Exhibit 13–3 Behavioral Observation Scale

PUNCH PRESS OPERATOR:

1. Checks press for loose dies or other parts.						
Almost never	5	4	3	2	1	Almost always
2. Cleans all machine parts with proper solvents.						
Almost never	5	4	3	2	1	Almost always
3. Leaves machines when not using it.						
Almost never	5	4	3	2	1	Almost always
4. Wears all safety equipment and clothing.						
Almost never	5	4	3	2	1	Almost always
5. Feeds machine so as to prevent jamming or other malfunctioning.						
Almost never	5	4	3	2	1	Almost always

From: *Performance Appraisal and Review Systems,* by Carroll and Schneier. Copyright © 1982 by Scott, Foresman and Company. Reprinted by permission.

[22]F. J. Landy and J. L. Farr, "Performance Rating," *Psychological Bulletin,* 1980, pp. 72–107.

[23]Carroll and Schneier, *Performance Appraisal.*

Weighting is another problem in rating scales. If factors overlap in the behavioral domain that they measure, then some dimensions of performance may be inadvertently overweighted. Appraisal rating scales are similar to the scales used in job evaluation. In our discussion of the point system in chapter 10 we pointed out that the actual weighting of the scales may be quite different from the weights specified when the system was developed. Thus weights should be applied *after* the ratings (both job evaluation and performance appraisal) have been completed and checked statistically.

The most common criticisms of rating scales, particularly the graphic ones, is the set of *constant* errors that occur in rating. The first of these errors is rating everyone too leniently or severely. The second is central tendency. Here the rater overuses the middle of the scale, making it hard to distinguish among employees. The third error is the halo effect. Raters tend to have a global impression of an employee, and this impression colors how they rate all factors. Different levels of performance on different factors are not recorded. Last, and connected with the halo error, are proximity and logical errors. Factors that are next to each other on the rating form are likely to correlate just because of this. Logical errors occur when the rater assumes that two factors are similar and should therefore be rated the same.[24]

A final area of concern in rating scales is the choice of factors. Advocates of BARS have questioned two things about the factors used in graphic rating scales. The first is the factors themselves. The BARS indicates by its name that it is behaviors that should be used as factors. As will be seen, users of MBO say that outcomes or goals should be used. Both are reasonable approaches. Graphic rating scales are criticized where they use personal characteristics as factors. Research has shown that the closer the factors are to actual behaviors and/or results, the more raters will agree on their evaluations.[25] A focus on behavior and/or results improves the actual observation ability of the raters; they can focus on what they have observed. All this indicates that systems that have included the participants in their development will have a better chance of success.

The second criticism from BARS advocates is that using a single rating scale over a large number of jobs is not useful since the behavioral dimensions of jobs differ greatly. This is a dilemma. While the criticism is valid, the solution—that of having many different scales—has its own difficulties. It is expensive and time-consuming to develop a series of rating scales. This is a major complaint with BARS. Employing many scales also makes it more difficult to directly compare employees in different jobs.

Despite all of these criticisms of rating scales, the compensation administrator has to be able to use them in a pay-for-performance program since this is the most common program used by organizations. Where there are common factors and a summated score the task is easy, if not always accurate, since all employees can be placed upon a single ranking, making the performance axis complete. If constant errors are prevalent in the rating process, the responses may need to be statistically spread out on the scale. The best results can be obtained if (1) unambiguous descriptions of factors and degrees are developed,

[24]Cascio, *Applied Psychology.*

[25]J. P. Campbell, M. D. Dunnette, E. E. Lawler, and K. E. Weick, *Managerial Behavior, Performance, and Effectiveness* (New York: McGraw-Hill, 1970).

(2) evaluations are not shared with the ratee, and (3) the raters have been trained.

Behavioral Checklists.   A behavioral checklist is a set of statements about behaviors that an employee might engage in on the job. The rater's task is to indicate whether the employee does or does not engage in the behavior. This puts the rater in the position of recording behavior more than evaluating it, and should lead to more reliable reporting. A behavioral checklist can be made more complex by requiring the rater to indicate how much the employee engages in the behavior.

A special form of a behavioral checklist is *forced choice*. In this method the rater is presented with a set of behaviors and is requested to choose the most descriptive and least descriptive behaviors of the employee. In a set of four items, two appear favorable and two unfavorable. But only one of the favorable items adds to the total score and only one of the negative ones detracts from it. The value of the items is determined statistically by an item analysis of successful and unsuccessful employees. The scores are not known to the rater, who is in essence rating blind. This last feature is intended to reduce the constant errors of rating scales.

The forced-choice method was developed by the armed forces, where the problem of leniency had led to everyone being rated excellent. The method does reduce error and has the advantage of having the rater record rather than evaluate. But forced choice also has some strong disadvantages. The secrecy feature leaves raters questioning how they in fact rated the employee. This is uncomfortable and leads to resistance to and subversion of the method. As a method of providing feedback to the employee, forced choice is not useful since neither rater nor ratee knows what the important behaviors are. In fact, the armed forces have abandoned its use.

Nevertheless, for use in pay-for-performance programs any behavioral checklist that evaluates employee behaviors so as to provide an overall score would be useful in establishing the relative performance of employees.

The Critical-Incident Method.   The critical-incident method involves determining those behaviors that are critical to success or failure on the job. When the rater observes these behaviors in the employee he or she records them, along with the date, and places the data in the employee's performance record. This method was also developed to overcome the constant errors of rating scales.

An informal version of this method is often used in other performance appraisal formats where the rater is asked to indicate what the person's job is and how well the person is doing it. In some cases this format is just one part of the system, but in others it constitutes all of it. The newer methods of performance appraisal, such as BARS and BOS, use critical incidents as their items.

The primary advantage of the critical-incident approach and the accompanying performance record is the amount of observable information that is available for feedback and judgments. Equally important, it gives the manager a means of observing and encouraging employees.

The usefulness of the critical-incident method in a pay-for-performance program, however, may be minimal. The method typically does not offer any way to summate the rating of an employee, so the ranking of employees would be a qualitative exercise. The method is also costly to develop, install, and operate since it requires managers to keep a record on each employee. This record keeping in turn fosters the negative feeling among employees that big brother is watching them.

Appraisal by Objectives.   This approach, more commonly called *management by objectives* (MBO), compares the employee against a standard of expected results. It clearly differs from behavioral checklists and the critical-incident methods, which focus on behavior. MBO requires three things: (1) a set of clearly defined goals, (2) participation of both manager and employee in setting the goals, and (3) feedback to the employee as to how well he or she is progressing toward the goals.[26] Theoretically, MBO ought to be an effective method of appraising employees and, as its name implies, managing people. Its principles virtually coincide with Locke's goal theory of motivation.[27] And from a practical standpoint it is job outcomes that are important to the organization, for it is these outcomes that the organization probably wishes to pay for.

So why doesn't MBO always work? There are a number of practical problems. One set of difficulties comes from trying to make goals clear and explicit. Not all goals that are important—for instance, qualitative goals—can be neatly defined. Vagueness in goals may give employees the maneuverability they need to get the job done in a dynamic environment. In fact, in a dynamic environment attempts to set goals may be futile. Finally, focusing on particular goals may lead employees to ignore other parts of the job.

A second area of concern is the participation of manager and employee in goal setting. This requires a level of trust that is hard to achieve in a situation of uneven power. Joint goal setting can be perceived as manipulative by the employee if the relationship with his or her manager is not good. In addition, a natural tension exists if we assume that goal theory is operating. According to goal theory, more productivity is a result of higher goals being set and accepted by the employee alone. Goal setting is a difficult task to handle within the supervisor–subordinate relationship. Participation takes a great deal of both parties' time. One or both may feel the time can be better spent.

Third, the information required to provide feedback to the employee may not be developed in the organization or may be impossible because of the nature of the task. MBO also assumes that the outcomes of work are the only important variables to consider in defining *good* performance. Often, however, how the work is done is as important as what is accomplished. The former variable is hard to program into MBO.

As a performance appraisal method for a pay-for-performance program, MBO is not very useful. There is no way other than qualitative judgments to decide who is doing better or worse other than accomplishing or not accomplishing goals. This leads to a nominal measurement, but more is needed for the program to operate. MBO is much better suited to bonus or incentive systems, which we describe in the next chapter.

[26]S. J. Carroll and H. L. Tosi, Jr., *Management by Objectives* (New York: Macmillan, 1973).
[27]G. P. Latham and E. A. Locke, "Goal Setting: A Motivational Technique That Works," *Organizational Dynamics*, 1979, pp. 68–80.

COMPARISON WITH EMPLOYEES. Employee comparison systems compare employees directly with each other and not against any standard of performance. This gives the organization a relative positioning of all rated employees. Although it is possible to rate employees against each other on a number of factors, employee-comparison systems typically rely on a global evaluation of employees.

The simplest form of employee comparison is *rank-order rating* which requires the rater to rank all the employees from best to worst. This method certainly has the advantage of simplicity. It also is not unrealistic, since, as discussed, most uses of rating scales have a global impression that influences their ratings anyway. Ranking is facilitated by providing raters with a pack of cards, one for each employee. The rater then numbers the cards in sequence. A major drawback to this system is the difficulty of keeping the performance of many employees in mind at one time. Ranking systems often involve a number of raters ranking their employees and then amalgamating their lists into a master list. This is usually done by having all raters meet together with their manager as arbitrator.

One response to the size problem just noted is *alternation ranking.* In this method the rater indicates the best performer, the worst, the next best, the next worst, and so on until all employees have been rated. More complex is the *paired-comparison method* (discussed in chapter 10 among the ranking methods of job evaluation). The advantage of paired comparison is that the rater makes a judgment about two employees and not an employee and all others. The problems with paired comparison are the large number of comparisons required when the number of employees exceeds about six and the complexity of the data analysis that follows all the comparisons.

The product of all these methods is a rank ordering of all employees rated. Rank ordering works best where all employees occupy similar jobs. Large engineering organizations are likely to use this kind of ranking for all their engineers. Like all sets of rankings, these rankings order employees by their performance but tell the organization nothing about how much better one person's performance is than any other's. They also tend to make some very fine distinctions that may not actually exist. Scores can be obtained in these methods if the employees are rated on a number of factors or if they are rated by more than one rater.

A major variation of employee-comparison systems is the *forced-distribution system.* Here the rater distributes all employees among finite performance categories such that a prescribed percentage of employees are in each category. A typical distribution would be (1) the bottom 10 percent, (2) the next 20 percent, (3) middle 40 percent, (4) the next 20 percent, and (5) the top 10 percent. Again, this may be done globally or for a number of factors. Note that this system assumes that employees form a normal distribution in terms of their performance.

Advantages and Disadvantages. As indicated, a major advantage of employee-comparison systems is their simplicity. Because of this it has also been claimed that they are more accurate. Moreover, it is easier to make relative judgments than to make a comparison against a standard. Finally, these methods take advantage of, instead of fighting, raters' tendency to make a global judgment.

In pay-for-performance systems either rankings or forced distribution works well. Either provides a relative positioning of employees that can be compared with their relative position in the pay range. In fact, all the methods of comparison with a standard must eventually arrive at a ranking or a forced distribution.

But for other purposes employee-comparison systems fall short. Other than the ranking itself there is a definite lack of information to provide a basis for discussion with the employee. Where a global ranking is used there is no agreement as to what the appropriate criteria are. The forced-distribution system does provide a standard, but it is the group average, which offers little help to the manager who needs to discuss performance with an employee.

A disadvantage shared by all employee-comparison systems is that of employee comparability. This has two aspects. The first has been mentioned: are the jobs sufficiently similar? The second is whether employees are rated on the same criteria. It is likely that one employee rates high for one reason and another rates low for an entirely different reason. Another disadvantage is that raters do not always have sufficient knowledge of the people being rated. Normally the immediate supervisor has this knowledge, but in large ranking systems supervisors two and three levels removed often have to do the rating. The very size of units also poses a problem. The larger the number of employees to be ranked, the harder it is to do so; on the other hand, the larger the number in the group, the more logical it is that there is a normal distribution. This brings up one last problem. If the manager knows that some employees must be rated below average, he or she will start thinking of those employees that way. This leads to a self-fulfilling prophecy: the manager now treats them as if they cannot do well, and they respond by not doing well.[28]

Administration of Performance Appraisal

Unlike job evaluation, which is clearly a responsibility of the compensation department, performance appraisal, since it is used in most personnel functions, may be housed in a number of places within the personnel department. In addition, the decision making in performance appraisal is done by the manager and not the personnel specialist. Personnel typically designs the system and oversees its operation. This is not an easy task. Performance appraisal is not something that managers look forward to, and thus they will put it off unless required to do it. To the extent that they see the process as belonging to personnel and offering little help in managing their employees, managers not only avoid it but regret the time taken to do the appraisals.

Besides the design of the performance system itself, the major administrative questions that arise are when it should be done, by whom it should be done, and how its operation can be improved.

TIMING. Ideally performance feedback should occur as the job is being performed. If adequate feedback occurs a great deal of the emphasis on

[28]P. H. Thompson and G. W. Dalton, "Performance Appraisal: Managers Beware," *Harvard Business Review*, January-February 1970, pp. 149–57.

the performance interview would be unnecessary. There is also the question of when formal ratings need to be done in order to be coordinated with pay increases. One argument is that the two should take place as close in time as possible. This way the performance–reward connection is clear in the minds of the employees. The greater the time lag, the less likely an employee will see that what he or she did was related to the pay increase. On the other hand, some argue that close timing makes it difficult to create a meaningful change in the employee's behavior, because he or she will be very defensive if there is negative feedback. Regardless, a current performance appraisal must be available for all employees when the time comes to allocate increases under a pay-for-performance program.

RATERS.   The clear answer to who should do the rating is the person who best knows the employee's performance and is in a position to judge. But this could be the supervisor, a peer, or even a subordinate. Almost all formal appraisals in organizations are made by the supervisor. But often this is not the person who knows what the employee is doing, or how well. The best argument for having the supervisor do the rating is that this is the person whom the organization wishes to be seen by the employee as having the power of reward and punishment.

Studies have shown that there is a great deal of reliability, validity, and freedom from bias in peer ratings.[29] Despite this they present problems. For one thing, they tend to be even more global than supervisory ratings, making differentiation among factors difficult. Mainly, though, all parties resist the idea. Supervisors do not like giving up their power, and employees are concerned that their peers will have their own interests at heart if they perceive the situation as a zero-sum game.

Others who might serve as raters are a subordinate, the person himself, or a client. Each has unique information that might be useful in a complete evaluation but that by itself might be incomplete or biased. Lawler has therefore suggested that all these sources be used. Each has something different to contribute that would add to the overall evaluation.[30]

IMPROVING PERFORMANCE RATINGS.   The research evidence that the average of ratings made by several raters is superior to the rating made by one person tends to support the multi-rater approach just discussed. The problem often is to determine who the second or third rater should be. If there is less emphasis on selecting raters only from the organizational hierarchy, it may be easier to identify those who are capable of judging. It is important to identify what behaviors a prospective rater knows about. For instance, customers have the best perspective on the selling behaviors of salespeople.

Higher-level supervisors may also be useful raters—assuming they have a chance to observe the employee's behavior. Like the other sources, their advantage is a different perspective. A supervisor one or two levels removed is

[29]J. S. Kane and E. E. Lawler, "Performance Appraisal Effectiveness: Its Assessment and Determinants," *Research in Organizational Behavior,* 1979, pp. 425–78.

[30]E. E. Lawler, "The Multitrait-Multirater Approach to Measuring Managerial Job Performance," *Journal of Applied Psychology,* October 1967, pp. 369–81.

less likely to be influenced by immediate events and is more likely to look at the employee's customary behavior or beliefs.

Ratings can also be improved by increasing their frequency. Since current events outweigh past events the more often ratings are given, the less important events will be lost in the shuffle. Perhaps six months is the longest that should elapse between ratings. Some jobs, however, have a long time span, such that a six-month limit may not make much sense.

A powerful device for improving performance ratings is rater training. Discussions of the meaning of the factors and the definitions of scale positions along with practice in rating help improve the reliability of ratings. There are two types of training programs. The first is directed at reducing the response errors discussed earlier, such as the halo effect. This is called *rater-error training* (RET). The second type of training is aimed at developing observational skills that improve the accuracy of ratings. This is called *rater-accuracy training* (RAT). Studies show that RET does reduce error and bias but does not improve accuracy; RAT is better than RET at improving accuracy but was not superior to a control group given no training.[31] These results seem to indicate that with training raters can reduce errors but not necessarily improve their accuracy. Despite these mixed results, the weight of evidence is that training improves performance rating. Given the importance of good ratings in a pay-for-performance program, it seems absolutely necessary that raters be trained.

SUMMARY

The purpose of having rate ranges is so the organization can reward employees for factors other than the value of the job. Performance is a primary factor other than the job for which organizations wish to reward employees. This chapter suggests a method for clearly rewarding performance within the confines of the typical wage structure, that of a pay-for-performance program. Such programs, however, need to be approached cautiously. Paying for performance is not always possible nor desirable. The advantages and the costs of such a program should be carefully considered before installing such a program.

Pay-for-performance programs operate by relating all wage increases resulting from adjustments to the wage structure on the basis of performance. The goal is to correlate the position of the employee in the rate range with their relative position on a performance scale. The result of the program is this: employees whose wage rate is at the low end of the range and whose performance is high receive large increases, those whose performance matches their place in the rate range receive average increases, and those whose performance falls below their place in the rate range receive no increase. These results differ greatly from the usual distribution of wage increases given by an organization.

A pay-for-performance program requires the organization to have a good performance evaluation system. Where possible, performance should be measured. But this requires that there be some clear outcome from the job that

[31]H. J. Bernardin and E. C. Pence, "Effects of Rater Training: Creating New Response Sets and Decreasing Accuracy," *Journal of Applied Psychology*, 65:1980, pp. 60–66.

is the result only of the labors of the person on that job; this is clearly not very likely in an organizational setting. Performance appraisal is the most common form of performance evaluation. Methods of appraisal involve comparing the employee's performance to some standard. This may be some form of rating scale, standard of performance, goals and objectives, or other employees' performance. No one method can be said to be superior, and all methods have problems that put their use into question. Constant attention to performance appraisal results is necessary if the pay-for-performance program is to be seen by employees as a fair and reasonable way to allocate increases.

14

Incentive Plans

This chapter takes the concept of pay for performance one step further. A standard pay-for-performance plan relies on the job as the base unit of pay and adds a performance component to that base. An incentive plan starts with a person's performance and uses the job only as a reference. An incentive plan, often called *payment by results*, is "a payment system under which money rewards vary with measured changes in performance according to predetermined rules."[1] This type of compensation program makes the basic assumption that employees are interested in money and are willing to put forth more effort for more money.

Thus organizations utilizing incentive plans believe that they are offering performance rewards and providing performance motivation by focusing on performance, defined as output, rather than on the job, as the basic unit of payment. As we will see in this chapter, this contention may or may not be true. Well-planned incentive plans can yield substantial increases in productivity and lowered costs to organizations together with increased earnings for employees. But they may also lead to increased employee earnings with no in-

[1]International Labour Office, *Payment by Results* (Geneva, 1984). This publication is a major source in the development of this chapter. It is recommended for anyone interested in incentive plans.

crease in performance, together with increased costs and numerous employee-relations problems.

Incentive plans elicit strong feelings. Opponents variously claim that performance is a function of the organization of work and management practices rather than employee effort, and that incentives do not work and cause more problems than they solve.[2] Many proponents of incentive plans believe that a fair day's work is not normally attainable without an incentive plan because time workers produce only about 50 to 60 percent of the output of incentive workers.[3] Although they admit that some incentive plans malfunction, they insist that this is usually due to poor installation and maintenance rather than shortcomings of the concept of incentive.

This chapter examines some of the background factors in incentive plans, the dimensions of the plans, their design, and the problems with the plans.

BACKGROUND

To understand why incentive plans are so controversial, let's examine incentives and their use before turning to the characteristics of incentive plans. In this section, therefore, we will discuss incentive contributions, compare them with two motivation models, look at the results of incentive plans, and assess the prevalence of these plans.

Incentive Contributions

The wage system discussed in this book up to now essentially pays people for the time they contribute. If we assume that the job is the major determinant of the wage, then it is a person's occupancy of that job for which the organization pays. Performance and/or any other factor may also enter into the equation, but the time spent on the job is the primary consideration. To some degree, then, an organization wishing to attain increased performance has a choice of using a pay-for-performance system (see chapter 13) or some form of incentive plan. Both may reward performance, but the incentive plan does so more directly. In addition, the effects of payment by results and payment by time on the organization's cost structure are different. Payment by results leads to variable labor costs, since these attach directly to output. Payment by time makes labor costs fixed, since they are the same in any period, regardless of output.

Our model of the employment exchange specifies that it is contributions that lead to rewards; the question is the units in which performance is determined. Payment on the basis of time allows for a large number of unspecified contributions to be included. Payment for output requires that contributions produce measurable results before they are recognized as contributions.

---

[2] See, for example, AFL–CIO, "Decline of Wage Incentives," *Collective Bargaining Report,* November 1960; and R. Marriott, *Incentive Payment Systems,* 3rd ed. (London; Staples Press, 1968), p. 259.

[3] H. K. von Kass, *Making Wage Incentives Work* (New York; American Management Assn., 1971), p. 11.

In practice, however, payment for results often turns out to be payment for one contribution—effort; other contributions required by the organization are often ignored.

The measure of distribution does not have to be either output or time. The two can more reasonably be viewed as the two ends of a continuum on which various wage systems can be placed. At the time extreme is a system of automatic rate adjustment. At the other end is a piece-rate system, which pays a set amount for each unit produced. Other systems would fall at various places in between. This continuum is illustrated in figure 14–1. Where along this scale an organization's wage system should be is a matter of a large number of factors.

The work itself is a major determinant of whether to pay for time or output. The work characteristics to consider include (1) measurability of output; (2) the relationship between effort and output; (3) the degree of standardization; (4) requirements for quality as well as quantity; and (5) competitive conditions, which make it imperative that unit labor costs be definitely known and fixed before production.

General expectations are also very important. Community attitudes and the expectations of employees, both as individuals and as expressed through their union, affect attempts to install an incentive plan and certainly its chances of success.

Technological considerations may, of course, enter into the decision. To the degree that machines set the pace for the work, the employee loses control over determining the number of units that will be produced. The ability to change output through increased effort is critical in incentive plans. Also, incentive plans are more likely to be successful in industries with a stable technology than in those undergoing continual technological change.

The decision to pay for output instead of time is partially based upon the rational factors just discussed and is partially a matter of faith. If an organization is convinced that incentives are the way to go, then a way will be found to apply incentives to the work. The varieties of incentive plans and the kinds of contributions are so numerous that desire is more important than a precise fit of job and incentive standards.

Incentive Plans and the Motivation Models

Since organizations believe that incentive plans motivate performance, the evidence for this should be reviewed. Research shows that this belief has a foundation: incentive plans can increase performance above that attainable at a fixed pay rate. But as we have noted, incentive plans do not always result in increased performance. In fact, numerous studies have shown that incentive plans can also result in restriction of output and cause employee-relations prob-

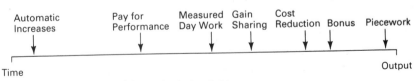

Figure 14–1 A continuum of time and output systems

lems. Also, it has been shown that the different kinds of incentive plans produce different results. Thus it seems useful to examine incentive plans in terms of the performance-motivation and membership models outlined in chapter 4.

THE PERFORMANCE-MOTIVATION MODEL. According to this model, for an incentive plan to motivate performance, employees must (1) believe that good performance will lead to more pay, (2) want more pay, (3) not believe that good performance will lead to negative consequences, (4) see that other desired rewards besides pay result from good performance, and (5) believe that their efforts do lead to improved performance. Although the model specifies that the relationship among these variables is multiplicative (anything multiplied by a zero yields a zero), the first variable is clearly the most important.

Incentive plans do foster the belief that good performance leads to more pay. But some plans do this better than others. Specifically, plans that relate the individual's pay to his or her output do better than plans applied to groups or other larger units. And plans based on objective standards and measurements create a stronger belief in the performance–pay relationship than plans based on less objective standards. With plans involving less objective standards, the belief is based in part on the employee's confidence that the measurements do reflect his or her performance.

Since people do attach different values to pay, the second condition—desiring more pay—is variable. If employees do want more pay and nothing about the plan serves to reduce its importance to them, this part of the model is met. If, however, an incentive plan is applied to employees who don't want more pay or who don't want their pay based on their performance, it is not.

The belief that negative consequences will result from good performance is quite possible under incentive plans. It has been shown that employees can believe that rates will be cut if they produce too much and that social rejection by peers, working themselves out of a job, or even getting fired if they fail to meet the standard can be anticipated. Thus, in some plans it is quite possible that the perceived negative consequences could offset the perceived positive consequences.[4] A major negative consequence is the competitiveness inspired by incentive plans. Where cooperation, not competition, is required, an incentive plan can lead to many dysfunctional behaviors.

The belief that other desired rewards result from good performance is more likely to appear where the competitive nature of the plan is minimized.[5] In some plans good performance is likely to result in social acceptance, esteem, respect, and feelings of achievement. If a person feels that he or she benefits from another's good performance and it becomes the norm of the group to perform well, then the possibilities of good performance are increased.

Employee perceptions that the contributions they believe they are contributing to the organization are in fact those being rewarded may be the weakest link in incentive plans.[6] If employees feel that the performance measured is affected by so many things beyond their control that their efforts have little

[4]W. F. Whyte, "Skinnerian Theory in Organizations," *Psychology Today*, April 1972, pp. 67–68.

[5]H. Meyer, "The Pay for Performance Dilemma," *Organizational Dynamics*, Winter 1975, pp. 22–38.

[6]Ibid.

effect, this belief in the contribution–reward connection will be weak. If employees feel that the performance measure does not reflect a number of contributions that they make and that they feel the organization needs, the belief is likewise weak. If the incentive plan is based on such a limited conception of employee contributions that employees believe that it reflects neither the contributions they make nor those that the organization really requires, not only will the incentive plan not work, it may weaken membership motivation because of resentment.

THE MEMBERSHIP MODEL.   If incentive plans work by creating or confirming beliefs, they can also affect the beliefs and perceptions that form the basis of membership motivation. If the incentive plan signals employees that more of the rewards they want are available in this employment exchange in return for the contributions they want to make, their commitment to the exchange is likely to increase. If, however, the plan signals that additional money is the only reward available for increased performance and they don't want more money; that other rewards they value will be reduced by good performance; that only those contributions resulting in the measured performance result in more rewards but they do not want to provide more of those contributions; or that the contributions they wish to increase are not going to result in higher rewards, then their commitment to the employment exchange may be significantly depressed. In fact, the employee may seek an employment exchange that meshes more closely with their contribution–reward desires.

Thus attempts to improve performance motivation may weaken membership motivation. This is an example of the dilemmas faced by organizations in compensation administration. Fortunately, it is usually possible to treat different employee groups differently in matters of pay.

Results of Incentive Plans

Most reports of experience with incentive plans suggest that wage incentives result in greater output per hour worked, lower unit costs, and higher employee earnings. Typically, these reports come from company experience with incentive plans and do not attempt to determine the source of change or to compare results of incentive workers with those of a control group. When incentive plans are installed, many changes are made in the conditions of work, and if no effort is made to determine the effects of each, the changes observed may be due to something other than the incentive plan. It is quite possible, for example, that the results obtained are attributable to changed management practices employed as a prerequisite to installation of an incentive plan.

Reports of incentive plan results often cite employee earnings increases of 10 to 70 percent and cost decreases of 25 to 65 percent. A survey of the results of 2500 incentive plans reported an average productivity increase of 63.5 percent and an average savings in unit labor costs of 25.9 percent.[7] Although these surveys imply that the observed results are attributable to the incentive plan, no attempt was made to determine whether the source of improvement was better management, increased employee effort, or other changes accompanying installation. Evidence that not all the improvement re-

---

[7]"Wage Incentives and Productivity," *Personnel,* May-June 1955, pp. 4–5.

sults from the incentive plan is available from the experience of a five-plant company. Two plants had incentive plans and three measured daywork (production standards but no wage incentive). The most and least efficient plants, their performance separated by a wide margin, were the two incentive plants.[8]

Two authors have reviewed incentive plan results in detail. Lawler conservatively estimates that individual incentive plans result in a productivity increase of 10 to 20 percent.[9] Locke and associates examined experiments that compared the effects of individual incentive plans with those of time-based pay plans. The average increase in performance was 30 percent, with a range of 3 to 49 percent.[10]

Under an incentive plan increased productivity should result in higher wages for employees. This indeed seems to be the case. In one study of manufacturing organizations the earnings of those workers under incentive plans were significantly higher than those paid by time plans.[11]

Prevalence of Incentive Plans

Given the good fit between the performance-motivation model and incentive plans and the positive results of incentive plans, it would seem logical that a large proportion of employees would be working under incentive plans of some sort. But this is not true, at least not in the United States. There may even be a trend away from incentive plans in the United States.[12] In the period 1961–1963 about 26 percent of American workers were under incentive plans. This figure dropped to 20 percent in 1967–1968 and then to 18 percent in 1973–1980.[13] In other countries incentive plans often apply to a majority of employees, and in some their use is expanding. Overall, however, there has been either a slowdown of the movement toward incentive programs internationally or a retreat such as that in the United States.[14]

This decline in the use of incentive plans has a number of causes, but three stand out. First, the emphasis of American, and to a lesser degree European, economies has been changing from manufacturing to *services*. Service industries and jobs are harder ones in which to relate performance directly to rewards or even to clearly define performance in a measurable fashion. Second, the *complexity of production* has increased, in both methods and technology, so that the individual relationship between effort and output has been

---

[8]S. H. Slichter, J. J. Healy, and E. R. Livernash, *The Impact of Collective Bargaining on Management* (Washington, D.C.: Brookings Institution, 1960), p. 49.

[9]E. E. Lawler, *Pay and Organizational Effectiveness: A Psychological View* (New York: McGraw-Hill, 1971), p. 124.

[10]E. A. Locke, D. B. Feran, V. M. McCaleb, K. N. Shaw, and A. T. Denny, "The Relative Effectiveness of Four Methods of Motivating Employee Performance," in *Changes in Working Life*, ed. K. D. Duncan, M. M. Greenberg, and D. Wallace, (New York: John Wiley, 1980), pp. 363–388.

[11]L. E. Badenhoop and A. N. Jarrel, "Wages and Related Practices in the Machine Industries," *Monthly Labor Review*, August 1956, p. 912.

[12]J. H. Cox, "Time and Incentive Practices in Urban Areas," *Monthly Labor Review*, December 1971, pp. 53–56.

[13]N. W. Carlson, "Time Rates Tighten Their Grip on Manufacturing Industries," *Monthly Labor Review*, May 1982, pp. 15–22.

[14]International Labour Office, *Payment by Results.*

obscured. Third, society has displayed an increased concern for *equity* as opposed to performance. Incentive plans assume that the primary virtue is productivity and that equity may be absent.

The incidence of incentive plans varies greatly with the type of worker. Very few office workers, for instance, work under incentive plans.[15] Although incentive plans are more prevalent in manufacturing than in nonmanufacturing, there is a great deal of variation by industry and area. For example, in the textile, clothing, cigar, and steel industries the proportion of covered employees is over 60 percent, whereas in the aircraft, bakery, beverage, chemical, and lumber industries the proportion is less than 10 percent. Area variation is just as great. In some cities in the Northeast and the North Central States, from 35 to 40 percent of plant workers work under incentive plans; in the South some cities range from 20 to 25 percent; on the West Coast the percentage is less than 10. Even within these areas there is wide variation. Forty percent of plant workers in Waterloo, Iowa, work under incentive plans, but only 4 percent in Detroit. Even within an industry the variation by area is substantial.[16]

One analysis of incentive plans dealt with some correlates of these variations. The first correlate found was with *labor costs*. Where labor costs are high, incentive plans are likely to be used. The second correlate was a *product market* that is cost-competitive. Remember that for these two correlates incentive plans can change labor costs from fixed to variable. The third correlate was a slow advancement of *technology*. This would be consistent with our previous observation that the prevalence of incentive plans has declined with modern techniques and technology. Fourth, if there was a high probability of *production breakdowns,* then incentive plans were not as likely to be used. Clearly, incentive plans need to have an atmosphere of continuous activity if employees are to associate their activity with the output.[17] In a further study the type of incentive plan and the incidence of incentives were found to be related to unionization, the type of technology, and the amount of supervision. Unionization discouraged group incentive plans. Continuous-process technology and close supervision reduced the incidence of incentive plans in general.[18]

The move away from incentive plans may be in the process of being reversed. With competition from other countries, American industry is renewing its emphasis on employee productivity. In addition, there is more emphasis on having the employee perceive the connection between his or her efforts and the fortunes of the organization. These developments indicate that there is likely to be a renewal of incentive plans, but their form may well be changed more to group- and organization-wide plans that use profits and other organizational measures, such as cost savings, as the measures of performance. The current name for these new programs is *gain sharing,* which implies that the employee will share in any organizational gain resulting from the plan. Another sign of the renewal of incentive plans is the recognition of their value by

[15]Cox, "Time and Incentive Practices."

[16]U.S. Department of Labor, *Area Wage Surveys, Selected Metropolitan Areas, 1968–1969, Bulletin no. 1625–90* (Washington, D.C. U.S. Printing Office, 1970).

[17]R. B. McKersie, C. F. Miller, and W. E. Quarterman, "Some Indicators of Incentive Plan Prevalence," *Monthly Labor Review,* March 1964, pp. 271–76.

[18]F. W. Pryor, "Incentives in Manufacturing: The Carrot and the Stick," *Monthly Labor Review,* July 1984, pp. 40–43.

academicians. For instance, Lawler has recently stated that "there is some evidence that the absence of (incentive pay) is a disincentive."[19]

DIMENSIONS

To be effective an incentive plan should fit the circumstances of the organization. The great variety of incentive plans that are possible can be classified by a number of variables, specifically the level of aggregation, the performance definition, and the reward determination method. This section examines these variables, and the following section will look into the necessary considerations in designing an incentive plan.

Level of Aggregation

The level of aggregation defines the unit for which performance or output will be determined. In turn this defines the unit that will receive the organization's reward. Three levels of aggregation are usually defined—the individual, the group, and the organization.

INDIVIDUAL INCENTIVE PLANS.   This is still the most popular form of incentive plan. In this type of plan each person's output or performance is measured and the rewards the person receives are based upon this measurement. Clearly this is the type of incentive plan most likely to establish a clear performance–reward relationship in the mind of the employee. The purpose of the plan is to increase the pace of work or the effort the individual is willing to contribute in order to receive higher rewards. The most common individual incentive plan is the *piecework* system, wherein the employee is paid a set amount for each unit of production.[20] The organization expects to receive more output than it would if the employee were paid under a time-based system. In addition, the organization knows clearly the labor cost associated with that unit of output.

One assumption of these plans is that the employee is an *independent operator,* that he or she alone can carry out all the activities required to achieve the performance measure. In this way performance is a function of the employee's effort. The performance standard must be clearly defined and measurable if such a plan is to be useful. Also, the job must be relatively stable: the output required from the job should be consistent and the inputs to the job should arrive in such a way that the employee can work continuously.

GROUP PLANS.   Where it is impossible to relate output to an individual employee's efforts it may be possible to relate it to the efforts of the work group. If, in addition, cooperation is required to produce the desired output, then a group incentive plan may be the best alternative. *Interdependence of work,* then, is a major reason for choosing a group plan over an individual one. A group incentive plan can reward things that are very different from what an

[19]E. E. Lawler, "Whatever Happened to Incentive Pay?" *New Management,* 1984, p. 37–41.

[20]P. Schwinger, *Wage Incentive Systems* (New York: Halstead, 1975).

individual plan rewards, in particular cooperation, teamwork, and coordination of activities. Where these are highly valued a group plan is most appropriate. As organizations become more complex and the production process more continuous, group incentive plans can be expected to become more popular.

Group plans are also useful where performance standards and measures cannot be defined as objectively. In a group setting variations tend to average out, so no one gets as hurt by random variation or lack of continuity. Group plans and individual ones are of the same type, and almost any individual plan can be adapted to a group setting. Thus the focus in group plans is still higher level of effort.

The primary disadvantage of the group plan is that it weakens the relationship between the individual's effort and performance. Where there is likely to be wide variation in the efforts of group members, a group incentive may lead to more intragroup conflict than cooperation. In group plans it is also more difficult to monitor performance standards and measures. Finally, group norms play an expanded role, both positive and negative, in group plans. They are stronger and more controlling on the individual. Where the group norms are congruent with management's goals, this is a plus; but where the two differ, it can harm the chances of success of the incentive plan.

PLANT AND ORGANIZATION-WIDE PLANS.   Organization-wide plans are expanding under the name of *gain sharing*.[21] These types of plans are both old and new. The *Scanlon Plan* is one of the oldest incentive plans in continuous use in organizations.[22] New plans are cropping up. Organization-wide plans differ significantly from individual plans. In essence they reward different things. As indicated, most individual and group plans attempt to increase effort. Most organization-wide plans, however, reward an increase in *organization-wide outcomes* that directly affect the cost and/or profit picture of the organization. Usually these plans reward increases in productivity of the plant or organization as measured by reduction of organizational costs in comparison with some measured "normal" cost or increased output with the same or fewer inputs.

A major feature of organization-wide incentive plans is a change in the relationship between management on the one hand and employees and their representative body, the union, on the other. Rather than the traditional adversarial relationship between the two, most organization-wide plans require a high degree of cooperation. This is because both groups must focus on the desired cost savings and listen to the other party. All this requires a degree of trust that is hard to achieve in American labor relations. Failures of the Scanlon Plan have been attributed most often to the inability of management to take employee input seriously.[23]

Profit sharing is another popular organization-wide program that is often classified as a gain-sharing plan. This type of plan can be made much more simple than a cost-savings plan. Nor does it require the revolution in em-

[21]See B. E. Graham-Moore and T. L. Ross, *Productivity Gainsharing* (Englewood Cliffs, N.J.: Prentice-Hall, 1983).

[22]See F. G. Lesieur, *The Scanlon Plan: A Frontier in Labor–Management Cooperation* (New York: John Wiley, 1958).

[23]R. A. Ruh, R. L. Wallace, and C. F. Frost, "Management Attitudes and the Scanlon Plan," *Industrial Relations*, 12:1973, pp. 282–88.

ployee–management relationships that cost-savings plans do. With profit sharing management hopes to change employee attitudes toward the organization without a concomitant change in managerial attitudes toward the employee. The idea behind profit sharing is to instill in the employee a sense of partnership with the organization. But most plans go beyond this and use profit sharing as a way to keep valuable employees and to encourage thrift in employees.

Clearly the relationship between effort and performance becomes very tenuous in any organization-wide incentive plan. Even if the performance (profit or cost savings) and the reward (an amount of the profit or savings based on salary) are clear, their connection with what the employee does every day is not clear. In fact, most organization-wide plans fit the membership model better than they do the performance-motivation model.

This enhanced membership motivation appears to be the greatest strength of profit sharing. The profit-sharing objective of instilling a sense of partnership is met to the extent that employees want to continue their membership and to make the additional contributions that enhanced membership implies. Improved performance may result not because employees see a performance–reward relationship but because they want to broaden and deepen the employment exchange by increasing their contributions in return for more intrinsic and perhaps extrinsic rewards.

Performance Definition

The definition of performance is probably the most important step in establishing any incentive plan. It tells the employee what output or behavior the organization considers important enough to reward—that is, to spend its money on. The point is that the employee's attention is directed to accomplishing a particular objective or group of objectives at the expense of others that might also be accomplished on the job. So the definition of performance should be complete, or the organization will not obtain the outcomes it needs from its employees. This section will examine the range of factors that is often used as the definition of performance in incentive plans.

OUTPUT.   The most common definition of performance, and in many ways the best, is the intended output of the job. In some situations this can be made an explicitly measurable item, such as the number of electronic assemblies produced. In many jobs in organizations, however, it is hard either to define exactly the output desired or to measure that output. An incentive plan is not well suited to these circumstances.

The most common incentive plan that uses an output measure is the piecework plan.[24] In this plan, as we have seen, a set reward value is attached to each unit of output; the employee's pay is that value times the number of units produced. This plan clearly connects performance and reward and allows the employee to know at all times exactly how much reward he or she is receiving. Since the piecework system emphasizes quantity, quality can be a problem unless it is also built into the determination of units produced.

[24]T. H. Patten, *Pay: Employee Compensation and Incentive Plans* (New York: Free Press, 1977).

Straight piecework can intimidate employees because it places them under considerable pressure to produce, which they may have difficulty doing consistently. Also, since failure to meet the standard may cause the employee to earn below the minimum wage, most piecework plans establish a minimum standard for a set wage and pay a premium for units produced above that minimum. Employees who regularly do not make the standard are reviewed to see if they are properly placed.

TIME.   Time is often employed in definitions of performance. Amount of production and amount of time are two variables that are always considered together in individual incentive plans. In piecework the amount of production is the measure put before the employee and time is used to determine the value of the output. In time-based rates the expected production is stated as a function of the time taken to produce that output, so the output is expressed as a function of time and not money.

The most common form of time rate individual incentive is the *standard-hour* plan.[25] As in piecework, the employee is paid according to output. However, in the standard hour plan a *standard time* is allowed to complete a job and the employee is paid a set amount for the job if completed within that time. For instance, an auto mechanic may be assigned to tune an automobile, a task for which the standard time is two hours. If the mechanic completes the task in an hour and a half, he or she is paid for two hours. If the job takes two and a half hours, the mechanic is paid for that time. Continually failing to make the standard time would result in examination of either the time standard or the employee.

Another form of time rate is *measured daywork*.[26] Under this plan formal production standards are determined for the job and employee performance is judged relative to those standards. Evaluation is done at least quarterly, and the employee's pay rate may be adjusted according to how well he or she has performed in comparison with the standard. This plan looks very much like the pay-for-performance system discussed in the last chapter. The real differences are in the measured daywork formality of production standards and shorter period of performance review. However, with the measured daywork plan, pay rates may go down as well as up. Measured daywork is advantageous where there are numerous unstandardized conditions in the work that make judgment of performance more important. Sometimes measured daywork utilizes the time standards but does not include the incentive feature.

Measured daywork and the standard hour plan also lend themselves to the use of *bonuses*. A bonus is a one-time payment to the employee that is not built into his or her pay rate. The basis of the bonus may be any performance desired by the organization, and the payment schedule can be designed like that of the standard hour or measured daywork. But a bonus system can be used in much broader circumstances. An advantage to a bonus is that it may be a reward for any behavior or outcome deemed important to the organization; it does not have to cover all relevant parts of the job. An example of this is a

[25]See T. H. Patten, op. cit.

[26]A. Shaw, "Measured Daywork: One Step toward a Salaried Workforce," in *Payment Systems*, ed. T. Lupton (Harmondsworth, England: Penguin, 1972), pp. 143–65.

series of programs designed to reduce absenteeism in organizations through the use of behavior-modification principles.[27]

MULTIPLE PERFORMANCE DIMENSIONS.   Any incentive plan is designed to focus the employee on particular desired outcomes or activities. The effect of this is that any job dimensions not included in the definition of performance are not likely to be performed. Thus it is important to include all important job dimensions in performance definition. A single dimension, such as units produced in a piecework plan, is appealing in terms of simplicity and clear performance–reward connections but is often dysfunctional to genuine productivity. The clearest example of this is the problem of quality in a piecework plan. If the number of units is the only performance standard, the employee is encouraged to turn out a lot of units but they will likely be substandard.

Many incentive plans, then, employ multiple performance definitions, and the question becomes how to combine them. The simplest way, if possible, is to use a *composite score*. The values of the various performance variables are added together. This in turn leads to the question of the weight each variable is accorded. This process is much like the use of a number of compensable factors in job evaluation (see chapter 10). A second method is the *multiple-hurdle approach*, in which a minimum level must be reached on each performance dimension before any incentive is paid. A third approach is a series of *mini–incentive plans*, one for each performance dimension.

GAIN SHARING.   This approach, broader than the use of output and time standards, rewards outcomes that are direct measures of the success of the organization as opposed to the success of the individual employee. As we have noted, gain-sharing plans are more appropriate to organization-wide incentive plans. The purpose of gain sharing is to tie the employee to the performance measures by which top management is judged and by which society defines a successful organization. Although clear performance–reward connections can be made in these circumstances, it is difficult to make a performance–effort connection.

A number of different performance measures can be used in gain sharing, but all share a common dimension: a baseline standard must be established to determine where the organization is "at the present time." The value of improvements in future measures of the performance are then shared with the employees. One set of performance definitions rewards *reductions in costs* or *improvements in productivity*.

The most popular gain-sharing plan is the Scanlon Plan.[28] In this plan employees are paid a bonus if costs remain below preestablished standards. The standards have been set by studies of past cost averages. Ways to reduce costs are developed by a series of committees throughout the organization and a plantwide screening committee that reviews and implements changes. Although Scanlon developed this plan in 1937, these committees look much like

---

[27]L. M. Schmitz and H. G. Heneman III, "Do Positive Reinforcement Programs Reduce Employee Absenteeism?" *Personnel Administrator*, September 1980, pp. 87–93.

[28]B. E. Moore and T. L. Ross, *The Scanlon Way to Improve Productivity* (New York: Wiley-Interscience, 1978).

the *quality-control circles* that are popular today.[29] The Scanlon Plan is built on a philosophy of labor–management cooperation and consequently a trust relationship. Such cooperation is hard to develop in our society, where the relationship between management and labor, particularly when a union is involved, is perceived as adversarial.

The Scanlon Plan is not the only organization-wide plan, but it is the best known. Others that have been successful in the United States include the *Rucker Share-of-Production, Kaiser,* and *Nunn-Bush* plans. A more recent plan is *Improshare,* of which more than 100 had been adopted as of the early 1980s.[30] Although these plans differ in details, all rely on a definition of productivity improvements wholly measured by some time period and pay bonuses for savings. Further, most depend upon labor–management cooperation which represents a change in the relationship between management and labor.

PROFIT SHARING.   A further attempt to tie employees to the economic success of the organization is to grant them a share of the profits of the organization. Obviously, this type of incentive is useful only in a for-profit organization. Profit sharing has not always been carefully delineated. The Council of Profit Sharing Industries categorizes plans for cost-savings sharing as profit sharing, although they pay off whether or not the organization makes a profit.

Increased production has been cited as one of the goals of profit sharing, and reported results include increased efficiency and lower costs. Many early reports of profit-sharing results attributed large increases in production to the plan.[31] More recent reports find profit-sharing companies more successful financially than non-profit-sharing companies but are more careful in attributing the difference to profit sharing.[32] Profit sharing is popular for organizations, from both a practical standpoint and a philosophical one. Management often feels that having the employee focus on profits is useful and will lead to higher organizational profits. In recent years the Employee Retirement Income Security Act (ERISA), variations in profits, and the advent of employee thrift plans have blunted the growth of profit-sharing plans.

Profit sharing can be useful to an organization for a number of reasons. For example, the following objectives of profit sharing were compiled from a survey of 298 profit-sharing companies: (1) to instill a sense of partnership, (2) to serve as a group incentive, (3) to provide employee security, (4) to be fair, (5) to provide benefits beyond basic wages without incurring fixed commitments, (6) to attract desirable employees and reduce turnover, and (7) to encourage employee thrift. These objectives are listed in order of the frequency in which they appeared in the survey.[33]

Profit-sharing plans are typically differentiated on the basis of when profit shares are distributed. *Cash* plans (known also as *current-distribution plans*)

[29]M. Zippo, "Productivity and Morale Sagging? Try the Quality Circle Approach," *Personnel,* May–June 1980, pp. 43–45.

[30]Graham-Moore and Ross, *Productivity Gainsharing.*

[31]*Sharing Profits with Employees,* Studies in Personnel Policy no. 162 (New York: National Industrial Conference Board, 1957).

[32]B. L. Metzger and J. A. Colletti, *Does Profit Sharing Pay?* (Evanston, Ill.: Profit Sharing Research Foundation, 1971).

[33]P. A. Knowles, *Profit Sharing Patterns* (Evanston, Ill.: Profit Sharing Research Foundation, 1954), p. 55.

pay out profit shares at regular intervals as earned. *Deferred plans* put the profits to be distributed in the hands of a trustee, and distribution is delayed until some event occurs. This type of plan is ordinarily tied into a retirement plan (see chapter 16). *Combination plans* distribute part of the profit share as earned and defer distribution of the balance.

Perhaps the most famous of the current-distribution profit sharing-plans is that of the Lincoln Electric Company of Cleveland. This incentive system consists of a number of plans, of which a year-end bonus based on profits is only one. Most employees are on piecework with a guarantee. In addition, profits above 6 percent are distributed each year among employees in accordance with their merit rating. Since 1934 the year-end bonus has not been less than 20 percent of annual wages and has often been well over 100 percent.

The famous Sears, Roebuck plan is a deferred-distribution plan under which company and employee contributions combine to provide very satisfactory retirement benefits. One of the features of this plan has been the limitation of employee contributions, which effectively equalizes the participation of lower- and higher-salaried employees. It is quite apparent that this plan has succeeded in attracting and holding employees.

Profit-sharing plans vary widely in provisions concerning organization contributions, employee allocation, eligibility requirements, payout provisions, and other administrative details. Two thirds of the plans define the contribution of the organization by a formula; in the balance this amount is determined by the board of directors. Most formulas specify a straight percentage of before-tax profit after reservations for stockholders and reserves. The amounts allocated to employees or their accounts are usually based on their compensation but may also be influenced by their length of service, contributions, performance, or responsibility. In most plans all full-time employees are eligible immediately or after a short waiting period, but a substantial minority of plans exclude union employees or are limited to specific employee groups. Payout provisions are usually determined by plan designation (cash, deferred, or combination), but deferred and combination plans are increasingly incorporating vesting provisions and payout under a wide variety of circumstances.

Our discussion of profit sharing suggests that it does not closely fit the performance-motivation model. Profits are influenced by so many variables that it is very difficult for an individual to feel that his or her contributions have organization-wide results. Thus, it is difficult for employees to believe that their profit share is related to their performance. It may be possible for small organizations with cash plans and continuous communication efforts to maintain their employees' belief in the performance–reward relationship, but such a belief is vulnerable to any reduction in profits that occurs while the employee is maintaining his or her performance level. Larger organizations with cash plans are less likely to be able to foster this belief in the first place and may be even more vulnerable to changing circumstances. Deferred plans involve the additional hurdle of payment that is delayed, often for years. Under such plans employee belief in the performance–reward relationship may be impossible, even in small organizations.

On the other hand, profit sharing may closely fit the membership-motivation model, even in large organizations, at least for certain groups of employees. The promise to provide additional economic rewards when profits of the organization permit it and the implied acceptance of all employee contributions that will advance the profit goal serve to increase both the numerator and the denominator of the membership-motivation model. In this way employees may enlarge their commitment to the organization.

Reward Determination

A major assumption of the performance-motivation model is that the person must desire the reward being offered. Since money is considered the most desired reward, it is far and away the most important reward offered in incentive plans. The idea of an incentive plan relies heavily on the value of money to the employee. Although there are few employees who would claim that money is unimportant, the degree to which money is important to people varies with their circumstances. So incentive plans are likely to be of major importance to only some employees. Those whose wages are low and those whose wages are high are most likely to be attracted to incentive plans, but for different reasons. More money, itself, is attractive to those whose wages are low. To the person who has high wages, money becomes a symbol of success. Two aspects of money need to be considered by the administrator of an incentive plan—when and how much of it is granted.

TIMING. We have seen that the reward may be granted anywhere from immediately after the accomplishment to many years later. From a motivational standpoint, the closer the reward is to the desired performance the stronger its motivational value. This is because the person can more easily attribute the reward to a particular performance. Incentive plans vary greatly in their timing of the reward. Those such as piecework make the connection every payday. Others, such as bonus plans, may grant the reward quarterly or semiannually. Under deferred plans it may be years before the person receives any value.

AMOUNT. The reward must be perceived as worth the additional effort. An incentive plan that requires considerable effort and luck to achieve a substantial amount of extra money will probably not lead to extra effort; the employees will feel that the probabilities of gaining additional income are not worth it. Where the incentive plan is an adjunct to the regular wage, the amount possible to receive under the plan must be a large enough percentage of base pay to entice the person to put forth extra effort. Again, the amount or percentage that will be perceived as significant varies with the person.[34]

NONFINANCIAL REWARDS. Not all incentive plans focus on money as the reward. *Time* can be a significant reward to many people. Incentive plans can provide time off the job as well as more pay. To many people in our society, defining what needs to be done and then letting the person complete it in whatever time is comfortable provides not only free time but a sense of freedom as well.

Some incentive plans avoid any involvement with the pay system by developing contests in which employees receive *prizes* of value to them. These

[34]L. A. Krefting, "Differences in Orientation toward Pay Increases," *Industrial Relations,* 19:1977, pp. 81–87.

prizes can range from merchandise to vacation trips. Of course the prize must be something the recipient desires. Otherwise there is no incentive to perform. Incentive plans such as this can also be dysfunctional if the reward is for something that is peripheral to the job. The focus on the contest may remove attention from the basic purpose of the job.

DESIGN

In the previous section we discussed the two basic parts of an incentive plan—the performance definition and the reward. In this section we discuss how these two are put together in an incentive plan. Specifically, the jobs to be included, relating performance to reward, and the administration and control of incentive plans are examined.

Jobs to Be Included

Not all people or all jobs should be placed under an incentive plan. Jobs in particular vary in appropriateness of incentive plans. Further, the variety of incentive plans and the variation in effectiveness of those in operation suggest that there are conditions under which a particular plan is applicable and conditions that make for the success or failure of incentive plans in general.

JOB CONDITIONS. The kind of work being performed is a major variable in choosing which incentive plan if any, is the most applicable.[35] A plan suited to highly repetitive, standardized, short-cycle manual operations is unlikely to fit less structured work. Highly variable, unstandardized work may make incentives unworkable.

The major job variables that need to be examined in determining the applicability of incentives are (1) standardization of the job, (2) repetitiveness of the operations, (3) rate of change in operations, methods, and materials, (4) control of the work pace, and (5) measurability of job outcomes. If these variables are placed at the ends of a scale as in exhibit 14–1, then the more each is true for the job, the more individual incentive plans that focus on job outcomes, such as piecework or standard-hour plans, are appropriate. If these

Exhibit 14–1 Applicability of Incentive Plans to Work Conditions

INDIVIDUAL INCENTIVE PLAN	GROUP INCENTIVE PLAN	ORGANIZATION INCENTIVE PLAN	NO INCENTIVE PLAN
1. Standardized jobs		1. Variable jobs	
2. Repetitive work		2. Novel work	
3. Stable methods		3. Changing methods	
4. Worker control of pace		4. Machine control of pace	
5. Measurable outcomes		5. Judged outcomes	

[35]H. K. von Kaas, *Making Wage Incentives Work* (New York: American Management Assn., 1971).

conditions are not met and variability is introduced, group- or organization-wide plans are more appropriate. These types of plans can smooth out the variations that occur in jobs that fall between the two extremes illustrated in exhibit 14–1. At the other end of the scale are jobs that are largely inappropriate for incentive plans because of their lack of standardization and repetitiveness, frequent changes in methods, lack of worker control, and difficulty in measurement.

Most organizations have jobs that fall into all of these categories. Thus an organization desiring to place all or most employees on incentives may find that a plantwide plan is most feasible. Some organizations, because of the value of incentives, choose to invest a great deal of time in developing an individual incentive plan in a variable situation, but most choose to install a number of different plans, each geared to a limited segment of the organization, or an organization-wide plan.

It is seldom mentioned in reports of experience with incentive plans, but pointed out increasingly by others,[36] that work often requires workers to cooperate rather than compete with one another and with other organization units. Such requirements, which are becoming the norm in complex organizations, argue against individual incentive plans and in favor of group and organization-wide plans. Obtaining cooperation among interdependent workers and among organization units is difficult under the best conditions and logically impossible when the reward system encourages competition.

ORGANIZATIONAL CONDITIONS.   The *size* of the organization may affect the chances of success of incentive plans. A large organization can typically make the administrative commitment required to support an individual incentive plan. Plantwide plans apparently require fairly small organizations in order to be successful. Thus large organizations would seem to be limited to individual or small-group incentive plans or to none at all, and small organizations with limited staff expertise would seem to be limited to plantwide plans.

Also involved is the proportion of total costs represented by *labor costs*. If labor costs are a high proportion of total costs, placing labor costs on a variable-cost basis is worth considerable effort. But if labor costs are a small proportion of total costs, incentive plans will appear less attractive to management.

Management attitudes constitute a major variable in incentive plan success. Unless management is committed to maintaining the relationship between performance and pay and backs this commitment with the necessary administrative expenditures and organization of work, an individual incentive plan can fail or become obsolete very quickly. Management attitudes will depend in part on the nature of competition in the industry and on business conditions, but the real variable is the trust management has in employees to guide and direct their own activities. This is true of both individual and organization-wide incentive plans.

Union–management relationships also determine the kind of incentive plan, if any, that is feasible. A hostile relationship argues against any incentive plan, because the union may be motivated to use it as an additional arena of controversy. A formal, arms-length relationship suggests limiting incentive coverage to situations where sufficient objectivity can be achieved to preclude dis-

[36]For example, Lawler, in *Pay and Organizational Effectiveness*.

agreement. If, however, the relationship is characterized by mutual respect and trust, incentive plans dictated by technical conditions may be employed. For example, a gain-sharing plan based on imperfect measurement may be employed if the work requires it.

INCENTIVE PLAN APPLICABILITY.   There is a tendency to think of incentive plans as being applicable primarily to direct production jobs, with pay for performance plans the appropriate method for other employees. This tendency applies primarily to individual and small-group incentives rather than to plantwide or organization-wide incentives, which ordinarily cover all employees.

The fact is, however, that individual and small-group incentive plans are applied to almost all varieties of work. What is required is a willingness to engage in the expense and administration required to make the program work. From this standpoint, there is scarcely any job that someone has not successfully measured, and applied a reasonably successful incentive plan to.

The premise for this reasoning may be simply stated. All tasks, jobs, or functions must have a purpose. Better performance of this purpose is worth money to the organization. Devising a yardstick to measure this improved performance will therefore permit rewarding the individual or group who achieve it.

The general approach in all these applications of incentive systems has been (1) identifying measurable work as a yardstick of performance, (2) setting standards on the basis of this yardstick, (3) measuring performance against these standards, and (4) providing extra pay for performance above standard. It has been found in all of these applications that certain aspects of work results can be measured.

The widely varied applications of incentive plans prove that with diligence and ingenuity it is possible to find and measure aspects of work. But it may be useful to remember that the kind of behavior measured is the kind of behavior that people exhibit.[37] Thus, organizations must be certain that incentive plans are based on measures of output that they require rather than merely on those that can be measured. If what is measured is related only peripherally to organization goals and if what is not measured remains undone and neglected by employees, the incentive plan impedes attainment of organization goals.

Relation of Performance to Reward

The central imperative in an incentive plan is that the person being paid understand that a particular outcome or behavior, when compared successfully with the performance standard, will lead to a specified reward. In this section we will cover the development of this relationship. In order to develop this relationship, the performance standard must be clearly stated and the ratio between it and the reward delineated.

SETTING PERFORMANCE STANDARDS.   An incentive plan must contain a clear performance standard. As we have seen, a number of definitions of performance are used in incentive plans. These include the output of the job, the

---

[37]Ibid.

time taken to complete a task, the efficiency with which the job or organization operates, and the profit derived from the operation of the organization.

Setting performance standards in terms of outputs would seem the easiest since it taps the purpose of the job. But in many jobs it is difficult or impossible to quantify the output. Further, output can be defined in terms of the number of units, the quality of those units, and/or the time taken to complete the units.

The most common way of determining a performance standard for production jobs is to conduct a *time and motion study*. This technique estimates the time normally required to produce a unit. In turn, a study of the job in operation in which the exact motions required to perform the task and the time required to do so is made. Thus, each activity or element that goes into producing the unit of production is timed and a total time is developed under which a normal worker working at a normal pace would complete a unit of production.[38] The equitable relationship between the unit of production and pay can then be arrived at by finding the market rate for the job or through bargaining. The focus of a time and motion study can be either the output or the time taken to complete the task. Thus both piecework and standard-hour incentive plans tend to use this technique.

Nonproduction jobs can also be paid under an incentive plan based upon outputs. Sales jobs are a case in point: the salesperson is paid on the basis of sales volume. Regardless of the job, the major requirement of setting performance standards is to define the value of a unit of production or performance. In order to do this there must be some idea of a normal output and an equitable wage for achieving that output.

Incentive plans focusing on efficiency, or cost reduction, involve defining a standard or normal cost and then rewarding employees on a schedule that is achieved at less than this standard cost. The cost definition varies with the plan. In a Scanlon Plan the typical cost standard is labor costs as a percentage of sales. The Rucker Plan uses value added by manufacture for each dollar of payroll costs measured by the difference between sales income from goods produced and the costs of materials, supplies, and services consumed in production. In Improshare, the focus is on the hours saved in producing a given output. Production standards are developed from past production records.

Profits are a clear-cut measure, but as a performance standard in a profit-sharing plan they require two decisions. The first is to set the percentage of the profits that will go into the profit-sharing plan in each time period allocated. This percentage can be fixed, such as 10 percent, or established anew for each period by management decision. The second decision is the proportion of the total allocation that each person receives (distribution). This is ordinarily done by calculating an employee's base pay as a percentage of total payroll and giving the employee that percentage of the total profit-sharing allocation.

PROPORTION OF EARNINGS.   Incentive plans can range from being the basis for all of the employee's pay to being an insignificant percentage of it. In a straight piecework plan the employee is paid for the number of units produced. There is no guarantee of how much the employee will make in a time period; that is up to the employee. A keypunch operator who is paid a certain

---

[38]See, for example, S. Konz, *Work Design* (Columbus, Ohio: Grid Publishing, 1979).

amount for each 100 cards would be an example. At the other extreme might be a profit-sharing plan that provides no additional money, beyond base pay, to the employees in a year in which the organization does not make a profit. Clearly, in these two cases the importance of the incentive plan to the employee and its motivational effect is very different.

Both of these situations are likely to be unacceptable to the employee, but for different reasons. The straight incentive plan makes the employee feel insecure. In the second case there is supposed to be an incentive, but none is forthcoming or it is so small that it means nothing. The employee feels cheated. The lessons from this are that some guarantees should be built into the incentive plan on one hand and the incentive plan should be a significant proportion of the employee's total pay on the other.

Rather than a straight incentive plan most plans contain a guaranteed base pay. This is usually the market rate or some proportion of the job's market rate. This guarantee is associated with an output standard that matches the guaranteed rate. The incentive plan then really operates only if the employee exceeds the performance standard; for all time periods in which he or she does not "meet standard," the pay is the base guaranteed pay. In this way employees are protected from circumstances beyond their control that limit production in a particular period. If an employee continually fails to meet standard, management must decide whether the standard is incorrect or whether the employee is not capable of performing the job.

As we have seen, for a reward to be of value to a person, it must be perceived as significant enough to expend effort on. Ordinarily, an incentive plan that yields a small proportion of the employee's earnings or a plan in which the probability of attaining the reward is low does not energize the employee to expend effort. Thus it is unlikely that the organization will attain the performance it desires. One exception may be bonus plans that reward a very specific behavior that is an out-of-the-ordinary outcome of the job. A *suggestion system* is an example.

PERFORMANCE–REWARD RATIO. Basic to the performance–reward connection is the ratio of reward to performance. This ratio can take a number of forms. The most common is the *straight-proportional ratio*. This is the type used in piecework and standard-hour plans. It provides a one-for-one proportion between performance and reward. A second possibility is the *geared ratio*. In this case the ratio of reward to performance units varies at different levels of production. The proportional change may be *less* or *more* than the proportional change in output. These three possibilities are illustrated in figure 14–2 (p. 298). Note that this illustration assumes that there is a base rate of production and reward after which the incentive system takes hold.

These three examples do not exhaust the types of performance–reward ratio. Three more, based on the geared ratio, are illustrated in figure 14–3 (p. 298). In a *progressive ratio* the reward increases with higher production. This type of system is most likely to be useful where higher levels of production become increasingly difficult to achieve. A *regressive ratio* is the opposite: higher levels of production lead to less proportionate reward. This may be appropriate where higher levels require help of others in the organization to achieve. The final ratio is not really a ratio but a *fixed amount* if a standard is exceeded. This arrangement is often found in a fixed bonus system.

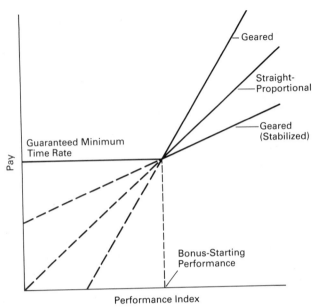

Figure 14–2 Performance-reward ratios
(Source: *Payment by Results,* International Labour Office, Geneva, 1984, p. 11.)

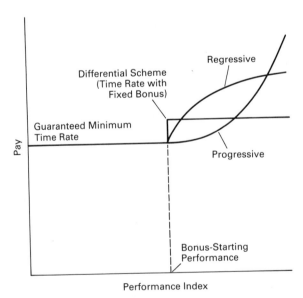

Figure 14–3 Three geared ratios
(Source: *Payment by Results,* International Labour Office, Geneva, 1984, p. 12.)

POSITIVE-REINFORCEMENT PLANS.   To some degree all incentive plans are based upon the principles of *behavior modification*. Some organizations, however, have developed incentive plans that specifically use these principles. Emery Air Freight was one of the first to develop such a plan. Its procedure was as follows:

1. Define the performance variables of importance and conduct an audit to see how well the organization is doing.
2. Establish specific goals for each employee, using employee input.
3. Have each employee keep records on how he or she is doing.
4. Praise positive results and ignore substandard work.[39]

Many other companies have developed this kind of plan.[40] A major use of these programs has been to reduce absenteeism.[41] Although praise is the basic ingredient in many positive-reinforcement plans, there is increasing pressure to include money in them.

Administration and Control

Careful attention to incentive policies and procedures is a necessary prerequisite for the installation and successful operation of any incentive plan. Wide participation in the development of these policies and procedures, including union–management negotiation, also increases the possibilities of success. A careful statement of policy goes far toward preventing situations in which rewards are offered for results not desired by either the organization or employees. Participation in policy making helps ensure both the commitment of resources and energy required by management and the favorable attitudes of employees and the union on which the success of the incentive plan depends.

ADMINISTRATIVE SUPPORT.   Incentive plans require expert staff support for proper operation, especially a heavy commitment of resources to industrial engineering. Unless the industrial engineers can carry out the standardization and measurement work as well as plan maintenance, the incentive plan will quickly become obsolete.

There is also likely to be pressure to expand incentive coverage to other workers in order to bring their earnings up to the level of those of incentive plan workers. Ensuring that such expansion is economically justified requires expert administrative support and upper-management decision making based upon the value of incentive plans and not upon other organizational political considerations.

SUPERVISION.   Incentive plans require good supervision. This requirement may mean selecting more capable supervisors. But it certainly means training supervisors to understand the workings of wage incentives and,

[39]W. C. Hamner and E. P. Hamner, "Behavior Modification on the Bottom Line," *Organizational Dynamics*, Spring 1976, pp. 8–9.
[40]Ibid.
[41]Schmitz and Heneman, "Positive Reinforcement Programs."

equally important, showing supervisors that wage incentives are an important means of obtaining the quality, cost, and output objectives that are their responsibility and the basis of their rewards. Unless supervisors acquire the necessary skills and a strong interest in making the plan work, the incentive plan will quickly deteriorate.

The role of the supervisor changes when an incentive plan is installed. The control function is lessened since the incentive plan builds in a control mechanism. On the other hand, the supervisor must ensure that the production process runs smoothly, with a minimum of down time, so that the employees may produce according to the plan. Supervisors spend more time in liaison and training and less in directing their workers.

EMPLOYEE PERCEPTIONS.   Employees and their union representatives must *accept* the incentive plan as *fair* if it is to work. In nonunion organizations, obtaining this belief may require a continuing communications effort. In unionized organizations, union help in explaining the plan may ease this task. Emphasizing the prospects for steady employment and allaying other fears of employees is necessary to obtain their belief in the fairness of the plan.

Standards must be accepted by employees, who in turn must be guaranteed that the standards will not be changed except under agreed-on conditions. Employee fear of *rate cutting* is the force behind restricted output and employee distrust of incentive plans. Accepted standards require capable administrative staff and supervisors who are not only technically competent but able to secure employee approval of standards and the standard-setting process. Successful incentive plans emphasize measurement rather than negotiation in the setting of standards. Obviously, acceptance of measurements requires confidence in management's fairness and good labor relations.

Keeping the incentive plan *simple and understandable* to employees is essential. All procedures should be as simple as possible. Complicated earnings formulas should usually be avoided. Employee trust requires that employees understand how the plan works and affects their pay.

ESTABLISHMENT OF PERFORMANCE STANDARDS.   As indicated, performance standards lie at the heart of any incentive plan. How these standards are set goes a long way toward achieving their acceptance. *Participation* is one way to aid in acceptance. Unions often have time-study experts who work with the organization's staff to set standards. Standards disputes are typically settled between the union time-study expert and the industrial engineer on the basis of the results of a joint study. The solutions must be acceptable to employees, the union, and the organization.

Developing acceptable original standards is not as difficult as obtaining acceptance of *changes in standards.* Because of employees' fear of rate cutting and union insistence on protecting employees' interests, any change in standards is likely to be resisted, no matter how justified. But changes in materials, methods, and equipment require changes in standards if the incentive plan is not to become uneconomical for the organization. Still, any changes in standards should be a last resort and should be carefully explained to employees.

Failure to meet or exceed standards should be carefully investigated, and the reasons found and corrected. The failure may be due to poor standardization of materials and equipment, in which case employees have the right to request a revision of the standard. Or it may be due to inadequate training or failure to follow the prescribed methods. Each of these cases calls not for a revision of the standard but for better supervision and training. Paying the worker "average earnings" if he or she fails to reach standard rather than finding and correcting the reason for the failure weakens incentive plans.

As indicated, most incentive plans contain a *base rate* that guarantee the employee a base salary regardless of his or her production. The relationship among base rates should be determined by job evaluation and market rates, just as with any other job in the organization.

ORGANIZATIONAL PAY RELATIONSHIPS. Pay relationships between jobs become more important when there is an incentive plan in the organization. If earnings of low-skilled employees on incentive exceed those of high-skilled employees not on incentive, a perception of inequity is created that will lead to pressure for increases in wages for those not under the incentive plan whether or not there is any basis for these increases. Under individual and small-group incentive plans continually monitoring pay relationships involves an additional commitment of resources.

As we have noted, extra earnings under the plan must be sufficient to provide incentive for extra effort. With reasonable effort most workers should be able to attain some incentive earnings. The average worker on incentive is usually expected to earn a 25-to-30 percent bonus. Individual workers are expected to vary around the normal bonus rate. Theoretically, of course, there is no ceiling on earnings, and establishing one would in essence cut rates and reduce the plan's incentive value for high producers.

INCENTIVE PLAN MAINTENANCE AND AUDIT. More incentive plans fail because of inadequate maintenance than for any other reason. There is a constant tendency for incentive plans to erode.[42] Although changing the plan has its hazards, as just indicated, ignoring the constant changes that occur in the organization is most likely to lead to a situation where the standards are too loose and the incentive plan is costing too much and not providing the incentive for extra effort.

Many organizations with successful incentive plans audit all phases of their incentive operation at regular intervals of one year or less. Standards are audited by analyzing an operation selected at random, almost as if an original standard were being developed: materials, methods, operator proficiency, and equipment are checked and compared with the existing standard. The timekeeping and reporting systems are also audited, as are earnings relationships among individuals and groups. The latter are subjected to statistical analysis of earnings distributions.

An advantage of the periodic audit is the assurance that high earnings are not used as a signal to revise standards but that every standard is periodically audited and revised up or down as prevailing circumstances dictate. Union officials, recognizing the desirability of a consistent rate structure and the elimination of inequities, find the approach logical. Employees are less likely to

---

[42]International Labour Office, *Payment by Results.*

resent changes wrought by an agreed-on system than by an individual making decisions that affect them.

PROBLEMS

Although there is a great deal of evidence that incentive plans can improve employee performance, there is also much evidence that they have dysfunctional consequences. If this were not true, incentive plans would undoubtedly be more popular than they are. The problems of incentive plans fall into two categories—practicality and perception.

Problems of Practicality

With incentive plans there are many things that might be possible to do but not worth doing because they cost too much, either directly or indirectly. There is a tremendous amount of evidence, for example, that incentive plans, especially individual ones, result in *restriction of output*. Such studies show that this phenomenon is widespread and results in productivity considerably below worker capability.[43]

The reason for restriction of output has been shown to be worker beliefs that additional productivity will lead to a rate cut or to their working themselves out of a job.[44] These beliefs presumably result in group pressures to restrict output.

It has also been shown that the competition created by individual incentive plans can cause serious problems if the work calls for cooperative effort. People can be expected to exhibit behavior that is rewarded, and cooperative behavior is not rewarded or recognized under an individual incentive plan. In fact, it has been suggested that incentive plans cause employee resentment because they reward only effort, although employees know that many other contributions are required by the organization.

A problem implied above is the high administrative costs of an incentive plan. Although there is no question that determining standards, measuring output, and maintaining the plan are more costly than administering a pay-for-time-worked plan, there are no studies that accurately show the costs of installing and operating an incentive plan. Studies cited earlier concerning cost reductions under incentives suggest that productivity increases often offset the additional costs.

Still another problem of incentive plans, noted earlier, is the tendency for internal wage and salary relationships to be distorted such that lower-skilled incentive-based workers may earn more than high-skilled workers not under the plan. Interestingly, this problem as well as intergroup conflict has been

[43]There are many illustrations of this problem in management literature. See, for example, O. Collins, M. Dalton, and D. Roy, "Restrictions of Output and Social Cleavage in Industry," *Applied Anthropology,* Summer 1946, pp. 1–14; M. Dalton, "The Industrial Rate Buster: A Characterization," *Applied Anthropology,* Winter 1948, pp. 5–18; D. Roy, "Quota Restriction and Gold Bricking in a Machine Shop," *American Journal of Sociology,* March 1952, pp. 427–42; and W. F. Whyte, ed. *Money and Motivation* (New York: Harper, 1955).

[44]D. J. Hickson, "Motives of People Who Restrict Their Output," *Occupational Psychology,* July 1961, p. 110–21.

credited with the move toward expanding incentive-based plans at the plant and organizational level.

Several of these problems, especially the last one and the need for co-operation between workers on interdependent jobs, have encouraged the adoption of group and plantwide incentive plans. Although the studies to date have not proved that these broader plans avoid these problems, there is evidence that they can encourage cooperation and offer suggestions (not proof) that output restriction is less likely. The numerous changes that accompany the installation of a companywide plan make determining the source of results especially difficult. At any rate, there is no reliable evidence comparing the relative effectiveness of individual, group, and companywide plans.

Problems of Perception

The performance-motivation model is a perceptual model: it states that people will behave in a given way provided they perceive certain things. This section will reexamine this model to see what problems of perception incentive plans can have.

THE IMPORTANCE OF PAY.   Incentive plans rely on pay as being an important reward for the employee. This is undoubtedly true. But pay is not the *only* reward that is important to employees. There are many nonfinancial rewards that employees need and desire in their work relationship. Incentive plans not only ignore most of these other rewards but often thwart their satisfaction. The discussion on restriction of output and its causes is a good example. The reasons that incentive plans have problems of this kind is that they prevent employees from satisfying their social needs. Where desires for different rewards come into conflict the motivational strength of the plan is diminished.

THE PERFORMANCE–REWARD CONNECTION.   As we have seen, the most important aspect of incentive plan design is the determination of the performance standards and the ratio of rewards to those standards. This is easy to say and hard to do. Performance is hard to define for all jobs. It is even harder to define all the performance variables and relate them to the rewards. What occurs is a dilemma. In order to include all the variables and make the connections the plan becomes complex. This in turn violates the simplicity principle and increases the probability that the employee will not understand the plan.

Establishing performance standards is a continual problem. To the degree that it is done by management for the employee, its acceptance by the employee depends upon the faith that the employee has in management. The constant fear of the employee, as we have noted, is of rate cutting. Thus any change in the standards whether justified or not, will be viewed with suspicion. Again, incentive plans require trust between management and labor, something that is not common in our society. Even where there is trust the process of setting standards is judgmental, suggesting that there is always the possibility of error. It is therefore wise to have a formal appeal system, whether there is a union or not. Further, the definition of performance by management in some cases is seen by employees as breaking down the skill requirements of the job and thereby making the job less intrinsically appealing.

Although the connection between performance and reward is clear in the short run, it may not be so in the long term. As we have seen, the employee may perceive that to produce above the standard is to work oneself out of a job. This becomes a further reason to restrict output and to encourage others to do likewise. A further concern along these lines, by employees, may be that the proportion of the gain made under the incentive plan goes mostly to the organization and not to the employees.

THE PERFORMANCE–EFFORT CONNECTION.   The final part of the performance-motivation model is the connection between performance and effort. The purpose of incentive plans is to increase the effort of employees and thereby their output. Obviously, this assumes that the employee's effort makes a difference in the output, but this is not always true, at least not in a proportion that allows the performance–effort connection to operate.

Employees have concerns about attempts to increase effort. They may feel that management is trying to get more than a *fair day's work for a fair day's pay*. Or they may feel that incentive plans are excuses for a *speedup* by management. At the extreme the pressure for more effort may lead to stress and fatigue.

In order to have high earnings the employee under an incentive plan must put out a consistently high level of effort. This may not be a natural pace for people. Most of us are able to work faster at certain times of the day than at others, so a constant high level of effort is almost impossible to maintain. Employees who cannot keep up are going to feel a great deal of frustration and concern for their continued employment.

Furthermore, base rates in incentive plans that are established through industrial engineering assume that all people have the same ability to achieve the standard or higher. This is not true. Thus there are some employees for whom the performance–effort connection is low because they are easily able to meet the standard, and others for whom the connection is low because they must put forth too much effort to meet it. But it is impossible to have different standards, since that would be perceived as unfair.

All of these perceptual concerns by employees serve to lower the contingencies required for the performance-motivation model to operate and therefore reduce the effectiveness of an incentive plan. Management and the compensation staff need to recognize the possible presence of these concerns and deal openly with them through communication programs with the employees.

SUMMARY

Incentive plans are the ultimate in pay-for-performance. After a considerable period of decline in their usage in the United States, new interest is being shown in developing incentive plans for a wide range of jobs, many of which were considered inappropriate jobs for incentive plans in the past. However, with the need to focus on productivity and the known positive results of incentive plans, many new ideas in incentive plans are being tried. The use of incentive plans comes the closest to using the performance-motivation model in the design of the compensation plan.

There are three essential elements to incentive plans. First, the unit of the incentive plan, called the level of aggregation, is determined. Incentive plans are ordinarily categorized into individual, group, or plant wide (organizational). Each of these levels defines the level at which output or productivity is defined and the group that receives the rewards. Second, and most important, a performance standard is set. In individual and group plans the standard is usually some statement of output or time or both. In organizational plans, standards of performance are based on reductions in cost, improvements in overall productivity, increased profits, or a combination of all three factors. Third, rewards are offered. The rewards are usually money, but time can also be a potent reward. Money needs to be in significant quantity to the extra effort required by the employee and received in a timely fashion so the connection is clear.

Designing incentive plans requires making a further set of decisions. The first of these is the jobs to be included. This is important because some jobs are not amenable to incentive plans. The second set of decisions has to do with organizational conditions such as size of organization, labor costs, and managerial attitudes. Determining the applicability of incentives is a third decision. In general, in the past, applicability has been too narrowly defined. A fourth decision has to do with the manner in which performance and reward are connected. This requires a clear definition of performance, a ratio between performance and reward, and determination of the proportion of total pay controlled by the incentive plan. Finally, incentive plans require well-devised administration and constant surveillance for optimum operation.

Incentive plans are not always popular because they have problems that may make them not worth their advantages. The assumption that workers operate only on an economic level is not supported when one sees the restriction of output that often occurs in incentive plans. Incentive plans also require considerable administrative costs, take control away from supervisors, and require a supportive climate within management. Further, the inability to define performance in a way that is complete and acceptable often has doomed incentive plans. Changing the conditions of the plan once established is very difficult as it is often seen as taking away things from the employee. Finally, incentive plans for one group in the organization may be perceived as inequitable by other groups in the organization.

PART V

THE WAGE FORM DECISION

> "Why are they so anxious to offer improved maternity benefits in the health program? After all at fifty I'm not likely to care about that!"
>
> "What do you think the union is going to demand in new benefits this time around?"
>
> "It sure is hard to have a pension plan when you have to meet all these government requirements!"
>
> "Why should we worry when there is Social Security?"
>
> "We have got to do something to get the medical program costs under control. I want a plan by next week!"

Essentially the wage form decision is a choice between taking payment in a periodic paycheck or deferring it in some form of benefit. Either one is a cost to the organization. There are reasons, however, from both an organizational and a personal standpoint, that some proportion of the total wages paid to employees should be in the form of benefits. The reasons for having benefits, their administration, their integration with pay, and their types are the subjects of the next two chapters. With the addition of benefits, the total compensation package for the individual employee has been determined.

15

Benefit Programs

The total wage cost of an employee to the organization is far more than the pay rate of that employee. Likewise, the total compensation reward of the employee exceeds his or her take-home pay. Total compensation consists partly of the pay of the employee and partly of a set of other rewards that are loosely called *benefits*. The addition of these items to the compensation package complicates the administration of compensation considerably. Benefits are unlike base pay in that they are awarded for different things, they are not periodically given, they are sometimes deferred rather than current, and they require different types of administration. The basic decision in this part of the book is called the wage form decision because, since pay and benefits together make up the wage costs of the organization, there is a trade-off between direct pay and benefits that determines how much of each of these forms of compensation will go into the person's total compensation. Benefits are becoming more important in compensation administration as they become a larger proportion of total compensation and as the necessity of properly managing them has become clear.[1]

   Benefits are important as a reward in that organizations wish to reward employees not only for their job and performance but for their membership in the organization. The rewards discussed in this and the next chapter are

[1]*Employee Benefits, 1979* (Washington, D.C.: Chamber of Commerce of the United States, 1980), p. 27.

ordinarily available to the employee on the basis of being a member of the organization and not on the basis of the job held or performance on that job.

BACKGROUND FOR WAGE FORM DECISIONS

Organizations need to have jobs completed within required performance standards. But they also need continuity to accomplish organizational goals. So there is a need for rewards for more than the job and how well it is done. These are called *membership rewards*. As the embodiment of these rewards, benefits are not a clear-cut body of rewards but rather a collection of ill-defined rewards.

Membership Rewards

The emergence of membership rewards attests to the differences between the employment exchange and the economic exchange as it is narrowly conceived. These rewards indicate that organizations are aware that in the employment exchange they are purchasing not only labor services but also organizational attachment sufficient to provide the continuity required to accomplish their goals. Thus, membership rewards are evidence that organizations take a broader view of the employment exchange than is traditionally embodied in wage and salary administration.

If this view is correct, membership rewards in organizations would be expected to vary with the breadth of the organization's view of the employment exchange. Viewing the employment exchange strictly in economic terms would be expected to lead to few membership rewards and to temporary employment by the employee. This is very much the situation in a secondary labor market. On the other hand, viewing the employment exchange in a broader sense should lead to a broad base of membership rewards as the organization attempts to secure long-term commitment from its employees. This situation is much more typical in a primary labor market.[2]

Employees too find it useful to broaden the definition of the employment exchange and seek membership rewards from their employer. Those employee groups with the strongest commitment to the organization have always received membership rewards. When groups are requested by the organization to increase their organizational commitment they typically request more membership rewards. Thus organizations which request and/or require high levels of commitment over time find considerable pressure from employees for membership rewards. Fortunately, this thought process does not have to be conscious on the part of either the organization or the individual to be valid.

THE DIVERSITY OF MEMBERSHIP REWARDS. Unlike establishing a specific wage rate for a person, the determination of membership rewards is fragmented rather than unitary. It represents a hodgepodge of economic rewards, most of which are awarded on the basis of the person accepting the role of be-

[2]P. B. Doeringer and M. J. Piore, *Internal Labor Markets and Manpower Analysis* (Lexington, Mass.: Heath, Lexington Books, 1971).

ing an employee. Unfortunately, none of the parties to the exchange has a clear definition of the boundaries of this set of rewards. There is a lack of agreement on what is or is not to be included, the purposes to be served, responsibility for programs, the cost and value of the various elements, the units of measurement for determining worth, and the criteria to be used. As a result decisions in the area of membership rewards are more complex and confusing than those involved in determining wages and salaries.

This complexity is increased by the ambivalence shown by both organizations and employees toward membership rewards. As stated, organizations find that consideration of membership rewards is outside of their typical economic definition of the employment exchange. So while they perceive the need for these rewards, they do not fit them into their definition of the exchange. Employees and their representatives also have ambivalent feelings. Membership rewards are often viewed by employees not so much as rewards for membership as a right accompanying employment. Indeed this position is supported by much of the legislation in the field.

Terminology

Just as the particular rewards that constitute membership rewards are diverse, so is their terminology. *Fringe benefits* is the most common name given to this set of rewards, but *indirect compensation, wage supplements, nonwage benefits, social wages, supplementary employee remuneration, supplementary compensation,* and *indirect payments* have also been used. In this chapter the simple term *benefits* will be used.

All of these terms suggest that these rewards are ancillary and not a significant part of total compensation. Neither is true. As indicated, membership rewards are important in maintaining a consistent work force. These rewards can no longer be considered a small part of the total compensation package when their total cost approaches 50 percent of direct wage payments.[3]

There is no common definition of what is included in the benefit package. But since two organizations (the U.S. Chamber of Commerce and the Bureau of Labor Statistics) have been conducting surveys of benefit costs for about 30 years, it could be argued that benefits are what these organizations include in their surveys.[4] But even here there is a lack of agreement. Both include social insurance, private welfare plans, and paid leave. The BLS also includes premium pay and the Chamber of Commerce includes company-paid time off the job and certain employee services.

There are other classifications of benefits. A common one is offered by Sargent and has the following categories: (1) pay for time not worked; (2) monetary rewards and prizes for special activities and performance; (3) bonuses, contributions, and profit sharing; (4) payments for employee security; and (5) practices and services that benefit employees.[5] This categorization is broader

[3]*Employee Benefits, 1979.*

[4]H. Fox, "Comparing the Cost of Fringe Benefits," *Conference Board Record,* May 1967, pp. 29–35.

[5]C. W. Sargent, *"Fringe Benefits": Do We Know Enough about Them?* (Hanover, N.H.: Amos Tuck School of Business Administration, Dartmouth College, 1963).

than the one to be discussed in this chapter and the next. In particular, categories 2 and 3 were covered in the previous chapter, on incentives.

Organizations differ considerably in what they include in their own definitions. For instance, some will include legally required benefits and others only the ones that are voluntary. Unions and management also often differ, with unions often excluding employee services, premium pay, and paid leave.[6]

Some of these differences as to what constitutes benefits are a function of whether certain costs are seen as obligations of employers for the social welfare of their employees and therefore not perceived as rewards at all.[7] A basic premise of this viewpoint is that unions turned to employers to provide benefits when it became apparent that they would not be provided through social legislation. These benefits do not constitute rewards as much as *rights* of the employed individual. If this analysis is valid, we could expect increased pressure on organizations to provide benefits as long as the atmosphere in Washington remains as it is now. The current push for day care can be seen as an expression of this viewpoint.

The confusion in benefit definition does not provide organizations with a good way of defining the benefit package. A better way is to work backwards from the total cost of having a person on the payroll. Benefits would then be all costs beyond the direct wage paid to the individual. The BLS has defined total compensation as all payments to employees subject to income-tax withholding and all payments made by the employer to government agencies, insurance companies, or trustees for insurance and welfare. This would leave out employee services, which probably should be added if the organization wishes to get a complete picture of employee cost. Exhibit 15–1 is a list of items that might be included as benefits.

None of the above discussion describes the purpose for the organization providing the reward. The viewpoint of this book is that the major purpose of all this hodgepodge of rewards is to increase the attractiveness of the organization to the individual so that he or she will continue as an employee. Remember, however, that for a reward to be a part of the employment exchange it must be perceived and considered relevant. Unlike the paycheck, many of these benefits are hidden from the employee, especially if they are deferred for long periods. This suggests that benefit administration requires a large component of communication.

THE GROWTH OF BENEFITS

Originally membership rewards were called fringe benefits because they were only a small portion of the total compensation package. Not so today. The growth of benefits has far exceeded the increase in wages, even during inflationary periods, for the past 30 years. In fact, the growth has been three times that of wages and salaries.[8] The Chamber of Commerce found that by 1980

[6]N. M. Bortz, "The Measurement of Fringe Benefit Expenditures," *Personnel,* July 1956, pp. 87–94.

[7]D. Allen, *Fringe Benefits: Wages or Social Obligation?* (Ithaca, N.Y.: Cornell University Press, 1964).

[8]T. J. Gordon and R. E. LeBleu, "Employee Benefits, 1970–1985," *Harvard Business Review,* January-February 1970, pp. 93–107.

Exhibit 15–1   Examples of Benefits

1. *Extra payments for time worked:*

   Holiday premiums
   Overtime premiums

   Shift premiums
   Weekend premiums

2. *Nonproduction awards and bonuses:*

   Anniversary awards
   Attendance bonus
   Christmas bonus
   Quality bonus
   Safety awards

   Service bonus
   Suggestion awards
   Waste-elimination bonus
   Year-end bonus

3. *Payments for time not worked:*

   Call-back pay
   Call-in pay
   Clean-up time
   Clothes-changing time
   Dental care time
   Down time
   Family allowances
   Holidays paid for but not worked
   Jury duty time
   Lay-off pay
   Medical time
   Military induction bonus
   Military service allowance
   National Guard duty
   Paid death-in-family leave

   Paid lunch periods
   Paid sick leave
   Portal-to-portal pay
   Religious holidays
   Reporting pay
   Reserve military duty
   Rest periods
   Room and board allowances
   Severance pay
   Supper money
   Time spent on contract negotiation
   Time spent on grievances
   Vacation pay
   Voting time
   Witness time

4. *Payments for employee security:*

   Contributions toward:
     accident insurance
     disability insurance
     hospitalization insurance
     life insurance
     medical insurance
     surgical insurance

   Contributions to State disability insurance
   OASI contributions
   Contributions to unemployment compensation
   Supplements to unemployment compensation

   Contributions to workmen's compensation
   Supplements to workmen's compensation
   Contributions to employee thrift plan
   Contributions to employee stock purchase plans
   Credit union
   Employee loan association
   Health and welfare funds
   Home financing
   Mutual benefit association
   Payment of optical expenses
   Pensions
   Savings Bond administration

5. *Payments for employee services:*

   Annual reports to employees
   Beauty parlors
   Cafeteria
   Canteen service
   Charm courses
   Company athletic teams
   Company housing
   Company orchestra
   Company stores

   Income tax service
   Information racks
   Legal aid
   Lunch period entertainment
   Medical examinations (voluntary)
   Music at work
   Nursery
   Paid club memberships
   Paid subscriptions to magazines

Exhibit 15–1   Examples of Benefits (continued)

5. *Payments for employee services* (continued)

Cooking schools	Parking space operation
Dietetic advice	Purchasing service
Educational assistance	Reading room facilities
Employee counselling	Recreational facilities
Employee discounts on purchases	Rest room facilities
Employee parties	Safety clothes at company expense
Employee pleasure trips	Safety programs
Employee publications	Scholarships
Financial advice	Shower and locker rooms
Flowers for ill and deceased employees and families	Transportation
	Vacation facilities
Free laundry	Visiting nurse
Free meals	Vitamins and salt tablets
Functions for retired employees	Wedding gifts
Health education	Work clothes at company expense
Hospital facilities	

benefits were accounting for 36.9 percent of payroll, or an average of $6084 per employee. The total benefit bill in the country ran about $435 billion in 1980.[9] Nor does there seem to be any significant lessening of this growth. The increases have come about in two ways. First, there has been a considerable increase over time in the number of benefits offered by employers. Second, the cost of the benefits themselves has risen dramatically. Health insurance is the prime example of the latter.

The figures just cited, however, are averages and do not represent the amounts spent on benefits by particular organizations or industries. There exists a good deal of variation between industries, as well as within industries by firm, in expenditures on benefits. The petroleum industry spends almost half of its total compensation dollar on benefits; hospitals spend a little over a quarter. Traditionally, government organizations have offered higher benefits or at least are perceived as doing so.[10] These variations may represent a number of differences in compensation policy, including the emphasis placed upon the value of continuity in membership.

This dramatic growth in benefits has come about for a number of reasons. These include (1) changes in the economy, (2) social responsibility, (3) government influence, (4) union demands, and (5) employee interests.

Changes in the Economy

The continuing industrialization in modern times, or more accurately the move toward a postindustrial society, has created changes that encourage organizations to provide more benefits to employees. One of the effects of an increasing standard of living is that people's desire for leisure increases in proportion to their desire for more wages. In economic terms, the elasticity of the supply of labor is such that as wages rise there is a point at which leisure be-

---

[9]*Employee Benefits 1980* (Washington D.C.: Chamber of Commerce of the United States, 1981).

[10]Ibid.

comes more appealing than more work, even work at a higher wage. At this point there is a demand for more time off by the employee.[11]

Continuing industrialization and consequent changes in modes of living have brought new risks to the employee and increased old ones at the same time that increased productivity has afforded programs that provide security against these risks. Economic security in a society in which most individuals are employees depends on finding and keeping a job. Any threat to continuing employment becomes a risk to the employee and the family and creates a demand for insurance against such risk. The result is that at least a portion of individual compensation represents protection against insecurity.

Social Responsibility

Social responsibility may not be the best name for the response by employers to the needs of their employees, but it does get across the point. As far back as the 1920s, organizations began to realize that their employees were assets that needed to be preserved rather than exploited. This awareness has varied over time. At first there was a reaction to unions that created an era of paternalism that encouraged providing many employee services in the hope that employees would see that their employer had their best interests at heart and would not join a union.[12]

Recently there has been a new trend in providing employee services, but the motivation is different. Today it is seen that an employee who is healthy, both physically and mentally, is a more productive person. This has led to a series of employee services, such as athletic facilities and counseling in areas such as smoking and drug abuse, intended to create and maintain a healthy work force.[13]

A current issue in this area is whether employers have a responsibility to provide care for children of employees. With the increase in the number of women in the work force, the number of working women who are the only support of their families, and the need for both partners in the marriage to work, the demand for day-care facilities for children has increased dramatically. There is presently considerable debate as to who is going to provide these facilities, but it is clear that employers will play an important part. There is evidence that facilities close to the work site provide a better solution than those near the home.[14]

Government Influence

The influence of government on benefits has come in three ways—directly through legislation and attempts to control the economy and indirectly through the tax laws. In the 1930s there was a flurry of legislation that pro-

[11]D. S. Hamersmesh and A. Rees, *The Economics of Work and Pay*, 3rd ed. (New York: Harper & Row, 1984).

[12]H. Eilbert, "The Development of Personnel Management in the United States," *Business History Review*, Autumn 1959, p. 352.

[13]G. T. McIlroy, "Health Care Cost Containment in the 1980's," *Compensation Review*, fourth quarter 1983, pp. 15–31.

[14]O. Ornato and C. Buckham, "Day Care: Still Waiting Its Turn as a Standard Benefit," *Management Review*, May 1983, pp. 57–62.

duced organizational requirements in the areas of worker's compensation, unemployment compensation, and social security, old age and survivors' benefits, and disability insurance. More recently, some state legislation has provided for employer and employee contributions toward nonwork accidents and illnesses.

Since the 1960s there has been a new flurry of legislation, designed not to create new benefits but to control programs currently offered by organizations. The most critical of these acts are the Employee Retirement Income Security Act (ERISA), dealing with pensions; the Civil Rights Act, which affects all areas of benefits; the Occupational Safety and Health Act (OSHA), which deals with safety standards on the job; and the Consolidated Omnibus Reconciliation Act (COBRA), which deals with health insurance. All these laws will be dealt with in more detail in the next chapter.

At times, usually wartime, the government has imposed wage and price controls. These controls have given a strong impetus to the growth of benefits by permitting improvements in benefits while discouraging wage and salary increases on the grounds that the latter would contribute to inflationary pressures while the former would not. Clearly, this view is that benefits are *fringes*.

An equally important, but indirect, influence of the government on benefits has been income-tax legislation. High corporate income-tax rates make it advantageous for employers to include as business expenses a wide range of benefits, particularly those to executives. Since most of these benefits are not taxed as income, provision of these benefits results in huge savings for the employer. The future of this reason for benefits is in doubt. Most suggestions for income-tax reform contain restrictions on what organizations can write off as expenses and propose to tax at least some benefits.

Union Demands

Union demands have served to increase benefits as a proportion of total pay. The growth of the unions during the 1930s occurred largely in the mass-production industries. Workers in these industries were much more prone to the risks of industrial life than were craft workers, and so the leaders of industrial unions made it a point to demand protection from insecurity for their members.

In this way union leaders of industrial unions have fostered member interest in programs providing protection from insecurity. Sometimes a benefit has been demanded to establish a principle of employer responsibility for risks facing workers. The UAW's fight for the guaranteed annual wage is a case in point: the union felt that a large portion of the down time in model changeovers could be reduced by management. At other times benefits have been sought when pay increases appeared infeasible. Ross has suggested that unions have sought to expand benefits for a number of reasons, including their desire for (1) increased status, (2) security, (3) a shorter work week, (4) more strength in the eyes of its members, and (5) the development of the plant as a community.[15]

---

[15]A. M. Ross, "Fringe Benefits Today and Tomorrow," *Labor Law Journal*, August 1956, pp. 467–82.

Employee Interest

To the employee, the advantages of benefits are many. Certainly the two most prevalent are the tax advantages mentioned and the lower cost of receiving the benefit by belonging to a group. The fact that over half of all benefits are intended to reduce economic insecurity suggests that both employers and employees are aware that life in an industrial society requires these protections.

At best, however, employee attitudes toward benefits are ambivalent. On one hand, people seem very interested in benefits, since this is a major item of consideration in the recruiting process. On the other hand, most employees do not know what benefits the organization is providing them and particularly the cost to the organization of those benefits. In a way benefits appear to be a classic case of what Herzberg calls a *hygiene factor* or *dissatisfier*.[16] When the benefit is absent the person wants it. When it is present it has no positive motivational force.

Early studies of benefits found that they were not very important to employees.[17] More recent studies have shown a consistent upturn in interest in benefits. The increasing standard of living would suggest this, given the preceeding analysis of the value of money versus benefits at high levels of income. Newer studies have shown that employees place a high value on benefits even beyond their tax advantages and reduced price. Employees differ understandably in their demand for benefits and even more clearly in the types of benefits they demand. This seems to vary most noticeably with the personal circumstances of the employee. Young employees desire fewer benefits compared with wages and time off. Employees with dependents value medical benefits greatly, and the desire for good pension benefits understandably rises with age.[18] In all these cases it should be noted that employees base their decision on their perceived need and not on the cost to the organization of the benefit.

The demographics of an organization's employees offer a hint as to the needs and preferences of its members, but they are not an infallible guide. Glueck, in a review of employee-preference studies, found that some demographic characteristics, particularly age and marital status, were good predictors of benefit preference but that others, such as sex, age, and occupation, were not.[19] Clearly there is a ranking of desirability of benefits by individuals, but it is not wholly predictable by employee characteristics.

Why Benefits?

The use of benefits in the compensation package makes the process of compensating employees much more complex. As indicated, benefits are a hodgepodge of items, and planning and administering them is time-consuming and costly and now takes an expertise not available in many organizations. So the question can be raised whether it is worth it to include benefits in the com-

[16]F. Herzberg, *Work and the Nature of Man* (Cleveland: World Publishing, 1966).

[17]L. G. Reynolds, *The Structure of Labor Markets* (New York: Harper, 1951), p. 94.

[18]S. M. Nealey, "Pay and Benefit Preferences," *Industrial Relations*, October 1963, pp. 17–28.

[19]W. F. Glueck, *Personnel: A Diagnostic Approach* (Dallas: Business Publications, 1978).

pensation package. The discussion thus far in this section provides a base for stating why benefits are here to stay. In summary the following reasons can be put forth as to why organizations have benefits in their compensation package:

1. They are required by law. Most employees are covered by a number of federal and state laws requiring that the organization provide a minimum level of benefits as a condition of employing people.
2. They are desired by employees. Despite the misunderstanding and ambivalence of employees toward benefits, employees insist upon them and they are a major recruiting tool. Benefits probably increase the satisfaction of employees or at least reduce dissatisfaction. The effect of this has been shown to be lower turnover.
3. They are demanded by unions. Benefits provide alternative bargaining chips when direct confrontation over wages is not feasible or desirable.
4. They help to develop an atmosphere of trust in the organization. Taking care of employees through benefit programs increases the feeling that the relationship between the organization and the individual goes beyond an economic transaction.
5. They provide more stability in the economy. The more that benefits are oriented toward reduction of insecurity among employees, the more stable is the economic environment.

BENEFIT PLANNING

Decisions with respect to benefits are made more complex because of confusion of purpose, lack of agreement on which benefits do and do not constitute compensation, and the rapid growth of benefits and their costs. Perhaps the only point of agreement is that benefit administration is changing.

To the employer, decisions on benefits represent a large and growing proportion of compensation expenditures and thus a large part of the organization's contribution to the employment exchange. To the union, benefits are often perceived as a social obligation of the employer and a right of the employee. To the employee, they represent protection from insecurity and a reward for continuing their employment with the organization.

The process of benefit planning, then, is one of deciding why benefits are being offered, what benefits to offer, and to whom? The first of these, the why question, was discussed in the preceding section. The other two questions are examined in this section.

What Benefits to Offer

Superficially, benefit decisions are similar to wage level decisions. In both instances, the basic issue to the employer is that of labor cost. The employer decision involves expenditures resulting from the employment exchange, and from a cost standpoint the organization is indifferent as to whether these costs are in the form of wages or benefits. The tendency to talk about wages and benefits as a *package* reinforces this view.

Actually, however, decisions on benefits involve a number of decisions different from other wage decisions. Benefits are not unitary, as are wages. There are many choices to make as to which ones to offer, and there are a number of influences on this decision. Unions sometimes do and sometimes do not consider benefits to be pay equivalents. As indicated, employees value benefits differently, but they do this not only on the basis of their own needs but also upon being convinced of their importance by the union and management. Organizations differ greatly in the composition of their work force and thus on the needs and desires of their employees. The purpose served by the benefit decision—that of membership—is different from the job and performance considerations in the wage decision. Some of the considerations in deciding what benefits to offer are treated in the rest of this section.

LEGISLATION.   Social legislation requires that the employer make expenditures for the health and safety of employees and for various forms of insurance to indemnify employee loss of income from illness and injury, unemployment, and old age. The law also determines how the organization will develop and operate specific benefits, particularly pensions. These expenditures are required whether or not the employer wants to make them and whether or not the employee desires the resultant benefit.

It might be argued that these expenditures are not truly compensation based upon the employment exchange but are merely a convenient method whereby society insures that its members are protected from certain risks. But to the employer they are expenditures that arise from hiring people, they are of benefit to the employees, and they do substitute for, or at least diminish the ability to pay, direct wages.

It may be possible, however, that these benefits are not benefits in the eyes of the·employee. The employment exchange requires that the person be aware of and consider as relevant any item for it to be a part of the exchange. So if an employee is not aware of the employer's expenditure or does not care for the benefit, the employer is making a contribution to the exchange for which the organization is not receiving a return. The only alternative for the organization is to try to convince the employee of the importance of the benefit.

Legally required benefits currently cost employers an average of 10 percent of their payroll. These are the direct payments made and do not include administrative costs or costs of legal requirements affecting the workplace.[20]

BENEFIT SURVEYS.   Another consideration in benefit planning is industry and area practice regarding benefits. In order to keep employees the organization must remain competitive for labor services, and knowing what benefits other employers are offering is necessary for decisions about what benefits to offer. Surveys of benefits, then, are conducted for the same reason as wage and salary surveys—to obtain information on the conditions prevailing in the labor market. Community wage surveys conducted by the Bureau of Labor Statistics include a number of benefits practices. Employer-association wage and salary surveys customarily include benefit-program information. Without this

[20]*Employee Benefits, 1979.*

information the wage rate information received in surveys may be misleading. The usual benefits survey seeks prevailing practice in the form of enumeration of the programs offered and descriptions of those programs and their coverage. Tabulations consist of the number of responding organizations having each type of program and, if possible, variations in programs by employee group.

These benefit surveys show employer concern with the membership rewards of labor-market competitors. They also accord with union interest in prevailing benefit practice. But it should be noted that the information obtained in benefit surveys differs significantly from that received in wage and salary surveys. Wage survey results record wage costs. Benefit surveys record practice, and the costs of that practice to different organizations may be very different. This difference can result from differences in the organization's work force or in the methods used to finance the benefits.

Ideally, an organization would know both the benefits offered by competitors and the competitors' costs for those benefits. But the cost figures are hard to get. It is difficult to cost out individual benefits, and accounting practices vary considerably. As indicated, some organizations see an item as a benefit and others do not. Cost information on individual benefits may not be useful, since the composition of the work force in each organization differs. What is probably more important is to know the total benefit costs of your organization and others.[21]

Other organizations' benefit practices and costs may not be relevant to your organization unless you know that your employees desire the benefits that others are offering. The next section discusses internal surveys of employee benefit needs and desires. Even if the benefit is desired by your employees it is the cost to you and not other organizations' practice that may be most important. This suggests that the prevailing practice identified in surveys of other organizations should be costed out for your organization and this information used, along with employee preferences, in benefit decisions.

This section reinforces the complexity of benefit decisions. Compensation decision makers are charged with making sure that all expenditures for compensation benefit the organization. As benefits become a larger proportion of total compensation, the impact of benefit decisions is greater and more care must be taken with these decisions. In wage decisions, comparison with other organizations may be an important consideration in order for the organization to be competitive in the labor market. In benefit decisions, however, although benefit practices of other organizations are one consideration, they are less important than the total cost of benefits and employee preferences. Unless employees want a particular benefit, they are unlikely to consider it a reward, and expenditures for that benefit do not enter the employment exchange and would therefore not create value for the organization.

ORGANIZATIONAL BENEFIT PLAN ANALYSIS. Surveys of prevailing benefits may have the dysfunctional consequence of encouraging particular benefit programs simply because they exist in other organizations and not be-

[21]M. T. Wermel and G. M. Beidman, *How to Determine the Total Cost of Your Employee Benefit Program: A Guide for a Company Survey* (Pasadena: Industrial Relations Section, California Institute of Technology, 1960).

cause they are wanted or needed by the organization's employees. The present benefit structure in this country suggests that benefit decisions have been motivated by competition based on a vague feeling that more benefits help an organization attract and retain employees rather than by a careful analysis of employee needs and preferences.

Internal organizational analysis of benefit practices would seem to require a comparison of current benefit offerings with the needs and preferences of employees. Our designation of benefits as membership rewards is an aid in this analysis in that it specifies the organization's purpose for engaging in these programs as obtaining and retaining employees. But the analysis gets complex because individual employees and groups have different needs and preferences.

So the internal organizational analysis of benefits focuses on the needs and preferences of employees. Organizations differ in the demographic makeup of their work force, and this should in turn create differences in the types and levels of benefits that organizations offer. As discussed, there are some predictable differences based upon factors such as age and marital status, but the situation is so complex that it is hard to predict the exact benefit needs and preferences just from a knowledge of the organization's demographic makeup.

A survey of employee preferences for benefits can be done by developing and administering a questionnaire within the organization. This questionnaire need not be very complex and can consist of a listing of possible benefits that are to be ranked in importance by the employee or rated on a scale of very important to very unimportant. It is useful to have the respondents also indicate their own characteristics so that the organization can determine if particular employee groups have predictable preferences.

From the results of the questionnaire the desired and present benefits package can be compared. Unmet needs of employees may call for additional benefits. But overlapping benefits that provide more protection than is needed are a waste of resources. One of the most pressing problems in benefits today is that of overlapping benefits provided the two-career family. When both members of the family work they are often covered under each other's benefit program. The result is that neither spouse's employing organization is receiving the maximum value out of providing the benefits, and the employees are frustrated because they are receiving too much of things they have only so much need for.

ORGANIZATIONAL FINANCIAL ANALYSIS.   A further part of the organization analysis is a comparison between direct wages and benefits, in terms of both cost and employee need. This comparison is needed for a couple of reasons. The first is to maintain a balance between direct wages and benefits. Granting wage increases and benefit changes independently can lead to excessive increases in payroll costs without anyone controlling the situation. Second, changes in wages directly affect the cost of benefits in areas such as vacation costs and holiday pay.

A further part of the organization's financial analysis is like a consideration in the wage level decision—the employer's ability to pay. We have indicated that benefit programs are most often viewed as a package of individual benefits. The emphasis on employee needs and preferences encourages this view of benefits. Decision making from this approach ordinarily focuses on identifying what the employee group needs and then finding out the current cost of that benefit. When installed, the benefit is then based upon the *level of benefit* and not the level of cost to the employer. In the field of medical insurance this has had a disastrous effect on employer costs. The focus on the level of coverage in benefits leads employees to form their impressions of the employment exchange in terms of this level of coverage and not on the cost of that coverage. This makes it hard for the employer to lower the level of coverage subsequently as the costs rise beyond the value of the benefit.

The other problem with the coverage approach is that it is only the employer who is concerned with the problem of rising costs. Yet it is the employee who is in the position of helping to control costs but has no incentive to do so.

A cost-based approach can use data from other companies, but such costs are likely to vary between organizations not only because of the different work-force characteristics described earlier but also because of other factors, such as ratio of labor cost to total cost, variability of demand, technical considerations requiring round-the-clock operations, and profitability. Companies with high profits tend to have high benefit costs, as do larger organizations, unionized organizations, and organizations in low-labor-cost industries. Benefit expenditures vary also by geography and community size.

All the analysis discussed in this section and the previous one suggests that organizations would be advised to have on their compensation staff experts in performing benefit analysis. Such benefit analyses require a knowledge of a specialized field. This is particularly true of the organization's insurance programs. The increased cost of medical insurance and the legislative demands on pension programs has made it imperative that organizations have a high degree of technical expertise available to them.

COLLECTIVE BARGAINING AND BENEFITS. In unionized organizations the decision making just discussed is done largely at the bargaining table. If it is assumed that union demands reflect employee preferences and that organizations have analyzed their own position, the results of collective bargaining can be advantageous to all parties. The employees should be receiving the benefits they want, and unions are motivated to convince employees of the value of the benefits bargained for.

Unfortunately, unions often have goals that do not reflect employee preferences in particular organizations. The union may be striving to institute a benefit in the whole industry or to satisfy a majority of the total union. Because of the political nature of unionism, there is always pressure to achieve gains for the members, and benefits can often appear to be a big gain when pay increases are hard to bargain for. Further, union leaders often are caught in the same problem that management is in an organization with a diverse work force: there is no consensus on what the real needs and preferences of employees are.

Furthermore, if Donna Allen[22] is correct in concluding that benefits are perceived by unions not as compensation but as the social responsibility of employers, to be obtained at the bargaining table because they could not be ob-

[22]Allen, *Fringe Benefits.*

tained through social legislation, then unions have no reason for considering the needs and desires of particular employees and organizations. By this reasoning, benefits become prerequisite to the employment exchange rather than rewards from it, and unions may seek to attain them by calling them wages or nonwages, whatever strategy works. In this view unions represent all employees and not just their own constituency.

Who Receives Benefits?

If benefits are truly membership rewards and not job- or performance-related, then they should be equally available to all employees. This is provided that continuity in employment from all employee groups is equally important to the organization. However, if the organization needs continuity of employment from only some groups and doesn't care about turnover in other groups, a case can be made for having different packages of benefits for different employee groups. This is an extension of the cost/benefit argument—that these expenditures, like all others, should clearly bring something of value to the organization.

The costs of having different benefit packages for different employee groups are many. First, this creates a status ladder in the organization in which there are the haves and the have-nots. This can create morale problems within the have-not group and tensions between the groups when they must work together to accomplish organizational goals. Second, there are administrative problems, such as deciding exactly which job titles fall into which categories and setting up a number of different plans. Third, there are external problems with insurance carriers when only some employees are covered and fourth, legal problems with qualifying programs for tax purposes if only some employees are involved.

Despite these problems, most organizations have at least two benefits packages, one for executives and one for all other employees. Many organizations also pull out other groups for special consideration, such as sales personnel and technical employees. Some of these considerations are covered in chapters 17 and 18.

The trend toward using part-time employees rather than full-time employees is based partly on the cost of benefits. Using part-time employees, the employer can reduce the legally required benefits somewhat and other benefits entirely if the organization so wishes. Although this is the ultimate in different status for different employee groups, many organizations feel that the cost savings are worth the price.

THE CAFETERIA APPROACH.   Different benefit programs for employee groups will be functional to the employment exchange to the extent that the group as a whole wants the set of benefits. But as discussed, employee groups are not always a good indicator of differences in benefit preferences of individuals. The only effective way to deal with individual variability in benefit preferences is to have each person decide what benefits to include and how much to allocate to each. This is called the *cafeteria approach*. The employee is assigned a dollar amount of compensation or a set of credits based on salary, seniority, and age that he or she can divide among a variety of benefit options; cash is sometimes included as an option.[23]

From the discussion thus far in this chapter the cafeteria approach would seem to be an ideal approach to maximizing the employment-exchange potential. From the employee's standpoint needs and preferences can be accommodated. Further, the employee is making the decisions and so should be more aware of and committed to the outcome. From the employer's standpoint there is a clear focus on the total cost of benefits for each employee. This cost can be more easily controlled by assigning a dollar amount to each person. There is a potential for tying rewards more closely to the behavior—membership, in this case—desired by management.

Despite these apparent advantages, thus far few organizations have seriously undertaken a cafeteria benefits program although this may be changing. There are a number of reasons for this slow acceptance of the idea. The first is an accounting problem. The payroll is made much more complex with each person having different deductions. Automated payroll programs, however, should be able to handle this situation. Second, insurance carriers develop their programs on the assumption that all employees will be covered. When all employees do not choose the option the cost goes up for those who do choose it. Third, there is considerable concern about employee decision making. This concern runs in opposite directions. First, there are concerns that the employee will choose very few benefits and focus on maximum cash, which will cause them regret if they become sick and when they get older. There are some benefits, especially the pension, that people must invest in long before they are likely to perceive the benefit of it. On the other hand, there is a concern that employees may choose too many benefits and thereby distort the membership rewards vis-à-vis the job and performance rewards.

Last, there is a concern that unions will not accept the concept of the cafeteria approach, and that leaves the technique to nonunion organizations or to the nonunion sector of the organization. This concern appears to be based upon the feeling that unions try to have everyone treated alike.[24]

A compromise position of the cafeteria approach is to develop a number of optional benefit programs and allow the employee to choose the one that best fits his or her needs. These options could be developed through a survey method, as described earlier. One author suggests that a number of packages be developed that follow what he calls the *stages-of-man approach:* each package would fit a person's situation for a five-year period. Each program would be equal in overall cost but differ in its coverage for each benefit.[25] Concerns for protection from insecurity could be taken care of in this alternative by building these benefits into all packages.

---

[23]B. N. Fragner, "Employees 'Cafeteria' Offers Insurance Options," *Harvard Business Review*, November-December 1975, pp. 7–10.

[24]For discussion of these concerns see D. J. Thomsen, "Introducing Cafeteria Compensation in Your Company," *Compensation Review*, first quarter 1978, pp. 56–63; and L. M. Baytos, "The Employee Fringe Benefit Smorgasbord: Its Potentials and Limitations," *Compensation Review*, first quarter 1970, pp. 16–28.

[25]J. Taylor, "A New Approach to Compensation Management," *Compensation Review*, first quarter 1969, pp. 22–30.

Unintended Effects of Organizational Benefits

In any planning process it is useful to look as broadly as possible at the effects of the decisions being made. This section briefly examines some of the issues that face employing organizations, unions, the economy, and society because of the method we have chosen to solve the problem of employee insecurity in this country.

ORGANIZATIONAL EFFECTS.   Americans have chosen to solve the problems of insecurity arising from an industrial society very largely by private means. This protection varies by industry and area as well as with organization size and unionization. Thus, employees of large, unionized organizations in metropolitan areas are well protected from insecurity and receive a large amount of leisure both on and off the job. On the other hand, employees of small, nonunion organizations may have only the limited protection provided by social legislation. Employees of many small organizations are not even covered by social legislation. This range between the haves and the have-nots grows wider with the growth of benefits, which shows no signs of abating.

A continuing disparity of this kind is an invitation to create public programs to redress the inequality. The development of such programs brings into question how these required benefits are perceived by the employee. If, as Allen suggests, benefits that are required of the organization become social responsibilities and are thereby taken out of the employment exchange, the organization may lose a reward that constitutes a large percentage of the total compensation program.[26]

Benefits have a very definite place in the motivational scheme of the organization. They are a major motivator of continuing membership, but are not as useful for other purposes. This is an effect of the way they are administered, being available on the basis of being employed and/or length of service. Organizations may be wise to keep it this way. Making different motivational connections would be difficult and place the organization in the position of doing things that their employees perceive as illegitimate. Furthermore, it may be functional to clearly delineate these rewards for membership so that the employee knows why certain rewards are being offered. But all this is predicated on employees' seeing these rewards as relevant to them; otherwise the benefit does not enter the employment exchange at all.

Benefit programs greatly increase the responsibility of employing organizations. Underlying membership rewards is the assumption that the organization desires long-term employment and will provide it. This commitment can reduce the ability of the organization to adapt to changing circumstances. In addition, with the constant increase in benefits the organization must be even more careful that additional employees are worth hiring. As pointed out, there is now a trend toward using part-time and temporary employees because the commitment to full-time employees is so great; this is creating a new group of organizational have-nots.

UNION EFFECTS.   Benefit program decisions also increase the responsibilities of unions. With each additional benefit, union responsibility for ensur-

[26]Allen, *Fringe Benefits*.

ing value to members would seem to increase along with the difficulties of carrying out this responsibility. The same type of benefit analysis and expertise discussed earlier for organizations is probably required in unions as well. Also, although the political nature of unionism may explain obtaining benefits that some members may not need, it does not remove the moral issue. Furthermore, the tendency for unions to demand benefits obtained by other unions has resulted in benefits crossing industry lines, perhaps destroying economically justifiable differentials. More serious for unions in partially unionized industries, the larger benefit programs in unionized firms appear to have intensified union–nonunion competition to the disadvantage of the union. In the past few years this has taken on an international scope as American firms are having trouble competing with foreign companies. Multiple employer plans and direct-service health plans may have the effect of creating a union paternalism that resembles the employer paternalism of the past.

ECONOMIC AND SOCIAL EFFECTS.   Benefit decisions of employers and unions may have unintended consequences for our economy. Our method of providing benefits by private means may have reduced our ability to compete in foreign markets. Although other industrialized nations have equal or higher benefits, their cost incidence is quite different. Although it can be argued that these benefits are social costs, paid in their entirety by the worker, regardless of how they are provided, the effect on the employer's labor costs is quite different. In this country, benefits are provided through employment and these costs appear in employer labor costs. In many other countries, benefits are largely provided by employee contribution and general tax revenue and thus do not appear in the employer's labor costs. Also, there appears to be a more selective approach to granting benefits only to those who need them rather than the more general approach taken in the United States. For both of these reasons our competitiveness may be decreasing.

Benefit decisions can also harm price stability. When total compensation gains exceed productivity gains in the economy, inflation is the consequence. Benefit costs are often not given their full weight in calculating total compensation and so amount to a hidden inflationary tendency.

Benefit decisions may have two different effects upon employment. The first is to encourage organizations to work employees overtime since this does not significantly change the other benefit costs. The effect of this, of course, is to lower the employment level. The second effect is to encourage organizations to hire part-time and temporary employees to whom the organization does not have to pay these expensive benefits.

Another area in which there is a great deal of potential impact on benefit decisions is labor mobility. Although logic and some studies suggest that benefits are among the factors that tie people to organizations,[27] it has not been shown conclusively that pension plans do so.[28] The most accurate statement is

[27]H. Folk, *Private Pension Plans and Manpower Policy*, U.S. Department of Labor Bulletin No. 1359 (1963).

[28]H. S. Parnes, "Labor Force and Labor Markets," in *A Review of Industrial Relations Research*, ed. W. L. Ginsburg et al. (Madison Wisc.: Industrial Relations Research Assn., 1970), p. 51.

probably that benefits are one of a number of factors in the employment exchange that tie people to organizations.

The issue of whether protections from insecurity provided through employment have weakened community efforts to stimulate citizen participation in programs designed to provide group protection would seem to deserve more attention. In order to be protected one must be employed, but it is when one is not employed that there is the greatest need. Also, like the problem within the organization of having all employees in the program, when those not covered are those not employed they represent a group whose cost to cover is much higher than the average.

ADMINISTRATION OF BENEFITS

Benefit administrators do more than plan what benefits to offer and to whom. They must take care of the benefit package that is in effect. This administrative task consists of processing claims related to the benefits, communicating the benefit package to the employees, and monitoring the changing environment of benefits.

Processing Claims

Employees ordinarily have to request that benefits be invoked, and it is up to the organization or others, such as insurance companies, to decide if the request is legitimate. That is, someone has to determine if the act that is claimed has occurred, if the employee is covered for this act, and if so what payment is appropriate. This work can be time-consuming but does not necessarily require highly technical skill to perform. The knowledge of a number of different areas, particularly insurance, is the main concern in this task. Counseling employees who have been turned down for a claim and showing them why they did not qualify requires good interpersonal skills.

This is one area in which a benefits administrator can show his or her worth to the organization in concrete terms. Proper claims processing and monitoring can make savings in benefit costs of up to 15 percent.[29]

Communication of Benefits

The employment-exchange model points out that to be considered rewards, benefits must be recognized and perceived as relevant by the employee. The experience of many organizations is that employees are unaware of what benefits the organization offers and not at all aware of the cost of these benefits even after extensive efforts have been made to inform them.[30] Further, although it can be said that employees certainly value benefits,[31] it is not clear that they desire the particular set of benefits that the organization offers. These

[29]T. Fannin and T. Fannin, "Coordination of Benefits: Uncovering Buried Treasure," *Personnel Journal*, May 1983, pp. 386–91.

[30]A. A. Sloane and E. W. Hodges, "What Workers Don't Know about Employee Benefits," *Personnel*, November-December 1968, pp. 27–34.

[31]R. A. Lester, "Benefits as a Preferred Form of Compensation," *Southern Economic Journal*, April 1967, pp. 488–95.

two concerns indicate that organizations need a well-devised communications program both to inform employees of what their benefits are and to persuade them that they are valuable rewards.

Communicating benefits is harder than communicating wage information. Each payday the employee receives feedback regarding wages. But benefits may or may not be visible to the employee over a long time period. Pensions are a good example. To a young person this is something rarely thought about or discussed, so the chances are slight that he or she is aware of the organization's pension program. Further, there is little perceived relevance of a pension to young people; retirement is the least of their concerns. To complicate matters, many benefits are difficult to explain and pension plans are among the worst. The technical language of insurance and pension plans makes it difficult for employees to understand what they are entitled to, even if they show an interest.

Communicating benefit information takes a planned and continuous approach if employees are to know and understand their benefit package. Some ideas that organizations use are as follows:

1. Develop a benefits manual that explains the benefits that are provided to employees. This can consist of one master manual or a series of brochures for each benefit. It is important that any manual keep jargon to a minimum. In addition, some organizations have prepared videotapes describing their benefit programs, to be shown to groups of employees.

2. Periodically send each employee a benefits report that explains the level of coverage the employee has for all benefits, the value of the benefits to him or her, and the cost of these provisions to the organization.

3. Make a benefits presentation to all employees in small groups. This can be done by the expert in benefits or the supervisor supported by the expert.

4. Have a counseling line and/or hotline for individual questions. This is an attitudinal requisite as well as a formal device. It should be clear that the organization encourages employees to ask questions about their benefits.

Monitoring Benefits

The field of benefits is changing rapidly. It is necessary for the organization to keep careful track of what is happening both externally and internally. The needs and preferences of employees are likely to change because the organization's work force is constantly changing. Surveying employee needs and preferences should be a continuing exercise and not a one-time project. The practices of competition in the labor market need to be monitored on the same basis as they do for wage information. But what has become most complex for the organization to monitor is the changing costs of those benefits provided by outside organizations such as insurance companies. Organizations that have been monitoring what has happened in this area have begun to develop alternative ways of providing these benefits to employees at a lower or stable cost. Last, legislation in this field is changing every day and administrators need to examine these acts to see if the organization is meeting legal requirements and taking proper advantage of changes in the law.

SUMMARY

A major continuing change in compensation administration is the increase of benefits as a part of total compensation. Benefits are a different form of compensation from direct pay, discussed in the two previous chapters. The focus in benefits is the membership model of motivation. Benefits provide a reason to join and remain a member of the organization. Benefits are a wide variety of inducements offered to employees with little in common except that they are not "paid" to the person each payday. This makes terminology and categorization of benefits difficult.

There has been a growth of benefits for a number of reasons. Industrialized society makes it difficult for people to provide themselves with needed protection from the vicissitudes of the economy. Thus, organizations are often seen as having a social responsibility to provide these protections, both to care for their employees and to provide a service to society. Unions have also found it useful to demand benefits. They see the need to provide protection for their members, and the organization is the group that they can directly affect. Employees, too, are interested in benefits. Tax advantages and cost savings are two reasons, but changes in lifestyle make items like time off more appealing.

In the past, a major problem with benefits has been their disorganized growth. Organizations are finding that it is becoming more necessary to carefully plan out benefit packages both to optimize their motivational impact and to reduce costs. The first decision an organization makes is what benefits to offer. Some are required by law, some are bargained for by unions, others are needed to be competitive, and others meet the needs of the employees. All these must be integrated into the organization's ability to pay. The second decision is who is to receive what benefit. A recent trend in this area is to involve the employee by instituting a *cafeteria benefits* plan. In planning benefit programs it is also wise to consider some broader issues of the effects of benefits on the organization, unions, the economy, and society. The way the United States handles employee protection and benefits is peculiarly American.

The administration of benefits is becoming much more important in organizations; staff specialists are assigned to this function. Planning out the program is not the only requirement; control of costs is becoming a major goal. To maximize the impact of benefit plans, organizations are developing sophisticated communication programs to explain to employees the advantages of their benefits.

16

Characteristics of Benefits

Employee benefits consist of a large number of diverse organizational rewards. This diversity makes it difficult to categorize and discuss the characteristics of benefits in general, since each one needs to be dealt with independently. In fact, benefits administration has become a specialized function within organizations in the past few years that requires specific training and experience. This chapter will use the categories used by the U.S. Chamber of Commerce in its benefits survey to discuss the characteristics of most of the common benefits provided by organizations today. One should be cautioned that this field is changing very rapidly due to legal and other environmental pressures, so there may be major differences in the common benefits and/or their characteristics discussed, by the time you read this chapter.

CONSIDERATIONS IN BENEFIT ANALYSIS

Although it is hard to develop commonalities among benefits, there are a number of considerations which affect or need to be considered when discussing any benefit. Those to be examined briefly here are purpose, legal requirements, contribution, and cost.

Purpose

In the last chapter it was made plain that the central purpose of benefits in the employment exchange is to foster membership or continuity of employment. There was also a focus on the fact that security is a major theme in benefits. So although the major overall aim of benefits from the employer's standpoint is membership, some other advantages can adhere to the employer from granting benefits. In order for a person to concentrate on performing well, he or she must be able to concentrate upon the job. Having protection from uncertainty provides this ability to concentrate. Benefits provide security in three areas: age, unemployment, and sickness and accident.

But security is an after-the-fact type of protection. There are also benefits that employers provide with the expectation that their provision will improve or maintain the current level of performance of the employee. These benefits are largely in the form of time off, which is expected to help the employee recuperate or to reduce fatigue on the job; programs to improve the health of the employee, and programs to improve the employee's future worth to the organization, such as educational reimbursement.

Legal Requirements

Laws affect benefits in two ways, through requiring that certain benefits be provided by the employer and by monitoring or directing the way benefits are administered. The first of these, requiring certain benefits, consists of a series of benefits that employers must grant as a price of hiring employees. As discussed in the previous chapter, these may or may not be considered benefits, but since they are a definite wage cost the position taken in this book is that they are a major form of benefit provided to employees. These benefits are the topic of the first category of benefits discussed below.

There are also laws regulating how benefits are to be administered. ERISA is probably the best example, although many tax laws also direct organizations in how they administer benefits. These benefits are not ordinarily required by law, but if offered are controlled by law. These laws are discussed as the type of benefit they affect is dealt with.

Contribution and Cost

The costs of providing the benefit are a major consideration of all benefits discussed in this chapter. Further, for some of them there is a discussion of methods of controlling the cost of the particular benefit. This contrasts somewhat with the focus in the last chapter on controlling overall benefit costs. Most benefit administrators can show that they are cost-effective by the savings that they can attain through proper administration of particular benefits.

A final consideration is who should pay for the benefits, or more likely, how much each partner to the employment exchange should contribute to the cost of the benefit. To the degree that the employee pays for the benefit the employer cannot claim it as his or her contribution to the employment exchange. But there are good reasons to share the cost of particular benefits. The employee *sees* the benefit more clearly as a part of the employment exchange when costs are shared and has a larger and more direct stake in keeping benefit costs down when both parties are contributing to the cost of the benefit.

Types of Benefits

Although there is no set way of classifying benefits, the U.S. Chamber of Commerce has been surveying and reporting on benefits for many years and uses the five categories of benefits shown in exhibit 16–1. This breakdown will be used in this chapter as we discuss the major features of today's most common benefits. Some of the benefits (profit sharing and suggestion awards) listed in section 5 of the exhibit were discussed in chapter 14 as incentives. These are awarded for people's performance and not for their membership. As such we would not consider them benefits.

LEGALLY REQUIRED BENEFITS

There are some benefits that employers must provide by law. This section will examine the three major benefits required by federal and state law: Social Security, unemployment compensation, and worker's compensation. All three are based upon laws passed quite a while ago, but changes both in the law and in society make them problematic today.

Social Security

Social Security benefits are based upon the Social Security Act of 1935. Social Security's original intent was to encourage workers to retire at the age of 65 by providing payments to them. At the time of the depression this was done to attempt to remove these people from the work force and thereby lower unemployment. The act provides for the employer and the employee as well as the self-employed to pay for these benefits. This is an important point: Social Security taxes current workers and employers to pay for former workers who have left the work force.

COVERAGE.   Over the years Social Security coverage has changed. In addition to old-age benefits Social Security now also provides disability benefits, aid to dependents and survivors, medical insurance, and death benefits. As with most such laws, the proportion of the work force covered has also ex-

---

Exhibit 16–1   Categorization of Employee Benefits

Type of Benefit
1. Legally required payments (employer's share only)
   a. Old-age, survivors, disability, and health insurance (FICA taxes)
   b. Unemployment compensation
   c. Worker's compensation (including estimated cost of self-insured)
   d. Railroad retirement tax, railroad unemployment and cash sickness insurance, state sickness benefits insurance, etc.
2. Pension, insurance, and other agreed-upon payments (employer's share only)
   a. Pension plan premiums and pension payments not covered by insurance-type plan (net)
   b. Life insurance premiums; death benefits; hospital, surgical, medical, and major medical insurance premiums, etc. (net)
   c. Salary continuation or long-term disability
   d. Dental insurance premiums

Exhibit 16–1   Categorization of Employee Benefits (continued)

___

  e. Discounts on goods and services purchased from company by employees

  f. Employee meals furnished by company

  g. Miscellaneous payments (compensation payments in excess of legal requirements, separation or termination pay allowances, moving expenses, etc.)

3. Paid rest periods, lunch periods, wash-up time, travel time, clothes-change time, get-ready time, etc.

4. Payments for time not worked

  a. Paid vacations and payments in lieu of vacation

  b. Payments for holidays not worked

  c. Paid sick leave

  d. Payments for National Guard (or army or other reserve duty); jury, witness, and voting pay allowances; payments for time lost due to death in family or other personal reasons, etc.

5. Other items

  a. Profit-sharing payments

  b. Contributions to employee thrift plans

  c. Christmas or other special bonuses, service awards, suggestion awards, etc.

  d. Employee education expenditures (tuition refunds, etc.)

  e. Special wage payments ordered by courts, payments to union stewards, etc.

___

Source: Reprinted with the permission of the Chamber of Commerce of the United States of America from *Employee Benefits 1984*, ©1986 Chamber of Commerce of the United States of America.

panded over time.[1] In order to pay for this expansion the tax has gone up over the years and today stands at 7.05 percent; it is scheduled to rise to 7.65 percent by 1990. The wage base has also been moving upward. In 1983 it was $35,700 and this is adjusted upward each year for inflation.[2]

     PROBLEMS.   The Social Security program encountered problems in 1981-1982. Expenses in the old-age benefits, aid to survivors, and medical insurance parts of it have risen faster than has income to the program; there was talk of the program being bankrupt. Indeed, the combination of asking the program to do more than it started out to do, the increasing longevity of people, the increased level of benefits, the tying of benefit levels to the Consumer Price Index, and the decline in the proportion of the population paying into Social Security led to a projected deficit in the program. For instance, in 1950 there were 14 active workers supporting each retiree; by 1990 there will be a projected two active workers for each retiree. A number of amendments to the Social Security Act made in 1983 have purportedly solved the financial problem for 75 years. To the degree that some of the problem was the age distribution of the work force, in the next number of years the problem may reverse as the depression babies reach retirement age and the baby boomers their peak earning period.

     These changes and problems of Social Security have implications for the employer and the employment exchange. As the costs of Social Security

___

[1]W. J. Cohen, "The Evolution and Growth of Social Security," in *Federal Policies and Worker Status since the Thirties*, ed. J. P. Goldberg, E. Ahern, W. Haber, and R. A. Oswald (Madison, Wisc.: Industrial Relations Research Assn., 1976), p. 62.

[2]*What the New 1983 Social Security Law Means to You and Your Employees*, Personnel Management-Compensation Report Bulletin 4 (Englewood Cliffs, N.J.: Prentice-Hall, 1983).

have risen, so automatically has the employer's contribution to the employment exchange. Social Security is seen positively by almost all employees. Only the youngest age group (those 25 to 35) show less confidence in the future of the system.[3] Since Social Security is not going to go away, it may be incumbent upon employers to work with employees to develop a realistic concept of Social Security.

In the recent past there was a feeling among many employees that Social Security would take care of retirement, so further saving was unnecessary. Likewise, among employers there was the development of pension programs without any consideration of Social Security. The crisis in Social Security provided an opportunity to coordinate Social Security, employer pension programs, and employee savings programs to provide realistic protection for the employee during retirement.

Unemployment Insurance

Protection against loss of income from losing one's job was another protection included in the Social Security Act of 1935. The administration of this program, however, is separate from that of Social Security, being a combination of state and federal administration.

FINANCING.   Also unlike Social Security, unemployment insurance is paid for in most states entirely by employer contributions, making it much less visible to the employee. The tax to pay for this benefit is 3.4 percent of the first $6000 of the employee's wages. Of this amount 2.7 percent stays with the state for operation of its unemployment commission and the remaining 0.7 percent goes to the federal government. The rates in some states are higher than 2.7 percent, but all states allow for experience rating—lower rates for employers who have few claims made by former employees.[4]

COVERAGE AND ELIGIBILITY.   Unemployment benefits are intended to be available to employees who become unemployed through no fault of their own. All workers are covered by the provisions except for some agricultural and domestic workers. However, in order to be eligible upon becoming unemployed a worker must:

1. be able, available, and seeking work;
2. not have refused suitable work;
3. not be unemployed because of a labor dispute (there are exceptions to this);
4. not have left the job voluntarily;
5. not have been terminated for gross misconduct; and
6. have been employed in a covered industry, and earned a designated minimum amount for a certain period of time.

[3]D. Yankelovich, A. B. Skelly, and A. B. White: *A 50-Year Report Card on the Social Security System,* August 1985.

[4]C. A. Williams, J. S. Turnbull, and E. F. Cheit, *Economic and Social Security,* 5th ed. (New York: John Wiley, 1982).

These requirements reduce the segment eligible for unemployment insurance substantially.[5]

BENEFITS.   An unemployed worker who qualifies under these requirements is entitled to 26 weeks of unemployment payments. These payments are supposed to be half of the person's lost wages. In fact, it often amounts to more, since these payments are not taxable.[6] During periods of high unemployment the government often extends the payment period beyond the 26 weeks.

COST CONTROL.   As indicated, employers are *experience-rated.* That is ex-workers who apply and are granted unemployment benefits are charged against the employer. This increases the cost of unemployment insurance to the employer, so it is in the organization's best interest to see that claims for unemployment are legitimate. A further and more positive approach is to reduce terminations within the organization. The total cost of terminating people is quite high, and programs of intervention before termination are necessary and worthwhile. Also, it is important that production methods and practices that encourage alternating hiring and layoffs of personnel be examined and their full costs be apparent to management.[7]

EMPLOYEE MOTIVATION.   A final concern about unemployment insurance is its effect on the will to work. All of us are aware of or have heard about people who really are not trying to seek work while collecting unemployment insurance. Empirical studies do show that those workers covered by unemployment insurance do remain unemployed for a somewhat longer period. But it may also be that covered workers are less likely to become unemployed. Overall, unemployment insurance may have more of an effect on the composition of the unemployed than on the level of unemployment. The law may well have the intended effect of keeping low-level and entry-level positions unattractive to highly skilled and experienced workers and allowing new entrants into the work force even when unemployment is high.[8] An intended effect of this program is to allow unemployed workers to improve their labor-market status while unemployed. The small disincentive effect of unemployment insurance is offset by its value as worker protection in our industrialized world.

Worker's Compensation

Worker's compensation is a program that provides benefits for employees injured on the job. It is based on state laws, so the requirements vary considerably from state to state.[9] All states do have a law, however. This fact is a

[5]G. S. Fields, "Direct Labor Market Effects of Unemployment Insurance," *Industrial Relations,* February 1977, pp. 33–44.

[6]M. Feldstein, "The Economics of the New Unemployment," *Public Interest,* Fall 1973, pp. 3–42.

[7]A. Janoff, "You Can Control Your Unemployment Taxes," *Personnel Administrator,* January 1976, pp. 29–30.

[8]C. Vickery, "Unemployment Insurance: A Positive Reappraisal," *Industrial Relations,* Winter 1979, p. 18.

[9]M. W. Elson and J. F. Burton, Jr., "Workers Compensation Insurance: Recent Trends in Employer Cost," *Monthly Labor Review,* March 1981, pp. 45–50.

statement about how prevalent industrial injury has been and how little protection was available to workers before passage of these laws.[10]

LEGAL REQUIREMENTS.   Worker's compensation laws require that covered employers provide insurance to pay for expenses resulting from work-related accidents, injury, or disease. There is no determination of fault in worker's compensation. The employer pays fully for this insurance coverage. The insurance is carried through private carriers or in some cases the states themselves. Some states provide a *second injury fund* to protect a present employer from paying for a previously covered injury.

Worker's compensation also requires employers to have medical facilities available in case of injury on the job. This has been one of the more successful aspects of the program. However, part of the law that seeks to reduce accidents through reporting and study has not been nearly as effective. At least the passage of Occupational Safety and Health Act (OSHA) would indicate that there is still a perceived problem of industrial injury.[11]

COVERAGE.   Injured employees are covered both for the costs of the injury and for the time lost off the job. In this regard worker's compensation is a combination of medical insurance and disability insurance. The injured employee typically receives 50 to 67 percent of lost income. But there are indications that this is not always the case.[12] Injury and permanent-disability payments are usually paid out on a schedule.

EMPLOYER CONCERNS.   The cost of worker's compensation is a major concern of the employer. This type of insurance is experience-rated, so it pays the employer to keep the number of injuries to a minimum. Where this is done through safety programs and education all parties benefit. However, all injuries must be reported and dealt with.

Of recent concern has been the broadening of the definition of what constitutes a work-related injury or disease. Where the injury is clearly physical and the cause and effect immediate there is little problem. But there are increasing claims for mental and emotional injury as well as claims in which the time lag may be several years from the incident to the disease.

RETIREMENT PROGRAMS

This category of benefits, and the next (insurance), validates the statement in the last chapter that in the United States employee-protection arrangements have been left to organizations rather than government. Most of the programs covered in this section are similar to those in the last section but are not required by law. However, they often are controlled by law when they are offered by the organization.

---

[10]H. Pelling, *American Labor* (Chicago: University of Chicago Press, 1960).

[11]R. J. Paul, "Worker's Compensation: An Adequate Employee Benefit?" *Academy of Management Review*, October 1976, pp. 112–18.

[12]Ibid.

Pension Programs

A major benefit requirement is to provide economic security for employees upon retirement. This can be accomplished in a number of ways. In essence all methods of providing economic stability in later life is done by deferring current compensation to some future time, but some programs do this more obviously than others. The least visible form to the employee is the pension program. In a pension program money is put away in a fund each year for the employee's eventual retirement. At retirement the employee begins to receive the money put away for him or her. Thus a pension program is a trade-off between current income and future security. It is not strange, then, that desire for and interest in pension programs increases with age. The problem is that in order to have a retirement income that is satisfactory one must be concerned about it from a young age.

Pension programs have been a part of organization benefit packages for a long time. During the early 1970s there was a great deal of concern about pension programs as it became clear that many employees who thought they were covered by such programs discovered that they were not. This was partially an administrative situation involving very complicated plans and partially an economic problem where organizations had not funded the retirement programs and could not meet the demands of retirees.[13] The result of these problems was the Employee Retirement Income Security Act (ERISA), which sets forth the standards that the organization's pension program must meet. The act does not say that the organization must have a pension program but does say that if it does have a pension program the program must meet certain standards.

In addition to ERISA, the tax laws affect the development and administration of pension programs. Since there is a deferral of income from today to tomorrow, the IRS is interested in seeing that this deferral is not abused to avoid taxation. In addition, the tax laws are concerned with treating all employees in the organization in a nondiscriminatory manner. What this means is that pension plans cannot be established that benefit only a portion of the organization's employees, usually executives, if the plan is to qualify for the above-mentioned tax advantages.

The design of a pension program calls for identifying who, when, and how.

WHO IS IN THE PROGRAM.   Our placement of benefits as membership rewards in the employment exchange would suggest that a pension program include all employees. But this may ignore two factors—length of time in the organization and the value of the reward in retaining different groups of employees. If the program is to encourage continued membership, then a waiting period before entrance into the program makes sense. Likewise, certain groups, particularly executives, have needs that are different from those of other employee groups.

ERISA and the tax laws have some rules regarding who shall be in the program. The law requires that any employee who (1) has been employed for

---

[13]R. D. Paul, "The Impact of Pension Reform on American Business," *Sloan Management Review,* 17:1976, pp. 56–62.

one year or (2) is 21 years of age, whichever occurs later, must be included. The tax consideration has to do with whether the program is *qualified*. Participation eligibility must be 70 percent and participation at least 80 percent of the eligible population. The importance to the employee of the plan being qualified is that the monies placed in the fund for the employee are not counted as income to the employee in that year. Thus, in order to be qualified pension programs must benefit only employees and their beneficiaries and not discriminate in favor of particular employee groups, such as executives.

VESTING. A second part of the who question involves the idea of vesting. The term *vesting* means that the employee has an interest in the accrued benefits of the pension program that cannot be taken away even if he or she quits or is fired. This is a requirement of ERISA and was placed in the law because organizations would avoid paying pensions by letting people go before their retirement age. Also, having to stay all of one's working life with a particular organization in order to receive a pension reduces labor mobility drastically.

ERISA defines three different methods of calculating the maximum vesting period:

1. Graduated 15-year vesting: An employee has a 25 percent vested right after 5 years, an additional 5 percent for each of the next 5 years, and an additional 10 percent for each of the last 5 years, so that at the end of 15 years the employee is fully vested.
2. Ten-year vesting: After 10 years of service the employee would have a 100 percent vesting right. Any percentage of vesting, or none, may take place during the 10 years.
3. Rule of 45: An employee with at least 5 years of service must have a 50 percent vesting right when the sum of the employee's age and service equals 45. For each succeeding year of service the percentage goes up 10 points, so that after 5 more years of service the employee has a 100 percent vested pension right.

Vesting allows the employee to have a stated interest in a pension program after a specific period. But it is clear that this is not a full interest until some time after 10 years. Since the number of years in the pension program is a major determinant of the value of the interest in the program, vesting alone may not provide the person with a very substantial retirement income. One suggested answer to this would be to make pensions portable. That is, the person could transfer his or her value to the new employer's pension program. This idea has not gotten very far because the administrative problems are great and it defeats the basic idea that benefits should be rewards for continuing membership.[14]

WHEN ARE BENEFITS PAID? The easy answer to this is when the employee retires. But this answer hides more than it reveals. When is retirement?

[14]S. M. Phillips and L. P. Fletcher, "The Future of the Portable Pension Concept," *Industrial and Labor Relation Review*, January 1977, pp. 194–201.

Ordinarily pension programs assume a retirement age of 65. This standard is under pressure from both directions today. On one hand the Age Discrimination Act says that employers cannot force a person to retire before 70, and some states have abolished mandatory retirement entirely. On the other hand, there is a trend toward early retirement of employees before the age of 65. Most organizations stay with the 65 figure as a model one and adjust the payments made to people who retire early or late actuarially. An alternative way of dealing with this question is to define a number of years of service in the organization before the person is able to obtain full pension benefits.

There are two circumstances other than retirement, death, and disability in which there is a payout from the pension plan. Upon the employee's death the usual practice is to provide the deceased's beneficiary with the money that is in trust for the deceased. Most retirement programs also have a disability-retirement clause that, much like an early-retirement provision, pays the employee a proportion of the amount that the employee would be entitled to had he or she stayed employed until the normal retirement date.

How Much?   This is the most complex question to answer, and one that is affected by at least two major variables. The first of these is the contributor. In some plans only the employer contributes; in others both employer and employee contribute. Employee contribution plans tend to pay more than noncontributory ones. On top of Social Security a further deduction from the paycheck may seem like a lot to the employee and certainly reduces his or her options for putting money away in other ways. But it also makes the pension program more visible to the employee and makes it a shared contribution to the employment exchange.

The second variable is the type of program—defined benefit or defined contribution. These are so different that they are discussed separately.

Defined-Benefit Plans.   A defined-benefit plan is one in which the employee upon retirement is guaranteed a set income for as long as he or she lives. There is usually also a clause that allows a percentage continuance beyond that for the person's spouse. This is the most common form of pension program. The exact benefit amount is determined by the employee's income and the number of years of service. The current wage rate or an average of the wage rate for a previous time period forms the base for determining the amount to be paid.

The length of service determines the percentage of the base pay that will be paid out each month. This figure is ordinarily some small percentage per year, from 1 to 5 percent. An employee with 30 years of service and a 3 percent accrual per year is entitled to 90 percent of base pay. This percentage need not be the same each year. A *front-loaded program* gives a person a higher percentage in the early years of coverage and a lower percentage in later years. A *back-loaded program* does just the opposite. The two have very different consequences for employee retirement thoughts. A front-loaded plan makes early retirement attractive since additional years do not add much to the person's retirement income. A back-loaded program makes staying on the job to the normal retirement time more attractive, since it is the last few years that make a large difference in retirement income.

Under ERISA the employer must contribute to the pension fund enough monies each year to fund the additional interest that the employee has gained in the pension program. In a defined benefit plan there is a problem in determining what this amount should be. It is a complex actuarial decision that must be made by an expert.

Three other considerations with defined benefit plans need to be discussed. The first is the effects of inflation. If the plan provides a certain income at retirement without a way of adjusting to inflation, the value of the pension can decline rapidly in a few years after retirement. This is very difficult if the former employee has planned a reasonable retirement program and finds it is inadequate. On the other hand, automatic adjustments tied to the CPI can break the program, so most pension programs are granting ad hoc increases as deemed necessary.

A second consideration is male–female discrimination. Women live longer, so there have been attempts over the years to either lower the payment amounts to women or to make women contribute more to the program. Both alternatives have been ruled out by the Supreme Court, so pension programs may make no distinction because of sex.

The third consideration is the possibility of integrating the pension program with Social Security. This can be a cost-cutting strategy for the organization since benefit levels can be lowered if Social Security benefits are taken into account in determining the benefit levels that are appropriate for the organization's employees.[15]

DEFINED-CONTRIBUTION PLANS. In a defined-contribution plan employees do not know what income they will receive upon retirement but do know how much money there is in the pension fund earmarked for them. Upon retirement the person can take that money out and develop a retirement-income program. This is usually done by going to an insurance company and buying an annuity.

The money in the defined-contribution plan comes from employer contributions, the growth and interest earned on those contributions, and possibly employee contributions. The employer contributions can be determined in a number of ways. The easiest is a percentage of the person's pay each year. More complex, but of more interest to many organizations, is the combination of a defined-contribution plan with a profit-sharing program, as discussed in chapter 14.

Defined-contribution plans are not as numerous as defined-benefit plans but are growing at a faster rate. Part of the reason is their comparative simplicity. The employer contribution is much easier to calculate and understand under a defined-contribution plan. Also, the ability to combine the program with profit sharing is becoming more attractive as these programs gain attention.

401K PLANS. One of the offshoots of the Social Security program's problems of the early 1980s and the dramatic inflation rates of the late 1970s is the realization by more people that they must plan for their own future re-

[15]R. Frumkin and D. Schmitt, "Pension Improvements Since 1974 Reflect Inflation, New Tax Law," *Monthly Labor Review*, April 1979, pp. 18–22.

tirement and not depend upon the government to take care of them. This trend has been encouraged by the government, which has established a number of programs to allow individuals to invest money and defer the taxes on that money until retirement.

401K plans are the best example of this trend.[16] They are a defined-contribution plan that if properly administered and sold to the employees is a qualified plan under the tax laws. A 401K plan allows the employee to put aside up to $7000 of his or her income per year. The organization may provide matching funds if it wishes. This matching can be one for one, some percentage, or tied to profits. The monies collected may go into a single fund or may be allocated among a number of funds by the employee, and if there are multiple funds the employee can switch funds as needed. These plans may also have a loan program that allows the employee to take money out for emergencies without having the money become taxable. 401K plans require considerable thought and communication by management if they are to be effective, since a major problem can be the discrimination tests that require that the participants be spread out over all employees of the organization and not just the executives.[17] Despite these requirements, 401K plans are the fastest-growing pension benefit today.

ESOPs, TRASOPs, AND PAYSOPs. Employee stock-ownership plans (ESOP) are also a form of defined-contribution program. The idea of these plans is that the employer puts aside for the employee money, which is used to purchase stock in the company. These ESOPs are attractive to organizations because they can borrow money to purchase the stock and pay off the loan and interest with taxable income. Banks are permitted to exclude 50 percent of interest on ESOP loan value from taxable income. If the company does well these plans are seen positively by employees, but if the company does not do well the employee receives little value. TRASOPs and PAYSOPs are more recent forms of ESOPs allowed under recent tax laws.[18]

SEPs. A new form of retirement program allowed by law is the simplified employee pension (SEP). This is a form of individual retirement account (IRA) in which the employer is allowed to contribute up to 15 percent of the employee's income or $30,000, whichever is less, into a savings account. This is a popular form of pension program because it requires little administration. It is particularly valuable to small organizations.[19]

SAVINGS PROGRAMS. Savings programs are similar to 401K plans and allow the organization and the employee to work together to achieve the

[16]T. Benna, *Cash or Deferred (Sec. 401[k]) Plans: Adding Flexibility to Your Benefits Program,* Personnel Management-Compensation, Report Bulletin 7 (Englewood Cliffs, N.J.: Prentice-Hall, 1983).

[17]H. E. Moody and E. D. Higgins, "Selling the 401(k) Plan to Employees," *Harvard Business Review,* November-December 1984, pp. 68–73.

[18]J. Hoerr, G. Stevenson, and J. R. Norman, "ESOP's: Revolution or Ripoff?" *Business Week,* April 15, 1985, pp. 94–108.

[19]J. S. Rosenbloom and G. V. Hallman, *Employee Benefits Planning* (Englewood Cliffs, N.J.: Prentice-Hall, 1981).

employee's retirement goals. In a saving plan the employee can contribute up to 6 percent of his or her pay to the plan; the employer can match this amount or contribute some percentage of the employee's contribution. These programs have the same restrictions as discussed for pension programs as to membership in the program and vesting of employer contribution.

Some programs have a limited option for investment of the funds collected, typically in company stock. Most programs in large companies at least provide investment options which vary in the amount of risk of the portfolio from which the employee may choose.

INSURANCE PROGRAMS

Organizations typically offer insurance benefits for employees in three categories, health and medical, disability, and life. There are two major benefits from having the organization provide this insurance, as opposed to having the employees obtain it themselves—taxability and group rates. As a benefit, payments made by the employer for the insurance are not considered to be income to the employee. But this may be a short-lived advantage: Congress is examining ways to tax these benefits. The employer acting as a representative of the group of employees can obtain a better rate for all employees by putting them into a group program. This is a very real advantage and one that will continue to be effective.

One consideration that runs through all these types of insurance programs is the question of employee contribution. Traditionally, medical programs have been paid for by the employer, life programs are variable between organizations, and disability is usually paid by the employee. When the employee pays for all or some of the cost of the insurance, the value of the benefit in the employment exchange goes down but the attention that the employee gives to the benefit goes up.

Health/Medical Programs

The purpose of health insurance programs is to provide protection from the costs, sometimes enormous, of sickness and accident to the employee and his or her family. This is done in two ways, an insurance plan or a health maintenance program (HMO).

INSURANCE PROGRAMS.   Insurance programs collect money from the employer into a fund and pay it out as employees and their families have health needs. The amount that the employer puts into the fund must, over time, equal the claims against the fund plus the administrative costs of operating the fund. Rates go up when this does not happen. The program must define the health charges that will be accepted for payment and determine what proportion of the costs the insurance program will cover. As an alternative the program determines the amount that will be paid for any particular service.

Although there are some variations within insurance programs, the major change to take place in this area in the past few years has been to self-insure. This means that the organization provides the agreed-upon coverage to employees out of its own assets instead of turning over a sum of money to the insurance company. This has been a way in which organizations have been able to reduce their health insurance costs. Of course, in doing so they are moving the risk from the insurance company to themselves.

HEALTH MAINTENANCE ORGANIZATIONS. An HMO is an organization that combines being an insurance company and providing health care. It offers comprehensive health care, both inpatient and outpatient. Like an insurance plan, it charges a fixed fee. HMOs are supposed to focus on preventive medicine as well as taking care of current health problems. In this they seem somewhat successful, for hospital days per member are lower than the national average.[20]

Under the HMO Act of 1973 an HMO option is required of the employer should an HMO approach the organization for recognition and the organization is offering health insurance. HMOs sometimes do cost less than other health alternatives but almost always provide more coverage for the money.[21]

OTHER HEALTH-RELATED INSURANCE. Most health insurance plans limit the area of health covered. In particular, dental and eye care are usually excluded. These are now becoming popular as new benefit programs.[22]

HEALTH CARE COVERAGE. Health care programs usually cover all employees. However, many organizations exclude part-time employees from coverage. In some cases organizations have different plans for different employee groups; managers and executives often have plans that include wider coverage. The Consolidated Omnibus Reconciliation Act of 1985 (COBRA) requires that employees, their spouses, and their children must be covered after the employee is no longer with the organization. The coverage is for 18 to 36 months, depending on the circumstances. The employer is allowed to charge the covered person 102 percent of the premium cost.

CONTAINMENT OF HEALTH CARE COSTS. Health care is a good example of a fringe benefit that has gotten out of control. When organizations first started offering health insurance it was cheap and health-care costs were relatively low. In addition, organizations began offering the benefit in terms of coverage and not in terms of cost. Then came the dramatic increase in the costs of health care. From 1968 to 1985 the proportion of GNP devoted to health care rose from 6.7 percent ($58 billion) to an estimated 10 percent ($460 billion) in 1985. The cost of health-care coverage to the organization has likewise risen as the organization had agreed to provide health care coverage regardless of cost. At this point organizations have started looking toward ways of controlling health-care costs. Some of these alternatives have already been mentioned: HMOs and self-insuring were some of the first to appear.[23]

[20]J. Ross, "Attacking Soaring Health Benefit Costs," *Pension World*, November 1978, pp. 51–58.

[21]"Doctors Are Entering a Brave New World of Competition," *Business Week*, July 16, 1984, pp. 56–61.

[22]D. R. Bell, "Dental and Vision Care Benefits in Health Insurance Plans," *Monthly Labor Review*, August 1982, pp. 22–26.

[23]"The Upheaval in Health Care," *Business Week*, July 25, 1983, pp. 44–56.

A new cost-control method using the insurance approach is the *preferred-provider organization* (PPO). This is an organization that contracts with a group of doctors and hospitals to provide services at a discounted price. This is attractive to the providers because it produces a consistent flow of patients. The PPO is halfway between a regular insurance plan and an HMO. The employee is free to go to any doctor or facility on the list.[24]

Probably the most successful technique in cost containment is sharing the cost with the employee. This can be done at two points. The first is to share the premium costs of the insurance. The second is to share the health-care charges. This can be done by having deductibles for overall services or for specific service events. This may take place informally in nonunion organizations or as a part of collective bargaining in unionized organizations.[25]

Close administration of health-care programs is also necessary. Knowing who is being paid and for what can lead to identification of abuses in the system. Claims control is important, allowing administrators to see that the providers are charging correctly and that employees are properly making claims on the program. Communication and education can alert the employee to the costs the employer must put into this area and therefore not into others. Further, educational efforts directed to promoting health reduce claims and provide a better-performing employee.[26] Finally, some organizations reward employees for savings in insurance programs by returning a portion of unused self-insured pooled funds to the employees at the end of each fiscal year.

Disability Insurance

Worker's compensation takes care of disability resulting from injury on the job, and health insurance takes care of the medical costs of non-work-related injuries. But a person who is out of work because of a non-work-related injury faces a loss of income at the very time that it is important to have full income. Disability insurance is designed to fill this need. At present five states and Puerto Rico have a legal requirement for disability protection for the employee.

The immediate form of disability coverage is *sick leave*. This is not really insurance but payment for time not worked. But the effect is the same: the employee's salary is continued while he or she is ill. From the organization's standpoint it is like self-insurance. Long-term disability is taken care of by an insurance program that specifically pays a proportion of the employee's salary for a specified period. This is commonly an option the employee may choose if he or she is willing to pay for it.

Life Insurance

Life insurance is one of the most common benefits offered by organizations. The insurance is usually of the group-term type, which provides coverage

---

[24]"A New Cure for Health-Cost Fever," *Business Week,* September 20, 1982, p. 117; and *PPO Alternatives: A New Approach to Health Care Delivery* (Chicago: A. S. Hanson, 1984).

[25]"Trying to Curb Health Care Costs at the Bargaining Table," *Business Week,* September 19, 1983, pp. 73–76.

[26]R. M. McCaffery, *Managing the Employee Benefits Program* (New York: American Management Assn., 1972).

for a certain period with no cash surrender value or investment value. The amount of coverage is geared to the salary rate of the employee: the higher the salary the more insurance the employee is allowed to obtain. Organizations vary as to whether the premiums for this insurance are paid by the employee or by the organization.

PAYMENT FOR TIME NOT WORKED

This category of benefits includes a number of situations in which the employee is paid but is not actually working. It can include both time at the workplace and time away from the workplace.

Time Not Worked on the Job

Included in this category of benefits are arrangements for rest periods, lunch breaks, and various preparatory activities and cleanup activities at the end of the day. Most of these arrangements have come about historically and are informal. In some cases they are predicated on state laws requiring breaks after a certain work time or negotiated as part of a labor contract.

Time Off the Job

This is a category of benefits that many employees look forward to. It includes vacations, holidays, sick leave, and personal leave.

VACATION.   The purpose of vacation is to give the employee time away from the job for rest and recreation. Over time there has been a trend toward granting more vacation time. This trend, if not being currently reversed, is clearly on hold. The practice seems to be to start with two weeks and work up to four weeks' vacation at around 15 years.[27] The major issues in vacation policy are whether the vacation time can be carried over, if so how much, and whether to pay the employee off if the vacation time is forfeited. Allowing employees to build up a bank of vacation time creates a large potential cost to the organization and destroys the purpose of vacation—to get away from the job. So most companies have a policy limiting the amount of vacation time that can be stored.

HOLIDAYS.   The common number of paid holidays per year ranges from 9 to 12. Some of these are legally defined and others are the product of tradition and bargaining. Recent downturns in the economy and concession bargaining have reduced the number of holidays in many industries.

SICK LEAVE.   This topic was introduced in our discussion of disability insurance. The most common amount of sick leave is a day a month, amounting to 12 days a year. There are two opposing concerns with sick leave. The first is the person who abuses sick leave by taking it whether really sick or not.

[27]*Personnel Management-Compensation* (Englewood Cliffs, N.J.: Prentice-Hall, 1982), pp. 50(301)-50(313).

This employee then has no sick leave available when it is needed. The opposite problem is those employees who take no sick leave and thereby build up a large potential cost to the organization. This can be quite costly, since employees could build up their reserve while their salary rate is low and then use it when their salary rate is much higher. Every time the wage structure is adjusted this affects the total potential cost of sick leave. To get around this problem organizations are limiting the buildup of sick leave just as they are vacations.

PERSONAL LEAVE.   This is a grab bag of time off for various reasons, such as death in the family, military leave, and jury duty. Many organizations are setting up a general category of personal leave rather than having a series of special circumstances that lead to different interpretations throughout the organization.

In fact, one trend that is starting to take hold is to combine all the time-off categories just discussed and grant a certain number of days off per year for paid time off the job. It is left up to the employee to decide how these days are to be distributed.

EMPLOYEE SERVICES

A number of other benefits are often granted to employees because they are of value to the employee and the employer or while not of great value to the employer it is the employer who can arrange for the service. The latter category contains a wide range of services where the employer can group employees to provide an economic advantage in dealing with the suppliers of the service, much as is done in insurance. Examples of this are credit unions, food services, recreational facilities, and discount tickets to entertainment events.

The former category consists of services that are needed by the employee but also enhance the value of the employee to the organization at the same time. The three best examples of this are reimbursement for educational expenses, health-club or recreational-club memberships, and day care for children. In each of these cases the employer is spending money to provide the employee with a service that will improve the ability of that person to accomplish his or her job.

Educational expense reimbursement has been popular for a long time, particularly among professional and managerial employees who are seeking advanced degrees. The organization ordinarily pays the tuition of the employee provided the educational experience relates to the job. In addition, adjustment of the working day is often required to allow part-time students to attend classes. Increasingly, this benefit is being taxed.

Health-club memberships or the development of a health facility on plant premises is increasing with the knowledge that a healthy person is a more productive employee. The movement toward concern with health in the United States has spurred this trend. Many organizations claim that this, plus a campaign to promote wellness among employees, reduces absenteeism, increases productivity, and lowers medical-insurance costs.

Day care represents one of the newest and hardest-to-solve problems of the work force today. The problem is a result of the twin work-force trends of two-paycheck families and single-parent families. Both of these trends call for adequate child care to be available to parents. Organizational contentions that this is the employee's problem or society's problem disregards much of the rationale for the benefits described in this chapter. It is in fact when employees need something and society is not in a position to provide it that organizations have been called upon to provide the service, either voluntarily or under the law.[28]

The problem actually concerns two groups of children. The first are preschool children who require all-day care. The second are school-age children who need care after school—the *latch key children*. The latter group is seemingly being dealt with by government and private organizations to a greater degree than the preschooler.[29]

SUMMARY

Benefits represent a wide variety of rewards granted to employees for a number of reasons; the two major ones are these: the benefit is mandated by law and protection is provided for the employee. Each benefit requires discussion, since the administration of each is different. This chapter groups benefits by categories and examines their characteristics.

The first category is legally required benefits. These include Social Security, Unemployment Compensation, and Workers Compensation. All three of these were begun in the depression to provide employees with protection against old age, unemployment, and job-related injury. The employer pays part or all of the cost of these benefits. Social Security has come under attack in recent years for being unable to provide required benefits, and workers compensation has been expanding the definition of "job related."

A second category of benefits is retirement programs. The passage of ERISA has made an enormous impact on the design and administration of retirement programs through the requirements for funding, vesting, and reporting. Retirement programs are either defined benefit or defined contribution plans. The latter is becoming more popular because of the funding requirements of ERISA. Tax laws have encouraged a number of new types of plans in recent years including 401Ks, ESOPs and their cousins, and SEPs.

A third category of benefits is insurance programs. These include health/ medical plans, disability, and life insurance. Medical plans have been the most troublesome in recent years as costs have risen significantly. A major concern in organizations today is reducing these costs. Some ways of doing this have been use of HMOs and PPOs, self-insuring, close administration, and cost sharing with the employee.

A fourth category of benefits is for time not worked, including vacation, holidays, sick and other leave days. A final category of benefits is employee services, which can include an unbelievable variety of services depending on the organizational circumstance. The current concern in this category is the provision of day care for children of employees.

[28]S. L. Burud et al., *Child Care: The New Business Tool* (Pasadena, Calif.: National Employer Sponsored Child Care Project, 1983).

[29]See S. Koepp, "Make Room for Baby," *Business Week*, September 3, 1984, p. 61; and "Business Group Leads Schools in Starting Child Care Programs," *Impact*, September 12, 1984 (Englewood Cliffs, N.J.: Prentice-Hall), p. 6.

PART VI

THE WAGE TREATMENT DECISION

> "Do you think we get our money's worth out of our sales commission plan?"
>
> "I don't understand why we can't treat the engineers just like everyone else around here!"
>
> "Our division managers need to keep better track of the expenses they run up. Do you have any ideas as to how we can get their attention?"
>
> "If we start sending these people over to Asia, what problems does this create for paying them?"

Not all employees are the same, nor are the jobs they hold. Some groups in organizations need special wage systems in order to take advantage of the type of person in their jobs and the special characteristics of those jobs. The four groups that organizations typically find it useful to have special wage programs for are sales, professional, managerial, and international employees. Programs for these four groups are covered in the next two chapters.

17

Compensation of Sales and Professional Employees

This book has suggested that compensation programs consist of a series of decisions that form a framework for rewarding employees for their participation and productivity resulting in ongoing and successful performance of the organization. Since each person is different, these decisions must be able to be applied in varying circumstances while retaining the consistency required for equity. In this way, the employment exchange is an individual exchange between the person and the organization based upon the variations in perception of each. In some cases, groups of employees have similar circumstances and/or perceptions that have led organizations to develop compensation programs that contain enough special characteristics to be dealt with separately. This chapter will discuss two such groups in organizations: sales and professional employees.

Different compensation programs for these groups is based to some degree upon traditions within organizations and to a larger degree upon differences in the jobs and the people in these jobs. Jobs vary in measurability of their product and therefore in ease of establishing a clear measure of performance necessary for an incentive program. Jobs also differ in their importance to organizational goals and therefore in the degree to which it is profitable to the organization to expend the energy necessary to develop special programs. Further, some jobs operate independently, so the identification of cause and effect is easier and more reasonable. In highly interdependent jobs there is a dysfunctional effect from creating competition. Finally, some jobs require a great deal of contact with individuals outside the organization, making the employee a representative of the organization. This often leads to a feeling in the organization that such a job has a special status.

People also vary in their expectations of what contributions they deem important. Personal attributes are perceived as important by some groups, and much less so by others. Much loyalty is expected of some groups, little of others. Although most people in organizations work in similar conditions, some work in such different circumstances that these are seen as an important part of the employment exchange. When these differences in jobs and their incumbents become great enough, organizations respond by specializing the compensation decisions for the group involved.

Some of these differences were recognized in the Fair Labor Standards Act, which classified as nonexempt certain groups of employees within the organization. That is, these employees did not fall under the provisions of the act. These groups are the ones to be discussed in this chapter and the next. The reasons for making these groups exempt may have been those discussed here, but what is clear is that this classification by the FLSA has encouraged the continued separation of compensation for these groups.

PROGRAMS FOR SALES EMPLOYEES

In most organizations the compensation program for sales personnel is different and separate from that of other employees. This different treatment has to do with the nature of the job, the importance of the job, and the nature of sales personnel. The dominant feature of sales compensation is the use of incentives. Whereas incentive plans may be becoming more popular for a wide range of employee groups in this time of emphasis upon productivity, the sales group has always been paid on incentive and the nature of the work makes sales incentive plans different from other such plans in the organization. In addition, the use of incentives in sales compensation has been the result of tradition: that is how it has been done in the past. However, to the degree that the organization of sales activity in organizations is changing, the use of incentives may need to be examined closely.

The concept of the employment exchange again seems a useful way of examining the compensation of this group of employees. The contributions of the job and the person is examined first, and then the design of the reward systems based upon these contributions.

The Sales Job

Sales work involves working with customers—people outside the organization—to convince them to order the products or services of the organization. The importance of this activity is obvious. Except in the odd circumstance where the organization's product sells itself, this activity is vital to the continuing operation of the organization. Furthermore, this importance of the job is highly visible in the organization, making the impact of the job even clearer. But an in-depth analysis shows two things about sales work that should be kept in mind: not all of the salesperson's activities are sales work, and not all sales activity is carried out by personnel labeled sales personnel.

SALES ACTIVITY.   Most sales jobs include activities such as soliciting orders, servicing customers, seeking out buyers, obtaining information, and performing *missionary work* such as cold calls and product promotion. Some sales personnel also engage in credit-information collection and analysis, product modification, customer-personnel training, and technical advice and assistance. All sales jobs require that the salesperson perform some administrative work, such as making reports and keeping records. Depending upon the market, the products, and the organization, various aspects of these activities are more or less important in particular sales jobs. Further, although some of these activities are important and necessary, they may not really be sales work, indicating that sales personnel do more than just sell.[1]

This variety of sales activities suggests that it is necessary to develop job descriptions for sales jobs that describe clearly the contributions required of the employee. When the salesperson is paid on an incentive basis the nonselling activities can often be neglected unless they are clearly spelled out as a part of the job. These descriptions are most useful where there are a number of different types of sales positions in the organization. Sales job descriptions typically include not only information about activities but also information about number of customers, volume of sales, diversity of products sold, and geographical area covered.

SALES SUPPORT.   The typical picture of the salesperson is someone operating alone with the customer. This is often inaccurate, however. Sales work requires the support of others in the organization. At one level there is administrative support enabling the salesperson to operate in the field. Some of this support is clerical, but a larger part in today's complex economic environment is support of the field sales effort by inside sales personnel. Many sales situations also require help in the form of technical expertise that is available from others in the organization. All of this support both changes the picture of a salesperson as an independent operator and has a considerable impact on developing incentive programs, which assume that it is the activity of the salesperson that brings in the sales orders.[2]

CHARACTERISTICS OF SALES JOBS.   Despite these complexities there are a number of dimensions of sales jobs that make establishing incentive programs useful and perhaps necessary. The first of these, importance of the function, has already been discussed. The others are independence, boundary spanning, and measurability.

Independence.   As indicated, the typical picture of the salesperson is one of working one to one with a customer outside the organization. For many sales positions this is still an accurate picture. Direct supervision and control of the

---

[1]"The Death (or Transfiguration) of the Field Salesperson," *Sales and Marketing Management,* April 5, 1982, p. 133.

[2]P. Kotler, *Marketing Management: Analysis, Planning and Control,* 2nd ed. (Englewood Cliffs, N.J.: Prentice-Hall, 1972).

salesperson in this circumstance is therefore very difficult. The traditional reliance on tools such as performance appraisal does not work as well since the supervisor does not *see* the salesperson in action. This makes reliance on the outcomes of the job more attractive. It should be noted, however, that the degree of independence of salespeople varies with the job situation. There is a great deal of difference between a salesperson who is on the road and one who operates in a store where the supervisor is present.[3]

Where the employee is autonomous, control of behavior must be more internalized. One way of doing this is to reward the desired activities or the outcomes of the activities. In the case of sales personnel the outcomes are desired, and rewarding these keeps the person attempting to achieve them. The problem is to have the salesperson achieve the outcome without doing so in an unacceptable manner.

Boundary spanning.   The salesperson represents the organization to the customer. Likewise he or she represents the customer to the organization. This creates a position within the organization with split loyalties, some to the organization and some to the customer. This is the classic dilemma of a boundary-spanning role—representing the other party to whomever you are presently in contact with.[4] Often it is the salesperson who is the organization to people outside the organization. This makes the sales position an important one for the organization's reputation.

Boundary spanners must be able to see both groups' point of view and to collect and transmit information between groups. Within the organization the salesperson is often seen as giving trouble to other employees inside the organization in order to serve the customer. Thus, the loyalty of the salesperson to the organization is likely to be perceived as less than that of other employees. This puts pressure on the compensation program since it is compensation that is the major method of maintaining a positive membership decision.[5]

Measurability.   These characteristics of sales jobs make incentive programs an attractive way to compensate salespeople. That the results of sales work are highly measurable makes the incentive idea possible. Sales volume, either in units or monetary, is easily measurable and is connected with the efforts and ability of the salesperson. There is also considerable variation among salespeople in volume of sales—an important consideration in establishing an incentive program. Further, the salesperson expects to be rewarded by the use of an incentive program.

Using sales volume alone, though, can be a problem in rewarding salespeople. As indicated in chapter 14, connecting performance and reward focuses the person on the performance factor to the exclusion of other job activities. If the organization wants activities other than just sales volume, it is not

[3]R. B. Marks, *Personal Selling* (Boston: Allyn & Bacon, 1985).

[4]J. S. Adams, "The Structure and Dynamics of Behavior in Organizational Boundary Roles," in *Handbook of Industrial and Organizational Psychology*, ed. M. D. Dunnette (Chicago: Rand McNally, 1976), pp. 1175–99.

[5]K. R. Davis, "Are Your Salesmen Paid Too Much?" in *Salesmanship and Salesforce Management*, ed. E. C. Bursk and G. S. Hutchinson (Cambridge, Mass.: Harvard University Press, 1971).

likely to get them if only sales volume is rewarded. Thus, salespeople have a reputation for not doing their paperwork correctly or not doing other things, such as making cold calls or giving product presentations, that do not in the salesperson's eyes clearly lead to more sales volume. So most sales compensation programs need to reward more than just sales volume.

Last, there is the problem of connecting performance with effort. Sales jobs differ greatly in the degree to which the effort of the individual salesperson influences the measured output. If the sales effort is a group affair or the sale takes the efforts of other jobs in the organization, then using simple output measures may not be appropriate.

The Salesperson

Salespeople are often perceived as extroverts who can meet and deal with strangers and friends alike and get them to do what they want them to do. This, of course, is a stereotype. Like all stereotypes it has some truth to it, but overall it is too simplistic. Some sales positions do require the aggressive extrovert. But others require a high degree of technical skill and a great deal of patience to sell highly complex organizational outputs one order of which may take years to complete. Studies do show, however, that successful salespeople are relatively aggressive, outgoing, self-motivated, and materially oriented.[6]

TOLERANCE FOR AMBIGUITY. The rewards of sales work, both extrinsic and intrinsic, are not constant or consistent, as they are in many other organizational jobs. Some days the salesperson comes home feeling that much has been accomplished, since in selling one can see positive results immediately. Other days there is no positive feedback: there have been no successful sales efforts, or other activities have prevented the salesperson from spending time on sales efforts. Thus, the salesperson experiences wide swings of positive and negative feedback. He or she must be able to adapt to this variation in reward structure. In fact the stimulation and uncertainty act as stimuli to the salesperson.

The nature of sales work also leads to ambiguity. The lack of performance feedback from the supervisor, the focus on outcomes and the consequent uncertainty of how to perform the job, and the lack of participation in decision making all lead to a lack of role clarity for the sales job, and the salesperson experiences this as an ambiguous situation.[7] Added to this is the boundary-spanning aspect of the job, which creates role conflict as well as ambiguity.[8]

ACHIEVEMENT DRIVE. McClelland has studied a number of socially derived needs of individuals.[9] One of the most-studied of these is the drive

[6]L. M. Lamont and W. J. Lundstrom, "Identifying Successful Salesmen by Personality and Personal Characteristics," *Journal of Marketing Research*, 16:1977, p. 525.

[7]R. K. Teas, J. G. Wacker, and R. E. Hughes, "A Path Analysis of Causes and Consequences of Salespeople's Perceptions of Role Clarity," *Journal of Marketing Research*, August 1979, pp. 355–69.

[8]D. A. Whetten, "Coping with Incompatible Expectations: An Integrated View of Role Conflict," *Administrative Science Quarterly*, 23:1978, pp. 254–71.

[9]D. C. McClelland, *The Achieving Society* (New York: Free Press, 1961).

to achieve. A person with a high achievement drive has a number of distinctive characteristics. The first of these is a desire to take moderate risks and to decide upon these for oneself. These risks are achievable but not easy to reach, and in this way provide a challenge rather than discouragement. The second characteristic is the need for immediate feedback. The person must be able to see that he or she is moving toward the goal. Third, the high achiever finds the path to the goal as rewarding as the extrinsic reward at the conclusion of the activity. Last, the high achiever is preoccupied with the task, focusing on the goal and keeping at it until it is achieved. If we put the last two together we can see why the high achiever often feels a letdown upon reaching the goal: it was the pursuit and not the product that was stimulating.

These characteristics would seem to fit the type of job that sales is and the compensation program typically developed for sales work. Sales allows one to set one's own challenging goals, there is immediate feedback, and one can immerse oneself in the process of the sale and enjoy that process. In fact, McClelland found that the most likely place in the organization for high achievement drive to show up is in sales personnel. There appears to be a self-selection process whereby those with a high need for achievement find sales work to be most satisfying.

Sales Payment Plans

As indicated, the dominant feature of sales compensation is the use of incentive plans. However, not all sales personnel are paid on the basis of incentive plans, and fewer still are on plans that are totally incentive-based. A recent survey of sales pay plans showed that 27.3 percent of the companies surveyed used only a straight salary, 52.2 percent used some combination of salary and incentive, and the remaining 20.5 percent used a straight incentive or commission approach.[10] Thus, incentives are clearly important but not exclusive in paying salespeople. In this section each of the three options mentioned in the survey just cited is considered.

STRAIGHT SALARY. As indicated, a little over a quarter of the sales compensation plans surveyed pay sales personnel a straight salary without any incentive plan. This makes setting wage rates for sales jobs similar to setting wage rates for other jobs in the organization. The process of arriving at ranges would follow the process developed in part III of this book, although the process is probably more influenced by the economics of the organization than it is for most other jobs in the organization.

Sales pay ranges are affected by the same forces that influence other wages within the organization. The labor market is a major influence. Surveys of sales compensation are made by trade associations, consultants, and the organization itself. Variations in salary rates, however, tend to be larger for sales jobs than for other jobs.

Salary relationships within the organization also influence sales wage rates. The sales-manager position and sales-support positions in the organization often are used as buffer positions; they can be compared with both the sales job and other organizational jobs. Sales jobs are often more influenced by

[10]"Study of Sales Income," *American Salesman*, April 1982, pp. 40–41.

the incumbent than are other organizational jobs. The skills and abilities of the individual often dictate the particular activities that constitute a particular sales job.

Straight-salary plans do not preclude the use of performance motivation. A pay-for-performance program [see chapter 13] can be used to focus the salesperson on high performance levels. The sales job has the advantage of having a more measurable standard than other jobs, so the performance measurement is less judgmental. The danger is that the sales volume alone will be used as the measure of performance when other job factors may also contribute to the definition of performance.

Equity is always a problem in sales compensation. When sales personnel are paid a straight salary the comparison with other organizational jobs through job evaluation reduces the equity problem within the organization. But it increases the equity problem with other sales jobs that are paid on an incentive basis. It is difficult to compare sales positions paid on a commission and straight salary, for they often involve quite different work. What is clear, however, is that they are paid quite different amounts: salespeople on commissions are paid up to a third more than those on straight salary.[11]

There are a number of circumstances that make straight salary advantageous. These all center in the inability to connect either performance and reward or effort and performance. Where the product is highly complex, the time taken to culminate a sale is long, and/or the sales effort is a team affair, an incentive program is infeasible. In some sales jobs the nonsales aspects are of primary importance to the organization, and these factors are difficult to measure. An incentive program may be unfair to new salespeople, who do not know the job or the customers well enough to meet sales goals. In general, the less impact the salesperson has upon the sales results, the less argument there is to establish an incentive program.

A straight-salary program has certain advantages to the organization, the salesperson, and the customer. From the salesperson's standpoint, a straight salary takes the ambiguity out of how much salary he or she is receiving. Some people are very uncomfortable not knowing how much they will make next month, or are unable to budget the good times to cover the bad times. For the organization, a straight salary plan is much simpler. In addition, it gives the organization more control over the salesperson. One of the aspects of placing a person on incentives is that the person feels much more independent of organizational control. It has also been found that salespeople under a straight-salary plan are more willing to perform the nonsales aspects of the sales job.[12] From the standpoint of the customer, the sales person on a straight salary is more likely to provide service and less likely to pressure the person into a sale and move on.

The disadvantages of a straight-salary program reverse the advantages above. They center in the lack of connection between performance and reward and therefore suggest that motivation levels among salespeople paid in this manner can be expected to be lower than those of salespeople on incentives.

[11]R. C. Smyth, "Financial Incentives for Salesmen," *Harvard Business Review,* January-February 1968, pp. 109–17.

[12]G. Canning, Jr., and R. Berry, "Linking Sales Compensation to the Product Life Cycle," *Management Review,* July 1982, pp. 43–46.

Also, as indicated, from the salesperson's standpoint, wage rates tend to be lower. From the organizational viewpoint, sales salaries are a fixed cost rather than a variable cost, making sales salaries a burden in times of low sales. Poor performance must be dealt with administratively, a requirement that is becoming more difficult each year.

Whether the use of straight salary is increasing or decreasing seems uncertain. A study by the Conference Board in 1972 showed a trend away from straight-salary plans.[13] The recent focus on performance and the bringing of more and more employees under incentives would seem to be expanding this retreat from straight salary. Sibson, on the other hand, indicates that there is a trend toward straight-salary plans.[14] The arguments for this direction are the increasing sales job complexity and the need for non-sales-related tasks in the sales job. This trend may also be a reflection of the organization's recognizing that marketing and not just selling is the important aspect of keeping its output moving.

COMMISSION PLANS. A straight commission plan is like a straight piecework plan in that the salesperson's earnings are in direct proportion to his or her sales. It is probably the oldest form of compensation program for sales personnel. Establishing a commission plan, then, will be similar to establishing an incentive plan, as described in chapter 14. As indicated, about a fifth of the sales compensation plans surveyed are strictly commission-based. However, a commission or bonus is also an integral part of combination plans discussed next.

In theory, a commission plan is very simple. A commission is ordinarily defined as a percentage of the sales price of the product.[15] The exact percentage is highly variable with the product being sold, the industry practice, and the organization's economic situation. It also varies with internal organizational factors and the exact nature of the sales job. For instance, the directness of the relationship between the salesperson's efforts and the sales volume usually affects the percentage given to the salesperson.

Two things need to be noted about providing a percentage of the sale to the salesperson. First, the percentage need not be the same at all levels of sales; it may increase or decrease with volume. (This point was discussed in chapter 14.) This increase or decrease can be related to the effort the salesperson must exert to increase the sales volume. The second point is that sales may be stated as sales price, sales units, or some other measure that reflects the variation in sales. In particular, the point in the sale process when the sale is counted is important. Sales percentages calculated at the point of sale versus the point of delivery are different figures and occur at different times for the salesperson.

The effects of the commission system need to be examined before it is put into operation. The basic calculation that needs to be made is an estimate of what amounts will be paid to sales personnel in the form of commissions. This information should be used in a number of ways. First, it should be used

[13]*Compensating Salesmen and Sales Executives, 1972* (New York: Conference Board, 1972).

[14]R. E. Sibson, *Compensation*, rev. ed. (New York: American Management Assn., 1981).

[15]J. W. Barry and P. Henry, *Effective Sales Incentive Compensation* (New York: McGraw-Hill, 1981).

in the pay level sense of determining the total cost of selling the product. Here the concern is whether sales costs are in line with other costs of production. Second, estimates of commissions should be used in a wage structure sense of determining whether wages paid to salespeople are in line with wages paid other jobs in the organization and with those paid sales jobs in other organizations. Third, these estimates should be used to determine the expected income to the sales personnel. An incentive program may look like a good plan, but unless a sufficient percentage of the sales force are likely to make above a minimum amount over expectations, the incentive value of the program may be negative.[16]

The performance-motivation model specifies that for an incentive plan to be effective the following conditions must be met:

1. Employees must believe that good performance leads to more pay. A commission plan should clearly do this by its construction. This belief is strengthened because the measurement of results is clear and objective. If there is a long time between point of sale and delivery or if many sales are not converted to delivery, this relationship can be weakened.

2. Employees must desire more pay. This seems obvious, but it is more complex than that. First, people differ in their desire for more pay, although sales personnel are reputed to be a group that strongly desires pay.[17] Second, the increased pay must be worth the foregone opportunities: if more sales, and therefore more pay, means more hours at work or evening hours, some people will choose not to pursue more pay. Organizations may be safe in assuming that through self-selection those who enter sales work highly desire pay, but as sales jobs become more complex and technical this assumption may become less valid.

3. Employees must not believe that good performance will lead to negative consequences. Unfortunately, this is a likely consequence of commission plans. Sales incentive plans are often changed by the organization. These frequent changes are perceived as ways to solve two opposite problems—lack of sales and perceived overpayment of sales personnel. From the salesperson's viewpoint these changes create confusion in the performance–reward connection and a feeling that the organization is *cutting the rate*. Further, many sales incentive plans are so complex that the salesperson becomes confused as to what will happen if he or she takes certain actions. So some actions are avoided because the salesperson does not know what the consequences of taking action will be. Last, the sales incentive plan can put the salesperson in conflict with the rest of the organization. Difficulties between sales personnel and credit, finance, manufacturing, and shipping are everyday events in many organizations.

[16]B. Ellig, "Sales Compensation: A Systematic Approach," in *Compensation and Benefits: Design and Analysis*, ed. B. Ellig (Scottsdale, Ariz.: American Compensation Assn., 1985), pp. 36–45.

[17]D. L. Thompson, "Stereotype of the Salesman," *Harvard Business Review*, January-February 1972, pp. 20–36.

4. Employees must see that other desired rewards besides pay result from good performance. Sales incentive plans are mixed on this. Feelings of achievement, esteem, and respect are quite likely to occur along with high incentive pay for most sales personnel.[18] On the other hand, high pay restricts long-term movement within the organization. Sales positions are often perceived as having little career-growth opportunity.[19]

5. Employees must believe that their efforts lead to good performance. This perception probably varies widely among sales incentive plans. Where certain activities clearly lead to sales then this perception is strengthened. However, there are a number of hinderances to this connection. Since sales are highly affected by the economy, the product, past relationships, and other factors beyond the salesperson's control, the connection is often tenuous. The sales incentive plan itself may be perceived as not rewarding important efforts of the salesperson or rewarding efforts that are of little importance. The problem is that if the plan includes a wide range of relevant efforts then it becomes so complex that the performance–reward connection is not clear and the dysfunctions of condition 3 operate.

COMBINATION PLANS.   As indicated, a little over half of the sales compensation plans surveyed are some sort of combination of base salary and incentive. The reasons given for developing combination plans are that (1) the salesperson is not the only influence on the sales volume, and (2) some parts of the sales job do not involve direct selling and these need to be rewarded also. Done properly, a combination plan should contain the advantages of both straight-salary and incentive plans. On the other hand, such plans can also be seen as management indecision as to what they want of salespeople, and they can confuse the salesperson as to what is important in the job.[20]

All combination plans involve the establishment of a sales standard— the expected volume of sales for a particular time period. In the sales field this standard is usually called a *sales quota*. But the standard may be broader than just sales volume: other factors, such as obtaining new customers, retaining customers over time, and doing missionary work, can be included. The advantage of including a number of variables in the standard is that the plan then more clearly covers the whole sales job. The disadvantage is that the complexity of the plan is increased and the salesperson may become confused about what he or she is being paid for.

This establishment of a standard or quota is like setting production standards discussed in chapter 14. The basis for developing the standard is the level of sales and other factors that the salesperson can be expected to achieve. Establishing this standard is more difficult here than it is in most incentive plans in a number of ways. Sales jobs tend to be individual, in terms of both the salesperson and the customers dealt with. Also, outside influences can easily affect the sales volume. In setting sales quotas it is useful to consider the past

[18]Marks, *Personal Selling.*

[19]J. K. Moynahan, *Designing an Effective Sales Compensation Program* (New York: American Management Assn., 1980).

[20]Ibid.

year's performance, economic conditions, technological changes, and competitors' strategies. For these reasons setting the expected volume is more often a figure negotiated with the individual salesperson than a standard for all salespeople to meet.

The standard generally sets the level at which the salesperson's straight salary is considered *covered* by the sales volume. But this can vary, with the incentive starting after some percentage of the standard has been reached. Straight salary usually constitutes around 75 percent of the total salary in combination plans, but this percentage can be planned as high or as low as desired. The incentive portion will be lower where the direct contribution of the salesperson to sales volume is low, where nonsales activities are valued by management, and where there are considerable variations in sales over time and between sales areas.[21]

There are a number of ways of establishing the incentive portion of sales compensation. Probably the simplest system is to use a commission combined with a *draw*. The salesperson receives a specified salary each payday. At periodic times, such as each quarter, the total commissions due the salesperson are calculated. The amount taken as a draw is deducted from this and the salesperson then receives the remainder. If the draw exceeds the commission, the organization must decide whether to reduce the draw or carry over the deficit, and/or whether to retain the salesperson in the position.

A *bonus system* provides incentive payments after a given level of sales has been reached. These plans can be quite simple or very complex. Simple ones resemble a commission-draw system with a percentage payment made for sales above a standard. More complex plans have payment schedules that vary with sales volume or payments for a variety of things beyond sales volume, such as obtaining new accounts, reducing sales expenses, improving market penetration, and increasing order size. A variation on the more complex bonus plans is the *point plan*. Here the salesperson receives points for meeting and exceeding goals or quotas in a number of areas. These points are then converted to monetary values.

Completing the Sales Compensation Package

Sales compensation considerations do not end with the design of the direct pay system. There are other aspects of sales compensation that differ from the compensation of other employee groups. These differences are both in further incentives, in the form of contests, and in differences in benefits.

CONTESTS. One of the more unique reward techniques that the nature of the sales job allows for is the development of sales contests. The measurable-output aspect allows the organization to design a short-term reward system that gives prizes for accomplishing certain quotas or selling more than all others. This is often attractive to the type of person who enjoys sales work. The prizes can be either monetary or nonmonetary but more often are not direct pay. Most popular are nonmonetary prizes such as vacation trips or goods such as golf clubs or other recreational equipment.

[21]Ibid.

These contests have a number of advantages. First, they provide a very visible reward. Records of who is winning what can be placed on bulletin boards and put in the newsletter. It is interesting that this publicity seems natural for a contest but out of place for direct pay. Second, a contest, like any bonus, is a one-shot affair: it does not add to the overall wage costs beyond the time of the contest. This allows the rewards to be large and still not have a detrimental effect on labor costs. Last, contests extend to the salesperson's family more clearly than direct pay. Such awards as vacations are shared with family members, ideally creating company loyalty within the family as well as the salesperson.

Contests also have some disadvantages. The publicity can be very discouraging to those salespeople who perceive they have no chance to accomplish the level of sales necessary to win an award. Not only is one not receiving a reward but all one's colleagues are aware of one's shortfall. This is particularly hard on new sales personnel or those in difficult territories. Contests may also shift the focus from the main job to side issues. If the awards are for selling items that are not important to the overall sales effort, then the total sales of the company may actually decline as a result of the contest.[22]

BENEFITS.   Salespeople used to be perceived almost as independent contractors. As such they were not included in benefit programs to the same extent as other employee groups. This situation has changed, and sales personnel are now recipients of the regular organizational benefit program and at times more.[23] This inclusion in benefits programs should have the effect of increasing the commitment of the salesperson to the organization.

Sales personnel are usually granted two benefits that are not common to other employees. The first of these is an automobile. For the salesperson traveling to the customer's site this is an important benefit. It is also one that the IRS is looking at more closely these days. The salesperson must keep records as to exactly what use is being made of the car. The second benefit is an expense account. Ordinarily, the only other group to have this benefit is the executive group. This benefit is necessary as a part of the boundary-spanning aspect of the sales job. But this is one of those situations where the organization perceives it is granting a reward and the salesperson sees it as a part of the job that breaks even with no advantage to him or her. Expense accounts also have the potential for abuse and are also being watched more closely by the IRS.

PROGRAMS FOR PROFESSIONAL EMPLOYEES

The compensation of professionals represents a considerably different problem than that of sales personnel. As with sales personnel the employment exchange in the case of professionals is more tenuous than it is with other employee groups, but for somewhat different reasons. The professional is tied to the job

[22]T. R. Wotruba and D. J. Schoel, "Evaluation of Salesforce Contest Performance," *Journal of Personal Selling and Sales Management,* May 1983, pp. 1–10; and D. Hampton, "Contests Have Side Effects, Too," *California Management Review,* Summer 1970, pp. 86–94.

[23]Barry and Henry, *Effective Sales Incentive Compensation.*

first and the organization second. This means a heavier role for the intrinsic rewards of the job as opposed to the extrinsic rewards that are the heart of the traditional compensation program. Thus, compensation, as defined in this text, has a more limited role in the membership and performance decisions of professionals. This does not mean that monetary compensation is unimportant or that special programs cannot achieve a better match of the professional with the organization. With the increasing numbers of professionals in organizations, developing compensation programs that meet their needs takes on increased importance. This section discusses some of the important aspects of professional work, professionals themselves, the adaptation to professionals of standard compensation plans, and special compensation plans.

The Professional's Job

A professional job is one that "involves the application of learned knowledge to the solution of enterprise problems and the achievement of enterprise goals."[24] This learned knowledge is ordinarily acquired through a college education or some other extended period of formal study. Professional work is mental, requiring the person to apply specialized knowledge to decision making. It is difficult to manage professional work, since management often does not have the same knowledge and is therefore dependent on the judgment of the professional. The training of the professional develops a sense of independence that does not jibe well with traditional management techniques.

True professional jobs are nonsupervisory. They include such areas as engineers, scientists, attorneys, economists, physicians, psychologists, and editors. Sibson suggests that these professions can be classified into three groups.[25] The first comprises professions that require advanced knowledge in a specific academic field, such as engineers. The second group consists of professions that require original and creative work, such as artists and designers. The third group requires a knowledge of business disciplines, such as finance, and includes mainly staff groups. Of these three groups, the first has the characteristics and numbers that call for special compensation programs.

Professional work is often hard to describe in the way that most organizational jobs are described. Different levels of professionals are not doing different tasks but are applying more expertise to the same kinds of problems. In addition, the exact project, set of activities, and organization goal pursued changes often, so typical descriptions get out of date rapidly.

In order to overcome these problems, organizations have developed generalized job descriptions for engineers and scientists. One type is called *functional* job descriptions. The tasks described are typical of persons at that level but may not be the exact job of a certain person at a certain time. A second type, *generic* job descriptions, is similar in that it describes in broad terms the work involved in a series of levels of work. Sometimes the specific task is made an attachment to these descriptions. A third type is the *work-sample* description. It describes the past assignments of the person, highlighting the ones that demonstrate the highest level of work he or she is capable of performing.[26]

[24]Sibson, *Compensation*, p. 189.
[25]Ibid., p. 190.
[26]Ibid., p. 193.

The Professional Worker

From the discussion thus far it can be seen that professionals are educated and independent and have a close association with their job and profession. In some ways the ideas of being a professional and working in an organization are antithetical. The professional is an independent agent and the organization is a client. This is an extreme and traditional notion of the professional, but the vestiges of it remain with the *organizational professional*. The feeling of independence from organizational constraints still creates a tension between the organization and the professional. Certainly professionals perceive that their most important input to the employment exchange is the knowledge and skill they bring to the job.

Organizational commitment, or the membership decision, is lower in professionals than in other employee groups. Gouldner classified employees into cosmopolitans and locals.[27] Cosmopolitans look to their work and outside to their profession for rewards. Locals associate their goals with those of the organization and are responsive to those rewards the organization has to offer. Although professionals are not wholly cosmopolitan, they are more so than other employee groups.[28] Such people know more about market conditions, and because of their lower organizational commitment the organization needs to have a compensation program that is very responsive to market conditions.

In some professional areas, particularly the sciences, the knowledge of the new college graduate is worth a lot to the organization since the technical field is changing rapidly. It becomes hard for older professionals to keep up in the field as they gain experience. This is a situation almost opposite that of other employee groups, and the career pay curves of professionals reflect this difference. Scientists and engineers are hired at higher-than-average wages. They then progress fast in the first few years, because progression takes place within the technical field. At midlevel in their career their pay curve begins to flatten out considerably. This is the result of obsolescence combined with the organizational dynamic of going as far as one can within the professional area. Those who break out of the flat curve move into management.[29]

Adapting the Compensation Program to the Professional

All three of the major compensation decisions require some rethinking and adaptation to accommodate professional employees within the regular compensation program. Each of these will be considered in turn.

WAGE LEVEL DECISION.   In most organizations that use large numbers of professionals, particularly scientists and engineers, these employees are central to the successful functioning of the organization. Therefore it is likely that the organization will choose a strategy of leading or, at a minimum, meeting

[27]A. W. Gouldner, "Cosmopolitans and Locals: Toward an Analysis of Latent Social Roles: I" *Administrative Science Quarterly,* December 1957, pp. 281–306.

[28]R. Ritti, *The Engineer in the Industrial Corporation* (New York: Columbia University Press, 1971).

[29]D. W. Pelz and F. Andrews, *Scientists in Organizations* (Ann Arbor: Institute of Social Research, University of Michigan, 1976).

the market in paying this group of employees. This decision may be different for other employee groups in the organization whose jobs do not represent the same importance. In addition, the labor market for professionals is more clearly defined. Knowledge of the market can be gained from college graduates' salaries, since the major entrance into the market is the campus.

Information about wages in professional areas is widely disseminated in professional literature. In fact this is a major problem for the compensation administrator. Much of the information published about wage rates in professional literature does not meet the collection and analysis standards discussed in chapter 6, so the accuracy of the data is suspect. But the fact is that the professional feels just as inequitably paid after examining that information as if it had been accurate.

Salary surveys for professionals are difficult to construct and use. On one hand, obtaining information about wage rates for a category of professionals, such as engineers or accountants, may be easy in general but it is not enlightening. As discussed, professionals may appear to be doing the same thing but, depending upon their experience level, be paid very differently. Also, a close examination of professionals' jobs shows that they are doing considerably different things requiring different types of experience. All this makes it difficult to determine comparability for the wage survey. An answer to this is to collect data in terms of the skill and experience level of the professional, as a maturity-curve approach does. This alternative is considered in more detail shortly.

Finally, labor markets for some professional groups have been very volatile. Changes occur more rapidly there than in most labor markets. Combine this with the lower level of organizational commitment and there can be a high turnover of professionals spearheaded by a group who are very mobile and move often to take advantages of changes in the labor market faster than organizations can adjust to these changes.

THE WAGE STRUCTURE DECISION.   Evaluation of professional jobs is difficult. Particularly in scientific and artistic areas it takes long exposure of the compensation specialist to the language of the field before accurate judgments can be made. The use of a body of knowledge is the primary task of the professional. This is not always a factor in job evaluation, and it is not always weighted as heavily as it ought to be to accurately evaluate the professional's job. There is a great deal of freedom as to how work is done by the professional. But this factor can be overweighted, since the control on the professional is more internal than external. All this leads to difficulty in determining the proper level of the professional's job within the job hierarchy. Higher-level professionals do not do different things but apply more experienced judgment to the decisions they are asked to make.

The career pattern just discussed affects the nature of the wage structure. Professionals, most of them college graduates, enter the organization at an advanced wage rate. Typically organizations have a series of levels, five to seven, within which the professional may move without leaving professional work. These levels overlap the lower and middle managerial levels of the organization, peaking at around 30 percent of the CEO's salary.[30] So the regular

---

[30]J. W. Crim, *Compensating Non-Supervisory Professional Employees* (Ann Arbor, Mich., UMI Research Press, 1978).

wage structure can usually accommodate the professional career pattern but may have some aspects of inequity for other employee groups, who do not have this high-level *escalator* of pay ranges.

Many organizations recognize this limited career-growth pattern, which flattens out the professional's pay curve at an early age, and attempt to create a longer career path through the use of a *dual-career ladder*.[31] In this system the professional may continue to do technical work while moving into pay grades that are parallel to managerial levels, as illustrated in figure 17–1. But dual-career ladders have come under attack on a number of grounds. Professionals may be too stunted in growth to be able to move beyond technical expertise,[32] it is not realistic to separate technical and professional decision making at higher levels,[33] and execution is often poor, because qualifications and performance criteria are not made explicit.[34]

A major problem with using the regular organizational wage structure for professionals is the dynamic character of the labor market for professionals. When market rates change faster for professionals than for other employee groups, the rate ranges become obsolete in determining professional wage rates. The response to this is *grade creep*—the placement of the professional in a higher grade level than deserved at the present time in order to meet the market rate.

THE PAY SYSTEM DECISION.   Unlike the other special groups discussed in this part of the book, professional groups are not commonly placed under incentive plans, nor do such plans seem appropriate for them. Both within-grade movement and promotion are important ways of rewarding the professional. The criteria used for both of these decisions are mixed, since performance is often hard to judge for this group of employees. Time and experience are major considerations. It is assumed that performance improves with experience in professionals, at least in the early years, and that they can undertake

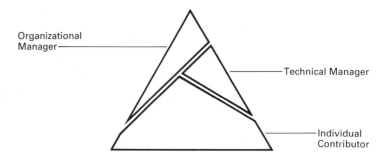

Figure 17–1   A dual career ladder
Source: E. S. Brown and W. H. Hoffman, "Multiple Career Paths: An Organizational Concept," in *Human Resource Planning*, vol 5(4):1982, p. 213. Reprinted by permission.

[31]H. G. Kaufman, *Obsolescence and Professional Career Development* (New York: American Management Assn., 1974).

[32]G. Dalton, P. Thompson, and R. Price, "The Four Stages of a Professional Career," *Organizational Dynamics*, 5:1977, pp. 19–42.

[33]Ritti, *Engineer*.

[34]L. Roth, *A Critical Examination of Dual Ladders* (New York: Career Center of Columbia University, 1982).

higher-level jobs as they gain experience. Promotion and movement within grade appears, then, almost automatic for at least a few levels. Later, obsolescence leads to the problem of professionals occupying levels above their usefulness to the organization.[35]

Movement within grade is also affected by the fast-changing conditions of professional labor markets. Since professionals are more cognizant of labor market conditions and are likely to move when better offers are advanced, making changes in salary to counteract these offers is a typical procedure. Thus, movement within grade often looks more like a bargaining situation than a reward situation.

To the degree that contribution is high in the new professional and levels off with time, there is a lag between performance and reward. It is impossible to reward the new professional to the full extent of his or her contribution. This would entail wage levels that would be considered inequitable by long-term employees. Further, there would be no room for the professional for growth within the wage structure. So the increases are spread out and the person appears to be receiving automatic increases when in fact the wages are catching up with the contributions already given. In this regard the organizational professional is like the professional athlete.[36]

Maturity Curves

The employment-exchange model suggests that there are three major categories of contributions—the job, performance, and personal characteristics. The model of compensation programs developed in this book indicates that organizations start with the job in setting wage level and structure and include performance and perhaps personal characteristics to some degree in individual pay determination. This model does not fit the professional well if what the organization is paying for is the use of the professional's knowledge and skill, and this is the contribution that the professional perceives as the most important.

An alternative system for compensating employees was explored at the end of chapter 11—that of payment for skills and knowledge. This type of system seems particularly appropriate for rewarding professionals, since their job emphasizes the personal contribution of skill and experience and downplays the impact of the job on pay. For professional employees this type of system is called a *maturity curve*. A maturity curve is a deceptively simple device. As indicated in chapter 6, it is a set of curves that record the progression of professional salaries in terms of years of experience, usually defined as years since college or last degree. Figure 17–2 (p. 368) illustrates a maturity curve.

The data for the curve is derived from a salary survey usually conducted by professional societies. Salary figures for the professional group are collected by years since college. For any year this will be a range of salaries. This range is illustrated in figure 17–2 by the vertical distribution at year 10. The curve represents a particular proportion of the distribution for each year. For instance, the middle curve in figure 17–2 is ordinarily either the mean or

---

[35]G. Dalton and P. Thompson, "Accelerating: the Obsolescence of the Older Engineer," *Harvard Business Review*, September-October 1971, pp. 57–67.

[36]Pelz and Andrews, *Scientists in Organizations*.

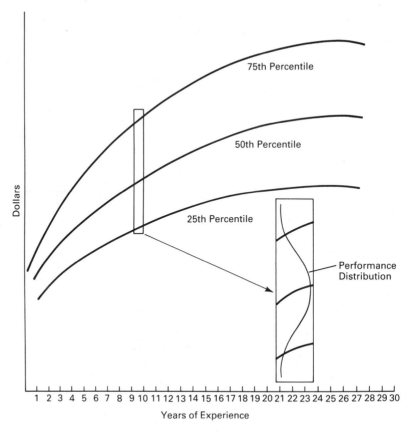

Figure 17–2 A maturity curve

median for each year's distribution. The other curves can represent percentiles, proportions, or standard deviations. Note that the shape of these curves reflects the nature of career pay for professionals, starting high, moving rapidly in early years, and flattening out in later years as obsolescence takes over.

So instead of a pay range based upon the market value of the job, a maturity curve suggests a pay range based on the market value of the professional's experience level. This pay range can then be used in conjunction with a pay-for-performance system (chapter 13). The professional's position in the pay range should then match his or her position in the performance ratings. A professional who is at the 67th percentile in performance should then be paid at the 67th percentile of the range of wages for his or her years of experience on the maturity curve. Many large organizations that employ large groups of professionals in particular categories, such as engineers or programmers, find it useful to use a ranking system of performance appraisal to coordinate the performance ratings with the maturity curve. Given the difficulties of determining performance previously discussed, the ranking technique may be useful in this circumstance.

The maturity-curve technique leaves the job out of the direct compensation determination process. The assumption is that management will assign the professional to the best and highest use of which he or she is capable. When this in fact occurs the labor costs of the organization are kept to a minimum, but when this is not the case labor costs are higher, since the professional is not being employed at the level of work for which he or she is being paid.

Benefits for Professionals

Interest in benefits by professionals is similar to that of managers. They are well paid, so they receive maximum amounts of those benefits that are tied to salary level. In most cases, since benefit desires are tied to personal circumstance and not to the job, professionals exhibit a cross section of interest in types of benefits. The one area in which professionals show the most interest as a group is benefits tied to *education*. This benefit is tied both to their own desires to advance in their profession and to the problem of obsolescence that confronts them if they do not continue their education.

This desire for continuing education can take a number of forms. The first is *reimbursement for tuition*. Many organizations pay for the tuition and book costs of having the employee pursue an advanced degree. This may also entail adjusting work schedules to enable the employee to attend class. A second area of benefit in the professional's education is *attendance at professional conferences*. This is more of an incentive than a benefit for some professionals, such as those in research. Regardless, attending conferences is seen as a benefit by many professionals because it allows them to interact with others in the same job and find out what is new in the field. The third possible benefit in education is the application of the *sabbatical* to some professionals, and perhaps managers. The purpose of the sabbatical is to free the person from organizational pressures for a period of time and allow him or her to examine a particular problem in depth.

SUMMARY

Organizations identify certain groups in order to establish special compensation programs for them. They do this for a number of reasons including organizational tradition, employee expectations, importance and centrality of the job, and the law. This chapter covers two such groups: salespeople and professional employees. The next chapter will continue by dealing with managerial employees and international employees.

Salespeople are paid primarily on an incentive basis. There are a number of reasons for this, not the least of which is organizational tradition. Sales jobs tend to be central to the organization, are carried out away from direct supervision, have measurable outcomes, require the person to be a boundary-spanner, and attract people who find incentive programs attractive. Sales compensation plans may be straight salary, straight commission, or a combination of these two. The latter is the most common. Since sales incentive plans are ordinarily individual plans there is an assumption that it is the sales person's efforts that makes the difference. This assumption is called into question more often as selling becomes more of a team effort. Commission plans have the same advantages and disadvantages as individual incentive plans. Sales compensation plans also may include competitive contests and special benefits, such as a car.

Professionals are another important group of organizational employees who have different needs. Professional jobs tend to be hard to define and evaluate with other organizational jobs. Professional workers are more independent and have strong allegiance to their profession and less to the organization. Thus, professional employee compensation requires adaptation of the organization's program. The labor market for professional groups has been volatile in recent years, leading to a high wage level strategy. The wage structure is influenced by the fact that education and training are more important than job assignments for these employees, leading to the development of *maturity curves* as a way of determining pay rates. *Dual career ladders* are another feature of professional groups attempting to keep the professional using his or her skill instead of having to move into management in order to move up. Last, professionals have clear desires for somewhat different benefits in educational advancement and attending conferences.

18

Managerial and International Employees' Compensation

This chapter covers the special compensation programs of two of the more important groups in organizations, employees in foreign countries and managers. Managerial employees represent the most common group to be identified as requiring special compensation programs. This group easily meets the requirements discussed in the last chapter for special consideration in regards to compensation. Managers are a small part of the total number of employees in any organization but represent a disproportionately high percentage of total wage costs. They are a group of vital importance to the operation of the organization, and it is important to attempt to individualize compensation for each manager, particularly each executive. It is possible to develop measures of individual performance such that incentives are appropriate and desirable, since it is of utmost importance that managers associate themselves with organizational success.

Compensation of employees assigned to foreign operations—*expatriates*—is becoming a major concern in many American organizations with the continuing trend toward internationalization of industry and the advent of the multinational organization. Moving employees between countries leads to a number of questions of equity in pay for both the employees who are moved and the employees in the host country. Although this is an extremely complex compensation problem, this chapter will attempt to outline the major concerns and practices.

MANAGERIAL COMPENSATION

Managers are probably the most important group for which special compensation programs are established. The importance of the management job demands that special consideration be given to this group. Managerial compensation plans are also a very sensitive subject. It is, after all, the managers who make the compensation decisions in organizations, so any special plans need to be clearly delineated so there is no appearance of taking advantage of the situation. The public watches closely what is being done in managerial compensation, particularly at the executive level, and in publicly held companies this information must be made public.

This section examines the managerial job, the characteristics of managers, and the plans that organizations develop to compensate the job and the person.

The Managerial Job

Presthus identified one of the basic patterns by which people accommodate themselves to working in organizations to be that of the upward-mobile. This person accommodates by associating his or her goals with those of the organization.[1] The major group of people in organizations who meet this description are its managers. This connection that these people make between themselves and the organization needs to be enhanced and encouraged through the compensation plan. This section will discuss the managerial role, the characteristics of managerial work, and the differences in levels of managerial work.

THE MANAGERIAL ROLE. In a way all managers are like what has been said of the foremen, they are the people *in the middle*.[2] This emphasizes the fact that managers have to please a number of constituencies in order to get their work done. Broadly speaking, managers have an *internal* role and an *external* role.[3] The internal role has to do with directing an organizational unit. In interpersonal terms, Katz sees this as a *leadership* function.[4] The external role requires the manager to deal with people outside the organizational unit to accomplish the unit's work. This role is not as clearly defined as the internal role but involves developing relationships, gathering information, and deciding where the organization is going and how to get there. In this, the manager is often like the salesperson—on the margin of the organization. To the extent that this is the case, incentive plans would seem appropriate.

Mintzberg has elaborated further upon the roles of a manager.[5] He has developed ten roles, divided into three categories—interpersonal roles, infor-

[1]R. Presthus, *The Organizational Society* (New York: Knopf, 1962).

[2]F. J. Roethlisberger, "The Foreman: Master and Victim of Double Talk," *Harvard Business Review*, Spring 1945, pp. 285–94.

[3]T. J. Atchison and W. W. Hill, *Management Today: Managing Work in Organizations* (New York: Harcourt Brace Jovanovich, Inc., 1978).

[4]R. L. Katz, "The Skills of the Effective Administrator," *Harvard Business Review*, September-October 1974, pp. 90–102.

[5]H. Mintzberg, *The Nature of Managerial Work* (New York, Harper & Row, Pub. Inc., 1973).

mational roles, and decisional roles. Each of these categories has roles that can be considered internally and externally oriented, as illustrated in figure 18–1. Externally, the manager represents the organization to the world, deals with the world, and decides the direction the organization needs to take. Internally, the manager directs organizational activity and allocates resources to accomplish goals. All this is central to the organization's success. Not all managerial jobs contain all ten roles equally, nor do all managers perform all roles equally. This leads to a great deal of variety in the definition of the managerial job, with the manager having a good deal of influence over their definition.

A somewhat different view of the managerial job was raised in chapter 9, in our discussion of the Management Position Description Questionnaire (MPDQ). The variables that this questionnaire taps are similar to those just discussed, despite the different approaches taken by Mintzberg and MPDQ. The variables in the MPDQ tend to be more specific, such as internal business control, but they can generally be placed within the categories developed by Mintzberg. Both observational techniques and questionnaires may be useful in describing managerial jobs.

CHARACTERISTICS OF MANAGERIAL WORK. Mintzberg goes on to point out that managerial activity has three basic characteristics: *brevity, variety,* and *fragmentation.* Managers deal with a great many things each day—sometimes a hundred or more—and these things cover a wide variety of topics. Managers are active people. They perform a large quantity of work and find it hard to leave it behind when they leave the office. In this they are like professionals. Further, managers are not able to concentrate their energies on a single project until it is completed; instead they jump from one thing to another all day long, leading to the feeling of fragmentation. This makes the job very ambiguous to the manager.

It is no wonder that Sayles finds that managers have a hard time describing what they do to others in meaningful terms and that what comes out sounds like a lot of little unconnected items.[6] Thus, describing the managerial

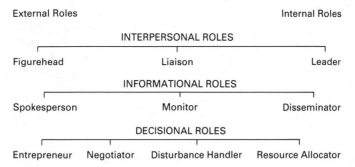

Figure 18–1 The internal and external roles of the manager
Source: T. J. Atchison and W. W. Hill, *Management Today,* New York: Harcourt Brace Jovanovich, Inc., 1978, p. 7.

[6]L. Sayles, *Leadership: What Effective Managers Do and How They Do It* (New York: McGraw-Hill, 1980).

job can be very difficult, partly because the manager has trouble defining what he or she does and partly because it is hard to make sense of what is done. Developing useful job descriptions is difficult in this circumstance. Since most compensation programs need job descriptions for evaluation purposes, this problem may change the way managerial compensation is handled.

These characteristics of the managerial job are tied to the activities of managers just discussed. Since managerial jobs differ in the degree to which certain activities take place in the job, the characteristics also vary. For instance, managerial jobs such as sales or marketing positions are more subject to brevity and fragmentation than some other managerial jobs.[7]

LEVELS OF MANAGERIAL WORK.   Organizations are hierarchical, which is what creates the managerial role in the first place. Large organizations have a number of managerial levels. In fact, the organization chart is usually a chart of the managerial jobs in the organization. Compensation plans for the managers in an organization generally follow this organizational hierarchy closely. The hierarchy contains three levels of managers: top management (executives), middle management, and lower management (supervisors).

Top Management.   Executives are those at the top of the organizational hierarchy, usually the top 1 percent of the organization's work force.[8] Their view is looking out of the organization to the environment. They are charged with developing the goals and strategies required to keep the organization effective. The owners, through the board of directors, see these people as the trustees of their resources. Thus compensation for this group is closely associated with the success of the organization as a whole.

Ordinarily, top management is responsible for the total operations of the organization (the CEO and executive VPs), a major segment of the organization (an operating division with a set of products), or a major organizational function (such as finance). The results of these units are measurable, and it is usually assumed that these managers had a significant impact on these results and therefore should be rewarded on the basis of the results.

Lower Management.   At the other end of the hierarchy are the supervisors. They are first-line managers. That is, they direct the work of nonmanagerial employees. This job is more internally oriented, in two ways. First, the supervisor is more intimately concerned with a small group of workers and the work of that unit. Second, although the supervisor's external contacts are outside the organizational unit, they are still within the organization itself. The pressures of the first-line supervisor are immediate and influence today's results, in considerable contrast with the top manager, who is concerned mostly with problems extending years into the future. Because supervisors are so close to their workers, the job comparison for first-line supervisors is often the worker in the organizational unit. Thus the supervisor's wages are some percentage over those of the workers. In fact a series of studies show that employ-

[7]W. Whitely, "Managerial Work Behavior: An Integration of Results from Two Major Approaches," *Academy of Management Journal*, June 1985, pp. 344–62.

[8]A. Patton, *Men, Money, and Motivation* (New York: McGraw-Hill, 1961).

ees have a definite idea about the "appropriate" distance between organizational levels. Mahoney's review of these concepts and studies indicates that about a 33 percent distance between organizational levels feels right to people.[9] A study by one of the authors shows a lower differential at the supervisory level, closer to 20 percent.[10]

Middle Management.   As the name implies, this consists of the organizational levels between the two so far discussed. These managers manage other managers and act as an information channel between top management and supervisors. Their perspective is ordinarily intermediate. They are usually responsible for a specific function in the organization and spend much of their time coordinating this function with other groups in the organization. A great number of the contacts of this group are lateral, so that getting work done is through means other than the use of authority.[11] This creates considerable ambiguity for the middle manager, a feeling that he or she is responsible but does not have the necessary control. These contacts make peer comparisons important for this group. Compensation for this group is often related to the function that is being managed, and since there are large enough numbers of managers, managerial wage surveys make sense.

Managers

It is difficult to identify any particular personality pattern as being common to managers. However, there are a number of aspects of managers relevant to the development of a compensation program for them that need to be explored. These are their commitment, decision orientation, and power needs.

COMMITMENT.   From the discussion thus far it should be clear that commitment is one thing managers have and organizations need. Managers associate themselves with the organization and spend a great deal of time at their work, usually up to 60 hours a week. But even if they are not formally working, managers find it is hard to turn off the job. They think about their job even when they are supposed to be at leisure. In terms of the membership model, these people have high inputs and will therefore expect high outcomes from the organization.

DECISION ORIENTATION.   Managers are action-oriented. Mintzberg found that managers had a preference for live action and the use of verbal media.[12] This often gives them the appearance of being intuitive rather than analytical in their decision making.[13] This is in contrast with the reasons why the

[9]T. A. Mahoney, "Organizational Hierarchy and Position Worth," in *Compensation and Reward Perspectives,* ed. T. A. Mahoney (Homewood, Ill.: Richard D. Irwin, 1979), pp. 194–200.

[10]T. J. Atchison, F. W. Koetter, and P. Wright, "Compensation and Job Input Factors in the Determination of an Appropriate Distance between Adjacent Job Levels" (paper presented at the annual meeting of the Academy of Management, Western Division, Reno, 1986).

[11]L. Sayles, *Managerial Behavior: Administration in Complex Organizations* (New York: McGraw-Hill, 1964).

[12]Mintzberg, *The Nature of Managerial Work.*

[13]J. P. Kotter, *The General Managers* (New York: Free Press, 1982).

professional, who is analytical, is valuable to the organization. The manager ensures that things keep moving and get done. Decisions are the heart of the manager's job.[14] In a way this is what the manager is paid for. Certainly the time span of descretion, by which Jaques measures job level, implies that decisions are central to defining managerial jobs.[15] Likewise, the Hay system of job evaluation, the one most commonly used to evaluate managerial jobs, focuses upon three aspects of decisions: know-how, problem solving, and accountability.[16] So an orientation to decision making is probably useful in trying to evaluate managerial jobs and performance. Furthermore, both Kotter and Mintzberg find that being knowledgeable about the business and organization and having a wide set of contacts in order to collect information are important aspects of the manager's job.[17]

Managerial decision making is not like technical decision making. Katz points out that as managers move up the organizational hierarchy they need to have higher levels of *conceptual skill*. This skill requires the manager to think in terms of general trends rather than specifics and to be able to see the forest for the trees.[18] This skill may be related to the idea of left-brain thinking.[19] The point is that managers as they move up in the organization need to be able to think and make decisions using a much broader framework and be able to deal with high levels of uncertainty. These skills may be in very short supply within the society, creating demand higher than supply.[20]

POWER NEEDS. McClelland found that, unlike sales personnel, managers do not have a high achievement drive. This is not to say that they do not focus on accomplishing things or are not ambitious; they do and are.[21] But they do not match the careful definition developed in the last chapter of achievement drive. What McClelland did find out about managers is that they have a high power need.[22] They enjoy controlling a situation and having a strong influence on the outcome of events. This desire for power can take two different forms, power *over* and power *to*. The former is a personal definition of power that taps the unsavory aspects of the idea of power. The power *to* is a more institutional expression of power that focuses on getting the job done in the organization within the rules of the organization. Compensation programs for managers need to encourage this type of power drive.

[14]H. A. Simon, *The Shape of Automation for Men and Management* (New York: Harper & Row Pub. Inc., 1965).

[15]E. Jaques, "Preliminary Sketch of a General Structure of Executive Strata," in *Glacier Project Papers*, ed. W. Brown and E. Jaques (London: Heinemann, 1965), pp. 114–29.

[16]Hay Associates, *The Guide-Chart Profile Method of Job Evaluation* (Philadelphia: Hay Associates, 1981).

[17]Kotter, *The General Managers;* and Mintzberg, *The Nature of Managerial Work.*

[18]Katz, "Effective Administrator."

[19]H. Mintzberg, D. Raisinghani, and A. Theoret, "The Structure of Unstructured Decision Processes," *Administrative Science Quarterly*, 21:1976, pp. 246–75.

[20]E. Jaques, *Levels of Abstraction in Logic and Human Action* (London: Heinemann, 1978).

[21]Kotter, *The General Managers.*

[22]D. McClelland and D. Burnham, "Good Guys Make Bum Bosses," *Psychology Today*, December 1975, pp. 42–43.

This power aspect of the manager indicates that managers have and need considerable interpersonal skill. Most studies show that this is true.[23] Katz sees that this interpersonal skill takes on two forms, supervisory and peer. Supervisory skill has to do with the leadership of the people in the manager's organizational unit. Peer skill has to do with the myriad contacts the manager must engage in outside the organizational unit in order to get the work done.[24]

Also connected to power is the idea of status. Managers spend a great deal of time on the job, are committed to the organization, and carry heavy responsibility. They must find it worth doing. Beyond the high wages there are a number of other extrinsic and intrinsic rewards available to managers. The management job is held in esteem within the organization, if not in society as a whole. But there is a hierarchy of managers in the organization, with those further up having more status than those lower down. The measure of status is most often reflected in the wages of the person. Thus, managerial compensation is a reflection not only of job worth but of the rank and status of the manager.

Managerial Base Pay

Most discussions of managerial pay divide the total amount of pay into two categories, base pay and incentive pay. This section examines the base-pay component of managerial pay and the next two, short- and long-term incentives. Base pay of managers can represent as much as two thirds of their pay or as little as one third. The percentage tends to vary with organization level. The higher the level, the lower the percentage of total pay represented by base pay. The base pay of managers is set using the model developed in this book. However, there are some special considerations for management pay, so each of the three core decisions is examined in turn.

THE WAGE LEVEL DECISION. The managerial group in the organization has a number of characteristics that affect the pay level decision in the direction of paying this group at or preferably above market. First, this group of jobs is very important to the organization. The people in these jobs are highly skilled and replacement can be difficult. These factors would call for a wage level decision that emphasizes being at or above market in order to be able to recruit and retain these employees. Tied to these factors is a second consideration, the sunk costs that the organization has in the manager. Ordinarily the manager is a person who has worked for the organization a number of years, and the odds are good the organization has spent considerable money in training this person as he or she has moved up the managerial ranks.

A third consideration that supports a high wage level decision is that this is a small group of employees. So even if wages are high for the group, their overall impact on total wage costs of the organization may be small. Fourth, managers are in contact with the outside world a great deal. This means that they are more likely to be aware of the market rates for their jobs than other employee groups and that other organizations would be more aware of managers and be inclined to make an employment offer to them. Any group

[23]Kotter, *The General Manager.*
[24]Katz, "Effective Administrator."

that is both important and visible, as is this group, will have to be paid competitively in order to hold down turnover. A final consideration that calls for an aggressive pay level decision is the relatively small supply of managers as compared with other employee groups. There is evidence that although a large number of students are going on to college and obtaining degrees, many do not desire managerial positions as much as professional ones.[25]

The criteria used to determine wage level also differ somewhat from those used in the regular compensation program. In particular, organization size has been shown to be a major criterion in determining top management pay.[26] Organizational performance in the form of profit levels, sales, market share, and other measures are also criteria that are often used and always talked about for use in deciding top-management pay. Although it is logical that these would be major criteria, studies show that the proportion of top-management pay explained by these factors is not as high as might be expected.[27]

Middle-management pay criteria are more likely to be influenced by internal organizational factors, particularly the organization chart and the salary of the top executive. The organization chart becomes a guide for determining the appropriate internal references—those at the same organizational level. The top executive's pay becomes a ceiling in the organization: all other managerial positions can be measured in terms of their percentage of that person's pay. This is a common way in which managerial pay is reported.[28] For instance, the Conference Board's biennial report on executive compensation reports the top five levels of executive pay as a percentage of the top executive's pay. This is illustrated in table 18–1.

Table 18–1   Pay of Top Five Executives in Selected Industries

	MANUFACTURING		RETAIL TRADE		UTILITIES	
Highest	$408,000		$310,000		$228,000	
Two	278,000	69%	221,000	75%	151,000	67%
Three	221,000	54	163,000	60	128,000	55
Four	190,000	47	137,000	50	112,000	50
Five	167,000	41	115,000	43	99,000	45

	BANKING		CONSTRUCTION	
Highest	$220,000		$198,000	
Two	150,000	68%	147,000	75%
Three	111,000	54	116,000	65
Four	96,000	46	99,000	56
Five	87,000	42	85,000	50

Source: *Top Executive Compensation*, 1985 ed., Report no. 854 (New York: Conference Board, 1984).

[25]J. B. Miner, *The Challenge of Managing* (Philadelphia: Saunders, 1975).
[26]W. Lewellen and B. Huntsman, "Managerial Pay and Corporate Performance," *American Economic Review*, 60:1970, pp. 710–20.
[27]H. Fox, *Top Executive Compensation* (New York, Conference Board, 1980).
[28]E. F. Finkin, "How to Figure Out Executive Compensation," *Personnel Journal*, July 1978, pp. 371–75.

Pay ranges for the lowest managerial levels tend to be set as a percentage above those of the employees being supervised.[29] This percentage increase seems to be fairly constant, averaging about 30 percent.[30] This differential is supposed to reflect the complexity of the managerial task. Organizations can use both the top-down and bottom-up approaches but they may find that there is a compression problem, or the opposite, a gap in the grade levels. This is because the starting points at the top and at the bottom are using different criteria, so that where the results of these calculations come together there can be either a gap or an overlap.

These various criteria used for managerial jobs should not be interpreted to mean that market rates for managerial jobs cannot be obtained. In fact, there are many managerial wage surveys. These can be both general managerial surveys and industry-specific surveys. Examples of the major general surveys are listed in exhibit 18–1. Most industries, through their associations, also conduct and distribute managerial wage surveys. The advantage of these industry surveys is that they provide information on jobs that reflects the way organizations in the industry organize. For instance, the banking surveys provide information on jobs such as loan officer and branch manager. Often these surveys will provide information on wages for the overall sample and use major breakdowns, such as geographical regions and size of organization. A problem with some of these data is the sample size. Since most times there is only one position for a particular job title per organization, if the sample is subdivided the number of positions included can become quite small and the data not as usable.

THE WAGE STRUCTURE DECISION.   The first consideration in the application of wage structure decisions to managerial employees is whether there should be a separate wage structure for managers or whether the top of the regular wage structure will be satisfactory. Many organizations have a separate wage structure for managerial employees. Some of these structures include more than just managers: they include other groups, particularly professionals. These wage structures often include all exempt employees. The main rationale for this separation of wage structures is that the pay-policy lines for exempt and nonexempt are so different that combining them leads to a false straight-

---

Exhibit 18–1   Managerial Wage Surveys*

Hay Associates: Point Survey
Management Compensation Services (Hewitt Associates): Project 777 Survey
Sibson and Co.: Management Compensation Survey
Towers, Perrin, Foster and Crosby: Management Regression Analysis
Wyatt Co.: Executive Compensation Service

Personnel Management-Compensation (Englewood Cliffs, N.J.: Prentice-Hall) contains addresses and further information about these and other specialized management surveys.

---

[29]H. A. Simon, "The Compensation of Executives," *Sociometry,* March 1957, pp. 32–35.
[30]T. A. Mahoney, "Organizational Hierarchy and Position Worth," *Academy of Management Journal,* December 1979, pp. 726–37.

line function, the relationship between market wages and the job evaluation system being curvilinear in this case.

As indicated, managerial jobs tend to be difficult to describe, and thus although job descriptions are used for managers they often are not taken as seriously in determining wages. Management job descriptions are typically written in terms of broad functions, areas of responsibility, scope and impact of assignments, degree of accountability, and the extent and nature of supervision and influence involved. This is in contrast with the focus on tasks and activities performed in a standard job description. Since there is only one job incumbent in most managerial jobs, each job is unique and the impact of the manager on the nature of the job can be great. Properly developed managerial job descriptions are useful for organizational and personnel planning as much as they are for compensation.

Organizations often have a different job evaluation plan for management. This is probably useful only in large organizations, given the cost of developing a separate system. But some organizations find that the factors that are relevant in evaluating a managerial job are significantly different from those that are relevant for other jobs. The different focus noted above in job descriptions illustrates the different factors that would be relevant. The Hay system with its focus on know-how, problem solving, and accountability is widely and successfully used for managerial jobs. In general, there is an emphasis in managerial job evaluation factors on mental activities—decision making. This is consistent with our discussion of the nature of managerial work.

The job evaluation methods used do not vary much from those used with other employee groups, but the program tends to be more tailor-made to the organizational situation. Schuster found that about half of the plans used in the high-technology industries are of a point-system variety. Another quarter of the plans are a *rank-to-market plan,* wherein the organization compares its jobs with one or more compensation surveys to determine if there is a good match. In this type of plan the structure is designed first and then jobs slotted into appropriate ranges depending upon their market value.[31]

The difficulty in using job evaluation in managerial positions leads some experts to question whether it is useful to evaluate managerial jobs at all. The basic argument is that the person and not the job is the important ingredient in the management situation. Managers should be paid as a function of their impact on the organization's success. This argument seems more appropriately directed at the proportion of the manager's total pay that is determined by the job and how much is provided through bonuses.

The wage structure for managerial jobs is characterized by wide ranges and broad grades. Ranges may be typically 50 to 60 percent wide, but 100 percent is also quite common.[32] The arguments for this are (1) that the evaluation of managerial jobs is not as precise as it is for lower-level jobs and thus a broader range allows for variation, and (2) that there is more possible variation in performance of managerial jobs, so the use of wider ranges allows the organization to recognize this greater variation. Grades and ranges are more likely

[31]J. Schuster, *Management Compensation in High Technology Companies* (Lexington, Mass.: Heath, Lexington Books, 1984).
[32]R. C. Smyth, *Financial Incentives for Management* (New York: McGraw-Hill, 1960).

to be seen as guidelines in managerial compensation rather than as strict rules. The midpoint is important since it reflects the labor-market value. Minimums are less likely to be used, since rarely would a person who is minimally qualified be placed in the job. Maximums are not held to because the performance or value of a particular manager supersedes and exceeds the structure.[33]

THE WAGE SYSTEM DECISION. Everything discussed so far has indicated that managers have more-than-average ability to affect their performance. Further, there are measures that can be used to determine this impact on the job. Therefore, pay for performance would seem to be highly appropriate for managerial positions. Most organizations indeed claim that they pay managers in terms of performance, both that of the individual and that of the organization. If there is a difference between pay-for-performance systems for managers and those for other groups it lies in defining performance in organizational and not personal terms. This difference increases as the job moves toward the top of the organization. This is true for both basic wage increases and bonuses. This emphasis on organizational measures of success is functional since managers feel that organizational success is their success. But as in most pay-for-performance systems, the correct performance standards must be the focus of the system. Schuster found that those managerial pay systems that were ineffective were those that did not focus on critical organizational outcomes.[34]

Where an individual definition of performance in managerial jobs is developed it is most often done through *management by objectives* (MBO). The measurable standards that are developed are done jointly by the manager and his or her boss. At the end of the time period, performance is evaluated by both parties in a joint meeting in terms of how well the objectives were met. This system can work well where each party respects the other and does not play power games with the setting and evaluation of objectives. There are two main problems in MBO from the standpoint of tying it into wage increases. The first is that there is not much comparability between individuals, so that judgments about how much one person should receive versus another are not clear. The second is that the world may be too dynamic to set objectives and have them mean anything in a month, much less six months. Thus, MBO may be restrictive and hold managers to objectives that are out of date.

Two concerns with pay for performance for managers are (1) Is pay contingent on performance? and (2) Does it make any difference in performance when pay and performance are connected? Lawler found almost no relation between pay and performance measures on a sample of 600 middle- and lower-level managers. However, those managers that were most highly motivated did exhibit two crucial attitudes. First, they felt that pay was important to them (the first condition in the performance-motivation model). Second, they did feel that good performance would lead to higher pay. So the perception is more important than the fact. Lawler went on to explain why it is hard for managers to always see the performance–reward connection. First, many of the rewards are deferred, so that the time frame is too long. Second, the goals are

[33]R. E. Sibson, *Compensation*, rev. ed. (New York: American Management Assn., 1981).
[34]Schuster, *Management Compensation*.

not always clearly expressed, so the manager does not know what he or she or the organization needs to achieve. Third, the secrecy that surrounds pay increases reduces the knowledge that the individual manager has as to how he or she has done comparatively.[35]

The answer to the second concern may not be any more positive. In one of the few studies that examined an organization throughout a period of time in which a merit-pay system was installed, it was found that the system had no effect at all on organizational performance.[36] Although there may be a number of explanations of these results, the fact is that we cannot take it for granted that paying for performance is worth doing.

Short-Term Incentives

Base pay may represent almost all of total pay for lower-level managers to as little as a third of top managers' total pay. The difference is made up in incentive bonuses, associated with both short-term and long-term performance. This section discusses short-term managerial bonuses.

The use of bonuses varies greatly with industry, but more than 50 percent of organizations have some sort of managerial bonus plan.[37] Those organizations with bonus plans tend to pay somewhat less in base pay than those without them. Bonus plans can be divided into immediate-cash plans and deferred plans. Since short-term plans are usually immediate-cash plans, they are covered here and the deferred plans under the long-term plans are discussed in the next section.

BONUS STANDARDS.   The manager who receives a bonus receives it because some standard was met during the past time period, typically a year. As indicated, in pay for performance this standard may be either organizational or job-related. The most common form of managerial bonus is based upon organizational profits. But there are a number of other possible organizational measures, such as sales, productivity, or cost savings of one sort or another (see chapter 14). Individual job-related standards may relate to job outcomes or to the performance of particular activities beyond minimum expectations.

Bonus standards may be either single or multiple. Profit sharing is a single standard. Organizations may choose to focus managers on a number of variables that they feel are important measures of success. These may include combining organizational and job measures. Each variable must be weighted when multiple criteria are used. The problems with multiple plans are that they are more complex and therefore not as understandable and the manager may have a hard time knowing what he or she will receive, since the factors may overlap or cancel each other out. Although profits may be the most popular organizational measure there are a number of other ones; exhibit 18–2 defines four of the more popular.

[35]E. E. Lawler, *Pay and Organizational Development* (Reading, Mass.: Addison-Wesley, 1981).

[36]J. L. Pearce, L. B. Stevenson, and J. L. Perry, "Managerial Compensation Based on Organizational Performance: A Time Series Analysis of the Effects of Merit Pay," *Academy of Management Journal,* June 1985, pp. 261–78

[37]Fox, *Top Executive Compensation.*

Exhibit 18–2 Four Common Financial-Performance Criteria

1. *Earnings per Share:* the organization's net income divided by the average number of shares of common stock outstanding.
2. *Return on Equity:* the organization's net income divided by the average of shareholders' equity (common and preferred stock plus retained earnings).
3. *Return on Capital:* the organization's net income divided by its average capital (shareholders' equity plus outstanding loans).
4. *Return on Assets:* the net income of the organization divided by the net assets of the organization.

BONUS FORMULA.   Most managerial short-term bonuses are established on the basis of a formula that operates at given levels of profit or other measures, such as those described in exhibit 18–2. It is possible, however, to establish a totally discretionary plan in which the board of directors determine each year whether a bonus will be given for the past year's performance, and if so how much. The arbitrary nature of this procedure and the lack of knowledge by the manager of the effect of his or her actions ahead of time makes the incentive value of a discretionary plan low.

Ordinarily, a managerial bonus is based upon the base pay of the manager. When profit sharing is used, a percentage of total profits is placed in a fund and each manager shares in the fund in the proportion of total managerial base pay represented by his or her base pay. When other measures are used, such as those illustrated in exhibit 18–2, goals are established for each of the appropriate measures. If the organization achieves or exceeds the goal, the managers would receive a percentage of their base pay. For instance, assume that the organization wished to maintain a minimum return on assets of 10 percent. The managers may receive 20 percent of base pay if the organization achieves a 10 percent return on assets and an additional 5 percent of base pay for each 5 percent increase in return on assets over 10 percent. These calculations could be made for one measure or for a number of measures. Further, the measures could be independent, or any bonus at all could depend upon maintaining a minimum level of performance on all measures. Often limits are placed on the percentage above base pay that can be earned, such as 50 percent.

ELIGIBILITY.   Bonus plans are usually based on a formula designed to reflect the participant's contribution to profits or other organizational measures of success. The motivational value of the plan depends in large part on whether the manager's actions do have an impact on these measures. Members of top management seem to meet these requirements, and thus such incentive plans would seem ideal for this group. For middle management the connection is not as clear, but the possibility of earning a substantial amount over base pay may keep these managers' attention on and increase their interest in the organization's goals. For lower-level management the case for incentives tied to organizational performance is hard to make. The amounts these managers typically receive are small and the connection of their actions to the performance standard nonexistent. Incentive plans for lower-level managers should be based more upon establishing job-related measures of performance that the organization believes will also relate to organizational success.

Long-Term Incentives

Long-term managerial incentives are usually restricted to top management, the 1 percent at the top of the organization. In contrast to short-term incentives, which are ordinarily paid in cash, long-term incentives are usually deferred. The purpose of long-term incentives is to tie the executive into the long-term success of the organization. In today's competitive business climate, when American business is being criticized for its focus on short-term profits, these longer-term incentives take on added importance. These incentives usually involve the granting of rights to the executive to become a stockholder of the organization at a reasonable cost today so that if the organization does well in the future the stock will be of significant value.

This form of incentive has become more popular in recent years because of the concern with the performance of American business and because of the tax advantages that can be achieved through this form of incentive.[38] One of the problems has been that the tax laws have changed over time, and plans that are attractive and useful today may no longer qualify under tomorrow's tax laws. There are a number of ways in which these programs operate, which are covered in this section, but there is no guarantee that they will stay useful with future changes in the tax laws.

STOCK-OPTION PLANS. Basically under a stock-option plan the manager is offered stock at a set price. He or she may purchase that stock at any time within a period specified by the plan. If the value of the stock rises, the manager has a considerable value in the right without having had to put out any money. Exercising the option does take money, however, and this is often a problem for the manager. Taxation is another problem. The income derived is straight income under the new tax law of 1986. Finally, the executive may not always be able to take advantage of increases in the price of the stock since he or she may not use insider information when selling the stock.

Under the Economic Recovery Act of 1981 *incentive stock options* (ISOs) became popular. Earlier versions of stock options became obsolete when they were no longer considered qualified under tax laws. Under an ISO the manager is given a right to purchase common stock for a specified period and at a specified price. The length of time is a maximum of ten years from shareholder approval, and the price must not be less than fair market value on the date of award. Limitations on the plan are that grants are limited to $100,000 of stock and the manager must exercise the grant within ten years. Under the Tax Equity and Fiscal Responsibility Act of 1982 (TEFRA) the gain from exercising these options is taxable at from 20 to 40 percent. With the Tax Reform Act of 1986, ISOs may not be as popular as they have been in previous years. The $100,000 limit has been modified so that an unlimited number of options may be granted in any one year, but these may only be exercised up to an initial value of $100,000 per year. Despite this change, other types of bonus programs are likely to become more popular.

[38]M. Bentson and J. Schuster, "Executive Compensation and Employee Benefits," in *Human Resources Management in the 1980's,* ed. S. Carroll and R. Schuler (Washington, D.C.: Bureau of National Affairs, 1983), pp. 6.1–6.33.

STOCK APPRECIATION RIGHTS (SARS).   These types of plans work like stock options, but the manager does not have to buy the stock. As with a stock option, the manager is granted an option at a stated price. The manager then may call in that option at any time during an established period. But rather than having to purchase the stock the manager receives from the organization the difference between the current market value of the stock and the stated option value of the stock. This saves the manager from having to come up with the cash necessary to purchase the stock. However, many plans restrict the amount of possible gain to 50 to 60 percent of growth in the stock's value. The gain is taxed as ordinary income to the manager when received, but there is no tax obligation when the rights are offered. This incentive plan provides a cash incentive over a longer period but no ownership advantages.

RESTRICTED STOCK PLANS.   In this type of plan the manager is granted a certain number of shares of stock as a bonus but may not sell those shares until certain conditions have been met. These conditions usually involve holding the stock for a period of time and remaining employed with the organization during that period. Another condition may be meeting some performance objectives on the job. As far as taxes are concerned, the lifting of the restrictions creates an ordinary income liability for the difference between the current value and employee cost. The manager may choose, at the time of the award, to be taxed on the current value of the stock, but any appreciation would be taxed at time of sale.

PHANTOM STOCK PLANS.   In some circumstances it is impossible or undesirable to allow managers to have stock. This may be because of ownership dilution or a closely held organization. Phantom stock plans can work well in these circumstances. In these plans the manager is awarded units that represent shares of stock. These units typically mature at some time, ordinarily four to six years. At maturity the manager is paid the then-current value of the stock or the difference between original value and current value. Obviously, the manager does not have to invest in the stock in this case. Again, the award is treated as ordinary income when received. Determining the current value of the stock can be a problem. Where the stock is not widely traded there is no real market value. Sometimes a number of other financial measures, such as those illustrated in exhibit 18–2, are used as surrogates of the stock value and the rise in them is assumed to create a higher value in the stock.

PERFORMANCE SHARE PLANS.   In this type of plan the manager is granted performance units that represent shares of common stock. He or she earns these shares through the performance of the organization. For instance, a manager might be granted 100 units, and if the organization's earnings per share were 10 percent the manager would receive 25 percent of the shares and up to 100 percent if the earnings per share were 15 percent averaged over five years. Typically the payoff in this type of program is 50 percent stock and 50 percent cash based upon the current value of the stock. The manager is taxed on both the cash and the value of the stock as ordinary income.

In all these plans there are three common themes. One is to reward the manager for organizational success. The second is to establish performance goals for the manager that reflect this success. The third is to try to maximize the value of the reward to the manager by taking advantage of the tax laws. The first two are relatively stable goals, but the third is constantly changing. The value of and interest in different long-term managerial incentives will continue to change with changes in the tax laws. Perhaps it is wiser to focus on the first two goals and minimize the evaluation of the worth of long-term incentives based on the third criterion.

Benefits and Perquisites

Managers, particularly top managers, are often granted additional benefits. The rationale for additional benefits is that retention of this group of employees is very important to the organization, so enhancing the membership decision is an important compensation goal. These additional benefits are often termed *golden handcuffs*. Some of these extra benefits are increases in the benefits available to all employees and some are special benefits to this group. One particular group of the latter are called *perquisites*.

MANAGERIAL BENEFITS.   Retirement benefits of managers tend to be the maximum available within the organization's plan since managers are usually the highest-paid employees and have long service—the two criteria that determine benefit levels. In addition, long-range incentives also provide the manager with a source of retirement income. Sometimes top executives also have an employment contract that limits the organization's ability to fire the executive without providing him or her with a financial advantage. These guarantees are called *golden parachutes*.

Insurance coverage for managers is high since again the criterion is most often salary. Top executives are often given additional life insurance and special types of insurance, such as travel insurance. Although their time-off provisions are the same or higher, managers tend not to take advantage of them as readily as other groups. It is sometimes necessary to insist that managers take the time off that is available to them, both because they need that time off and because a large liability can be created for the organization if a category such as vacations is allowed to accumulate.

MANAGERIAL PERQUISITES.   This is a set of special benefits available to managers, primarily top managers, that are designed to satisfy the special needs of this group. There are a number of perquisites. The first category is *internal*. These perquisites consist of items that are part of the work setting of the manager, such as special offices and furniture that distinguishes the status of the manager. A second category, *external* perquisites, has to do with conducting business outside the organization, such as a car, entertainment expenses, and club memberships. The last category is *personal* perquisites. This category consists of a wide variety of items, such as free medical examinations, low-cost loans, and financial or legal counseling. The last group is distinguished from the first two in that it is usually taxable to the employee.

Managerial Pay Reform?

An issue that periodically catches the attention of the public is whether executives in the United States are overpaid. This question gets raised whenever large pay raises or bonuses are awarded to executives at a seemingly inappropriate time. This can be examined using both of the motivation models outlined in this book.

THE EQUITY MODEL. The public looks at the high salaries of executives as a problem of equity and asks, Is this person worth this much more than other people? If the rewards are this high then the contributions must be equally great.[39] It is not easy to prove that the executive is in fact worth that much more than others. Some people would claim that this much difference in contribution and therefore reward is not possible. It is difficult to describe the contribution made by the executive to those outside the organization. The visibility of the executive can be easily exploited by the press, making this figure even more public and pointing out the supposed discrepancy.

THE PERFORMANCE-MOTIVATION MODEL. Each of the three major facets of the performance-motivation model provide a question regarding the size of executive salaries. As we have seen, the first part of the model is valence, or the attractiveness of the reward. Clearly the reward is attractive, but does it take this much to be attractive? Critics point out that executives in Europe and Japan do not get these large salaries but still perform very well. One response is that there are more alternatives in the United States for these talented people to go out on their own and make high incomes in an entrepreneurial manner.

The performance–reward connection questions whether there is in fact such a connection in executive salaries. As discussed in this chapter, there is evidence that this connection is tenuous at best. So this may be a major area in which pay reform is needed. However, a recent study does show a high relationship between both short- and long-term incentives and shareholder interests.[40] If American organizations need to improve their performance, assuring this connection would seem to be a high priority.

The performance–effort connection questions whether it is the executive or other environmental factors that lead to the organizational results for which the executive is rewarded. At times it may be true that the executive gains from improvement in the general economy rather than from his or her efforts. Of course, the reverse is also true—the executive gets blamed for poor performance that may not be his or her fault—so this may even out.

INTERNATIONAL COMPENSATION

Paying employees assigned to foreign countries clearly calls for a special compensation plan. This situation is one of the most complex in the field of

[39]D. Kraus, "Executive Pay: Ripe for Reform?" *Harvard Business Review,* September-October 1980, pp. 78–85.

[40]K. J. Murphy, "Top Executives Are Worth Every Nickel They Get," *Harvard Business Review,* March-April 1986, pp. 125–32.

compensation. This section does not pretend to develop a complete plan for compensating organizational employees who are assigned overseas. Rather the basic problems are explored and the approaches to these problems mentioned. In contrast with managerial and sales compensation, the emphasis in international compensation is upon equity. What most international compensation plans attempt to do is to *keep the employee whole*. This means that the plan attempts to see that the employee maintains a standard of living that he or she would have if occupying the same job in the United States. But in doing this the organization may create inequities with other employees of the organization, in particular those from the host country and those from a third country. So there are comparisons between the expatriate and employees at home doing the same work, between the expatriate and local nationals, and between the expatriate and organizational employees from a third country. All these possibilities are illustrated in figure 18–2.

Components

As in most compensation plans, international pay is basically for the job, so the first component of international compensation is base pay. But this base pay needs to be adjusted for a number of factors if the concept of keeping the employee whole is to be followed. So a second part of international com-

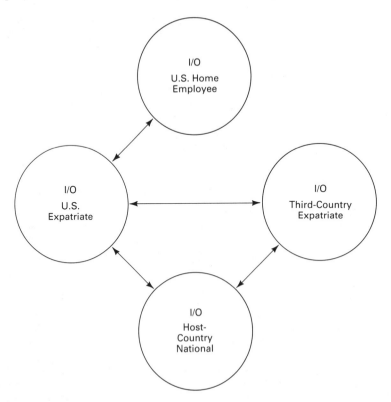

Figure 18–2 Comparison groups in international compensation

pensation is an equalization premium. Third, in order to make the overseas assignment attractive, some incentive is required. Last, there are some benefits that differ for employees assigned overseas.

BASE PAY. The base pay of the expatriate employee should be in the same range as that of a comparable employee working in the United States. The rating of the job can be done by job evaluation and the job placed in the appropriate pay grade. A major problem with trying to evaluate the overseas job is to determine comparability, since there are some factors that are different for the overseas job, in particular the degree of supervision. But it is important to try to keep the employee in the appropriate pay grade since when he or she returns there can be a problem with pay rates in the new job at home if the base pay of overseas jobs is inflated.

Movement within range should also be handled the same as with employees at home and at the same times. One of the fears of expatriates is that since they are so far away they will be forgotten in the compensation process. It is often hard, however, to evaluate performance, since the employee may be far removed from his or her supervisor or anyone who knows clearly what the employee is doing. So, as with salespeople, there is more emphasis for this group on results and less on behavior.

EQUALIZATION PREMIUM. Paying overseas employees just their base pay would not meet the conditions of keeping them whole, since there are differences in costs and complexities that are not present in the domestic situation. Thus, the organization would have a difficult time recruiting domestic employees for overseas assignments. The purpose of equalization premiums is to enable expatriate employees to equalize their living costs so that they can maintain the same standard of living they had at home. Such premiums may be required even if the country to which the employee is assigned has a high standard of living, since there are costs that are different for the expatriate than for the local employee. The most common premiums are related to taxes, housing, education, cost of living, and exchange rates.

Taxes. Income earned in a foreign country by a United States citizen is usually subject to taxation by both the foreign country and the United States. If overseas employees are left to fend for themselves, their taxes are likely to be higher than those of domestic employees even with the tax credits in the United States tax code. So organizations attempt to make the tax liability what it would be in the United States alone by providing a premium in the salary to pay for foreign taxes. The calculation of the amount of this premium is complex, because the premium itself and the others to be discussed are also considered income. So there is a multiplier effect that makes the decision as to the proper amount difficult to calculate. Tax equalization has been needed less since the passage of the Economic Recovery Act of 1981, which put in a $75,000 exclusion on income earned in a foreign country.

Housing, education, and cost of living. Housing costs for living in housing equivalent to that in the United States are usually greater overseas. Some organizations guess at the relative costs, some determine the premium by surveys of housing costs, and some provide an equal percentage of a total income formula. Two types of educational expenses are likely to be incurred by the expatriate and his or her family—learning a second language and attending private schools. The latter is required where local public schools are not as good as American ones or where the lack of language skill requires the child to attend an English-speaking school. Besides these special areas there may be an overall difference in the cost of living by American standards. This may be because goods and services common in the United States are hard to obtain in these countries. The U.S. State Department maintains an index of comparative living costs that is helpful.

Exchange rates.   The expatriate earns income in United States dollars. But he or she spends money in the host country, using the currency of that country. So the American paycheck has to be exchanged each pay period. The problem is that exchange rates fluctuate, so the person may receive more or less each pay period. Also, the value of the foreign currency may vary since the inflation rate in that country may not be the same as that in the United States. These fluctuations may make keeping the person whole just about impossible.[41]

INCENTIVE PREMIUM.   All of these adjustments assume that it is possible to make living abroad like living in the United States. This is often not possible, so there is a need for an incentive bonus to make the foreign assignment attractive. This incentive is for accepting an assignment that puts the person in a different situation, both on the job and personally. The job may require less supervision, contact with unfamiliar customs, a different language, and the role of sole representative of the organization.[42] The living situation may be unattractive and local customs may restrict the employee and his or her family in how they behave and live. This incentive is ordinarily a percentage of base pay, and the U.S. State Department is a good source of information as to how much, if anything, such an incentive should be.

BENEFITS.   In a number of ways benefits must be adapted for expatriates. Insurance costs, both medical and life, may be considerably higher in other countries. House hunting is usually more difficult, so there are allowances for time to do this as well as temporary locations for family, either in the foreign country or at home. Transportation of household goods is more expensive. Vacation time is often made longer to provide home leave, and transportation costs are sometimes paid.

Some benefits are a function of the overseas assignment. Emergency evacuation plans would be a prime example. Another is granting personal leave for family emergencies in the States. Where the assignment is dangerous so that family cannot go along, there are the costs of maintaining two residences. Personnel in this situation are most often treated as if they were on a temporary travel status with the organization.

[41]See the Prentice-Hall *Personnel Management-Compensation* (Englewood Cliffs, N.J.) for a discussion of this issue.

[42]C. G. Howard, "Overseas Compensation Policies of U.S. Multinationals," *Personnel Administrator*, July 1975, pp. 50–55.

Many countries to which the expatriate could be assigned have much higher benefits required by law. Even if the expatriate does not fall under the law of the host country, his or her fellow workers are being granted these benefits and this makes for negative comparisons. Where the benefits are required there is a question as to whether these extra benefits should be subtracted from base pay.

Maintaining International Equity

Thus far we have discussed mainly how to keep American expatriate employees equitably rewarded in comparison with their fellow employees in the United States or to their situation were they working in the United States for the organization. This is one of the possible comparisons illustrated in figure 18–2. The other two comparisons are those with local nationals and those with expatriates of a third nation. As organizations become multinationals, with employees in and from many of the world's nations, these comparisons are becoming more frequent. Maintaining equity in these comparisons is even harder than maintaining equity in the United States comparison. If the standard to be used is the job, then all three employees should receive the same pay. But the standard of keeping the expatriate employees whole in comparison with home-country employees leads to all three earning very different wages.

Organizations adopt both the job-comparison strategy and the making-whole strategy. The latter, however, is the more prevalent.[43] This leads to plans that include a number of the allowances just discussed in order to maintain a *balance-sheet* approach—one that neither overrewards nor hurts the employee for accepting overseas work in the organization.[44] The job-comparison strategy is easier to implement but harder to encourage the American employee to accept.[45]

These international compensation practices are expensive and complex. But they may not be as necessary in the future. Differences in living costs between countries are declining, making a major form of allowance less necessary. This is particularly true between the United States and Western Europe. Many countries limit the number of expatriates who can be in the organization's local facility and allow expatriates to train locals only on a temporary basis. The emergence of the multinational organization creates a group of people who really do not have a home country to be compared with in order to make them whole. These people will probably be paid highly for their mobility and commitment to the organization.

SUMMARY

Managers are probably the most important group of employees in the organization. While they represent a small percentage of the workers, they represent a major portion of the cost of compensation. It is important to develop a compensation program for this group that both obtains the most from these employees and keeps the costs within reason. The managerial job is one of high

[43]M. R. Foote, "Controlling the Cost of International Compensation," *Harvard Business Review,* November-December 1977, p. 123.

[44]B. Teague, *Compensating Key Personnel Overseas* (New York: Conference Board, 1972).

[45]Ibid.

stress, a great deal of variety, and the need to exercise considerable judgment. Managers are highly committed to the organization, have an action orientation, and a need to express their power motive.

Compensation programs for managers are a combination of base pay and incentive pay. Given the importance of this group, its high visibility, and easy movement to other organizations it is usual to use a high-paying wage level strategy for this group. Job evaluation is not as accurate for this group, which leads to the development of a separate wage structure or a broadening of the wage structure, both horizontally and vertically, at the top end. Individual pay determination is most typically dominated by pay-for-performance with management by objectives used as a basis for measuring performance.

Managerial incentives programs are divided into short and long range. Short-range programs are typically rewards for performance in a particular year based on how well the manager did in achieving his or her goals but with a measure of overall organizational performance forming the base of the bonus pool from which these funds emanate. Long-term managerial incentives are intended to tie the executive into the organization, both so the executive will stay with the organization and continue to perform highly. Most of these plans are a variation of a stock option plan that grants stock or money, based on overall organizational worth, to the executive over a long time period. These plans are typically deferred income. Managers are also granted a variety of benefits and perquisites that are not available to other employee groups.

International compensation is a very complex topic, and the coverage in this chapter is intended to merely introduce the reader to the main concerns, mostly of equity issues that are involved. The main concern of most organizations when they send an employee to another country is to *keep the person whole.* This is very complex, since there are varying standards of living involved, taxation and other legal problems in both countries, exchange rates, and a major question of the expatriate's wages as compared to the wages of the national worker. Extra benefits to international employees are usually extra vacation to come home and travel allowances.

THE WAGE ADMINISTRATION DECISION

"How much money should we allocate to each department this year considering we are moving the pay policy line by 7.5 percent?"

"How can I get my people to cooperate if I have to grant different increases and I have so little to work with?"

"How are we doing in controlling our labor costs this year?"

"What do you think will happen with the tax reform movement in Congress this year?"

"Why are all the secretaries suddenly asking for pay raises all the time?"

"Have you noticed that we seem to hire women for this job at a lower starting wage than men?"

This book concludes with two chapters on the administration of compensation programs. The planning and control of compensation is becoming more important for two reasons. The first is the increased sophistication of planning and control in organizations that is moving into the area of human-resource administration. The second reason is that with the high cost of American labor, controlling this cost in the competitive environment of today is critical. Chapter 19 covers the way in which compensation can be planned and controlled. Chapter 20 deals with a major issue in the administration of compensation—discrimination.

19

Planning and Control of Compensation Programs

The compensation decisions that have been discussed and described in this book are very important organizational decisions since all employees of the organization are vitally affected by them, as is the economic health of the organization itself. Thus, it is extremely important that these decisions be made professionally and that as a whole the compensation program achieve the goals set out for it. Like all organizational activity, the compensation program needs to be well thought out and planned and then followed up on and controlled in order to insure that the activities that take place are those that were intended and that they do, in fact, lead toward accomplishing the organization's goals. This chapter covers the tools and techniques required to carry out this important and final aspect of compensation administration.

One of the most difficult aspects of managing is to put an activity in the context of the overall functioning of the organization, particularly when the activity requires a lot of subactivities and is important to the organization and others in it. Compensation is just such an activity.

Further, compensation requires that many technical activities, described in this book, be carried out by a compensation staff. These activities become important to this staff for their own sake and it is important to keep in mind why the activities were instituted and what they are to achieve. Employees find compensation decisions both important and frightening. How much one is paid by the organization is of extreme importance, but often how the decision is arrived at seems mystical. Supervisors need compensation to create a climate in their work unit that is individually and collectively conducive to completing that unit's work. The organization needs to be competitive both in the labor market and the product market, and these two things may not be consistent. The force of all these pressures on compensation is to make it difficult to optimize the potential of compensation to energize organizational activity toward organizational goals.

INTEGRATION OF ORGANIZATIONAL AND COMPENSATION GOALS

Organizations are collectivities of people brought together to accomplish goals that an individual would not be able to accomplish alone. Organizations must accomplish goals of these individuals as well as their own in order to be attractive to the individual. In order to accomplish organizational goals the people must channel their energies toward activities that are important to the organization. Thus, the primary goal of compensation is the control of behavior of organizational participants. This behavior is of two types, membership and performance. However, the source of these two different kinds of behavior is different.

Membership Behavior

Membership is a behavior required in order to provide a continuity of activity over time. Without it the resources of the organization would be constantly expended in recruitment, selection, training, and development of employees. Organizations require long-term membership from most employees but only short-term membership from others. Regardless, the requirements are the same. Individuals must perceive that their rewards at least equal and preferably exceed their contributions. Likewise the organization must perceive these individual's contributions as at least equal to the value received from these contributions by the organization.[1]

To obtain this continuity in membership organizations must see that individuals obtain the rewards that they desire and are able to make the contributions that are needed. *Able* has both the meaning that the person is capable and the meaning that the organization creates the circumstances that allow the person to express that capability. These rewards and contributions can be expected to differ among employee groups. Some groups may want only economic rewards in exchange for minimal effort on their part while others may want intrinsic rewards and be willing to contribute not only continuity but commitment. Short-term employees often fall into the former category and managers and professionals the latter.

Organizations that require continuing membership must ensure that employees perceive that rewards do exceed contributions on a continuing basis. Because the employment exchange is perceptual, changes—real or imagined—

---

[1]D. W. Belcher and T. J. Atchison, "Compensation for Work," in *Handbook of Work, Organization, and Society,* ed. R. Dubin (Chicago: Rand McNally, 1976), pp. 567–611.

in the environment can strengthen or weaken it. In the extreme an employee who perceives much better opportunities for his or her contributions in the labor market will quit. On the other hand, employees who perceive that other jobs are not readily available will increase the perceived value of their rewards, making the exchange stronger. Although the former action is relatively permanent, the latter is not, so changes in the environment can rapidly change the perceptions of the employment exchange among current employees. Also, a cumulative effect can take place: little irritations and changes can build up until the perceptual field of the employees takes a turn around; although nothing dramatic has changed externally, the employee's perceptions have changed dramatically.[2]

A positive change in the employment-exchange balance—that is, rewards perceived as exceeding contributions—causes the person to wish to make and/or continue the exchange. But it goes beyond this simple fact. It also increases or broadens what Barnard calls the *zone of indifference*.[3] This means that the employee is more willing to perceive a wider variety and intensity of demands or contributions as legitimate parts of the employment exchange. The effect can be a positive spiral in which more contributions lead to higher rewards, which again strengthens the exchange in the eyes of the employee.

A negative change in the perceived balance of contributions and rewards leads to an uncomfortable feeling in the employee, which he or she attempts to alleviate either by direct action, ranging from asking for a raise in pay to quitting, or by perceptually manipulating either contributions or rewards in such a way as to realign the balance. Direct action is used where the employee feels that there is a positive environment outside the organization, and perceptual manipulation is more likely in a situation where movement is unlikely as an alternative. Even if the employee perceptually manipulates the exchange to create a positive balance there is likely to be a feeling of resentment that can carry over into future changes in the employment exchange.[4]

In summary, a perception of fairness in the employment exchange can lead to a strengthening of the exchange and continuing employment of the person. The organization gets continuing membership. Reductions in the perceptions of fairness in the exchange lead to dysfunctional behaviors on the employee's part, ending in a severance of the employment exchange. Employee groups may differ in what they desire and in how they perceive the environment for themselves, so the organization must be sensitive to how each of these groups is seeing its relationship to the organization. The reward to the organization for this vigilance is a continuing group of employees who understand the terms of the exchange under which they operate.

Performance Behavior

Organizations also require performance from employees. But obtaining performance behavior involves different requirements than obtaining member-

[2]P. R. Timm, "Worker Responses to Supervisory Communication Inequity: An Exploratory Study," *Journal of Business Communications,* Fall 1978, pp. 11–24.

[3]C. I. Barnard, *The Functions of the Executive* (Cambridge, Mass.: Harvard University Press, 1938).

[4]E. Walter, E. Berscheid, and G. V. Walster, "New Directions in Equity Research," *Journal of Personality and Social Psychology,* February 1973, pp. 151–76.

ship does. The simplest way is to build performance requirements into the job: the specific contributions and rewards are spelled out in the employment exchange at the time of its inception. Thus, just doing the job will lead to the required level of performance. This approach is most commonly seen in collective bargaining although it is also seen in most assembly-line situations, where management defines rather precisely what is to be done and how.

A second way of achieving desired performance levels was discussed in chapter 3 in terms of expectancy theory. The requirements of this method are that the organization:

1. provide to the employee rewards that he or she wants;
2. make a connection between these rewards and the desired performance in such a way that more performance leads to more reward; and
3. make a connection between the employee's effort and performance, so that the employee is sure that it is he or she that has influenced the outcome.

The second and third steps emphasize the need to make the definition of performance clear to the employee. Although this method of obtaining performance is currently becoming more popular, it should be noted that it greatly increases the level of complexity of compensation administration.

From the viewpoint of the organization, using this method of obtaining performance implies an additional employment exchange beyond membership. Applying this method to all employees may be difficult. Organizationally, it may be impossible to define performance standards as clearly as this method requires. Performance must be measured, and often the measurement is not a close fit with the desired outcome. Organizations typically require a number of contributions, not one or two, and establishing performance standards for all contributions that do not conflict and that are all measurable is at best difficult. Further, convincing employees of the intended connections may also be very difficult.[5]

Employees differ in their desire to engage in this further exchange. There is a range of how interested various employees are in the rewards that the organization is offering, and some find it hard to contribute the further effort required to engage in this exchange. The requirements demanded may not be "worth it" to some employees, and trying to change them may be seen by them as a continual haggle over the terms of employment.[6] However, if the zone of indifference discussed above is operative, then the attractiveness of this second exchange is enhanced and this new commitment welcomed. For those employees who find their job intrinsically satisfying the second exchange operates unconsciously, at least on the part of the organization.

Within limits, organizations can influence individuals to accept a broader definition of the employment exchange just as individuals can influence the organization to offer broader exchanges. Organizations can teach em-

[5]S. J. Carroll and C. E. Schneier, *Performance Appraisal and Review Systems* (Glenview, Ill.: Scott, Foresman, 1982).

[6]H. Behrend, "The Effort Bargain," *Industrial and Labor Relation Review,* July 1957, pp. 503–15.

ployees to value rewards that they have to offer and to contribute what they need.[7] Likewise, individuals can influence organizations to offer things that they need and accept contributions that they are willing to make.

Organizational Costs

Despite the behavioral overtones to the employment exchange, it is still an exchange that has instrumental aspects to it on both sides. The organization needs the employee's contribution, not for its own sake but in order to create something that is desired by society and that therefore allows the organization to survive. Likewise, with the exception of intrinsic rewards, the employee values the outcomes of the exchange for what these outcomes provide him or her outside of the workplace.

Thus, like all exchanges, both parties attempt to gain the maximum for themselves while providing the minimum to the other. This is possible to some extent because each party places different values on the respective contributions and rewards.[8] In the case of the organization, and examining the exchange in economic terms, further contributions required to gain higher outcomes from employees increase the cost of labor to the organization. There is a trade-off point between costs and the additional value received by the organization from the employee. As with all things, there is a point of diminishing returns in attempts to improve the employment exchange of the employee. The compensation planning and control process should be designed to deal with this trade-off and to balance the costs of compensation with the contributions received from employees.

Compensation administrators should keep clearly in mind the objectives of compensation while they are engaged in the everyday activities of compensation. There is a tendency to evaluate an activity on its own merits without examining how it fits into the overall scheme. The result of this is a great number of activities that fragment the efforts of the organization rather than focus and conserve activity to achieve organization goals.

COMPENSATION STRATEGY

There is no "one best" compensation program. Each organization's compensation program must match the circumstances of that particular organization. This process is one of matching organizational and environmental characteristics with the numerous options that have been presented in this book. Here are some of these options.

Wage Level Options

In chapter 5, we suggested that organizations could choose to pay above market, lower than market, or at the market level. Organizations differ in their ability and desire to use these options.

---

[7]S. Krupp, *Patterns in Organizational Analysis: A Critical Examination* (New York: Holt, Rinehart & Winston, 1961).

[8]Belcher and Atchison, "Compensation for Work."

HIGH-WAGE OPTION. Organizations can choose to pay, on average, better than their competitors for employees. They may wish to do so expecting to get better employees and keep turnover to a minimum. Organizations choosing this option are likely to be large organizations, that have high profit margins, produce well-differentiated products, maintain labor costs as a low percentage of total costs, and occupy a market niche such that keeping costs low is not a major consideration. Human resources are usually important in a high-paying organization. Often they are highly technological in nature and use many professional employees. Obtaining and retaining this group of employees is difficult, both because they have less organizational commitment and because the labor market is so dynamic that there are many opportunities for them.

LOW-WAGE OPTION. In contrast, some organizations choose or are forced to pay less than others for the same workers. Such organizations can expect to obtain a lower quality of employee and to be more subject to fluctuations in the labor market. Thus, in a tight labor market these organizations must spend more time recruiting employees and may have to train people for even low-level jobs.

Low-paying organizations tend to be in industries where there are undifferentiated products, considerable competition, easy entry for firms into the field, high wage costs to total costs, and low profit margins. But organizations operating at the fringe of any market are likely to fall into this category. The employees sought by these organizations tend to be less technical and often represent the secondary labor market. The minimum wage is a constraint on these organizations since they may wish to pay less for labor than they are allowed.

MARKET-WAGE OPTION. Most organizations claim that they attempt to pay market rates to their employees. Organizations possessing the characteristics of either of the two previously mentioned groups may choose to pay market rate for a number of reasons. They may feel that maintaining this position will allow them to attract and retain adequate employees while at the same time not raise labor costs too high. This strategy must work well because it is very popular, but it does seem to place the organization in a catch-up position when the labor market becomes tight. By the time that the organization recognizes that the market is tightening up, they may have lost many good employees.

Wage Structure Options

Strategic options in the design of wage structures are not as clearly defined as for the wage level, but two such areas can be identified: (1) market versus internal orientation and (2) design of the wage structure.

MARKET VERSUS INTERNAL ORIENTATION. Some organizations find that they must be or choose to be responsive to the marketplace over the total range of organizational jobs. These organizations tend to have jobs that are common in the marketplace, and they choose to recruit at all levels from the market. These organizations often pay less attention to internal movement of employees and do not have clearly defined career ladders. In these circumstances the organization usually designs its wage structure in such a way as to respond to the market first or, in the extreme, not to use job evaluation at all but to establish a wage structure that has market rates on both the horizontal and vertical dimensions.

Other organizations find that the internal structure of jobs as derived through job evaluation is an important variable on the wage structure that they develop. Organizations that have jobs for which there is no labor market comparison must pay more attention to internally developed structures. These organizations also tend to have staffing strategies that limit recruitment from outside to a few entry points and use internal promotion as the major way that positions are filled within the organization. In these organizations, use of market rates become guides for the overall structure and determinants only for those positions where recruitment from the outside is done.

WAGE STRUCTURE DESIGN.   Wage structures can be designed so that they have many levels, often with narrow rate ranges and a considerable overlap between levels. They can also be designed with the opposite characteristics. Organizations that have a highly developed promotion ladder and a narrow definition of jobs tend to go for the first option. These organizations are often more mechanistic and are concerned with bureaucratic procedures. Organizations that are in a dynamic environment, are more organic in nature, and where careful job definition is not possible given the rapid change that occurs, will tend to have wage structures that have fewer grades, wider rate ranges, and less overlap between levels.

Wage System Options

The basic option in the development of wage systems is how much the organization is going to pay for performance. It might seem that all organizations would opt for pay for performance but this may not be possible or desirable; reasons for this were discussed in chapter 13. In contrast to the options in wage level and structure, the determinants here are much more internal than external. While outside influences affect this choice in organizations today, particularly the focus on competition in American industry, most of the forces that decide the emphasis on performance are internal.

A major influence is the ability to define performance and to isolate the performance effects of a particular job. Organizations are becoming more complex and interdependent. This makes the determination of individual performance more difficult. Within organizations there is also considerable ambivalence about the use of variable performance as a guide to assigning different wage rates to employees. Unions have always opposed this on the grounds that it is a judgment that leads to management favoritism. But even supervisors find it hard to place a heavy emphasis on relative performance, partly because this is hard to define and partly because this emphasis gets in the way of the cooperation needed in the organizational unit.

A renewed emphasis on incentive plans is a symbol of the increased emphasis on performance. Interestingly, in this area one sees that there is a stronger emphasis on plans that focus on or at least include organizational performance in the measurement of performance.

These options do not exhaust the choices open to those designing compensation programs. This section is intended to suggest that one needs to look at most of the decisions elucidated in this book as opportunities to accomplish the goals of the organization by matching the compensation program to the environmental and organizational circumstances that exist.

COMPENSATION PLANNING

Planning is the process of determining *what* you want to do and *how* you are going to get it done. It is a process that is done all the time in order to keep the organization moving toward its goals. But the process may not be a conscious one or well thought out. In compensation, formal planning processes are a recent and necessary addition to compensation administration.

Determining what to accomplish and how to accomplish it has two concerns. The first is that the environment outside may make achieving goals either more or less difficult. So the planner must have some estimate of the interaction between the organization's actions and the environment. Second, there is an interaction between the what and the how. The planner must estimate whether the actions taken—the how—will in fact create the desired state—the what.

Compensation planning must answer four questions: (1) What is the current status of the program? (2) What do we want the program to do? (3) What is likely to happen? and (4) What action do we take to get the program to do what we want?[9]

Where Are We Now?

This first question might be considered an audit of the present compensation program.[10] It is necessary because in order to know where you wish to go you first need to know where you presently are. This question in turn has a number of aspects. The planner needs to know where the compensation program is in relation to the market, the job and wage structures, and individual wage rates.

KNOWLEDGE OF THE MARKET.   The organization is always in some sort of relationship to the market in regards to wages. It is necessary to have a wage survey to compare with the pay rates within the organization to determine the current position of the organization vis-à-vis the market. The main thing that this will tell the planner is the current pay level of the organization. It can also identify particular jobs that seem to be out of line with the market such that the job or wage structure needs to be altered.

Another source of information is the recruiting and retention information within the organization. If the discussion at the beginning of this chapter

[9]T. J. Atchison and W. W. Hill, *Management Today: Managing Work in Organizations* (New York: Harcourt Brace Jovanovich, Inc., 1978).

[10]R. J. Greene, "Auditing Your Pay Programs: Are They Equitable, Competitive and Defensible?" *1982 Conference Proceedings* (Scottsdale, Ariz.: American Compensation Assn., 1982), pp. 29–42.

is accurate, then turnover and retention rates should be a good indication of the labor market and of employees' knowledge of and response to changes in it. It may be necessary not only to find out the turnover statistics but to get a picture of the ability of the organization to recruit and retain the quality of personnel that the organization needs.[11]

KNOWLEDGE OF THE JOB AND WAGE STRUCTURE. The wage structure consists of a series of progressive pay grades. Each grade has a range, which can be viewed in terms of its maximum, midpoint, and minimum. The planner needs to know how these ranges are working. For the ranges in general it is useful to know how many jobs are being paid out of range. For each rate range it is necessary to know what the distribution of people is within the range. For instance, if everyone is at the bottom of the range it may indicate high turnover rates and problems with the membership decision. Everyone at the top of the range may dictate a slowdown of intergrade progression within the organization.

A major tool in compensation planning and control is a statistic called the *compa-ratio.* The compa-ratio tells the planner how the distribution of jobs or people's wages in the pay range compares with the midpoint of the range. A compa-ratio of 1 indicates that the average of the pay rates is the same as the midpoint of the range. Here is the formula for the compa-ratio:

$$\text{Compa-ratio} = \frac{\text{average rates actually paid}}{\text{midpoint of the range}}$$

If the compa-ratio is a figure such as 1.06, the average of the wages paid in that pay range exceeds the midpoint. By itself this tells the planner very little. The reason to focus on this statistic goes back to the assumption made in chapter 11 that the midpoint of the pay range is where the "average" performer is to be paid and that given a number of people in a pay range the average should therefore be the midpoint of the range. Actually a compa-ratio of more than 1 can be the result of a conscious decision by the organization to pay above average, a long tenure of people in the pay range, superior performance of these people, or a number of other reasons. A compa-ratio is a signal that things need to be looked at and not that things are wrong.

Compa-ratios may be used at a number of levels besides examination of the wage structure if we simply replace the numerator in the preceding equation. For instance, replacing the average pay rate with any individual pay rate allows the planner to see how each person's wage relates to the pay range. Or the numerator could be replaced with the market rate to examine competitiveness. So compa-ratios can be calculated for organizations, for any subunit of the organization, for job categories, or for individual jobs.

KNOWLEDGE OF INDIVIDUAL PAY RATES. This information is the pay rate and actual pay received by employees in the organization. This is necessary both in aggregate amounts and individual amounts. At this point the planning

[11]T. Hestwood and B. D. Biswas, "Human Resource Planning and Compensation: A Developing Relationship," *1979 National Conference Proceedings* (Scottsdale Ariz.: American Compensation Assn., 1979), pp. 22–35.

process moves from an internal examination of the way in which compensation operates to how compensation decisions relate to the rest of the organization. The actual pay rates are necessary for budgeting the amounts required in the future at all levels, from the individual employee to the total wage cost of the organization.

Where Do We Want to Be?

This second question of the planning process involves the policy decisions that have been discussed throughout this book. They are at three levels— wage levels, wage structure, and individual pay decisions.

WAGE LEVEL POLICIES.   Wage level policies deal with the relationship between the organization and the external labor market. The basic decision is whether the organization wishes to lead, lag, or meet the market (chapter 5). The higher the organization is willing to go against the market, the better the quality of employee the organization can expect to attract and retain.

This basic pay level decision may be made for the organization as a whole, for subunits of the organization, or for particular job categories. Some jobs may be considered more important to the success of the organization, so those are paid higher relative to the market than are other jobs in the organization. Such a policy, however, can lead to feelings of inequity in the nonfavored groups in the organization and in some circumstances could lead to charges of discrimination if the groups were separated by race or gender.

WAGE STRUCTURE POLICIES.   In the establishment of the wage structure the major policy decision deals with the weight that market and organizational factors will have in determining the shape of the wage structure. As indicated in chapter 11, the wage structure is a combination of the job structure and the labor-market data. Which will prevail when there is a disagreement is a policy question. Organizations that are market-sensitive probably have to put the market first, whereas organizations that are insulated from the market, such as through internal labor markets, will probably put the job structure first.

A second major policy decision involves the number of pay ranges and the overlap between them. This decision reflects the attitudes of the organization toward promotion and transfer within the organization. Wide pay ranges and few grades mean that employees will spend a long time in a particular pay grade before being promoted. The number of grades should also be coordinated with the shape of the organization. A tall, thin organization with many organizational levels calls for a wage structure that looks the same way.

Adjusting the wage structure also involves some policy considerations. When a new wage structure is being implemented the survey data must be updated. The decision as to how to do this affects the true degree to which the wage level decision is implemented. In addition, the wage level decision is interpreted in terms of when during the year the organization will maintain its chosen competitive stance. A decision to match the market at the beginning of the year is very different from saying that you will meet the market at the end of the year.

PAY SYSTEMS POLICIES. Individual pay determination deals with two questions: how much to pay a new hire and how much of a pay increase to give an employee this year. The answer to the latter question is based upon what determines movement within the pay range—performance, seniority, or other contributions. The answer to the first question is greatly affected by the labor-market conditions. These conditions, in turn, affect the internal pay system if hiring rates must be raised to close to or above the pay rates of current employees, creating a compression problem.

As discussed in part V, another policy consideration is what proportion of total pay goes to direct wages and what to benefits. In addition, the individual pay decision criteria are likely to differ with employee groups, as was seen in part VI.

What Is Likely to Happen?

To develop an idea of what will happen is to *forecast*. As indicated, two types of forecasts are required. The first is of environmental conditions that will influence the compensation plan and the other is whether the actions under the plan accord with the policy statements developed above. These two types of forecasts may be considered external and internal forecasting.[12]

EXTERNAL FORECASTING. A wage survey presents a picture of the labor market at the time the survey is taken. But by the time the organization adjusts its wage structure those data may be out of date. Therefore, in adjusting the wage structure one must take into account the expected changes in the labor market during the period the wage structure will be in effect. As pointed out in chapter 11, this is done in two ways. The first is to age the survey data from the time the survey was taken until the time the wage survey is effective. This means that upward or downward movements in wages, either observed or predicted, are included in the wage structure by adjusting the pay-policy line by the amount of the change in the labor market.

At this point the wage structure would be accurate as of the moment it was put into effect. But it is to be used for some period of time, typically one year. During this year the labor market will continue to change, and it is this forecast that is most important and most difficult. The planner must estimate the amount of change that will occur in the labor market during the next year and again change the pay-policy line by that amount. This may involve both an overall percentage change and/or a change in specific job categories that will change the slope of the pay-policy line or bring some jobs into or out of line with the wage structure. Last, the adjustment for the pay level policy decided upon in the second stage of planning above needs to be built in before a finished wage structure can be developed. Thus, an operational wage structure is not just a reflection of the wage survey that was done but is also a sophisticated forecast of the labor market and organizational goals for the next time period.

COST OF LIVING. This discussion assumes that the organization adjusts its wage structure based upon labor-market information in the form of wage

[12]T. E. Milne, *Business Forecasting: A Managerial Approach* (London: Longman, 1975).

surveys. Employees only rarely have access to wage surveys or know how to interpret them. What they do see and hear about all the time is the change in the cost of living. During times of high inflation, when the news bombards everyone with the large and rapid changes in the cost of living, employees can feel that they are falling behind considerably if the wage structure adjustments are not of the same magnitude as the changes in the cost of living. The wage structure appears to get out of date quickly and by quite a bit. In response, many organizations adjust their wage structures by changes in the cost of living and not by wage survey data.[13] In many collective bargaining contracts this is built in in the form of cost-of-living-adjustment (COLA) clauses.[14]

The basic purpose of adjusting the wage structure is to remain competitive for the type of workers that the organization wishes to recruit and retain. Does adjusting the wage structure using the cost of living do this? Milkovich and Newman point out that there are three different but overlapping concepts here: the cost of living, changes in the prices of products and services, and changes in wages in the labor market.[15] Changes in wages in the labor market are measured by wage surveys, as discussed in chapter 6, and, as indicated above, are ordinarily used to adjust the wage structure. This is reasonable if the goal is to be competitive in the labor market.

But employees do not see wage survey figures and do not feel changes in others' wages as directly as they do changes in the prices they pay for groceries. Changes in prices of goods and services are measured by the Consumer Price Index (CPI) and it is this figure that the press picks up and that is seen on television and in newspapers.

The CPI is a government-developed figure intended to record changes in a hypothetical market basket of the goods and services most likely to be used by an average family. The current index was developed in 1972–1973 from a study of the buying habits of a sample of 30,000 individuals. From this study the percentage of total expenditures for a number of categories of goods and services was developed. As surveys were run over time of the changes in the cost of these items, the change is recorded in the overall change of the CPI.

The accuracy of the CPI has come under attack in recent years, when it has been used more and more to adjust wages and other payments, such as retirement benefits and Social Security. Does it accurately reflect changes in the cost of living? Three criticisms have been made. First, there is a substitution effect that is not recorded in the CPI. If an item goes up dramatically in price, as beef did a few years ago, people substitute cheaper goods for it. But the CPI keeps the previous weight of the expensive item. Second, the weights given items has been challenged. For instance, housing prices in recent years rose dramatically, and for a person who had to buy a new home these increases were traumatic. But for those who did not buy a new home there was little

[13]J. E. Reiter, G. R. Koester, and B. H. Kloecker, "Compensation of Non-Exempt Salaried Employees during Inflationary Periods: Pay Unitil It Hurts," *1980 Regional Conference Proceedings* (Scottsdale, Ariz.: American Compensation Assn., 1980).

[14]D. J. B. Mitchell, "Should the Consumer Price Index Determine Wages?" *California Management Review*, Fall 1982, pp. 5–19.

[15]G. T. Milkovich and J. M. Newman, *Compensation* (Plano, Tex.: Business Publications, 1984).

change in housing costs. The CPI, until recently, measured housing prices rather than costs. The third criticism is that the group used to develop the weights of items and the items themselves may not be representative of the buying public today.[16]

In general, these criticisms may suggest that the use of the CPI to adjust wages or other payments overstates the change in the living costs of the people affected. Given those criticisms, it is apparent that changes in the CPI will only imperfectly reflect changes in the employee's cost of living. For some groups, such as middle-age employees whose children are grown and who remain in the same home, changes in the CPI may have almost no effect. On the other hand, young employees starting families may be very affected by changes in the CPI, particularly when the change is caused by factors such as food.

INTERNAL FORECASTING.   Inside the organization forecasting is concerned with the effects of individual wage determination. The organization is concerned with the costs of the total wage bill created by hiring and retaining employees. In order to do this the organization must make estimates of which employees will stay with the organization, which job rates these employees will have, which employees will leave the organization, their pay rates, and which new employees will have to be hired and the pay rates of these employees. This is essentially the function of human-resource planning, a topic in personnel administration that can take up a whole book of its own.[17]

The reason this information is required is changes: growth, decline, and turnover change the average wage bill of the organization and its subunits. In general, growth and turnover will lower the average wage. This is because new employees are hired at or near the bottom of the pay range whereas senior employees are at or above the midpoint of the pay range. So replacing or adding people lower in the range will lower the average of that group of employees. Decline and slow turnover have the opposite effects. If there is no growth and no turnover, the average wage of the group will move upward by at least the amount that the wage structure was adjusted. For example, in school districts in which movement within grade has traditionally been by seniority and/or the taking of more advanced courses, the decline in the need for teachers in the latter 1970s created a situation where almost all teachers were at the top of the pay range; even reductions in force had little effect on the overall wage bill of the district.

Another set of changes that can have a considerable effect on the average wage bill are technological changes. Growth and decline resulting from technological change is like any other change unless the skills now required are different. If skill levels rise with the technological change, the average wage bill may rise even if the total number of employees declines. Typically, however, the average skill level does not change dramatically with technological change, but the distribution of skill changes considerably. Computerization in particular seems to have more higher- and lower-skill requirements and fewer midrange

---

[16]Ibid.

[17]Hestwood and Biswas, "Human Resource Planning and Compensation."

requirements. Thus, even if the average wage of the group does not change, the pressures placed upon the wage structure increase.[18]

What Action Is Required?

This final step of compensation planning involves implementing the policies developed in step two, taking into account the information gathered in step one and the projections from step three. The product is a pay rate for each employee developed within the framework of the pay level policies and the newly adjusted wage structure. The latter provides a framework for the determination of the actual pay rates to be assigned but allows a great deal of judgment as to these rates. It is these rates that in the aggregate make up the total wage costs of the organization.

By adjusting the wage structure in line with the pay level policies the organization has indicated the total amount by which it wishes to adjust its wage costs either up or down. On the other end of the spectrum there are a myriad decisions to be made about what wage rate to assign to each employee, again within the constraints of the wage structure and the policies of governing individual pay determination. These two approaches may not lead to the same amount of change in the total wage costs unless the two approaches are coordinated. This is the function of the compensation budget.

BUDGETING. From the above it is clear that there can be two approaches to developing a compensation budget. The first is from the *bottom up*.[19] In this approach the organization has each supervisor indicate the wage change that will be assigned to each employee during the year. These changes are then reviewed up the organizational ladder for congruence with pay level and structure policies and the amounts summed to find out the total change in wage costs.

In practice the process is not this simple, mainly because of the factors discussed in the section on internal forecasting. It is not enough to indicate the new wage rate for each current employee. There are a number of other factors to consider:

1. When will the change in wage rate be made? Assuming a yearly budget starting the first of the year, a 5 percent increase on January 1 amounts to a 5 percent increase for the year in that employee's salary. But a 5 percent increase given on July 1 is a 2.5 percent increase for the year. Note, however, that although the increase given in the middle of the year is 2.5 percent the first year, it builds in 5 percent for the next year.

2. Whose wages will be adjusted? This is the *participation rate*. If all employees are to receive an increase in wages, this will lead either to less for each employee or to a higher overall increase for the organization. New employees are often not eligible for an increase for a period such

---

[18]W. Skinner, "The Impact of Changing Technology on the Working Environment," in *Work in America: The Decade Ahead,* ed. C. Kerr and J. M. Rosow (New York: Van Nostrand Reinhold, 1979), p. 218.

[19]Atchison and Hill, *Management Today.*

as six months, or, conversely, they must be given an automatic increase at some similar period depending on organizational policy.

3. Will the organization (or unit) grow or decline? And when? The number of employees in the unit has an obvious effect on the total wage costs of the organization. But *when* changes take place also affects how the change must be accounted for in estimating wage costs, as when wage increases are granted.

4. What turnover will take place? This is hard to estimate in each organizational unit but easier to do at the overall organizational level. In general, new employees brought in to replace old ones are hired at a lower rate than the old employee had attained, and thus turnover lowers the average wage costs.

5. What changes in the types of jobs will occur in the organization (or unit)? Higher skills lead to more employees at higher pay grades, and lower skills the opposite. But changing current employees to new job titles may not have its full effect immediately, for wage increases for upgrades may not be much more than regular pay increases in the first year and a downward movement is often restricted entirely.

These questions can be answered in each organizational unit and the adjusted figures passed upward, or rough estimates can be made in the subunits and then adjustments made at the organizational level.

A second approach to budgeting is from the *top down*. In this approach an overall amount of change is dictated for the organization as a whole and this change in turn is apportioned to each organizational unit. This may, in fact, take place through a number of organizational levels so that the allocation process may be done a number of times with smaller and smaller amounts. Each manager ends up with a given amount of money to allocate to wages, or more likely a percentage by which last year's wage costs may change. The product is again the proposed wage rate for each employee. When the product is a percentage the organization starts with the change in wage structure and accounts for the factors that were discussed immediately above in adjusting the percentage to a *planned level rise*.

An alternative to this method that incorporates the ability to give varying amounts to different organizational units is to budget by using each organizational unit's compa-ratio. This approach assumes that each organizational unit should have an overall average wage rate and that this rate should be the midpoint of the pay range. So those units whose compa-ratio is lower than 1 would be allowed to give higher increases than those who at present have a compa-ratio of more than 1. However, it is not necessary to strive for or achieve a compa-ratio of 1 in all organizational units. The organization as a whole may wish to have a compa-ratio of more or less than 1 depending on its pay level policies. In addition the organization may wish to keep one or more units' compa-ratio over 1 and others under 1 for reasons such as importance of the function to the organization or competition for the skills in the labor market.

A final reminder needs to be interjected here. This discussion has dealt with direct wage costs, and the budgets are for those costs. In order to develop total wage costs of the organization the indirect or benefit costs must be added in. These are often hard to coordinate with the direct costs at the unit level because benefits are not allocated in the same manner as are direct costs. Managers in this situation often feel that an added burden is being placed on them over which they have no control.

COMPENSATION CONTROL

Control is the process of seeing that the plans that have been developed are carried out. It is an after-the-fact process in that it reviews what went on to see if it conformed with the plan. The formal control process in organizations involves (1) establishing a standard of performance and a measure of that performance, (2) comparing actual behavior with the standard, and (3) taking corrective action if there proves to be a difference between the two.[20] The first step, establishing standards, is what was done in our discussion of planning; the plan is the standard since that is what we want to have happen. If the plan has been formalized there should be sufficient measurement standards to provide for comparisons.

Actual behavior that needs to be monitored is of two types, external and internal. In developing the compensation plan a number of assumptions or forecasts were made of the labor market, particularly the rate and type of change in wage rates. The actual changes need to be monitored to see if the predictions were accurate. The internal information is of two types, that dealing with the accuracy of internal forecast assumptions, such as turnover, and that dealing with the behaviors that take place as a result of acting upon the plan. These two sets of internal information also need to be monitored.

The purpose of the monitoring is to make a comparison between the plan and the action. But the action to take, assuming that the two do not match, depends on where the differential occurs. If the action that is supposed to take place under the plan is not occurring, then the behavior in question needs changing. But if at the same time the assumptions upon which the plan was devised also show a differential, it is most probable that the behavior is correct and that it is the plan that needs to be changed. Plans should be guides to action and not rigid prescriptions never to be violated.[21]

Finally, this change in the plan represents a closing of the planning and control cycle. The examination of what has happened is, in fact, the same as the first step in the planning process. So planning and control are not done once a year and then forgotten but rather constitute a continuing process carried out along with the daily activity of compensation.

Achieving Control

Control is not easy to achieve in organizations. There are a number of forces that make maintaining control difficult and at times dysfunctional. These problems center in the different control processes, the effects of control on people, and measurement dysfunctions.

MANY CONTROL PROCESSES.   To a degree everyone attempts to control everyone else. In an organization where people have to interact to get their

[20]See Atchison and Hill, op. cit.
[21]Ibid.

work done and each participant is also there to achieve his or her personal needs, there is considerable pressure being applied by everyone on others and on the organization itself. No small part of this is the need and desire of all of us to feel in control of our environment. Actually, there are three major types of control operating in organizations: (1) formal organizational controls, such as those proposed above; (2) social control by groups or by one person on another; and (3) self-control, in which the other is one's self and the control is internalized.[22] Good control would require all three of these types of control to be congruent and to direct the same thing for the person. The chances of this are small so that the person is in the position of having to choose between conflicting forces. The result is less-than-perfect organizational control. Resistance to control is often in reality a reaction to these cross-pressures on the person.

CONTROL AND PEOPLE.   Organization controls work better on some groups of employees and jobs than on others. For example, if tasks can be programmed and performed independently and have a short time cycle, organization controls can work very well. They also work better if the person wants and needs control, as in the case of a new employee who does not know the job well. But if the job requires years of training and interdependent action over an extended period before results appear, then organization controls do not work well. It is in these circumstances, however, that social control and self-control are most likely to be congruent and provide good guides. Also, these controls are not seen as controls by the individual, so the negative aspect of feeling that one is not in control is not present. This puts a premium on hiring or developing employees who have a built-in control system.[23]

MEASUREMENT DYSFUNCTIONS.   It is often hard or impossible to observe the actual behavior desired, such as making a proper decision. Therefore, organizations develop measures of the desired behavior. This is functional for control purposes but leads to the employee focusing on the measurement and not on the goal. For instance, a manager may rate all employees as outstanding, not because they are but because only those employees rated as outstanding are eligible to receive a 10 percent raise and he or she wishes to give a 10 percent raise.

The advantage of developing a measurement of a performance standard is that it is precise. But sometimes it is not desirable to make things clear and unambiguous. Vagueness also has its value. Where flexibility is required a vague standard is more useful than a precise one. Also, where there are conflicting standards to be achieved vagueness allows the manager to pursue both without failure.[24]

Methods of Control

Organization control of the compensation program emphasizes the three decision areas of wage level, wage structure, and individual wage determination.

---

[22]P. Blau and W. R. Scott, *Formal Organizations* (San Francisco: Chandler, 1967).

[23]G. W. Dalton and P. R. Lawrence, *Motivation and Control in Organizations* (Homewood, Ill.: Richard D. Irwin, 1971).

[24]Atchison and Hill, *Management Today*.

WAGE LEVEL CONTROL.   Control measures for wage level are both external and internal. The external control standards have to do with whether the organization is remaining competitive. In some cases this means doing spot checks of a wage survey to see if the market is behaving as expected. An internal indicator that is often used as a signal is the turnover rate, overall or particularly in important job titles. The beginning of a rise in these turnover figures is a signal to find out what the change in wage rates really is. The problem with this is that it is uni-directional; it tells the organization when the market has gone up faster than planned but not when it is going up slower than planned.

Internal wage level control takes place through total payroll expenditures and comparisons between the budgeted payroll amounts and actual payroll expenditures. As indicated, a discrepancy does not necessarily mean that expenditures must be reduced; it can mean that the assumptions of the plan were inaccurate. One problem here is that expenditures can be brought down in the future but not in the past. So overexpenditures, if the organization were to insist on a return to the original budget levels, would require lower expenditures than planned for the remainder of the budget period.

JOB AND WAGE STRUCTURE CONTROL.   Wage structure control involves determining if the relationships between jobs in the organization are proper and reflect the values intended by the organization. Perhaps the ultimate standard for wage structure control is employee acceptance of internal pay relationships.

Measurement of wage structure control is not as easy as that of wage level control since the wage structure, being predicated upon the job structure of the organization, provides a framework for the planning process but is not a direct part of the planning. Periodic audits of job evaluation is one way of finding out if job relationships are sound. Wage survey results may be signals that the nature of jobs has changed or that relationships need altering due to market forces. Complaints about job evaluation in the form of requests for reclassification of jobs or grievances in a union setting are signals of wage structure anomalies.

Perhaps the biggest problem in the job structure, *grade creep,* is a result of these requests for reclassification. This is often used by managers to pay a valuable employee more money than the structure allows. But as one job is reclassified another manager will decide his or her jobs are underpaid in relation to the newly reclassified job and so request reclassification. This leads to a spiral of changes in the evaluation of jobs, which eventually moves all jobs into a higher grade.

Two final aspects of control having to do with jobs are the total number and types of jobs. Both have a considerable influence over the total wage bill. Organizations appear to have an inevitable drift toward overstaffing. Control of this can be done mainly through examining the relative percentages of expense devoted to different organizational activities over time.[25]

CONTROL OF INDIVIDUAL PAY.   Control of individual pay rates involves ensuring that employee's pay is fair and within the guidelines established

[25]M. T. Steele, "Productivity through Manpower Expense Control," *1982 Conference Proceedings* (Scottsdale, Ariz.: American Compensation Assn., 1982), pp. 48–54.

through the budgeting process. Most of budgeting has to do with individual pay determination, making this area the most developed for control purposes. The reasons for this are that (1) this part of the control process is clearly distinct from general management controls, (2) uncontrolled individual pay decisions have large cost and equity implications, and (3) this is an area that is rather easy to control.

Decisions about individual pay occur both when the employee is first hired and at the time of subsequent changes, and include both the amount and the timing of such changes. The amount of pay the person is offered at the time of hiring is governed partially by the job, particularly the minimum of the pay range for the job. But this is also a time when the personal qualifications of the individual are a prominent consideration.

Decisions regarding pay after hire are a result of a complex of policies about pay level, pay structure, and individual pay determination. In the last category in particular, the criteria for movement within grade (chapter 12) are important. The measurement of control of individual pay is the position of the individual in relation to the pay range. Again the compa-ratio is a useful measure when the individual's pay is used as the numerator.

Most organizations have specific rules for employee pay raises. These can include not only periodic pay adjustments but hiring rates and all movements within the organization. These guidelines usually specify minimum increases, sometimes maximum increases, and the frequency of these increases. Increase amounts usually increase with the level of the job in the pay grades and organization, and frequency decreases with these same factors.

Most organizations also have policies regarding wage increases as a function of promotion. These guidelines usually specify that the new rate be at least the minimum of the pay grade and a specified minimum and/or maximum over current salary. Many organizations also have ground rules for demotion. One alternative is to reduce the employee's pay to the maximum of the new pay grade immediately. Another is to freeze the employee's present pay rate as a *red-circle rate* and wait for the adjustments of the pay structure to bring the employee's pay into range.

Although organizations appear to believe that individual pay increases are designed to provide performance motivation, a review of the control process for these increases shows mixed evidence of channeling employee behavior toward increased performance.[26] Although most organizations use the term *merit* to describe the basis of pay adjustments, there is little in the control process to ensure that large pay increases go to the best performers and small or no increases to poor performers. Even if this is the case, there is no way of knowing if the employees perceive this connection.

These individual pay decisions are most often the purview of the individual manager. There are a number of pressures on managers that make it difficult for them to carry out this connection between performance and reward successfully. In particular there is the problem that with differential reward under the budget process, giving a large increase to one employee automatically means a reduction in the amounts available to others. This

[26]W. C. Hamner, "How to Ruin Motivation with Pay," *Compensation Review,* third quarter 1975, pp. 26–34.

competitive situation is antithetical to the development of cooperation within the work group.[27]

INCENTIVE PLAN CONTROL. A properly designed incentive plan makes control easier because the control is built into the program and can rely less on organization control and more on self-control. The mechanism for feedback to the employee is immediate, so there is no trouble with perceptions of the performance–reward connection. Performance standards and the measurement of the standard are an integral part of the design of the incentive program and so are much more advanced than in other compensation practices. In addition, most incentive plans develop further standards for monitoring the program on an ongoing basis.

BENEFITS CONTROL. No area of compensation has as great a need for control as benefits. The problems of benefit costs were discussed in chapters 15 and 16. Most of the problems in this area have been perceived as uncontrollable. That is, they are a function of the environment and not of the organization. However, as pointed out, much of the current situation in benefits derives from the unplanned way in which they were developed in the past. So, much of the problem of control is more correctly seen as a failure to plan. Benefits are not technically difficult to control from a measurement standpoint. It is the forecasting and acceptance of the forecasts that are difficult. Where forecasts are unacceptable the organization is required to take a proactive stance and make changes in the environment. This is exactly what is happening in the field of benefits as organizations seek alternatives that reduce the cost of benefits.

RESPONSIBILITY FOR COMPENSATION ADMINISTRATION

Compensating employees is a managerial process that requires considerable expertise. This skill is not typically one that most managers possess. Thus, it is likely that much of the work and decisions of compensation in any good-sized organization will be performed by a compensation staff. On the other hand, compensation requires many decisions that a staff group is not in a position to make. Since the goal is to determine a pay rate for the employee, it is the employee's manager who has the necessary information. Also, since compensation is a major motivational tool, the determination of compensation should be seen as emanating from the manager. Further, many compensation decisions involve considerable costs that affect the economic health of the entire organization. For these decisions top management needs to be involved so that compensation is integrated into the overall planning of the organization. Compensation, then, requires decisions to be made by staff and all levels of management working together for an optimum program to operate in the organization.[28]

---

[27]See Hamner, op. cit..

[28]J. A. Fossum, "Why Compensation Practices Often Seem to Interfere with Accomplishing New Goals," *1984 Conference Proceedings* (Scottsdale Ariz.: American Compensation Assn., 1984), pp. 8–11.

Staff–Line Integration

As in all staff–line situations, compensation can create a good deal of organizational conflict. The goals of line managers and the compensation staff are quite different and this can lead to each party feeling that the other does not understand the situation. The compensation staff are assigned to collect the necessary labor-market information and decide the wage structure and administration of the policies of top management. Line management, on the other hand, while given compensation policies, is directed to accomplish the mission of its organizational unit. These two different sets of direction from top management invariably conflict with each other, creating the feeling among managers that compensation is some sort of black magic done behind closed doors and a corresponding feeling among the compensation staff that line managers are trying to subvert the compensation program to solve their short-run motivation problems.

Although this staff–line conflict can never be completely solved, it can be lessened and controlled. First, the roles of each party can be spelled out,[29] and in the rest of this section this is further explored. Second, all parties need to recognize that each has special knowledge that the others do not and that decisions are best made where the information comes together. Third, the compensation staff have a greater burden in reducing this conflict, which they can do by helping to educate line management so that the image of compensation being mysterious disappears.

Top-Management Responsibility

Top management has ultimate responsibility for the total compensation program. But this is delegated partially to line management and partially to the compensation staff. Typically, the compensation staff are delegated the task of developing and maintaining a compensation program whereas line management makes the pay decisions within the program's guidelines. Top management is more involved in certain aspects of compensation decisions than in others. All policy areas are or should be the decision of top management. Thus, top management will be more involved with pay level considerations than with wage structure or individual pay decisions, since the pay level decision sets the framework for these other decisions.

Even if top management does not directly make all compensation decisions it needs to exercise a control function. This is done in a number of ways.[30]

APPROVAL.   Approval calls for assent to action before the action is to take place. The chief advantage of this approach is that it ensures that policies are followed as top management wishes them to be. Clearly this approach is limited, since if all decisions in organizations were made in this manner there would be little need for staff or lower-level managers and top management would be completely overwhelmed with decisions to approve. Also top management does not always have the appropriate information, such as individual

---

[29]W. Brown, *Explorations in Management* (New York: John Wiley, 1960).

[30]The four categories that follow were taken from R. E. Sibson, *Compensation*, rev. ed. (New York: American Management Assn., 1981).

performance data. This approach should be reserved for those decisions top management feels are most important and of a policy nature.

BUDGETS.   A budget allows top management to delegate the day-to-day decisions while retaining a say in the overall impact of these decisions. Budgetary controls permit measurement against a standard *before* decisions are made. Budgets are the best way to control the individual pay decisions without having to look at each decision.

STATISTICS.   A major function of the compensation staff is to provide statistical information to top management, which records compensation activities and results. Analysis of these reports can often be a source of standards. Even in the absence of standards, reports often suggest problem areas to be explored before they get out of hand. These reports are best at appraising actions that have taken place.

INTERNAL CONTROL.   Internal control involves helping individual managers make sound and consistent compensation decisions regarding their employees. This approach requires carefully developed policies and procedures known and understood by line managers. It also requires training managers in the organization's objectives in compensation. Furthermore, all line managers are provided information they need to make compensation decisions, the time to make them, and the staff to help them. Finally, all line managers are held accountable for the compensation decisions they make.

The emphasis that top management places on these various approaches varies widely by organization. Organizations where employees seek to expand the employment exchange can probably rely heavily on internal control. But even here budgets and statistics play a major role. In compensation it is extremely important that the employees receive consistent signals as to what is desired and what to expect. So coordination and consistency are important goals.

Line-Management Responsibility

The major decisions made by the line managers are the individual pay decisions for their employees. In addition, where there is a bottom-up budgeting system the line manager is involved in establishing the budget for his or her unit. These decisions are constrained by the policies and procedures established by top management and the compensation staff. Very often these constraints leave line managers feeling that it is impossible to reward their employees in a way that will obtain the motivational results they desire.

The major problem with line managers making these individual pay decisions is consistency. If the policies and other control techniques are strong enough to ensure consistency, then the individual manager does not have enough discretion to adequately discriminate among the various performances that take place in his or her unit. But unless there are very clear performance standards established and communicated in the organization, each manager is free to interpret performance as he or she sees fit. Given the state of the art in performance appraisal, consistency will continue to be a problem and the discretion of line managers will not be highly compromised. The problem of maintaining consistency is probably best approached through the internal control procedure.

Line managers are also concerned with job evaluation, because this has a major impact upon the wage rates of their employees. In this area, however, it is not typical for the line manager to have the final decision. The manager's job is most often that of designing the job; the compensation staff then determines the appropriate pay range for the job. This can lead to considerable jockeying of job tasks in an organizational unit solely to obtain the job rates that are desired.

Compensation-Staff Responsibility

The compensation staff are the people who have expertise in compensation and can carry out the technical functions of the area. These technical functions are expanding each year and becoming more complex. Nowhere is this more evident than in benefits administration. The last decade has seen this area go from a neglected one to an area that, well managed, can save the organization millions of dollars a year in costs. Further, changing legal patterns are making it necessary for organizations to have compensation expertise available in order to make sure that decisions made about compensation are legal.

The technical functions that compensation professionals typically carry out are performing job analysis and evaluation, conducting and analyzing wage surveys, developing and adjusting the wage structure, and of course advising line and top management on compensation matters. Clearly these decisions involve mainly the job and wage structure decisions of the compensation program. They set the framework for the decisions made by the line managers, so the feeling of the line manager can easily be one of frustration unless he or she understands what it is the compensation specialist is doing.

The compensation staff have a large role in the planning and control processes. The information needed for developing compensation plans is centralized in the compensation staff. They are also the group that has the time and interest to develop these plans. Often the policies of top management are results of the compensation staff's efforts. Most statistics and other information about compensation is provided by the compensation staff. To the degree that information is power, the compensation staff can develop power by the way they handle the information available to them. Control in the area of job structure is the most noticeable, since the standards are well developed, usually by the compensation staff. Control in the area of individual pay decisions is possible but for political reasons is often not well developed.

The compensation staff also have an important role in coordinating efforts with other staff groups. In particular three groups are important. The first is the financial staff. This is a result of the budgetary process, since the finance department is ordinarily in charge of budgets and the financial resources of the organization are controlled by this staff group. Second, as indicated earlier in this chapter, much of the information for internal forecasting comes from human-resource planning. So other parts of personnel are important information sources for the compensation staff. This relationship is reciprocal, since employment needs the input of compensation in order to carry out its function. Lastly, in those organizations that have a union, coordination between the compensation staff and labor relations is very important. The union contract represents one more level of constraint on how compensation decisions are made in the organization.

Clearly managers and staff have different roles in different compensation decisions. Top management is most concerned with pay level decisions in order to maintain organizational competitiveness and with overseeing and generally controlling other decision areas. Line managers are most concerned with the actual pay rates of their employees in order to keep and motivate them. The compensation staff are concerned mainly with developing a framework within which to make compensation decisions, collecting information for use in compensation decisions, and overseeing the total process within the organization. These different roles are summarized in figure 19–1.

SUMMARY

The pieces of the organization's compensation program and the various influences on those parts have been discussed in each chapter of this book. These pieces must be put together into a coherent whole that integrates the parts with each other and with the environment as well as accomplishing the goals of compensation. The goals of any compensation program must be to provide a system that is perceived as fair and to attract and retain employees. It must also motivate those employees to produce and contribute extra efforts at a level required by the organization. All this needs to be done with an eye to keeping costs to a minimum.

Compensation programs of different organizations will and should be different. Each organization must develop a compensation strategy that fits its

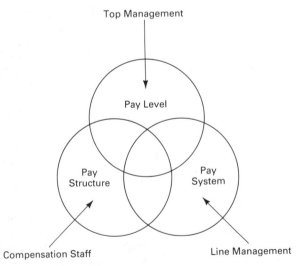

Figure 19–1 Relationships of top management, line management, and the compensation staff in compensation decisions

circumstances. Developing this strategy is done through compensation planning. The planning process consists of these four phases: first, know what is presently being done and what the current environment is like. Second, make decisions about what the compensation program ought to look like from the strategy formulation. Third, examine what is likely to happen that will influence the organization's ability to move from what it is presently doing to what it wishes to do. (This phase is largely a matter of forecasting.) Finally, develop an action plan that accomodates the first three phases and goes on to design the kind of compensation program that the organization needs.

Control of compensation is needed to see that things go as planned or that plans can be changed to accommodate changes in the environment. Achieving control is difficult, since there are so many different control procedures and the information needed is not always present. Control processes differ considerably depending on whether the control is on wage level, wage structure, or wage system. Control of individual wage adjustments is particularly difficult since it is so decentralized in the organization.

The compensation program is not the total responsibility of any one group in the organization. Top management must be involved in establishing the goals and policies of compensation. The compensation staff provides the expertise and can do the technical aspects of compensation. The supervisors are the people who must see that the system is perceived as fair and will motivate their employees. All three must be working together for a compensation program to achieve its goals.

20

Discrimination in Pay

Developing compensation programs that have as a major goal the creation of *equity in pay* has been a focus in this book. This final chapter deals with equity as it applies to the problem of discrimination in pay, particularly toward women. Attaining equity in pay is a difficult goal to achieve, for a number of reasons. The first is that equity is cognitive: it depends on the perceptual field of the person for its definition. It may vary between the two parties in the exchange or with observers to the exchange. Second, equity in pay may conflict with other goals of compensation. In particular, equity is often seen as conflicting with the competitiveness of the organization in the marketplace. Third, the legal environment, while encouraging equity in some ways, makes it a burden and defines the process to be followed in cumbersome ways. Fourth, the organization may find itself as a leader of social change rather than a follower. This makes the perceptual problem just cited particularly difficult to deal with, for different groups of employees have very different ideas about what is equitable. When one group sees that equity is being gained at its expense, the organization is placed in the middle.

In a way, consideration of discrimination in pay is an issue whose time has come. For the past 20 years organizations have been made more aware, through legislation and pressures from civil rights groups, of the way in which they discriminate against certain groups in their personnel practices. But the thrust of this pressure until recently has been on employment practices. Although no one would claim that discrimination in employment does not exist today, there are clear guidelines as to how organizations are to act. This level of sophistication has not been arrived at in discrimination in pay. It is not as clear whether there is a problem or, if there is, what action organizations should take to solve it. This chapter examines the problem of discrimination in pay and describes ways in which organizations can deal with it.

DISCRIMINATION AS A VIRTUE

Discrimination in pay is inevitable and indeed desirable in organizations.[1] All organizations pay differently for different jobs and in consequence pay people different amounts of money. Even if an organization were to pay all employees the same, some employees would unquestionably claim that this kind of equality is discrimination. So the problem is not *whether* to discriminate in pay but rather *how* organizations go about discriminating.

Compensation, as a reward in organizations, is intended to create behaviors that lead to the accomplishment of organizational goals. When differentials in payment are based upon this principle then the organization may be seen as *discriminating* in the best sense of the word. In this book it has been suggested that the basis of pay differentials should be the nature of the job, the performance of the job, and the personal attributes that enable the person to do the job.[2] In the Equal Pay Act four factors are defined as appropriate differences: skill, effort, responsibility, and working conditions. These four are similar to the three just cited, although working conditions adds the idea that the context within which work is done may be a reasonable factor. Establishing pay differentials on the basis of these *job-related* factors is perceived by most employees as reasonable and fair. The way in which they are administered may lead to feelings of inequity, as will be discussed later in this chapter.

IMPROPER DISCRIMINATION

Discrimination can be improper in two senses. The first is that the differentials in pay are not related to factors that lead to behaviors on the employee's part that are in turn related to the accomplishment of organizational goals. In this instance it is the organization that is not receiving its money's worth when it pays its employees. Second, these irrelevant criteria may harm the employee. Paying employees different pay at random is silly, but the employee is likely to feel that it is just luck as to what he or she is paid. But paying one employee less than another on the basis of sex is a defeating experience for the lesser-paid person, since sex is not a characteristic that one can change and is not perceived by the person as relevant to performing the job. Legally, using certain

---

[1]The idea for this section came from R. K. Miller, "Discrimination Is a Virtue," *Newsweek*, July 21, 1980, p. 15.

[2]D. W. Belcher and T. J. Atchison, "Compensation for Work," in *Handbook of Work, Organization, and Society*, ed. R. Dubin (Chicago: Rand McNally, 1976), pp. 567–614.

factors to differentiate pay are illegal. The Civil Rights Act says that it is unlawful

> to discriminate against any individual with respect to compensation, terms, conditions of employment, because of such individual's race, color, religion, sex, or national origin. . . .

These factors are quite clear, but what is not clear is when these are the factors that are being used. If women are paid less because they are women then the wrong criteria of pay differentials are being applied, but if women are paid less because of the job they hold then the question of whether this is improper discrimination is not as clear.

PERSPECTIVES ON THE PROBLEM

Improper discrimination in pay by organizations appears to occur mostly on the basis of sex. The feminist movement has focused attention on this by popularizing the idea of the *.59 dollar*. By this they point out that women earn 59 cents for every dollar of income that men earn. Actually, the figure is more accurately 64 cents, which, though a bit better, is still not very close to equality.[3] This difference clearly represents a significant *earnings gap* between men and women workers.

The question, however, is why there is such an earnings gap. Is it that organizations consciously discriminate and pay women less than men, or is this an unplanned result of establishing pay differentials based on rational criteria? This is a complex question, and this section examines it from three perspectives—the economic, the legal, and the psychological—so that we can see how we arrived at this state and what is likely to happen.

The Economic Perspective

Economists have been very interested in studying the earnings gap between men and women. Their approach has mainly been to examine the problem from a macro perspective, attempting to see if there are differences in men and women workers overall that account for the lower average wages paid to women. Their studies indicate that a majority of the differential can be accounted for by a number of factors, discriminatory and nondiscriminatory,[4] which we will turn to next. These factors narrow the gap between men's and women's wages to around 12 cents.

PARTICIPATION RATE. The first and most dramatic factor affecting women's wages today is the increased participation rate of women in the work

[3] J. Norwood, "Perspectives on Comparable Worth: An Introduction to the Numbers," *Monthly Labor Review,* December 1985, p. 3.

[4] B. A. Nelson, E. M. Opton, and T. E. Wilson, "Wage Discrimination and the 'Comparable Worth' Theory in Perspective," *University of Michigan Journal of Law Reform,* Winter 1980, pp. 231–301.

force. There has been a steady increase in this rate since after World War II for all age groups of women, as can be seen in table 20–1. This change may well be the most dramatic change in the labor force in this century, but it has occurred so gradually that it has been called the *Subtle Revolution.*[5] By 1990, 61 percent of women in the United States are predicted to be in the labor force.[6] The expected effect of an increase in the supply of workers of this magnitude is to depress wages for that group of workers, and this has undoubtedly happened.

The reasons for this increase in participation are many and involve a drastic change in American society. Lower birth rates and improved technology in the home have made it easier for women to work. Increased education has made it more desirable for women to work. But the need for two paychecks in many families and the increase in the number of one-parent families, usually headed by a woman, have made it necessary for women to work. The single-adult family accounts for a rising proportion of America's poor families.[7] This trend has been called the *feminization of poverty.*

JOB SEGREGATION.   The increase in the participation rate might not by itself have reduced women's wage rates. If there were a single labor market, then an increase in the participation rate would simply mean an overall increase in the supply of labor and somewhat lower wage rates for all workers. But there are in actuality many labor markets, and women tend to be segregated into only a few of them. Figures show that whereas 50 percent of male workers have jobs in 63 occupations, 50 percent of women workers are concentrated into 17 occupations. In order to eliminate this segregation, it is estimated, almost three quarters of all working women would have to change their

Table 20–1   Female Labor Force Participation, 1955–1982

	AGE, years			
YEAR	20–24	25–34	35–44	45–54
1955	45.9	34.9	41.6	43.8
1960	46.1	36.0	43.4	49.8
1965	49.9	38.5	46.1	50.9
1970	57.7	45.0	51.1	54.4
1975	64.1	54.6	55.8	54.6
1980	69.0	65.4	65.5	59.9
1982	69.8	68.0	68.0	61.6

Source: *Employment and Training Report of the President, 1981.* Table A-5; and *Employment and Earnings,* January 1983, p. 145.

[5]R. Smith, ed., *The Subtle Revolution: Women at Work* (Washington, D.C.: Urban Institute, 1979).

[6]G. George, T. Silvestri, J. M. Lukasiewitz, and M. E. Einstein, "Occupational Employment Projections Through 1995," *Monthly Labor Review,* Nov 1983, pp. 37–50.

[7]Bureau of the Census, "Characteristics of the Population below the Poverty Level, 1983," *Current Population Reports,* series P-60, no. 147 (Washington, D.C.: U.S. Government Printing Office, 1985), pp. 1–6.

occupations.[8] Further, the occupations occupied by women are lower-paid than those dominated by men.[9] See figure 20–1.

Job segregation of women is not limited to occupational areas. Women tend more than men to enter industries that pay lower wages overall.[10] Even when women are in male-dominated occupational areas the specific jobs they hold are at the bottom of the wage ladder in that occupation. This may be partially a case of employment discrimination and partly because the increased participation of women means that they are young and concentrated in the beginning steps of an occupational ladder.[11] For those occupational areas in which women predominate there is one further problem: there is very little vertical movement within the occupation, and the range of salaries is therefore narrower.

Job segregation between men and women is a deep-seated sociological phenomenon. There are appropriate roles for men and women in all societies.

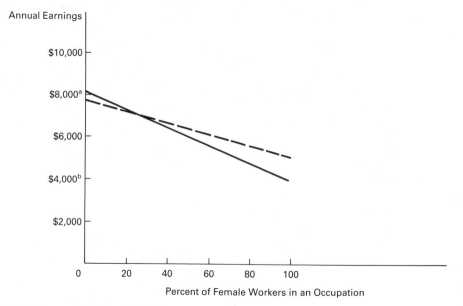

[a]Equivalent to $22,720 in 1984 dollars.
[b]Equivalent to $11,360 in 1984 dollars.

Figure 20–1   The relationship between occupational earnings and percentage of female workers
Source: D. J. Tremain and H. I. Hartmann, eds, *Women, Work, and Wages,* Washington, D.C., National Academy Press, 1981, p. 29.

[8]R. G. Blumrosen, "Wage Discrimination, Job Segregation, and Title VII of the Civil Rights Act of 1964," *University of Michigan Journal of Law Reform,* Spring 1979, pp. 397–502.

[9]J. Norwood, *The Female–Male Earnings Gap: A Review of Employment and Earnings Issues,* Bureau of Labor Statistics Report 673 (1982).

[10]G. T. Milkovich, "The Emerging Debate," in *Comparable Worth: Issues and Alternatives,* ed. E. R. Livernash (Washington, D.C.: Equal Employment Advisory Council, 1980), pp. 23–47.

[11]C. B. Bell, "Comparable Worth: How Do We Know It Will Work?" *Monthly Labor Review,* December 1985, pp. 5–12.

In the United States there is a blurring of these roles with increased participation of women in the work force, changing education patterns of women, and the effect of civil rights legislation. The changing nature of the economy, from manufacturing to service, encourages this trend.

Where men and women are working on the same job there is a dramatic narrowing of wage differentials, providing little evidence, either at the economy level or within organizations, of pay discrimination.[12]

EDUCATION AND EXPERIENCE.   Although the *level* of education of men and women in the United States does not differ, the *pattern* and *type* of education does. Women are more likely to finish high school and men more likely to go on to college. This pattern is changing, however, and women now constitute a majority of students in college today. In addition, men have traditionally majored in subjects that are more profession-oriented and lead directly to transferability into the labor market.[13]

Experience levels of women are affected by the tendency to drop out of the labor market for childbearing. At a minimum this means women have less experience than men the same age. In addition, dropping out may mean a lessening of skills in occupations that are changing rapidly. Further, employers are less likely to engage in training personnel whom they perceive as not being permanent employees, so even if women have the same level of experience they may have less training.[14]

UNIONIZATION.   Although the empirical evidence is not clear-cut on the subject, there is a widely held belief that unions have an upward impact on the wages of workers.[15] If this is so it represents another reason why women's wages might be lower than men's, since women are not as highly organized as men. In 1980, 31 percent of male workers belonged to unions, compared with 18.9 percent of female workers.[16] Reasons for this difference seem to be the types of jobs women typically hold—pink-collar jobs—and the lower likelihood of their seeing a union as a way of dealing with job dissatisfaction.

All this may be changing. The National Education Association (NEA) is now one of the largest unions in the country. It changed during the 1970s from a professional organization to a union when teacher salaries dropped relative to those of almost all other groups. The American Federation of State, County and Municipal Employees (AFSCME), the major union for government workers, is one of the few unions in the country currently growing stronger. Major thrusts of this union include the recruitment of women workers and concern with wage discrimination by calling attention to *comparable worth.* Also active in this area is the Service Employees International Union (SEIU).

[12]M. S. Seiling, "Staffing Patterns in Female–Male Earnings Gap," *Monthly Labor Review,* June 1984, p. 30.

[13]M. E. Gold, *A Dialogue on Comparable Worth* (Ithaca, N.Y.: ILR Press, 1983).

[14]J. Mincer and H. Ofek, "Interrupted Work Careers: Depreciation and Restoration of Human Capital," *Journal of Human Resources,* 17:1982, pp. 3–24.

[15]T. A. Kochan, "How American Workers View Labor Unions," *Monthly Labor Review,* April 1979, pp. 12–31.

[16]Bureau of Labor Studies, *Earnings and Other Characteristics of Organized Workers, May 1980,* Bulletin 2105 (Washington, D.C.: U.S. Government Printing Office, 1981).

AGE DISTRIBUTION OF WOMEN WORKERS.   A theme that runs through much of the discussion thus far is that there are two different groups of women workers, the young and the old. There is ample evidence that older women were discriminated against both in employment and in wages. The earnings potential of these workers has been stunted by this discrimination. They represent the most occupationally segregated group of women workers. They occupy jobs with little advancement possibilities and they are often underpaid for their experience level.

The young female worker is not as segregated in job choice but is new to the labor market and so is occupying the first steps of the career ladder. So, at present both groups are paid low. But this should change as the older workers retire and the younger workers move up in the occupational hierarchy. This is assuming, of course, that discrimination in promotion and internal organizational movement does not take place in the future as it did in the past.[17]

THE LABOR MARKET.   These factors, particularly the increased participation rate and job segregation, are likely to lead to a situation in which women's jobs are paid less in the marketplace. Since organizations need to be efficient, they should not pay any more than they have to for any resource, labor included. Viewed in this way, paying women less than men is simply following what the market dictates. It is claimed that administrative interference with wage setting would lead to inefficiency and would not work. For instance, in Australia there appears to have been a rise in female unemployment caused by raising women's wages artificially.[18]

As this book has pointed out, however, the labor market is not a perfect vehicle for determining wages. The going rate is not a point but a range of wages. Deciding what is the going rate is in itself an administrative decision. But most important, establishing wage structures is a process of integrating both internal and external wage pressures. Often it is the internal considerations that dominate in the wage-setting process. So the market is not a totally dominant force but rather one of the considerations the compensation specialist needs to keep in mind.[19]

SUMMARY.   Pay discrimination, as seen from an economic perspective, shows that women have entered the labor market in large numbers in the past 20 years but have been restricted to a small number of job areas. This has depressed any gains that might have occurred from the civil rights movement and has held women's wages at the same ratio to men's wages over this period. Gains can be expected in the future, however, as women move into male-dominated jobs and change their patterns of work life and education. The disparity may also shrink if women engage more actively in the union movement and if unions actively court the woman worker.

[17]J. P. Smith and M. P. Ward, *Women's Wages and Work in the Twentieth Century* (Santa Monica, Calif.: Rand Corporation, 1984).

[18]J. Bellace, "A Foreign Perspective," in *Comparable Worth, Issues and Alternatives*, ed. E. R. Livernash (Washington D.C. Equal Employment Advisory Council, 1980), pp. 137–172.

[19]Bell, "Comparable Worth."

The Legal Perspective

The legal perspective on discrimination in pay is based upon two doctrines, *equal pay* and *comparable worth*. The first is a product of the Equal Pay Act of 1963 and is well established in law. The second is based upon the Civil Rights Act of 1964 but is not well established in law at this time. This section will discuss each of these doctrines.

THE EQUAL PAY DOCTRINE.   The Equal Pay Act forbids pay discrimination

> between employees on the basis of sex when employees perform equal work on jobs in the same establishment requiring equal skill, effort, and responsibility and performed under similar working conditions. . . . Pay differences between equal jobs can be justified when the differential is based on (1) a seniority system; (2) a merit system; (3) a system measuring earnings by quality or quantity of production; or (4) any factor other than sex.

Equal in this law means *the same as* or, more accurately, *substantially similar.* That is, the work activities performed by male and female workers must be the same or almost the same. Where there are some activities carried out by males occasionally but not regularly this is not a basis for a differential in pay.[20] Further, it is the *actual* activities and not the formal stated ones that are considered.[21] This means that the job descriptions of the organization need to be kept current and reflect the activities of the employees in those jobs. The appropriate technique for evaluating equal pay is *job analysis.*

The determination of whether two jobs are substantially equal is based upon the four factors mentioned above in the Equal Pay Act. Guidelines for interpreting the law have evolved from court cases. The skill, effort, and/or responsibility involved in a job must be substantially greater than in another job for the two jobs to not be equal. The tasks involving this greater degree of the above must constitute a significant amount of the time of all employees in that job classification. The differential skill, effort, and responsibility should have a value commensurate with the pay differential that is in question. A further indication is different recruiting practices or training for the two jobs.

Differentials in pay for the same work are possible under the Equal Pay Act but must be for one or more of the four reasons stated above. As can be expected, it is this last exception that can cause the most trouble. In the Department of Labor guidelines these may include such things as shift differentials, temporary assignments, training programs, differential ability or training, or even a red-circle rate.

All in all, organizations must pay equal wages or at least have equal pay ranges for jobs that perform substantially the same work. It is the actual work that is done that controls this definition. This puts a weight on performing good job analysis in the organization, keeping job descriptions up to date, and having the compensation staff know what is happening in the organization.

[20]*Schultz* v.*Wheaton Glass Co.,* 421 F.2d 259 (3rd Cir. 1970).
[21]*Hodgeson* v. *Brookhaven General Hospital,* 436 F.2d 719 (5th Cir. 1970).

COMPARABLE WORTH. The concept of comparable worth takes the idea of equal pay for equal work one step further, comparing not only jobs that are the same but jobs that have the *same value* to the organization—that is, jobs that are comparable. This idea is not included in the Equal Pay Act, but proponents claim that it is inherent in the Civil Rights Act of 1964. As noted, it is unlawful to discriminate on the basis of sex and race as well as other factors in any terms of employment, including compensation. This is a much broader prohibition than that in the Equal Pay Act. At this time the courts have said that the Civil Rights Act may be invoked in compensation cases, but exactly how and to what degree are not clear.[22]

Comparable worth has caused much more argument than equal pay. Proponents point to the .59 dollar and claim that a major part of this discrepancy exists because women's jobs are undervalued by society in relation to men's jobs.[23] This has led feminist groups to claim that comparable worth is the women's issue of the 1980s. They feel that comparable worth will be served by comparing men's and women's jobs using job evaluation, and that if this is done it will show that women's jobs are indeed undervalued by society. In fact, where this has been done—Washington State, Los Angeles, and San Jose—there has been shown to be an undervaluing of women's jobs.

Thus, proponents of comparable worth point out that not only are women segregated into a few women's jobs but that because these jobs are occupied by women they are downgraded. Opponents answer that women can move into other jobs if they so wish. Proponents, in turn, point out that the training of women is provided in these women's jobs, that these jobs are intrinsically satisfying to women, and that women should not have to enter job arenas that are not as satisfying in order to gain pay equity.

Opponents of comparable worth have called it "the looniest idea since Looney Tunes," and this was from the chairman of the U.S. Civil Rights Commission. They contend, accurately, that the idea was rejected in the discussions that led to the passage of the Equal Pay Act and that Congress therefore did not wish to go this far in reducing inequality. The main problem that opponents see in comparable worth is that it ignores the labor market. They perceive organizations as merely paying market rates for jobs, and to do otherwise is to destroy the market mechanism. Further, the idea seems to them to be impractical. They see comparable worth as involving four elements that are objectionable and hard to achieve: (1) comparing dissimilar jobs, (2) comparing these dissimilar jobs on their so-called intrinsic value, (3) developing an unbiased job evaluation plan, and (4) requiring third-party intervention to make these determinations.[24] In short, opponents see comparable worth as impossible in the labor market and impractical in administration.

As in most emotionally charged issues, neither side is totally accurate. The proponents see the undervaluing of women's jobs as the major contributor to the .59 dollar. Given the analysis in our discussion of the economic perspective, this is not very likely. Part of the problem is undervaluation, but a fully

---

[22]See *Gunther* v. *County of Washington*, 1981 U.S. Supreme Court, 451 U.S. 161.

[23]Blumrosen, "Wage Discrimination."

[24]Association of Washington Business, "Comparable Worth in the Private Sector; A Debate—The Argument Against," *Pacific Northwest Executive*, July 1985, p. 20.

installed comparable worth program would not create equality of wages between men and women. Also, reliance on job evaluation ignores the fact that job evaluation does not create relative value of jobs in dollar terms, nor is there a conversion system other than using market rates.

On the other hand, opponents underestimate how much job evaluation can do. The argument that dissimilar jobs cannot be compared is contrary to the whole process of job evaluation in organizations. Likewise, the idea that organizations passively pay the market rate is inaccurate. As seen in this book, developing a wage structure is a process of integrating internal organizational value with the market value, and which is dominant depends on the jobs and the organization. Further, the measurement of the market rate is also a judgment that can influence the stated rate.

The legal status of comparable worth is not as clear as that for equal pay. The Civil Rights Act is a much broader act than the Equal Pay Act and has required a great deal of court interpretation in all areas. In the area of comparable worth there are likely to be more decisions in the future to define the limits and establish the process. At this time the following points seem to be established:

1. The Civil Rights Act may be used in a case of disparate compensation between men's and women's jobs.[25]
2. The *disparate impact* standard that is commonly used in civil rights cases can be a starting point, but it is necessary that *intent* also be shown. Where widespread sex discrimination has been shown in the organization or where the discrimination is blatant, comparisons of dissimilar male and female jobs were allowed, but discrimination caused solely by market forces is not a cause for action.[26]
3. Organizations must take action when they discover that there is discrimination in pay. Ignoring the results of studies showing that women's jobs are undervalued is a basis for legal action.[27]

But the courts are not the only arena in which the battle of comparable worth is being fought. Legislation on comparable worth is being sought in many states as well as in Congress. At least one state, Minnesota, has passed a Comparable Worth Act. There will be continuing pressure for such laws, particularly as applied to public employees.

Another arena for comparable worth is collective bargaining, particularly with public unions. As noted, the AFSCME has made comparable worth a major issue in its negotiations. In two major cases—San Jose and Los Angeles—it has won changes in wage schedules to upgrade women's jobs.[28] This movement is likely to increase in the near future as unions attempt to

[25]*Gunther* v. *County of Washington.*

[26]G. S. Sape, "Coping with Comparable Worth," *Harvard Business Review,* May-June 1985, pp. 145–52.

[27]Wilkins v. University of Houston.

[28]H. Bernstein, "Nurses Raise Women's Rights Flag," *Los Angeles Times,* January 24, 1982; and J. Picus, "Comparable Worth Concept Will Prevail," *Los Angeles Times,* September 12, 1985.

increase their membership by appealing to groups that they have ignored in the past. In 1981 the AFL–CIO adopted a resolution encouraging all national unions to (1) deal with sex-based pay inequities in contracts, (2) start pay-equity studies, either jointly or by the union, to identify wage discrimination, and (3) take any other action required to achieve comparable worth.[29] Success by the unions will in turn lead to changes in the relative values of men's and women's jobs in the labor market.

In summary, there is likely to be continuing pressure to examine discrimination in pay within organizations from a number of sources—feminist groups, unions, legislatures, and the courts. Organizations are going to have to defend the differentials in their organizations as being equitable.

The Psychological Perspective

Our discussion of comparable worth would indicate that there are considerably different perceptions about whether there is a problem of pay discrimination, about its nature, and about actions that should take place. These perceptions are likely to influence how people, in this case women, react to their compensation. Analysis of these reactions can be done by using the two models of motivation used in this book, the membership model and the performance model.

THE MEMBERSHIP MODEL. The membership model of motivation is based upon equity theory. This theory states that membership is a perceptual balance between the contributions required of the person and the rewards received by that person. If these are not in balance the person will take action to alleviate the resultant cognitive dissonance. In the case of pay discrimination of women, it would appear that there has been a change in their perceptions that has created or increased their dissonance in the past few years and that this dissonance will not go away without action taken by employing organizations.

Individuals feel equitably paid when they perceive that their rewards from work equal or exceed their contributions. In the case of women, there was in the past a tendency for them to undervalue their contributions and overstate their rewards. Women were likely to agree with the cultural norms and feel that their contributions to organizations were not as great as those made by men in terms of both the types of job contributions and the types of personal contributions, such as skill and training. In addition, they tended to increase their nonpay rewards by emphasizing the good working conditions of the office vis-à-vis the factory floor and the social aspects of the job.

This set of perceptions is changing. Women who are primary breadwinners are less interested in the nonpay aspects of the job and more interested in the pay they receive. The traditional position of not making more money than their husbands is disappearing: there often is not a husband and where there is this is less likely to be a consideration. As women's consciousness has been raised the value they place on their contributions to organizations is rising. They are now more likely to perceive that the skills they bring to the job are as valuable as male skills. However, organizations have not changed their

[29]W. Newman, "Pay Equity Emerges as a Top Labor Issue in the 1980's," *Monthly Labor Review*, April 1982, pp. 49–51.

perceptions as fast, leading to a situation in which women find that they have changed but their work situation has not, thereby creating feelings of inequity.

Furthermore, women are likely to respond to these feelings of inequity differently today. In the past, women were likely to reevaluate their contributions downward to agree with the cultural evaluation of women's work as not being as valuable. But today more women have the same background and skills as men, and those who have more traditional skills feel that those skills are as valuable as men's skills. The result is that women are more likely to try raising their pay in order to reduce their dissonance.

This pressure is not likely to go away, since women today are less likely to accept the traditional norms about women's work. In addition, organizations can expect women to now make men's jobs the comparison by which they judge whether they are being fairly rewarded. This puts organizations in an uncomfortable position. To the extent that men and the organization maintain the same perceptions that they have in the past, there is going to be tension between women and their employing organizations. This is the type of situation that has led to unionization of groups in the past, and unions are today attempting to take advantage of this disparity in perception.

THE PERFORMANCE-MOTIVATION MODEL.   Changes in perception are likely to effect the motivation to perform as well as create feelings of inequity. As we have seen, the performance-motivation model has three parts: the value of the reward, the performance–reward connection, and the performance–effort connection.

The value of the reward, pay in this case, appears to be going up for women. This should make it easier for organizations to get women to focus on working harder on the job, provided the other two parts of the model are fulfilled. The performance–reward connection is difficult in many women's jobs since women are more likely to provide a service rather than a product. In the past, there has been a tendency to shy away from making direct performance–reward connections in women's jobs. There appeared to be a feeling that they were inappropriate for that group of employees. As women move into men's jobs this distinction should lessen, but there are many women's jobs for which establishing a performance–reward connection is just beginning. Nurses and teachers are two such groups.

The performance–effort connection has also been tenuous in women's jobs. This is due partly because of the service type of work; again nurses and teachers are good examples. In neither of these areas is the person sure what impact she has had on the outcome. In fact, women in both professions find this a frustrating part of their job. There is also the problem that in women's jobs very often the performance–effort connection is purposely reduced by the organization; the woman is thereby not allowed the discretion necessary to make the connection. There is a catch-22 situation here. Where there is a perception by management that the person will not perform well unless her job is highly prescribed, they will define the jobs strictly. The person sensing this and finding the job dull will tend to put forth the minimum effort, leading to the validation of the managerial perception and in turn to even more prescriptions, and so on.

This analysis of the psychological perspective leads to the conclusion that there have been some clear changes in the perception of women about their jobs and their compensation. These perceptions are not likely to revert to more traditional perceptions, and therefore it is up to the organization to move toward the position of women employees in determining what is equitable. Further, organizations are in a position to move toward employing the performance-motivation model more clearly in women's jobs with an expectation that women will respond positively to these changes.

PAY DISCRIMINATION AND THE COMPENSATION DECISIONS

Until now we have examined the problem of pay discrimination from a societal viewpoint. This section looks at the issue of pay discrimination within the organization and makes suggestions as to how to find out if there is improper discrimination, either overt or unconscious, and how to improve compensation decisions so as to eliminate or at least reduce improper discrimination. We examine the three major compensation decisions—wage level, wage structure, and wage system.

Wage Level Decisions

The wage level decision has to do with who gets what, so it is very apropos when discussing discrimination. *Wage level* was defined in chapter 5 as the "average wage paid to workers at some level of analysis." In this case the level of analysis is the male and female employees in the organization. In most organizations this analysis will produce results like that for the society as a whole—that women are not paid as much as men in the organization. The differential may be less than 59 or 64 cents, but whatever it is the reasons for it need to be examined. The first level of analysis is the difference in male–female wage levels in parts of the organization and by job clusters. This analysis should reduce the differential. At the end this analysis should have been applied to each job category in the organization, and within these categories the only differences should be based on those criteria expressed in the Equal Pay Act—seniority, performance, and differences in quality or quantity of production.

The economic perspective discussed is a guide to why there may be a difference between male and female wages in the organization. Job segregation is a problem that is being worked on in most organizations through *affirmative action plans*. The dispersion of women into previously male-dominated jobs is a staffing issue rather than a compensation issue, but the movement will have considerable impact on the average wage paid to males and females in the organization.

The dual nature of women employees, young and old, is also a staffing concern, one that involves developing career paths for both young and old female employees. Not only are women segregated into certain jobs but most often in organizations these jobs have very little career progression. Organizations can do much to improve the possibilities for women to progress and thereby reduce their wage differential between men and women.

WAGE LEVEL POLICY FOR JOB GROUPS.   Organizations usually maintain different wage level strategies for different job groupings. These strategies are associated with the importance of the jobs to the organization. In an engineering organization, the wage level strategy is most likely to pay engineers somewhat above market while paying market or below to other jobs in the organization. They do this to ensure that the human resources most valuable to the organization, engineers in this case, are readily available and are the best that can be found. This differentiation of strategy among job groupings can exacerbate the discrimination problem where the jobs paid above average are male jobs and the jobs paid below average are female jobs. A common type of differentiating strategy is illustrated in figure 20–2. In this situation the organization has determined that it wishes to pay above average for the top jobs in the organization and below average for those at the bottom of the organization. If women predominantly occupy the lower-level jobs in this organization, then the differential between men and women will be enlarged by such a strategy.

WAGE SURVEYS AND THE LABOR MARKET.   The largest disagreement between the proponents and opponents of comparable worth lies with the function and use of the labor market as the determinant of wages. Opponents claim that wages should be whatever is the market rate. Proponents claim that

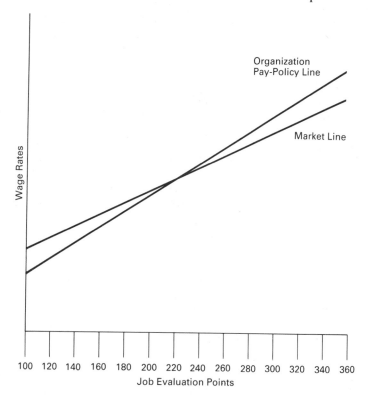

Figure 20–2   Organizational pay-policy line compared with market

the market rate for women's jobs is discriminatory and that therefore market rates should not be used. Both these positions are all-or-nothing positions. In fact, market rates are used for setting the value of jobs, but not exclusively, and jobs differ in the degree to which it is useful to try to determine market rates. So market rates are one factor in determining the wage rate for a job but not the only one. In some cases, this use of the labor market can increase the differential between men's and women's jobs. The effect of this can be lessened by aggregating men's and women's jobs' market rates together in establishing a wage structure.

The measurement of the labor market is done through wage surveys. At best, these surveys produce an estimate of the going rate. In chapter 6 it was noted that ranges of 100 percent to 200 percent in wages paid a particular job classification are commonly found in surveys so there is no one market rate but a rather wide range. This allows the decision maker considerable latitude in what he or she decides is the market rate. Further, the decision maker must analyze the market data. One of the authors recently participated in a study showing that 34 compensation analysts used almost 100 different methods in analyzing survey data and used that processed data for 48 separate purposes.[30] To say that the organization is just paying the market rate when this broad range of analysis is possible may be stretching reality. There are numerous ways to analyze sets of data to obtain desired results. In fact, this study found that only clerical wage rates were determined by simply taking the average of the total survey.[31] Developing a standard way of handling survey data may be a necessity in the future.

Wage Structure Decisions

The wage structure is a combination of the market rates as determined by the wage survey discussed above and the job structure of the organization. In turn the job structure is determined by job analysis and job evaluation. Both of these and the establishment of the wage structure can both help and hinder efforts to reduce wage rate differences between men and women.

JOB ANALYSIS.   Job analysis is the technique that is used in determining equal pay. Figuring out if two jobs are substantially the same involves finding out if they have the same tasks. This is a descriptive process, not an evaluative one. Since job analysis is supposed to be a descriptive process there should be little chance for discrimination to take place. But since the information is collected by humans there is always the possibility that the sex of the job incumbent and/or the job analyst can influence the data collection. This possibility has been investigated, with the conclusion that there does not appear to be much discrimination here. Arvey and colleagues did a study that had male and female analysts use the PAQ to analyze a job. Half the analysts viewed a man occupying the job and half a woman. There were no differences caused by the sex of the job occupant. There were marginal differences resulting from the sex of the analyst but these did not contribute to discrimination.[32] Another study, supervised by one of the authors, used the same technique but the analysts describes the jobs using other methods rather than the PAQ. The only difference was that male analysts tended to describe a task in sexist terms that the female analysts did not use.[33] This finding is consistent with the studies that show that the amount of information is a major variable in whether the sex of the person being analyzed enters into decision making. From this it appears that making sure that sufficient information is collected by the job analyst is necessary.

In a different approach, one of the authors examined whether men and women described their jobs differently. Incumbents of the same job title were asked to describe their activities, decisions, and interactions. The responses were content-analyzed. Major differences were found in the words men and women used to describe their activities, and these differences were found to be detrimental to women in that the words women used were evaluated lower.[34] It may be important, then, to look at how job descriptions have been developed for women's jobs to see if they are ready for job evaluation.

JOB EVALUATION. The question in the relationship of discrimination in pay and job evaluation is whether job evaluation is the solution or part of the problem. It appears to be a bit of both. A majority of organizations use some sort of job evaluation to establish a job structure. They most often use job evaluation because the market rates are unavailable or hard to obtain or because they wish to pay other than the going rate for some of their jobs. But job evaluation leads only to a job structure and not to a wage structure. There is no inherent worth developed through job evaluation.[35] What is established is a hierarchy of jobs within the organization which is then referred to the market values in order to establish pay rates for the job. So job evaluation, by itself, cannot establish the monetary value of the job to the organization or the economy.

However, job evaluation can develop the relative positioning that the organization establishes for jobs and can compare this positioning with that of the labor market. Where the two disagree the organization must determine whether it wishes to pay market rates or not. This decision does not always go in favor of the market rate, although it must take into account the effects of not paying the market rate. Organizations have different needs and values than the general economy does at a particular time. Thus, they may pay higher or lower than the market in order to most effectively pursue their own goals.

[32]R. D. Arvey, E. M. Passino, and J. W. Lounsbury, "Job Analysis Results as Influenced by Sex of Incumbent and Sex of Analyst," *Journal of Applied Psychology*, 62: 1977, pp. 411–16.

[33]M. E. Marcus, "Discrimination by Sex in Job Analysis and Job Description," (Master's thesis, San Diego State University, 1981).

[34]T. J. Atchison and C. Davis, "Male and Female Perceptions of Their Jobs" (paper presented to American Institute of Decision Sciences, Western Division, Monterey, Calif., 1985).

[35]D. P. Schwab, "Job Evaluation and Pay Setting: Concepts and Practices" in *Comparable Worth*, ed. Livernash, pp. 49–77.

Reducing the differential between male and female wages in the organization can reasonably be one of those goals.

In summary, job evaluation is a tool that can compare apples and oranges, which the opponents of comparable worth say cannot be done. Organizations can and do have job evaluation plans that rate *all* jobs within the organization. On the other hand, job evaluation cannot replace the use of market rates in setting wages, as is proposed by the proponents of comparable worth,[36] since the results of job evaluation are not stated explicitly in monetary terms, nor can any convenient ratio be assumed. Job evaluation can be used to rate and/or rank all organization jobs and to compare that ranking with market rates to establish the wage structure. For instance, if there is a 25 percent difference in the wages of two jobs, is this reflected in the differential developed through job evaluation? Where it is not, the organization must consciously decide whether to follow the market or its internal value determination. This is not a novel decision made only in the case of discrimination. Organizations are constantly faced with the issue of whether organizational value or market value should prevail.

Although job evaluation can be used as a partial solution to the pay discrimination problem, it is also a part of that problem. Job evaluation is a judgmental process and is subject to the human errors that can exist in any such process. As we have seen, the first step in job evaluation is determining the *compensable factors* to be used. Do some compensable factors discriminate against women, or are compensable factors that are important for women's jobs ignored in job evaluation plans? One study has shown that for some compensable factors the evaluation of male and female jobs did affect the ratings. But this effect was not strong.[37] However, this is a possibility that has not been thoroughly explored. Some important aspects of women's jobs may tend to be ignored in job evaluation. Interactions with others may be a case in point. Many women's jobs require considerable contact with others. This factor is ignored in most job evaluation plans and may be biased toward the kinds of interactions typical of men's jobs.

A second question relates to whether the type of job evaluation used makes a difference. Early studies comparing the results of job evaluation methods showed little difference between results obtained from different methods.[38] Two recent studies, one of which focused on the impact of different job evaluation plans on pay discrimination, show a considerable difference in the results of job evaluation plans.[39] Most of these differences were to the detriment of the evaluation of women's jobs.

[36]H. Remick, "The Comparable Worth Controversy" *Public Personnel Management Journal,* Winter 1981, pp. 371–82.

[37]R. Grams and D. P. Schwab, "An Investigation of Systematic Gender-Related Error in Job Evaluation," *Academy of Management Journal,* June 1985, pp. 279–90.

[38]T. J. Atchison and W. W. French, "Pay Systems for Scientists and Engineers," *Industrial Relations,* October 1967, pp. 44–56.

[39]L. R. Gomez-Mejia, L. R. Page, and R. C. Tornow, "A Comparison of the Practical Utility of Traditional, Statistical, and Hybrid Job Evaluation Approaches," *Academy of Management Journal,* December 1982, pp. 790–809; and R. M. Madigan and D. J. Hoover, "Effects of Alternative Job Evaluation Methods on Decisions Involving Pay Equity," *Academy of Management Journal,* 29:1986, pp. 84–100.

The third area where discrimination is likely to occur is in the actual evaluation of jobs. Most job evaluators, after they become experienced, find themselves using the formal plan to validate their initial impression of the job. To the extent that this impression is a result of knowledge of the job and the evaluation instrument, the results are probably accurate. But if the information is inadequate, as we have discussed, then the results are likely to be flawed. One study examined the influence of current wage rates on the evaluation process and found a significant effect.[40] Thus, the fact that women's jobs are paid less results in their being evaluated lower than men's jobs. All these criticisms indicate that job evaluation is not a perfect tool for determining whether women's jobs are underpaid vis-à-vis men's jobs. But since organizations have been using the technique with success for so long, it is reasonable to assume that job evaluation results can be one way of examining discrimination in pay.

Wage System Decisions

Wage systems decisions have to do with determining the wage rate of the employee within the guidelines of the wage structure. It is at this point that the personal contributions of the individual enter into the wage determination. The major discussion of pay discrimination has focused on jobs, but there is another series of studies that have examined the contributions of women in the workplace as compared with those of men. Economists claim that one of the reasons that women are paid less is that their contributions, defined as human capital, are less than men's. But are women's contributions valued as highly as men's? There are studies indicating that women and other minority groups earn less than white males of equivalent age, experience, and education.[41] This problem can be studied within the organization by developing a regression equation of the salaries of males based upon their age, experience, education, and any other relevant characteristics and using this equation to predict female salaries. This prediction can then be compared with women's actual salaries.[42] This process might look like figure 20–3 (p. 438).

Given this discussion and the process of individual pay determination the examination of discrimination in wage system decisions will focus on three areas: where the employee started in the pay range, how long the employee has been in the pay range, and the performance of the employee.

STARTING WAGES.   This may be an overlooked area in which pay discrimination occurs. The wage rate that a person accepts on his or her first job, and especially the first job with a particular organization, influences the wage rate of the employee from then on, since increases in pay are often a percentage increase over current wages. In the past, there was a tendency to offer

[40]Grams and Schwab, "Investigation."

[41]For example, F. H. Cassell, S. M. Director, and S. I. Doctors, "Discrimination within Internal Labor Markets," *Industrial Relations,* 14:1975, pp. 337–44; R. Buchele and M. Aldrich, "How Much Difference Would Comparable Worth Make?" *Industrial Relations,* 21:1982, pp. 222–33; and N. M. Gordon, T. E. Morton, and I. C. Braden, "Faculty Salaries: Is There Discrimination by Sex, Race, and Discipline?" *American Economic Review,* 64:1974, pp. 419–27.

[42]M. W. Gray and E. L. Scott "A Statistical Remedy for Statistically Identified Discrimination," *Academe,* May 1980, pp. 174–81.

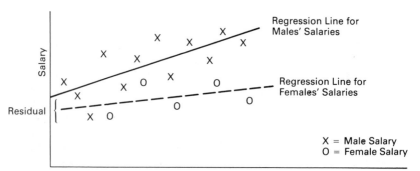

Figure 20–3   Predicted and actual salaries
Source: M. W. Gray and E. L. Scott, A 'Statistical' Remedy for Statistically Identified Discrimination, in *Academe,* May 1980, p. 177.

women not only lower-level jobs but lower wages on the same job. Although this practice is illegal under the Equal Pay Act, it is very hard to detect since job offers are clearly made within a particular pay range. The organization would need to keep track of the average pay offer for each job to men and women to control this tendency. Women aid in this process by being willing to accept lower pay than men for equivalent jobs. This may be particularly true for women reentering the work force after being out to raise children, for they may feel unsure of their talents at the time. Once they are back working and feel confident, they are still saddled with the decrement created by the salary at which they began.

One study in this area showed that women were offered lower wages on average than men for a particular job. To compound the error, they were more likely to be assigned more routine tasks and then given lower second-year increases than men.[43] Further, there has been a court case dealing with this problem of women getting behind men in wages based upon prior pay history. In the *Allstate* case women who were selected as sales agents from within the company had starting salaries lower than their male counterparts since they had come from lower-paid jobs. The trial court agreed with the women that the jobs they had come from were probably subject to discrimination and that the company should pay them on a par with the male sales agents. The appellate court, however, agreed with Allstate that its actions had a business reason and not a sex-biased reason.[44] Although Allstate won this case, it brings to light the problem of the variation in pay history between men and women.

TIME IN GRADE.   Two factors can hinder women in regard to time in grade. The first is the turnover rate. Many women's jobs have a high turnover. so few women get to the top of the range. This high turnover has to do mostly with the non-challenging way women's jobs are designed. The affect on the average wages paid to men and women in the organization is to lower women's average wages. The second factor is that women's jobs tend to be at the bottom

[43]J. R. Terborg and D. R. Ilgen, "A Theoretical Approach to Sex Discrimination in Traditionally Masculine Occupations," *Organization Behavior and Human Performance,* 14:1975, pp. 352–75.
[44]*Kouba and EEOC* v. *Allstate Insurance Co.,* 1982, 691 F.2d 873.

of the wage structure, which has pay ranges that are narrower than those at the top of the wage structure. So even if they did stay in the job they would not be able to move up as much as men.

PERFORMANCE. Discrimination can occur in a pay-for-performance plan if women's performance is viewed differently than men's performance. Studies on the effect of sex on performance ratings have varied widely in their results. Some show no effect, some a positive effect for men, and some a positive effect for women. The one thing that seems to account for these variations in results is the amount of information. That is, people rely on stereotypes when they do not have clear and objective information on which to make a judgment.[45]

There is evidence that women rate themselves lower than men and that women rate others higher than men do. Thus, women would be more likely to accept lower ratings than men, and supervisors would be more likely, therefore, to feel free to give lower ratings. Also since there are fewer women supervisors, their tendency to rate higher would not have a strong effect within the organization. However, one recent study did not support either of these contentions and showed both men and women rating themselves more highly than did their supervisors.[46]

Last, there may be some concern with the direction of performance rating and pay determination. It is probable that current pay affects the determination of performance. In order to be consistent supervisors in a pay-for-performance system are likely to rate employees high or low based upon where they are in the pay range presently. This smooths out the percentage increases that they give out to employees.

Reducing Pay Discrimination in Organizations

The responsibility for dealing with pay discrimination will fall on organizations in the end. Legislation and court decisions may provide guidelines, but the work will get done in individual organizations. Further, it will not be useful to ignore the question, since women are not likely to forget the problem and accept the current status of their earnings compared with those of males in the organization. Also, this is a problem that is perceived as best dealt with at the organizational level.[47] The areas that the organization can focus on to reduce discrimination are compensation-plan design, administration, and control.

COMPENSATION-PLAN DESIGN. Comparable worth is seen basically as an internal equity problem.[48] This suggests that job evaluation will always be important in determining whether discrimination is taking place in the organi-

---

[45]V. F. Niva and B. A. Gutek, "Sex Effects on Evaluation," *Academy of Management Review,* 5:1980, pp. 267–76.

[46]J. M. Shore and G. C. Thornton III, "Effects of Gender on Self and Supervisory Ratings," *Academy of Management Journal,* 29:1986, pp. 115–29.

[47]B. Rosen, S. Rynes, and T. Mahoney, "Compensation, Jobs, and Gender," *Harvard Business Review,* July-August 1983, pp. 170–90.

[48]Ibid.

zation. Most of the suggestions in the area of job evaluation are for the organization to have a *single* job evaluation plan for all jobs. This is not an uncommon practice, but it should be looked at seriously by those organizations using two or more plans. An alternative is to be able to compare the plans through the use of key jobs that can be evaluated in two plans to show if the results are the same in both cases.[49]

The job evaluation plan itself needs to be designed so as to minimize discrimination. The choice of compensable factors can help: factors that are clearly important to both men's and women's jobs would be preferable. Also suggested are plans that rely on more sophisticated procedures, such as factor comparison and point systems which are likely to give more accurate results and reduce the opportunity for intentional discrimination.[50]

Although external considerations appear secondary in comparable worth, it is necessary for the organization to minimize the discriminatory effects of the labor market. This can best be done by using key jobs in developing the pay-policy line that are both male and female jobs and using this single pay line in determining the value of all jobs.

Pay systems would be aided greatly by staffing and career changes in organization. Career paths for women's jobs need to be opened up so more movement can be made, but most important is to help reduce the job segregation of women by placing them in male-dominated jobs. This is seen by most people as the best way to reduce pay discrepancies.[51] Performance appraisal must also be designed to focus on behaviors that are important in both male and female jobs.

COMPENSATION-PLAN ADMINISTRATION.   Administration of compensation plans deal with a multitude of decisions made by many people in the organization. As with other parts of equal employment it is necessary to develop policies and procedures to guide this decision making. As indicated, the amount of information provided to decision makers is a major variable in whether they will use sex as a consideration in compensation decisions. Thus, it is imperative for the compensation staff to ensure that all the proper information is available and used in making pay decisions. It is particularly important to have sufficient information available for performance appraisal decisions, and setting pay rates for new hires are crucial points in ensuring that information is available.

COMPENSATION-PLAN CONTROL.   In order to see that progress is being made, the organization needs to keep some records of what is happening. Overall it is useful to know what the average wage is for men and women in the organization. This information can also be kept for organizational seg-

---

[49]T. J. Atchison, "Towards a Nondiscriminatory Measurement of Job Worth," in *Job Evaluation and EEO: The Emerging Issues* (New York: Industrial Relations Counselors, 1978).

[50]See, for example, J. Goodman, N. Fonda, and P. Glucklich, "Job Evaluation without Sex Discrimination," *Personnel Management*, February 1979, pp. 34–37; and J. R. Thomson, "Eliminating Pay Discrimination by Job Evaluation," *Personnel*, September-October 1978, pp. 11–22.

[51]Rosen, Rynes, and Mahoney, "Compensation, Jobs, and Gender."

ments, for groups of jobs, and for individual jobs. These figures can complement those kept for the distribution of men and women in job categories for affirmative action reasons. In job evaluation it is useful to keep track of whether the differentials paid to various jobs in the organization match the differentials indicated by job evaluation. This is an area on which many of the comparable worth suits are focusing.

Last, as suggested earlier, it is useful to keep track of whether the organization is valuing women's age, experience, and performance as highly as men's. This can be done by use of regression techniques, which can determine if both groups are being given the same weight for these factors.[52]

SUMMARY

Comparable worth has been called the "compensation issue of the 1980s." Certainly, it has been a topic in almost every meeting of compensation professionals and is constantly in the press. It may also prove to be the "issue of the 1990s" as it does not appear that the problem is going to be quickly solved. Further, comparable worth is only a part of the broader issue of discrimination in pay within organizations and this chapter examines this broader issue. Since discrimination in pay is inevitable, it is in the best interests of the organization and its employees to determine if the discrimination is illegal or not.

Discrimination in pay is largely a problem of women's pay in relation to men's pay. Women make somewhere around 64 cents for every dollar a man receives in the work force. We have attempted to examine this problem from three perspectives. The first is an economic one which attempts to explain why women do in fact make less than men. The combination of job segregation and the large influx of women into the work force accounts for a large proportion of the difference in pay rates. Other contributing factors are the education and skills obtained by women, the age mix of women in the work force, and the degree of unionization among women.

The legal perspective examines the doctrines of *equal pay* and *comparable worth*. The Equal Pay Act of 1963 requires that organizations pay men and women the same wages if their jobs are substantially similar. Comparable worth does not have the clear legal authority of equal pay laws. It would insist that men and women be paid the same wages if they have the same value to the organization regardless of job content. This latter concept is much more contentious but it is definitely gaining ground, if not in the courts certainly through union activity.

The psychological perspective focuses on the perceptions that have, in the past, made differences in pay between men and women seem correct and natural to both women and society. However, the debates about comparable worth are changing women's perceptions, and organizations are faced with either changing or engendering feelings of inequity within a large group of employees.

Discrimination in pay within the organization is more often unintentional and built into the compensation practices than it is overt and purposeful.

[52]Gray and Scott "A 'Statistical' Remedy."

Discrimination in wage level decisions can occur if different wage level policies are initiated for jobs held by women than are for jobs held by men. There has been very little evidence of discrimination in job analysis but there has been some in job evaluation. The use of different wage structures for male and female groups can lead to discrimination as can the choice of factors in the job evaluation plan. Pay discrimination most often occurs in the wage system decision since it relies on so many individual judgments of supervisors. Starting salaries and merit increases are both places where women can fall behind men in their wages over time. All of these areas can be controlled if the organization keeps track of the movement of men's and women's wages over time.

APPENDIX 1:
GOVERNMENT AGENCIES,
INDUSTRY GROUPS, AND CONSULTANTS
WHO CONDUCT WAGE SURVEYS

American Electronics Association
2600 El Camino Real
Palo Alto
California 94306

AMA's Executive Compensation Service
135 West 50th Street
New York
New York 10020

Bureau of Labor Statistics
U.S. Department of Labor
Washington, D.C. 20212

Bureau of National Affairs, Inc.
1231 25th Street, N.W.
Washington, D.C. 20037

Commerce Clearing House, Inc.
4025 West Peterson Avenue
Chicago
Illinois 60646

Compensation Practices Association
of San Diego County
P.O. Box 23757
San Diego
California 92123

Hansen Survey Group
A. S. Hansen, Inc.
1080 Green Bay Road
Lake Bluff
Illinois 60044

Hay Management Consultants
229 South 18th Street
Philadelphia
Pennsylvania 19103

Hewitt Associates
100 Half Day Road
Lincolnshire
Illinois 60015

Industrial Relations Counselors
P.O. Box 1530
New York
New York 10019

Merchants' and Manufacturers'
Association of Los Angeles
2300 Occidental Center
1150 South Olive Street
Los Angeles
California 90015

P-H Compensation Service
Prentice-Hall, Inc.
Englewood Cliffs
New Jersey 07632

APPENDIX 2: HAY GUIDE CHART

Source: © Hay Associates 1981. Used by permission.

ILLUSTRATIVE

GUIDE [HAY] CHART

KNOW-HOW

• • Human Relations Skills ⟶

	I. NONE OR MINIMAL — Performance or supervision of an activity (or activities) highly specific as to objective and content, with appropriate awareness of related activities.			II. RELATED — Operational or conceptual integration or coordination of activities which are relatively homogeneous in nature and objective.			III. DIVERSE — Operational or conceptual integration or coordination of activities which are diverse in nature and objectives, in an important management area.		
	1	2	3	1	2	3	1	2	3
A. BASIC — Basic work routines plus work indoctrination.	50	57	66	66	76	87	87	100	115
	57	66	76	76	87	100	100	115	132
	66	76	87	87	100	115	115	132	152
B. ELEMENTARY VOCATIONAL — Familiarization in uninvolved, standardized work routines and/or use of simple equipment and machines.	66	76	87	87	100	115	115	132	152
	76	87	100	100	115	132	132	152	175
	87	100	115	115	132	152	152	175	200
C. VOCATIONAL — Procedural or systematic proficiency, which may involve a facility in the use of specialized equipment.	87	100	115	115	132	152	152	175	200
	100	115	132	132	152	175	175	200	230
	115	132	152	152	175	200	200	230	264
D. ADVANCED VOCATIONAL — Some specialized (generally nontechnical) skill(s), however acquired, giving additional breadth or depth to a generally single functional element.	115	132	152	152	175	200	200	230	264
	132	152	175	175	200	230	230	264	304
	152	175	200	200	230	264	264	304	350
E. BASIC TECHNICAL - SPECIALIZED — Sufficiency in a technique which requires a grasp either of involved practices and precedents; or of scientific theory and principles; or both.	152	175	200	200	230	264	264	304	350
	175	200	230	230	264	304	304	350	400
	200	230	264	264	304	350	350	400	460
F. SEASONED TECHNICAL - SPECIALIZED — Proficiency, gained through wide exposure or experiences in a specialized or technical field, in a technique which combines a broad grasp either of involved practices and precedents or of scientific theory and principles; or both.	200	230	264	264	304	350	350	400	460
	230	264	304	304	350	400	400	460	528
	264	304	350	350	400	460	460	528	608
G. TECHNICAL - SPECIALIZED MASTERY — Determinative mastery of techniques, practices and theories ...	264	304	350	350	400	460	460	528	608
			350	400	460			528	700

• • BREADTH OF MANAGEMENT KNOW-HOW

Left margin labels: PRACTICAL PROCEDURES · SPECIALIZED TECHNIQUES

ILLUSTRATIVE

GUIDE **HAY** CHART

PROBLEM-SOLVING

● Thinking guided or circumscribed by:

THINKING CHALLENGE

THINKING ENVIRONMENT	1. REPETITIVE — Identical situations requiring solution by simple choice of learned things.	2. PATTERNED — Similar situations requiring solution by discriminating choice of learned things.	3. INTERPOLATIVE — Differing situations requiring search for solutions within area of learned things.	4. ADAPTIVE — Variable situations quiring analytical, terpretive, evaluat and/or construc thinking.
A. STRICT ROUTINE — Simple rules and detailed instructions.	10% / 12%	14% / 16%	19% / 22%	25% / 29
B. ROUTINE — Established routines and standing instructions.	12% / 14%	16% / 19%	22% / 25%	29% / 33%
C. SEMI-ROUTINE — Somewhat diversified procedures and precedents.	14% / 16%	19% / 22%	25% / 29%	33% / 38%
D. STANDARDIZED — Substantially diversified procedures and specialized standards.	16% / 19%	22% / 25%	29% / 33%	38% / 43%
E. CLEARLY DEFINED — Clearly defined policies and principles.	19% / 22%	25% / 29%	33% / 38%	43% / 50%
F. BROADLY DEFINED — Broad policies and specific objectives.	22% / 25%	29% / 33%	38% / 43%	50% / 57%
G. GENERALLY DEFINED — General policies and ultimate goals.	25% / 29%	33% / 38%	43% / 50%	57% / 66%
H. ABSTRACTLY DEFINED	29%	38%	50%	66%

APPENDIX 2: HAY GUIDE CHART (continued)

ILLUSTRATIVE

GUIDE **HAY** CHART

ACCOUNTABILITY

• • IMPACT OF JOB ON END RESULTS

INDIRECT
REMOTE: Informational, recording, or incidental services for use by others in relation to some important end and result.
CONTRIBUTORY: Interpretive, advisory, or facilitating services for use by others in taking action.

DIRECT
SHARED: Participating with others (except own subordinates and superiors), within or outside the organizational unit, in taking action.
PRIMARY: Controlling impact on end results, where shared accountability of others is subordinate.

• • • MAGNITUDE
• • IMPACT ——— AMI EQUIVALENT

AMI for use with 1982 dollars is 2.60.

	(1) VERY SMALL OR INDETERMINATE Under $100M				(2) SMALL $100M - $1MM				(3) MEDIUM $1MM - $10MM				
	R	C	S	P	R	C	S	P	R	C	S	P	R
A. PRESCRIBED These jobs are subject to: Direct and detailed instructions Close supervision	10	14	19	25	14	19	25	33	19	25	33	43	25
	12	16	22	29	16	22	29	38	22	29	38	50	29
	14	19	25	33	19	25	33	43	25	33	43	57	33
B. CONTROLLED These jobs are subject to: Instructions and established work routines Close supervision	16	22	29	38	22	29	38	50	29	38	50	66	38
	19	25	33	43	25	33	43	57	33	43	57	76	43
	22	29	38	50	29	38	50	66	38	50	66	87	50
C. STANDARDIZED These jobs are subject, wholly or in part, to: Standardized practices and procedures General work instructions Supervision of progress and results	25	33	43	57	33	43	57	76	43	57	76	100	57
	29	38	50	66	38	50	66	87	50	66	87	115	66
	33	43	57	76	43	57	76	100	57	76	100	132	76
D. GENERALLY REGULATED These jobs are subject, wholly or in part, to: Practices and procedures covered by precedents or well-defined policy Supervisory review	38	50	66	87	50	66	87	115	66	87	115	152	87
	43	57	76	100	57	76	100	132	76	100	132	175	100
	50	66	87	115	66	87	115	152	87	115	152	200	1
E. DIRECTED These jobs, by their nature or size, are subject to: Broad practice and procedures covered by functional precedents and policies Achievement of a circumscribed operational activity Managerial direction	57	76	100	132	76	100	132	175	100	132	175	230	1
	66	87	115	152	87	115	152	200	115	152	200	264	1
	76	100	132	175	100	132	175	230	132	175	230	304	1

FREEDOM TO ACT

446

APPENDIX 2: HAY GUIDE CHART (continued)

FREEDOM TO ACT

F. ORIENTED DIRECTION These jobs, by their nature or size, are broadly subject to: Functional policies and goals General managerial direction	87	115	152	200	115	152	200	264	152	200	264	200	264	350	200
	100	132	175	230	132	175	230	304	175	230	304	230	304	400	230
	115	152	200	264	152	200	264	350	200	264	350	264	350	460	264
G. BROAD GUIDANCE These jobs are inherently subject only to broad policy and general management guidance.	132	175	230	304	175	230	304	400	230	304	400	304	400	528	304
	152	200	264	350	200	264	350	460	264	350	460	350	460	608	350
	175	230	304	400	230	304	400	528	304	400	528	400	528	700	400
H. STRATEGIC GUIDANCE These jobs, by reason of their size, independent complexity and high degree of effect on Company results, are subject only to ... ience from top-most management.	200	264	350	460	264	350	460	608	350	460	608	460	608	800	460
	230	304	400	528	304	400	528	700	400	528	700	528	700	920	528
	264	350	460	608	350	460	608	800	460	608	800	608	800	1056	608
	304	400	528	600	400	528	700	920	528	700	920	700	920	1216	700

Index